Oracle Press™

OCP Oracle Database 12*c*: Advanced Administration Exam Guide

(Exam 1Z0-063)

ABOUT THE AUTHOR

Bob Bryla is an Oracle 9*i*, 10*g*, 11*g*, and 12*c* Certified Professional with more than 25 years of experience in database design, database application development, training, and Oracle database administration. He is the lead Oracle DBA and systems engineer at Epic in Verona, Wisconsin.

In his spare time, he has authored several Oracle DBA books such as *Oracle Database 12*c*: The Complete Reference* and *Oracle Database 12*c* DBA Handbook*. In addition, he has authored several certification study guides for Oracle Database 11*g* and 12*c*. He has also been known to watch science-fiction movies and dabble in videography in his spare time.

About the Technical Editor

Jeremy Russell (OCP) has been working with Oracle database products since the late 1980s, and his experience as a developer, database administrator, and instructor for Oracle University spans Oracle version 5 through Oracle 12*c*. He currently works on multiple Oracle databases in a 24/7 environment as a database administrator with Engility Corporation, a government contractor in the United States. He has a master's degree in IT from the University of Liverpool, United Kingdom, as well as industry certifications in Linux, security, and Oracle database products.

Oracle Press™

OCP Oracle Database 12*c*: Advanced Administration Exam Guide

(Exam 1Z0-063)

Bob Bryla

New York Chicago San Francisco
Athens London Madrid Mexico City
Milan New Delhi Singapore Sydney Toronto

Library of Congress Cataloging-in-Publication Data

Bryla, Bob.
OCP Oracle database 12*c* advanced administration exam guide (exam 1Z0-063) / Bob Bryla. — Third edition.
pages cm. — (Oracle press)
ISBN 978-0-07-182868-0

1. Oracle (Computer file) 2. Database management—Examinations—Study guides. 3. Electronic data processing personnel—Certification. I. Title.
QA76.9.D3B7978 2015
005.75'85—dc23

2015007035

McGraw-Hill Education books are available at special quantity discounts to use as premiums and sales promotions, or for use in corporate training programs. To contact a representative, please visit the Contact Us pages at www.mhprofessional.com.

OCP Oracle Database 12c: Advanced Administration Exam Guide (Exam 1Z0-063)

1 2 3 4 5 6 7 8 9 0 DOC/DOC 1 0 9 8 7 6 5

ISBN: Book p/n 978-0-07-183000-3 and CD p/n 978-0-07-182866-6
of set 978-0-07-182868-0

MHID: Book p/n 0-07-183000-6 and CD p/n 0-07-182866-4
of set 0-07-182868-0

Sponsoring Editor
Stephanie Evans

Editorial Supervisor
Jody McKenzie

Project Manager
Raghavi Khullar, Cenveo® Publisher Services

Acquisitions Coordinator
Mary Demery

Technical Editor
Jeremy Russell

Copy Editor
Kim Wimpsett

Proofreader
Susie Elkind

Indexer
Jack Lewis

Production Supervisor
George Anderson

Composition
Cenveo Publisher Services

Illustration
Cenveo Publisher Services

Art Director, Cover
Jeff Weeks

CONTENTS AT A GLANCE

CONTENTS

ACKNOWLEDGMENTS

Many technical books need the expertise of more than one person, and this one is no exception. Thanks to Stephanie Evans and Mary Demery for trying to keep me on schedule, and thanks to Jeremy Russell, who gave me good advice when the theoretical met the practical.

Many of my professional colleagues at Epic were a source of both inspiration and guidance, especially James Slager, Scott Hinman, and Justin Rush. In this case, the whole is truly greater than the sum of its parts.

If you have any questions or comments about any part of this book, please do not hesitate to contact me at rjbdba@gmail.com.

INTRODUCTION

If you're reading this book, you're well on your way to Oracle certification—one of the hottest certifications available for Oracle database professionals. You can achieve several certification tracks and three levels of certification: Oracle Certified Associate (OCA), Oracle Certified Professional (OCP), and Oracle Certified Master (OCM).

To earn the OCA, you've taken two exams so far and possibly some instructor-led or online courses. The next step, the OCP, requires one instructor-led or online course plus exam 1Z0-063: Oracle Database 12*c* Advanced Administration. This book covers all the requirements for 1Z0-063 and can be an invaluable supplement to the instructor-led training. The exam questions that appear at the end of each chapter mirror the actual exam's questions; the companion CD contains another sample exam; and after registering on our web site, you can take yet another bonus exam. After you've read this book cover to cover, tried all of the examples and exercises throughout the book, and passed the included exams, you are another step closer to passing exam 1Z0-063 and obtaining your OCP credential. Oracle Certified Professionals are among the best paid in the IT industry, more than Microsoft-, Sun-, and Cisco-certified professionals. Good luck with your certification journey!

In This Book

This book is organized to serve as an in-depth review for the Oracle Database 12*c* Advanced Administration exam (1Z0-063) for professionals who are already certified as OCAs. Each chapter covers a major aspect of the exam, with an emphasis on the *why* as well as the *how to*. All the objectives on the exam are carefully covered in the book.

On the CD-ROM

For more information about the CD-ROM, please see the appendix at the back of this book.

Exam Readiness Checklist

At the end of this introduction, you will find an Exam Readiness Checklist. This table allows you to cross-reference the official exam objectives with where they are covered in this book. The checklist also allows you to gauge your level of expertise on each objective at the outset of your studies in order to help you check your progress and make sure you spend the time you need on more difficult or unfamiliar sections. References are provided for each objective exactly as the vendor presents them, along with a chapter and page number.

In Every Chapter

Several components in each chapter call your attention to important items, reinforce important points, and provide helpful exam-taking hints. Take a look at what you'll find in every chapter:

- Every chapter begins with **certification objectives**—what you need to know to pass the section of the exam dealing with the chapter topic. The objective headings identify the objectives within the chapter, so you'll always know an objective when you see it!
- **Exam Watch** notes call attention to information about, and potential pitfalls on, the exam. These helpful hints are written by the authors, who have taken the exams and received their certification—who better to tell you what to worry about? They know what you're about to go through!

exam watch

Remember the precedence of the various points where globalization settings can be specified. On the server side, instance settings take precedence over database settings, but all the server settings can be overridden on the client side: first by the environment, then at the session and statement levels.

- **Step-by-step exercises** are interspersed throughout the chapters. These are typically designed as hands-on exercises that allow you to get a feel for the real-world experience you need in order to pass the exams. They help you master skills that are likely to be an area of focus on the exam. Don't just read through the exercises; they are hands-on practice that you should be comfortable completing. Learning by doing is an effective way to increase your competency with a product.

- **On the Job** notes describe the issues that come up most often in real-world settings. They provide a valuable perspective on certification- and product-related topics. They point out common mistakes and address questions that have arisen from on-the-job discussions and experience.
- The **Certification Summary** section offers a succinct review of the chapter and a restatement of salient points regarding the exam.

- The **Two-Minute Drill** section at the end of every chapter shows a checklist of the main points of the chapter. It can be used for last-minute review.

- The **Self Test** section offers questions similar to those found on the certification exams. The answers to these questions, as well as explanations of the answers, can be found at the end of each chapter. By taking the Self Test after completing each chapter, you'll reinforce what you've learned from that chapter while becoming familiar with the structure of the exam questions.

Some Pointers

After you've finished reading this book, set aside some time for a thorough review. You might want to return to the book several times and make use of all the methods it offers for reviewing the material.

- *Reread all the Two-Minute Drill sections or have someone quiz you.* You also can use the drills for a quick cram before the exam. You might want to make some flash cards out of 3-by-5 index cards with Two-Minute Drill material on them.
- *Reread all the Exam Watch notes.* Remember that these notes are written by authors who have already passed the exam. They know what you should expect—and what you should be on the lookout for.
- *Retake the Self Test exams.* Taking the tests right after you've read the chapter is a good idea because the questions help reinforce what you've just learned. However, an even better idea is to return later and consider all the questions in the book in one sitting. Pretend that you're taking the live exam. When you go through the questions the first time, you should mark your answers on a separate piece of paper. That way, you can run through the questions as many times as you need to until you feel comfortable with the material.

- *Complete the exercises*. Did you do the exercises when you read through each chapter? If not, do them! These exercises are designed to cover exam topics, and there's no better way to get to know this material than by practicing. Be sure you understand why you are performing each step in each exercise. If you are not clear on some particular item, reread that section in the chapter.

Exam 1Z0-063

Exam Readiness Checklist

Official Objective	Chapter #	Page #	Beginner	Intermediate	Expert
Explain Oracle backup and recovery solutions	1	2			
Configure and manage RMAN settings	2	36			
Configure the Fast Recovery Area	2	47			
Configure control files and redo log files for recoverability	2	54			
Back up and recover a NOARCHIVELOG database	2	59			
Create and use an RMAN Recovery Catalog	3	74			
Protect the RMAN Recovery Catalog	3	92			
Use various RMAN backup types and strategies	4	115			
Perform full and incremental backups	4	122			
Use techniques to improve backups	4	136			
Manage backups	4	153			
Perform backup of nondatabase files	4	158			
Describe and tune instance recovery	5	183			
Perform complete and incomplete recovery	5	185			
Perform recovery for SPFILEs, Password Files, Control Files, and Redo Log Files	5	204			
Perform recovery of index and read-only tablespaces and tempfiles	5	222			
Restore a database to a new host	5	224			
Describe the Automatic Diagnostic Workflow	6	248			

Exam Readiness Checklist

Official Objective	Chapter #	Page #	Beginner	Intermediate	Expert
Handle block corruption	6	258			
Create RMAN-encrypted backups	7	274			
Configure and use Oracle Secure Backup	7	279			
Tune RMAN performance	7	285			
Describe the Flashback technologies	8	309			
Use Flashback to query data	8	312			
Perform Flashback Table operations	8	317			
Perform table recovery from backups	8	334			
Describe and use Flashback Data Archive	8	337			
Perform Flashback Database	8	343			
Describe and use transportable tablespaces and databases	9	364			
Choose a technique for duplicating a database	9	382			
Create a backup-based duplicate database	9	383			
Duplicate a database based on a running instance	9	387			
Describe the multitenant architecture	10	405			
Explain pluggable database provisioning	10	409			
Configure and create a CDB	11	420			
Create a PDB using different methods	11	433			
Unplug and drop a PDB	11	441			
Migrate pre-12.1 non-CDB database to CDB	11	444			
Establish connections to CDBs and PDBs	12	454			
Start up and shut down a CDB and open and close PDBs	12	459			
Evaluate the impact of parameter value changes	12	468			
Manage permanent and temporary tablespaces in CDB and PDBs	12	470			
Manage common and local users	12	473			
Manage common and local privileges	12	475			

Exam Readiness Checklist

Official Objective	Chapter #	Page #	Beginner	Intermediate	Expert
Manage common and local roles	12	475			
Enable common users to access data in specific PDBs	12	478			
Perform backups of a CDB and PDBs	13	492			
Recover PDB from PDB datafiles loss	13	501			
Use Data Recovery Advisor	13	512			
Duplicate PDBs using RMAN	13	519			
Monitor operations and performance in a CDB and PDBs	14	530			
Manage allocation of resources between PDBs and within a PDB	14	537			
Perform Database Replay	14	543			
Use Data Pump	15	554			
Use SQL*Loader	15	562			
Audit operations	15	564			

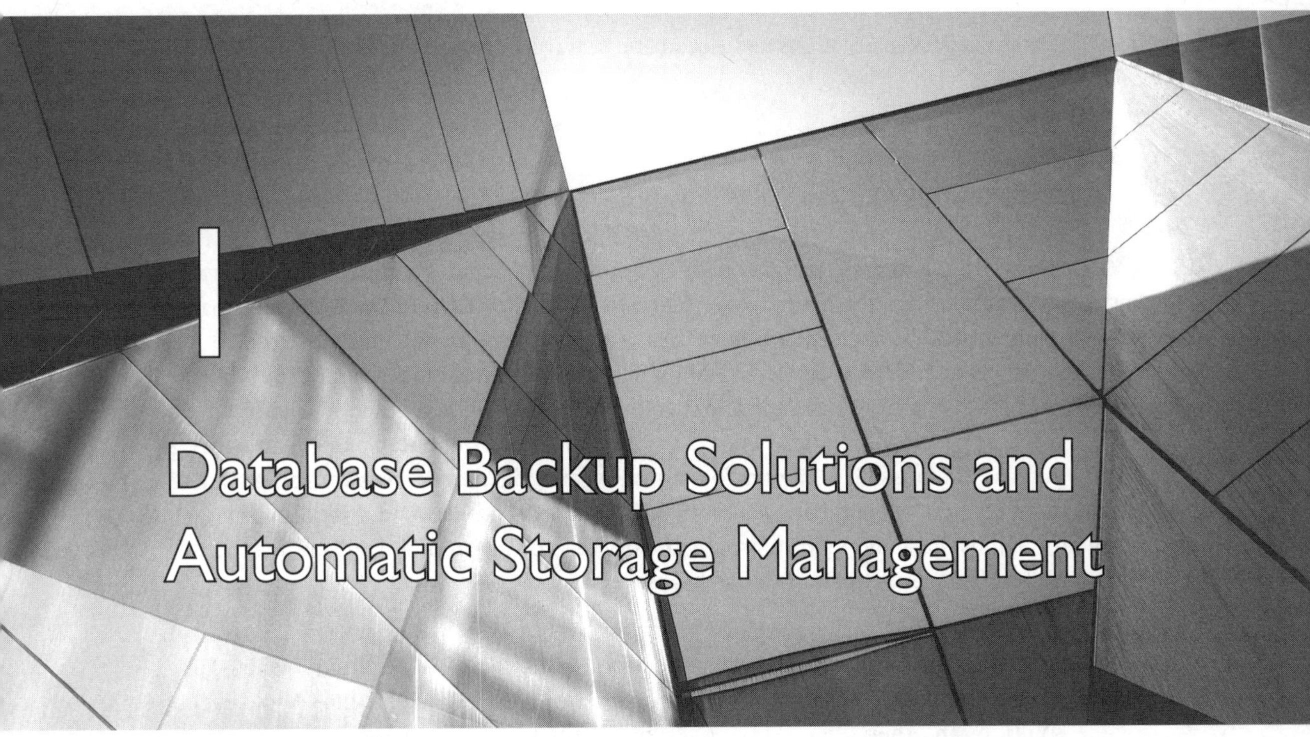

1

Database Backup Solutions and Automatic Storage Management

CERTIFICATION OBJECTIVES

1.01	Explain Oracle Backup and Recovery Solutions	✓	Two-Minute Drill
		Q&A	Self Test

Automatic Storage Management (ASM) is a key Oracle Database technology that you should be using in your environment, even if it has only one database and one database instance. ASM is the key to all robust and complete backup solutions. The integration of the server file system and a volume manager built specifically for Oracle Database files makes your disk management and tuning task a breeze: Every file object is striped and mirrored to optimize performance. In addition, nearly all ASM volume management tasks can occur while a volume is online. For example, you can expand a volume or even move a volume to another disk while users are accessing it, with minimal impact to performance. The multiplexing features of an ASM cluster minimize the possibility of data loss and are generally more effective than a manual scheme that places critical files and backups on different physical drives. And if that isn't enough, you can use an ASM instance and its disk groups to service more than one database instance, further optimizing your investment in disk hardware.

Before beginning a detailed explanation of how ASM works and how you can leverage it in your environment, this chapter discusses the available Oracle backup solutions and then offers a brief overview of the Oracle Database architecture, including instance memory structures, logical database structures, and physical database structures. A thorough understanding of the Oracle Database architecture (if you don't already have this from previous coursework) is required to fully understand and appreciate how ASM works and how ASM contributes to Oracle's extensive list of backup and recovery solutions.

CERTIFICATION OBJECTIVE 1.01

Explain Oracle Backup and Recovery Solutions

Before diving into the specifics of ASM and various backup and recovery scenarios in the following chapters, you must have a thorough understanding of Oracle Database and its associated memory and process structures. This section starts with the Oracle physical storage structures, including datafiles, control files, redo log files, and archived redo log files. It also covers the nondatabase files required to operate Oracle Database, such as initialization files and log files. Next, it reviews the key memory structures in an Oracle instance as well as the relationships between the physical storage structures and the memory structures. The last section of this chapter gives an overview of the Oracle-recommended backup and recovery solutions available in Oracle Database 12*c*.

Oracle Logical Storage Structures

The datafiles in Oracle Database are grouped together into one or more tablespaces. *Datafiles* are physical structures that are subdivided into *extents* and *blocks*. Each *tablespace* is a little like a logical wrapper for one or more datafiles. Within each tablespace are finer-grained logical database structures, such as *tables* and *indexes*. Another term used is *segments*, which in Oracle Database is used to describe the physical space occupied by a table or an index. The way in which Oracle Database is compartmentalized allows for more efficient control over disk space usage. Figure 1-1 shows the relationship between the logical storage structures in a database.

Tablespaces

An Oracle *tablespace* consists of one or more datafiles; a datafile can be part of one and only one tablespace. For an installation of Oracle Database 12*c*, a minimum of two tablespaces must be created: the SYSTEM tablespace and the SYSAUX tablespace. A default installation of Oracle 12*c* creates six tablespaces.

Oracle Database 12*c* (since Oracle Database 10*g*) allows you to create a special kind of tablespace called a *bigfile tablespace*, which can be as large as 128 terabytes

FIGURE 1-1 Logical storage structures

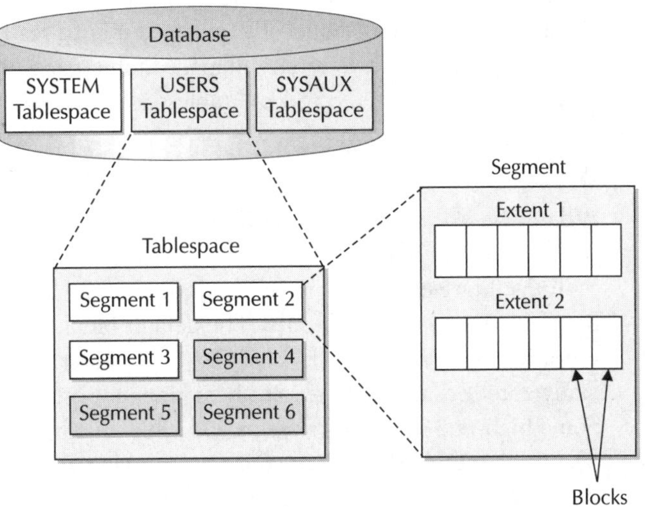

(TB). Using bigfiles makes tablespace management completely transparent to the database administrator (DBA); in other words, the DBA can manage the tablespace as a unit without worrying about the size and structure of the underlying datafiles.

Using Oracle Managed Files (OMF) can make tablespace datafile management even easier. With OMF, the DBA specifies one or more locations in the file system where datafiles, control files, and redo log files will reside, and Oracle automatically handles the naming and management of these files.

If a tablespace is *temporary*, only the segments saved in the tablespace are temporary; the tablespace itself is permanent. A temporary tablespace can be used for sorting operations and for table contents that exist only for the duration of the user's session. Dedicating a tablespace for these kinds of operations helps to reduce the I/O contention between temporary segments and permanent segments stored in another tablespace, such as tables.

Tablespaces can be either *dictionary managed* or *locally managed*. In a dictionary-managed tablespace, extent management is recorded in data dictionary tables. Therefore, even if all application tables are in the USERS tablespace, the SYSTEM tablespace will still be accessed for managing Data Manipulation Language (DML) on application tables. Because all users and applications must use the SYSTEM tablespace for extent management, this creates a potential bottleneck for write-intensive applications. In a locally managed tablespace, Oracle maintains a bitmap in the header of each datafile (inside a tablespace) to track space availability. Only quotas are managed in the data dictionary, dramatically reducing the contention for data dictionary tables.

Since Oracle Database 9*i*, if the SYSTEM tablespace is locally managed, then all other tablespaces must be locally managed if both read and write operations are to be performed on them. Dictionary-managed tablespaces must be read-only in databases with a locally managed SYSTEM tablespace.

Blocks

A database *block* is the smallest unit of storage in Oracle. The size of a block is a specific number of bytes of storage within a given tablespace, within the database.

To facilitate efficient disk I/O performance, a block is usually a multiple of the operating system block size. The default block size is specified by the Oracle initialization parameter DB_BLOCK_SIZE. Most operating systems will allow as many as four other block sizes to be defined for other tablespaces in the database. Some high-end operating systems will allow five block sizes. The blocks in the SYSTEM, SYSAUX, and any temporary tablespaces must be of the size DB_BLOCK_SIZE.

Extents

The *extent* is the next level of logical grouping in the database. An extent consists of one or more database blocks. When you enlarge a database object, the space added to the object is allocated as an extent. Extents are managed by Oracle at the datafile level.

Segments

The next level of logical grouping is the *segment*. A segment is a group of extents that form a database object that Oracle treats as a unit, such as a table or index. As a result, this is typically the smallest unit of storage that an end user of the database will deal with. Four types of segments are found in an Oracle database: data segments, index segments, temporary segments, and undo segments.

Every table in a database resides in a single *data segment* consisting of one or more extents; Oracle allocates more than one segment for a table if it is a partitioned table or a clustered table. Data segments include large object (LOB) segments that store LOB data referenced by a LOB locator column in a table segment (if the LOB is not stored inline in the table).

Each index is stored in its own *index segment*. As with partitioned tables, each partition of a partitioned index is stored in its own segment. Included in this category are LOB index segments. A table's non-LOB columns, a table's LOB columns, and the LOB's associated indexes can all reside in their own tablespace (different segments) to improve performance.

When a user's SQL statement needs disk space to complete an operation, such as a sorting operation that cannot fit in memory, Oracle allocates a *temporary segment*. Temporary segments exist only for the duration of the SQL statement.

From Oracle 10*g* onward, manual rollback segments exist only in the SYSTEM tablespace, and typically the DBA does not need to maintain the SYSTEM rollback segment. In previous Oracle releases, a rollback segment was created to save the previous values of a database DML operation in case the transaction was rolled back and to maintain the "before" image data to provide read-consistent views of table data for other users accessing the table. Rollback segments were also used during database recovery for rolling back uncommitted transactions that were active when the database instance crashed or terminated unexpectedly.

In Oracle Database 10*g* through 12*c*, Automatic Undo Management handles the automatic allocation and management of rollback segments within an undo tablespace. Within an undo tablespace, the undo segments are structured similarly to rollback segments, except that the details of how these segments are managed is under control of Oracle, instead of being managed (often inefficiently) by the DBA. Automatic undo segments were available starting with Oracle Database 9*i*, but manually managed rollback segments were still available in Oracle 10*g*. However, this functionality is deprecated as of Oracle 10*g* and later releases. In Oracle Database 12*c*, Automatic Undo Management is enabled by default; in addition, a Procedural Language/Structured Query Language (PL/SQL) procedure is provided to help you size the UNDO tablespace.

If you're starting out with Oracle Database 12*c*, all you really need to know is that manual rollback is redundant and will be unavailable in a future release. In addition, automatic undo is standard in Oracle Database 12*c*.

Oracle Physical Storage Structures

Oracle Database uses a number of physical storage structures on the disk to hold and manage the data from user transactions. Some of these storage structures, such as the datafiles, redo log files, and archived redo log files, hold real user data. Other structures, such as control files, maintain the state of the database objects. Text-based alert and trace files contain logging information for both routine events and error conditions in the database. Figure 1-2 shows the relationship between these physical structures and the logical storage structures reviewed in the section "Oracle Logical Storage Structures." A database file is one of either a control file, datafile, or online redo log file. All other files that are not important to the successful running of the database include parameter files, password files, backup files, archived redo log files, trace files, and alert log files.

Datafiles

Oracle Database must contain at least one *datafile*. One Oracle datafile corresponds to one physical operating system file on the disk. Each datafile in Oracle Database is a member of one and only one tablespace; a tablespace, however, can consist of many datafiles. The exception is a bigfile tablespace, which consists of exactly one datafile.

An Oracle datafile can automatically expand when it runs out of space, if the DBA created the datafile with the AUTOEXTEND parameter. A datafile can be manually expanded using the ALTER DATABABASE DATAFILE command. The DBA can limit the amount of expansion for a given datafile by using the MAXSIZE parameter. In any case, the size of the datafile is ultimately limited by the disk volume on which it resides.

FIGURE 1-2

Oracle physical storage structures

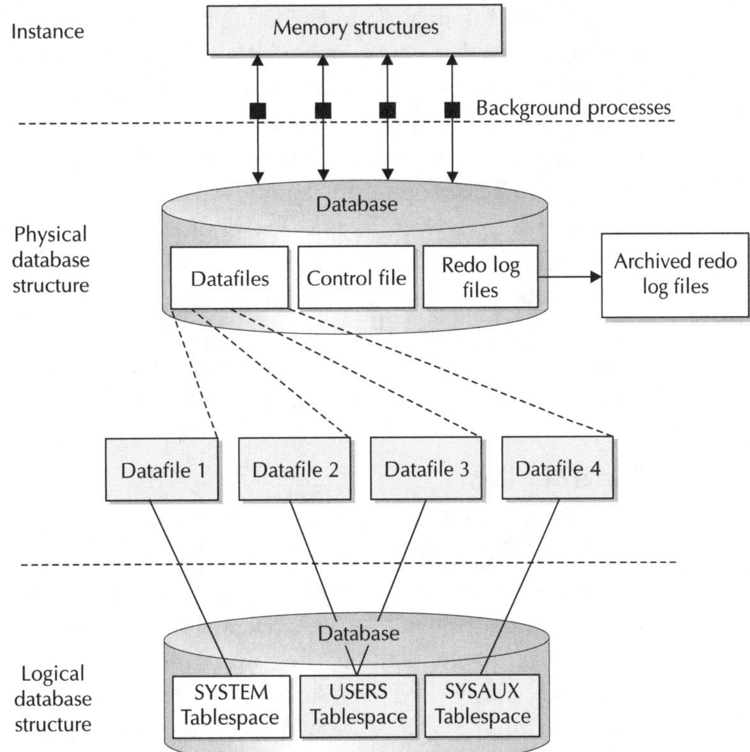

The datafile is the ultimate resting place for all data in the database. Frequently accessed blocks in a datafile are cached in memory. Similarly, new data blocks are not immediately written out to the datafile but are written to the datafile depending on when the database writer process is active. Before a user's transaction is considered complete, however, the transaction's changes are written to the redo log files.

Redo Log Files

Whenever data is added, removed, or changed in a table, index, or other Oracle object, an entry is written to the current *redo log file*. Oracle Database must have at least two redo log files because Oracle reuses redo log files in a circular fashion. When one redo log file is filled with redo log entries, the current log file is marked as ACTIVE, if it is still needed for instance recovery, or INACTIVE, if it is not needed for instance recovery. The next log file in the sequence is reused from the beginning of the file and is marked as CURRENT.

Ideally, the information in a redo log file is never used. However, when a power failure occurs or some other server failure causes the Oracle instance to fail, the new or updated data blocks in the database buffer cache might not yet have been written to the datafiles. When the Oracle instance is restarted, the entries in the redo log file are applied to the database datafiles in a *roll-forward* operation to restore the state of the database up to the point at which the failure occurred.

To be able to recover from the loss of one redo log file within a *redo log group*, multiple copies of a redo log file can exist on different physical disks. Later in this chapter, you will see how redo log files, archived log files, and control files can be *multiplexed* to ensure the availability and data integrity of the Oracle database. Multiplexing, in a nutshell, means you have more than one, or many more than one, copies of a structure for performance and availability.

Control Files

Oracle Database has at least one *control file* that maintains the metadata of the database. Metadata in the control file is the data about the physical structure of the database itself. Among other things, the control file contains the name of the database, when the database was created, and the names and locations of all datafiles and redo log files. In addition, the control file maintains information used by Recovery Manager (RMAN), such as the persistent RMAN settings and the types of backups that have been performed on the database. Whenever any changes are made to the structure of the database, the information about the changes is immediately reflected in the control file.

Because the control file is so critical to the operation of the database, it can also be multiplexed (one or more control files can be copied). However, no matter how many copies of the control file are associated with an instance, only one of the control files is designated as primary for the purposes of retrieving database metadata.

The ALTER DATABASE BACKUP CONTROLFILE TO TRACE command is another way to back up the control file. It produces a SQL script that you can use to re-create the database control file in case all multiplexed binary versions of the control file are lost because of a catastrophic failure.

You can also use this trace file, for example, to re-create a control file if the database needs to be renamed or to change various database limits that could not otherwise be changed without re-creating the entire database.

Archived Log Files

Oracle Database can operate in one of two modes: ARCHIVELOG or NOARCHIVELOG. When the database is in NOARCHIVELOG mode, the circular reuse of the redo log files (also known as the *online* redo log files) means that redo entries (the contents of previous transactions) are no longer available in case of a failure to a disk drive or another media-related failure. Operating in NOARCHIVELOG mode does protect the integrity of the database in the event of an instance failure or system crash because all transactions that are committed but not yet written to the datafiles are available in the online redo log files only. So, crash recovery is limited to entries currently in online redo logs. If your last backup of datafiles fails before your earliest redo log file, you cannot recover your database.

In contrast, ARCHIVELOG mode sends a filled redo log file to one or more specified destinations and can be available to reconstruct the database at any given point in time in the event that a database media failure occurs. For example, if the disk drive containing the datafiles crashes, the contents of the database can be recovered to a point in time before the crash, given the availability of a recent backup of the datafiles, the redo log files, and the archived log files that were generated since the backup occurred.

The use of multiple archived log destinations for filled redo log files is critical for one of Oracle's high-availability features known as *Oracle Data Guard*, formerly known as Oracle Standby Database.

Initialization Parameter Files

When a database instance starts, the memory for the Oracle instance is allocated, and one of two types of *initialization parameter files* is opened: either a text-based file called ***init<SID>.ora*** (known generically as **init.ora** or a PFILE) or a *server parameter file* (SPFILE). The instance first looks for an SPFILE in the default location for the operating system (**$ORACLE_HOME/dbs** on Unix, for example) as either ***spfile<SID>.ora*** or **spfile.ora**. If neither of these files exists, the instance looks for a PFILE with the name ***init<SID>.ora***. Alternatively, the STARTUP command can explicitly specify a PFILE to use for startup of Oracle.

Initialization parameter files, regardless of their format, specify file locations for trace files, control files, filled redo log files, and so forth. They also set limits on the sizes of the various structures in the System Global Area (SGA), as well as how many users can connect to the database simultaneously.

Until Oracle Database 9*i*, using the **init.ora** file was the only way to specify initialization parameters for the instance. Although it is easy to edit with a text editor, the file has some drawbacks. If a dynamic system parameter is changed at the command line with the ALTER SYSTEM command, the DBA must remember to change the **init.ora** file so that the new parameter value will be in effect the next time the instance is restarted.

An SPFILE makes parameter management easier and more effective for the DBA. If an SPFILE is in use for the running instance, any ALTER SYSTEM command that changes an initialization parameter can change the initialization parameter automatically in the SPFILE, change it only for the running instance, or both. No editing of the SPFILE is necessary or even possible without corrupting the SPFILE.

Although you cannot mirror a parameter file or SPFILE *per se*, you can back up an SPFILE to an **init.ora** file. Both the **init.ora** file and the SPFILE for the Oracle instance should be backed up using conventional operating system commands or, in the case of an SPFILE, using Recovery Manager.

When the Database Configuration Assistant (DBCA) is used to create a database, an SPFILE is created by default.

Alert and Trace Log Files

When things go wrong, Oracle can and often does write messages to the *alert log* and, in the case of background processes or user sessions, *trace log* files.

The alert log file, located in the directory specified by the initialization parameter BACKGROUND_DUMP_DEST, contains the most significant routine status messages as well as critical error conditions. When the database is started up or shut down, a message is recorded in the alert log, along with a list of initialization parameters that are different from their default values. In addition, any ALTER DATABASE or ALTER SYSTEM command issued by the DBA are recorded. Operations involving tablespaces and their datafiles are recorded here, too, such as adding a tablespace, dropping a tablespace, and adding a datafile to a tablespace. Error conditions, such as tablespaces running out of space, corrupted redo logs, and so forth, are also recorded here—all critical conditions.

The trace files for the Oracle instance background processes are also located in BACKGROUND_DUMP_DEST. For example, the trace files for PMON (process monitor) and SMON (system monitor) contain an entry when an error occurs or when SMON needs to perform instance recovery; the trace files for QMON (queue monitor) contain informational messages when it spawns a new process.

Trace files are also created for individual user sessions or connections to the database. These trace files are located in the directory specified by the initialization parameter USER_DUMP_DEST. Trace files for user processes are created in two situations: They are created when some type of error occurs in a user session because of a privilege problem, running out of space, and so forth. A trace file can be created for a user session on demand, to aid with problem diagnosis, with this command:

```
ALTER SESSION SET SQL_TRACE=TRUE;
```

Trace information is generated for each SQL statement that the user executes, which can be helpful when tuning a user's SQL statement.

The alert log file can be deleted or renamed at any time; it is re-created the next time an alert log message is generated. The DBA will often set up a daily batch job (through either an operating system mechanism, the Oracle Database internal scheduling mechanism, or Oracle Enterprise Manager's scheduler) to rename and archive the alert log on a daily basis.

As of Oracle Database 11*g* Release 1, the diagnostics for an instance are centralized in a single directory specified by the initialization parameter DIAGNOSTIC_DEST; USER_DUMP_DEST and BACKGROUND_DUMP_DEST are ignored.

Backup Files

Backup files can originate from a number of sources, such as operating system copy commands or Oracle RMAN. If the DBA performs a "cold" backup, the backup files are simply operating system copies of the datafiles, redo log files, control files, archived redo log files, and so forth.

In addition to bit-for-bit image copies of datafiles (the default in RMAN), RMAN can generate full and incremental backups of datafiles, control files, archived redo log files, and SPFILEs that are in a special format, called *backupsets*, readable only by RMAN. RMAN backupset backups are generally smaller than the original datafiles because RMAN does not back up unused blocks. RMAN is the standard for backup and recovery management, except in situations where RMAN backup processing has a detrimental effect on performance.

Oracle Memory Structures

Oracle uses the server's physical memory to hold many things for an Oracle instance: the Oracle executable code itself, session information, individual processes associated with the database, and information shared between processes (such as locks on database objects). In addition, the memory structures contain user and data dictionary SQL statements, along with cached information that is eventually permanently stored on disk, such as data blocks from database segments and information about completed transactions in the database. The data area allocated for an Oracle instance is called the *System Global Area (SGA)*. The Oracle executables reside in the software code area. In addition, an area called the *Program Global Area (PGA)* is private to each server and background process; one PGA is allocated for each user session or server process.

Figure 1-3 shows the relationships between these Oracle memory structures.

FIGURE 1-3 Oracle logical memory structures

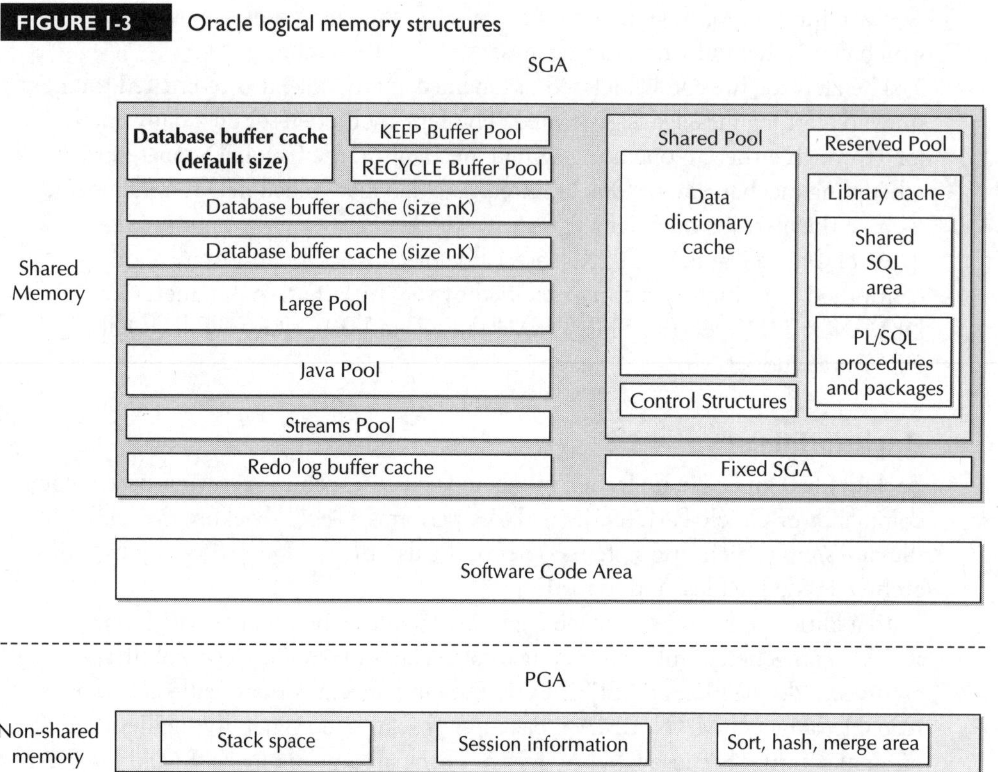

System Global Area

The SGA is a group of memory structures for an Oracle instance, shared by the users of the database instance. When an Oracle instance is started, memory is allocated for the SGA based on the values specified in the initialization parameter file or hard-coded in the Oracle software. Many of the parameters that control the size of the various parts of the SGA are dynamic (can be changed immediately while the instance is running); however, if the parameter SGA_MAX_SIZE is specified, the total size of all SGA areas must not exceed the value of SGA_MAX_SIZE. If SGA_MAX_SIZE is not specified but the parameter SGA_TARGET is specified, Oracle automatically adjusts the sizes of the SGA components so that the total amount of memory allocated is equal to SGA_TARGET. SGA_TARGET is a dynamic parameter; it can be changed while the instance is running. The parameter MEMORY_TARGET, new as of Oracle 11g, balances all memory available to Oracle between the SGA and the PGA to optimize performance.

Memory in the SGA is allocated in units of *granules*. A granule can be either 4MB or 16MB, depending on the total size of the SGA. If the SGA is less than or equal to 128MB, a granule is 4MB; otherwise, it is 16MB. The next few subsections cover the highlights of how Oracle uses each section in the SGA.

Buffer Caches The database *buffer* cache holds blocks of data from disk that have been recently read to satisfy a SELECT statement or that contain modified blocks that have been changed or added from a DML statement. As of Oracle Database 9*i*, the memory area in the SGA that holds these data blocks is dynamic. This is a good thing, considering that there may be tablespaces in the database with block sizes other than the default block size. Oracle allows for tablespaces with up to five different block sizes (one block size for the default and up to four others). Each block size requires its own buffer cache. As the processing and transactional needs change during the day or during the week, the values of DB_CACHE_SIZE and DB_*n*K_CACHE_SIZE can be dynamically changed without restarting the instance to enhance performance for a tablespace with a given block size.

Oracle can use two additional caches with the same block size as the default (DB_CACHE_SIZE) block size: the KEEP buffer pool and the RECYCLE buffer pool. As of Oracle Database 9*i*, both pools allocate memory independently of other caches in the SGA.

When a table is created, you can specify the pool where the table's data blocks will reside by using the BUFFER_POOL_KEEP or BUFFER_POOL_RECYCLE clause in the STORAGE clause. For tables that you use frequently throughout the day, it would be advantageous to place the tables into the KEEP buffer pool to minimize the I/O needed to retrieve blocks in the tables.

Shared Pool The *shared pool* contains two major subcaches: the library cache and the data dictionary cache. The shared pool is sized by the SHARED_POOL_SIZE initialization parameter. This is another dynamic parameter that can be resized as long as the total SGA size is less than SGA_MAX_SIZE or SGA_TARGET.

The *library cache* holds information about SQL and PL/SQL statements that are run against the database. In the library cache, because it is shared by all users, many different database users can potentially share the same SQL statement.

Along with the SQL statement, the execution plan of the SQL statement is stored in the library cache. The second time an identical SQL statement is run, by the same user or a different user, the execution plan is already computed, improving the execution time of the query or DML statement.

If the library cache is sized too small, then frequently used execution plans can be flushed out of the cache, requiring just as frequent reloads of SQL statements into the library cache.

The *data dictionary* is a collection of database tables, owned by the SYS and SYSTEM schemas, which contain the metadata about the database, its structures, and the privileges and roles of database users. The *data dictionary cache* holds a subset of the columns from data dictionary tables after first being read into the buffer cache. Data blocks from tables in the data dictionary are used continually to assist in processing user queries and other DML commands.

If the data dictionary cache is too small, requests for information from the data dictionary will cause extra I/O to occur; these I/O-bound data dictionary requests are called *recursive calls* and should be avoided by sizing the data dictionary cache correctly.

Redo Log Buffer The *redo log buffer* holds the most recent changes to the data blocks in the datafiles. When the redo log buffer is one-third full, or every 3 seconds, Oracle writes redo log records to the redo log files. Additionally, as of Oracle Database 10g, the Log Writer (LGWR) process will write the redo log records to the redo log files when 1MB of redo is stored in the redo log buffer. The entries in the redo log buffer, once written to the redo log files, are critical to database recovery if the instance crashes before the changed data blocks are written from the buffer cache to the datafiles. A user's committed transaction is not considered complete until the redo log entries have been successfully written to the redo log files.

Large Pool The *large pool* is an optional area of the SGA. It is used for transactions that interact with more than one database, message buffers for processes performing parallel queries, and RMAN parallel backup and restore operations. As the name implies, the large pool makes available large blocks of memory for operations that need to allocate large blocks of memory at a time.

The initialization parameter LARGE_POOL_SIZE controls the size of the large pool and is a dynamic parameter.

Java Pool The *Java pool* is used by the Oracle Java Virtual Machine (JVM) for all Java code and data within a user session. Storing Java code and data in the Java pool is analogous to SQL and PL/SQL code cached in the shared pool.

Streams Pool Starting with Oracle 10g, the *streams pool* is sized by using the initialization parameter STREAMS_POOL_SIZE. The streams pool holds data and control structures to support the Oracle Streams feature of Oracle Enterprise Edition.

Oracle Streams manages the sharing of data and events in a distributed environment. If the initialization parameter STREAMS_POOL_SIZE is uninitialized or set to zero, the memory used for Streams operations is allocated from the shared pool and can use up to 10 percent of the shared pool.

Program Global Area The PGA is an area of memory allocating dynamic sections of itself, privately for one set of connection processes. The configuration of the PGA depends on the connection configuration of the Oracle database: either *shared server* or *dedicated server*.

In a shared server configuration, multiple users share a connection to the database, minimizing memory usage on the server but potentially affecting response time for user requests. In a shared server environment, the SGA holds the persistent session information for a user instead of the PGA. Shared server environments are ideal for a large number of simultaneous connections to the database with infrequent or short-lived requests.

In a dedicated server environment, each user process gets its own connection to the database; the PGA contains the session memory for this configuration. The PGA also includes a sort area that is used whenever a user request requires a sort, bitmap merge, or hash join operation.

As of Oracle Database 9*i*, the PGA_AGGREGATE_TARGET parameter, in conjunction with the WORKAREA_SIZE_POLICY initialization parameter, can ease system administration by allowing the DBA to choose a total size for all work areas and let Oracle manage and allocate the memory between all user processes. As mentioned earlier in this chapter, the parameter MEMORY_TARGET manages the PGA and SGA memory as a whole to optimize performance. The MEMORY_TARGET parameter can help to manage the sizing of PGA and SGA as a whole. In general, PGA was automated starting in Oracle Database 9*i*. SGA was automated in 10*g*. Starting with Oracle Database 11*g*, the sum of SGA and PGA is now automated as well. Even experienced DBAs find that automated memory structuring is more effective at managing memory allocations.

Software Code Area Software code areas store the Oracle executable files that are running as part of an Oracle instance. These code areas are static in nature and change only when a new release of the software is installed. Typically, the Oracle software code areas are located in a privileged memory area separate from other user programs.

Oracle software code is strictly read-only and can be installed as either sharable or nonsharable. Installing Oracle software code as sharable saves memory when multiple Oracle instances are running on the same server, at the same software release level.

Background Processes

When an Oracle instance starts, multiple background processes start. A *background process* is a block of executable code designed to perform a specific task. Figure 1-4 shows the relationship between the background processes, the database, and the Oracle SGA. In contrast to a foreground process, such as a SQL*Plus session or a web browser, a background process works behind the scenes. Together, the SGA and the background processes make up an Oracle instance.

FIGURE 1-4 Oracle background processes

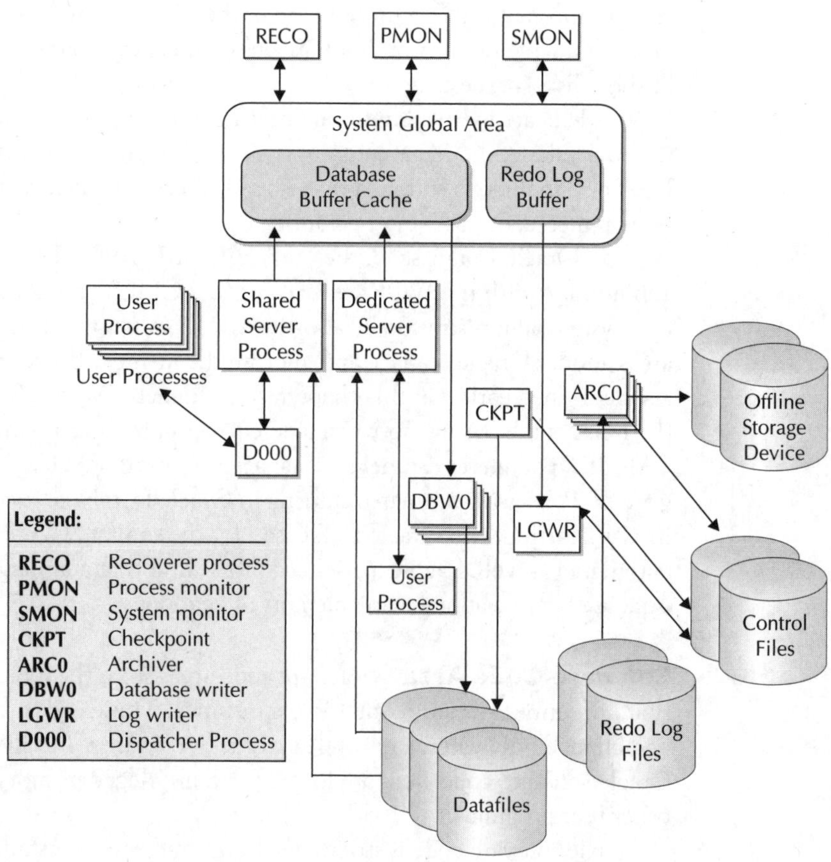

SMON In the case of a system crash or instance failure due to a power outage or CPU failure, SMON, the *system monitor* process, performs crash recovery by applying the entries in the online redo log files to the datafiles. In addition, temporary segments in all tablespaces are purged during system restart.

One of SMON's routine tasks is to coalesce the free space in tablespaces on a regular basis if the tablespace is dictionary managed (which should be rare or nonexistent in an Oracle Database or 12*c* database).

PMON If a user connection is dropped or a user process otherwise fails, PMON, the *process monitor*, does the cleanup work. It cleans up the database buffer cache along with any other resources that the user connection was using. For example, suppose a user session is updating some rows in a table, placing a lock on one or more of the rows. A thunderstorm knocks out the power at the user's desk, and the SQL*Plus session disappears when the workstation is powered off. Within milliseconds, PMON will detect that the connection no longer exists and perform the following tasks:

- Roll back the transaction that was in progress when the power went out
- Mark the transaction's blocks as available in the buffer cache
- Remove the locks on the affected rows in the table
- Remove the process ID of the disconnected process from the list of active processes

PMON will also interact with the listeners by providing information about the status of the instance for incoming connection requests.

DBW*n* The *database writer* process, known as DBWR in older versions of Oracle, writes new or changed data blocks (known as *dirty blocks*) in the buffer cache to the datafiles. Using a least recently used (LRU) algorithm, DBW*n* writes the oldest, least active blocks first. As a result, the most commonly requested blocks, even if they are dirty blocks, are in memory.

Up to 100 DBW*n* processes can be started: DBW0 through DBW9, DBWa through DBWz, and BW36 through BW99. The number of DBW*n* processes is controlled by the DB_WRITER_PROCESSES parameter.

LGWR LGWR, or *Log Writer*, is in charge of redo log buffer management. LGWR is one of the most active processes in an instance with heavy DML activity. A transaction is not considered complete until LGWR successfully writes the redo information, including the commit record, to the redo log files. In addition, the dirty buffers in the buffer cache cannot be written to the datafiles by DBW*n* until LGWR has written the redo information.

If the redo log files are grouped and one of the multiplexed redo log files in a group is damaged, LGWR writes to the remaining members of the group and records an error in the alert log file. If all members of a group are unusable, the LGWR process fails and the entire instance hangs until the problem can be corrected.

ARC*n* If the database is in ARCHIVELOG mode, then the *archiver process*, or ARC*n*, copies redo logs to one or more destination directories, devices, or network locations whenever a redo log fills up and redo information starts to fill the next redo log in sequence. Optimally, the archive process finishes before the filled redo log is needed again; otherwise, serious performance problems occur—users cannot complete their transactions until the entries are written to the redo log files, and the redo log file is not ready to accept new entries because it is still being written to the archive location. At least three potential solutions to this problem exist: make the redo log files larger, increase the number of redo log groups, and increase the number of ARC*n* processes. Up to 10 ARC*n* processes can be started for each instance by increasing the value of the LOG_ARCHIVE_MAX_PROCESSES initialization parameter.

CKPT The *checkpoint process*, or CKPT, helps to reduce the amount of time required for instance recovery. During a checkpoint, CKPT updates the header of the control file and the datafiles to reflect the last successful *system change number* (SCN). A checkpoint occurs automatically every time one redo log file fills and Oracle starts to fill the next one in a round-robin sequence.

The DBW*n* processes routinely write dirty buffers to advance the checkpoint from where instance recovery can begin, thus reducing the *mean time to recovery (MTTR)*.

RECO The *recoverer process*, or RECO, handles failures of distributed transactions (that is, transactions that include changes to tables in more than one database). If a table in the CCTR (contact center) database is changed along with a table in the WHSE (data warehouse) database and the network connection between the databases fails before the table in the WHSE database can be updated, RECO will roll back the failed transaction.

ASM Overview

ASM is a multiplexing solution that automates the layout of datafiles, control files, and redo log files by distributing them across all available disks. When new disks are added to the ASM cluster, the database files are automatically redistributed across all disk volumes for optimal performance. The multiplexing features of an ASM cluster minimize the possibility of data loss and are generally more effective than a manual scheme that places critical files and backups on different physical drives. One of the key components of an ASM disk is a *disk group*, a collection of disks that ASM manages as a unit.

When creating a new tablespace or other database structure, such as a control file or redo log file, you can specify a disk group as the storage area for the database structure instead of an operating system file. ASM takes the ease of use of OMF and combines it with mirroring and striping features to provide a robust file system and logical volume manager that can even support multiple nodes in an Oracle Real Application Cluster (RAC). ASM eliminates the need to purchase a third-party logical volume manager.

ASM not only enhances performance by automatically spreading out database objects over multiple devices but also increases availability by allowing new disk devices to be added to the database without shutting down the database; ASM automatically rebalances the distribution of files with minimal intervention.

The following sections review the ASM architecture, show you how to create a special type of Oracle instance to support ASM, and show how to start up and shut down an ASM instance.

ASM Architecture

ASM divides the datafiles and other database structures into extents, and it divides the extents among all the disks in the disk group to enhance both performance and reliability. Instead of mirroring entire disk volumes, ASM mirrors the database objects to provide the flexibility to mirror or stripe the database objects differently depending on their type. Optionally, the objects may not be striped at all if the underlying disk hardware is already RAID enabled, part of a storage area network (SAN), or part of a network-attached storage (NAS) device.

Automatic rebalancing is another key feature of ASM. When an increase in disk space is needed, additional disk devices can be added to a disk group, and ASM moves a proportional number of files from one or more existing disks to the new disks to maintain the overall I/O balance across all disks. This happens in the background while the database objects contained in the disk files are still online and available to users. If the impact to the I/O subsystem is high during a rebalance operation, the speed at which the rebalance occurs can be set using an initialization parameter.

ASM requires a special type of Oracle instance to provide the interface between a traditional Oracle instance and the file system; the ASM software components are shipped with the Oracle Database software and are always available as a selection when you're selecting the storage type for the entire database while creating a database.

Using ASM does not, however, prevent you from mixing ASM disk groups with manual Oracle datafile management techniques. For example, you might have all of your tablespaces in ASM storage but have one tablespace created on your server's file system to make it easier to transport to another database. Still, the ease of use and performance of ASM makes a strong case for eventually using ASM disk groups for all your storage needs.

Two Oracle background processes introduced in Oracle Database 10*g* support ASM instances: the rebalancer (RBAL) and ARB*n*. RBAL coordinates the disk activity for disk groups, performing rebalancing when a disk is added or removed. ARB*n*, where *n* can be a number from 0 to 9, performs the actual extent movement between disks in the disk groups.

For RDBMS instances that use ASM disks, two new background processes exist as of Oracle Database 10*g*: ASMB and RBAL. ASMB performs the communication between the database and the ASM instance, whereas RBAL performs the opening and closing of the disks in the disk group on behalf of the database. This is the same process as RBAL in an ASM instance but performs a different, but related, function. In other words, the process behaves differently depending on the type of instance.

EXERCISE 1-1

Find New ASM-Related Processes in ASM and RDBMS Instances

For this exercise, identify the new background processes on a Linux server for both the RDBMS instance and the ASM instance. On Linux, every Oracle process has its own thread. You can either join the Oracle dynamic performance views V$BGPROCESS and V$SESSION or use the Linux **ps -ef** command and search for command names containing either the ASM or the RDBMS instance names.

1. Query **/etc/oratab** for the name of the ASM and RDBMS instances:

```
[oracle@oel63 ~]$ tail /etc/oratab
#
# Multiple entries with the same $ORACLE_SID are not allowed.
#
#
+ASM:/u01/app/product/12.1.0/grid:N:          # line added by Agent
```

```
complref:/u01/app/oracle/product/12.1.0/dbhome_1:N:      # line added by Agent
cdb01:/u01/app/oracle/product/12.1.0/dbhome_1:N:    # line added by Agent

[oracle@oel63 ~]$
```

2. Set the ORACLE_SID environment variable for the RDBMS instance; in this case, choose **complref**:

```
[oracle@dw ~]$ export ORACLE_SID=complref
```

3. Connect to the RDBMS instance and query V$SESSION and V$BGPROCESS to get the list of running processes:

```
[oracle@dw ~]$ sqlplus / as sysdba

SQL*Plus: Release 12.1.0.1.0 Production on Sun Feb 2 22:40:52 2014

Copyright (c) 1982, 2013, Oracle.  All rights reserved.

Connected to:
Oracle Database 12c Enterprise Edition Release 12.1.0.1.0 - 64bit Produc-
tion
With the Partitioning, Automatic Storage Management, OLAP, Advanced
Analytics and Real Application Testing options

SQL> select sid, serial#, process, name, description
  2>    from v$session join v$bgprocess using(paddr);

       SID    SERIAL# PROCESS   NAME   DESCRIPTION
---------- ---------- --------- ------ --------------------------------
--
       237          1 2886      PMON   process cleanup
       1            1 2893      VKTM   Virtual Keeper of TiMe process
       119          1 2897      GEN0   generic0
. . .
       238          1 2899      MMAN   Memory Manager
       358          1 2912      DBW0   db writer process 0
       127          3 3005      TMON   Transport Monitor
       3            1 2914      LGWR   Redo etc.
      121           1 2916      CKPT   checkpoint
      6             7 3011      FBDA   Flashback Data Archiver Process
      4             1 2922      SMON   System Monitor Process
       362          1 3009      SMCO   Space Manager Process
. . .
       360          1 2928      RBAL   ASM Rebalance master
       5            1 2930      ASMB   ASM Background
       124          1 2942      MARK   mark AU for resync coordinator
       123          1 2932      MMON   Manageability Monitor Process
       242          1 2934      MMNL   Manageability Monitor Process 2

24 rows selected.
SQL>
```

Note the processes RBAL and ASMB near the end of the list.

4. You can use the PID column to identify the Linux process number and query the Linux process directly:

```
SQL> !ps -f -p 2928
UID        PID  PPID  C STIME TTY          TIME CMD
oracle    2928     1  0 21:31 ?        00:00:00 ora_rbal_complref
SQL>
```

5. Next, check for the ASM background processes by setting the ORACLE_SID environment variable for the ASM instance (+ASM):

```
[oracle@oel63 ~]$ . oraenv
ORACLE_SID = [+ASM] ? +ASM
```

6. Connect to the ASM instance and query V$SESSION and V$BGPROCESS to get the list of running processes:

```
[oracle@dw ~]$ sqlplus / as sysasm
. . .
SQL> select sid, serial#, process, name, description
  2>  from v$session join v$bgprocess using(paddr);

       SID    SERIAL# PROCESS  NAME  DESCRIPTION
---------- ---------- -------- ----- ------------------------------
       283          1 2810     PMON  process cleanup
       1            1 2814     VKTM  Virtual Keeper of TiMe process
       3            1 2832     CKPT  checkpoint
       4            1 2840     GMON  diskgroup monitor
       142          1 2818     GEN0  generic0
       425          1 2812     PSP0  process spawner 0
       145          1 2842     MMON  Manageability Monitor Process
       427          1 2830     LGWR  Redo etc.
       284          1 2820     MMAN  Memory Manager
       285          1 2828     DBW0  db writer process 0
       428          1 2838     RBAL  ASM Rebalance master
       287          1 2844     MMNL  Manageability Monitor Process 2
       144          1 2834     SMON  System Monitor Process
       143          1 2826     DIA0  diagnosibility process 0
       2            1 2824     DIAG  diagnosibility process
       286          1 2836     LREG  Listener Registration
       147          1 2868     ASMB  ASM Background
17 rows selected.
SQL>
```

Note the processes RBAL and ASMB in the list. The ARB*n* process starts when a rebalance operation is initiated.

Database Failures and Backup Solutions

Eventually, your database will have some kind of failure whether it be a network failure, user error, disk drive failure, or memory corruption issue causing an instance failure. The best way to prepare for this nearly inescapable occurrence is to have a backup and recovery plan in place. This backup and recovery plan should also be tested on a regular basis to make sure that the recovery techniques will be successful if they are ever needed.

To create a successful backup and recovery strategy, you must first understand the types of failures and how Oracle responds to each of them: Some require no immediate user intervention, and some do. Which backup and recovery solutions you leverage depend on many factors, including how fast you need to recover from a failure and how many resources you want to dedicate to the solution. Your investment in recovery infrastructure is proportional to the cost of lost productivity or business income if the database is unavailable for a day, an hour, or a minute.

Failure Categories

The types of failures or errors you may encounter fall into two general categories: physical and logical. Physical errors are generally hardware errors or software errors in the applications using the database, while logical errors are typically at the end user level (database users or administrators). The categories of failures are as follows:

- **Statement failure** A user's SELECT or DML statement failed because of permissions, syntax, or resource limits.
- **User error** The user mistakenly dropped a table or deleted the wrong rows in a table.
- **User process failure** The connection to the database failed because of a client disconnect or unexpected shutdown.
- **Network failure** As the name implies, the network connection between the client and the server (database) failed because of network hardware or protocol errors.
- **Instance failure** The database instance crashed because of a bug, OS errors, memory corruption, or even power loss to the server.
- **Media failure** There were disk drive physical errors or a controller hardware failure.

These failure categories are in the order of least serious and easiest to recover from to the most serious and harder to recover from. Specifically, statement failures are the easiest to recover from since they are almost always user managed: Rewrite the SELECT or INSERT statement so it does not generate a syntax error! Accidentally dropping an important table can be recovered by the user or by the database administrator depending on whether the dropped table is still in the recycle bin or whether the DBA has given the user privileges to use various flashback features. Recovery from network, instance, or media failure will necessitate varying actions, the choice of which will depend on the criticality and severity of any lost data.

Your backup and recovery strategy will need to account for all of these failures, even though some of these failures are easier to recover from than others. For example, an instance failure may be because of a power outage. The recovery of committed transactions is relatively painless and automatic as long as your online redo log files are intact and multiplexed.

Oracle Backup and Recovery Solutions

Your *recovery time objective* (RTO) is the target in which a recovery operation must be completed to meet your customer's or client's service level agreement (SLA). Various Oracle tools and technologies will apply depending on the RTO:

- **Days or hours** RMAN (and optionally Oracle Secure Backup) can recover your database in days or hours if the entire database is lost because of natural disaster or disk failures.
- **Hours or minutes** Various flashback technologies, either user-initiated or DBA-initiated, can recover database objects usually while the database is still available to other users. Although the database needs to be temporarily shut down, by using a flashback database the DBA can roll back the entire database to a point in time earlier in the day or even weeks ago depending on the storage available in the fast recovery area and the restore points defined.
- **Minutes or seconds** If the database must be available continuously with downtimes no longer than a few minutes, Oracle solutions such as Data Guard or Active Data Guard can fail over to a backup database with minimal or no intervention from the DBA.
- **Recovery analysis** Regardless of the type of failure or RTO, the Oracle Data Recover Advisor makes it easy to quickly determine the type of failure and the fastest way to recover from a specific type of failure.

Recovery Manager Recovery Manager is the primary tool you use to back up, restore, and recover database objects from the table level (new to Oracle Database 12*c*) to the datafile, tablespace, and of course database level. RMAN has many uses outside of backup and recovery, including the cloning or duplication of a database to another location.

A key component of RMAN is a special location for backup and recovery objects called the *fast recovery area* (FRA), explained in detail in Chapter 2. While this area is ideally a disk group in ASM, it can also be located in an operating system (OS) file system. Regardless of location, it is a centralized place for all backup and recovery objects. The FRA is managed based on size and your recovery objectives, whether that's based on the recovery window or on the number of backups you need to retain.

Oracle Secure Backup In conjunction with RMAN, Oracle Secure Backup (OSB) will take RMAN backups from the FRA and copy them to a tape device or to cloud storage to prevent loss of data from a catastrophic failure at a data center. OSB also provides an extension to RMAN at the OS level to back up Linux servers as well as any attached storage such as in a NAS appliance.

Oracle Data Guard Oracle Data Guard is one of Oracle's high-availability (HA) solutions to ensure near-real-time availability because of a failure of the primary database or to prevent database corruptions. A standby database receives archived redo log files from the primary database and maintains a secondary copy of the database that can be used in a number of scenarios beyond just disaster recovery. For example, during a scheduled maintenance window, the standby database can be switched to the role of primary database, while a new disk array is added to the primary database's server. A standby database can also play the temporary role of a read-only copy of the database for reporting purposes and therefore free up resources on the primary database for better response time in an OLTP environment. This configuration is a special type of Data Guard configuration called Active Data Guard.

One primary database can update up to 30 standby databases (31 if you count the local archived redo log destination defined by the LOG_ARCHIVE_DEST_*n* parameter). One standby database can be updated in real time; another standby database can be updated with a lag time of 30 minutes or more to guard against the propagation of logical errors from the primary database.

Another type of standby database is called a *logical standby database*. Instead of continuously applying archived redo log files to a physical copy of the primary database, a logical standby database receives only the equivalent DML SQL statements that were submitted to the primary database. Therefore, the standby database is *logically* equivalent to the standby database but will almost certainly not have the identical *physical* structure of the primary database.

CERTIFICATION SUMMARY

This chapter started with a review of the Oracle Database architecture. Some of this material has been covered in previous coursework, but a refresher course is always helpful for day-to-day database administration. More importantly, understanding the basic Oracle tablespace architecture is a prerequisite for understanding how ASM disk groups will store and manage Oracle tablespaces. In addition, understanding the basic Oracle background process architecture will dovetail nicely into a discussion of the ASM-related background processes available in both an ASM instance and an RDBMS instance.

Oracle provides a number of backup and recovery tools to meet the needs of any recovery time objective whether it be days, hours, or minutes. The tools center on Recovery Manager and include the fast recovery area and extensions to RMAN such as Oracle Secure Backup. Oracle Data Guard continuously protects a primary database by sending physical (archived redo log files) or logical (SQL DML statements) updates to one or more standby databases that can be used for both failover and offloading of reporting requests.

TWO-MINUTE DRILL

Explain Oracle Backup and Recovery Solutions

- ❑ Oracle database logical structures include tablespaces, segments, extents, and blocks, in order of increasing granularity.
- ❑ At a minimum, a database must have a SYSTEM tablespace and a SYSAUX tablespace.
- ❑ Oracle database physical structures include datafiles, redo log files, control files, archived log files, initialization parameter files, alert/trace files, and backup files.
- ❑ Oracle memory structures include the System Global Area, the Program Global Area, and the software code area.
- ❑ The primary Oracle background processes are SMON, PMON, DBW*n*, LGWR, ARC*n*, CKPT, and RECO.
- ❑ The background processes that support ASM instances are RBAL and ARB*n*; RDBMS instances that use ASM disks have the ASMB and RBAL background processes.
- ❑ ASM requires a dedicated instance for managing shared disks, called, not surprisingly, an ASM instance.
- ❑ Automatic rebalancing of disks in an ASM disk group happens in the background when disks are added or removed from an ASM disk group.
- ❑ The RBAL background process in an ASM instance coordinates disk activity for disk groups; the ARB*n* processes perform the actual extent movement between the disks in a disk group.
- ❑ The ASMB background process in an RDBMS instance performs the communication between the database and the ASM instance; the RBAL background process performs the opening and closing of the disks in the disk group for the RDBMS instance.
- ❑ An ASM instance has an initialization parameter file and a password file, but since there are no datafiles in an ASM instance, there is therefore no data dictionary; all connections to an ASM instance use operating system authentication.

- The new SYSASM privilege in an ASM instance facilitates the separation of database administration and storage administration in an ASM instance.
- Recovery Manager provides a flexible set of tools to back up and recover a database as well as to clone a database.
- Oracle Secure Backup can copy RMAN backups, local file systems, and objects from NAS devices to tape or cloud backup.
- Oracle Data Guard can send continuous changes from a primary database to up to 30 locations (standby databases) plus a local destination.
- Standby databases can be physical or logical. Active Data Guard (physical) databases are maintained with archived redo log files, whereas a logical standby database uses SQL DML statements.
- Active Data Guard databases can be used in read-only mode to support reporting requirements to free up resources on the primary database.

SELF TEST

The following questions will help you measure your understanding of the material presented in this chapter. Read all the choices carefully because there might be more than one correct answer. Choose all correct answers for each question.

Explain Oracle Backup and Recovery Solutions

1. Which of the following tablespaces are required in an installation of Oracle Database 12*c*? (Choose all that apply.)
   - A. USERS
   - B. SYSTEM
   - C. SYSAUX
   - D. TEMP
   - E. UNDOTBS1
   - F. RMAN
2. What is the maximum number of database writer processes (DBW*n*) in an Oracle database instance?
   - A. 1.
   - B. 100.
   - C. 20.
   - D. None; database writer processes exist only in an ASM instance.
3. Which of the following background processes exist in both an ASM instance and an RDBMS instance and also support ASM disk groups? (Choose all that apply.)
   - A. ASMB
   - B. RBAL
   - C. ARB*n*
   - D. LGWR
   - E. ARC*n*
4. At which level does ASM perform mirroring?
   - A. At the database object level.
   - B. At the tablespace level.
   - C. At the disk volume level.
   - D. ASM does not perform mirroring; it only supports disk hardware that is already RAID-enabled.

5. What is the value for INSTANCE_TYPE in the **init.ora** file or SPFILE for an ASM instance?

A. RDBMS.

B. ASM.

C. +ASM.

D. NOMOUNT.

E. There is no such initialization parameter INSTANCE_TYPE.

6. You connect to an ASM instance with connected RDBMS instances as SYSOPER and run this command:

```
SQL> shutdown immediate
```

What happens?

A. The ASM instance shuts down immediately, and all connected RDBMS instances shut down with the ABORT option.

B. The ASM instance shuts down immediately, and all connected RDBMS instances shut down with the IMMEDIATE option.

C. The command is ignored, since the SYSOPER privilege does not include starting up or shutting down an ASM instance.

D. The ASM instance is not shut down because there is at least one connected RDBMS instance.

7. The value of the initialization parameter ASM_DISKGROUPS on your ASM instance is the following:

```
DATA, RECOV, DATA2
```

What happens when the ASM instance starts? (Choose the best answer.)

A. Nothing happens until you issue ALTER DISKGROUP MOUNT commands.

B. The ASM instance automatically mounts the disk groups, and you can manually mount any disk groups not in the list.

C. ASM_DISKGROUPS is valid only for RDBMS instances.

D. The disk devices DATA, RECOV, and DATA2 are available to create new disk groups.

8. Which of the following parameters are required for an ASM instance? (Choose all that apply.)

A. INSTANCE_NAME

B. INSTANCE_TYPE

C. ASM_DISKGROUPS

D. ASM_POWER_LIMIT

E. ASM_PREFERRED_READ_FAILURE_GROUPS

9. Which of the following failures would be considered user errors? (Choose all that apply.)
   A. The intern just got a user account on the database and tries to update her own salary in the HR.EMPLOYEES table.
   B. Because of a power outage, the report server goes down during the overnight report batch window and is not able to generate most of the daily reports.
   C. Several users think the database has been upgraded to Oracle Database 12*c* and try to create a table with a VARCHAR2 column of more than 4,000 characters.
   D. The Linux administrator accidentally kills an OS process belonging to a database user who is trying to run a SELECT statement against the data warehouse.
   E. A data warehouse programmer enters the server room and removes a network card from the primary database server.

10. Which Oracle HA technology would be best suited for near-real-time failover in the case of a complete media failure of all disks in the primary database?
   A. Logical standby database
   B. Oracle Active Data Guard read-only access
   C. Oracle flashback database
   D. Oracle Active Data Guard physical standby

SELF TEST ANSWERS

Explain Oracle Backup and Recovery Solutions

1. ☑ **B** and **C.** Both the SYSTEM and SYSAUX tablespaces are required.
☒ **A, D, E,** and **F** are incorrect. While the USERS tablespace is highly desirable for placing application tables in its own tablespace, it is not required; TEMP, USERS, and UNDOTBS1 are created in a default installation of Oracle Database 11*g*. No RMAN tablespace is created, nor is it required in an installation of Oracle Database 11*g*.

2. ☑ **B.** The database writer processes are DBW0 through DBW9 and, if needed, DBWa through DBWz and BW36 through BW99 (for a total of 100) on most operating system platforms.
☒ **A, C,** and **D** are incorrect. Database writers exist only in an RDBMS instance.

3. ☑ **B.** Only the RBAL process exists in both ASM and RDBMS instances for ASM operations. RBAL coordinates the disk activity for disk groups in an ASM instance. RBAL performs the opening and closing of the disks in a disk group in an RDBMS instance, on behalf of the database.
☒ **A, C, D,** and **E** are incorrect. **A** is incorrect because ASMB exists only in an RDBMS instance that uses ASM disks. **C** is incorrect because ARB*n* exists only in an ASM instance and performs the extent movement between disks in disk groups. **D** is incorrect because LGWR exists only in an RDBMS instance and is not ASM related; it writes redo information to the online redo log files. **E** is incorrect because ARC*n* exists only in an RDBMS instance and is not ASM related; it writes online redo log files to archive redo log files when the database is in ARCHIVELOG mode.

4. ☑ **A.** ASM mirrors database objects only.
☒ **B, C,** and **D** are incorrect. ASM mirrors database objects to provide the flexibility to mirror or stripe each database object differently depending on their type. ASM does not need to mirror a given object if an underlying object is already mirrored by RAID hardware or the operating system.

5. ☑ **B.** As you might expect, INSTANCE_TYPE has a value of ASM for an ASM instance.
☒ **A, C, D,** and **E** are incorrect. **A** is valid only for an RDBMS (database) instance. **C** is the value for DB_UNIQUE_NAME in an ASM instance. **D** is an option to the STARTUP command. **E** is wrong because there is an initialization parameter called INSTANCE_TYPE and it defaults to RDBMS.

6. ☑ **D.** All connected RDBMS instances must be shut down before you can shut down an ASM instance with the IMMEDIATE option. If you stop an ASM instance with the ABORT option, all connected RDBMS instances are stopped.
☒ **A, B,** and **C** are incorrect. **A** is incorrect because RDBMS instances shut down with ABORT only if the ASM instance shuts down with the ABORT option or the ASM instance

crashes. **B** is incorrect because you must explicitly shut down connected RDBMS instances first. **C** is incorrect because the SYSOPER privilege, while not as powerful as the SYSDBA or SYSASM privilege, does have the power to start and stop ASM instances.

7. ☑ **B.** The ASM instance automatically mounts the specified disk groups, and you can manually mount any disk groups not in the list.
☒ **A, C,** and **D** are incorrect. **A** is incorrect because ASM_DISKGROUPS facilitates automatic mounting of the specified disk groups at startup. **C** is incorrect because ASM_DISKGROUPS is valid only for ASM instances. **D** is incorrect because the parameter ASM_DISKGROUPS contains existing disk groups, not raw devices available for disk groups.

8. ☑ **B.** Only the INSTANCE_TYPE parameter is required, and its value must be ASM.
☒ **A, C, D,** and **E** are incorrect. ASM_DISKGROUPS can be empty, but then you must mount disk groups manually after starting an ASM instance. ASM_POWER_LIMIT defaults to 1 if it is not set; ASM_PREFERRED_READ_FAILURE_GROUPS, new to Oracle Database 11*g*, specifies a preferred failure group that is closest to the instance's node to improve performance in a clustered ASM environment.

9. ☑ **A** and **C.** User errors are typically logical errors with SQL syntax, permissions on database objects, or trying to use features not available in the current version of the database.
☒ **B, D,** and **E** are incorrect. **B** is a process failure since the client (in this case, the batch report generator) has failed and disconnects from the database. **D** is a user process failure except that the user's process fails because of an OS administrator killing the incorrect process. If the OS administrator had killed a global database process, the failure would likely be considered an instance failure instead. **E** is a hardware or network failure, not a user failure. The user will likely be looking for a job somewhere else.

10. ☑ **D.** Oracle Active Data Guard physical standby continuously applies archived redo log files on one or more (up to 30) remote locations (standby locations) and can be configured to almost instantaneously take over the role of the primary database in case of a catastrophic failure of the primary database. Any standby location can be configured to apply the archived redo logs after a predefined delay to avoid potential logical corruptions to the database even if there is not a catastrophic failure of the primary database.
☒ **A, B,** and **C** are incorrect. **A** is suitable for read-write access to report writers or developers but will not be an exact physical copy of the primary database. **B** is incorrect because using an Active Data Guard database for read-only queries is not providing a failover after a catastrophic failure but instead supplements the primary database for offloading some or all of the reporting workload. **C** is a viable option for recovering a database, tablespace, or individual database object to a previous state but does not provide real-time failover from a failure of the primary database.

CERTIFICATION OBJECTIVES

2.01	Configure and Manage RMAN Settings	2.04	Back Up and Recover a NOARCHIVELOG Database
2.02	Configure the Fast Recovery Area	✓	Two-Minute Drill
2.03	Configure Control Files and Redo Log Files for Recoverability	Q&A	Self Test

Oracle provides a variety of backup procedures and options that help protect an Oracle database. If they are properly implemented, these options will allow you to back up your databases and recover them easily and efficiently. Since Oracle Database 10g, you can use Recovery Manager (RMAN) to execute nearly all of your backup and recovery operations. In situations for which you cannot use RMAN for recovery, such as for a database that is not in ARCHIVELOG mode, user-managed backup and recovery is discussed at the end of this chapter.

The first part of this chapter gives you a refresher on both types of backups available to you: *logical* and *physical*. A logical backup backs up individual objects, such as a table or a schema; a physical backup backs up objects with a granularity at the file system level, such as the datafiles that make up a tablespace. A physical backup of a database can occur while the database is either online or offline. You must use RMAN for all online backups except for backing up tablespaces using operating system commands while they are in backup mode (ALTER TABLESPACE BEGIN BACKUP).

This chapter provides a warm-up to RMAN; however, before you can use RMAN to back up or recover a database, you must perform a number of steps. First, your database must be in ARCHIVELOG mode or you must have the database shut down and started up in MOUNT mode. Then, you must ensure that the retention policy and the number of archived log file destinations are appropriate for your environment.

This chapter provides a brief overview of the RMAN commands you'll use on a regular basis. Performing maintenance on the RMAN catalog, creating RMAN backups, and using RMAN backups for recovery are covered in Chapters 3, 4, and 5, respectively. RMAN secure backups are covered in Chapter 7, and using flashback features is covered in Chapter 8. Chapter 9 shows you how to easily duplicate a tablespace to another database or duplicate the entire database.

CERTIFICATION OBJECTIVE 2.01

Configure and Manage RMAN Settings

There are two general categories of backups, regardless of the tools used to make the backups: logical and physical. As the name implies, *logical backups* make a copy of the rows in the table optionally including the indexes defined on the tables for improved retrieval of the rows in the table. A logical backup is independent of the physical storage characteristics of the tables on the disk and is therefore suitable for migration to a database on a different server, a database hosted by a different operating system, or a database stored on a server with a different architecture. Logical backups are most efficiently created and restored using the Oracle Data Pump utilities **expdp** and **impdp**.

In contrast, a *physical backup* copies and maintains the higher-level characteristics of the containers that comprise the tables and indexes in the database such as datafiles. Using physical backups makes the transfer of database tables to other servers much faster since the tables within a datafile and subsequently in a tablespace are exported and imported as a group without re-creating the relative locations of the tables and indexes within the tablespaces. For the same reason, physical backups make restore and recovery operations to the same database much faster.

The Oracle-recommended backup strategies for physical backups center on the Recovery Manager (RMAN) utility. RMAN commands can perform backups and recoveries in several ways depending on your backup retention policy, what you will use the backups for, and the resources available on the server itself such as the number of CPUs and the I/O characteristics. Understanding how to configure RMAN is just as important as performing the backup itself, so an overview of all RMAN commands is key to a robust and easily recoverable database environment.

Logical Backups

A logical backup of a database involves reading a set of database rows and writing them to a file. These records are read independently of their physical location. In Oracle, the Data Pump Export utility performs this type of database backup. To recover using the file generated from the Data Pump Export utility, you use the Data Pump Import utility.

Oracle's original Import and Export utilities (*imp *and* exp*), available prior to Oracle Database 10*g*, are still provided as part of the Oracle 12*c *installation but are no longer supported. Users of the old Export and Import utilities are encouraged to use Data Pump Export and Data Pump Import instead.

Oracle's Data Pump Export utility **expdp** queries the source database, including the data dictionary, and writes the output to a binary format file called an *export dump file*. You can export the full database, specific schemas or tablespaces, or specific tables. During exports, you can choose whether to export the data dictionary information associated with tables, such as grants, indexes, and constraints. The file written by Data Pump Export will contain the commands necessary to completely re-create all the chosen objects and data.

Once data has been exported via Data Pump Export, it can be imported into a target database using the Data Pump Import utility. Data Pump Import reads the dump file created by Data Pump Export and executes the commands found there. For example, these commands may include a CREATE TABLE command, followed by an INSERT command to load data into the table.

Data Pump Export and Data Pump Import can use a network connection for a simultaneous export and import operation, avoiding the use of intermediate operating system files and reducing total export and import time.

The data that has been exported does not have to be imported into the same database, or the same schema, that was used to generate the export dump file. You can use the export dump file to create and populate a duplicate set of the exported objects in a different schema in the same database or into a separate target database.

You can import either all or part of the exported data. If you import the entire export dump file from a full export, all the database objects, including tablespaces, datafiles, and users, will be created during the import. However, it is often useful to pre-create tablespaces and users in the target database in order to specify the physical distribution of objects in another database. This is one method of changing the physical structure of a database.

If you want to import part of the data from the export dump file, the tablespaces, datafiles, and users who will own and store that data should be set up in the target database prior to the import.

Physical Backups

Physical backups involve copying the files that constitute the database. These backups are also referred to as *file system backups* because they involve using operating system file backup commands. Oracle supports two types of physical file backups: *offline backups* and *online backups* (also known as *cold* and *hot backups*, respectively). You can (and as of Oracle Database 12*c*) use RMAN (covered in this chapter and in Chapters 3, 4, 5, 7, and 9) to perform all physical backups. You can optionally choose to write your own scripts to perform physical backups, but doing so will prevent you from obtaining many of the benefits of the RMAN approach.

Offline Backups

Consistent offline backups occur when the database has been shut down normally (that is, not because of instance failure) using the NORMAL, IMMEDIATE, or TRANSACTIONAL option of the SHUTDOWN command. While the database is offline, the following files should be backed up:

- All datafiles
- All control files
- All archived redo log files
- The **init.ora** file or server parameter file (SPFILE)
- Text-format files such as the password file and **tnsnames.ora**

on the Job

You should never want or need to back up online redo log files. While a slight time savings results from restoring from a cold backup after a clean shutdown, the risk of losing committed transactions outweighs the convenience. Your online redo logs should be mirrored and duplexed so that you effectively eliminate the chances of losing the current online log file.

Having all these files backed up while the database is closed provides a fixed or consistent image or snapshot of the database, as it existed at the time it was closed. The full set of these files could be restored from the backups on disk or tape at a later date, and the database would be able to function simply by restarting the database. It is *not* valid to perform a file system backup of the database while it is open or unless an online backup of tablespace datafiles is being performed with those tablespaces set into BACKUP mode.

A tablespace placed into BACKUP mode switches the tablespace datafiles offline for the purposes of reading and writing data. Any changes made to the tablespace while in backup mode will be wholly written to log files. This gives you datafiles that are static, can be copied to the file system, and can be used later for recovery and log entry restoration. When a tablespace is switched out of backup mode, all temporary changes made in log files will be applied to (recovered into) the datafile placed online.

Offline backups that occur following database aborts will also be considered inconsistent and can require more effort to use during recoveries—if the backups are usable. A database restarted after a crash needs the online redo log files for crash recovery, but since you do not back up online redo log files, data loss after restoring an inconsistent offline backup is virtually certain.

Online Backups

You can use online backups for any database that is running in ARCHIVELOG mode. In this mode, the online redo logs are archived, creating a log of all transactions within the database.

Oracle writes to the online redo log files in a cyclical fashion: After filling the first log file, it begins writing to the second, until that one fills; then it begins writing to the third, and so on. Once the last online redo log file is filled, the Log Writer (LGWR) background process begins to overwrite the contents of the first redo log file.

When Oracle is running in ARCHIVELOG mode, the ARC*n* (archiver) background processes make a copy of each redo log file before overwriting it. These archived redo log files are usually written to a disk device. The files can also be written directly to a tape device, but disk space is cheap enough that the additional cost of archiving to disk is offset by the time and labor savings when a disaster recovery operation must occur.

on the job

Most production databases, particularly those that support transaction-processing applications, must be run in ARCHIVELOG mode; using RMAN to back up the database while online requires that the database be in ARCHIVELOG mode.

You can perform file system backups of a database while that database is open, provided the database is running in ARCHIVELOG mode. An online backup involves setting each tablespace into a backup state, backing up its datafiles, and then restoring the tablespace to its normal state.

on the job

When using the RMAN utility, you do not have to manually place each tablespace into a backup state. RMAN reads the data blocks in the same manner Oracle uses for queries.

The database can be fully recovered from an online backup, and it can, via the archived redo logs, be rolled forward to any point in time before the failure. When the database is then opened, any committed transactions that were in the database at the time of the failure will have been restored, and any uncommitted transactions recorded in the redo log files and datafiles will have been rolled back.

While the database is open, the following files can be backed up:

- All datafiles
- All archived redo log files

- One control file, via the ALTER DATABASE BACKUP CONTROLFILE command
- The SPFILE

watch ***RMAN automatically backs up the control file and SPFILE whenever the entire database or the SYSTEM tablespace are backed up.***

Online backup procedures are powerful for two reasons: First, they provide full point-in-time recovery. Second, they allow the database to remain open during the file system backup. Even databases that cannot be shut down because of user requirements can still have recoverable backups taken. Keeping the database open also keeps the System Global Area (SGA) of the database instance from being cleared when the database is shut down and restarted. Keeping the SGA memory from being cleared will improve the database's performance because it will reduce the number of physical I/Os required by the database if it were restarted.

on the job ***You can use the FLASHBACK DATABASE option, introduced in Oracle Database 10g, to roll the database back in time without relying on physical backups. To use the FLASHBACK DATABASE command, you must have a fast recovery area defined, be running in ARCHIVELOG mode, and have issued the ALTER DATABASE FLASHBACK ON command while the database was mounted but not open. Logs written to the fast recovery area are used by Oracle during the FLASHBACK DATABASE operation. The configuration and use of the fast recovery area are covered in the "Configure the Fast Recovery Area" section of this chapter.***

RMAN Command Overview

You start RMAN from the operating system command line with, as you might expect, the RMAN command. (See the section "Configure the Fast Recovery Area" later in this chapter for instructions on using Enterprise Manager to perform RMAN operations in a GUI.) In the following sections, you'll learn how to start RMAN from the command line along with a brief overview of the command structure once you are at the RMAN> prompt. Typically, you will script your RMAN commands to avoid typing errors for repetitive operations. Most DBAs run ad hoc RMAN commands, especially when recovering a database.

Although you may not use them often, the RMAN commands for setting the RMAN backup retention policy must specify either the number of full backups to maintain or a window in which you need to be able to recover. You also want to ensure that your SLA for recoverability is met without using more disk space than you need.

Invoking RMAN

Here is a typical and simple invocation of RMAN that connects to a remote recovery catalog (recovery catalogs, schemas in other databases that store backup and structure information for your source database, are covered in Chapter 3):

```
[oracle@dw ~]$ rman target / catalog rman/rman@rac
```

In this example, the **target** option is used to connect to the database using operating system authentication, and the **catalog** option is used to connect to a recovery catalog in a different database. RMAN recovery catalog concepts are covered in painful detail in Chapter 3.

Although 16 different RMAN command-line options are available when you start RMAN, here are the most common ones:

- **target** Identifies the connect string for the Oracle database you want to back up
- **catalog** Specifies a recovery catalog database for backup information
- **nocatalog** Uses the control file for backup information
- **cmdfile** Specifies an input file containing a list of RMAN commands
- **log** Sets the name of the log file for RMAN messages

The **cmdfile** and **log** options make it easy to reuse a list of RMAN commands over and over and facilitate running RMAN from a batch process.

RMAN Command Types

The two basic types of RMAN commands are *standalone* commands and *job* commands. Standalone commands are executed only at the RMAN> prompt and are self-contained. Examples of standalone commands are CHANGE, CONNECT, CREATE SCRIPT, and CREATE CATALOG.

In contrast, job commands are usually grouped and run inside a command block using the RUN command. Within a command block, the failure of any command within the block terminates execution of the block. An example of an RMAN command that can be used only as a job command is ALLOCATE CHANNEL:

The channel allocation is valid only for the duration of the command block. (You would use CONFIGURE CHANNEL, a standalone command, to create a default channel.) An RMAN *channel* is one stream of data from the database to a device and corresponds to one database server session.

Here is an example of some commands run within a command block to back up the database, force the archiving of the current online redo log file, and remove obsolete backups:

```
RMAN> run
2> {
3>     backup as compressed backupset database;
4>     delete noprompt obsolete;
5> }
Starting backup at 15-MAR-13
using channel ORA_DISK_1
channel ORA_DISK_1: starting compressed full datafile backup set
. . .
```

Note that RMAN uses a default channel when you don't explicitly allocate a channel; in this case, it's the fast recovery area.

Some commands are both standalone and job commands; in other words, you can use them at the RMAN> command prompt or within a command block. For example, you can use BACKUP DATABASE as a standalone or within a command block; when you run BACKUP DATABASE as a standalone command, RMAN automatically allocates one or more channels based on defaults specified by CONFIGURE CHANNEL and whether you're using a fast recovery area.

Table 2-1 describes the RMAN commands you'll use on a regular basis, along with some common options and caveats for each command. For the complete list of all RMAN commands and their syntax, see *Oracle Database Backup and Recovery Reference, 12c Release 1*.

Using a Retention Policy

Backups can be automatically retained and managed using one of two methods: by a *recovery window* or by *redundancy*. Using a recovery window, RMAN will retain as many backups as necessary to bring the database to any point in time within the recovery window. For example, with a recovery window of seven days, RMAN will maintain enough image copies, incremental backups, and archived redo logs to ensure that the database can be restored and recovered to any point in time

TABLE 2-1 Common RMAN Commands

RMAN Command	Description
@	Runs an RMAN command script at the path name specified after the @. If no path is specified, the path is assumed to be the directory from which RMAN was invoked.
ADVISE FAILURE	Displays repair options for the failure found.
ALLOCATE CHANNEL	Creates a connection between RMAN and a database instance, initiating a database server session that performs the work of backing up, restoring, or recovering an RMAN backup.
BACKUP	Performs an RMAN backup, with or without archived redo logs. Backs up datafiles and datafile copies or performs an incremental level 0 or level 1 backup. Backs up an entire database or a single tablespace or datafile. Validates the blocks to be backed up with the VALIDATE clause.
CREATE SCRIPT	Creates a stored script in the recovery catalog.
CATALOG	Adds information about file copies and user-managed backups to the repository.
CHANGE	Changes the status of a backup in the RMAN repository. This is useful for explicitly excluding a backup from a restore or recovery operation or to notify RMAN that a backup file was inadvertently or deliberately removed by an operating system command outside of RMAN.
CONFIGURE	Configures the persistent parameters for RMAN. The parameters configured are available during every subsequent RMAN session unless they are explicitly cleared or modified.
CONVERT	Converts datafile formats for transporting tablespaces or entire databases across platforms.
CREATE CATALOG	Creates the repository catalog containing RMAN metadata for one or more target databases. It is strongly recommended that this catalog not be stored in one of the target databases.
CROSSCHECK	Checks the record of backups in the RMAN repository against the actual files on disk or tape. Objects are flagged as EXPIRED, AVAILABLE, UNAVAILABLE, or OBSOLETE. If the object is not available to RMAN, it is marked UNAVAILABLE.
DELETE	Deletes backup files or copies and marks them as DELETED in the target database control file. If a repository is used, the record of the backup file is removed.
DROP DATABASE	Deletes the target database from disk and unregisters it. The target database must be mounted in EXCLUSIVE mode. All datafiles, online redo logs, and control files are deleted. All metadata stored in the recovery catalog is removed.
DUPLICATE	Uses backups of the target database (or use the live database) to create a duplicate database.

TABLE 2-1 Common RMAN Commands (*Continued*)

RMAN Command	Description
FLASHBACK DATABASE	Performs a Flashback Database operation. The database is restored to a point in the past by System Change Number (SCN) or log sequence number using flashback logs to undo changes before the SCN or log sequence number, and then archived redo logs are applied to bring the database forward to a consistent state.
LIST	Displays information about backupsets and image copies recorded in the target database's RMAN repository (the catalog). See REPORT for identifying complex relationships between backupsets.
RECOVER	Performs a complete or incomplete recovery on a datafile, a tablespace, or the entire database. This can also apply incremental backups to a datafile image copy to roll it forward in time.
REGISTER DATABASE	Registers a target database in the RMAN repository.
REPAIR FAILURE	Repairs one or more failures recorded in the automated diagnostic repository (ADR).
REPORT	Performs a detailed analysis of the RMAN repository. For example, this command can identify which files need a backup to meet the retention policy or which backup files can be deleted.
RESTORE	Restores files from image copies or backupsets to disk, typically after a media failure. Can be used to validate a restore operation without actually performing the restore by specifying the PREVIEW option.
RUN	Runs a sequence of RMAN statements as a group when those commands are typed between braces: {***run this stuff***}. The braces form a group of commands, allowing you to override default RMAN parameters for the duration of the execution of the group.
SET	Sets RMAN configuration settings for the duration of the RMAN session, such as allocated disk or tape channels. Persistent settings are assigned with CONFIGURE.
SHOW	Shows all or individual RMAN configured settings.
SHUTDOWN	Shuts down the target database from within RMAN. Identical to the SHUTDOWN command within SQL*Plus.
STARTUP	Starts up the target database. This has the same options and function as the SQL*Plus STARTUP command.
SQL	Runs SQL commands in RMAN. Most SQL commands can be run in RMAN without the SQL qualifier unless there are both SQL and RMAN commands with the same name and you want to ensure that there is no ambiguity.
TRANSPORT TABLESPACE	Creates transportable tablespace sets from backup for one or more tablespaces.
VALIDATE	Examines a backupset and reports whether its data is intact and consistent.

within the last seven days. Any backups that are not needed to support this recovery window are marked as OBSOLETE and are automatically removed by RMAN if you are using a fast recovery area and disk space is needed for new backups.

In contrast, a redundancy retention policy directs RMAN to retain the specified number of backups (copies of datafiles and control file). Any extra copies or backups beyond the number specified in the redundancy policy are marked as OBSOLETE. As with a recovery window, obsolete backups are automatically removed if disk space is needed and the fast recovery area is used. Otherwise, you can use the DELETE OBSOLETE command to manually remove backup files and update the catalog.

If the retention policy is set to NONE, no backups or copies are ever considered obsolete, and the DBA must manually remove unneeded backups from the catalog and from disk. By default, the retention policy is a single copy (with the retention policy set to 1). You can set the retention policy to two copies using the following RMAN command:

```
RMAN> configure retention policy to redundancy 2;
```

The following example sets the retention policy to a recovery window of 4 days:

```
RMAN> configure retention policy to recovery window of 4 days;
old RMAN configuration parameters:
CONFIGURE RETENTION POLICY TO REDUNDANCY 2;
new RMAN configuration parameters:
CONFIGURE RETENTION POLICY TO RECOVERY WINDOW OF 4 DAYS;
new RMAN configuration parameters are successfully stored
RMAN>
```

Oracle best practices recommend using a recovery window, or a period of time in which it will be possible to uncover any problems with the database, such as an inadvertently dropped table or deleted rows in a table, and be able to perform a point-in-time recovery at just before the error occurred.

In some environments, you may want to disable the retention policy completely. This is useful in an environment where a backup system outside of RMAN stores the disk backups to tape and deletes them. As a result, RMAN does not need to decide when a backup is obsolete and therefore no retention policy is needed. As a result, the details of RMAN backups are maintained up to the time specified by the initialization parameter CONTROL_FILE_RECORD_KEEP_TIME. Here is how you can disable the retention policy:

```
RMAN> configure retention policy to none;
```

EXERCISE 2-1

Query and Change the Retention Policy

In this exercise, you will identify the current RMAN retention policy and change it.

Start RMAN without connecting to a **recovery catalog:**

```
[oracle@tettnang ~]$ rman target /

Recovery Manager: Release 12.1.0.1.0
       - Production on Mon Feb 10 12:44:11 2014

Copyright (c) 1982, 2013, Oracle and/or its affiliates.
   All rights reserved.
connected to target database: RPT12C (DBID=1766066998)
RMAN>
```

1. Show the existing retention policy:

```
RMAN> show retention policy;
using target database control file instead of recovery catalog
RMAN configuration parameters for database with db_unique_name RPT12C are:
CONFIGURE RETENTION POLICY TO RECOVERY WINDOW OF 4 DAYS;
RMAN>
```

2. Change the retention policy to a recovery window of ten days:

```
RMAN> configure retention policy to recovery window of 10 days;
old RMAN configuration parameters:
CONFIGURE RETENTION POLICY TO RECOVERY WINDOW OF 4 DAYS;
new RMAN configuration parameters:
CONFIGURE RETENTION POLICY TO RECOVERY WINDOW OF 10 DAYS;
new RMAN configuration parameters are successfully stored
RMAN>
```

CERTIFICATION OBJECTIVE 2.02

Configure the Fast Recovery Area

The *fast recovery area* (FRA), formerly known as the flash recovery area, available since Oracle Database 10*g*, is a unified storage location for all recovery-related files in an Oracle database. As the price of disk space drops, the convenience, increased availability, and decreased recovery times make a completely disk-based backup solution more desirable than tape backup.

Defining the Size and Location of the Fast Recovery Area

The fast recovery area can reside in a single file system directory or as an ASM disk group. In a default installation of Oracle Database 12*c*, you can easily configure the fast recovery area after you specify the location for the database's datafiles. Figure 2-1 shows the windows where you specify the location of the fast recovery area along with its size. In this example, the fast recovery area will reside in the ASM disk group +RECOV with a maximum size of 8GB.

All the files that you need to recover a database from a media failure or a logical error are contained in the fast recovery area. The files that can reside in the area are divided into two categories: *permanent* or *transient*. Permanent files are actively being

FIGURE 2-1 Storage Locations Recovery Related Files window

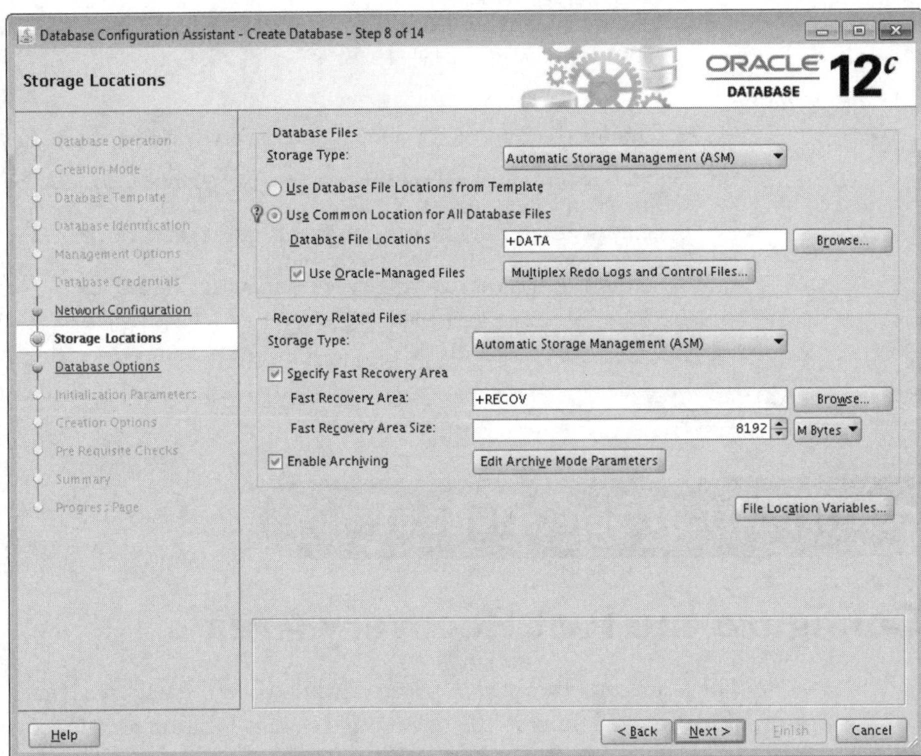

used by the database instance, and transient files are required only when you need to recover part of or the entire database.

The following permanent items are stored in the fast recovery area:

- **Control file** Oracle stores one or many copies of the control file in the fast recovery area during an installation.
- **Online redo log files** You can store one or more mirrored copies from each redo log file group in the fast recovery area.

The following transient items are stored in the fast recovery area:

- **Archived redo log files** When you configure the fast recovery area, one set of archived redo log files is stored in the fast recovery area.
- **Flashback logs** Flashback logs are stored in the fast recovery area when Flashback Database is enabled.
- **Control file copies** Control file copies are explicit (manual) backups of the control file.
- **Control file automatic backups** RMAN stores control file automatic backups in the fast recovery area. When RMAN backs up the first datafile, which is part of the SYSTEM tablespace, the control file is automatically included in the RMAN backup.
- **Datafile copies** When you use the RMAN command BACKUP AS COPY, the datafile copies are stored in the fast recovery area by default.
- **RMAN backupsets** Files created with the BACKUP AS BACKUPSET command are stored in the fast recovery area.
- **RMAN files** By default, RMAN uses the fast recovery area as a staging area for backup and recovery of the archive log files from disk or tape.

Three initialization parameters control the default locations for new control files, online redo log files, and datafiles: DB_CREATE_FILE_DEST, DB_RECOVERY_FILE_DEST, and DB_CREATE_ONLINE_LOG_DEST_*n*. DB_CREATE_FILE_DEST specifies the default location for Oracle-managed datafiles if you do not explicitly specify a destination. DB_CREATE_ONLINE_LOG_DEST_*n* specifies up to five locations for online redo log files; if this parameter is not specified and you create new or additional redo log files, Oracle uses DB_CREATE_FILE_DEST as the destination. Finally, DB_RECOVERY_FILE_DEST specifies the default location for the fast recovery area. If you use DB_RECOVERY_FILE_DEST, you must also specify DB_RECOVERY_FILE_DEST_SIZE. Here is an example of the values of these parameters in a default installation of Oracle Database 12*c*:

```
SQL> show parameter db_create

NAME                                 TYPE        VALUE
------------------------------------ ----------- ---------------
db_create_file_dest                  string      +DATA
db_create_online_log_dest_1          string
db_create_online_log_dest_2          string
db_create_online_log_dest_3          string
db_create_online_log_dest_4          string
db_create_online_log_dest_5          string

SQL> show parameter db_recovery

NAME                                 TYPE        VALUE
------------------------------------ ----------- ---------------
db_recovery_file_dest                string      +RECOV
db_recovery_file_dest_size           big integer 4800M
SQL>
```

Notice that none of the DB_CREATE_ONLINE_LOG_DEST_*n* parameters is specified. As a result, Oracle stores the online redo log files in the location specified by DB_CREATE_FILE_DEST. But there's only one set of online redo log files. You might ask whether this is inviting disaster if a case of media failure occurs. However, if the +DATA disk group is mirrored, you essentially have two or more copies of each online redo log file.

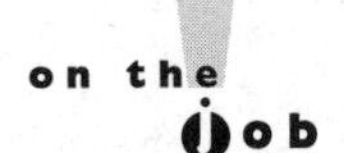

To further optimize the use of disk space for recovery operations, a fast recovery area can be shared by more than one database.

When the fast recovery area is configured, the initialization parameter LOG_ARCHIVE_DEST_10 is automatically set to the fast recovery area location. The corresponding ARC*n* background processes create archived log files in the fast recovery area and any other locations defined by the LOG_ARCHIVE_DEST_*n* initialization parameters.

If you do not specify a fast recovery area during installation, you can use Enterprise Manager Cloud Control 12*c* to create or configure the fast recovery area. From the home page, select the Availability tab and then click the Backup and Recovery link to open the Recovery Settings window, as shown in Figure 2-2.

FIGURE 2-2 Configuring the fast recovery area using Cloud Control 12*c* recovery settings

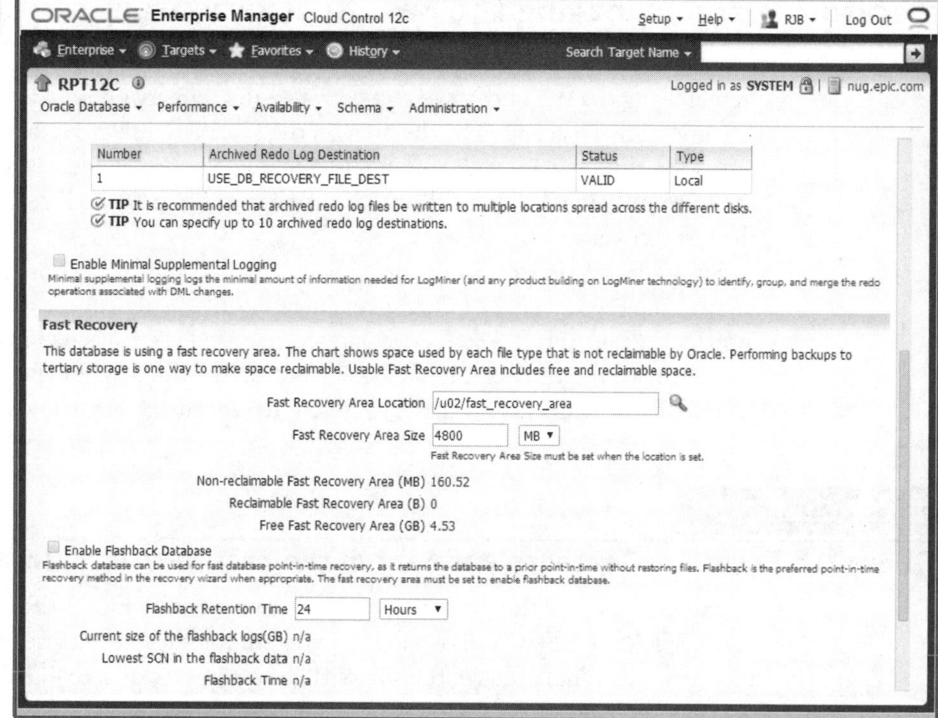

This Recovery Settings window not only allows you to adjust the location and size of the fast recovery area (in this case, 4800MB in the file system directory **/u02/fast_recovery_area**), but it also shows you the fast recovery area disk usage broken down by file type.

The recommended size of the fast recovery area is the sum of the database size, the size of incremental backups, and the size of all archived log files that have not been copied to tape or to another disk location (if they are copied at all). In addition, if you're using flashback logging, you want to have enough space to hold double the number of redo blocks times the flashback retention target. You can keep all of your recovery files in the fast recovery area depending on your recovery window. The minimum size of the fast recovery area should be at least large enough to hold all archived redo log files that have not been copied to tape or another disk location.

Monitoring and Managing the Fast Recovery Area

The initialization parameter DB_RECOVERY_FILE_DEST_SIZE can also assist in managing the size of the fast recovery area. Its primary purpose is to limit the amount of disk space used by the area on the specified disk group or file system directory. However, it can be temporarily increased once an alert is received to give the DBA additional time to allocate more disk space to the disk group or relocate the fast recovery area.

Short of receiving a warning or critical alert, you can be a bit more proactive in monitoring the size of the fast recovery area. Using the dynamic performance view V$RECOVERY_FILE_DEST, you can see the total used and reclaimable space on the destination file system. In addition, you can use the dynamic performance view V$FLASH_RECOVERY_AREA_USAGE to see a usage breakdown by file type.

EXERCISE 2-2

Query the Location, Contents, and Size of the Fast Recovery Area

In this exercise, use the dynamic performance views V$RECOVERY_FILE_DEST and V$FLASH_RECOVERY_AREA to determine the current size of the fast recovery area. Then, reduce the size of the fast recovery area to 4GB.

1. Query the view V$RECOVERY_FILE_DEST from SQL*Plus to see its location and maximum size:

```
SQL> select * from v$recovery_file_dest;

NAME         SPACE_LIMIT SPACE_USED SPACE_RECLAIMABLE NUMBER_OF_FILES
------------ ----------- ---------- ----------------- ---------------
+RECOV        8589934592 1595932672          71303168              13
```

The fast recovery area is less than 20 percent used.

2. Determine the breakdown of file usage within the fast recovery area using V$FLASH_RECOVERY_AREA_USAGE:

```
SQL> select * from v$flash_recovery_area_usage;

FILE_TYPE        PERCENT_SPACE_USED PERCENT_SPACE_RECLAIMABLE NUMBER_OF_FILES
---------------- ------------------ ------------------------- ---------------
CONTROL FILE                    .12                         0               1
REDO LOG                       1.87                         0               3
ARCHIVED LOG                    .83                         1               7
BACKUP PIECE                  15.75                         0               2
IMAGE COPY                        0                         0               0
FLASHBACK LOG                     0                         0               0
```

```
FOREIGN ARCHIVE                  0                    0          0
D LOG
AUXILIARY DATAF                  0                    0          0
ILE COPY

7 rows selected.

SQL>
```

3. Change the size of the fast recovery area to 4GB:

```
SQL> alter system set db_recovery_file_dest_size = 4g
scope=both;
System altered.
SQL>
```

Note that DB_RECOVERY_FILE_DEST_SIZE is a dynamic parameter and therefore takes effect immediately (without a database restart).

Oracle performs some automatic management of the space in the fast recovery area as well. Oracle does this by keeping track of which files are no longer needed for recovery or other flashback functions. If not enough free space exists for new files, Oracle deletes the oldest obsolete files and writes a message to the alert log. When disk space in the fast recovery area is low and insufficient space is free for new files, a message is written to the alert log, an alert is posted on the Enterprise Manager Cloud Control 12*c* home page, and a row is added to the data dictionary view DBA_OUTSTANDING_ALERTS. If the available free space is 15 percent or less (85 percent or more used), a warning message is issued. When the available free space reaches 3 percent or less (97 percent or more used), a critical warning is issued.

The column SUGGESTED_ACTION in the data dictionary view DBA_OUTSTANDING_ALERTS provides a possible corrective action for a disk space problem; however, for space pressure in the fast recovery area, your possible corrective actions fall into one of these categories:

- Add additional disk space to the fast recovery area and adjust DB_RECOVERY_FILE_DEST_SIZE.
- Back up files to a tertiary tape or disk device and remove the files from the fast recovery area.
- Review and delete files from the fast recovery area using the RMAN commands REPORT OBSOLETE and DELETE OBSOLETE.
- Change the RMAN retention policy.

Using RMAN with the fast recovery area is covered in more detail in Chapters 4 and 5.

CERTIFICATION OBJECTIVE 2.03

Configure Control Files and Redo Log Files for Recoverability

Oracle offers logical and physical backup capabilities. RMAN can perform either full or incremental logical and physical backups. You should understand the implications and uses of both physical and logical backups to develop the most appropriate solution for your applications.

A robust backup strategy includes both types of backups. In general, production databases rely on physical backups as their primary backup method, while logical backups serve as the secondary method. For development databases and for some small data movement processing, logical backups offer a viable solution.

Your backup and recovery plan should include, at a minimum, these tasks:

- **Configuration** Define backup destinations, encryption, and retention policies.
- **Scheduling** Automate backups to minimize human error and manual intervention.
- **Testing** Perform routine backup and recovery options to ensure that your backup plan works before you experience a real disaster.
- **Monitoring** Ensure that you minimize the resources used to perform a sufficient backup and minimize the impact to other database users.
- **Restoration** Restore your database files in the file system (datafiles, archive logs, and so on) from a previous backup.
- **Recovery** Perform a recovery of the database to the point of failure of the database by applying archived redo log entries to restored database files and rolling forward changes to your restored backup. Know how to recover your database.

Backup and recovery tools such as RMAN can be used in nonemergency situations as well. For example, you can take a snapshot of an entire database at one location and restore it to another location for developers or for testing.

The following sections present information on logical and physical backups, distinguishing between online and offline backups and focusing on online backups for the rest of this chapter and in the rest of this book. Finally, you'll get a brief overview of RMAN commands. Details of using RMAN for your backup and recovery environment are covered in Chapters 4, 5, 7, and 9.

Configuring ARCHIVELOG Mode

Consistent offline backups can be performed only while the database is shut down. However, you can perform physical file backups of a database while the database is open, provided the database is running in ARCHIVELOG mode and the backup is performed correctly. These backups are referred to as *online backups*.

Oracle writes to the online redo log files in a cyclical fashion: After filling the first log file, it begins writing to the second, until that one fills, and it then writes to the third, and so on. Once the last online redo log file is filled, the LGWR background process begins to overwrite the contents of the first redo log file.

When Oracle is run in ARCHIVELOG mode, the ARC*n* background process makes a copy of each redo log file after the LGWR process finishes writing to it. These archived redo log files are usually written to a disk device. They can instead be written directly to a tape device, but doing this can be operator intensive and will most likely slow down a busy database while waiting for the LGWR process to finish writing a redo log file to tape. Most likely, you will write your archived redo log files to disk and send the archived log files to tape or delete them once your retention policy is satisfied.

To make use of the ARCHIVELOG capability, you must first place the database in ARCHIVELOG mode. Before starting the database in ARCHIVELOG mode, make sure you are using one of the following configurations, listed from most to least recommended:

- Enable archiving to the fast recovery area only; use disk mirroring on the disks containing the fast recovery area. The DB_RECOVERY_FILE_DEST parameter specifies the file system location or ASM disk group containing the fast recovery area (see "Configure the Fast Recovery Area" later in this chapter).
- Enable archiving to the fast recovery area and set at least one LOG_ARCHIVE_DEST_*n* parameter to another location outside of the fast recovery area. (You'll learn how to leverage multiple archive destinations later in the chapter in the section "Leveraging Multiple Archive Destinations.")
- Set at least two LOG_ARCHIVE_DEST_*n* parameters to archive to other destinations than the fast recovery area.

The following examples assume that the best configuration, a single mirrored fast recovery area, has been selected. The following listing shows the steps needed to place a database in ARCHIVELOG mode; first, shut down the database, and then issue these commands:

```
SQL> shutdown immediate
SQL> startup mount
SQL> alter database archivelog;
SQL> alter database open;
```

on the job **_To see the currently active online redo log and its sequence number, query the V$LOG dynamic view._**

If you enable archiving but do not specify any archiving locations, the archived log files reside in a default, platform-dependent location; on Linux platforms, the default location is **$ORACLE_HOME/dbs**.

Each of the archived redo log files contains the data from a single online redo log. They are numbered sequentially, in the order in which they were created. The size of the archived redo log files varies, but it does not exceed the size of the online redo log files. When an online redo file reaches its specified maximum size, the redo log file is copied to a new archive log file, and the redo log file is then recycled for reuse by new redo log entries.

If the destination directory of the archived redo log files runs out of space, the ARC*n* processes will stop processing the online redo log data, and the database will stop until you free up space in the destination directory. Make sure you have enough space available in the destination directory.

This situation can be resolved by adding more space to the archived redo log file destination disk or by backing up the archived redo log files and then removing them from this directory. If you are using the fast recovery area for your archived redo log files, the database issues a warning alert (via e-mail or on the Enterprise Manager Cloud Control 12*c* home page) if the available space in the fast recovery area is less than 15 percent and issues a critical alert when the available space is less than 3 percent.

Taking action at the 15 percent level, such as increasing the size or changing the location of the fast recovery area, can most likely avoid any service interruptions, assuming that no runaway processes (such as untested SQL code running in production) are consuming space in the fast recovery area.

Leveraging Multiple Archive Destinations

You can use two different sets of archive-related initialization parameters, depending on the edition of the Oracle Database Server software you are using, the number of archived log file destinations you need, and whether the archived log file destinations are only local or both local and remote.

Local-Only Destinations

If you are using only local disk locations (in other words, you're not using a standby database as the destination for archived redo log files) and no more than two local disk locations, you can use the LOG_ARCHIVE_DEST and LOG_ARCHIVE_DUPLEX_DEST parameters. Here is an example of setting these two parameters to an archive location on two different disk drives:

```
LOG_ARCHIVE_DEST = '/u01/app/oracle/arch'
LOG_ARCHIVE_DUPLEX_DEST = '/u03/app/oracle/arch'
```

Note that the disk drives can be local to the server running Oracle Database 12*c*, or they can be on a network-based storage server hundreds of miles away.

EXERCISE 2-3

Identify the Archive Log File Destinations

In this exercise, you will identify the archived redo log file locations and determine the minimum number of required archive destinations.

1. Connect to your database with SQL*Plus and find the value of the LOG_ARCHIVE_* parameters:

```
SQL> show parameter log_archive_

NAME                                 TYPE        VALUE
------------------------------------ ----------- ---------------
log_archive_config                   string
log_archive_dest                     string
log_archive_dest_1                   string      SERVICE=RMT1
log_archive_dest_10                  string

log_archive_dest_11                  string

log_archive_dest_12                  string

log_archive_dest_state_1             string      enable
log_archive_dest_state_10            string      enable
log_archive_dest_state_11            string      enable
```

```
log_archive_dest_state_12            string       enable
. . .
log_archive_dest_state_2             string       enable
log_archive_dest_state_3             string       enable
log_archive_dest_state_4             string       enable
log_archive_dest_state_5             string       enable
log_archive_dest_state_6             string       enable
log_archive_dest_state_7             string       enable
log_archive_dest_state_8             string       enable
log_archive_dest_state_9             string       enable
log_archive_duplex_dest              string
log_archive_format                   string       %t_%s_%r.dbf
log_archive_local_first              boolean      TRUE
log_archive_max_processes            integer      4
log_archive_min_succeed_dest         integer      1
log_archive_start                    boolean      FALSE
log_archive_trace                    integer      0
SQL>
```

For this database, there appears to be only one archived log file destination, and it is a remote destination. Only one remote destination must succeed for archiving to be considered successful.

2. A second archived log file destination is available if a fast recovery area is defined. Query the fast recovery area–related parameters:

```
SQL> show parameter db_recov

NAME                                 TYPE         VALUE
------------------------------------ ----------- ---------------
db_recovery_file_dest                string       +RECOV
db_recovery_file_dest_size           big integer 8G
SQL>
```

on the job ***If you are using Oracle Database 12c Enterprise Edition, LOG_ARCHIVE_DEST and LOG_ARCHIVE_DUPLEX_DEST are deprecated in favor of the newer LOG_ARCHIVE_DEST_n parameters.***

Local and Remote Destinations

You can specify up to 31 archive log file destinations, either local or remote. If specified, you must use either the LOCATION parameter for a disk destination or the SERVICE parameter to specify a remote database instance as the destination.

In this example, you have two archived log file destinations on disk, and a third is a standby instance whose service name is STNDBY_CLEVELAND:

```
LOG_ARCHIVE_DEST_1 = 'LOCATION=/u01/app/oracle/arch'
LOG_ARCHIVE_DEST_2 = 'LOCATION=/u03/app/oracle/arch'
LOG_ARCHIVE_DEST_3 = 'SERVICE=STNDBY_CLEVELAND'
```

Defining Minimal Successful Destinations

Regardless of whether you use the LOG_ARCHIVE_DEST or the LOG_ARCHIVE_DEST_*n* parameter, you can use the LOG_ARCHIVE_MIN_SUCCEED_DEST parameter to specify the number of destinations to which the ARC*n* processes should successfully copy a redo log file to archive log files, before recycling the online redo log file for reuse. In other words, if you define several destinations, it may be acceptable from a recovery standpoint to have only two destinations available at any given time. Some destinations can temporarily be unavailable because of network issues or a failed standby server. In this case, two available destinations may be sufficient for a potential recovery scenario.

The value of the parameter LOG_ARCHIVE_MIN_SUCCEED_DEST cannot exceed the total number of enabled destinations. In addition, if you are using LOG_ARCHIVE_DEST_*n* with more destinations designated as MANDATORY than the number of destinations specified by LOG_ARCHIVE_MIN_SUCCEED_DEST, then the parameter LOG_ARCHIVE_MIN_SUCCEED_DEST is ignored.

In addition, if any archive log destination is designated as MANDATORY, a failure of this destination prevents the online log files from being overwritten until the failure is resolved. In this case, parameter LOG_ARCHIVE_MIN_SUCCEED_DEST is also ignored.

Finally, if you're using LOG_ARCHIVE_DEST, Oracle assumes that it is a MANDATORY location. The behavior will be the same as if you specified a destination using LOG_ARCHIVE_DEST_*n* with the MANDATORY parameter.

CERTIFICATION OBJECTIVE 2.04

Back Up and Recover a NOARCHIVELOG Database

Although the recommended database mode for production databases and even some development databases is ARCHIVELOG mode, you may not need Oracle's full availability and recoverability for a database and choose to use NOARCHIVELOG mode. One reason for choosing NOARCHIVELOG mode could be that the database is read-only and therefore recoverability is as easy as restoring from a full backup. Also, you may not have the disk space for the archived redo logs. Still, you need to have a backup of a database that is in NOARCHIVELOG mode and may need to restore and recover it in the case of disk corruption or datafile loss.

While the database is in NOARCHIVELOG mode, the database uses the online redo log files to ensure recovery only in case of instance failure. When you back up a database in NOARCHIVELOG mode, the database must be shut down and restarted in MOUNT mode to perform a full or incremental backup. Although you don't need to have disk space available for archived redo log files, your database availability is reduced while the database is being backed up. In addition, in a recovery scenario, you won't be able to recover the database to the last committed transaction but instead up to the last incremental backup.

CERTIFICATION SUMMARY

This chapter started with an overview of the types of backups you can and should perform on a regular basis: logical and physical. Physical backups can be either online or offline backups. However, because of the business demands of 100 percent uptime, the luxury of offline backups has given way to online backups, and the Oracle RMAN tool can be used to perform online backups.

Although RMAN is covered in much greater detail later in this book, this chapter presented an overview of how to start RMAN with some basic command-line options. RMAN commands fall into two broad categories, standalone and job commands, both of which you can execute at the RMAN command line or as a batch process. It also covered the types of retention policies you can configure within RMAN, depending on your availability and recovery requirements.

Next, you learned about the other prerequisites you need to fulfill before you can run your first RMAN command, such as configuring your database for ARCHIVELOG mode (if not already archived) and specifying the appropriate number and type of archive log file destinations.

Backing up your database in NOARCHIVELOG is possible, but the database must be shut down and restarted in MOUNT mode, which means that users cannot access the database during this time. Backing up in NOARCHIVELOG mode also means you will be able to restore and recover your database only to the point in time of the last incremental backup.

Finally, you reviewed the usage and configuration of the fast recovery area, how it automates backup and recovery operations, and how you can monitor the disk space available in the fast recovery area.

TWO-MINUTE DRILL

Configure and Manage RMAN Settings

- ❑ Oracle *logical* backups save the structure and contents of a table but not the physical format or location of the table on disk.
- ❑ Oracle *physical* backups save the physical files on disk containing the logical structures that define tables and indexes.
- ❑ An *online* backup performs a logical or physical backup while the database is open and available to users.
- ❑ An *offline* backup performs a logical or physical backup while the database is unavailable to users and is usually a physical backup.
- ❑ RMAN can retain and manage backups by using either a recovery window or by redundancy.
- ❑ Using a retention policy of NONE relies on an externally managed recovery window or redundancy.
- ❑ The default RMAN retention policy is a single copy.
- ❑ The initialization parameter CONTROL_FILE_RECORD_KEEP_TIME controls how long RMAN backup information is kept in the target database's control file if a recovery catalog is not used.

Configure the Fast Recovery Area

- ❑ The fast recovery area is a unified storage location for all recovery-related files in an Oracle database.
- ❑ All the files that you need in order to recover a database from a media failure or a logical error are contained in the fast recovery area.
- ❑ The permanent items kept in the fast recovery area are a copy of the control file and mirrored copies of the online redo log files.
- ❑ The transient items kept in the fast recovery area are the archived redo log files, flashback logs, control file automatic backups, datafile copies, and RMAN files used for staging a backup or recovery operation using archived log files.
- ❑ The initialization parameter DB_CREATE_FILE_DEST specifies the default location for database files that do not explicitly specify a location.

- The initialization parameter DB_CREATE_ONLINE_LOG_DEST_*n* specifies a default destination for one set of archived redo log files.
- The initialization parameter DB_RECOVERY_FILE_DEST specifies the location of the fast recovery area.
- The initialization parameter DB_RECOVERY_FILE_DEST_SIZE specifies the maximum size of the fast recovery area.
- When the fast recovery area is configured, the initialization parameter LOG_ARCHIVE_DEST_10 is automatically set to the fast recovery area location.
- The recommended size of the fast recovery area is the sum of the database size, the size of incremental backups, and the size of all archived log files that have not been copied to tape or to another disk location.
- The initialization parameter DB_RECOVERY_FILE_DEST_SIZE can be temporarily increased once an alert is received to give the DBA additional time to allocate more disk space to the disk group or relocate the fast recovery area.
- The dynamic performance view V$RECOVERY_FILE_DEST shows the total used and reclaimable space on the destination file system or fast recovery area.
- Oracle performs some automatic management of the space in the fast recovery area and keeps track of which files are no longer needed for recovery or other flashback functions.
- The data dictionary view DBA_OUTSTANDING_ALERTS contains a possible corrective action for space pressure in the fast recovery area when the amount of free space in the fast recovery area is 15 percent or less of the total fast recovery area size.

Configure Control Files and Redo Log Files for Recoverability

- Oracle's Data Pump Export utility queries the database, including the data dictionary, and writes the output to a binary file called an *export dump file*.
- Once data has been exported via Data Pump Export, it can be imported via the Data Pump Import utility.
- Physical backups involve copying the files that constitute the database.
- Consistent offline backups occur when the database has been shut down normally (that is, not because of instance failure) using the NORMAL, IMMEDIATE, or TRANSACTIONAL option of the SHUTDOWN command.

- ❑ You can use online backups for any database that is running in ARCHIVELOG mode.
- ❑ In ARCHIVELOG mode, the online redo logs are archived, creating a log of all transactions within the database.
- ❑ You can perform file system backups of a database while that database is open, provided the database is running in ARCHIVELOG mode.
- ❑ The database can be fully recovered from an online backup, and it can, via the archived redo logs, be rolled forward to any point in time before the failure.
- ❑ The two basic types of RMAN commands are *standalone* commands and *job* commands.
- ❑ The preparation for using RMAN in your environment consists of two basic steps: change your database to ARCHIVELOG mode (if it is not already), and configure the number and types of archive log destinations to maximize recoverability and availability.
- ❑ When Oracle is run in ARCHIVELOG mode, the ARC*n* background process makes a copy of each redo log file after the LGWR process finishes writing to it.
- ❑ Changing your database to ARCHIVELOG mode increases recoverability of your database and enables the use of RMAN as a backup and recovery tool for online backups.
- ❑ The initialization parameter DB_RECOVERY_FILE_DEST specifies the location of the fast recovery area, which can be on a file system or an ASM disk group.
- ❑ Set at least one LOG_ARCHIVE_DEST_*n* parameter to a location outside the fast recovery area.
- ❑ Set at least two LOG_ARCHIVE_DEST_*n* parameters to archive to destinations other than the fast recovery area.
- ❑ For one or two archived log file destinations, you can use LOG_ARCHIVE_DEST and LOG_ARCHIVE_DUPLEX_DEST.
- ❑ For more than two archived log file destinations with at least one remote destination, use LOG_ARCHIVE_DEST_*n*.
- ❑ Use LOG_ARCHIVE_MIN_SUCCEED_DEST to guarantee that a minimal number of archived log file destinations are accessible by ARC*n*.

Back Up and Recover a NOARCHIVELOG Database

- ❑ A database in NOARCHIVELOG mode does not need space for archived redo logs but must be shut down and unavailable to users during a full or incremental backup.
- ❑ Recovery to the last committed transaction is not available to a database in NOARCHIVELOG mode.

SELF TEST

The following questions will help you measure your understanding of the material presented in this chapter. Read all the choices carefully because there might be more than one correct answer. Choose all correct answers for each question.

Configure and Manage RMAN Settings

1. Which of the following RMAN commands does not correctly configure a retention policy? (Choose the best answer.)
   A. CONFIGURE RETENTION POLICY TO RECOVERY WINDOW OF 100 DAYS;
   B. CONFIGURE RETENTION POLICY TO NONE;
   C. CONFIGURE RETENTION POLICY TO REDUNDANCY WINDOW OF 2 DAYS;
   D. CONFIGURE RETENTION POLICY TO REDUNDANCY 2;
2. If you disable the RMAN retention policy, how long are the details of RMAN backups kept?
   A. Until the fast recovery area is full
   B. Up to the time specified by the initialization parameter CONTROL_FILE_RECORD_KEEP_TIME
   C. Until the database is shut down
   D. Indefinitely

Configure the Fast Recovery Area

3. Which of the following items are permanent and are stored in the fast recovery area? (Choose all that apply.)
   A. Control file
   B. Archived redo log files
   C. Online redo log files
   D. Control file backup
   E. RMAN backupsets
4. Which of the following items are transient and are stored in the fast recovery area? (Choose all that apply.)
   A. Control file
   B. Archived redo log files
   C. Online redo log files
   D. Control file backup
   E. RMAN backupsets

5. If you specify the initialization parameter DB_RECOVERY_FILE_DEST, what other initialization parameter must be set?
   A. DB_CREATE_FILE_DEST.
   B. DB_CREATE_ONLINE_LOG_DEST_*n*.
   C. DB_RECOVERY_FILE_DEST_SIZE.
   D. No other parameter needs to be set.
6. You have just received a pager alert indicating that the fast recovery area is below 3 percent free space. Which view and column can you query for a possible corrective action for this space condition? (Choose the best answer.)
   A. V$FLASH_RECOVERY_AREA_USAGE, PERCENT_SPACE_RECLAIMABLE
   B. DBA_OUTSTANDING_ALERT, SUGGESTED_ACTIONS
   C. DBA_OUTSTANDING_ALERTS, SUGGESTED_ACTIONS
   D. DBA_OUTSTANDING_ALERTS, SUGGESTED_ACTION
7. RMAN has several configuration settings related to space management. Which of the following settings directly control space management in the fast recovery area? (Choose all that apply.)
   A. RETENTION POLICY
   B. RECOVERY CATALOG
   C. CONTROLFILE AUTOBACKUP
   D. BACKUP OPTIMIZATION
   E. ARCHIVELOG DELETION POLICY

Configure Control Files and Redo Log Files for Recoverability

8. Which of the following statement is not true regarding database backups?
   A. A consistent offline backup occurs after a SHUTDOWN NORMAL, IMMEDIATE, or TRANSACTIONAL.
   B. As of Oracle Database 12*c*, RMAN supports only online backups.
   C. A physical database backup copies one or more files that constitute the database.
   D. A logical database backup reads a set of database rows and writes them to a file.
   E. A logical database backup reads a set of database rows and writes them to an ASM disk group.
   F. Online backups can occur only when your database is in ARCHIVELOG mode.
9. Which of the following objects can be backed up by RMAN while the database is open? (Choose all that apply.)
   A. Archived redo log files
   B. Online redo log files
   C. Password files

D. Tablespaces
E. Tables and indexes
F. Control files
G. Server parameter files (SPFILEs)
H. Datafiles

10. Which of the following are not RMAN standalone commands? (Choose all that apply.)

A. BACKUP DATABASE
B. ALLOCATE CHANNEL
C. CONNECT
D. CREATE CATALOG
E. CREATE SCRIPT

11. Choose the four best commands from the following list that you would use to enable ARCHIVELOG mode, and put them in the correct order:

1. STARTUP MOUNT
2. SHUTDOWN ABORT
3. ALTER DATABASE ARCHIVELOG;
4. STARTUP FORCE
5. ALTER DATABASE ENABLE ARCHIVELOG;
6. ALTER SYSTEM SWITCH LOGFILE;
7. SHUTDOWN NORMAL
8. ALTER DATABASE OPEN;
9. SHUTDOWN IMMEDIATE

A. 2, 1, 3, 8
B. 9, 3, 1, 8
C. 4, 5, 7, 6
D. 7, 1, 3, 8
E. 9, 1, 3, 8

12. Which of the following initialization parameters is not valid?

A. LOG_ARCHIVE_DEST_3 = '/rmtdisk/u01/app/oracle/flash'
B. LOG_ARCHIVE_DUPLEX_DEST = '+DATA'
C. LOG_ARCHIVE_DEST = 'SERVICE=RMTDB99'
D. LOG_ARCHIVE_DEST = '/rmtdisk/u01/app/oracle/flash'
E. LOG_ARCHIVE_DEST_10 = 'SERVICE=RMTDB99'
F. LOG_ARCHIVE_DEST_10 = '/rmtdisk/u01/app/oracle/flash'

13. Your SPFILE contains the following parameter values:
LOG_ARCHIVE_DEST_1 = 'LOCATION=/u01/app/oracle/arch'
LOG_ARCHIVE_DEST_2 =
'LOCATION=/u03/app/oracle/arch MANDATORY'
LOG_ARCHIVE_DEST_3 = 'SERVICE=STNDBY_CLEVELAND MANDATORY'
LOG_ARCHIVE_MIN_SUCCEED_DEST = 1
You are not using a fast recovery area. The disk drive containing the directory /u03/app/oracle/arch fails. What happens to the archive processes and the database?

A. The database pauses because LOG_ARCHIVE_DEST_2 is MANDATORY.

B. The database continues to run normally with the remaining two archive locations because at least one other destination is marked as MANDATORY.

C. The database continues to run normally with the remaining two archive locations because LOG_ARCHIVE_MIN_SUCCEED_DEST is 1.

D. The database will not start unless LOG_ARCHIVE_MIN_SUCCEED_DEST is set to at least the number of MANDATORY locations.

Back Up and Recover a NOARCHIVELOG Database

14. Which of the following are characteristics of a database in NOARCHIVELOG mode? (Choose all that apply.)

A. NOARCHIVELOG databases can recover to the last committed transaction as long as the online redo log files are available.

B. The database must be closed to perform a full backup in NOARCHIVELOG mode.

C. OLTP databases should be in NOARCHIVELOG mode to ensure that archived redo log file operations do not affect performance.

D. A NOARCHIVELOG database must be started in NOMOUNT mode after a full or incremental backup.

E. Test environments are good candidates for NOARCHIVELOG databases.

SELF TEST ANSWERS

Configure and Manage RMAN Settings

1. ☑ **C.** REDUNDANCY WINDOW OF 2 DAYS is syntactically incorrect.
☒ **A, B,** and **D** are incorrect. They are all valid RMAN commands. You can set the RMAN retention policy to the total number of copies of each database file, you can set it to the number of days in the past for which you can restore the database after a logical error, or you can disable the retention policy completely and manage the retention policy externally from RMAN.

2. ☑ **B.** When there is no retention policy, RMAN keeps the details of RMAN backups up to the time specified by the CONTROL_FILE_RECORD_KEEP_TIME initialization parameter.
☒ **A, C,** and **D** are incorrect. The control file or a recovery catalog still contain the information about RMAN backups, and this information is available until CONTROL_FILE_RECORD_KEEP_TIME.

Configure the Fast Recovery Area

3. ☑ **A** and **C.** A mirrored copy of the control file and one mirrored copy of each online redo log file are stored in the fast recovery area.
☒ **B, D,** and **E** are incorrect. They aren't considered permanent items.

4. ☑ **B, D,** and **E**. Archived redo log files, backups of the control file, and RMAN backupsets are considered transient and are stored in the fast recovery area.
☒ **A** and **C** are incorrect. They aren't considered transient items.

5. ☑ **C.** When you specify the location of the fast recovery area with DB_RECOVERY_FILE_DEST, you must also set the parameter DB_RECOVERY_FILE_DEST_SIZE to limit the amount of space used by the fast recovery area on the destination file system.
☒ **A, B,** and **D** are incorrect. **A** is incorrect because DB_CREATE_FILE_DEST specifies a default location for any database object created without an explicit location. **B** is incorrect since DB_CREATE_ONLINE_LOG_DEST_*n* specifies the location for new or additional online redo log files. **D** is incorrect since you must specify a size for the fast recovery area.

6. ☑ **D.** The REASON column in DBA_OUTSTANDING_ALERTS contains a description for the alert, and the SUGGESTED_ACTION provides a recommendation for corrective action. These descriptions also appear in the alerts section of the Enterprise Manager Database Control home page.
☒ **A, B,** and **C** are incorrect. **A** is incorrect since the column PERCENT_SPACE_RECLAIMABLE doesn't provide any recommendations, only an amount of disk space that can be reclaimable for objects that may be obsolete in the fast recovery area. **B** and **C** are incorrect because there is no such data dictionary view as DBA_OUTSTANDING_ALERT, and there is no such column as SUGGESTED_ACTIONS in the view DBA_OUTSTANDING_ALERTS.

7. ☑ **A** and **E.** The RETENTION POLICY setting will delete objects in the fast recovery area under space pressure when the object falls outside the number of copies or retention period of the retention policy.
   ☒ **B, C,** and **D** are incorrect. **B** is incorrect because the space in the recovery catalog is not controlled by the retention policy of the target database. **C** is incorrect because CONTROLFILE AUTOBACKUP specifies that the control file is backed up before the start of each backup and not how much space the control file takes in the fast recovery area. **D** is incorrect because backup optimization doesn't manage space directly but saves space and time when an exact copy of a file that is being backed up has been backed up before to the same device type.

Configure Control Files and Redo Log Files for Recoverability

8. ☑ **B.** RMAN can perform both online and offline backups.
   ☒ **A, C,** and **D** are incorrect. All other statements about online and offline backups are true.

9. ☑ **A, D, F, G,** and **H.** RMAN can back up archived redo log files and then delete them from the fast recovery area. Tablespaces can be backed up individually by RMAN. Control files are backed up either explicitly during an RMAN backup or implicitly when the SYSTEM tablespace is part of a backup, or they are backed up by setting RMAN control file autobackup with CONFIGURE CONTROLFILE AUTOBACKUP ON. The SPFILE, but not a static PFILE (text parameter file), can also be included in an RMAN backup. Individual datafiles can be backed up as well.
   ☒ **B, C,** and **E** are incorrect. **B** is incorrect because you should never back up online redo files, and RMAN will not back them up anyway. **C** is incorrect because RMAN will not back up an operating system file such as a password file; you can back up this file manually. **E** is incorrect because RMAN cannot back up individual tables and indexes. These types of objects are best backed up by a logical backup using **expdp**.

10. ☑ **B.** The ALLOCATE CHANNEL command can be used only in a command block; you can define a default channel for a standalone command using the CONFIGURE CHANNEL command.
    ☒ **A, C, D,** and **E** are incorrect. They are all standalone commands; BACKUP DATABASE can be used as a standalone command or as a job command.

11. ☑ **E.** The correct commands and sequence for enabling ARCHIVELOG mode are as follows:

```
SHUTDOWN IMMEDIATE
STARTUP MOUNT
ALTER DATABASE ARCHIVELOG;
ALTER DATABASE OPEN;
```

☒ **A, B, C,** and **D** are incorrect. All other combinations are either in the wrong order or have incorrect or unnecessary steps. You cannot use SHUTDOWN ABORT because this leaves the database in an unusable state until the database can be recovered (or restarted); thus, you cannot enable ARCHIVELOG mode without extra steps. STARTUP FORCE performs a SHUTDOWN ABORT and a STARTUP, which leaves you with the database in OPEN mode, and thus this command is not necessary. ENABLE ARCHIVELOG is not a valid keyword in the ALTER DATABASE command. SHUTDOWN NORMAL is one way to shut down the database gracefully, but then you must wait for all users to disconnect from the database. ALTER SYSTEM SWITCH LOGFILE is a valid command but is not part of the process of switching a database into ARCHIVELOG mode.

12. ☑ **C.** If you use LOG_ARCHIVE_DEST or LOG_ARCHIVE_DUPLEX_DEST, the locations must be a disk device (file system or ASM disk). The destination cannot be another Oracle instance.
☒ **A, B, D, E,** and **F** are incorrect. When you use LOG_ARCHIVE_DEST_*n*, the destination can be a file system or a database service. By default, if you have a fast recovery area defined, LOG_ARCHIVE_DEST_10 points to the fast recovery area; however, you can override this with any valid disk location or service.

13. ☑ **A.** All archive destinations marked as MANDATORY must be available when ARC*n* attempts to archive a filled redo log.
☒ **B, C,** and **D** are incorrect. **B** is incorrect because all MANDATORY locations must be available when ARC*n* needs to archive a filled redo log file. **C** is incorrect because all MANDATORY locations must be available and the number of available locations must be greater than or equal to the number of locations specified in LOG_ARCHIVE_MIN_SUCCEED_DEST. **D** is incorrect because LOG_ARCHIVE_MIN_SUCCEED_DEST can be any integer and is not related to how many LOG_ARCHIVE_DEST_*n* parameters are set to MANDATORY; both parameters work independently to ensure a minimum number of available archive locations.

Back Up and Recover a NOARCHIVELOG Database

14. ☑ **B** and **E.** A database must be shut down and opened in MOUNT mode to perform either a full or incremental backup. Databases with short lifetimes or mostly read-only databases with few updates are good candidates for NOARCHIVELOG mode.
☒ **A, C,** and **D** are incorrect. **A** is incorrect because committed transactions since the last backup are not available in a NOARCHIVELOG database. **C** is incorrect because OLTP databases, because of their continuous write activity, must be in ARCHIVELOG mode to be able to recover up to the last committed transaction after a database failure. **D** is incorrect because starting a database in NOMOUNT mode has no bearing on the recoverability of the database.

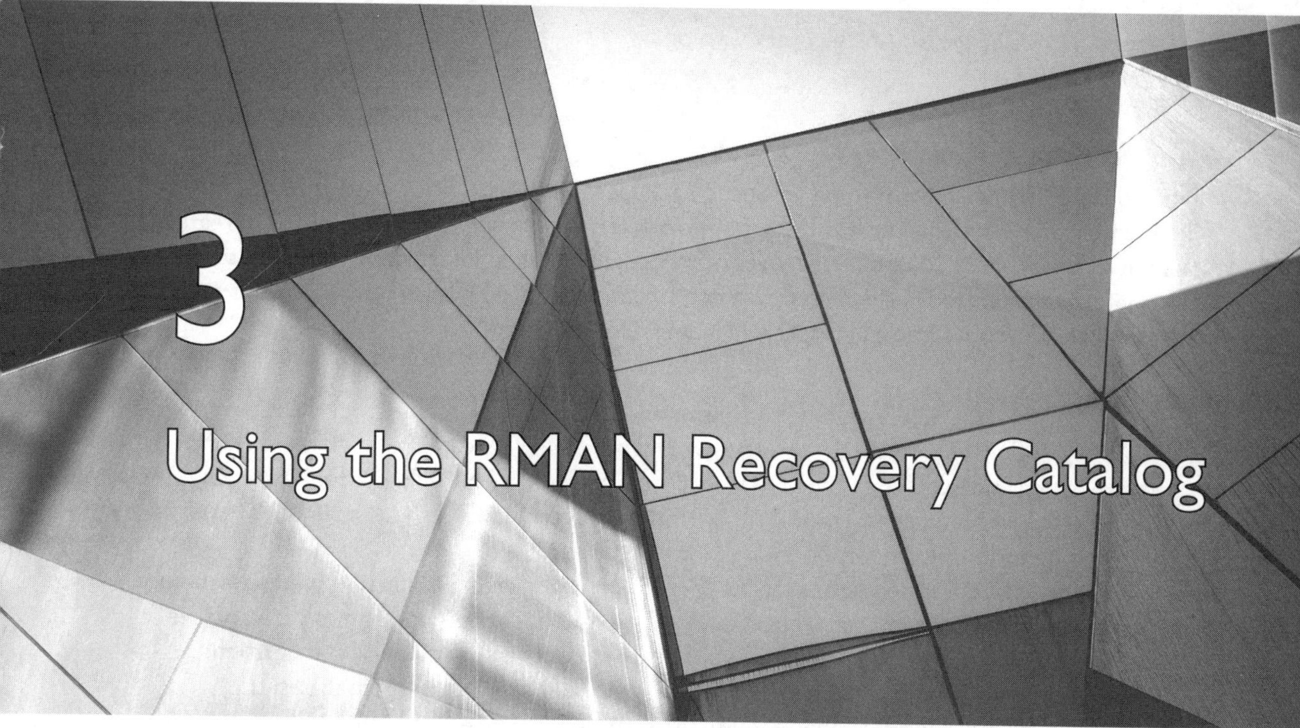

3

Using the RMAN Recovery Catalog

CERTIFICATION OBJECTIVES

3.01	Create and Use an RMAN Recovery Catalog	✓	Two-Minute Drill
3.02	Protect the RMAN Recovery Catalog	Q&A	Self Test

If you're ready to perform some advanced backups with RMAN, you'll have to wait until the next chapter. This chapter lays the groundwork for performing RMAN backups by creating the *recovery catalog*. Without a recovery catalog, your backup information is limited to the RMAN information stored in the target database's control file. You'll learn how to do this at the command line and from Oracle Enterprise Manager Cloud Control 12*c*.

Next, you'll learn how to register and unregister a database from the recovery catalog. Once a database is registered with a recovery catalog, you'll see scenarios for which you might need to resynchronize the RMAN backup information in the target database control file with the recovery catalog. In most cases, RMAN performs the synchronization automatically.

RMAN stored scripts makes your job easier by saving frequently used sequences of commands in a recovery catalog; using stored scripts is one of many advantages of using a recovery catalog for RMAN backups over a target database's control file.

Just as you need to back up and recover each of your target databases, the recovery catalog database itself must be backed up on a regular basis. I'll show you a couple ways to back up the recovery catalog database.

CERTIFICATION OBJECTIVE 3.01

Create and Use an RMAN Recovery Catalog

RMAN always stores its *metadata* (information about the database structure, backup sets, and image copies) in the target database's control file. However, there are several advantages, and a few disadvantages, to storing this metadata in a recovery catalog stored in a separate database. The following sections discuss the pros and cons of using a recovery catalog.

Using the Control File for RMAN Metadata

Oracle strongly recommends using a recovery catalog, but doing so has a few downsides. Whether you use a recovery catalog or not, the RMAN backup information is always stored in the control file of the target database. Although the RMAN information in the control file is aged out based on the value of the initialization parameter CONTROL_FILE_RECORD_KEEP_TIME, this might not be a problem if you use an RMAN retention policy that has a RECOVERY WINDOW that is less than CONTROL_FILE_RECORD_KEEP_TIME. In addition, using your control file as the only repository for RMAN information is easier to manage because you don't need a second database that, in turn, needs to be backed up. Finally, if you are mirroring your control file in several locations and you create an offsite backup of your control file after every database structure change or RMAN backup, then you will likely never lose your control file and will always be able to restore your database successfully from any media failure, even a complete loss of the database. Using a recovery catalog database also means you have another database to back up on a regular basis.

Using a Recovery Catalog for RMAN Metadata

If you manage more than one database in your environment and you want to keep your recovery information for a much longer time, then using a recovery catalog might be justified. A single recovery catalog can store RMAN information for a virtually unlimited number of target databases. In addition, all information in the control file of the target database resides in the RMAN recovery catalog after you perform the first RESYNC CATALOG operation.

Using stored scripts is another reason to use a recovery catalog; you cannot store scripts in the target database's control file. You can save a sequence of commands as a single script to make it easy to run the sequence of commands on demand or perhaps on a specific schedule. A script can be tied to a specific target database (a local script), or it can be available to all target databases (a global script).

Because you can put the metadata from several databases into a single recovery catalog, you can use the RC_ views, such as RC_ARCHIVED_LOG, RC_BACKUP_FILES, and RC_DATABASE, in the recovery catalog database to retrieve metadata for all target databases. Otherwise, when you're using the target database control file, you must connect to each target database separately and query the V$ views based on the target database's control file.

Finally, using a recovery catalog permits you to use the following RMAN commands:

- **BACKUP...KEEP UNTIL TIME** Keep a backup for a period of time that differs from the configured retention policy.
- **BACKUP...KEEP FOREVER** Keep a backup indefinitely or until you manually remove it.
- **REPORT SCHEMA...AT** Show the structure of the database at a specific time in the past.

Configure the Recovery Catalog Database

Starting out with available free space of 150MB for the recovery catalog repository will, in most cases, be sufficient for the first year, and enabling automatic extents of 50MB each will be sufficient in the long term depending on how many databases you manage in the recovery catalog. A minimum of 15MB is required for each database registered in the catalog. Overall, it's a small amount of disk space compared to your terabyte data warehouse!

Connect to the repository database (in this case, the RCAT database) with SYSDBA privileges and create the recovery catalog in the RMAN tablespace as follows:

```
[oracle@tettnang ~]$ . oraenv
ORACLE_SID = [oracle] ? rcat
The Oracle base remains unchanged with value /u00/app/oracle
[oracle@tettnang ~]$ sqlplus / as sysdba

SQL*Plus: Release 12.1.0.1.0 Production on Tue Feb 18 14:46:11 2014
Copyright (c) 1982, 2013, Oracle.  All rights reserved.
Connected to:
Oracle Database 12c Enterprise Edition Release 12.1.0.1.0 - 64bit Production
With the Partitioning, Automatic Storage Management,
   OLAP, Advanced Analytics and Real Application Testing options
SQL> create tablespace rman datafile '+data' size 150m
  2  autoextend on next 50m;
Tablespace created.
SQL>
```

Create the Recovery Catalog Owner

Creating the recovery catalog owner is as easy as creating any database user. In this example, you create the user RMAN to manage the recovery catalog. You could just as easily create a user called FRED to own the recovery catalog. Using RMAN as the catalog owner makes it easier to identify the purpose of the account:

```
SQL> create user rcat_owner identified by Rcat9095
  2  default tablespace rman
  3  quota unlimited on rman;
User created.
SQL> grant recovery_catalog_owner to rcat_owner;
Grant succeeded.
SQL>
```

The predefined role RECOVERY_CATALOG_OWNER includes these system privileges:

- ALTER SESSION
- CREATE CLUSTER
- CREATE DATABASE LINK
- CREATE PROCEDURE
- CREATE SEQUENCE
- CREATE SESSION
- CREATE SYNONYM
- CREATE TABLE
- CREATE TRIGGER
- CREATE TYPE
- CREATE VIEW

Later in this chapter, you'll learn how to create virtual catalog owners, each of which will own a virtual private catalog. This enables the division of responsibilities among many DBAs, allowing management of multiple databases using the same RMAN repository.

Create the Recovery Catalog

Now that the RMAN user account exists in the repository database, you can start RMAN, connect to the catalog, and initialize the repository with the CREATE CATALOG command:

```
[oracle@tettnang ~]$ rman catalog rcat_owner/Rcat9095@rcat
Recovery Manager: Release 12.1.0.1.0 -
   Production on Tue Feb 18 14:55:14 2014
Copyright(c) 1982, 2013, Oracle and/or its affiliates. All rights reserved.
connected to recovery catalog database
RMAN> create catalog;
recovery catalog created
RMAN>
```

From this point on, using a repository is as easy as specifying the repository username and password on the RMAN command line with the CATALOG parameter or using the CONNECT CATALOG command in an RMAN session.

FIGURE 3-1 Persisting RMAN repository credentials

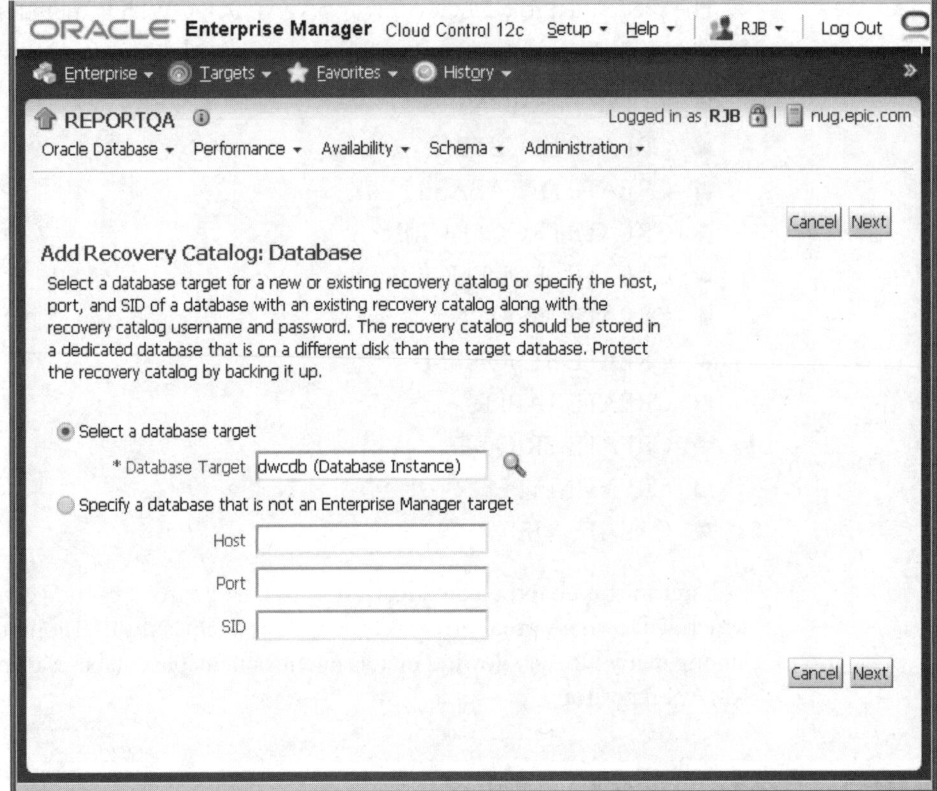

Within Oracle Enterprise Manager Cloud Control 12*c*, you can persist the repository credentials, as demonstrated in Figure 3-1. In this example, the database target dwcdb is a database monitored by Enterprise Manager Cloud Control. If the database is not being monitored, you can specify the host, port, and instance name of any database that will play the role of the recovery catalog database.

In future Cloud Control sessions, any RMAN backup or recovery operations will automatically use the recovery catalog.

Synchronize the Recovery Catalog

Now that you've set up your recovery catalog, you can register one or more of your databases with the recovery catalog. The registration process propagates backup information and the target database structure to the recovery catalog. In general, RMAN saves most information from the control file to the recovery catalog; however, a few operations require you to update the metadata manually in the recovery catalog.

The following sections cover topics related to recovery catalog synchronization: registering a database, unregistering a database, and resynchronizing a recovery catalog. In addition, you'll learn how to change the database identifier (DBID) of a duplicated database to permit you to register the duplicated database in the recovery catalog; the DBID of each database recorded in the recovery catalog must be unique.

Registering a Database

For each database for which RMAN will perform a backup or recovery, you must register the database in the RMAN repository; this operation records information such as the target database schema and the unique DBID of the target database. The target database needs to be registered only once; subsequent RMAN sessions that connect to the target database will automatically reference the correct metadata in the repository. The database must be in the MOUNT or OPEN state to be successfully registered.

The following example connects to the target database using operating system authentication and connects to the repository with password authentication:

```
[oracle@tettnang ~]$ rman target / catalog rcat_owner/Rcat9095@
rcat
Recovery Manager: Release 12.1.0.1.0 -
     Production on Tue Feb 18 21:20:26 2014
Copyright (c)1982, 2013, Oracle and/or its affiliates. All
rights reserved.
connected to target database: RPT12C (DBID=1766066998)
connected to recovery catalog database
RMAN> register database;
database registered in recovery catalog
starting full resync of recovery catalog
full resync complete
RMAN>
```

All databases registered with the repository must have unique DBIDs; trying to register the database again yields the following error message:

```
RMAN> register database;
RMAN-00571: ===========================================================
RMAN-00569: =============== ERROR MESSAGE STACK FOLLOWS ===============
RMAN-00571: ===========================================================
RMAN-03009: failure of register command on
     default channel at 02/18/2014 21:22:40
RMAN-20002: target database already registered in recovery catalog
RMAN>
```

As you might expect, you can use Cloud Control to register the database; Figure 3-2 shows the Recovery Catalog Settings page where you can specify a recovery catalog and register the database. If you do not include this step in the registration process, any backups you perform using EM will not be recorded in the recovery catalog.

Changing the DBID of a Database

In the preceding section, you attempted to register the same database in the recovery catalog twice. RMAN prevented the duplicated registration because a database with the same DBID already existed in the recovery catalog. But what if you duplicate a database and now want to use the same recovery catalog for both databases? You can use the DBNEWID utility, using the **nid** command at the command-line prompt.

Running **nid** without any parameters shows you the possible parameters:

```
[oracle@tettnang ~]$ nid
DBNEWID: Release 12.1.0.1.0 - Production on Tue Feb 18 21:37:46 2014
Copyright (c)1982, 2013, Oracle and/or its affiliates. All rights reserved.

Keyword     Description                    (Default)
----------------------------------------------------
TARGET      Username/Password              (NONE)
DBNAME      New database name              (NONE)
LOGFILE     Output Log                     (NONE)
REVERT      Revert failed change           NO
SETNAME     Set a new database name only   NO
APPEND      Append to output log           NO
HELP        Displays these messages        NO

[oracle@tettnang ~]$
```

TARGET specifies the username and password of the database, as you might expect. You can optionally specify DBNAME to create a new database name in addition to the DBID; if you want to change only the database name, you specify SETNAME=Y.

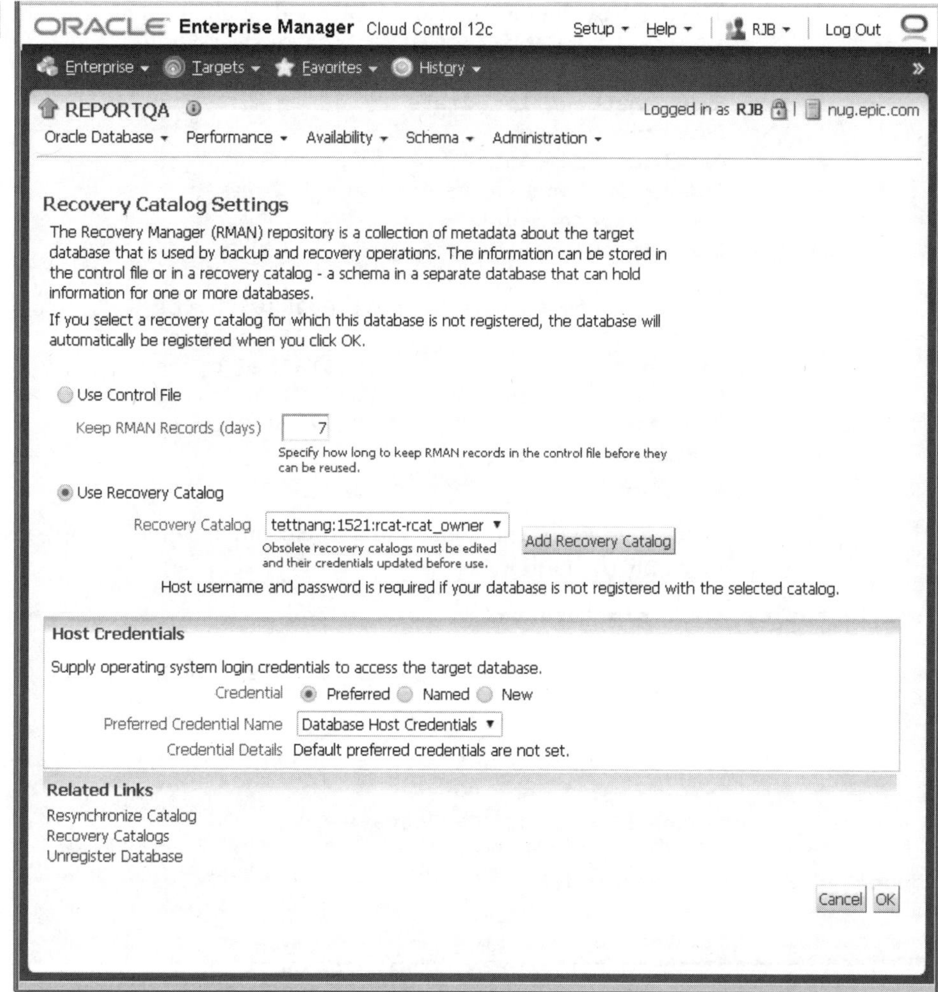

FIGURE 3-2 Specifying a repository and registering a database using EM

Here is the DBID for the RPT12C database before you change it:

```
SQL> select dbid, name from v$database;

      DBID NAME
---------- ---------
1766066998 RPT12C
SQL>
```

The database whose name and DBID will be changed must be shut down cleanly and restarted in MOUNT mode, as in this example:

```
SQL> shutdown immediate
Database closed.
Database dismounted.
ORACLE instance shut down.
SQL> startup mount
ORACLE instance started.

Total System Global Area 3140026368 bytes
Fixed Size                  2686512 bytes
Variable Size            1040187856 bytes
Database Buffers         2080374784 bytes
Redo Buffers               16777216 bytes
Database mounted.
SQL>
```

Next, you run the **nid** command at the command-line prompt; you want to change only the DBID:

```
[oracle@tettnang ~]$ nid target=/

DBNEWID: Release 12.1.0.1.0 - Production on Tue Feb 18 21:46:23 2014


Copyright (c)1982, 2013, Oracle and/or its affiliates. All rights reserved.

Connected to database RPT12C (DBID=1766066998)

Connected to server version 12.1.0

Control Files in database:
    +DATA/RPT12C/CONTROLFILE/current.261.826650871
    +RECOV/RPT12C/CONTROLFILE/current.256.826650871

Change database ID of database RPT12C? (Y/[N]) => Y

Proceeding with operation
Changing database ID from 1766066998 to 1779317104
    Control File +DATA/RPT12C/CONTROLFILE/current.261.826650871 - modified
    Control File +RECOV/RPT12C/CONTROLFILE/current.256.826650871 - modified
    Datafile +DATA/RPT12C/DATAFILE/system.258.82665079 - dbid changed
    Datafile +DATA/RPT12C/DATAFILE/example.266.82665088 - dbid changed
    Datafile +DATA/RPT12C/DATAFILE/sysaux.257.82665075 - dbid changed
    Datafile +DATA/RPT12C/DATAFILE/undotbs1.260.82665084 - dbid changed
```

```
    Datafile +DATA/RPT12C/DATAFILE/users.269.82693134 - dbid changed
    Datafile +DATA/RPT12C/DATAFILE/users.259.82665084 - dbid changed
    Datafile +DATA/RPT12C/DATAFILE/undotbs1.270.82693134 - dbid changed
. . .
    Datafile +DATA/RPT12C/TEMPFILE/temp1.381.82768161 - dbid changed
    Datafile +DATA/RPT12C/TEMPFILE/temp2.382.82768162 - dbid changed
    Datafile +DATA/RPT12C/TEMPFILE/temp3.383.82768162 - dbid changed
    Control File +DATA/RPT12C/CONTROLFILE/current.261.826650871 -
       dbid changed
    Control File +RECOV/RPT12C/CONTROLFILE/current.256.826650871 -
       dbid changed
    Instance shut down

Database ID for database RPT12C changed to 1779317104.
All previous backups and archived redo logs for this database are unusable.
Database is not aware of previous backups and archived logs
   in Recovery Area.
Database has been shutdown, open database with RESETLOGS option.
Successfully changed database ID.
DBNEWID - Completed successfully.

[oracle@tettnang ~]$
```

Finally, open the database with the RESETLOGS option:

```
[oracle@tettnang ~]$ sqlplus / as sysdba

SQL*Plus: Release 12.1.0.1.0 Production on Tue Feb 18 21:51:19 2014

Copyright (c) 1982, 2013, Oracle.  All rights reserved.

Connected to an idle instance.

SQL> startup mount
ORACLE instance started.

Total System Global Area 3140026368 bytes
Fixed Size                  2686512 bytes
Variable Size            1040187856 bytes
Database Buffers         2080374784 bytes
Redo Buffers               16777216 bytes
Database mounted.
SQL> alter database open resetlogs;

Database altered.
SQL>
```

Here is the DW database's DBID after you change it:

```
SQL> select dbid, name from v$database;

      DBID NAME
---------- ---------
1779317104 RPT12C

SQL>
```

Using the DBNEWID (**nid**) command has at least one downside. Since all backup files contain the old DBID, previous backups are unusable; after you change the DBID, you must open the database for the first time with the RESETLOGS option, as shown in the preceding example. In addition, you should perform a full backup of the database since you now have no usable previous backups.

Unregistering a Database

If you want to migrate your backup information from one recovery catalog to another, either because of space pressure on the existing catalog or an erroneously registered database, you can unregister a database from a recovery catalog using, as you might expect, the UNREGISTER command. In this example, you connect to the target database and the recovery catalog, and then you execute the UNREGISTER command:

```
[oracle@tettnang ~]$ rman target / catalog rcat_owner/Rcat9095@rcat

Recovery Manager: Release 12.1.0.1.0 -
     Production on Tue Feb 18 21:58:42 2014

Copyright (c)1982, 2013, Oracle and/or its affiliates.
     All rights reserved.

connected to target database: RPT12C (DBID=1779317104)
connected to recovery catalog database

RMAN> unregister database;

database name is "RPT12C" and DBID is 1779317104

Do you really want to unregister the database (enter YES or NO)? yes
database unregistered from the recovery catalog
RMAN>
```

After you unregister a database, your backup metadata is still stored in the control file for the number of days specified by the initialization parameter

CONTROL_FILE_RECORD_KEEP_TIME. If you reregister the database, Oracle populates the recovery catalog with the backup-related and database structure metadata from the control file. If you want to add information about any backups not in the control file at the time you reregister the database, you can manually add the backup metadata with the CATALOG command, as you will see in the next section.

Cataloging Additional Backup Files

If you have created backups outside of RMAN or you have registered your database and RMAN backups have already been aged out of the control file, you can use the CATALOG command to add these backups to the RMAN recovery catalog. The CATALOG command can add the following types of backup files to the recovery catalog with the associated keyword for the CATALOG command:

- **Datafile copies** DATAFILECOPY
- **Backup pieces** BACKUPPIECE
- **Control file copies** CONTROLFILECOPY
- **Archived redo log files** ARCHIVELOG

For example, you might want to record an additional archived log file destination in the recovery catalog, in addition to the archived log files in the flash recovery area that are already recorded. If you want to catalog a number of backup files in a specific Automatic Storage Management (ASM) disk group location or a file system location, you can use the START WITH option. This example uses the START WITH option to catalog all backup files in the ASM disk group +DATA2:

```
RMAN> catalog start with '+DATA2';
```

The filename or file path specified in the START WITH clause is only a prefix, and no wildcards are allowed.

EXERCISE 3-1

Cataloging Additional Backup Files

In this exercise, the COMPLREF database has an additional archived log destination at **/u00/oradata/arch/complref**, and these archived log files were created before the database was registered with the recovery catalog. Query the file system location using the Unix **ls** command, and add all archived log files in that location to the recovery catalog:

1. Query the file system for a list of backup files:

```
[oracle@oel63 complref]$ ls -l /u00/oradata/arch/complref
total 11120
-rw-r----- 1 oracle vboxsf 11375104 Feb 18 23:48
1_557_821312592.dbf
-rw-r----- 1 oracle vboxsf     1024 Feb 18 23:49
1_558_821312592.dbf
-rw-r----- 1 oracle vboxsf     1536 Feb 18 23:49
1_559_821312592.dbf
[oracle@oel63 complref]$
```

2. Connect to RMAN and use the CATALOG START WITH command to add these archived redo log files to the recovery catalog:

```
[[oracle@tettnang ~]$ rman target / catalog rcat_owner/
Rcat9095@rcat

Recovery Manager: Release 12.1.0.1.0 -
    Production on Tue Feb 18 21:58:42 2014

Copyright (c)1982, 2013, Oracle and/or its affiliates. All
rights reserved.

connected to target database: RPT12C (DBID=1779317104)
connected to recovery catalog database

RMAN> catalog start with '/u00/oradata/arch/complref';
searching for all files that match the pattern /u00/oradata/
arch/complref

List of Files Unknown to the Database
=====================================
File Name: /u00/oradata/arch/complref/1_557_821312592.dbf
File Name: /u00/oradata/arch/complref/1_558_821312592.dbf
File Name: /u00/oradata/arch/complref/1_559_821312592.dbf

Do you really want to catalog the above files (enter YES or
NO)? yes
cataloging files...
cataloging done
List of Cataloged Files
=======================
```

```
File Name: /u00/oradata/arch/complref/1_557_821312592.dbf
File Name: /u00/oradata/arch/complref/1_558_821312592.dbf
File Name: /u00/oradata/arch/complref/1_559_821312592.dbf
RMAN>
```

If you inadvertently or intentionally unregistered the database, you can reregister the database. However, some of your backup metadata might have been aged out of the control file because reregistration uses metadata from the control file. If you have a flash recovery area, you can easily recatalog all backups in the flash recovery area using the RECOVERY AREA option of the CATALOG command:

```
RMAN> catalog recovery area noprompt;
```

The NOPROMPT keyword, as you might expect, catalogs each backup without confirmation.

Manually Resynchronize the Recovery Catalog

In some situations, you need to resynchronize the metadata in the target database's control file with the recovery catalog. For example, the recovery catalog database might be unavailable for one or more of your backups because of a network problem or because the recovery catalog database is down. In this situation, RMAN records the backup information only in the target database control file. RMAN always records backup information in the control file even when the recovery catalog is unavailable!

exam watch

The RMAN recovery catalog records information about target database structures, archived redo logs, and backups when you run an RMAN BACKUP command or perform a manual resynchronization.

In addition, you may perform infrequent backups and rely on archived redo log files for a recovery scenario. This is not a problem per se, but the list of recent archived redo log files is not recorded automatically in the recovery catalog.

Finally, you may occasionally make changes to the physical structure of the target database. This information is automatically recorded in the target database control file but not in the recovery catalog.

Manually resynchronizing the recovery catalog is a straightforward process. After you start RMAN (and connect to a recovery catalog, of course), run the RESYNC CATALOG command, as in this example:

```
RMAN> resync catalog;
starting full resync of recovery catalog
full resync complete
RMAN>
```

Create and Use RMAN Stored Scripts

As mentioned earlier in this chapter, RMAN stored scripts help you automate repetitive groups of RMAN commands, easing the daily grind of being an Oracle DBA. Stored scripts are a good alternative to scripts you store on a traditional file system. Not only is the script stored with the recovery catalog (in other words, you won't lose it when you move the recovery catalog database), you can also control access to stored scripts by restricting a script to a single target database or to all databases managed within the recovery catalog.

Creating RMAN Stored Scripts

You create an RMAN script with the CREATE SCRIPT or CREATE GLOBAL SCRIPT command. The GLOBAL parameter specifies that the script is available to all RMAN target databases sharing this recovery catalog. To create a script as either global or local, you must be connected to the target database and the recovery catalog.

This example creates a global script called GLOBAL_BACKUP_DB that creates a full backup including archived log files:

```
RMAN> CREATE GLOBAL SCRIPT
2>        global_backup_db { BACKUP DATABASE PLUS ARCHIVELOG; }

created global script global_backup_db

RMAN>
```

If you wanted the script to be available to only one specific target database, you would omit the GLOBAL keyword. If you already have an RMAN script in a text file on a file system, you can import the script into an RMAN global or local script using this syntax:

```
RMAN> create script local_backup_db from file
2>        '/home/oracle/dbscripts/local_bak.rman';
```

Executing RMAN Stored Scripts

Running a global or local RMAN stored script is straightforward; however, you must execute the script within a RUN block. The syntax is as follows:

```
RUN
{   ...other commands...;
    EXECUTE [GLOBAL] SCRIPT scriptname;
    ...other commands...;
}
```

Here is how to run the global script you created in the previous section:

```
RMAN> run { execute script global_backup_db; }
```

You can also use parameters within an RMAN stored script. In other words, if one or two values will change within a script, such as the value for a particular channel or the value of an object to back up, then you can use the & character as a substitution indicator, much like you would in a SQL*Plus script.

EXERCISE 3-2

Creating a Parameterized Stored Script

In this exercise, you'll automate the backup of individual tablespaces. You will create an RMAN global script to accomplish this, with a parameter that will prompt you for a tablespace name.

1. Create a global stored script with the &1 parameter representing a tablespace name:

```
RMAN> create global script backup_ts
2>       {
3>           backup tablespace &1;
Enter value for 1: users
4>       }

created global script backup_ts

RMAN>
```

Notice that the default value for the tablespace parameter is USERS.

2. Run the stored script and override the default value assigned for the tablespace when you created the script with the SYSTEM tablespace:

```
RMAN> run {execute script backup_ts;}

executing global script: backup_ts

Enter value for 1: sysaux

Starting backup at 18-FEB-14
allocated channel: ORA_DISK_1
channel ORA_DISK_1: SID=517 device type=DISK
channel ORA_DISK_1: starting full datafile backup set
channel ORA_DISK_1: specifying datafile(s) in backup set
input datafile file number=00003
name=+DATA/RPT12C/DATAFILE/sysaux.257.826650753
channel ORA_DISK_1: starting piece 1 at 18-FEB-14
channel ORA_DISK_1: finished piece 1 at 18-FEB-14
piece handle=+RECOV/RPT12C/BACKUPSET/2014_02_18/
    nnndf0_tag20140218t222200_0.268.839888521
tag=TAG20140218T222200
    comment=NONE
channel ORA_DISK_1: backup set complete, elapsed time:
00:00:15
Finished backup at 18-FEB-14
RMAN>
```

Retrieving RMAN Stored Script Metadata

You can retrieve the contents of RMAN stored scripts using the PRINT and LIST commands: The PRINT command shows the contents of an individual script, and the LIST command shows the names of global scripts or both global and local scripts.

This example uses the LIST SCRIPT NAMES command to show both the local and global scripts:

```
RMAN> list script names;

List of Stored Scripts in Recovery Catalog

    Scripts of Target Database COMPLREF

        Script Name
```

```
        Description
        ----------------------------------------------------------
        local_backup_db

    Global Scripts

        Script Name
        Description
        ----------------------------------------------------------
        backup_ts

        global_backup_db

RMAN>
```

The LIST GLOBAL SCRIPT NAMES returns only the global script names.

To show the actual contents of a script, use the PRINT command. Because a global script and a local script can have the same name, you qualify the PRINT command with the GLOBAL option if you want to print the global version instead of the local version. This example retrieves the contents of the **global_backup_db** script:

```
RMAN> print global script global_backup_db;

printing stored global script: global_backup_db
{ BACKUP DATABASE PLUS ARCHIVELOG; }

RMAN>
```

You can spool the contents of a global or local script to a file using the TO FILE option of the PRINT command:

```
RMAN> print global script global_backup_db
2>         to file '/tmp/save_script.rman';

global script global_backup_db written to file /tmp/save_script.rman

RMAN>
```

Managing RMAN Stored Scripts

It's also easy to delete or replace stored scripts. To replace a stored script, use the REPLACE [GLOBAL] SCRIPT command. In this example, you want to modify the global script **backup_ts** to back up the SYSTEM tablespace in addition to the desired tablespace:

```
RMAN> replace global script backup_ts
2>    {
3>        backup tablespace system, &1;

Enter value for 1: users
4>    }

replaced global script backup_ts

RMAN>
```

As you might expect, you use the DELETE SCRIPT command to delete a global or local script:

```
RMAN> delete script local_backup_db;

deleted script: local_backup_db

RMAN>
```

CERTIFICATION OBJECTIVE 3.02

Protect the RMAN Recovery Catalog

Since the recovery catalog resides in an Oracle database, it must be backed up and restored just like any other database. You must know how to re-create a recovery catalog when your recovery catalog database backups are incomplete. In addition, you may be required to move the recovery catalog to another database and drop the recovery catalog from a database. These topics, in addition to upgrading a recovery catalog, are covered in the following sections.

Backing Up the Recovery Catalog

Even though this has already been mentioned in this chapter and in other chapters—and for that matter, in other books—it's worth another reminder: Don't keep your recovery catalog in the same database as your target database. If you lose the target database, you also lose your recovery catalog, and you must rely on a backup or multiplexed copy of the target database control file to re-create the recovery catalog and restore the database, assuming you have adequate backups and any structural changes to the target database were made within the window of the initialization parameter CONTROL_FILE_RECORD_KEEP_TIME.

Now that you've been reminded to keep the recovery catalog in a separate database, you should also remember to back up the database containing the recovery catalog, using RMAN, of course, to ensure that the recovery catalog metadata and backup information are recorded in the recovery catalog database's control file. Here is the Oracle-recommended configuration for ensuring a recoverable recovery catalog database:

1. Configure the database for ARCHIVELOG mode.
2. Set the RMAN parameter RETENTION POLICY to REDUNDANCY greater than 1.
3. Back up the recovery catalog to disk and tape after each target database backup (in other words, two separate media types).
4. Use BACKUP DATABASE PLUS ARCHIVELOG when you back up the recovery catalog.
5. Use CONFIGURE CONTROLFILE AUTOBACKUP ON to ensure that the control file is backed up after every RMAN backup.

This configuration ensures that a complete loss of either a target database or a recovery catalog database is completely recoverable. If you lose both the target database and the recovery catalog database at the same time, it's probably because you are using the target database for the recovery catalog. And, as a final reminder, *do not do that*!

Recovering from a Lost Recovery Catalog

In the event that you lose the recovery catalog database, the recovery operation is much the same as recovering any other database that has adequate backups (using RMAN) and is running in ARCHIVELOG mode. For example, you can restore a control file backup (or use a multiplexed control file) and then restore and perform a complete recovery using RMAN backups of the recovery catalog plus archived redo log files. If you have the luxury of having two recovery catalog databases, you can save the RMAN metadata for one recovery catalog in the database of the other recovery catalog.

If you have no backups of your recovery catalog database, your options are more limited, but hope is not lost. Here are the steps to follow to retrieve most, if not all, of the metadata for your target database backups:

1. Re-create the recovery catalog database from scratch.
2. Register the target database with the new recovery catalog.
3. Perform a RESYNC CATALOG operation to copy all available backup information from the target database control file.
4. Use the CATALOG START WITH command to add information about any available backups of the target database to the recovery catalog.

Since the previous physical backup files for your target database contain the target DBID and RMAN identifies each database in its recovery catalog with the DBID, the RMAN CATALOG START WITH command can easily assign each backup to its associated target database in the recovery catalog.

Exporting and Importing the Recovery Catalog

As you can with any database, you can use the Oracle Data Pump export and import utilities **expdp** and **impdp** to create logical backups of the recovery catalog. You can use this logical backup to move the recovery catalog to another database. Follow these general steps to move a recovery catalog to another database:

1. Use the **expdp** utility to copy the recovery catalog schema to an export dump file.
2. Create the recovery catalog owner on the target catalog database with the appropriate permissions; see "Create the Recovery Catalog Owner" earlier in this chapter.
3. Use the corresponding import utility to copy the recovery catalog schema to the target catalog database.

The next time you launch RMAN, you connect to the same target database but a different recovery catalog database. However, even though the recovery catalog database name is different, the target database's metadata is identical to the metadata in the previous recovery catalog.

You can also use transportable tablespaces to move a recovery catalog schema from one database to another.

You do not need to run an RMAN CREATE CATALOG command in this scenario; the tables, columns, and views are already in place from the source database.

Dropping a Recovery Catalog

After you have successfully moved the recovery catalog, you can drop the catalog from the previous recovery catalog database. As you might expect, you use the DROP CATALOG command to remove the catalog from the previous recovery catalog database. In fact, you need to run the command twice as a way of confirming your desire to delete, as in this example:

```
RMAN> connect catalog rcat_owner/Rcat9095@rcat

connected to recovery catalog database

RMAN> drop catalog;

recovery catalog owner is RCAT_OWNER
enter DROP CATALOG again to confirm catalog removal

RMAN> drop catalog;

recovery catalog dropped

RMAN>
```

Note that you do not need to connect to a target database to drop a recovery catalog. Also, to ensure that all traces of the recovery catalog owner are removed from the previous recovery catalog database, do not manually remove the recovery catalog owner's schema. Use the DROP CATALOG command instead.

Upgrading the Recovery Catalog

To support a newer RMAN client (for example, your RMAN recovery catalog is at version 11*g* and a new RMAN client is at version 12*c*), you use the UPGRADE CATALOG command to update the local packages and schema. As with the DROP CATALOG command, you are prompted twice, and you do not need to be connected to a target database. Here is an example:

```
RMAN> upgrade catalog;

recovery catalog owner is RCAT_OWNER
enter UPGRADE CATALOG command again to confirm catalog upgrade

RMAN> upgrade catalog;
```

```
recovery catalog upgraded to version 12.01.00.01
DBMS_RCVMAN package upgraded to version 12.01.00.01
DBMS_RCVCAT package upgraded to version 12.01.00.01
RMAN>
```

You receive an error message if you attempt to downgrade the recovery catalog version. However, if the version has not changed, the UPGRADE CATALOG command proceeds in case all required packages are not in place.

Create and Use a Virtual Private Catalog

In many organizations, one DBA cannot manage the RMAN backups for all databases within the organization. In addition, the Sarbanes-Oxley Act (2002) requires an IT shop to tighten up the security and access to each database so that a DBA can see only the databases and database backups for which they are responsible. As of Oracle Database 11g, you can create an RMAN *virtual private catalog* to facilitate and enforce these separations of duty. In the following sections, you'll get more details about RMAN virtual private catalogs, learn how to create and manage a virtual private catalog, and see a virtual private catalog in action.

Understanding Virtual Private Catalogs

A virtual private catalog is functionally identical to the recovery catalog discussed throughout this chapter; from the perspective of an individual DBA, it appears to be a single catalog containing only his or her databases' metadata and RMAN backup information. From this point on, the recovery catalog discussed earlier in the chapter will be called the *base catalog*. Each virtual private catalog is a logical partition of the base catalog. Each virtual catalog owner relies on a separate Oracle account and several views and synonyms in the recovery catalog database.

exam watch

Either the base recovery catalog owner or a virtual private catalog owner can query the DB_NAME column of the view DBINC to see a list of registered databases. The virtual private catalog owner will see only databases she has registered or to which she has been granted access.

As was already done earlier in this chapter, the base recovery catalog owner creates the base catalog and grants the RECOVERY_CATALOG_OWNER role to each Oracle account that will own a virtual private catalog. If databases are already registered in the base recovery catalog, the base catalog owner can grant access to a registered database for a virtual private catalog owner; alternatively, the base recovery catalog owner can grant the REGISTER privilege to the virtual private catalog owner so he or she can register a new database in the virtual private catalog.

Creating and Managing a Virtual Private Catalog

The following sections show you how to set up a virtual private catalog, create the virtual private catalog owner, and then grant the appropriate privileges to the virtual private catalog owner. Next, the virtual private catalog owner will create a virtual private catalog and register one or more databases. Alternatively, the base catalog owner can grant catalog privileges for an already registered database to a virtual catalog owner.

For the examples in the following sections, the base catalog owner RCAT_OWNER for the RCAT database will create a virtual private catalog owner VPC1 and grant the RMAN privilege REGISTER DATABASE to VPC1. The DBA of the CDB01 database on the server **oel63** will use VPC1 to create a virtual private catalog and register the CDB01 database.

Creating Virtual Private Catalog Owners

On the recovery catalog database, the first step is to create an Oracle account that will own the virtual private catalog:

```
[oracle@oel63 complref]$ sqlplus / as sysdba

SQL*Plus: Release 12.1.0.1.0 Production on Wed Feb 19 00:17:49 2014
Copyright (c) 1982, 2013, Oracle.  All rights reserved.
Connected to:
Oracle Database 12c Enterprise Edition Release 12.1.0.1.0 - 64bit Production
With the Partitioning, Automatic Storage Management,
     OLAP, Advanced Analytics and Real Application Testing options
SQL> create user vpc1 identified by vpc1
  2> default tablespace rman quota unlimited on rman;
User created.
SQL>
```

Granting Permissions to Virtual Private Catalog Owners

Next, you will grant the RECOVERY_CATALOG_OWNER privilege to VPC1, the owner of the new virtual private catalog:

```
SQL> grant recovery_catalog_owner to vpc1;
Grant succeeded.
SQL>
```

Note that the user VPC1 is not the owner of the entire recovery catalog; the role name is a bit misleading. Instead, it means that VPC1 can create his or her own private recovery catalog that is a logical subset of the base recovery catalog.

Optionally, the base recovery catalog owner can now grant permission on existing catalogs using the RMAN GRANT CATALOG command. In this example, the base catalog owner gives permission to VPC1 on the DW database that is already registered in the recovery catalog (note: RMAN must be connected to the recovery catalog, not necessarily the target database, before issuing this command):

```
RMAN> grant catalog for database cdb01 to vpc1;
Grant succeeded.
RMAN>
```

If the base recovery catalog owner wants the user VPC1 to register his or her own databases, the owner must grant the RMAN privilege REGISTER DATABASE to VPC1, as in this example:

```
RMAN> grant register database to vpc1;
Grant succeeded.
RMAN>
```

Creating a Virtual Private Catalog

Now that the user VPC1 has the appropriate privileges to create and populate a virtual catalog, the next step is to connect to RMAN as the user VPC1 and create the catalog.

For convenience, the user VPC1 connected to the target database HR at the same time that he connected to the recovery catalog. The next step is to create the virtual private catalog itself (this needs to be done only once, just like you need to register a database only once):

```
[oracle@oel63 complref]$ rman target / catalog vpc1/vpc1@rcat

Recovery Manager: Release 12.1.0.1.0 -
     Production on Wed Feb 19 00:27:27 2014
```

```
Copyright (c)1982, 2013, Oracle and/or its affiliates.  All
rights reserved.
connected to target database: CDB01 (DBID=1367268229)
connected to recovery catalog database

RMAN> create virtual catalog;
found eligible base catalog owned by RCAT_OWNER
created virtual catalog against base catalog owned by RCAT_OWNER
RMAN>
```

Dropping a virtual private catalog is the same as dropping a base catalog; just make sure you do not execute the DROP CATALOG command as the base catalog owner!

Using a Virtual Private Catalog

Now that all the permissions are granted and the virtual catalog has been created, the user VPC1 can register a database:

```
[oracle@oel63 complref]$ rman target / catalog vpc1/vpc1@rcat

Recovery Manager: Release 12.1.0.1.0 -
     Production on Wed Feb 19 00:30:59 2014
Copyright (c)1982, 2013, Oracle and/or its affiliates.  All
rights reserved.
connected to target database: CDB01 (DBID=1367268229)
connected to recovery catalog database


RMAN> register database;

database registered in recovery catalog
starting full resync of recovery catalog
full resync complete
RMAN>
```

To see which databases the user VPC1 can manage via the RMAN virtual private catalog, connect to the recovery catalog database and query the DBINC view:

```
[oracle@oel63 complref]$ sqlplus vpc1/vpc1@rcat
SQL*Plus: Release 12.1.0.1.0 Production on Wed Feb 19 00:33:25
2014
Copyright (c) 1982, 2013, Oracle.  All rights reserved.
Last Successful login time: Wed Feb 19 2014 00:31:00 -06:00
```

```
Connected to:
Oracle Database 12c Enterprise Edition Release 12.1.0.1.0 -
64bit Production

With the Partitioning, Automatic Storage Management,
     OLAP, Advanced Analytics and Real Application Testing
options

SQL> select distinct db_name from dbinc;
DB_NAME
--------
CDB01

SQL>
```

Note that you have to use DISTINCT in the SELECT statement. The DBINC view has one row for each incarnation of a target database; without the use of DISTINCT, more than one row per database will often appear.

CERTIFICATION SUMMARY

This chapter started with an overview of the advantages and disadvantages of using an RMAN recovery catalog over using only the control file for backup information. Although there is some extra work to maintain another database to store the recovery catalog information, this disadvantage is relatively minor compared to the advantages of ease of use and more robust recovery capabilities.

Next, assuming that you will eventually need and want a recovery catalog, you stepped through the process of creating a recovery catalog and registering one or more target databases with the recovery catalog. In addition, you learned how to include the metadata for backups created outside of RMAN (in the recovery catalog), further increasing the value of a central backup metadata repository.

Stored scripts, another feature available only with a recovery catalog, help you automate some routine tasks consisting of many steps or commands, all stored in a single command. Stored scripts can be either local (specific to one database) or available to all databases registered in the catalog.

In the event of a lost or corrupted recovery catalog (which should never happen because you back up your recovery catalog as often as you back up your target database), you reviewed a few different disaster recovery scenarios and learned ways to lessen the potential impact of a full or partial loss of the recovery catalog.

To facilitate the division of labor and responsibility when you have more than one DBA in your organization, you can use the concept of virtual private catalogs. Setting up a virtual private catalog for each DBA in your organization is straightforward and restricts access to only the databases for which the DBA is responsible, while at the same time keeping all database backup information in the same recovery catalog.

TWO-MINUTE DRILL

Create and Use an RMAN Recovery Catalog

- ❑ If your backups are simple and your database is not mission-critical, the control file is probably sufficient for your RMAN metadata.
- ❑ If you have several databases to back up and you want to use stored scripts, then a recovery catalog is highly recommended based on Oracle best practices.
- ❑ Having a centralized metadata repository permits easy backup reporting because you can use one set of RC_ views in one database to query backup information.
- ❑ Several useful RMAN commands such as BACKUP ... KEEP FOREVER are available only when you use a recovery catalog.
- ❑ The three basic steps for creating a recovery catalog are 1) configure a new or existing database, 2) create the recovery catalog owner, and 3) create the catalog.
- ❑ Only about 125MB of disk space is required for the initial deployment of a recovery catalog.
- ❑ The predefined role RECOVERY_CATALOG_OWNER includes all privileges necessary to manage a recovery catalog, such as ALTER SESSION, CREATE SESSION, and CREATE TABLE.
- ❑ You use the CREATE CATALOG command to create the recovery catalog.
- ❑ You can use Enterprise Manager to persist recovery catalog credentials.
- ❑ The initial synchronization of the recovery catalog uses the target database control file.
- ❑ Each database to be backed up needs to be registered with the recovery catalog using the REGISTER DATABASE command.
- ❑ The target database must be in the MOUNT or OPEN state to register successfully with the recovery catalog.
- ❑ You can use the DBNEWID utility (enter **nid** at the command line) to change the value of the DBID for a database. You can also change the database name as an additional option.
- ❑ After changing the DBID for a database, you must reopen it with RESETLOGS, and then you should perform a full backup of the database.

- ❑ You can unregister a database from a recovery catalog using the UNREGISTER DATABASE command.
- ❑ You can catalog several types of backup files with RMAN: datafile copies, backup pieces, control file copies, and archived redo log files.
- ❑ One of the many advantages to using a flash recovery area is that it makes it easy for you to recatalog all backup files in the area by using the CATALOG RECOVERY AREA command.
- ❑ Manual resynchronization of the recovery catalog is required when the recovery catalog is unavailable during an RMAN backup. This applies if you want to catalog archived redo log files or you make physical changes to the target database.
- ❑ You create stored scripts with either the CREATE SCRIPT or CREATE GLOBAL SCRIPT command.
- ❑ Local scripts are available only for the target database.
- ❑ Global scripts are available for any target database or even when you are not connected to any target database.
- ❑ You execute a global or local script within a RUN block.
- ❑ You execute scripts with the EXECUTE [GLOBAL] SCRIPT command.
- ❑ The substitution character & permits a default value that can be overridden when the script runs.
- ❑ The LIST [GLOBAL] SCRIPT NAMES shows a list of the global or global and local scripts in the repository.
- ❑ The PRINT command shows the contents of a global or local script.
- ❑ You can use REPLACE [GLOBAL] SCRIPT to replace the contents of a global or local script.
- ❑ DELETE SCRIPT deletes a script from the recovery catalog.

Protect the RMAN Recovery Catalog

- ❑ The recovery catalog database is backed up like any other database in your environment.
- ❑ The recovery catalog should be in ARCHIVELOG mode.
- ❑ The utilities **expdp** and **impdp** can create logical backups of the recovery catalog that can be used in a disaster recovery situation or to move the recovery catalog to another database.

- ❑ Using transportable tablespaces is another way to move the recovery catalog to another database.
- ❑ Use the DROP CATALOG command to drop a recovery catalog. Do not manually drop schemas and packages in the recovery catalog database.
- ❑ You run the UPGRADE CATALOG command to support an RMAN client that is at a later version than the recovery catalog database.
- ❑ A virtual private catalog facilitates the separation of duties among several DBAs.
- ❑ One or more virtual private catalogs share the same base recovery catalog.
- ❑ You grant the RECOVERY_CATALOG_OWNER role to each Oracle user account that will own a virtual private catalog.
- ❑ The base recovery catalog owner can grant permissions on existing registered databases to virtual private catalog owners using the GRANT CATALOG command.
- ❑ Once you grant a user the RECOVERY_CATALOG_OWNER role, the user creates the virtual catalog with the CREATE VIRTUAL CATALOG command.
- ❑ The virtual private catalog owner uses REGISTER DATABASE to register a new database, just like a base recovery catalog user would.
- ❑ You can query the DBINC data dictionary view to determine the databases accessible to the virtual private catalog owner.

SELF TEST

The following questions will help you measure your understanding of the material presented in this chapter. Read all the choices carefully because there might be more than one correct answer. Choose all correct answers for each question.

Create and Use an RMAN Recovery Catalog

1. Which of the following are good reasons to use a recovery catalog instead of the target database control file? (Choose three answers.)
   A. You can keep stored scripts in the recovery catalog.
   B. You save space in the control file of the target database used for RMAN backup information.
   C. A recovery catalog is easier to maintain than a control file in each target database.
   D. The recovery catalog can report on the tablespaces and datafiles in the target database at any point in time since the recovery catalog was created.
   E. A recovery catalog can be used to manage RMAN information for more than one database.

2. If you do not use a recovery catalog, what data dictionary or dynamic performance views must you query to retrieve RMAN backup information? (Choose the best answer.)
   A. The V$ views on each target such as V$BACKUP_SET and V$DATAFILE_COPY
   B. The RC_ views on each target
   C. The DBA_ views on each target
   D. V$CONTROLFILE

3. The net service name of your target database is DW, and the net service name of your recovery catalog database is RCAT. The environment variable ORACLE_SID has a value of RCAT. Which of the following sets of commands will successfully create a recovery catalog?
   A. connect catalog rman/rmanpass
      create catalog;
   B. connect catalog rman/rmanpass@rcat
      create catalog@rcat;
   C. connect catalog rman/rmanpass@dw
      create catalog;
   D. create catalog rman/rmanpass@rcat;

4. Which of the following roles should you grant to the recovery catalog owner? (Choose the best answer.)
   A. RECOVERY_CATALOG
   B. CATALOG_OWNER
   C. RECOVERY_CATALOG_OWNER
   D. DBA
5. Which of the following does not occur when you register a target database with the recovery catalog database using the REGISTER DATABASE command?
   A. The recovery catalog is synchronized with the structure of the database from the control file.
   B. Information about manual tablespace backups is registered in the recovery catalog.
   C. Data about recent backups is copied from the control file to the recovery catalog tables.
   D. Metadata rows are created for the target database in the recovery catalog.
6. What is the difference between a partial and a complete recovery catalog resynchronization? (Choose two answers.)
   A. A partial resynchronization occurs when RMAN records have been aged out of the target database's control file because of the value of CONTROL_FILE_RECORD_KEEP_TIME.
   B. A partial resynchronization uses the current target database control file, and a full resynchronization uses a backup control file.
   C. A full resynchronization uses the current target database control file, and a partial resynchronization uses a backup control file.
   D. A full resynchronization includes information about the database structure and not just recent backups.
7. What is the difference between an RMAN local script and an RMAN global script?
   A. A local script is available only for a single target database.
   B. A global script references a list of commands in an external file.
   C. A local script references a list of commands in an external file.
   D. A global script can execute commands against many target databases simultaneously.
   E. A local script is available only to the user who created it. A global script is available to all users.
8. You create and execute a stored local script using the following commands:

```
create script full_backup
{
   backup as compressed backupset database;
   delete noprompt obsolete;
}
execute script full_backup;
```

What happens when you run these commands?

A. The script is created but does not run successfully.

B. A full backup occurs, and all previous backups and archived redo logs outside of the retention period or retention policy are deleted.

C. The script creation step fails because you must explicitly allocate one or more channels with a stored script.

D. The script does not run because you must specify a target database when you use a local script.

Protect the RMAN Recovery Catalog

9. You have lost the most recent archived redo log files from the recovery catalog database as well as the tablespace containing the RMAN catalog. You can do an incomplete restore of the recovery catalog database to a point in time after the target databases were registered with the recovery catalog. What commands can you use to resynchronize the target database's metadata and backup information with the recovery catalog database?

A. Use the CREATE CATALOG command to re-create the recovery catalog database.

B. Use the REGISTER DATABASE command to reregister the target database control file records.

C. Use the RESYNC CATALOG command to update the recovery catalog with the latest records from the target database's control file and the CATALOG START WITH command to record any additional backups that are no longer in the target database's control file.

D. Use both the CREATE CATALOG and the REGISTER DATABASE commands to resynchronize the target database with the recovery catalog.

10. Under what circumstances would you use the RMAN command UPGRADE CATALOG?

A. When you have made structural changes to the recovery catalog database

B. When you are using a version of the recovery catalog that is older than that required by the RMAN target database client

C. When you are using a version of the RMAN target database client that is older than required by the recovery catalog

D. When you have made structural changes to the target database

11. You have created a virtual private catalog to separate your RMAN administration duties among several DBAs for 20 different databases. Which role must you grant to each virtual catalog owner to allow the person to access existing registered databases?

A. SELECT_CATALOG_ROLE

B. REGISTER_CATALOG_OWNER

C. VPC_OWNER

D. RECOVERY_CATALOG_OWNER

12. The virtual catalog database owner VPC1 has the RECOVERY_CATALOG_OWNER privilege on the database CATDB2 in addition to the RMAN REGISTER DATABASE privilege. Which of the following sets of commands will allow an 11g RMAN client to create a virtual catalog, register a new database DW, and create a full database backup?

A. RMAN> connect catalog vpc1/vpc1pwd@dw
RMAN> create virtual catalog;
RMAN> connect target system/syspwd@catdb2;
RMAN> register database;
RMAN> backup database;

B. RMAN> connect catalog vpc1/vpc1pwd@catdb2
RMAN> exec
catowner.dbms_rcvcat.create_virtual_catalog;
RMAN> connect target system/syspwd@dw;
RMAN> register database;
RMAN> backup database;

C. RMAN> connect catalog vpc1/vpc1pwd@catdb2
RMAN> create virtual catalog;
RMAN> connect target system/syspwd@dw;
RMAN> grant catalog for database DW to vpc1;
RMAN> backup database;

D. RMAN> connect catalog vpc1/vpc1pwd@catdb2
RMAN> create virtual catalog;
RMAN> connect target system/syspwd@dw;
RMAN> register database;
RMAN> backup database;

SELF TEST ANSWERS

Create and Use an RMAN Recovery Catalog

1. ☑ **A, D,** and **E.** Using a recovery catalog allows you to create and maintain stored scripts. In addition, it keeps a running history of all changes to the database tablespaces and datafiles since the recovery catalog was created. Finally, you can store recovery information for more than one database in a recovery catalog.
☒ **B** and **C** are incorrect. **B** is not a good reason to use a recovery catalog because the RMAN repository information is always stored in the control file even if you use a recovery catalog. **C** is also not a good reason because a recovery catalog requires more setup and maintenance in addition to a backup of another database. Also, the control file is simpler to manage, and its size can be controlled with the parameter CONTROL_FILE_RECORD_KEEP_TIME. It is much simpler to export a copy of the control file whenever the database structure changes using ALTER DATABASE BACKUP CONTROLFILE TO TRACE.

2. ☑ **A.** When you do not use a recovery catalog, information about RMAN backups is available on each individual target in dynamic performance views such as V$BACKUP_SET and V$DATAFILE_COPY. These views are sourced from the target database control file.
☒ **B, C,** and **D** are incorrect. **B** is incorrect because the RC_ views exist only in the database containing the recovery catalog. **C** is incorrect because the DBA_ views do not maintain RMAN information. **D** is incorrect because V$CONTROLFILE contains only the locations of each copy of the target database's control file.

3. ☑ **A.** The environment variable ORACLE_SID is set. Thus, the RMAN command CONNECT automatically uses the value of ORACLE_SID to connect to the recovery catalog.
☒ **B, C,** and **D** are incorrect. **B** is incorrect because you do not need to specify the name of the recovery catalog database in the CREATE CATALOG command. **C** is incorrect because it creates the recovery catalog in the target database. **D** is incorrect because you cannot combine the CONNECT CATALOG and CREATE CATALOG commands.

4. ☑ **C.** The predefined role RECOVERY_CATALOG_OWNER includes the system privileges ALTER SESSION, CREATE CLUSTER, CREATE DATABASE LINK, CREATE PROCEDURE, CREATE SEQUENCE, CREATE SESSION, CREATE SYNONYM, CREATE TABLE, CREATE TRIGGER, CREATE TYPE, and CREATE VIEW.
☒ **A, B,** and **D** are incorrect. **A** and **B** are incorrect because the RECOVERY_CATALOG and CATALOG_OWNER roles do not exist. **D** is incorrect because it provides the recovery catalog owner with more system privileges than necessary.

5. ☑ **B.** Any manual backups performed outside of RMAN or that were aged out of the target database control file before you create the recovery catalog must be manually registered with the recovery catalog.
☒ **A, C,** and **D** are incorrect. They are all steps that occur when you register a database with a recovery catalog.

6. ☑ **B** and **D.** A full resynchronization creates a control file snapshot and synchronizes database structure information as well as information about backups in the target database control file that are not in the recovery catalog. A partial resynchronization compares the target database's control file directly with the control file.
☒ **A** and **C** are incorrect. **A** is incorrect because RMAN records aged out of the control file can be added to the recovery catalog manually. **C** is incorrect because a full resynchronization uses a copy of the control file (a control file snapshot) for its comparison. A partial resynchronization does not.

7. ☑ **A.** A local script is available only to the database that was connected when the script was created.
☒ **B, C, D,** and **E** are incorrect. **B** and **C** are incorrect because both global and local scripts are stored in the recovery catalog. **D** is incorrect because any script operates on one database at a time. **E** is incorrect because both local and global scripts are available to any user who authenticates with the recovery catalog.

8. ☑ **A.** Stored scripts, whether they are local or global, must be run within a RUN block as follows:
run {execute script full_backup;}.
☒ **B, C,** and **D** are incorrect. **B** is incorrect because a script must be enclosed in a RUN block. **C** is incorrect because you can include a channel allocation or use the default channel in the RUN command containing the EXECUTE SCRIPT command. **D** is incorrect because both local and global scripts apply only to the currently connected target database.

Protect the RMAN Recovery Catalog

9. ☑ **C.** The RESYNC CATALOG command synchronizes the target database's control file information with the recovery catalog database, and the CATALOG START WITH command adds any backup information that is no longer in the target database control file.
☒ **A, B,** and **D** are incorrect. **A** is incorrect because you do not need to re-create the recovery catalog; you just need to resynchronize it. **B** is incorrect because the database itself is already registered with the recovery catalog. **D** is incorrect because you do not need to re-create the recovery catalog or reregister the target database.

10. ☑ **B.** When the recovery catalog schema version is less than the RMAN client version, you must use UPGRADE CATALOG.
☒ **A, C,** and **D** are incorrect. **A** and **D** are incorrect because structural changes to either database means you should back up your control file, but this does not trigger a recovery catalog upgrade. **C** is incorrect because you can use RMAN clients that are older than the recovery catalog database version, although some features of the newer RMAN client will not be available, such as flashback database.

11. ☑ **D.** To allow access to a virtual private catalog, you must grant the role RECOVERY_CATALOG_OWNER as a SQL command to each user who will access a virtual private catalog.
☒ **A, B,** and **C** are incorrect. **A** is incorrect because the SELECT_CATALOG_ROLE allows access to a database's data dictionary and does not control access to RMAN virtual catalogs. **B** and **C** are incorrect because these roles do not exist in a default installation of the database.

12. ☑ **D.** To create the virtual catalog, you connect to the base catalog, create the virtual catalog, connect to the target database, register the database, and finally back it up. You need to create the virtual catalog only once, and each target database needs to be registered only once. Subsequent backup operations can occur after connecting to the base catalog and the target database.
☒ **A, B,** and **C** are incorrect. **A** is incorrect because the base catalog and virtual catalog are on the instance with the service name CATDB2, not the target database DW. **B** is incorrect because EXEC CATOWNER.DBMS_RCVCAT.CREATE_VIRTUAL_CATALOG is only for pre-11*g* clients and must be run by the virtual catalog owner at a SQL> prompt. **C** is incorrect because GRANT CATALOG FOR DATABASE DW TO VPC1 must be run by the base catalog owner and only if the database is already registered in the base catalog.

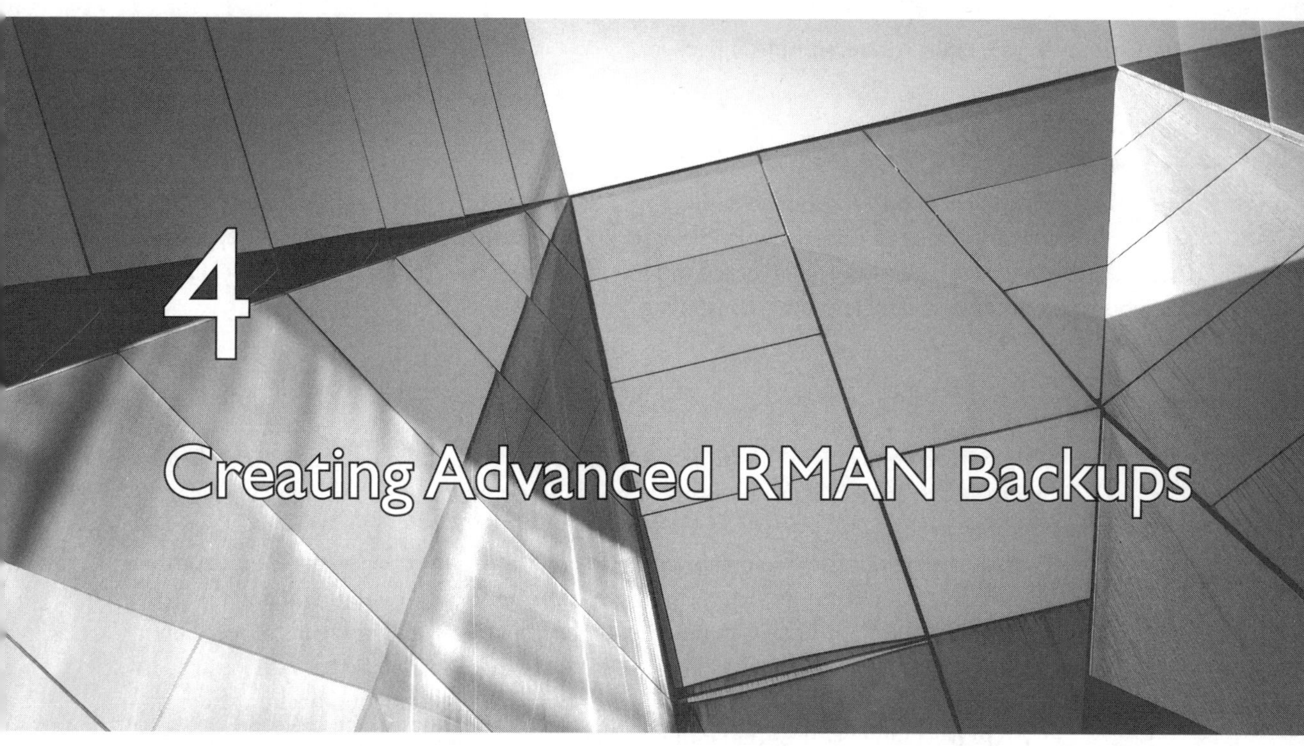

4

Creating Advanced RMAN Backups

CERTIFICATION OBJECTIVES

4.01	Use Various RMAN Backup Types and Strategies
4.02	Perform Full and Incremental Backups
4.03	Use Techniques to Improve Backups
4.04	Manage Backups
4.05	Perform Backup of Nondatabase Files
✓	Two-Minute Drill
Q&A	Self Test

Here's the part you've all been waiting for: You'll learn to create backups using Recovery Manager (RMAN). Needless to say, you can create many different types of backups using RMAN and leverage the many features new to Oracle Database 12*c* to make your backups smaller and less time-consuming.

RMAN supports a number of backup methods that can be used according to your availability needs, the desired size of your recovery window, and the amount of downtime you can endure while the database or part of the database is involved in a recovery operation. You'll learn more about configuring and using recovery in Chapter 5.

First, you'll learn how to create image file backups—in other words, exact copies of your database's datafiles. Even though you can make copies of your database files manually, RMAN provides a number of added benefits. You'll also get an overview of the other types of RMAN backups: standalone whole-database backups, as well as whole-database backups that you can use as part of an incremental backup strategy. RMAN has many features that can make an incremental backup run even faster, such as creating a block change tracking file to mark which datafile blocks have changed since the last backup.

Next, you'll learn how to create an archival backup for long-term retention. Business requirements and recent changes to record-keeping and privacy laws demand a retention period for corporate data that is frequently beyond the configured RMAN retention policy. An RMAN archival backup gives you a consistent and simple snapshot of your database at a point in time in the past.

I'll also review the configuration options available in RMAN when you are connected to a target database; each target database has its own set of configurable parameters, such as the compression level, automatic backups of the control file, and channel types.

As of Oracle Database 11*g*, RMAN provides enhancements such as multisection backups for very large database (VLDB) environments. In previous versions of RMAN, a bigfile tablespace took a long time to back up because RMAN could process the bigfile tablespace only serially. In Oracle Database 11*g* and 12*c*, RMAN can back up large datafiles as a multisection backup, leveraging multiple output devices (multiple channels either to disk or to tape) to dramatically reduce the time it takes to back up the datafile, among other advantages. RMAN's alternative compression techniques and encryption methods further reduce backup size and make the backups unavailable to unauthorized parties by using standalone passwords or the database's encryption wallet.

Finally, you'll get a whirlwind tour of RMAN reporting capabilities. As a robust backup tool, RMAN has a wealth of commands and many useful data dictionary views. This makes it easy for you to identify the state and contents of your backups, either on the target database or in the repository.

CERTIFICATION OBJECTIVE 4.01

Use Various RMAN Backup Types and Strategies

RMAN configuration settings can appear daunting at first, until you realize that the "out-of-the-box" settings for RMAN don't require many configuration changes to perform successful full and incremental backups to disk. The following sections reiterate some key RMAN concepts and capabilities, go into a bit more depth on how to specify alternative backup destinations, cover how to persist some RMAN settings, and show you how to ensure that the control file is backed up with every backup.

Types of RMAN Backups

RMAN supports a number of backup methods, depending on your availability needs, the desired size of your recovery window, and the amount of downtime you can endure while the database or part of the database is involved in a recovery operation.

Consistent and Inconsistent Backups

A physical backup can be classified as being a *consistent* or *inconsistent* backup. In a consistent backup, all datafiles have the same system change number (SCN). In other words, all changes in the redo logs have been applied to the datafiles, making the files into a synchronized set. Because an open database with no uncommitted transactions can have some dirty blocks in the buffer cache, it is rare that an open database backup can be considered consistent. As a result, consistent backups are taken when the database is shut down normally or in a mounted (MOUNT) state.

In contrast, an inconsistent backup is performed while the database is open and users are accessing the database. A recovery operation performed using an inconsistent backup must rely on both archived and online redo log files to bring the database into a consistent state before it is opened. This is because the SCNs of the datafiles typically do not match when an inconsistent backup takes place. As a result, a database must be in ARCHIVELOG mode to use an inconsistent backup method. Apart from that, backup mode tablespaces can produce a lot of redo log entries and recycled log entries could be lost.

Full and Incremental Backups

Full backups include all blocks of every datafile within a tablespace or a database; it is essentially a bit-for-bit copy of one or more datafiles in the database. Either RMAN or an operating system command can be used to perform a full backup, although backups performed outside of RMAN must be cataloged with RMAN before they can be used in an RMAN recovery operation. However, it is possible to recover a database manually without using RMAN. As of Oracle Database 12*c*, Oracle recommends that all backups be performed using RMAN; using OS commands to perform backups no longer has any significant advantages over the equivalent RMAN commands.

In Oracle 12*c*, incremental backups can be level 0 or level 1. A level 0 backup is a full backup of all blocks in the database that can be used in conjunction with differential, incremental, or cumulative incremental level 1 backups in a database recovery operation. A distinct advantage to using an incremental backup in a recovery strategy is that archived and online redo log files may not be necessary to restore a database or tablespace to a consistent state; the incremental backups may have some or all of the blocks needed. Incremental backups can be performed only within RMAN.

Image Copies

Image copies are full backups created by operating system commands or RMAN BACKUP AS COPY commands, at the database, tablespace, or datafile level. Although a full backup created with a Linux **cp** command can be later registered in the RMAN catalog as a database backup, performing the same image copy backup using RMAN has the advantage of checking for corrupt blocks as they are being read by RMAN and recording the information about the bad blocks in the data dictionary. Image copies are the default backup file format in RMAN.

This is a great feature of Oracle 12*c* RMAN for the following reason: If you add another datafile to a tablespace, you also need to remember to add the new datafile to your Linux script **cp** command. By creating image copies using the RMAN BACKUP AS COPY DATABASE command, all datafiles will automatically be included in the backup. Forgetting to add the new datafile to a Linux script will make a recovery situation extremely inconvenient at best and a disaster at worst.

Backupsets and Backup Pieces

In contrast to image copies, which can be created in most any backup environment, backupsets can be created and restored only with RMAN. A *backupset* is an RMAN backup of part or all of a database, consisting of one or more *backup pieces*. Each backup piece belongs only to one backupset and can contain backups of one or many datafiles in the database. All backupsets and pieces are recorded in the RMAN repository, the same as any other RMAN-initiated backup.

Compressed Backups

For any Oracle12*c* RMAN backup creating a backupset, compression is available to reduce the amount of disk space or tape needed to store the backup. Compressed backups are usable only by RMAN, and they need no special processing when used in a recovery operation; RMAN automatically decompresses the backup. Creating compressed backups is as easy as specifying AS COMPRESSED BACKUPSET in the RMAN BACKUP command.

RMAN Backup Destinations

RMAN backup destinations include a file system disk directory, a tape-based media library, or the flash recovery area. Oracle best practices dictate that you use a flash recovery area for many reasons; Chapter 2 covered the details of configuring and using the flash recovery area and the initialization parameters DB_RECOVERY_FILE_DEST and DB_RECOVERY_FILE_DEST_SIZE. One of the many benefits of a flash recovery area includes automatic filenaming for backup files. In addition, RMAN automatically deletes obsolete files in the flash recovery area when it's pressed for space.

To facilitate a completely disk-based recovery scenario, the flash recovery area should be big enough for a copy of all datafiles, incremental backup files, online redo logs, archived redo logs not on tape, control file autobackups, and server parameter file (SPFILE) backups. Using a larger or smaller recovery window or adjusting the redundancy policy will require an adjustment in the size of the flash recovery area. If the area is limited in size because of disk space constraints, at a minimum enough room should be available to hold the archived log files that have not yet been copied to tape. The dynamic performance view V$RECOVERY_FILE_DEST displays information about the number of files in the flash recovery area, how much space is currently being used, and the total amount of space available in the area.

The flash recovery area automatically uses Oracle Managed Files (OMF). As part of Oracle 12*c*'s simplified management structure, you do not need to set any of the LOG_ARCHIVE_DEST_*n* initialization parameters explicitly if you need only one location for archived redo log files; if the database is in ARCHIVELOG mode and a flash recovery area is defined, then the initialization parameter LOG_ARCHIVE_DEST_10 is implicitly defined as the flash recovery area.

As you have seen in many examples, RMAN uses the flash recovery area in an organized fashion—with separate directories for archived logs, backupsets, image copies, block change tracking files, and automatic backups of the control file and SPFILE. In addition, each subdirectory is named with the date of the backup (for example, **+RECOV/rpt12c/autobackup/2014_7_28**), making it easy to find a backupset or image copy when the need arises.

Multiple databases, even a primary database and a standby database, can share the same flash recovery area. Even with the same DB_NAME, as long as the DB_UNIQUE_NAME parameter is different, no conflicts will occur. RMAN uses the DB_UNIQUE_NAME to distinguish backups between databases that use the same flash recovery area.

Persisting RMAN Settings

To make the DBA's job easier, a number of RMAN settings can be *persisted*. In other words, these settings will stay in effect between RMAN sessions. In the example that follows, the SHOW ALL command is used to display the default RMAN settings:

```
RMAN> show all;

RMAN configuration parameters for database with db_unique_name RPT12C are:
CONFIGURE RETENTION POLICY TO RECOVERY WINDOW OF 10 DAYS;
CONFIGURE BACKUP OPTIMIZATION OFF; # default
CONFIGURE DEFAULT DEVICE TYPE TO DISK; # default
CONFIGURE CONTROLFILE AUTOBACKUP OFF; # default
CONFIGURE CONTROLFILE AUTOBACKUP FORMAT FOR DEVICE TYPE DISK TO '%F';
           # default
CONFIGURE DEVICE TYPE DISK PARALLELISM 1 BACKUP TYPE TO BACKUPSET; # default
CONFIGURE DATAFILE BACKUP COPIES FOR DEVICE TYPE DISK TO 1; # default
CONFIGURE ARCHIVELOG BACKUP COPIES FOR DEVICE TYPE DISK TO 1; # default
CONFIGURE MAXSETSIZE TO UNLIMITED; # default
CONFIGURE ENCRYPTION FOR DATABASE OFF; # default
CONFIGURE ENCRYPTION ALGORITHM 'AES128'; # default
CONFIGURE COMPRESSION ALGORITHM 'BASIC' AS OF RELEASE 'DEFAULT'
      OPTIMIZE FOR LOAD TRUE ; # default
CONFIGURE RMAN OUTPUT TO KEEP FOR 7 DAYS; # default
CONFIGURE ARCHIVELOG DELETION POLICY TO NONE; # default
CONFIGURE SNAPSHOT CONTROLFILE NAME TO
   '/u00/app/oracle/product/12.1.0/dbhome_1/dbs/snapcf_RPT12C.f'; # default

RMAN>
```

Any parameters that are set to their default values have **# default** at the end of the configuration setting. These parameters are easy to review and change using Enterprise Manager (EM), as demonstrated in Figure 4-1.

The next few sections review a few of the more common RMAN persistent settings.

Retention Policy

Backups can be automatically retained and managed using one of two methods: by a *recovery window* or by *redundancy*. Using a recovery window, RMAN will retain as many backups as necessary to bring the database to any point in time within the recovery window. For example, with a recovery window of seven days, RMAN will maintain enough image copies, incremental backups, and archived redo logs to ensure that the database can be restored and recovered to any point in time

FIGURE 4-1

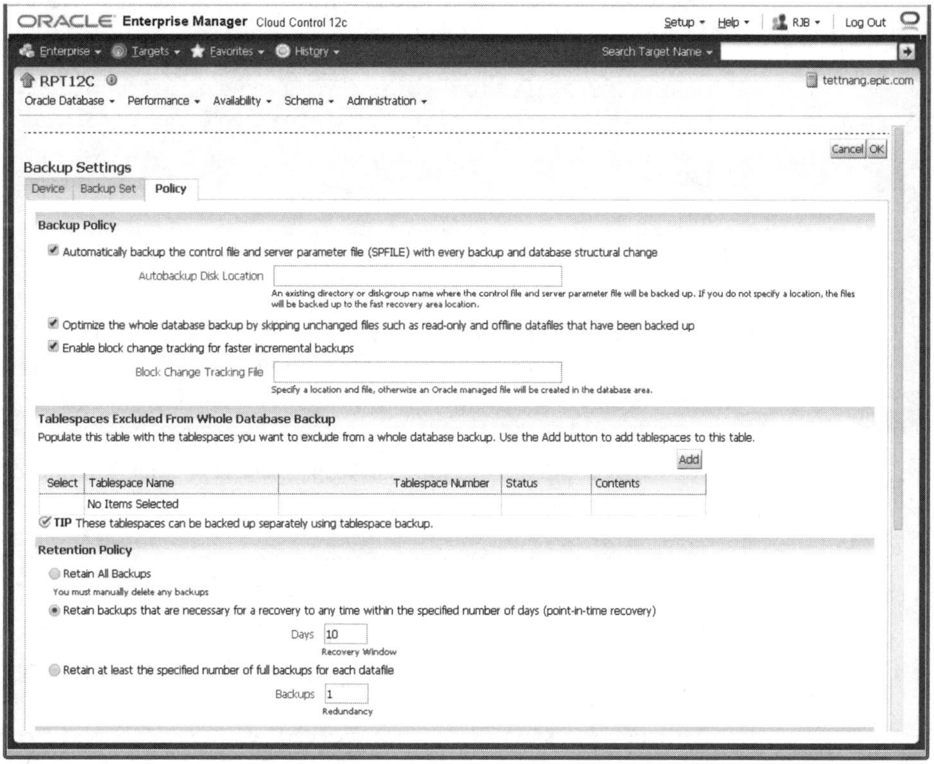

RMAN persistent parameters in Cloud Control 12*c*

within the last seven days. Any backups that are not needed to support this recovery window are marked as OBSOLETE and are automatically removed by RMAN if a flash recovery area is used and disk space is needed for new backups.

In contrast, a redundancy retention policy directs RMAN to retain the specified number of backups or copies of each datafile and control file. Any extra copies or backups beyond the number specified in the redundancy policy are marked as OBSOLETE. As with a recovery window, obsolete backups are automatically removed if disk space is needed and a flash recovery area is used. Otherwise, you can use the DELETE OBSOLETE command to remove the backup files and update the catalog.

If the retention policy is set to NONE, no backups or copies are ever considered obsolete, and the DBA must manually remove unneeded backups from the catalog and from disk.

The following example sets the retention policy to a recovery window of four days (from a default redundancy policy of one copy):

```
RMAN> configure retention policy to recovery window of 4 days;

new RMAN configuration parameters:
CONFIGURE RETENTION POLICY TO RECOVERY WINDOW OF 4 DAYS;
new RMAN configuration parameters are successfully stored

RMAN>
```

Device Type

If the default device type is set to DISK and no path name parameter is specified, RMAN uses the flash recovery area for all backups; you can easily override the disk backup location in EM, as you can see in Figure 4-2. As with many of the simplified administration tasks in Oracle 12*c*, there is no need to allocate or deallocate a specific channel for backups unless you're using a tape device.

Although configuring a tape device is specific to your installation, in general terms, you configure a tape device as follows:

```
RMAN> configure channel device type sbt
2>       parms='ENV=(<vendor specific arguments>)';
```

sbt is the device type used for any tape backup subsystem, regardless of vendor.

Although you can use the flash recovery area to restore and recover your database entirely from disk, at some point it becomes inefficient to keep all your backups on

FIGURE 4-2 Configuring backup destination using Cloud Control 12*c*

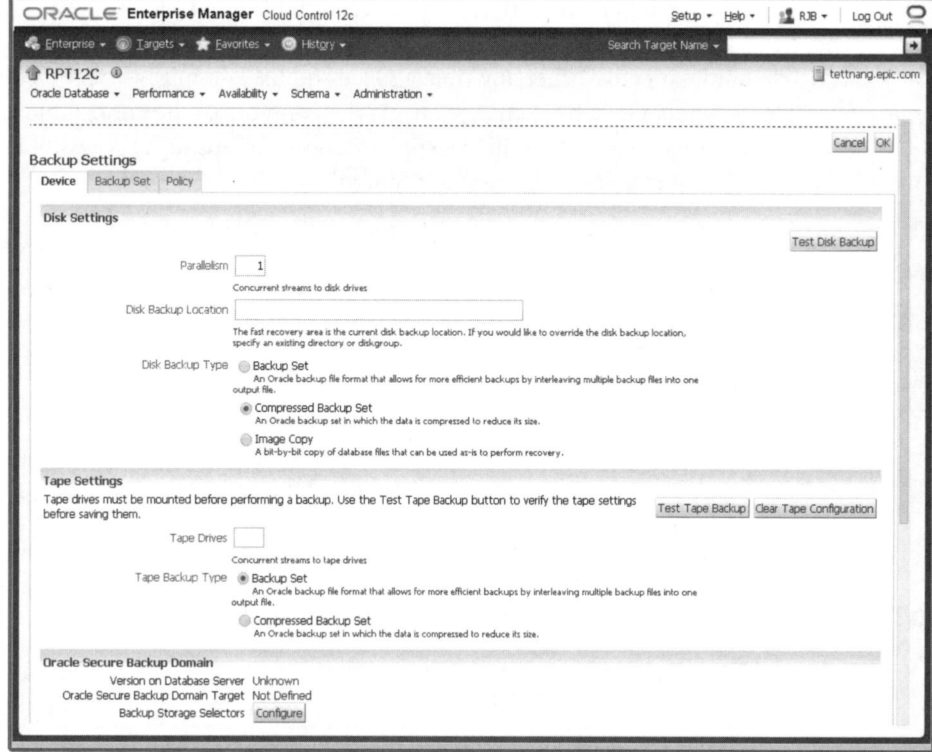

disk, especially if you have a large recovery window or you use archival backups. As a result, you can make copies of your backup files to tape, and RMAN will dutifully keep track of where the backups are in case you need to restore or recover the database from tape or in case you need to restore archived redo logs to roll forward an image copy in the flash recovery area.

Control File Autobackups

Because of the importance of the control file, you should back it up at least as often as it changes due to modifications in the structure of the database. By default, the backup of the control file does not occur automatically. This is a strange default, considering the importance of the control file and how little disk space it takes to back it up. Fortunately, RMAN can easily be configured to back up the control file automatically, either any time a successful backup must be recorded in the repository or when a structural change affects the contents of the control file (in other words, cases when a control file backup must occur to ensure a successful recovery if and when a recovery operation is required):

```
RMAN> configure controlfile autobackup on;

new RMAN configuration parameters:
CONFIGURE CONTROLFILE AUTOBACKUP ON;
new RMAN configuration parameters are successfully stored

RMAN>
```

Every RMAN backup from this point on will automatically include a copy of the control file. The control file is also backed up whenever a new tablespace is created or another datafile is added to an existing tablespace.

Allocating Channels to Use in Backing Up

You can allocate channels in two different ways in RMAN: You can set channels with the CONFIGURE command, or you can set them by using the ALLOCATE CHANNEL within a RUN block to override the default channel or if no default channel is defined. As mentioned earlier in the chapter, you don't have to specify any channels if your destination is a disk location.

Here is the line from the SHOW ALL command that specifies the default device type. Note that no default channel is defined since the default device type is DISK:

```
CONFIGURE DEFAULT DEVICE TYPE TO DISK; # default
```

CERTIFICATION OBJECTIVE 4.02

Perform Full and Incremental Backups

You'll find few reasons to not use RMAN as your main tool for managing backups. The following are some of the major features of RMAN, which either are unavailable with traditional backup methods or are limited by significant restrictions using traditional backup methods:

- **Skipping unused blocks** Blocks that have never been written to, such as blocks above the high water mark (HWM) in a table, are not backed up by RMAN when the backup is an RMAN backupset. Traditional backup methods have no way to know which blocks have been used.
- **Backup compression** In addition to skipping blocks that have never been used, RMAN can also use one of four Oracle-specific binary compression modes to save space on the backup device. Although operating system–specific compression techniques are available with traditional backup methods, the compression algorithms used by RMAN are customized to maximize the compression for the typical kinds of data found in Oracle data blocks. Although a slight increase in CPU time is required during an RMAN compressed backup or recovery operation, the amount of media used for backup can be significantly reduced, as well as network bandwidth reduction if the backup is performed over the network. Multiple CPUs can be configured for an RMAN backup to help alleviate the compression overhead.
- **Open database backups** Tablespace backups can be performed in RMAN without using the BEGIN/END BACKUP clause with ALTER TABLESPACE. Whether using RMAN or a traditional backup method, however, the database must be in ARCHIVELOG mode.
- **True incremental backups** In any RMAN incremental backup, unchanged blocks since the last backup will not be written to the backup file. This saves a significant amount of disk space, I/O time, and CPU time.
- **Incrementally updated backups** For restore and recovery operations, RMAN supports *incrementally updated backups*. Data blocks from an incremental backup are applied to a previous backup to potentially reduce the amount of time and number of files that need to be accessed to perform a recovery operation. You'll see an example of an incrementally updated backup later in this chapter.
- **Block-level recovery** To help avoid downtime during a recovery operation, RMAN supports *block-level recovery* for recovery operations that need to restore or repair only a small number of blocks identified as being corrupt during the backup operation. The rest of the tablespace and the objects within the tablespace can remain online while RMAN repairs the damaged blocks.

The rows of a table not being repaired by RMAN are even available to applications and users. You'll learn about block-level recovery in Chapter 5.

- **Multiple I/O channels** During a backup or recovery operation, RMAN can utilize many I/O channels using separate operating system processes, thus performing concurrent I/O. Traditional backup methods, such as a Unix **cp** command, are typically single-threaded operations.
- **Platform independence** Backups written with RMAN commands are syntactically identical regardless of the hardware or software platform used. In other words, RMAN scripts are portable and platform-independent. The only difference will be the media management channel configuration. If you don't use RMAN, something like a Unix script containing lots of **cp** commands will not run at all if the backup script is migrated to a Windows platform.
- **Tape manager support** All major enterprise backup systems are supported within RMAN by a third-party media management driver, which is provided by a tape backup vendor.
- **Cataloging** A record of all RMAN backups is recorded in the target database control file and optionally in a recovery catalog stored in a different database. This makes restore and recovery operations relatively simple compared to manually tracking operating system–level backups using "copy" commands. The benefits and reviewed catalog configuration were discussed in Chapter 3.
- **Scripting capabilities** As you saw in Chapter 3, RMAN scripts can be saved in a recovery catalog for retrieval during a backup session. The tight integration of the scripting language, the ease of maintaining scripts in RMAN, and the Oracle scheduling facility make RMAN a better choice compared to storing traditional operating system scripts in an operating system directory with the operating system's native scheduling mechanisms.
- **Encrypted backups** RMAN uses backup encryption integrated into Oracle Database 12*c* to store encrypted backups. Storing encrypted backups on tape requires the extra-cost Advanced Security option.

In a few limited cases, a traditional backup method can have an advantage over RMAN. For example, RMAN does not support the backup of password files and other nondatabase files, such as the networking control files **tnsnames.ora**, **listener.ora**, and **sqlnet.ora**. However, these files are relatively static in nature, and they can be easily backed up and restored using a traditional backup method, such as the Unix **cp** command.

RMAN supports a number of different backup methods. The choice of method depends on your availability needs, the desired size of your recovery window, and the amount of downtime you can endure while the database (or part of the database) is involved in a recovery operation.

An RMAN backup can be one of five types:

- A whole-database backup
- A full backup
- An incremental level 0 backup
- A differential incremental level 1 backup
- A cumulative incremental level 1 backup

RMAN stores its backups in one of two formats: backupsets or image copies. This section highlights and defines the differences between the two, and more examples of each backup type are provided later in this chapter.

Creating Backupsets

A *backupset* is an object specific to RMAN; only RMAN can create and read backupsets. As you learned in Chapter 3, a backupset is a set of files called *backup pieces* that can be stored on a file system or ideally on an Automatic Storage Management (ASM) disk. Each backup piece can contain one or more database file backups. All backupsets and pieces are recorded in the RMAN repository, the same as any other RMAN-initiated backup.

By default, any backups to disk default to a backupset backup type:

```
CONFIGURE DEVICE TYPE DISK PARALLELISM 1 BACKUP TYPE TO
     BACKUPSET; # default
```

As a result, the following backup command does not need the AS BACKUPSET qualifier, but you can specify it anyway, especially if it's in a global script that could be run in an RMAN session with different defaults:

```
RMAN> backup as backupset format '/u00/rpt12c/backups/auxbak.set'
2>        tablespace sysaux;
```

The FORMAT clause can use substitution variables to differentiate backupsets by database, by piece, and so forth. Here are a few sample substitution variable types:

- **%d** Database name

- **%e** Archived log sequence number
- **%f** Absolute file number
- **%F** Combines the database identifier (DBID), day, month, year, and sequence number, separated by dashes
- **%c** Copy number for multiple copies in a duplexed backup
- **%I** DBID
- **%n** Database name padded to eight characters
- **%p** Piece number within the backupset
- **%s** Backupset number
- **%t** Backupset timestamp
- **%U** System-generated unique filename (the default)

EXERCISE 4-1

Create a Compressed Backupset

In this exercise, you'll create an RMAN backup to the directory **/u02/oradata/rman/rpt12c** that includes the database name, the backupset number, a backupset timestamp, and a piece number within the backupset. You'll create a second RMAN backup using the default backup location and backupset format.

1. Connect to the target database and the recovery catalog on the RPT12C database:

```
[oracle@tettnang rpt12c]$ rman target / catalog rcat_owner/
Rcat9095@rcat
Recovery Manager: Release 12.1.0.1.0 -
     Production on Tue Feb 25 01:13:39 2014
Copyright (c) 1982, 2013, Oracle and/or its affiliates.
     All rights reserved.
connected to target database: RPT12C (DBID=1779317104)
connected to recovery catalog database

RMAN>
```

2. Run the RMAN backup and explicitly specify AS COMPRESSED BACKUPSET, even if this is already the default:

```
RMAN> backup as compressed backupset
2>       format '/u02/oradata/rman/rpt12c/rman_%d_%s_%t_%p.bkupset'
```

```
3>        tablespace users;

Starting backup at 25-FEB-14
using channel ORA_DISK_1
using channel ORA_DISK_2
using channel ORA_DISK_3
using channel ORA_DISK_4
channel ORA_DISK_1: starting compressed full datafile backup set
channel ORA_DISK_1: specifying datafile(s) in backup set
input datafile file number=00005
name=+DATA/RPT12C/DATAFILE/users.269.826931347
channel ORA_DISK_1: starting piece 1 at 25-FEB-14
channel ORA_DISK_2: starting compressed full datafile backup set
channel ORA_DISK_2: specifying datafile(s) in backup set
input datafile file number=00006
name=+DATA/RPT12C/DATAFILE/users.259.826650843
channel ORA_DISK_2: starting piece 1 at 25-FEB-14
channel ORA_DISK_1: finished piece 1 at 25-FEB-14
piece handle=/u02/oradata/rman/rpt12c/rman_RPT12C_31_840418162_1.
bkupset
tag=TAG20140225T012921 comment=NONE
channel ORA_DISK_1: backup set complete, elapsed time: 00:00:01
channel ORA_DISK_2: finished piece 1 at 25-FEB-14
piece handle=/u02/oradata/rman/rpt12c/rman_RPT12C_32_840418162_1.
bkupset
tag=TAG20140225T012921 comment=NONE
channel ORA_DISK_2: backup set complete, elapsed time: 00:00:01
Finished backup at 25-FEB-14

RMAN>
```

3. Run the RMAN backup again, this time backing up the SYSAUX tablespace and using the default location and format:

```
RMAN> backup as compressed backupset tablespace sysaux;

Starting backup at 25-FEB-14
using channel ORA_DISK_1
using channel ORA_DISK_2
using channel ORA_DISK_3
using channel ORA_DISK_4
channel ORA_DISK_1: starting compressed full datafile backup
set
channel ORA_DISK_1: specifying datafile(s) in backup set
input datafile file number=00003
name=+DATA/RPT12C/DATAFILE/sysaux.257.826650753
channel ORA_DISK_1: starting piece 1 at 25-FEB-14
```

```
channel ORA_DISK_1: finished piece 1 at 25-FEB-14
piece handle=+RECOV/RPT12C/BACKUPSET/2014_02_25/
     nnndf0_tag20140225t013056_0.268.840418257
tag=TAG20140225T013056
     comment=NONE
channel ORA_DISK_1: backup set complete, elapsed time:
00:01:35
Finished backup at 25-FEB-14

RMAN>
```

The FORMAT parameter can be provided in two other ways: in the ALLOCATE CHANNEL and as part of the CONFIGURE commands. The default FORMAT applies only to the control file autobackup, as in this example:

```
CONFIGURE CONTROLFILE AUTOBACKUP FORMAT FOR
     DEVICE TYPE DISK TO '%F'; # default
```

Creating Image Copies

An *image copy* is an exact copy of a tablespace's datafile, an archived redo log file, or a control file. Although you can use an operating system command to perform the copy, using the RMAN command BACKUP AS COPY provides the additional benefits of block verification and automatically recording the backup into the control file and the recovery catalog (if you have configured a recovery catalog). Another spin-off benefit to making image copies is that the copies can be used "as is" outside of RMAN if, for some reason, a recovery operation must occur outside of RMAN.

A restriction applies when you're using image copies in that image copies can be written only to disk. This can turn out to be a benefit, however: Although disk space may be at a premium compared to tape storage, restoration time is considerably less because the file used for recovery is already on disk.

You can use a disk image copy in a recovery scenario using two different methods: using an RMAN command or using a SQL command. If you are in RMAN, you use the SWITCH command. In the next example, you lose the disk containing the tablespace STAR_SCHEMA and you want to switch to a backup copy:

```
RMAN> sql "alter tablespace star_schema offline immediate";
RMAN> switch tablespace star_schema to copy;
RMAN> recover tablespace star_schema;
RMAN> sql "alter tablespace star_schema online";
```

Starting with Oracle Database 12c RMAN, you do not need to use the sql " " construct to run commands that you would otherwise run in SQL*Plus unless there is a command with the same name in both RMAN and SQL*Plus that could cause some ambiguity. You can, however, still use sql " " to make it crystal clear that you are not running an RMAN command.

Alternatively, at the SQL> prompt, you can use the ALTER DATABASE RENAME FILE command, as long as the tablespace containing the datafile is offline or the database is in MOUNT mode.

Finally, note that an image copy of a tablespace or archived redo log file contains all blocks in the tablespace or archived redo log file. An image copy of a datafile can be used as a full or incremental level 0 backup as long as you add the INCREMENTAL LEVEL 0 parameter:

```
RMAN> backup incremental level 0
2> as copy
3> tablespace sysaux;

Starting backup at 25-FEB-14
allocated channel: ORA_DISK_1
channel ORA_DISK_1: SID=1281 device type=DISK
allocated channel: ORA_DISK_2
channel ORA_DISK_2: SID=1029 device type=DISK
allocated channel: ORA_DISK_3
channel ORA_DISK_3: SID=1274 device type=DISK
allocated channel: ORA_DISK_4
channel ORA_DISK_4: SID=523 device type=DISK
channel ORA_DISK_1: starting datafile copy
input datafile file number=00003
name=+DATA/RPT12C/DATAFILE/sysaux.257.826650753
output file name=+RECOV/RPT12C/DATAFILE/sysaux.288.840446473
tag=TAG20140225T092112 RECID=1 STAMP=840446486
channel ORA_DISK_1: datafile copy complete, elapsed time:
00:00:15
Finished backup at 25-FEB-14
RMAN>
```

Whole-Database Backups

A whole-database backup includes a copy of all datafiles in the database plus the control file. You can also include archived redo log files and the server parameter file (SPFILE).

If your default backup device is disk, the following command will back up your database as image files, including all database files, the control file, all archived redo log files, and the SPFILE:

```
RMAN> backup as copy database spfile plus archivelog;
```

Even if CONTROLFILE AUTOBACKUP is OFF, RMAN backs up the current control file whenever datafile #1 (SYSTEM) is included in the backup. Backing up the entire database in a whole-database backup includes datafile #1 and, as a result, backs up the control file. Additionally, setting CONTROLFILE AUTOBACKUP to ON results in no significant performance hit to any RMAN backup unless disk space is extremely tight and the control file is very large after many RMAN backups and a long control file retention period.

If you add the DELETE INPUT clause to the preceding BACKUP command, RMAN deletes the archived log files from all destinations after they are backed up. If you are using a flash recovery area, this clause is generally unnecessary because RMAN automatically deletes obsolete files in the flash recovery area when space is running low.

Finally, you can back up a previous backup of a database (either image copies or backupset) to another location (such as tape) by using this command:

```
backup copy of database;
```

Full Backups

A full backup is different from a whole-database backup. A full backup can consist of a single datafile or tablespace, while a whole-database backup includes all datafiles in a database. For full backups of tablespaces or archived redo log files, RMAN copies all data blocks into a backupset; blocks that have never been used are skipped. For an image copy, all blocks are included whether or not they have been used.

on the job

A full backup of an individual database object is a logical subset of a whole-database backup. When performing database recovery, RMAN may use a more recent full backup of a tablespace rather than the most recent backup piece, which RMAN uses from an older backup of a whole-database backup. This is because a whole-database backup is a snapshot of the entire database. You plug in a datafile and let the automated recovery process resynchronize between data in datafiles, redo log entries, and the control file.

You perform a full backup of an individual database object much like a whole-database backup, except that you use the TABLESPACE keyword instead of the DATABASE keyword in the BACKUP command. This is because you are backing up tablespaces individually.

EXERCISE 4-2

Perform a Full Backup of Two Tablespaces

In this exercise, you'll perform a full backup of the USERS and SYSAUX tablespaces in the same BACKUP command.

1. Connect to RMAN and run the BACKUP command with the tablespaces separated by commas:

```
RMAN> backup tablespace sysaux, users;

Starting backup at 25-FEB-14
using channel ORA_DISK_1
using channel ORA_DISK_2
using channel ORA_DISK_3
using channel ORA_DISK_4
channel ORA_DISK_1: starting compressed full datafile backup set
channel ORA_DISK_1: specifying datafile(s) in backup set
input datafile file number=00003
     name=+DATA/RPT12C/DATAFILE/sysaux.257.826650753
channel ORA_DISK_1: starting piece 1 at 25-FEB-14
channel ORA_DISK_2: starting compressed full datafile backup set
channel ORA_DISK_2: specifying datafile(s) in backup set
input datafile file number=00005
     name=+DATA/RPT12C/DATAFILE/users.269.826931347
channel ORA_DISK_2: starting piece 1 at 25-FEB-14
channel ORA_DISK_3: starting compressed full datafile backup set
channel ORA_DISK_3: specifying datafile(s) in backup set
input datafile file number=00006
     name=+DATA/RPT12C/DATAFILE/users.259.826650843
channel ORA_DISK_3: starting piece 1 at 25-FEB-14
channel ORA_DISK_2: finished piece 1 at 25-FEB-14
piece handle=+RECOV/RPT12C/BACKUPSET/2014_02_25/
     nnndf0_tag20140225t092602_0.286.840446763
tag=TAG20140225T092602
     comment=NONE
channel ORA_DISK_2: backup set complete, elapsed time: 00:00:01
channel ORA_DISK_3: finished piece 1 at 25-FEB-14
piece handle=+RECOV/RPT12C/BACKUPSET/2014_02_25/
     nnndf0_tag20140225t092602_0.285.840446763
tag=TAG20140225T092602
     comment=NONE
```

```
channel ORA_DISK_3: backup set complete, elapsed time: 00:00:01
channel ORA_DISK_1: finished piece 1 at 25-FEB-14
piece handle=+RECOV/RPT12C/BACKUPSET/2014_02_25/
    nnndf0_tag20140225t092602_0.287.840446763
tag=TAG20140225T092602
    comment=NONE
channel ORA_DISK_1: backup set complete, elapsed time: 00:01:35
Finished backup at 25-FEB-14

RMAN>
```

Note that the control file and SPFILE are not included in this backup unless you have CONTROLFILE AUTOBACKUP set to ON or datafile #1 is included in the backup; by default, it is set to OFF, as in this example.

A full backup cannot participate in an incremental backup strategy; in other words, a full backup stands alone regardless of other incremental backups you are performing for the same objects. You'll see how to set up an incremental backup strategy in the next section.

Incremental Backups

As mentioned in Chapter 3 and earlier in this chapter, an incremental backup can be one of two types: level 0 or level 1. A level 0 incremental backup includes all blocks in the specified datafiles except for blocks that have never been used. In addition, a level 0 backup is physically identical to a full backup of the same datafiles, except that a full backup cannot be used in an incremental backup strategy—it stands alone. A level 1 backup can be one of two types: either a differential backup that backs up changed blocks since the last backup at level 0 or level 1 or a cumulative backup that backs up all changed blocks since the last level 0 backup.

You use the following keywords in the RMAN BACKUP command to specify an incremental level 0 or level 1 backup:

```
INCREMENTAL LEVEL [0|1]
```

You'll learn how to set up an incremental backup strategy for the USERS tablespace in the following sections.

Level 0 Incremental Backups

A level 0 backup includes all blocks in a database object except for blocks that were never used above the HWM. Subsequent level 1 backups use the most recent level 0 backup as the base for comparison when identifying changed blocks.

How often you perform a level 0 backup depends on how much the database object, such as a tablespace, changes between backups. A tablespace containing tables that are completely replaced on a weekly basis would most likely have more frequent level 0 backups than a tablespace containing tables that your applications change infrequently—for example, only 5 percent of the table's rows every week, but the changes might depend on the block distribution of those rows.

In this example, you perform the first level 0 backup of the USERS tablespace in your incremental backup strategy:

```
RMAN> backup incremental level 0 tablespace users;

Starting backup at 25-FEB-14
using channel ORA_DISK_1
using channel ORA_DISK_2
using channel ORA_DISK_3
using channel ORA_DISK_4
channel ORA_DISK_1: starting compressed incremental level 0
     datafile backup set
channel ORA_DISK_1: specifying datafile(s) in backup set
input datafile file number=00005
      name=+DATA/RPT12C/DATAFILE/users.269.826931347
channel ORA_DISK_1: starting piece 1 at 25-FEB-14
channel ORA_DISK_2: starting compressed incremental level 0
     datafile backup set
channel ORA_DISK_2: specifying datafile(s) in backup set
input datafile file number=00006
     name=+DATA/RPT12C/DATAFILE/users.259.826650843
channel ORA_DISK_2: starting piece 1 at 25-FEB-14
channel ORA_DISK_1: finished piece 1 at 25-FEB-14
piece handle=+RECOV/RPT12C/BACKUPSET/2014_02_25/
     nnndn0_tag20140225t093233_0.288.840447153
tag=TAG20140225T093233
     comment=NONE
channel ORA_DISK_1: backup set complete, elapsed time: 00:00:01
channel ORA_DISK_2: finished piece 1 at 25-FEB-14
piece handle=+RECOV/RPT12C/BACKUPSET/2014_02_25/
nnndn0_tag20140225t093233_0.268.840447153 tag=TAG20140225T093233
     comment=NONE
channel ORA_DISK_2: backup set complete, elapsed time: 00:00:01
Finished backup at 25-FEB-14

RMAN>
```

Subsequent level 1 backups will use this backup as the starting point for identifying changed blocks.

Differential Incremental Backups

A *differential* backup is the default type of incremental backup that backs up all changed blocks since the last level 0 or level 1 incremental backup. Again using the USERS tablespace, here's how you perform an incremental backup:

```
RMAN> backup incremental level 1 tablespace users;

Starting backup at 25-FEB-14
using channel ORA_DISK_1
using channel ORA_DISK_2
using channel ORA_DISK_3
using channel ORA_DISK_4
channel ORA_DISK_1: starting compressed incremental level 1
   datafile backup set
channel ORA_DISK_1: specifying datafile(s) in backup set
input datafile file number=00005
     name=+DATA/RPT12C/DATAFILE/users.269.826931347
channel ORA_DISK_1: starting piece 1 at 25-FEB-14
channel ORA_DISK_2: starting compressed incremental level 1
     datafile backup set
channel ORA_DISK_2: specifying datafile(s) in backup set
input datafile file number=00006
     name=+DATA/RPT12C/DATAFILE/users.259.826650843

channel ORA_DISK_2: starting piece 1 at 25-FEB-14
channel ORA_DISK_1: finished piece 1 at 25-FEB-14
piece handle=+RECOV/RPT12C/BACKUPSET/2014_02_25/
nnndn1_tag20140225t093513_0.315.840447313 tag=TAG20140225T093513
     comment=NONE
channel ORA_DISK_1: backup set complete, elapsed time: 00:00:01
channel ORA_DISK_2: finished piece 1 at 25-FEB-14
piece handle=+RECOV/RPT12C/BACKUPSET/2014_02_25/
nnndn1_tag20140225t093513_0.284.840447313 tag=TAG20140225T093513
     comment=NONE
channel ORA_DISK_2: backup set complete, elapsed time: 00:00:01
Finished backup at 25-FEB-14

RMAN>
```

Differential is the default incremental backup type. Unlike most Oracle commands that allow you to use a keyword that is the default, DIFFERENTIAL cannot be specified for the RMAN BACKUP command.

Cumulative Incremental Backups

Cumulative incremental backups back up all changed blocks since the last level 0 incremental backup. You perform a cumulative incremental level 1 backup the same way you perform a differential level 1 backup, except that you specify the CUMULATIVE keyword, as in this example:

```
RMAN> backup incremental level 1 cumulative tablespace users;

Starting backup at 25-FEB-14
using channel ORA_DISK_1
using channel ORA_DISK_2
using channel ORA_DISK_3
using channel ORA_DISK_4
channel ORA_DISK_1: starting compressed incremental level 1
     datafile backup set
channel ORA_DISK_1: specifying datafile(s) in backup set
input datafile file number=00005
     name=+DATA/RPT12C/DATAFILE/users.269.826931347
channel ORA_DISK_1: starting piece 1 at 25-FEB-14
channel ORA_DISK_2: starting compressed incremental level 1
     datafile backup set
channel ORA_DISK_2: specifying datafile(s) in backup set
input datafile file number=00006
     name=+DATA/RPT12C/DATAFILE/users.259.826650843
channel ORA_DISK_2: starting piece 1 at 25-FEB-14
channel ORA_DISK_1: finished piece 1 at 25-FEB-14
piece handle=+RECOV/RPT12C/BACKUPSET/2014_02_25/
     nnndn1_tag20140225t093821_0.283.840447501
tag=TAG20140225T093821
     comment=NONE
channel ORA_DISK_1: backup set complete, elapsed time: 00:00:01
channel ORA_DISK_2: finished piece 1 at 25-FEB-14
piece handle=+RECOV/RPT12C/BACKUPSET/2014_02_25/
     nnndn1_tag20140225t093821_0.282.840447501
tag=TAG20140225T093821
     comment=NONE
channel ORA_DISK_2: backup set complete, elapsed time: 00:00:01
Finished backup at 25-FEB-14

RMAN>
```

The decision whether to use a cumulative or differential backup is based partly on where you want to spend the CPU cycles and how much disk space is available. Using cumulative backups means that each incremental backup will become progressively larger and take longer until another level 0 incremental backup is performed. This can be beneficial in that only two backupsets will be required during a restore and recovery operation. On the other hand, differential backups record only the changes since the last backup, so each backupset might be smaller or larger than the previous one, with no overlap in data blocks backed up. However, a restore and recovery operation can take longer if you have to restore from several backupsets instead of just two.

CERTIFICATION OBJECTIVE 4.03

Use Techniques to Improve Backups

In Oracle Database 12*c*, RMAN has many different methods to make your backups smaller, faster, and easier to manage. For example, RMAN supports *backup optimization*. In other words, the RMAN BACKUP command skips backups of one or more files when identical files have already been backed up to the specified device, such as disk or tape. RMAN takes into consideration the retention policy and the backup duplexing capabilities of RMAN to determine whether enough backups of a particular file already exist. Backup optimization was covered in Chapter 3.

Another way to improve the performance of incremental backups is to enable *block change tracking*. For a traditional incremental backup, RMAN must inspect every block of the tablespace or datafile to be backed up to see whether the block has changed since the last backup. For a very large database, the time it takes to scan the blocks in the database can easily exceed the time it takes to perform the actual backup.

By enabling block change tracking, RMAN knows which blocks have changed within a datafile by using a *change tracking file*. Although a slight overhead is incurred in space usage and maintenance of the tracking file every time a block is changed, the trade-off is well worth it if frequent incremental backups are performed on the database.

Once block change tracking is enabled, RMAN can perform fast incremental backups. In addition, database recovery is faster because fewer changed blocks need to be applied to a restored datafile. The following sections explain how block change tracking works, show you how to enable block change tracking and fast incremental backups, and show you how to monitor how well block change tracking is working in your database.

RMAN provides a number of options to make multiple copies of your backup simultaneously, to create backups of your existing backupsets, and to skip unnecessary backups of read-only tablespaces. Each of these topics is covered in the following sections along with relevant examples.

As your database grows in size, you inevitably have some really big datafiles that will take a long time to back up as part of a full database backup if backed up as a whole. In previous versions of RMAN (before Oracle Database 11*g* and 12*c*), using bigfile tablespaces had one big advantage and one big disadvantage. The big advantage was that you could have a database with a much larger size than in previous versions of Oracle (up to 1,022 bigfile tablespaces of 128TB each). The big disadvantage was that backing up a single bigfile tablespace took a long time because RMAN could back up a bigfile tablespace only using a single channel. In general, backing up four 32TB datafiles in parallel took less time than backing up a single 128TB datafile. As a result, some organizations (with a lot of data) were somewhat restricted to how big they could make their bigfile tablespaces. Therefore, RMAN supports multisection backups so that a very large datafile can be backed up in pieces in parallel.

Archival backups, new as of Oracle Database 11*g*, give you the flexibility to take a snapshot of the database and retain it indefinitely or for a specific period of time. I'll explain how archival backups work, how to perform an archival backup, and how to manage archival backups using the CHANGE command.

Finally, you need to know how to compress your backups with several compression algorithms. Which algorithm you use depends on how much disk space you have and how many CPU resources you can use to compress and decompress the backup. You also will learn how to ensure the privacy of the data in your backup by encrypting backups using two different methods.

Understanding Block Change Tracking

Once you create a block change tracking file for your database, the maintenance of the tracking file is automatic and transparent. The size of the tracking file is proportional to the size of your database, the number of instances if you have a Real Application Cluster (RAC) database, and the number of previous backups maintained in the block change tracking file. (Oracle maintains up to eight previous backups in the block change tracking file.) The first incremental level 0 backup reads every block in the datafile, and subsequent incremental level 1 backups use the block change tracking file.

Updates to the block change tracking file occur in parallel with redo generation to the online redo log files. Figure 4-3 shows a committed transaction in the SGA that both generates redo in the online redo log files and is processed by the CTWR (Change Tracking Writer) process and recorded in the change tracking file.

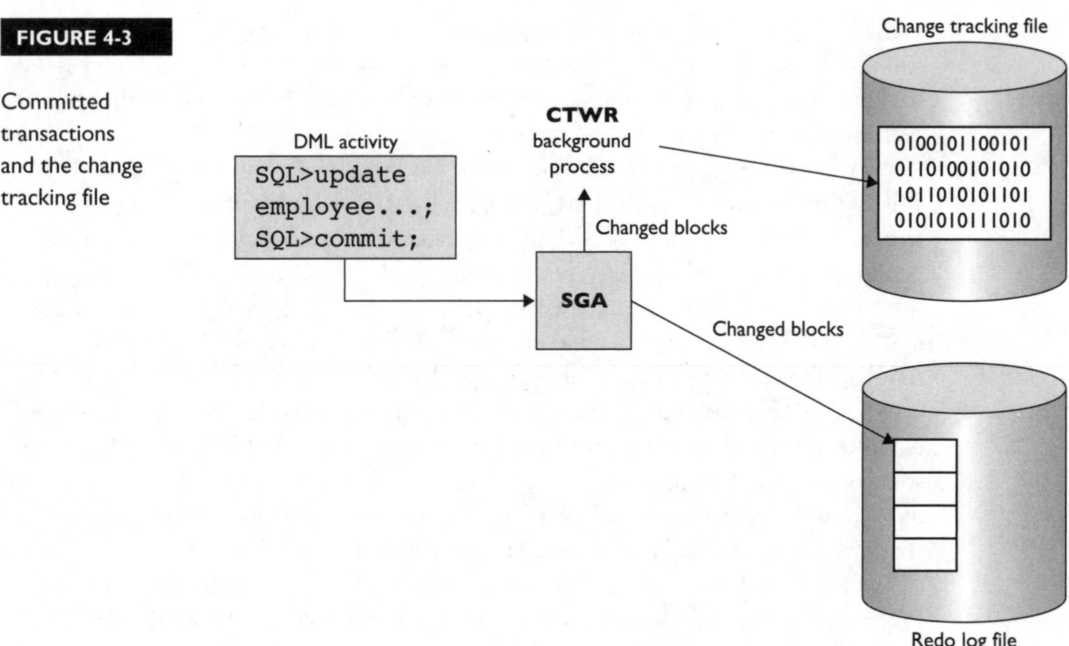

FIGURE 4-3 Committed transactions and the change tracking file

Enabling Fast Incremental Backup

You enable or disable block change tracking with the ALTER DATABASE command. In its simplest form, the following command is used to create and enable block change tracking:

```
alter database enable block change tracking;
```

If you do not specify a filename for the tracking file, Oracle creates it in the location specified by the initialization parameter DB_CREATE_FILE_DEST as an Oracle Managed File (OMF). If you want to explicitly specify the name and location of the tracking file, use the USING FILE clause. This example creates a block change tracking file in the DATA disk group and enables block change tracking:

```
SQL> alter database enable block change tracking
  2      using file '+DATA';
Database altered.
SQL>
```

Since the tracking file now exists in an ASM disk group, you can discover its size and where it is located within the DATA disk group by using the **asmcmd** utility:

```
[oracle@dw ~]$ asmcmd
ASMCMD> cd +data/RPT12C
ASMCMD> ls
CHANGETRACKING/
CONTROLFILE/
DATAFILE/
ONLINELOG/
PARAMETERFILE/
TEMPFILE/
spfileRPT12C.ora
ASMCMD> cd changetracking
ASMCMD> ls -s
Block_Size  Blocks     Bytes     Space  Name
       512   22657  11600384  12582912  ctf.420.840447821
ASMCMD>
```

The next time a level 1 incremental backup is performed after an initial level 0 backup, RMAN will have to use only the contents of the file ctf.420.840447821 (an OMF-named file in the RPT12C/CHANGETRACKING directory of the DATA disk group) to determine which blocks need to be backed up. The space needed for the block change tracking file is approximately 1/30,000 the size of the database.

You turn off block change tracking by using this command:

```
alter database disable block change tracking;
```

This ALTER DATABASE command drops the block change tracking file. If you re-create it later, you will have to create another level 0 incremental backup before RMAN can use the block change tracking file, which minimizes the number of blocks that have to be read for the next level 1 incremental backup.

Finally, you can rename the tracking file by using the same command you use to rename any database file: ALTER DATABASE RENAME. Your database must be in the MOUNT state to rename a tracking file.

Monitoring Block Change Tracking

The dynamic performance view V$BLOCK_CHANGE_TRACKING contains the name and size of the block change tracking file plus the status of change tracking:

```
SQL> select filename, status, bytes from v$block_change_tracking;

FILENAME                                        STATUS          BYTES
----------------------------------------------- ---------- ----------
+DATA/RPT12C/CHANGETRACKING/ctf.420.840447821 ENABLED      11599872

SQL>
```

To see the benefits of block change tracking, you can use the following query on the dynamic performance view V$BACKUP_DATAFILE to calculate the percentage of blocks read and the number of blocks backed up during an incremental level 1 backup:

```
select file#, avg(datafile_blocks) blocks,
  avg(blocks_read) blocks_read,
  avg(blocks_read/datafile_blocks)*100 pct_read,
  avg(blocks) blocks_backed_up
from v$backup_datafile
where used_change_tracking = 'YES'
  and incremental_level = 1
group by file#
order by file#
;
```

The dynamic performance view V$BACKUP_DATAFILE contains one row for each datafile backed up using RMAN. This query further refines the results to pick the backups that used block change tracking during an incremental level 1 backup.

Creating Duplexed Backupsets

To make multiple backups of the same backupset simultaneously, you can configure RMAN to make up to four duplexed copies of each backup piece. As with most RMAN commands, you can specify a default value for the COPIES parameter using the CONFIGURE command, as in this example:

```
RMAN> configure datafile backup copies
2>        for device type sbt to 3;

new RMAN configuration parameters:
CONFIGURE DATAFILE BACKUP COPIES FOR DEVICE TYPE 'SBT_TAPE' TO
3;
new RMAN configuration parameters are successfully stored
starting full resync of recovery catalog
full resync complete

RMAN>
```

Duplexing has a few restrictions: You cannot duplex backups to the flash recovery area, and you cannot duplex image copies—only backupsets. For duplexed disk backups, you specify multiple locations for a backup using the FORMAT clause. You can specify multiple locations either in the BACKUP command or when setting default values for device type DISK in the CONFIGURE command.

In this example, you back up the USERS tablespace to two different disk locations simultaneously:

```
RMAN> backup as compressed backupset
2>       device type disk
3>       copies 2
4>       tablespace users
5>       format '/u01/oradata/bkup/%U', '/u04/oradata/bkup/%U';
```

Note that even though you have the same format for each copy of the backupset, RMAN's default format, %**U**, is a shorthand for %**u**_%**p**_%**c**. As you may remember from the discussion on RMAN substitution variables, %c translates to a copy number in a duplexed backup operation.

Creating Backups of Backupsets

One option for creating a second copy of a backup is to create a backup of existing backupsets. This is especially useful if you forgot to duplex a previous backup and you don't want to perform a time-consuming backup again. If your backupsets are on disk (you cannot back up existing backupsets that are on tape), you can use the BACKUP . . . BACKUPSET command to copy all backupsets on one disk, to another disk, or to tape. This command copies all existing disk-based backupsets to the default tape device and channel:

```
RMAN> backup device type sbt backupset all;
```

If you want to keep recent backupsets on disk and older backupsets on tape, you can use the COMPLETED and DELETE INPUT options. In the following example, all backupsets older than two weeks are backed up to tape and deleted from the disk:

```
RMAN> backup device type sbt backupset
2>        completed before 'sysdate-14'
3>        delete input;
```

Backing Up Read-Only Tablespaces

As you might expect, backing up a read-only tablespace needs to happen often enough to satisfy the retention period configured in RMAN. You can force RMAN to skip a read-only tablespace by using the SKIP READONLY option of the BACKUP command.

If you configured RMAN for backup optimization (covered in Chapter 3), RMAN backs up read-only tablespaces only when there are not enough backups of the tablespace to satisfy the retention policy.

Understanding Archival Backups

By default, RMAN keeps your backups and archived log files not only to satisfy the configured retention policy but also to provide a mechanism to restore your database to any point in time between the backup and the present. RMAN uses a combination of full backups, incremental backups, and archived redo log files.

In certain situations, you may want only a snapshot of the database at a certain point in time for archival or regulatory purposes. This causes two complications with the default RMAN configuration: First, your snapshot will most likely fall outside of your retention policy, and you certainly don't want your yearly database snapshot to disappear before the end of the week! Second, you don't want RMAN to maintain one, two, or more years' worth of archived redo log files if you are not going to restore your database to a point in time between the snapshot and the current time.

RMAN addresses the need for a database snapshot by supporting an *archival backup*. If you label a backup as an archival backup, RMAN does not consider the backup to be obsolete using the configured retention policy; instead, RMAN marks an archival backup as obsolete after the amount of time you specify. Alternatively, you can specify that RMAN keep the archival backup indefinitely.

on the job

You can use an archival backup to migrate a copy of the database to another system for testing purposes without affecting the retention policy of the original database. Once you have created the database on the test system, you can delete the archival backup.

Performing an Archival Backup

One restriction for archival backups is that you cannot use the flash recovery area to store an archival backup. If you have a flash recovery area configured, you will have to use the FORMAT parameter to specify an alternative disk location for the backup. Additionally, a tape device might be the best option for long-term storage of archival backups.

This example creates an archival backup to be retained for one year using the KEEP UNTIL clause:

```
RMAN> backup as compressed backupset
2>      database format '/u02/oradata/rman/archback/%U'
3>      tag save1yr
4>      keep until time 'sysdate+365'
5>    ;

Starting backup at 25-FEB-14
starting full resync of recovery catalog
full resync complete
current log archived

using channel ORA_DISK_1
backup will be obsolete on date 25-FEB-15
archived logs required to recover from this backup will be
backed up
. . .
channel ORA_DISK_1: backup set complete, elapsed time: 00:00:02

using channel ORA_DISK_1
using channel ORA_DISK_2
using channel ORA_DISK_3
using channel ORA_DISK_4
backup will be obsolete on date 25-FEB-15
archived logs required to recover from this backup will be
backed up
channel ORA_DISK_1: starting compressed full datafile backup set
channel ORA_DISK_1: specifying datafile(s) in backup set
including current control file in backup set
channel ORA_DISK_1: starting piece 1 at 25-FEB-14
channel ORA_DISK_1: finished piece 1 at 25-FEB-14
piece handle=/u02/oradata/rman/archback/2bp1gfdd_1_1
     tag=SAVE1YR comment=NONE
channel ORA_DISK_1: backup set complete, elapsed time: 00:00:01
Finished backup at 25-FEB-14

RMAN>
```

Since the RPT12C database has a flash recovery area defined, you use the FORMAT clause to specify a location in which to store the archival backup. Note also that RMAN backs up any archived logs, which would be required to use the backup in a possible future recovery scenario.

Alternatively, you can perform the same backup but retain it indefinitely:

```
 RMAN> backup as compressed backupset
2>       database format '/u02/oradata/rman/archback/%U'
3>       tag saveforever
4>       keep forever;
. . .
using channel ORA_DISK_1
backup will never be obsolete
archived logs required to recover from this backup will be
backed up
. . .
```

Managing Archival Backups

In some situations, you might want to change the status of a backup. For example, you might want to change an archival backup's retention period, change an archival backup to a standard backup, or change a consistent backup to an archival backup. As you might expect, you can use the CHANGE command to accomplish this task. Although the CHANGE command has many other uses (such as to change the availability of a backup or to change the priority of failures in the database), the CHANGE command in relation to archival backups is covered here.

This example changes the backup created earlier with the tag SAVEFOREVER to fall under the existing retention policy instead:

```
RMAN> change backup tag 'saveforever' nokeep;

starting full resync of recovery catalog
full resync complete
using channel ORA_DISK_1
keep attributes for the backup are deleted
backupset key=3321 RECID=26 STAMP=654037077
keep attributes for the backup are deleted
backupset key=3344 RECID=27 STAMP=654037106
keep attributes for the backup are deleted
backupset key=3345 RECID=28 STAMP=654037128
keep attributes for the backup are deleted
backupset key=3346 RECID=29 STAMP=654037151

RMAN>
```

Depending on the retention policy and the other older or newer backups for this database, the backup could be deleted the next time RMAN starts. The backup could be retained longer if the configured retention policy needs this backup to fulfill the retention policy.

You can also use the CHANGE command to change all backups of a certain type. For example, if you want to remove the archive flag from all image copies of the database, you use the NOKEEP parameter:

```
change copy of database nokeep;
```

Creating a Multisection Backup

Creating a multisection backup is easy, but you must specify the section size with each BACKUP command. In addition, you can run the RMAN VALIDATE command by section. New data dictionary views, both the V$ and RC_ views, help you to identify which backups are multisection and how many blocks are in each section of a multisection backup.

Specifying the Section Size

To create a multisection backup, you add the SECTION SIZE parameter to the BACKUP command. The section size can be specified in kilobytes, megabytes, or gigabytes. Here is the general syntax for specifying a multisection backup:

```
BACKUP <backup options> SECTION SIZE <size> [K|M|G]
```

In this example HR database, the USERS tablespace is approximately 25MB, and you want to back it up with a section size of 10MB:

```
RMAN> backup tablespace users
2>       section size 100m;

Starting backup at 25-FEB-14
using channel ORA_DISK_1
using channel ORA_DISK_2
using channel ORA_DISK_3
using channel ORA_DISK_4
channel ORA_DISK_1: starting compressed full datafile backup set
channel ORA_DISK_1: specifying datafile(s) in backup set
input datafile file number=00005
     name=+DATA/RPT12C/DATAFILE/users.269.826931347
backing up blocks 1 through 12800
channel ORA_DISK_1: starting piece 1 at 25-FEB-14
channel ORA_DISK_2: starting compressed full datafile backup set
channel ORA_DISK_2: specifying datafile(s) in backup set
```

```
input datafile file number=00006
     name=+DATA/RPT12C/DATAFILE/users.259.826650843
channel ORA_DISK_2: starting piece 1 at 25-FEB-14
channel ORA_DISK_3: starting compressed full datafile backup set
channel ORA_DISK_3: specifying datafile(s) in backup set
input datafile file number=00005
     name=+DATA/RPT12C/DATAFILE/users.269.826931347
backing up blocks 12801 through 25600
channel ORA_DISK_3: starting piece 2 at 25-FEB-14
channel ORA_DISK_4: starting compressed full datafile backup set
channel ORA_DISK_4: specifying datafile(s) in backup set
input datafile file number=00005
     name=+DATA/RPT12C/DATAFILE/users.269.826931347
backing up blocks 25601 through 32000
channel ORA_DISK_4: starting piece 3 at 25-FEB-14
channel ORA_DISK_1: finished piece 1 at 25-FEB-14
piece handle=+RECOV/RPT12C/BACKUPSET/2014_02_25/
     nnndf0_tag20140225t101644_0.278.840449805
tag=TAG20140225T101644
     comment=NONE
channel ORA_DISK_1: backup set complete, elapsed time: 00:00:01
channel ORA_DISK_2: finished piece 1 at 25-FEB-14
piece handle=+RECOV/RPT12C/BACKUPSET/2014_02_25/
     nnndf0_tag20140225t101644_0.277.840449805
tag=TAG20140225T101644
     comment=NONE
channel ORA_DISK_2: backup set complete, elapsed time: 00:00:01
channel ORA_DISK_3: finished piece 2 at 25-FEB-14
piece handle=+RECOV/RPT12C/BACKUPSET/2014_02_25/
     nnndf0_tag20140225t101644_0.276.840449807
tag=TAG20140225T101644
     comment=NONE
channel ORA_DISK_3: backup set complete, elapsed time: 00:00:01
channel ORA_DISK_4: finished piece 3 at 25-FEB-14
piece handle=+RECOV/RPT12C/BACKUPSET/2014_02_25/
     nnndf0_tag20140225t101644_0.275.840449807
tag=TAG20140225T101644
     comment=NONE
channel ORA_DISK_4: backup set complete, elapsed time: 00:00:01
Finished backup at 25-FEB-14

RMAN>
```

This backup created three backup pieces: the first two of 100MB each, and the third piece approximately 50MB, which is the remainder of the datafile.

Don't use a high value for parallelism in your multisection backups to back up a large file on a small number of disks. The I/O contention of multiple RMAN threads accessing the same disk will erase any time savings gained by using a high value for parallelism.

Validating a Backup with a Section Size

You can also use the SECTION SIZE parameter with the VALIDATE command. The benefits of parallel operations for datafile block validation are the same as the benefits of using the BACKUP command: It will take you significantly less time to ensure that a datafile's blocks are readable and have valid checksums. This example validates the datafile backed up in the previous section:

```
RMAN> validate tablespace users
2>      section size 100m;

Starting validate at 25-FEB-14
using channel ORA_DISK_1
using channel ORA_DISK_2
using channel ORA_DISK_3
using channel ORA_DISK_4
channel ORA_DISK_1: starting validation of datafile
channel ORA_DISK_1: specifying datafile(s) for validation
input datafile file number=00006
     name=+DATA/RPT12C/DATAFILE/users.259.826650843
channel ORA_DISK_2: starting validation of datafile
channel ORA_DISK_2: specifying datafile(s) for validation
input datafile file number=00005
     name=+DATA/RPT12C/DATAFILE/users.269.826931347
validating blocks 1 through 12800
channel ORA_DISK_3: starting validation of datafile
channel ORA_DISK_3: specifying datafile(s) for validation
input datafile file number=00005
     name=+DATA/RPT12C/DATAFILE/users.269.826931347
validating blocks 12801 through 25600
channel ORA_DISK_4: starting validation of datafile
channel ORA_DISK_4: specifying datafile(s) for validation
input datafile file number=00005
     name=+DATA/RPT12C/DATAFILE/users.269.826931347
validating blocks 25601 through 32000
```

```
channel ORA_DISK_1: validation complete, elapsed time: 00:00:02
List of Datafiles
=================
File Status Marked Corrupt Empty Blocks Blocks Examined High SCN
---- ------ -------------- ------------ --------------- ----------
6    OK     0              16           257             15654354
  File Name: +DATA/RPT12C/DATAFILE/users.259.826650843
  Block Type Blocks Failing Blocks Processed
  ---------- -------------- ----------------
  Data       0              30
  Index      0              5
  Other      0              205

channel ORA_DISK_2: validation complete, elapsed time: 00:00:02
channel ORA_DISK_3: validation complete, elapsed time: 00:00:03
channel ORA_DISK_4: validation complete, elapsed time: 00:00:03
List of Datafiles
=================
File Status Marked Corrupt Empty Blocks Blocks Examined High SCN
---- ------ -------------- ------------ --------------- ----------
5    OK     0              31873        31998           1991172
  File Name: +DATA/RPT12C/DATAFILE/users.269.826931347

  Block Type Blocks Failing Blocks Processed
  ---------- -------------- ----------------
  Data       0              0
  Index      0              0
  Other      0              125

Finished validate at 25-FEB-14

RMAN>
```

Multisection Data Dictionary Views

The views V$BACKUP_SET and RC_BACKUP_SET have a MULTI_SECTION column that indicates whether the backup is a multisection backup. Similarly, the V$BACKUP_DATAFILE and RC_BACKUP_DATAFILE views have a SECTION_SIZE column that indicates the number of blocks in each piece of a multisection backup. Remember that the V$ views exist on the target database and the RC_ views exist on the recovery catalog database.

Compressing Backups

In addition to skipping unused blocks during a backup, RMAN can also apply one of two compression methods to the used blocks in a backup when you specify the COMPRESSED parameter with one of four values:

- **BASIC** Similar to MEDIUM compression but uses more CPU
- **LOW** Fastest but lower compression ratios
- **MEDIUM** Moderate CPU usage, good for network bandwidth constraints
- **HIGH** Most CPU usage, ideal for network bandwidth constraints

The default compression level is set to BASIC.

```
CONFIGURE COMPRESSION ALGORITHM 'BASIC'; # default
```

All compression methods except for BASIC require the Advanced Compression option.

The HIGH algorithm, as you might expect, creates much smaller backups but requires more CPU time to compress the blocks. If not too many other server processes are demanding CPU resources when your backups run, use MEDIUM or HIGH. On the other hand, if a lot of disk space is available and the network path from the database to your backup location is not congested, it might take less time overall not to use compression.

Regardless of what compression method you use, restoring a compressed backup requires no knowledge of the compression method used during the original backup. RMAN automatically detects the compression method used and decompresses accordingly.

Encrypting Backups

To ensure the security and privacy of your backups, you can encrypt them in one of three ways: via transparent encryption, password encryption, or dual mode encryption. By default, encryption is turned off:

```
CONFIGURE ENCRYPTION FOR DATABASE OFF; # default
CONFIGURE ENCRYPTION ALGORITHM 'AES128'; # default
```

In the following sections, you'll learn how to enable each type of encryption.

Using Transparent Encryption

You can set transparent (wallet-based) encryption as the default RMAN encryption method using the CONFIGURE command as follows:

```
RMAN> configure encryption for database on;

starting full resync of recovery catalog
full resync complete
new RMAN configuration parameters:
CONFIGURE ENCRYPTION FOR DATABASE ON;
new RMAN configuration parameters are successfully stored
starting full resync of recovery catalog
full resync complete

RMAN>
```

Keep in mind that your database wallet must be open as well. If it is not open, you might think that everything is going as planned—until the encryption process attempts to start. This is shown by the backup failure error message in the following output:

```
RMAN> backup as compressed backupset tablespace users;

Starting backup at 25-MAY-14
allocated channel: ORA_DISK_1
channel ORA_DISK_1: SID=106 device type=DISK
channel ORA_DISK_1: starting compressed full datafile backup set
channel ORA_DISK_1: specifying datafile(s) in backup set
input datafile file number=00004 name=+DATA/RPT12C/datafile/
      users.259.632441707
channel ORA_DISK_1: starting piece 1 at 25-MAY-14
RMAN-00571: ===========================================================
RMAN-00569: ============ ERROR MESSAGE STACK FOLLOWS ==========
RMAN-00571: ===========================================================
RMAN-03009: failure of backup command on
ORA_DISK_1 channel at 05/25/2014 20:04:31
ORA-19914: unable to encrypt backup
ORA-28365: wallet is not open

RMAN>
```

Opening the wallet at the SQL> prompt makes everything work a lot more smoothly:

```
SQL> alter system set encryption wallet open
  2      identified by "fre#3dXX0";
```

```
System altered.

SQL>
. . .
RMAN> backup as compressed backupset tablespace users;

Starting backup at 25-MAY-14
using channel ORA_DISK_1


. . .


channel ORA_DISK_1: starting piece 1 at 25-MAY-14
channel ORA_DISK_1: finished piece 1 at 25-MAY-14
piece handle=+RECOV/dw/backupset/2014_05_25/
      nnndf0_tag20080509t201659_0.550.654293845
tag=TAG20080509T201659
      comment=NONE
channel ORA_DISK_1: backupset complete, elapsed time: 00:00:16
Finished backup at 25-MAY-14

RMAN>
```

As you might expect, even if transparent encryption is not the default, you can turn it on just for the duration of a single backup. As in the previous example, the database wallet must be open. Here is an example:

```
RMAN> set encryption on;
executing command: SET encryption
RMAN> backup as compressed backupset tablespace users;

Starting backup at 25-MAY-14
using channel ORA_DISK_1


. . .
channel ORA_DISK_1: backupset complete, elapsed time: 00:00:09
Finished backup at 25-MAY-14

RMAN> set encryption off;
executing command: SET encryption
RMAN>
```

To restore or recover from an encrypted backup, the database wallet must be open, and either the encryption default must be ON or you must use SET ENCRYPTION ON before the recovery operation.

Using Password Encryption

To enable password encryption for a specific backup, use the SET ENCRYPTION command as follows:

```
RMAN> set encryption identified by "F45$Xa98";

executing command: SET encryption

RMAN> backup as compressed backupset tablespace users;
. . .
```

on the job

Password encryption is inherently less secure and reliable than transparent (wallet-based) encryption because a password can be lost, forgotten, or intercepted easily. Use password encryption only when backups must be transportable to a different database.

When you want to restore this backup, either to the same database (if wallet-based encryption is off) or to a different database, you must specify the decryption password with SET DECRYPTION:

```
RMAN> set decryption identified by "F45$Xa98";
executing command: SET decryption
RMAN>
```

If you are recovering one or more tablespaces or the entire database from backups that have different passwords, you can conveniently specify all the passwords at once with SET DECRYPTION.

```
RMAN> set decryption identified by "F45$Xa98", "XX407$9!@";

executing command: SET decryption

RMAN>
```

RMAN will try each password in turn for every encrypted backup until it finds a match. RMAN will terminate with an error only if no passwords match any of the passwords in any of the backups.

Using Dual Mode Encryption

You can use both transparent encryption and password encryption at the same time. This is useful if your backup might be used to restore or recover within the same database, and on occasion it can be used to recover another database. When both methods are in effect, you can use either the password or the database wallet to restore the backup. When recovering to a remote database, you must specify the password before recovering, as follows:

```
RMAN> set encryption on;

executing command: SET encryption

RMAN> set encryption identified by "F45$Xa98";

executing command: SET encryption

RMAN>
```

If you want to use only password-based encryption for a backup, add the ONLY clause to SET ENCRYPTION:

```
RMAN> set encryption identified by "F45$Xa98" only;
```

As a result, even if ENCRYPTION defaults to ON (and therefore uses the wallet), all subsequent backups use password encryption only until you turn off password encryption or exit RMAN altogether.

CERTIFICATION OBJECTIVE 4.04

Manage Backups

Once you have successfully completed your backups, you will probably need to find out which backups are available, which backups are obsolete, and which backups need to occur to satisfy your retention policy. RMAN has the LIST and REPORT commands to help you extract this metadata from the recovery catalog or the target database control file.

The LIST command provides basic information about the backupsets, image copies, proxy copies, and stored scripts recorded in the recovery catalog. In contrast, the REPORT command provides a more detailed analysis of the backup information in the recovery catalog. For example, the REPORT NEED BACKUP command lists all datafiles that don't have enough backups to satisfy the database's retention policy. In contrast, the REPORT OBSOLETE command identifies files that are no longer needed to satisfy the database's retention policy, such as extra datafile copies or archived redo log files that are superseded by a more recent datafile backup. If you are low on disk space, you can use DELETE OBSOLETE to remove these files.

Occasionally, you can lose a disk containing backups because of a hardware failure. Also, tapes containing backups can sometimes wear out and are no longer writeable or readable. As a result, you should run the CROSSCHECK command on a regular basis to ensure that the recovery catalog reflects the existence and integrity of these backups. Files that are no longer available for recovery are marked as EXPIRED, and you can remove them with the DELETE EXPIRED command.

The following sections describe each of these commands with numerous examples.

Using the LIST Command

The LIST command displays information about backupsets and image copies in the repository and can also store the contents of scripts stored in the repository catalog. The following example shows a summary of the backups and then lists the stored script names:

```
RMAN> list backup summary;

starting full resync of recovery catalog
full resync complete

List of Backups
===============
Key     TY LV S Device Type Completion Time #Pieces #Copies Compressed Tag
------- -- -- - ----------- --------------- ------- ------- ---------- ---
786     B  F  A DISK        25-FEB-14       1       1       YES        TAG20140225T012351
787     B  F  A DISK        25-FEB-14       1       1       YES        TAG20140225T012351
788     B  F  A DISK        25-FEB-14       1       1       YES        TAG20140225T012351
789     B  F  A DISK        25-FEB-14       1       1       YES        TAG20140225T012351
790     B  F  A DISK        25-FEB-14       1       1       YES        TAG20140225T012351
791     B  F  A DISK        25-FEB-14       1       1       YES        TAG20140225T012351
792     B  F  A DISK        25-FEB-14       1       1       YES        TAG20140225T012351
793     B  F  A DISK        25-FEB-14       1       1       YES        TAG20140225T012351
794     B  F  A DISK        25-FEB-14       1       1       YES        TAG20140225T012351
. . .
1546    B  A  A DISK        25-FEB-14       1       1       YES        SAVE1YR
1559    B  F  A DISK        25-FEB-14       1       1       YES        SAVE1YR
1583    B  F  A DISK        25-FEB-14       3       1       YES        TAG20140225T101644
1584    B  F  A DISK        25-FEB-14       1       1       YES        TAG20140225T101644

RMAN> list script names;

List of Stored Scripts in Recovery Catalog
```

```
    Scripts of Target Database RPT12C

       Script Name
       Description
       ---------------------------------------------------------
       local_backup_db


    Global Scripts

       Script Name
       Description
       ---------------------------------------------------------
       backup_ts

       global_backup_db

RMAN>
```

Another variation on the LIST command is LIST FAILURE, which displays database failures; LIST FAILURE, ADVISE FAILURE, and REPAIR FAILURE are covered in Chapter 6.

Using the REPORT Command

In contrast to the LIST command, the REPORT command performs a more detailed analysis of the information in the recovery catalog, such as which files need more backups to comply with the defined retention policy. The next example changes the retention policy to four copies and then queries the recovery catalog to see which datafiles don't have four copies:

```
RMAN> configure retention policy to redundancy 4;

old RMAN configuration parameters:
CONFIGURE RETENTION POLICY TO REDUNDANCY 2;
new RMAN configuration parameters:
CONFIGURE RETENTION POLICY TO REDUNDANCY 4;
new RMAN configuration parameters are successfully stored
starting full resync of recovery catalog
full resync complete

RMAN> report need backup;

RMAN retention policy will be applied to the command
RMAN retention policy is set to redundancy 4
```

```
Report of files with less than 4 redundant backups
File #bkps Name
---- ----- -----------------------------------------------------
1    2     +DATA/RPT12C/DATAFILE/system.258.826650799
2    2     +DATA/RPT12C/DATAFILE/example.266.826650883
3    2     +DATA/RPT12C/DATAFILE/sysaux.257.826650753
4    2     +DATA/RPT12C/DATAFILE/undotbs1.260.826650845
5    3     +DATA/RPT12C/DATAFILE/users.269.826931347
6    3     +DATA/RPT12C/DATAFILE/users.259.826650843
7    2     +DATA/RPT12C/DATAFILE/undotbs1.270.826931347
. . .
96   2     /u02/oradata/xport.dbf
97   2     +DATA/RPT12C/DATAFILE/users9.404.832157465
98   2     +DATA/RPT12C/DATAFILE/users9.405.832159845
99   2     +DATA/RPT12C/DATAFILE/users4.407.834660445
100  2     +DATA/RPT12C/DATAFILE/users5.408.834661423

RMAN>
```

As this report indicates, the datafiles for the USERS and SYSAUX tablespaces have enough backup copies to satisfy the retention policy.

This REPORT command finds out what the datafiles looked like back on 8/30/2013:

```
report schema at time='30-aug-2013';
```

Using the DELETE Command

Once you have identified which datafiles and archived redo log files are obsolete (as defined by your database's retention policy), you can remove them manually with the DELETE OBSOLETE command. You can either remove obsolete files one at a time or remove all obsolete backups using this command:

```
RMAN> delete noprompt obsolete;
```

Note that if you are using a flash recovery area, RMAN automatically removes obsolete files when the free space in the flash recovery area is low.

Using the CROSSCHECK Command

On occasion, a backup tape can get lost or a disk containing backup files can fail. To keep the recovery catalog up to date, you can use the CROSSCHECK command to mark the missing backups as EXPIRED. In the following example, a backup directory on the /u05 file system has failed. A backup of the USERS tablespace on this file system and the backup are recorded in the recovery catalog. To synchronize the recovery catalog with the backups that are still valid and exist, use the CROSSCHECK command:

```
RMAN> crosscheck backup;

using channel ORA_DISK_1
crosschecked backup piece: found to be 'AVAILABLE'
backup piece
handle=+RECOV/RPT12C/backupset/2014_05_25/
     nnndf0_tag20080509t234534_0.430.654306351 RECID=590
STAMP=654306351
crosschecked backup piece: found to be 'AVAILABLE'
. . .
Crosschecked 7 objects

RMAN>
```

RMAN may identify some backups as EXPIRED. Once you have marked expired backups as EXPIRED in the recovery catalog with the CROSSCHECK command, you can remove the entries in the recovery catalog by using the DELETE EXPIRED command:

```
RMAN> delete expired backup;

using channel ORA_DISK_1

List of Backup Pieces
BP Key  BS Key  Pc# Cp# Status      Device Type Piece Name
------- ------- --- --- ----------- ----------- ----------
4560    4557    1   1   EXPIRED     DISK
                                    /u05/oradata/rmtbak/jojg18cv_1_1

Do you really want to delete the above objects (enter YES or NO)? yes
deleted backup piece
backup piece handle=/u05/oradata/rmtbak/
                jojg18cv_1_1 RECID=595 STAMP=654352823
Deleted 1 EXPIRED objects

RMAN>
```

Note that you don't always have to delete expired backups. If the disk or tape becomes available in the future, you can run CROSSCHECK again. RMAN will find the backup and mark it as AVAILABLE; as a result, it can be used again in a recovery operation.

CERTIFICATION OBJECTIVE 4.05

Perform Backup of Nondatabase Files

Nondatabase files such as the control file, archived redo log files, and ASM metadata need to be backed up too. If there are backups that are not registered in the database control file or recovery catalog, you can use the RMAN CATALOG command to make those backups available for future recovery scenarios.

Backing Up the Control File

Although the control file is one of the smaller files in your database environment, it is critical to the operation of the database because it contains the metadata for all objects in your database. The control file contains datafile locations, online redo log file locations, and so forth. Therefore, it is wise not only to multiplex the control file in several locations but to back it up frequently. Backing up the control file for a database running in ARCHIVELOG mode produces the same end result as the method you use in NOARCHIVELOG mode.

The primary method for backing up a control file in ARCHIVELOG mode is to create an exact copy (in binary format) of the current control file to a location you specify:

```
SQL> alter database backup controlfile to '/u02/oradata/rman/
ctl.bkup';

Database altered.

SQL>
```

The other method creates an editable script that re-creates the control file. Here is the command:

```
SQL> alter database backup controlfile to trace;

Database altered.

SQL>
```

Oracle creates the script in the location where all trace files reside, which by default for the HR database is **$ORACLE_BASE/diag/rdbms/rpt12c/RPT12C/trace**. Here is an excerpt from the generated script:

```
. . .
-- The following commands will create a new control file and use it
-- to open the database.
-- Data used by Recovery Manager will be lost.
-- Additional logs may be required for media recovery of offline
-- Use this only if the current versions of all online logs are
-- available.
-- After mounting the created controlfile, the following SQL
-- statement will place the database in the appropriate
-- protection mode:
--  ALTER DATABASE SET STANDBY DATABASE TO MAXIMIZE PERFORMANCE
STARTUP NOMOUNT
CREATE CONTROLFILE REUSE DATABASE "RPT12C" NORESETLOGS  ARCHIVELOG
    MAXLOGFILES 16
    MAXLOGMEMBERS 3
    MAXDATAFILES 100
    MAXINSTANCES 8
    MAXLOGHISTORY 584
LOGFILE
  GROUP 1 (
    '+DATA/RPT12C/ONLINELOG/group_1.262.839886709',
    '+RECOV/RPT12C/ONLINELOG/group_1.257.839886709'
  ) SIZE 50M BLOCKSIZE 512,
  GROUP 2 (
    '+DATA/RPT12C/ONLINELOG/group_2.263.839886709',
    '+RECOV/RPT12C/ONLINELOG/group_2.258.839886709'
  ) SIZE 50M BLOCKSIZE 512,
  GROUP 3 (
. . .
```

Backing Up ASM Metadata

Backing up the database files stored in one or more ASM disk groups (and you should be using ASM unless you have a good reason not to!) is the most important component of ensuring recoverability, as well as making sure that the structure of the ASM disk groups is retained in case of media failure. If you don't have a metadata backup file, the disk groups must be re-created manually before performing a restore and recover operation on one or more datafiles. Even with a relatively simple disk group configuration (such as DATA and RECOV), it will add a significant amount of time to the recovery operation.

To perform the ASM metadata backup, you use the **asmcmd** utility with the **md_backup** command. You can use the **–G** option of the **md_backup** command to export the metadata for specific disk groups. In this example, you connect to the ASM instance and export the metadata for all mounted disk groups to **/home/oracle/asm_config.out**:

```
[oracle@tettnang ~]$ . oraenv
ORACLE_SID = [RPT12C] ? +ASM
The Oracle base remains unchanged with value /u00/app/oracle
[oracle@tettnang ~]$ asmcmd
ASMCMD> md_backup /home/oracle/asm_config.out
Disk group metadata to be backed up: RECOV
Disk group metadata to be backed up: DATA
Current alias directory path: RPT12C/CONTROLFILE
Current alias directory path: RPT12C/BACKUPSET/2014_02_18
Current alias directory path: RPT12C
. . .
Current alias directory path: XSAH2014/TEMPFILE
Current alias directory path: ASM/PASSWORD
Current alias directory path: RPT12C/CONTROLFILE
Current alias directory path: XSAH2014/PARAMETERFILE
Current alias directory path: RCAT/ONLINELOG
Current alias directory path: DWCDB
Current alias directory path: RCAT/CONTROLFILE
ASMCMD>
```

Looking at the file **asm_config.out**, you see this:

```
@diskgroup_set = (
                   {
                     'ATTRINFO' => {
                                     '_._DIRVERSION' => '12.1.0.0.0',
                                     'COMPATIBLE.ASM' => '12.1.0.0.0',
                                     'PHYS_META_REPLICATED' => 'true',
                                     'COMPATIBLE.RDBMS' => '10.1.0.0.0'
                                   },
                     'DISKSINFO' => {
                                       'RECOV_0000' => {
                                                          'RECOV_0000' => {
'TOTAL_MB' => '51199',
'FAILGROUP' => 'RECOV_0000',
'NAME' => 'RECOV_0000',
'DGNAME' => 'RECOV',
'PATH' => '/dev/oracleasm/disks/ASM05'
. . .
```

```
                                        },
                                 '5' => {
                                         'DGNAME' => 'DATA',
                                         'STRIPE' => 'COARSE',
                                         'TEMPNAME' =>
'AUTOLOGIN_KEY_STORE',
                                         'REDUNDANCY' => 'UNPROT',
                                         'SYSTEM' => 'Y'
                                        }
                                }
             }
          );
```

Even with a relatively small set of databases stored in this ASM configuration, you can see that it is much easier to perform a metadata backup than to re-create the configuration from scratch.

Cataloging Additional Backup Files

Cataloging additional backup files was covered in Chapter 3. You can catalog datafile copies, backup pieces, control file copies, and archived redo log files. Here is a sample CATALOG command that adds any datafiles in the +DATA2 disk group that are not recorded in the RMAN catalog:

```
RMAN> catalog start with '+DATA2';
```

CERTIFICATION SUMMARY

First, you were introduced to RMAN backup types and configuration settings, including how to persist RMAN settings, such as device types and channels, and you also learned how to ensure that the control file is backed up on a regular basis.

The first part of the chapter covered the basics of creating a backupset (the default) or image copies. You can create image copies of database datafiles and archived redo logs using operating system commands. However, RMAN provides a number of advantages when performing an image copy, such as block verification and backupset compression and decompression. When compressing a backup, RMAN provides four different encryption methods (all new to Oracle Database 12*c*) depending on your available disk space and CPU contention.

Next, the chapter explained the somewhat subtle distinctions between a whole-database backup, a full backup, and an incremental backup. A whole-database backup is a snapshot of all datafiles, the control file, and all archived redo log files. In contrast, a full backup is a complete backup of one or more individual database objects and cannot participate in an incremental backup strategy. Incremental backups can be level 0 or level 1. Level 0 backups are logically equivalent to full backups but can be used as the base for level 1 incremental backups, which can be either cumulative or differential.

RMAN has a number of features to make your backups more reliable and take less time to complete. Incremental backups use a block change tracking file to identify which data blocks have changed since the last incremental backup. As a result, RMAN does not have to read all blocks in every datafile to successfully back up only the changed blocks. Duplexed backups decrease the amount of time it takes to make simultaneous multiple copies of datafiles. You can send one copy to a local disk at the same time you send another copy to an offsite disk, all in less time than it takes to make two sequential backups or a local backup, followed by a copy of the backup to an offsite location. To further decrease the time it takes to complete your backups, RMAN can skip backing up a read-only tablespace by using the SKIP READONLY option or by configuring backup optimization.

Archival backups, another new RMAN feature since Oracle Database 11g, are backups that never expire and provide a snapshot of your database for regulatory compliance. Because they provide a snapshot of your database at a point of time in the past with a specific retention time or an indefinite retention time, you keep your recovery area clean of archived redo log files that would otherwise have to remain in your flash recovery area for an equivalent recovery window.

Multisection RMAN backups give you the flexibility to back up and validate backups of very large datafiles in sections. In previous versions, large datafiles (such as those found in bigfile tablespaces) took a prohibitively long amount of time to back up because RMAN could allocate only one thread to back up the datafile sequentially.

To enhance the security of your backups, RMAN can use either password-based or wallet-based encryption, or it can use both at the same time. Wallet-based encryption is the preferred method, but in cases where you must restore your datafiles to another database, providing a strong password keeps the backup secure until you are ready to restore it into a target database.

For the purposes of managing and reporting on backups, you were introduced to two commands used to query the contents of your recovery catalog: LIST and REPORT. The LIST command gives you a high-level view of your backups, including backupsets, image copies, and stored scripts. The REPORT command gives you a more in-depth analysis of your backups, such as identifying missing backups or database objects that need to be backed up again to satisfy your configured retention policy. Once you identify any extra backups, you can use the DELETE command to remove them. You can also use the DELETE command to remove backups from the recovery catalog that have been identified as missing with the CROSSCHECK command.

You also saw several ways to optimize your backups, reducing both disk space and elapsed time. For example, backup optimization reduces the number of times that a read-only tablespace needs to be backed up.

Finally, you need to back up and potentially recover nondatabase files. These nondatabase files include control files, archived redo log files, and ASM metadata. You may also want to catalog additional backup files that are not in the control file or recovery catalog.

TWO-MINUTE DRILL

Use Various RMAN Backup Types and Strategies

- RMAN backups can be full or incremental.
- Incremental backups can be level 0 or 1. Level 0 backups are full backups that you can use as part of a differential, incremental, or cumulative incremental level 1 backup strategy.
- RMAN image copies are exact copies of datafiles. Using RMAN to make copies of datafiles has the additional advantage of checking for corruption in each block read.
- RMAN can use backup compression to save space on the destination device, and RMAN automatically decompresses the backup during a recovery operation.
- Using a flash recovery area for RMAN has two advantages: RMAN automatically names backup files in the flash recovery area, and it automatically deletes obsolete backup files when there is space pressure in the flash recovery area.
- More than one database can use the flash recovery area.
- The RMAN command SHOW ALL lists all persistent RMAN settings.
- Use CONFIGURE CONTROLFILE AUTOBACKUP ON to ensure that a backup copy of the target database control file exists after each backup.

Perform Full and Incremental Backups

- RMAN backups are either backupsets or image backups.
- Backupsets can be created only by RMAN and can be read only by RMAN.
- The FORMAT clause of the BACKUP command specifies the substitution variables for the destination backup filename.
- You can create image copies of datafiles, archived redo log files, and control files.
- Image copies can be written only to disk.
- You can use the SWITCH command to quickly and easily switch between a datafile and its image copy during a recovery operation.

- A whole-database backup includes all datafiles plus the control file.
- A full backup of a datafile is a logical subset of a whole-database backup.
- A full backup cannot be used as the basis for an incremental backup strategy.
- An incremental backup is level 0 or level 1.
- An incremental level 0 backup can be used as the basis for an incremental backup strategy.
- Differential backups back up all changed blocks since the last level 0 or level 1 incremental backup.
- Cumulative incremental backups back up all changed blocks since the last level 0 backup.
- Enable fast incremental backup by creating a block change tracking file.
- Perform a level 0 incremental backup before configuring RMAN to use a block change tracking file.
- The data dictionary view V$BLOCK_CHANGE_TRACKING provides the name and status of the block change tracking file.
- Duplexed backupsets can significantly reduce the time it takes to create multiple copies of the same backup.
- Backups cannot be duplexed to the flash recovery area, and you cannot duplex image copies.
- Use the BACKUP . . . BACKUPSET commands to create a copy of an existing RMAN backup to disk or tape.
- RMAN will skip the backup of read-only tablespaces if you use SKIP READONLY in the BACKUP command.
- If you configure RMAN for backup optimization, RMAN will back up only additional copies of read-only tablespaces to satisfy the configured retention policy.
- An archival backup is a snapshot of the database at a certain point in time created to satisfy archival or regulatory purposes.
- Archival backups make it easy to migrate a copy of the database to another system without affecting the retention policy of the original database.
- To create an archival backup, you specify either the KEEP UNTIL TIME or KEEP FOREVER option in the BACKUP command.

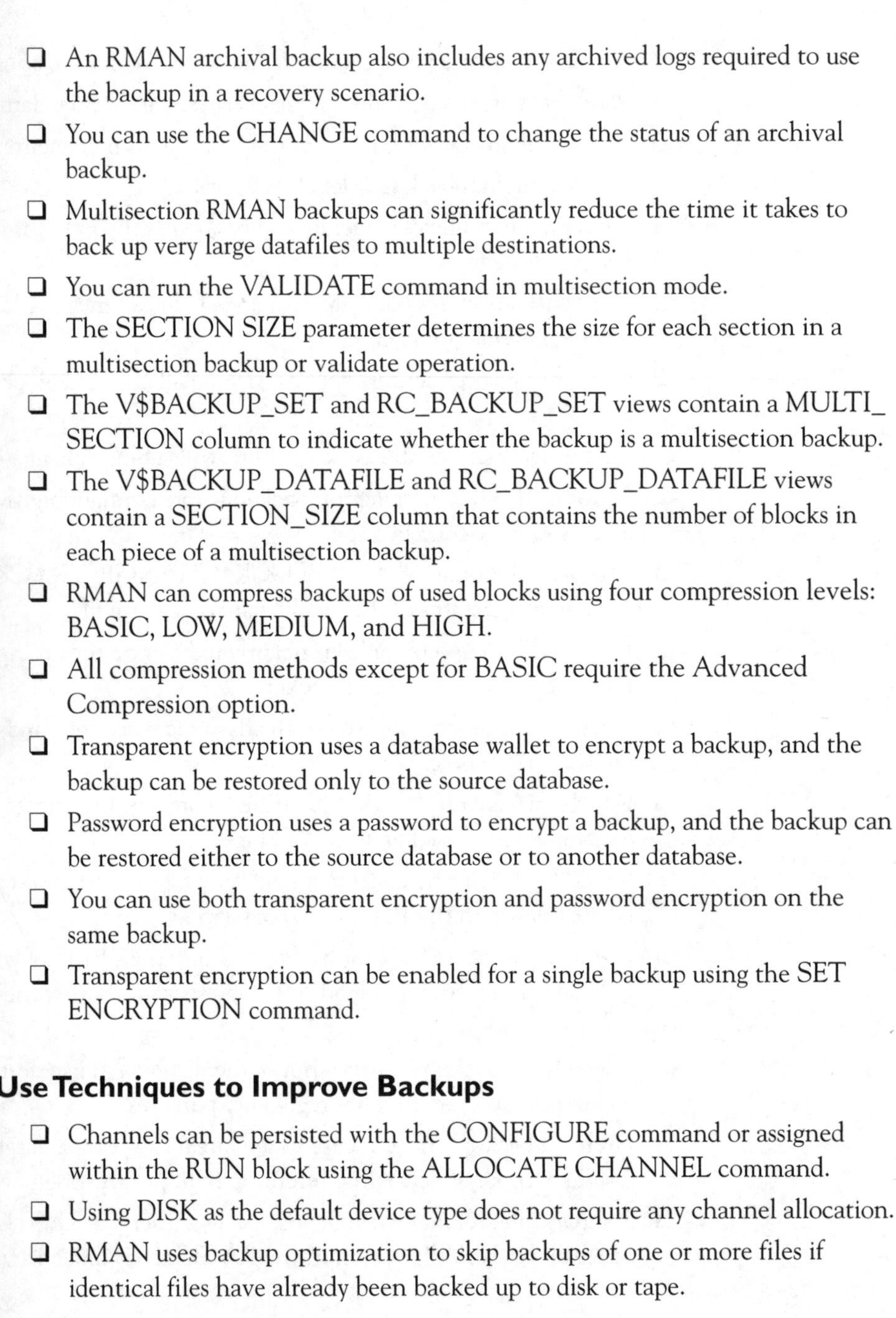

- An RMAN archival backup also includes any archived logs required to use the backup in a recovery scenario.
- You can use the CHANGE command to change the status of an archival backup.
- Multisection RMAN backups can significantly reduce the time it takes to back up very large datafiles to multiple destinations.
- You can run the VALIDATE command in multisection mode.
- The SECTION SIZE parameter determines the size for each section in a multisection backup or validate operation.
- The V$BACKUP_SET and RC_BACKUP_SET views contain a MULTI_SECTION column to indicate whether the backup is a multisection backup.
- The V$BACKUP_DATAFILE and RC_BACKUP_DATAFILE views contain a SECTION_SIZE column that contains the number of blocks in each piece of a multisection backup.
- RMAN can compress backups of used blocks using four compression levels: BASIC, LOW, MEDIUM, and HIGH.
- All compression methods except for BASIC require the Advanced Compression option.
- Transparent encryption uses a database wallet to encrypt a backup, and the backup can be restored only to the source database.
- Password encryption uses a password to encrypt a backup, and the backup can be restored either to the source database or to another database.
- You can use both transparent encryption and password encryption on the same backup.
- Transparent encryption can be enabled for a single backup using the SET ENCRYPTION command.

Use Techniques to Improve Backups

- Channels can be persisted with the CONFIGURE command or assigned within the RUN block using the ALLOCATE CHANNEL command.
- Using DISK as the default device type does not require any channel allocation.
- RMAN uses backup optimization to skip backups of one or more files if identical files have already been backed up to disk or tape.

- ❑ Backup optimization takes into account duplexing and retention policies before skipping a source file.
- ❑ You set backup optimization in RMAN with the command CONFIGURE BACKUP OPTIMIZATION ON.

Manage Backups

- ❑ The LIST command provides basic information about the availability of backupsets, image copies, proxy copies, and stored scripts.
- ❑ The REPORT command provides a more detailed analysis of the backup information in the recovery catalog.
- ❑ You can use the REPORT command to identify obsolete backups.
- ❑ You can use the REPORT command to identify datafiles that need more backup copies to satisfy the retention policy.
- ❑ The CROSSCHECK command validates the backup entries in the recovery catalog versus the existence of the actual backups on disk or tape.
- ❑ The DELETE OBSOLETE command removes obsolete backups from the recovery catalog and the backup location.
- ❑ You can remove EXPIRED backups with the DELETE EXPIRED command.

Perform Backup of Nondatabase Files

- ❑ If you want to back up your control file while the database is open, you can do it with two different SQL commands: ALTER DATABASE BACKUP CONTROLFILE TO <*filename*> and ALTER DATABASE BACKUP CONTROLFILE TO TRACE.
- ❑ ALTER DATABASE BACKUP CONTROLFILE TO <*filename*> creates an exact binary copy of the control file at the specified location.
- ❑ ALTER DATABASE BACKUP CONTROLFILE TO TRACE creates an editable script that re-creates the control file in the directory **$ORACLE_BASE/diag/rdbms/<*database*>/<*instance*>/trace**.
- ❑ Losing all copies of the online control file does not lose any committed transactions if you have a recent backup copy of the control file and both the datafiles and online redo log files are intact.

- You do not have to open the database with RESETLOGS after restoring your control file if you manually create the replacement control file using CREATE CONTROLFILE or you use a version of the control file script that you created with ALTER DATABASE BACKUP CONTROLFILE TO TRACE.
- When using the **asmcmd** utility for an ASM instance, you can run the **md_backup** command to export the disk group metadata for recovery purposes.

SELF TEST

The following questions will help you measure your understanding of the material presented in this chapter. Read all the choices carefully because there might be more than one correct answer. Choose all correct answers for each question.

Use Various RMAN Backup Types and Strategies

1. You run the following RMAN command:

```
RMAN> configure controlfile autobackup on;
```

Under what conditions does RMAN back up the control file and the SPFILE? (Choose all that apply.)

A. When an RMAN backup completes
B. When you start RMAN
C. When you connect to a target database
D. When you back up the SYSTEM tablespace
E. When you run the command BACKUP CURRENT CONTROLFILE;
F. When any of the DBA passwords change
G. When you change the size of the flash recovery area
H. When you add a tablespace

2. Which of the following objects cannot be backed up by RMAN using the RMAN BACKUP command? (Choose all that apply.)

A. DATAFILE
B. DATABASE
C. INSTANCE
D. CURRENT CONTROLFILE
E. SPFILE
F. TABLESPACE
G. ARCHIVELOG
H. CONTROLFILE
I. REDOLOG

3. Identify the statements in the following list that are true about managing RMAN persistent settings. (Choose all that apply.)
   A. SHOW ALL lists all current settings for the connected target database.
   B. You can use the CONFIGURE . . . CLEAR command to set a configuration value to an empty string.
   C. SHOW ALL shows the configuration values that apply to all target databases.
   D. You can use the CONFIGURE . . . CLEAR command to set a configuration value to its default value.
   E. SHOW ALL lists all RMAN settings that are different from the default value.

Perform Full and Incremental Backups

4. Which of the following is the default substitution variable for the FORMAT clause of the BACKUP command?
   A. %t
   B. %d
   C. %u
   D. %U
   E. %I
5. Which of the following are candidates for RMAN image copies? (Choose two answers.)
   A. Datafiles
   B. Archived redo log files
   C. Online redo log files
   D. Password files
6. The tablespace BI_HR in your database is on a disk that has crashed, but you have an image copy plus all required redo log files in the flash recovery area. Put the following sequence of RMAN commands in the correct order to recover the BI_HR tablespace successfully:

```
1. recover tablespace bi_hr;
2. sql "alter tablespace bi_hr online";
3. switch tablespace bi_hr to copy;
4. sql "alter tablespace bi_hr offline immediate";
```

   A. 4, 3, 2, 1
   B. 4, 3, 1, 2
   C. 3, 4, 1, 2
   D. 4, 1, 3, 2

7. You run the following command to create a whole-database backup:

```
RMAN> backup as copy database spfile plus archivelog delete input;
```

What does the DELETE INPUT clause do?

A. After the backup completes, RMAN deletes the archived log files from all archived log file destinations except for the flash recovery area.

B. After the backup completes, RMAN deletes the archived log files from the flash recovery area only.

C. After the backup completes, RMAN deletes the archived log files from the flash recovery area and any other archived log file destinations.

D. RMAN deletes all obsolete copies of database backups after the backup completes.

8. What is the difference between a full backup and a whole-database backup? (Choose the best answer.)

A. A whole-database backup can be used as the basis for an incremental backup strategy, but a full database backup cannot.

B. A full database backup can be used as the basis for an incremental backup strategy, but a whole-database backup cannot.

C. A whole-database backup can be only an image copy. A full backup can be an image copy or a backupset.

D. A full backup consists of a backup of one or more datafiles or tablespaces, whereas a whole-database backup contains all datafiles, for all tablespaces plus the control file.

9. What is true about a level 0 incremental backup? (Choose all correct answers.)

A. A level 0 backup includes all blocks in a datafile, including blocks that have never been used.

B. A level 0 backup includes all blocks in a datafile, except for blocks that have never been used.

C. A level 0 backup can be used with a level 1 cumulative backup.

D. A level 0 backup can be used with a level 1 differential backup.

E. A level 0 backup of a datafile has additional information that differentiates it from a full backup of the same datafile.

10. Identify the true statement regarding incremental and differential backups.

A. A differential backup is the default type of incremental backup and backs up all changed blocks since the last level 0 or level 1 incremental backup.

B. A cumulative backup is the default type of incremental backup and backs up all changed blocks since the last level 0 or level 1 incremental backup.

C. A differential backup is the default type of incremental backup and backs up all changed blocks since the last level 0 incremental backup.

D. A cumulative backup is the default type of incremental backup and backs up all changed blocks since the last level 1 incremental backup.

11. What method does RMAN use to enable fast incremental backup? (Choose the best answer.)
    A. It uses differential incremental level 1 backups.
    B. It uses a block change tracking file.
    C. It uses duplexed backupsets.
    D. It uses whole-database backups as the basis for an incremental backup.

12. You create a block change tracking file for your database. What happens if you run the following command? (Choose the best answer.)

```
RMAN> backup incremental level 1 database;
```

    A. The command fails because you need to run a level 0 backup first to initialize the block change tracking file.
    B. A level 0 incremental backup automatically runs before the level 1 backup so that RMAN initializes the block change tracking file.
    C. RMAN generates a warning message indicating that the block change tracking file needs to be initialized.
    D. The backup runs successfully but does not use the block change tracking file.

13. When you want to create a duplexed backupset, what is the maximum number of copies of each backup piece you can create with one BACKUP command?
    A. Two for disk locations and four for tape destinations.
    B. A maximum of four.
    C. Two for tape locations and four for disk locations.
    D. The maximum is limited only by the number of destination disks or tape drives.

14. Which of the following duplexed backups will run successfully? (Choose all correct answers.)
    A. An image copy duplexed to four tape drives
    B. A backupset duplexed to two tape drives
    C. A backupset duplexed to eight NAS disks
    D. An image copy duplexed to four disk drives
    E. A backupset duplexed to two file systems on different servers

15. Identify the true statements regarding archival backups. (Choose all correct answers.)
    A. Archival backups can be retained indefinitely.
    B. You can drop an archival backup using the CHANGE . . . DROP command.
    C. Archival backups include all archived redo logs from the archival date to the present.
    D. Once you create an archival backup, you must either keep it for the retention period specified or drop it.

E. You can use an archival backup to migrate a copy of the database without affecting the retention policy.

F. You can change the retention period of an archival backup once it has been created.

16. You have a datafile from the smallfile tablespace USERS that has a size of 90MB, and you run the following RMAN command:

```
RMAN> backup tablespace users section size 40m;
```

How many sections does this backup create?

A. The command does not run because multisection backups apply only to bigfile tablespaces.

B. Two sections of 45MB each.

C. Two sections of 40MB each and one section of 10MB.

D. The command does not run because you can back up the entire database only as a multisection backup.

17. Identify the true statement about the dynamic performance and data dictionary views related to multisection backups.

A. The views V$BACKUP_SET and RC_BACKUP_SET have a column named MULTI_SECTION. The views V$BACKUP_DATAFILE and RC_BACKUP_DATAFILE have a column named SECTION_SIZE.

B. The views V$BACKUP_SET and RC_BACKUP_SET have a column named SECTION_SIZE. The views V$BACKUP_DATAFILE and RC_BACKUP_DATAFILE have a column named MULTI_SECTION.

C. The views V$BACKUP_SET and V$BACKUP_DATAFILE have a column named MULTI_SECTION. The views RC_BACKUP_SET and RC_BACKUP_DATAFILE have a column named SECTION_SIZE.

D. The views V$BACKUP_SET and V$BACKUP_DATAFILE have a column named SECTION_SIZE. The views RC_BACKUP_SET and RC_BACKUP_DATAFILE have a column named MULTI_SECTION.

Use Techniques to Improve Backups

18. What happens when you run the following RMAN commands?

```
RMAN> run
{ configure channel ch2 device type disk;
   backup database; }
```

A. A full database backup is created in the flash recovery area.

B. The database is backed up to all default channels configured outside of the RUN block plus the additional channel within the RUN block.

C. The command fails because you cannot use CONFIGURE within a RUN block.

D. The command fails because you cannot use BACKUP within a RUN block.

19. You have configured backup optimization for your database using CONFIGURE BACKUP OPTIMIZATION ON. For which of the following commands will RMAN not skip a backup if the files are identical?

A. BACKUP DATABASE;

B. BACKUP TABLESPACE USERS;

C. BACKUP ARCHIVELOG ALL;

D. BACKUP BACKUPSET ALL;

Manage Backups

20. Which RMAN command would you use to find out which datafiles need another backup to satisfy the retention policy?

A. REPORT NEED BACKUP

B. LIST NEED BACKUP

C. CROSSCHECK NEED BACKUP

D. CONFIGURE RETENTION POLICY

21. One of your backups to disk is missing, and after you run the CROSSCHECK command, this backup is marked as EXPIRED. Later, you find the backup file on another disk and move it back to its original location. You run the CROSSCHECK command again. What is the status of the backup?

A. The backup is marked as OBSOLETE.

B. The backup is marked as AVAILABLE.

C. The backup is still marked as EXPIRED until the next incremental backup.

D. You cannot change the status of a backup unless it is stored in the flash recovery area.

Perform Backup of Nondatabase Files

22. Which of the following commands does not back up the current control file?

A. `SQL> ALTER DATABASE BACKUP CONTROLFILE TO TRACE;`

B. `SQL> ALTER SYSTEM BACKUP CURRENT CONTROLFILE;`

C. `RMAN> BACKUP CURRENT CONTROLFILE;`

D.
```
SQL> ALTER DATABASE BACKUP CONTROLFILE TO
'/U08/BACKUP/CTL.BAK';
```

23. You have lost all online control files. Specify the correct order for the following tasks:

1. Restore the control file from backup or run CREATE CONTROLFILE.
2. Start database recovery and specify the keywords BACKUP CONTROLFILE.
3. Start up the database in MOUNT mode.
4. Open the database with RESETLOGS.
5. Shut down the database.

A. 5, 1, 3, 2, 4

B. 1, 5, 3, 2, 4

C. 5, 1, 3, 4, 2

D. 1, 5, 3, 4, 2

SELF TEST ANSWERS

Use Various RMAN Backup Types and Strategies

1. ☑ **A, E,** and **H.** RMAN backs up the current control file and the SPFILE (if you use one) after a successful backup, when you explicitly back up the current control file, and when the structure of the database changes.
☒ B, C, D, F, and G are incorrect. RMAN does not back up the control file under any of these circumstances.

2. ☑ **C, H,** and **I. C** cannot be backed up because RMAN backs up databases; an instance comprises the Oracle memory structures and cannot be backed up. **H** cannot be backed up because CONTROLFILE is not a valid option; you must use CURRENT CONTROLFILE to back up the control file. **I** cannot be backed up because you should never, ever back up the online redo log files, and therefore BACKUP REDOLOG is syntactically incorrect.
☒ A, B, D, E, F, and G are incorrect because they can all be backed up. All other objects listed (the current control file, the SPFILE, the entire database, an individual datafile, an individual tablespace, or one or more archived redo log files) can be backed up by RMAN.

3. ☑ **A** and **D.** The SHOW ALL command shows all settings for the connected target; you can use CONFIGURE . . . CLEAR to reset a configuration value to its default.
☒ **B, C,** and **E** are incorrect. **B** is incorrect because CONFIGURE...CLEAR resets the configuration setting to its default value. **C** is incorrect because SHOW ALL works only when you are connected to a target database. **E** is incorrect since SHOW ALL lists all configuration values regardless of whether they have been changed from the default.

Perform Full and Incremental Backups

4. ☑ **D.** %U is the default and is a system-generated unique filename that is equivalent to %u_%p_%c.
☒ **A, B, C,** and **E** are incorrect. These choices are valid in the FORMAT command but are not the default.

5. ☑ **A** and **B.** In addition to datafiles and archived redo log files, you can also create image copies of control files.
☒ **C** and **D** are incorrect because they cannot be backed up as image copies. In fact, they cannot be backed up using RMAN.

6. ☑ **B.** All of these commands can be run at the RMAN prompt and successfully make the BI_HR tablespace once again available to users.

☒ **A, C,** and **D** are incorrect. They do not correctly recover the tablespace using image copies. **A** is incorrect because the tablespace contents must be recovered *before* bringing the tablespace back online. **C** is incorrect because the tablespace must be taken offline *before* switching to use the copy. **D** is incorrect because you can't recover the tablespace until it is switched.

7. ☑ **C.** When the backup completes successfully, RMAN deletes all archived redo log files from all destinations including the flash recovery area.
☒ **A, B,** and **D** are incorrect. **A** and **B** are incorrect because RMAN deletes archived redo log files from all destinations. **D** is incorrect because the DELETE INPUT command applies only to archived redo log files that apply to this backup.

8. ☑ **D.** A whole-database backup can also include archived redo log files and the SPFILE.
☒ **A, B,** and **C** are incorrect. **A** and **B** are incorrect because either can be the basis for an incremental backup strategy as long as you use the INCREMENTAL LEVEL 0 parameter in the BACKUP command. **C** is incorrect because both a whole-database backup and a full backup can be image copies or backupsets.

9. ☑ **B, C,** and **D.** A level 0 backup includes all blocks in a datafile, except for blocks that have never been used. It also can be used with both cumulative and incremental level 1 backups.
☒ **A** and **E** are incorrect. **A** is incorrect because a level 0 backup excludes blocks that have never been used. **E** is incorrect because a level 0 backup is physically identical to full backup of the same datafile; the differentiation is the metadata stored in the recovery catalog.

10. ☑ **A.** A differential backup is the default and backs up all changed blocks since the last level 0 or level 1 backup. You cannot specify the DIFFERENTIAL keyword, which is the default.
☒ **B, C,** and **D** are incorrect. **B** is incorrect because a cumulative backup is not the default and it backs up only changed blocks since the last level 0 backup. **C** is incorrect because differential backups also back up changed blocks from the last level 1 incremental backup. **D** is incorrect because a cumulative backup is not the default type of incremental backup and it backs up only changed blocks since the last level 0 backup.

11. ☑ **B.** RMAN uses a block change tracking file to indicate which blocks need to be backed up since the last level 0 incremental backup.
☒ **A, C,** and **D** are incorrect. **A** is incorrect because even though differential incremental backups reduce the backup time, this is not the mechanism for determining which blocks have been changed since the last level 0 backup. **C** and **D** are incorrect for the same reason.

12. ☑ **D.** Even though the block change tracking file exists, RMAN does not use it until after you run the first level 0 incremental backup.
☒ **A, B,** and **C** are incorrect. **A** is incorrect because even though the block change tracking file is not used, the backup still runs successfully. **B** is incorrect because RMAN will not automatically run a level 0 backup. **C** is incorrect because RMAN uses or does not use the block change tracking file transparently.

13. ☑ **B.** RMAN creates a maximum of four copies for disk or tape locations.
☒ **A, C,** and **D** are incorrect. There is no differentiation between tape and disk for duplexed backups, and the range is from two to four.

14. ☑ **B** and **E.** Duplexed backups can include only backupsets and cannot reside in the flash recovery area.
☒ **A, C,** and **D** are incorrect. **A** and **D** are incorrect because you cannot duplex image copies. **C** is incorrect since you can duplex only four copies in one backup.

15. ☑ **A, E,** and **F.** Archival backups can be kept for an indefinite period of time or retained for a specific period of time using the KEEP UNTIL clause. In addition, you can use an archival backup to migrate a database, and you can change the retention period as many times as you need to after you create it.
☒ **B, C,** and **D** are incorrect. **B** is incorrect since the correct clause is CHANGE . . . NOKEEP. **C** is incorrect because only the archived redo logs necessary for the snapshot are included in the backup. **D** is incorrect because you can easily change the retention period for any archival backup.

16. ☑ **C.** RMAN backs up the datafile in multiples of the section size, and any remainder resides in the last section.
☒ **A, B,** and **D** are incorrect. **A** is incorrect because you can use multisection backups for any type of tablespace. **B** is incorrect because RMAN does not round up the section size to create equal section sizes in the output. **D** is incorrect because you can back up either an individual tablespace or the entire database as a multisection backup.

17. ☑ **A.** SECTION_SIZE indicates the section size for the backup piece. MULTI_SECTION has a value of YES or NO to indicate whether the backup is a multisection backup.
☒ **B, C,** and **D** are incorrect. Each of these answers has an invalid combination of columns and their associated views.

Use Techniques to Improve Backups

18. ☑ **C.** You can use CONFIGURE only at the RMAN command prompt to set default values, and it cannot be used within a RUN block.
☒ **A, B,** and **D** are incorrect. **A** is incorrect because the CONFIGURE command cannot be used within a RUN block. **B** is incorrect for the same reason; additionally, any channels allocated within a RUN block override the default channel. **D** is incorrect since you can use BACKUP either as a standalone command or within a RUN block.

19. ☑ **B.** Backup optimization is not used for backing up individual tablespaces.
☒ **A, C,** and **D** are incorrect. Backup optimization is used for all of these commands.

Manage Backups

20. ☑ **A.** The REPORT NEED BACKUP command identifies any datafiles that need at least one additional backup to satisfy the configured retention policy.
☒ **B, C,** and **D** are incorrect. **B** and **C** are syntactically incorrect. **D** defines the retention policy for your database but does not determine which datafiles do not have enough backups to satisfy the retention policy.

21. ☑ **B.** When the CROSSCHECK command runs again, it finds the file in its original location and marks it as AVAILABLE.
☒ **A, C,** and **D** are incorrect. **A** is incorrect because backups are marked as OBSOLETE only when a more recent backup runs and identifies older backups as outside of the retention policy. **C** is incorrect because the CROSSCHECK command immediately changes the status for any backups that are now available. **D** is incorrect because a backup's status is independent of where it is stored.

Perform Backup of Nondatabase Files

22. ☑ **B.** There is no such command.
☒ **A, C,** and **D** are incorrect. **A** creates a text-based file containing two different CREATE CONTROLFILE commands, depending on the availability of your datafiles and online redo log files. **C** is one of many ways that RMAN backs up the control file. **D** creates a binary copy of the control file at the specified location.

23. ☑ **A.** The first step is to shut down the database (with ABORT), and the last step is to open the database with RESETLOGS (if you used a backup control file or you do not have current online redo logs or datafiles).
☒ **B, C,** and **D** are incorrect because first the database must be shut down. After that, you restore the control file, start the database in MOUNT mode, recover using BACKUP CONTROLFILE, then finally open the database with RESETLOGS.

CERTIFICATION OBJECTIVES

5.01	Describe and Tune Instance Recovery
5.02	Perform Complete and Incomplete Recovery
5.03	Perform Recovery for SPFILEs, Password Files, Control Files, and Redo Log Files
5.04	Perform Recovery of Index and Read-Only Tablespaces and Tempfiles
5.05	Restore a Database to a New Host
✓	Two-Minute Drill
Q&A	Self Test

In this chapter, you will learn how to use RMAN in a recovery scenario. This is required if you have lost a noncritical datafile, a critical datafile, a control file, or possibly the entire database.

This chapter addresses recovery scenarios for a database running in ARCHIVELOG mode. Of course, if it isn't apparent by now, you should be running in ARCHIVELOG mode, considering all the advantages and the relatively few disadvantages presented in previous chapters. However, if you are not running in ARCHIVELOG mode, your recovery options are also presented as well as those for NOARCHIVELOG mode.

Even in NOARCHIVELOG mode, you can rest assured that Oracle instance recovery will bring your database back to a consistent state after an instance crash due to factors external to the database. How soon you want your instance to be available has to be balanced with how much extra work you want to do to keep the database in a "recovery ready" state by keeping the checkpoint advanced as far as possible in the redo log files.

Image copies play an important role in your backup and recovery scenarios. You'll learn how to recover an image copy to make it even faster to recover your database in case of media failure. In addition, you'll see how to switch to an image copy and then switch back.

Once you create your backups, you want to make sure that you can use them to recover your database. You'll learn how to restore a database to a new host either to test your recovery scenarios or to move a production database to the new host.

Next, you'll learn how to perform incomplete recovery and recover your database up to a point in time in the past. This is useful when you have logical corruption in your database, including but not limited to user errors or DBA errors that would merely be re-created with a full recovery. An incomplete recovery also assumes that you cannot use other less drastic options, such as using Oracle's flashback table functionality or using SELECT . . . AS OF (to perform a query on data as of a previous time).

Data loss or corruption usually falls into one of three categories: user error, application error, or media failure. User error occurs when a DBA or system administrator inadvertently deletes or replaces a datafile or other Oracle-related file. Application errors, such as a backup script with a logic error, may back up the wrong file or delete a file that should be kept. Media failure applies to hardware failures that make a datafile either temporarily or permanently unavailable. This includes but is not limited to controller failures, disk failures, and network failures. For all three categories, the procedures for recovery are the same after any hardware problems are resolved.

It's important to know the distinction between the *restore* and *recover* steps when a datafile is lost or damaged. From an industry point of view, bringing your database back online from a disaster is typically known as *recovery*. However, Oracle naming conventions subdivide this process into two steps, restore and recover. In summary, the restore process copies a backup file into place if, for example, a datafile is lost or damaged. The restored file will contain data rows at the point in time that the backup was taken. Recovery then applies archived and perhaps online redo log information to bring the state of the database back to the point of time of the failure or to any point before the point of failure.

Another important distinction when considering database failures is *critical* versus *noncritical* failures. For noncritical failures, the database can continue to operate for all or most users. For example, you may lose only one copy of a multiplexed redo log group or a datafile from a tablespace used by only one application. Critical failures prevent the database from running, which occurs with, for example, the loss of a datafile from the SYSTEM tablespace or all control files.

The second part of this chapter shows you how to recover from the loss of one or more datafiles in a temporary tablespace, which is a noncritical failure since you can accomplish this without shutting down the database. Similarly, you'll learn how to recover from the loss of a redo log group member or an entire redo log group (a redo log group can have one or more members, each of which is a redo log file).

Finally, you'll learn how to recover from the loss of one or more control files, potentially a critical failure. Ideally, you have mirrored your control file several times, However, if the worst comes to pass, you can use a backup control file while minimizing or eliminating downtime and data loss.

CERTIFICATION OBJECTIVE 5.01

Describe and Tune Instance Recovery

Database failures often have nothing to do with the database itself (for example, Oracle bugs, programmer errors, or media failures) but instead may be caused by failures at the OS level or transient hardware issues such as power failures or network outages. When these events occur, the Oracle database will not be shut down gracefully, meaning that all of the dirty blocks in the buffer cache have not been written to disk and the headers of each datafile are not in sync. This type of failure requires *instance recovery*, also known as *crash recovery*, which occurs when the transient problems have been fixed and the database is restarted.

Because this type of failure is not a media failure, some of your committed transactions are only in the online redo log files and not in the datafiles. In addition, you may have transactions that had not been committed at the time of the instance failure and must be rolled back and removed, if those blocks had already been written to their respective datafiles. The system change number (SCN) in the header of each datafile must match the latest SCN in the control file (to synchronize the data and control files).

When the database is restarted, the Oracle kernel checks the headers of each datafile, and if they are not the same as the SCN in the control file, then Oracle initiates instance recovery. Note that this is an automatic operation: Oracle will use the online redo log files to roll forward and ensure that all committed transactions are written to their respective tables in each tablespace and then roll back any transactions containing changes to tables in each datafile that were never committed as of the instance crash. This is automatic; no intervention by the DBA is required. Here are the phases of instance recovery:

1. At instance startup, the datafiles are out of sync.
2. Roll forward by applying redo log file records (both committed and uncommitted data is now in the datafiles).
3. The database is opened.
4. Uncommitted transactions are rolled back (the database is now both consistent and synchronized); this part of the process continues while the database is already open and accessible to users and applications.

Note that by using the online redo log files, all transactions including uncommitted transactions are applied to the database up to the time of failure. After the database is open, the uncommitted transactions are rolled back using the undo segments in the UNDO tablespace. This is why the records in the UNDO tablespace are key to instance recovery.

The *checkpoint* process (CKPT) updates the control file with the position in the redo log file at which all previous data blocks in the redo log file have been successfully written to the datafiles. Figure 5-1 shows the contents of the current redo log file and the checkpoint position within the redo log file.

The highlighted blocks between the two arrows of Figure 5-1 have not yet been written to the datafiles. The checkpoint position is always right behind the oldest unwritten block. To control how fast the database is available after an instance

FIGURE 5-1

Checkpoint position in the redo log files

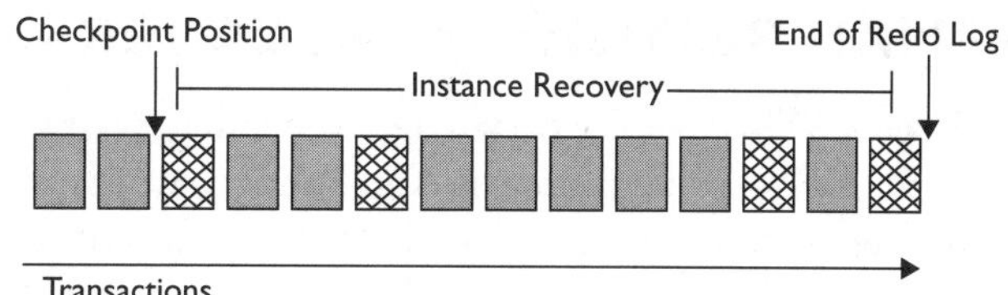

crash, the administrator uses the parameter FAST_START_MTTR_TARGET. The lower the value of this parameter, the faster the instance will recover, but as a result, the DBW*n* processes must perform more frequent but smaller writes. This may have an impact on OLTP system performance.

Setting the parameter FAST_START_MTTR_TARGET enables the MTTR advisor to adjust other parameters to meet the instance recovery time specified by FAST_START_MTTR_TARGET:

```
SQL> alter system set fast_start_mttr_target=100;
System altered.
SQL>
```

The range of FAST_START_MTTR_TARGET is from 0 to 3600. Setting it to zero disables the MTTR advisor; setting a value of 1 is possible but not usually achievable given the other events that occur during database startup.

CERTIFICATION OBJECTIVE 5.02

Perform Complete and Incomplete Recovery

In the following sections, you'll learn how to use the RESTORE and RECOVER commands for a database running in ARCHIVELOG mode. First, you'll read about the basic functions of RESTORE and RECOVER and how they work. Next, you'll see how to recover both a noncritical and a critical datafile successfully. You'll use incomplete recovery when either more recent archived redo logs are not available or you want to restore and recover to a time in the past before some kind of logical error occurred.

Using the RMAN RESTORE and RECOVER Commands

In general, recovering from a database failure is a two-step process: restoring one or more database files from a backup location, which is the restore phase, and applying archived and online redo log files to bring the entire database or individual datafile up to the specified SCN (usually the most recent SCN, or the last committed transaction), which is the recovery phase.

The RESTORE command is the first step in any recovery process. When you issue a RESTORE command, RMAN retrieves one or more datafiles from disk or tape along with any archived redo log files required during the recovery operation. If your backup files are on tape, you will need to allocate the necessary tape channels as well.

When you issue the RECOVER command, RMAN applies the committed changes in the archived and online redo log files to the restored datafiles. A disaster recovery operation is called for when most database datafiles are lost or corrupted. The recovery process can be as simple as the following example (the command output is excluded for clarity):

```
SQL> shutdown immediate;
SQL> startup mount;
[oracle@srv04 ~]$ rman target / catalog rman/rman@rcat
RMAN> restore database;
RMAN> recover database;
RMAN> sql 'alter database open';
```

The recovery process is slightly different, depending on whether you lose a critical or a noncritical datafile. If you lose a critical datafile, you must shut down and start up the database in MOUNT mode before you can recover the database. For a noncritical datafile, you can perform the recovery while users are connected and using other available datafiles.

Performing Complete Recovery of a Noncritical Datafile

If you lose a datafile that is not a part of the SYSTEM or UNDO tablespace, the datafile is considered noncritical (although the users of the lost datafile might disagree with this assessment). When the database is in ARCHIVELOG mode, a corrupted or missing datafile that is not part of the SYSTEM or UNDO tablespace affects only objects in that datafile.

The general steps to recover a datafile from a noncritical tablespace are as follows:

1. If the database is open, take the tablespace containing the corrupted or missing datafile offline with the ALTER TABLESPACE command.

2. Use the RMAN RESTORE command to load the datafiles for the tablespace from the backup location.
3. Use the RMAN RECOVER command to apply archived and online redo log files to the restored datafiles.
4. Bring the tablespace back online.

Because the database is in ARCHIVELOG mode, recovery up to the last committed transaction is possible. In other words, users do not have to reenter any data for previously committed transactions.

EXERCISE 5-1

Restore and Recover the USERS Tablespace

In this exercise, the datafile for the USERS tablespace was accidentally deleted by the system administrator. Restore and recover the tablespace while the database is still open for access to the other tablespaces.

1. Connect to RMAN and take the USERS tablespace offline:

```
RMAN> sql "alter tablespace users offline immediate";
sql statement: alter tablespace users offline immediate
RMAN>
```

on the job

Starting with Oracle Database 12c, you can run most SQL commands within RMAN without using the RMAN* sql *command. However, you may still choose to use the* sql *command to make it clear that you are running a non-RMAN command.

Any users trying to access the tablespace while it is offline will receive a message similar to the following:

```
SQL> select * from sales_data;
                        *
ERROR at line 1:
ORA-00376: file 4 cannot be read at this time
ORA-01110: data file 4: '/u01/app/oracle/oradata/hr/users01.dbf'

SQL>
```

2. Restore the USERS tablespace:

```
RMAN> restore tablespace users;

Starting restore at 12-MAR-14
allocated channel: ORA_DISK_1
channel ORA_DISK_1: SID=129 device type=DISK

channel ORA_DISK_1: starting datafile backup set restore
channel ORA_DISK_1: specifying datafile(s) to restore from backup set
channel ORA_DISK_1: restoring datafile 00004 to
       /u01/app/oracle/oradata/hr/users01.dbf
channel ORA_DISK_1: reading from backup piece
/u01/oradata/bkup/1sjh6l0u_1_1
channel ORA_DISK_1: piece handle=/u01/oradata/bkup/1sjh6l0u_1_1
                           tag=TAG20080524T170221
channel ORA_DISK_1: restored backup piece 1
channel ORA_DISK_1: restore complete, elapsed time: 00:00:15
Finished restore at 12-MAR-14
RMAN>
```

3. Recover the USERS tablespace to apply the archived and online redo log files:

```
RMAN> recover tablespace users;

Starting recover at 12-MAR-14
using channel ORA_DISK_1

starting media recovery
media recovery complete, elapsed time: 00:00:00

Finished recover at 12-MAY-14

RMAN>
```

4. Bring the USERS tablespace back online:

```
RMAN> sql "alter tablespace users online";

sql statement: alter tablespace users online

RMAN>
```

5. Confirm that users can once again access the USERS tablespace:

```
SQL> select * from sales_data;

SALES_ID SALE_DATE TRAN_AMT
-------- --------- --------
     202 11-MAR-14  1402.12
. . .
```

Performing Complete Recovery of a Critical Datafile

The procedure for recovering a critical datafile is similar to that of a noncritical datafile, except that the database must be shut down and opened in the MOUNT state to perform the recovery operation. If the lost datafile is from the SYSTEM tablespace, the instance will most likely crash or shut down automatically. Here are the steps you use to recover a critical datafile:

1. Shut down the database with SHUTDOWN ABORT if it is not already shut down.
2. Reopen the database with STARTUP MOUNT.
3. Use the RMAN RESTORE command to copy (restore) the datafile(s) for the critical tablespace from the backup location.
4. Use the RMAN RECOVER command to apply any archived or online redo log files.
5. Reopen the database for users with ALTER DATABASE OPEN.

All committed transactions are recovered up until the time of failure, so users will not have to reenter any data. In the case of the SYSTEM tablespace, you should not have any user transactions, and you will not lose any new objects created since the last backup.

Performing Incomplete Recovery Using RMAN

On occasion, you might need to restore a database to a point of time in the past. For example, applications could have made numerous erroneous changes to the database in the last 24 hours, and you may not be able to reverse errors easily with a table flashback, or you do not have flashback configured for the database.

Using restore points makes it easier to perform point-in-time recovery, whether you're performing incomplete recovery in RMAN or flashback database. After you learn about restore points, you'll perform an incomplete recovery using a restore point.

Creating Restore Points

You can create two types of restore points—either as of a specific time or with an SCN number in the past. Which type you use depends on your environment and which option is the more convenient. If you do not specify either option, Oracle uses the current SCN and assumes you want the restore time to be the current time. Remember that you can retrieve the current SCN from V$DATABASE:

```
SQL> select current_scn from v$database;

CURRENT_SCN
-----------
   34674668

SQL>
```

To create a restore point for the present time or SCN, use this format of the CREATE RESTORE POINT command:

```
SQL> create restore point good_for_now;

Restore point created.

SQL>
```

To create a restore point for a particular SCN, use the AS OF syntax:

```
SQL> create restore point good_for_now as of scn 34674668;

Restore point created.

SQL>
```

Restore points are also useful when you want to use Oracle's flashback technology to flash back a table or the database to a point in time in the past.

Oracle keeps restore points for at least as long as the time specified in the CONTROL_FILE_RECORD_KEEP_TIME initialization parameter. If you explicitly want to keep a restore point longer, use the PRESERVE keyword when you create the restore point:

```
SQL> create restore point good_for_now preserve;

Restore point created.

SQL>
```

As you might expect, you can explicitly remove a restore point with the DROP RESTORE POINT command:

```
SQL> drop restore point good_for_now;

Restore point dropped.

SQL>
```

Performing Server-Managed Incomplete Recovery

To perform server-managed (RMAN) incomplete recovery (user-managed recovery is not recommended and deprecated in Oracle Database 12*c*), use the following steps:

1. Determine the target point for the restore (SCN, time, restore point, or log sequence number).
2. Set the NLS variables at the operating system prompt if you are using time-based incomplete recovery:
   - NLS_LANG
   - NLS_DATE_FORMAT
3. Stop and restart the database in MOUNT mode.
4. Using an RMAN RUN block, use the SET UNTIL, RESTORE, and RECOVER commands.
5. Optionally, open the database in READ ONLY mode to verify that the restore point was the desired restore point.
6. Open the database using RESETLOGS.

It's important to specify the correct NLS variables so that RMAN will interpret the date strings you provide correctly; here are some sample values:

```
$ export NLS_LANG = american_america.us7ascii
$ export NLS_DATE_FORMAT = "Mon DD YYYY HH24:MI:SS"
```

Also note that opening the database as READ ONLY after your incomplete recovery gives you the opportunity to run another incomplete recovery for a different SCN or time. Once you open the database for read-write with RESETLOGS, the current log sequence is set to 1, and any redo information not applied during recovery is discarded. This prevents you from performing another recovery using a redo generated after the SCN or timestamp of your incomplete recovery.

EXERCISE 5-2

Perform Incomplete Recovery to Restore the USERS Tablespace

In this exercise, you will create a restore point and use it later to recover from the inadvertent deletion of tables and views in the EXAMPLE tablespace.

1. Create a restore point for the current SCN:

```
SQL> create restore point before_disaster_strikes;

Restore point created.

SQL>
```

2. "Accidentally" drop some tables and views in the EXAMPLE tablespace:

```
SQL> drop table hr.job_history;

Table dropped.

SQL> drop view hr.emp_details_view;

View dropped.

SQL>
```

3. Shut down the instance and restart the database in MOUNT mode:

```
SQL> shutdown immediate
Database closed.
Database dismounted.
ORACLE instance shut down.
SQL> startup mount
ORACLE instance started.

Total System Global Area  636100608 bytes
Fixed Size                  1301784 bytes
Variable Size             490734312 bytes
Database Buffers          138412032 bytes
Redo Buffers                5652480 bytes
Database mounted.
SQL>
```

4. At the RMAN prompt, create a RUN block that uses the restore point created earlier to restore and recover the database to the time of the restore point:

```
RMAN> run
2>    {
3>      set until restore point before_disaster_strikes;
4>      restore database;
5>      recover database;
6>    }

executing command: SET until clause
starting full resync of recovery catalog
full resync complete

Starting restore at 13-MAR-14
allocated channel: ORA_DISK_1
channel ORA_DISK_1: SID=151 device type=DISK
channel ORA_DISK_1: starting datafile backup set restore
channel ORA_DISK_1: specifying datafile(s) to restore from backup set
channel ORA_DISK_1: restoring datafile 00001 to
      /u01/app/oracle/oradata/hr/system01.dbf
channel ORA_DISK_1: restoring datafile 00002 to
      /u01/app/oracle/oradata/hr/sysaux01.dbf
channel ORA_DISK_1: restoring datafile 00003 to
      /u01/app/oracle/oradata/hr/undotbs01.dbf
channel ORA_DISK_1: restoring datafile 00004 to
      /u01/app/oracle/oradata/hr/users01.dbf
channel ORA_DISK_1: restoring datafile 00005 to
      /u01/app/oracle/oradata/hr/example01.dbf
channel ORA_DISK_1: reading from backup piece
/u01/oradata/bkup/1ujh9bkl_1_1
channel ORA_DISK_1: piece handle=/u01/oradata/bkup/1ujh9bkl_1_1
                 tag=TAG20080525T174036
channel ORA_DISK_1: restored backup piece 1
channel ORA_DISK_1: restore complete, elapsed time: 00:03:27
Finished restore at 13-MAR-14

Starting recover at 13-MAR-14
using channel ORA_DISK_1

starting media recovery
media recovery complete, elapsed time: 00:00:12

Finished recover at 13-MAR-14

RMAN>
```

5. Open the database with RESETLOGS:

```
SQL> alter database open resetlogs;

Database altered.

SQL>
```

6. Verify the existence of the dropped table:

```
SQL> select * from hr.job_history;

EMPLOYEE_ID START_DAT END_DATE  JOB_ID     DEPARTMENT_ID
----------- --------- --------- ---------- -------------
        102 13-JAN-93 24-JUL-98 IT_PROG               60
        101 21-SEP-89 27-OCT-93 AC_ACCOUNT           110
        101 28-OCT-93 15-MAR-97 AC_MGR               110
        201 17-FEB-96 19-DEC-99 MK_REP                20
        114 24-MAR-98 31-DEC-99 ST_CLERK              50
        122 01-JAN-99 31-DEC-99 ST_CLERK              50
        200 17-SEP-87 17-JUN-93 AD_ASST               90
        176 24-MAR-98 31-DEC-98 SA_REP                80
        176 01-JAN-99 31-DEC-99 SA_MAN                80
        200 01-JUL-94 31-DEC-98 AC_ACCOUNT            90

10 rows selected.

SQL>
```

Note that several less draconian methods are available to restore and recover these tables and views, such as using a flashback database, restoring and recovering each tablespace while the database is still online, or retrieving the tables from the recycle bin. Each recovery situation must be evaluated separately, balancing these factors:

- The time required to obtain the backup files needed for recovery. If backup files are on a tape offsite, then the time required could be unacceptable.
- The time to restore and recover the entire database once the recovery files are available.
- The time the DBA must spend to perform the recovery.
- The time the users must spend to reenter lost data.
- The tolerance of users for database downtime.

Recovering Using Incrementally Updated Backups

Using image copies in your backup and recovery strategy significantly reduces the time it takes to restore a datafile or the entire database. Image copies are already in the native Oracle datafile format and do not need to be re-created from a compressed or uncompressed RMAN backupset. RMAN can improve on this even more because you can incrementally update an image copy using an incremental backup. In the following sections, you'll learn more about how to recover an image copy, and you'll review a sample image copy strategy.

To clarify, you're creating image copies, but going forward you're keeping that image copy up to date incrementally. You're not actually using this image copy to recover your live database but instead using online and archived redo log files to recover the *copy* of a datafile so it's ready to use if and when disaster strikes.

Recovering Image Copies

When you update an image copy with an incremental backup, any recovery scenario that uses the image copy needs to apply only the archived and online redo log files since the last incremental backup. There is no longer any need to perform another full image copy of the datafile or database. The incremental recovery of each datafile is indistinguishable from a full image copy.

If more than one image copy of a datafile exists, RMAN automatically determines which one to use—usually the most recently created or incrementally updated version. If the recovery process for an image copy fails when applying an incremental backup, such as the temporary unavailability of the incremental backup, just restart the recovery process when the incremental backup is available again. RMAN picks up where it left off.

Implementing an Image Copy Strategy

Here is a sample RMAN script to implement an incrementally updated image copy strategy on a daily basis, after you've created the image copy of the entire database:

```
run {
      recover copy of database
         with tag 'inc_upd';
      backup incremental level 1
         for recover of copy
         with tag 'inc_upd'
         database;
    }
```

Here's a breakdown of what happens in this RUN block. The first time you run it, there is no level 0 image copy to restore and, similarly, no level 0 incremental backup yet, so you get these messages:

```
Starting recover at 13-MAR-14
using channel ORA_DISK_1
no copy of datafile 1 found to recover
no copy of datafile 2 found to recover
no copy of datafile 3 found to recover
no copy of datafile 4 found to recover
no copy of datafile 5 found to recover
Finished recover at 13-MAR-14

Starting backup at 13-MAR-14
using channel ORA_DISK_1
no parent backup or copy of datafile 2 found
no parent backup or copy of datafile 1 found
no parent backup or copy of datafile 3 found
no parent backup or copy of datafile 5 found
no parent backup or copy of datafile 4 found
channel ORA_DISK_1: starting datafile copy
. . .
```

RMAN automatically creates a level 0 backup whenever a level 1 backup occurs and there is no level 0 backup. The next time you run the script, the level 0 backup exists but no incremental level 0 backup exists yet. So, the RECOVER command in the RUN block still generates these messages:

```
Starting recover at 13-MAR-14
using channel ORA_DISK_1
no copy of datafile 1 found to recover
no copy of datafile 2 found to recover
no copy of datafile 3 found to recover
no copy of datafile 4 found to recover
no copy of datafile 13-MAR-14

Starting backup at 13-MAR-14
using channel ORA_DISK_1
channel ORA_DISK_1: starting incremental level 1 datafile backup
set
. . .
```

On the third and successive invocations of this RUN block, the RECOVER command updates the image copy with the latest level 1 backup, and another level 1 incremental backup occurs. This will be applied the next time this RUN block is executed. As a result, any recovery operation after the third invocation of this script will involve no more than the image copies, one incremental backup, and any archived and online redo logs generated since the last level 1 incremental backup.

on the job

Be sure to use tags with an incrementally updated image copy strategy. Without tags, a more recent, and possibly incorrect, incremental backup would be used to recover the image copies.

Switching to Image Copies for Fast Recovery

Once you've starting making image copies, and even incrementally updating them, you can use them in a restore and recover operation to quickly recover some or your entire database. To recover your database even faster, you can perform a fast switch to image copies. In other words, you can use the image copies directly, skip the restore step, and apply only the recovery step. After the original datafiles are repaired or restored, you can easily switch back with little or no impact to users who are using other datafiles. The database does not need to be shut down unless you are switching to the image copies of the critical SYSTEM or UNDO tablespace datafiles.

Using the SET NEWNAME command within the RUN block to specify an alternative location for the replacement image copy allows RMAN to make the switch to image copies even easier.

Performing a Fast Switch to Image Copies

When disaster strikes and you lose a single datafile or even all datafiles, having image copies available significantly reduces the time required to recover your database. Once you've switched to an image copy, you will most likely want to switch back to the original datafile locations after the media failure has been repaired. Here you'll learn how to switch to an image copy and then switch back.

Switching to an Image Copy The steps to switch to a datafile copy are straightforward. This assumes, of course, that you have image copies of the damaged or lost datafile, as well as all archived and online redo log files since the image copy was created. Here are the steps:

1. Take the tablespaces containing the missing datafiles offline. You can use one of the dynamic performance views V$RECOVER_FILE, V$DATAFILE_HEADER, or V$TABLESPACE to identify which datafiles need recovery.

The RMAN SWITCH command is equivalent to the SQL command ALTER DATABASE RENAME FILE.

2. Use RMAN SWITCH . . . TO COPY to point to the image copy of the missing datafiles.
3. Recover the datafiles using the RMAN RECOVER command.
4. Bring the tablespaces back online.

EXERCISE 5-3

Use the SWITCH Command to Recover a Datafile Quickly

The datafile for the USERS tablespace mysteriously disappears. Users start to complain immediately, reporting this message when they try to create or update a table:

```
ERROR at line 1:
ORA-01116: error in opening database file 4
ORA-01110: data file 4: '/u01/app/oracle/oradata/hr/users01.dbf'
ORA-27041: unable to open file
Linux Error: 2: No such file or directory
Additional information: 3
```

In addition, you see this message in the alert log. This alert should also be visible as an alert on the Enterprise Manager home page:

```
Fri Mar 14 19:45:13 2014
Checker run found 1 new persistent data failures
```

Find out what datafile number you need to restore, switch to an image copy, and then recover the datafile and bring the tablespace back online:

1. Since you already know that datafile #4 is having problems, query V$TABLESPACE to confirm that the USERS tablespace is the culprit:

```
SQL> select ts#, name
  2  from v$tablespace
  3  where ts# = 4;

       TS# NAME
---------- --------------------
         4 USERS

SQL>
```

The dynamic performance view V$DATAFILE_HEADER shows the error as well but does not always identify the tablespace name:

```
SQL> select file#, status, error, recover, tablespace_name, name
  2  from v$datafile_header
  3  where recover = 'YES'
  4     or (recover is null and error is not null);

     FILE# STATUS  ERROR              REC TABLESPACE_NAME NAME
---------- ------- ------------------ --- --------------- ------
         4 ONLINE  CANNOT OPEN FILE

SQL>
```

2. Take the USERS tablespace offline at the SQL> prompt:

```
SQL> alter tablespace users offline immediate;

Tablespace altered.

SQL>
```

Alternatively, you can take the tablespace offline using the RMAN SQL command.

3. Switch to the datafile copy for the USERS tablespace:

```
RMAN> switch tablespace users to copy;

datafile 4 switched to datafile copy
    "/u01/oradata/bkup/data_D-HR_I-3318356692_TS-USERS_FNO-4_37jhmn1m"
starting full resync of recovery catalog
full resync complete

RMAN>
```

Note that you can use the SWITCH command with either the DATAFILE or TABLESPACE parameter, whichever is easier or more convenient. Note also that you don't need to know where your datafile copy is. RMAN knows where it is and will switch it and update the control file and recovery catalog automatically with the new location.

4. Recover the USERS tablespace using the recent archived and online redo log files:

```
RMAN> recover tablespace users;

Starting recover at 14-MAR-14
using channel ORA_DISK_1
```

```
starting media recovery
media recovery complete, elapsed time: 00:00:20

Finished recover at 14-MAR-14

RMAN>
```

5. Bring the USERS tablespace back online:

```
RMAN> sql "alter tablespace users online";

sql statement: alter tablespace users online

RMAN>
```

Alternatively, you can bring the tablespace back online using the SQL> prompt.

Switching Back to Original Location Once your database is back up and running after switching to an image copy, you will likely want to switch the datafile back to its original location after the source disk has been repaired. This is especially true if the image copy you switched to resides in the flash recovery area. Flash recovery is used primarily for recovery and storage of multiplexed control files and archived redo log files, and it may reside on a slower disk. To move the tablespace and its associated datafiles back to the original location, follow these steps:

1. Create an image copy of the datafiles in the original location.
2. Take the tablespace offline.
3. Use the SWITCH TO . . . COPY command to switch back to the restored (re-created) datafile.
4. Recover the datafiles.
5. Bring the tablespace back online.

Note that you can perform most of these steps while the users are still using the original image copy. The tablespace will once again be unavailable during recovery. This step should be short if not many archived redo log files have been created since the image copy was made in the original location.

EXERCISE 5-4

Use the SWITCH Command after Creating the USERS Tablespace's Datafile in the Original Location

In this exercise, you'll switch the datafile for the USERS tablespace back to its original location after the source disk has been repaired (or you have figured out why datafiles are disappearing from the source disk). The datafile locations for each tablespace are currently as follows:

```
SQL> select file#, df.name, ts#, ts.name
  2  from v$datafile df join v$tablespace ts using(ts#);

     FILE# NAME                                 TS# NAME
---------- ------------------------- ---------- -------------
         1 /u01/app/oracle/oradata/h          0 SYSTEM
           r/system01.dbf
         2 /u01/app/oracle/oradata/h          1 SYSAUX
           r/sysaux01.dbf
         3 /u01/app/oracle/oradata/h          2 UNDOTBS1
           r/undotbs01.dbf
         4 /u01/oradata/bkup/data_D-          4 USERS
           HR_I-3318356692_TS-USERS_
           FNO-4_37jhmn1m
         5 /u01/app/oracle/oradata/h          6 EXAMPLE
           r/example01.dbf
SQL>
```

1. Create an image copy of the datafile at the original location:

```
RMAN> backup as copy tablespace users
2>      format '/u01/app/oracle/oradata/hr/users01.dbf';

Starting backup at 14-MAR-14
using channel ORA_DISK_1
channel ORA_DISK_1: starting datafile copy
input datafile file number=00004
   name=/u01/oradata/bkup/data_D-HR_I-3318356692_TS-USERS_
FNO-4_37jhmn1m
output file name=/u01/app/oracle/oradata/hr/users01.dbf
tag=TAG20080530T211450 RECID=36 STAMP=656111726
channel ORA_DISK_1: datafile copy complete, elapsed time:
00:00:16
Finished backup at 14-MAR-14

RMAN>
```

Note that you can name the image copy anything you want. In this case, you'll use the original name of the datafile to be consistent with the other datafile names.

2. Take the USERS tablespace offline in preparation for the SWITCH command:

```
RMAN> sql "alter tablespace users offline";

sql statement: alter tablespace users offline
starting full resync of recovery catalog
full resync complete

RMAN>
```

3. Switch to the newly created copy:

```
RMAN> switch tablespace users to copy;

datafile 4 switched to datafile copy
        "/u01/app/oracle/oradata/hr/users01.dbf"
starting full resync of recovery catalog
full resync complete

RMAN>
```

4. Recover the datafile in its new location:

```
RMAN> recover tablespace users;

Starting recover at 14-MAR-14
using channel ORA_DISK_1

starting media recovery
media recovery complete, elapsed time: 00:00:00

Finished recover at 14-MAR-14

RMAN>
```

5. Bring the USERS tablespace back online:

```
RMAN> sql "alter tablespace users online";

sql statement: alter tablespace users online
```

```
starting full resync of recovery catalog
full resync complete

RMAN>
```

6. Confirm that the datafile for the USERS tablespace is back in its original location:

```
SQL> select file#, df.name, ts#, ts.name
  2  from v$datafile df join v$tablespace ts using(ts#)
  3  where ts.name = 'USERS';

     FILE# NAME                                 TS# NAME
---------- ------------------------- ---------- -------------
         4 /u01/app/oracle/oradata/h          4 USERS
           r/users01.dbf

SQL>
```

7. Create a new image copy to be ready when or if the datafile disappears again, although you could also use the image copy you just switched from:

```
RMAN> backup as copy tablespace users;

Starting backup at 14-MAR-14
starting full resync of recovery catalog
full resync complete
using channel ORA_DISK_1
channel ORA_DISK_1: starting datafile copy
input datafile file number=00004
name=/u01/app/oracle/oradata/hr/users01.dbf
output file name=/u01/oradata/bkup/
  data_D-HR_I-3318356692_TS-USERS_FNO-4_39jhn16a
tag=TAG20080530T220810 RECID=38 STAMP=656114935
channel ORA_DISK_1: datafile copy complete, elapsed time:
00:00:26
Finished backup at 14-MAR-14

RMAN>
```

Using the RMAN SET NEWNAME with Fast Switch

One of the many options for the SET command in RMAN is the SET NEWNAME command. Inside a RUN block, SET NEWNAME makes it easy to specify one or more new datafile destinations in preparation for subsequent RESTORE and SWITCH commands. Here is an RMAN RUN block to specify a new location for the restored datafile of the USERS tablespace:

```
run {
   sql "alter tablespace users offline immediate";
   set newname
       for datafile '/u01/app/oracle/oradata/hr/users01.dbf'
           to '/u06/oradata/users01.dbf';
   restore tablespace users;
   switch datafile all;
   recover tablespace users;
   sql "alter tablespace users online";
}
```

Note that the SWITCH command is used in much the same way as it's used in the preceding section. The difference is that this example restores a datafile from a backup (most likely a backupset) to an alternative location instead of switching to an existing image copy. The result of the SWITCH command, whether in a RUN block or as a standalone command, is to update the control file (and the recovery catalog if you're using one) with the new filenames.

If you did not specify the SET command in the preceding example, RMAN would restore the datafile for the USERS tablespace to its original location, and the SWITCH command would not perform any useful action.

CERTIFICATION OBJECTIVE 5.03

Perform Recovery for SPFILEs, Password Files, Control Files, and Redo Log Files

In rare instances, you may lose all copies of the current control file. This is rare because you should have the control file multiplexed to several locations. Even if you do lose all copies of the current control file, you should have at least one autobackup of the control file from the most recent RMAN backup. In addition, if you are using a recovery catalog, all metadata within your most recent control file resides in the recovery catalog.

The SPFILE is also susceptible to loss if it does not reside on a mirrored external file system or on a mirrored ASM disk group. When RMAN performs a control file autobackup, both the current control file and the SPFILE are backed up.

In the following sections, you'll learn how to recover both the control file and the SPFILE if all online versions of either of these files are lost.

Restoring the SPFILE from the Autobackup

To restore the SPFILE from the autobackup, first set the database ID (DBID) if the instance is not running when the SPFILE is lost:

```
RMAN> set dbid 3318356692;
```

Next, restart the database with a default SPFILE (you will do something similar later in the chapter when recovering to a new host):

```
RMAN> startup force nomount;
```

Next, restore the SPFILE from the autobackup to the original location:

```
RMAN> restore spfile from autobackup;
```

Finally, start the database:

```
RMAN> startup force;
```

Restoring the Control File from the Autobackup

Restoring the control file from an autobackup is similar to the steps you use to restore an SPFILE from an autobackup. Here are the sample RMAN commands:

```
RMAN> startup nomount;
RMAN> restore controlfile from autobackup;
RMAN> alter database mount;
RMAN> recover database;
RMAN> alter database open resetlogs;
```

Note that since there is no control file, you have to open the database with NOMOUNT and then restore the control file. After you mount the database with the restored backup control file, you must recover the database because the backup control file contains information about an older version of the database. For the same reason, you must open the database with RESETLOGS.

RMAN restores the control file to all locations specified by the initialization parameter CONTROL_FILES. If one or more of those locations are still not available, you will have to edit the CONTROL_FILES parameter to specify alternative locations or temporarily restore the control file to a different location:

```
RMAN> restore controlfile to '/u06/oradata/rest_cf.dbf'
from autobackup;
```

EXERCISE 5-5

Restore the Control File from an Autobackup

In this exercise, all copies of the control file were accidentally deleted by an overly eager system administrator trying to free up disk space. Restore and recover the database with a control file restored from a control file and SPFILE autobackup:

1. Identify the control file locations where all copies of the control file used to reside:

```
SQL> show parameter control_files

NAME                                 TYPE        VALUE
------------------------------------ ----------- ------------------------------
control_files                        string      /u01/app/oracle/oradata/hr/con
                                                 trol01.ctl, /u02/app/oracle/or
                                                 adata/hr/control02.ctl, /u03/a
                                                 pp/oracle/oradata/hr/control03
                                                 .ctl
SQL>
```

2. Shut down the instance (if it is not already down) and reopen it in NOMOUNT mode:

```
SQL> connect / as sysdba
Connected.
SQL> shutdown immediate;
ORA-00210: cannot open the specified control file
ORA-00202: control file: '/u01/app/oracle/oradata/hr/control01.ctl'
ORA-27041: unable to open file
Linux Error: 2: No such file or directory
Additional information: 3
SQL> startup force nomount;
ORACLE instance started.

Total System Global Area  636100608 bytes
Fixed Size                  1301784 bytes
```

```
Variable Size              448791272 bytes
Database Buffers           180355072 bytes
Redo Buffers                 5652480 bytes
SQL>
```

3. Start RMAN and restore the control file from autobackup to the original locations:

```
[oracle@srv04 ~]$ rman target / catalog rman/rman@rcat

Recovery Manager: Release 12.1.0.1.0 -
   Production on Thu Mar 13 10:15:42 2014

Copyright (c)1982, 2013, Oracle and/or its affiliates. All
rights reserved.

connected to target database: HR (not mounted)
connected to recovery catalog database

RMAN> restore controlfile from autobackup;

Starting restore at 14-MAR-14
allocated channel: ORA_DISK_1
channel ORA_DISK_1: SID=152 device type=DISK

recovery area destination: /u01/app/oracle/flash_recovery_
area
database name (or database unique name) used for search: HR
channel ORA_DISK_1: AUTOBACKUP
/u01/app/oracle/flash_recovery_area/HR/autobackup
   /2008_05_31/o1_mf_s_656205340_4448nf6k_.bkp found in the
recovery area
channel ORA_DISK_1: looking for AUTOBACKUP on day: 20140314
channel ORA_DISK_1: restoring control file from AUTOBACKUP
/u01/app/oracle/flash_recovery_area/HR/autobackup
   /2014_03_14/o1_mf_s_656205340_4448nf6k_.bkp
channel ORA_DISK_1: control file restore from AUTOBACKUP
complete
output file name=/u01/app/oracle/oradata/hr/control01.ctl
output file name=/u02/app/oracle/oradata/hr/control02.ctl
output file name=/u03/app/oracle/oradata/hr/control03.ctl
Finished restore at 31-MAY-08

RMAN>
```

A few points are worth noting here. RMAN can connect to the instance even if it is not mounted. In fact, RMAN has to connect to an unmounted database to be able to restore the control file. RMAN finds the control file autobackup in the flash recovery area and writes it to the three control file destinations specified by the CONTROL_FILES initialization parameter.

4. Mount the database, recover the database (to synchronize the datafiles with the restored control file), and open the database with RESETLOGS:

```
RMAN> alter database mount;

database mounted
released channel: ORA_DISK_1

RMAN> recover database;

Starting recover at 14-MAR-14
Starting implicit crosscheck backup at 14-MAR-14
allocated channel: ORA_DISK_1
channel ORA_DISK_1: SID=152 device type=DISK
Crosschecked 11 objects
Finished implicit crosscheck backup at 14-MAR-14

Starting implicit crosscheck copy at 14-MAR-14
using channel ORA_DISK_1
Crosschecked 1 objects
Finished implicit crosscheck copy at 14-MAR-14

searching for all files in the recovery area
cataloging files...
cataloging done

List of Cataloged Files
=======================
File Name:
/u01/app/oracle/flash_recovery_area/HR/autobackup
         /2014_03_14/o1_mf_s_656205340_4448nf6k_.bkp

using channel ORA_DISK_1

starting media recovery

archived log for thread 1 with sequence 20 is already on disk
as file
         /u01/app/oracle/oradata/hr/redo02.log
```

```
archived log file name=/u01/app/oracle/oradata/hr/redo02.log
         thread=1 sequence=20
media recovery complete, elapsed time: 00:00:01
Finished recover at 14-MAR-14

RMAN> alter database open resetlogs;

database opened
new incarnation of database registered in recovery catalog
RPC call appears to have failed to start on channel default
RPC call OK on channel default
starting full resync of recovery catalog
full resync complete

RMAN>
```

Recovering from a Lost Redo Log Group

The loss of a redo log group or a redo log group member can mean data loss and a significant recovery effort. It can also mean no data loss and a minimal recovery effort, depending on the status of the redo log group and whether you lose the entire log group or only a member of a log group. The following sections review how log groups work and how the different log group statuses change as redo is written to the group, how the database switches to the next log group, and how a filled log group is copied to an archive location.

Let's review the types of log group failures and how to recover from each one. In most scenarios, data loss is minimal or nonexistent, especially if you mirror your log groups.

Understanding Log Group Status

A redo log group can have one of six statuses in the view V$LOG, described in Table 5-1.

At any given point in time, the most common statuses are CURRENT, ACTIVE, and INACTIVE. A redo log group is in the UNUSED state after creation, and once it's used, it will never return to that state. The CLEARING and CLEARING_CURRENT states exist when you re-create a corrupted log file, which ideally will not occur often!

TABLE 5-1 Log File Status in V$LOG

Log File Status	Status Description
CURRENT	Oracle is writing to this log group, and this group is needed for instance recovery.
ACTIVE	This log group is needed for instance recovery, but Oracle is not writing to this log group. It may or may not be archived yet.
INACTIVE	The log group is not needed for instance recovery, may be in use for media recovery, and may or may not be archived.
UNUSED	The log group has not been used yet.
CLEARING	The log is being cleared by ALTER DATABASE CLEAR LOGFILE. After being cleared, the status changes to UNUSED.
CLEARING_CURRENT	An error has occurred during ALTER DATABASE CLEAR LOGFILE.

The sample database has three redo log file groups, and this query of V$LOG shows the status of each log:

```
SQL> select group#, sequence#, archived, status
  2  from v$log;

    GROUP#  SEQUENCE# ARC STATUS
---------- ---------- --- ----------------
         1         88 NO  CURRENT
         2         86 YES INACTIVE
         3         87 YES INACTIVE
SQL>
```

The two log file groups with a status of INACTIVE have been archived. Depending on the I/O load of the system and other factors, the ARCHIVED status will be NO until the log file has been successfully written to all mandatory archived log file destinations.

Recovering from Log Group Member Failures

If one member of a log group becomes damaged or is lost, the Log Writer (LGWR) process continues to write to the undamaged member, and no data loss or interruption in service occurs. However, it is imperative that you correct this problem as soon as possible, because the log group with only one member is now the single point of failure in your database. If it is lost, your recovery efforts will increase, and loss of committed transactions is likely.

In this example, the second member of the third redo log file group becomes damaged. These error messages should appear in the alert log. You will see similar messages on the Enterprise Manager Database Control home page if it is configured:

```
Fri Mar 14 11:13:16 2014
Errors in file /u01/app/oracle/diag/rdbms/hr/hr/trace/hr_
arc2_5718.trc:
ORA-00313: open failed for members of log group 3 of thread 1
ORA-00312: online log 3 thread 1: '/u06/app/oracle/oradata/hr/
redo03.log'
ORA-27046: file size is not a multiple of logical block size
Additional information: 1
```

You can also identify the lost or damaged redo log file member using the V$LOGFILE view:

```
SQL> select group#, status, member from v$logfile;

    GROUP# STATUS  MEMBER
---------- ------- ----------------------------------------
         3         /u01/app/oracle/oradata/hr/redo03.log
         2         /u01/app/oracle/oradata/hr/redo02.log
         1         /u01/app/oracle/oradata/hr/redo01.log
         1         /u06/app/oracle/oradata/hr/redo01.log
         2         /u06/app/oracle/oradata/hr/redo02.log
         3 INVALID /u06/app/oracle/oradata/hr/redo03.log

6 rows selected.
SQL>
```

The solution to this problem is straightforward. Drop the invalid member and add a new member to the group, as in this example:

```
SQL> alter database drop logfile member
  2      '/u06/app/oracle/oradata/hr/redo03.log';

Database altered.

SQL> alter database add logfile member
  2      '/u06/app/oracle/oradata/hr/redo03a.log'
  3      to group 3;

Database altered.

SQL>
```

Note that the redundancy provided by the repaired redo log file group will not be available until the next time this log file group is active. If the destination disk itself is not damaged and the original redo log file is logically corrupted from user error or a rogue process, you can reuse the original redo log file by specifying the REUSE clause as follows:

```
alter database add logfile member
   '/u06/app/oracle/oradata/hr/redo03.log'
   reuse to group 3;
```

Recovering from Loss of an Entire Log Group

The loss of all members of a redo log group may have no effect on the database or may cause loss of committed transactions, which depends on the state of the redo log group. The three possible states of a log file group are INACTIVE, ACTIVE, and CURRENT.

Recovering from a Lost INACTIVE Redo Log Group

The loss of all members of a redo log group marked INACTIVE is the most benign redo log group failure, although you must act quickly before the Oracle database processes need to use the redo log group again. If Oracle needs to use the redo log group before it is repaired, the database halts until the problem is fixed. The group is not needed for crash recovery because it is INACTIVE. Therefore, you can clear the group using the ALTER DATABASE CLEAR LOGFILE command.

A damaged redo log group with a status of INACTIVE may or may not be archived yet. The archival status determines which form of the ALTER DATABASE CLEAR LOGFILE command to use.

Clearing an Archived Inactive Redo Log Group If a damaged inactive redo log group has been archived, you can identify the group number of the damaged group from the alert log or from the dynamic performance view V$LOGFILE. Remember that you can look at the ARCHIVED column in the dynamic performance view V$LOG to determine whether the log group has been archived yet.

In this example, redo log group #1 is damaged but has been archived. Use the ALTER DATABASE command as follows:

```
SQL> alter database clear logfile group 1;

Database altered.

SQL>
```

If the instance is down, start the database in MOUNT mode and run this command. Otherwise, you can run the command when the database is OPEN. All members of the redo log file group are reinitialized. If any or all of the redo log group members are missing, they are then re-created, provided that the destination directories are available.

The redo log group has been archived. Thus, no data loss will result, and all backups in combination with archived redo log files can be used for complete recovery of the database. Until the database reuses the redo log file group, it has a status of UNUSED, as you can see in this query:

```
SQL> select group#, sequence#, archived, status from v$log;

    GROUP#  SEQUENCE# ARC STATUS
---------- ---------- --- ----------------
         1          0 YES UNUSED
         2         98 NO  CURRENT
         3         96 YES INACTIVE

SQL>
```

Clearing a Nonarchived Inactive Redo Log Group If you have a nonarchived inactive redo log group, you will not lose any committed transactions. However, you must perform a full backup after clearing the redo log group to ensure that you can perform a complete recovery. You will have a gap in archived redo log files. Therefore, you will be able to perform only incomplete recovery up to the SCN of the last transaction in the archived redo log file created before the missing log file.

To clear the second unarchived log group, start the database in MOUNT mode (if it is not already up) and use the following command:

```
alter database clear logfile unarchived group 2;
```

Note the UNARCHIVED keyword in this command. It performs the same action that occurs when you cleared an archived redo log group, but this is Oracle's way of forcing you to acknowledge that you will have a gap in your archived redo log files.

After clearing the log file group, perform a full backup using operating system commands (remember, this is user-managed recovery, not system-managed recovery using RMAN). This provides a backup that you can use for complete recovery along with all successive archived redo log files.

A complicating factor to consider when you're clearing a nonarchived inactive redo log group is whether an offline datafile needs the cleared log file group before it can be brought online. In this scenario, you must drop the tablespace containing the offline datafile and re-create it using logical backups or some other method. You cannot recover the datafile, and therefore the tablespace containing the datafile, because the redo required to bring the datafile back online is gone. Oracle makes you acknowledge that your datafile is unrecoverable in this scenario as well, and you must use the UNRECOVERABLE DATAFILE keywords when you clear the log file group:

```
alter database clear logfile unarchived group 2
unrecoverable datafile;
```

The final step after clearing the redo log file group and creating a backup is to back up the control file to a specific directory or to the trace file directory:

```
alter database backup controlfile to trace;
```

Recovering from a Lost ACTIVE Redo Log Group

If a damaged redo log group is in the ACTIVE state, Oracle is not currently writing to it, but it is needed for instance recovery. Try this command:

```
alter system checkpoint;
```

If it runs successfully, all committed changes are written to the datafiles on disk.

Next, clear the redo log file group as you did with an inactive redo log group, and you will not lose any transactions. In addition, your archived redo log file stream will be intact.

If the checkpoint fails, you must perform an incomplete recovery using Flashback Database or an incomplete recovery using all archived and online redo log files up to but not including the damaged redo log group.

Recovering from a Lost CURRENT Redo Log Group

A lost redo log group in the CURRENT state is currently being written to by the LGWR process—or it *was* being written to at the time of failure. The instance will crash, and your only option is to perform incomplete recovery using Flashback

Database. Again, you can do likewise with all archived and online redo log files up to but not including the damaged redo log group.

After performing incomplete recovery with the database in MOUNT mode, open the database with RESETLOGS:

```
alter database open resetlogs;
```

If the location for the damaged online redo log file group is available, Oracle will reinitialize the log file group along with all other groups, resetting the log sequence number to 1 and starting a new incarnation. If the location is no longer available, rename the online redo log files and point them to a new location as in this example, while the database is mounted and before opening the database with RESETLOGS:

```
alter database rename file '/u01/app/oracle/oradata/hr/redo02.log'
   to '/u02/app/oracle/oradata/hr/redo02.log';
alter database rename file '/u06/app/oracle/oradata/hr/redo02.log'
   to '/u07/app/oracle/oradata/hr/redo02.log';
```

When you open the database with RESETLOGS, Oracle re-creates and initializes any missing online redo log files.

Recover from the Loss of the Password File

The loss of an Oracle password file is rather trivial compared to the loss of a datafile, a redo log file, or a control file. It won't cause the database to shut down but will prevent some or all DBAs from connecting to the database when it is not open. Although the password file is relatively easy to re-create, be sure that you make a backup copy of the password file using an operating system copy utility whenever it changes.

In the following sections, you'll get a brief refresher course on how the password file authenticates privileged users; then you'll learn how to re-create the password file when and if it becomes lost or corrupted.

Understanding the Password File

The system initialization parameter REMOTE_LOGIN_PASSWORDFILE controls how the password file is used for the database instance. It has three possible values: NONE, SHARED, and EXCLUSIVE.

If the value is NONE, Oracle ignores any password file that exists. Any privileged users must be authenticated by other means, such as by OS authentication, which is discussed in the next section.

With a value of SHARED, multiple databases can share the same password file. However, only the SYS user is authenticated with the password file, and the password for SYS cannot be changed (unless you re-create the password file). As a result, this method is not the most secure, but it does allow a DBA to maintain more than one database with a single SYS account.

on the job

If a shared password file must be used, ensure that the password for SYS is at least eight characters long and includes a combination of uppercase and lowercase alphabetic, numeric, and special characters to fend off a brute-force attack such as a dictionary attack.

A value of EXCLUSIVE binds the password file to one database only, and other database user accounts can exist in the password file. As soon as the password file is created, use this value to maximize the security of SYSDBA, SYSOPER, or SYSASM connections.

The dynamic performance view V$PWFILE_USERS lists all the database users who have SYSDBA, SYSOPER, or SYSASM privileges, as shown here:

```
SQL> select * from v$pwfile_users;

USERNAME                       SYSDB SYSOP SYSAS
------------------------------ ----- ----- -----
SYS                            TRUE  TRUE  FALSE
RJB                            TRUE  FALSE FALSE
```

Re-creating a Password File

A default installation of the Oracle database using the Oracle Universal Installer with a seed database, or using the Database Creation Assistant, will automatically create a password file. However, on some occasions you might need to re-create a password file if it is accidentally deleted or damaged. The **orapwd** command will create a password file with a single entry for the SYS user and other options when you run the **orapwd** command without any options:

```
[oracle@dw ~]$ orapwd
Usage: orapwd file=<fname> entries=<users> force=<y/n> asm=<y/n>
       dbuniquename=<dbname> format=<legacy/12> sysbackup=<y/n> sysdg=<y/
n>
       syskm=<y/n> delete=<y/n> input_file=<input-fname>

Usage: orapwd describe file=<fname>
```

```
  where
    file - name of password file (required),
    password - password for SYS will be prompted
               if not specified at command line.
               Ignored, if input_file is specified,
    entries - maximum number of distinct DBA (optional),
    force - whether to overwrite existing file (optional),
    asm - indicates that the password to be stored in
          Automatic Storage Management (ASM) disk group
          is an ASM password. (optional).
    dbuniquename - unique database name used to identify database
                   password files residing in ASM diskgroup only.
                   Ignored when asm option is specified (optional),
    format - use format=12 for new 12c features like SYSBACKUP, SYSDG and
             SYSKM support, longer identifiers, etc.
             If not specified, format=12 is default (optional),
    delete - drops a password file. Must specify 'asm',
             'dbuniquename' or 'file'. If 'file' is specified,
             the file must be located on an ASM diskgroup (optional),
    sysbackup - create SYSBACKUP entry (optional and requires the
                12 format). Ignored, if input_file is specified,
    sysdg - create SYSDG entry (optional and requires the 12 format),
            Ignored, if input_file is specified,
    syskm - create SYSKM entry (optional and requires the 12 format),
            Ignored, if input_file is specified,
    input_file - name of input password file, from where old user
                 entries will be migrated (optional),
    describe - describes the properties of specified password file
               (required).
  There must be no spaces around equal-to (=) characters.
[oracle@dw ~]$
```

The default location for the password file is **$ORACLE_HOME/dbs** on Linux and **%ORACLE_HOME%\database** on Windows. The name of the password file is the string "**orapw**" plus the name of the instance in lowercase. For example, the password file for the DW database would be **$ORACLE_HOME/dbs/orapwdw** and for Windows, the default is **PWD<*sid*>.ora**.

Once you've re-created the password file, you will have to grant the SYSDBA, SYSOPER, or SYSASM privileges to database users who previously had those privileges. In addition, if the password you provided in the **orapwd** command is not the same password that the SYS account uses in the database, this is not a problem. When you connect using CONNECT / AS SYSDBA, you're using operating system authentication. When you connect using CONNECT SYS/<*syspassword*>

AS SYSDBA, the password <*syspassword*> is the password for SYS in the database. And just to reiterate, if the database is down or in MOUNT mode, you must use operating system authentication or the password file. Also worth noting again is that operating system authentication takes precedence over password file authentication, so as long as you fulfill the requirements for OS authentication, the password file will not be used for authentication even if it exists.

on the job

As of Oracle Database 11g, database passwords are case-sensitive. To disable case-sensitivity, set the SEC_CASE_SENSITIVE_LOGON initialization parameter to FALSE.

EXERCISE 5-6

Re-create the Password File after Accidental Deletion

In this exercise, you'll re-create the password file for the HR database using the **orapwd** command and add the user RJB to the list of users in the SYSDBA group. Additionally, you'll give the user SCOTT the SYSOPER privilege:

1. Create the new password file with ten entries and a new password for the SYS account:

```
[oracle@srv04 ~]$ orapwd file=$ORACLE_HOME/dbs/orapwhr \
     password=bigsys entries=10
```

2. Connect as SYS and grant the SYSDBA privilege to the user RJB and the SYSASM privilege to SCOTT:

```
[oracle@srv04 ~]$ sqlplus sys/bigsys as sysdba

SQL*Plus: Release 12.1.0.1.0 Production on Thu Mar 13
10:30:08 2014

Copyright (c) 1982, 2013, Oracle.  All rights reserved.

Connected to:
Oracle Database 12c Enterprise Edition Release 12.1.0.1.0 -
64bit Production
With the Partitioning, Automatic Storage Management, OLAP,
Advanced Analytics
and Real Application Testing options
SQL> grant sysdba to rjb;
```

```
Grant succeeded.

SQL> grant sysoper to scott;

Grant succeeded.

SQL>
```

3. Confirm that the users RJB and SCOTT have the new privileges:

```
SQL> select * from v$pwfile_users;

USERNAME                       SYSDB SYSOP SYSAS
------------------------------ ----- ----- -----
SYS                            TRUE  TRUE  FALSE
RJB                            TRUE  FALSE FALSE
SCOTT                          FALSE TRUE  FALSE

SQL>
```

Recovering the Control File

Chapter 2 covered a scenario in which one of your multiplexed control files is lost. The recovery process in this scenario is straightforward because you can replace the missing copy by copying one of the multiplexed copies and then restart the database. However, even if you multiplex your control file in several locations, it is still possible that all copies of the control file can be lost because of a catastrophic failure of all disks containing the control file. In this event, you will have to use a backup copy of the control file created with one of the methods discussed in the preceding section (with hopes that not all backups failed during the hypothetical catastrophic event).

Depending on the status of the online redo log files and the status of the datafiles, you perform slightly different actions. In most cases, you must open the database with RESETLOGS after the recovery operation. Table 5-2 describes the actions you must perform for each combination of online redo log and datafile availability.

In each of the scenarios in Table 5-2, you perform the following steps:

1. Shut down the database with SHUTDOWN ABORT (if it has not already crashed).
2. Restore the control file from backup.

TABLE 5-2 Control File Recovery Scenarios

Availability of Online Redo Log Files	Availability of Datafiles	Recovery Procedure
Available	Current	Recover the database with a restored copy of the control file, applying online redo logs if necessary. Open the database with RESETLOGS.
Unavailable	Current	Re-create the control file and open the database with RESETLOGS.
Available	Restored from Backup	Restore a control file from backup, perform complete recovery, and then open the database with RESETLOGS.
Unavailable	Restored from Backup	Restore a control file from backup, perform incomplete recovery, and then open the database with RESETLOGS.

3. Start up the database in MOUNT mode.
4. Start database recovery and specify BACKUP CONTROLFILE in the RECOVER command.
5. Open the database with RESETLOGS.

If the following conditions are true, you do not have to open the database with RESETLOGS, and you will not lose any committed transactions:

- You manually ran CREATE CONTROLFILE or have a backup of the control file created with ALTER DATABASE BACKUP CONTROLFILE TO TRACE.
- All online redo log files are available.
- All datafiles are current.

All other scenarios, including using a backup control file with undamaged online redo log files and datafiles, will require opening the database with RESETLOGS.

A RECOVER command using a backup copy of the control file will look like this:

```
SQL> recover database using backup controlfile until cancel;
```

Even if all archived and online redo log files are intact, the RECOVER command will prompt for a missing archived redo log file. This indicates that unarchived changes existed in the online redo log files. In this scenario, you must manually specify the locations of each online redo log file until the RECOVER command finds the required redo information.

EXERCISE 5-7

Recover from the Loss of All Control Files

In this exercise, you'll use a backup copy of the control file to recover from the loss of all online control files.

1. Shut down the database if it has not already crashed after the inadvertent deletion of all online control files:

```
SQL> startup
ORACLE instance started.

Total System Global Area  636100608 bytes
Fixed Size                  1301784 bytes
Variable Size             490734312 bytes
Database Buffers          138412032 bytes
Redo Buffers                5652480 bytes
ORA-00205: error in identifying control file, check alert log
for more info

SQL> shutdown abort
ORACLE instance shut down.
SQL>
```

2. All online redo log files and datafiles appear to be intact, along with the disks containing the original copies of the control file. Use operating system copy commands to restore a backup of the control file to the original locations:

```
SQL> ! cp /u06/backup/control01.ctl
/u01/app/oracle/oradata/hr/control01.ctl
SQL> ! cp /u06/backup/control01.ctl
/u01/app/oracle/oradata/hr/control02.ctl
SQL> ! cp /u06/backup/control01.ctl
/u01/app/oracle/oradata/hr/control03.ctl
SQL>
```

3. Open the database in MOUNT mode and perform non-AUTOMATIC recovery so that you can manually specify online redo log files, if so required:

```
SQL> recover database using backup controlfile until cancel;
ORA-00279: change 5625919 generated at 03/10/2014 11:48:28
     needed for thread 1
```

```
ORA-00289: suggestion :
/u01/app/oracle/flash_recovery_area/HR/archivelog/
    2014_03_10/o1_mf_1_1_472fxokb_.arc
ORA-00280: change 5625919 for thread 1 is in sequence #1

Specify log: {<RET>=suggested | filename | AUTO | CANCEL}
. . .
Media recovery complete.
SQL>
```

4. Finally, open the database with RESETLOGS:

```
SQL> alter database open resetlogs;

Database altered.

SQL>
```

CERTIFICATION OBJECTIVE 5.04

Perform Recovery of Index and Read-Only Tablespaces and Tempfiles

Although the loss of a temporary tablespace is not critical, it will likely affect the performance of your database immediately. The same goes for index tablespaces: You don't require an index tablespace (or indexes at all), but the loss of a tablespace containing indexes will have a significant adverse effect on database performance in an OLTP environment.

Recovering from a Lost Tempfile

Recovering from the loss of one or more tempfiles is a straightforward process. Remember that a tempfile is identical to a datafile except that it belongs to a temporary tablespace. The impact to a running database is minimal depending on the query mix. In all cases, you can recover the tempfile while the database is up, even if the original file location is not available.

Losing a Tempfile

One of the consequences of losing a tempfile is that any SQL statements that need temporary disk space for sorting (in other words, insufficient memory is available in Oracle's memory space) will fail. If one or all of the datafiles for the TEMP tablespace is deleted at the operating system level, you can create a new tempfile in the same directory as the original one using the ALTER TABLESPACE command. If the original directory location is not available, you can create it in a different location. After that, you can drop the original tempfile using a similar ALTER TABLESPACE command.

EXERCISE 5-8

Create a Replacement Tempfile for the TEMP Tablespace

In this exercise, the tempfile for the TEMP tablespace was accidentally deleted, so you must create another tempfile to replace it while the database is still running.

1. Identify the name of the tempfile for the TEMP tablespace:

```
SQL> select file#, name from v$tempfile;

     FILE# NAME
---------- --------------------------------------------------
         1 /u01/app/oracle/oradata/hr/temp01.dbf

SQL>
```

2. Create a new tempfile with a different name for the TEMP tablespace:

```
SQL> alter tablespace temp add tempfile
  2      '/u01/app/oracle/oradata/hr/temp02.dbf'
  3      size 25m;

Tablespace altered.

SQL>
```

3. Drop the previous tempfile. This will update only the control file because the original tempfile is missing:

```
SQL> alter tablespace temp drop tempfile
  2      '/u01/app/oracle/oradata/hr/temp01.dbf';

Tablespace altered.

SQL>
```

4. Confirm that the TEMP tablespace contains only the newly created tempfile:

```
SQL> select file#, name from v$tempfile;

     FILE# NAME
---------- --------------------------------------------------
         2 /u01/app/oracle/oradata/hr/temp02.dbf

SQL>
```

Starting a Database Without a Tempfile

Recovering from the loss of a tempfile is even easier if you start the database with a missing tempfile. The database starts, and if the original disk directory location is available, Oracle re-creates all missing tempfiles, as you can see in this excerpt from the alert log:

```
Re-creating tempfile /u01/app/oracle/oradata/hr/temp02.dbf
Re-creating tempfile /u01/app/oracle/oradata/hr/temp03.dbf
```

If the original disk directory location is no longer available, the database still starts, and you can use the steps from the preceding section to re-create the tempfiles manually for the TEMP tablespace.

CERTIFICATION OBJECTIVE 5.05

Restore a Database to a New Host

RMAN can make it easy to restore a database to a new host in a number of ways, and a number of motives exist for restoring a database to a new host. The following sections delve into the reasons you should and should not restore and recover a database to a new host. In addition, you'll learn the steps for preparing the host and performing the actual restore and recovery operation.

Understanding Restoration to a New Host

If you want to perform a disaster recovery test to another host or you want to move a database permanently to another host, then using the RMAN RESTORE and RECOVER commands is the best method to use. However, using the procedures outlined in the following sections will keep the original database identifier and will therefore cause a conflict in the RMAN repository because the restored database with the same DBID will be considered the current target database. As a result, these procedures should not be used to create a permanent second database—use the RMAN DUPLICATE command for that. The procedures for using DUPLICATE are detailed in Chapter 9.

Preparing the New Host

To prepare the new host to receive the restored and recovered database, follow these steps:

1. Record the DBID of the source database. Use this command to query the DBID:

```
SQL> select dbid from v$database;

      DBID
----------
3318356692

SQL>
```

2. Copy the initialization parameter file from the source database to the new host.
3. Make sure that all source database backups are available to the new host. Do *not* connect to the recovery catalog.

Restoring and Recovering on the New Host

Although a lot of steps are required to restore and recover to the new host, each step is straightforward:

1. Configure environment variables on the new host.
2. Connect to the new target database with NOCATALOG.
3. Set the DBID.
4. Start the instance with NOMOUNT.
5. Restore the SPFILE from backup.
6. Shut down the new instance.
7. Edit the PFILE.
8. Start the instance with NOMOUNT (again).
9. Create an RMAN RUN block to restore the control file.

10. Create an RMAN RUN block to restore and recover the database.
11. Open the database with RESETLOGS.

The following sections offer a brief overview of each step.

1. Configure environment variables on the new host. Define the environment variable (on Unix or Linux systems) ORACLE_SID:

```
[oracle@srv04]$ export ORACLE_SID=hr
```

2. Connect to the new target database with NOCATALOG. Connect to the new target database but not the recovery catalog, as in this example:

```
[oracle@srv04]$ rman target /
```

3. Set the DBID. From within RMAN, set the DBID. You found the DBID earlier by querying V$DATABASE:

```
RMAN> set dbid 3318356692;
```

4. Start the instance in NOMOUNT mode. Start the database in NOMOUNT mode:

```
RMAN> startup nomount
```

RMAN will return a warning message and use a default parameter file because the parameter file has not been restored yet.

5. Restore the SPFILE. Within an RMAN RUN block, restore the SPFILE using a command similar to the following:

```
RMAN> restore spfile to pfile '?/oradata/testrecov/initorcl.ora'
  2      from autobackup;
```

Note that you're restoring the SPFILE to a PFILE, so you can make edits later.

6. Shut down the new instance. Shut down the new instance with either SHUTDOWN IMMEDIATE or SHUTDOWN ABORT. Since ABORT requires recovery on restart, IMMEDIATE is the preferable option.

7. Edit the PFILE. Edit the newly created PFILE to change any server-specific locations for initialization parameters such as these:

IFILE
LOG_ARCHIVE_DEST_*
CONTROL_FILES

8. Start the instance in NOMOUNT mode. Start the instance in NOMOUNT mode again. You use the edited control file because you don't have the control file restored yet:

```
SQL> startup force nomount pfile = '?/oradata/testrecov/initorcl.ora';
```

9. Create an RMAN RUN block. Now that the database is using the restored and edited parameter file, you can execute an RMAN RUN block to restore the control file and change the restored database to MOUNT mode:

```
run {
   restore controlfile from autobackup;
   alter database mount;
}
```

RMAN will restore the control file to the location specified for CONTROL_FILES in the initialization parameter file. Remember that many commands, such as ALTER DATABASE, work identically at both a SQL> prompt and an RMAN> prompt—convenient but sometimes confusing.

10. Create and run the RMAN recovery script. Create an RMAN RUN block that contains the appropriate SET NEWNAME commands to specify the new locations for each datafile, such as in this example:

```
set newname for datafile 1 to '?/oradata/testrecov/users01.dbf';
```

The script should also include any ALTER DATABASE . . . RENAME commands for the online redo log files:

```
sql "alter database rename file
         ''/u01/app/oracle/oradata/orcl/redo01.log'' to
         ''?/oradata/testrecov/redo01.log'' ";
```

Limit the recovery to the last archived redo log file, because the online redo log files for the new instance are not valid. RMAN will fail if it tries to recover past the last archived redo log file:

```
set until scn 49382031;
```

Finally, restore the database. Then use the SWITCH command to switch the datafile names in the control file to their new names and locations and then recover the database:

```
restore database;
switch datafile all;
recover database;
```

11. Open the database with RESETLOGS. Finally, open the database with the RESETLOGS option and you can proceed with testing the restored and recovered database:

```
RMAN> alter database open resetlogs;
```

CERTIFICATION SUMMARY

Oracle can recover from an instance failure or crash automatically when the online redo logs and all datafiles are intact and the failure was due to external factors such as a power outage or temporary hardware failure. You can adjust parameters like FAST_START_MTTR_TARGET to control how long an instance recovery should be with the caveat that the shorter this time is the more time the database must spend during normal operations to keep the checkpoint advanced in the redo log files.

Next, you saw a few more complicated scenarios involving redo log file failures. Losing one member of a redo log file group, even if it is active, is easy to repair and does not impact users and their transactions. Recovering from the loss of an entire redo log group is a bit more complicated. This is because loss of committed transactions is possible if the database is currently attempting to write to the lost redo log file group.

The password file is critical to the database in that it controls the authentication of DBAs who want to connect to the database as SYSDBA. It is easy to re-create the password file, but you should back it up using operating system commands whenever you add or remove SYSDBA, SYSOPER, or SYSASM privileges for a DBA.

You can perform some backups while the database is online, either backing up one tablespace at a time or backing up all datafiles in the database. If you are running your database in NOARCHIVELOG mode, the only way you can create a consistent backup without archived redo log files is to perform the backup while the database is shut down. You learned about several user-managed methods to back up and recover your database whether you are in ARCHIVELOG or NOARCHIVELOG mode.

One of the more straightforward recovery techniques is to replace a lost tempfile. The impact to the user is temporary, the database remains open, and you can create another tempfile within minutes of discovering the problem.

Finally, you saw some techniques that can be used to recover your database with a backup control file if all current copies of the control file are lost or damaged. If you frequently back up your control file (for example, after every structural database change), there is no loss of committed transactions if the datafiles and online redo log files are intact.

We also described one of the most basic types of recovery operation for a database in ARCHIVELOG mode. For a noncritical datafile, you take the tablespace containing the datafile offline, restore the missing or damaged datafile, and then recover the datafile using archived and online redo log files. For a critical datafile, the procedure is much the same, except that you must shut down the database and start it in MOUNT mode before starting the recovery operation.

On some occasions, you'll want to perform an incomplete recovery, typically because you want to roll back the database in time permanently due to numerous erroneous changes to the database that cannot be reversed using Oracle Flashback technology. You learned how to create a restore point as a marker for an SCN or a point in time and then how to use that restore point later for an incomplete recovery operation.

Image copies should play an important role in your disaster recovery plan. To speed up the recovery process even more, you can apply subsequent incremental backups to an image copy so that any recovery operation using the image copy has to use only the archived and online redo log files to recover the database. You saw a script that you can use to keep your image copies up to date with every incremental backup.

Once you create your image copies and keep them updated with incremental updates, you want to be ready to use them. Typically, you will restore a backupset or image copy. An even faster method is to use the image copy in place and apply any recent incremental updates and archived redo log files. You learned how to switch to an image copy, recover the image copy, and switch it back to its original location.

When using an RMAN RUN block, you can use the SET NEWNAME command to specify an alternative location for a datafile during a restore operation. Once

RMAN restores the datafile, you use the SWITCH command to update the control file and the recovery catalog with the new location for the datafile.

If you are not permanently moving a database to a new host, you can use the RMAN RESTORE and RECOVER commands to create a copy of the database on a new host quickly and easily. You use the original DBID on the copied database and make sure you don't connect to a recovery catalog with the copied database. Otherwise, you will compromise the integrity of the source database's backup metadata.

Next, you saw the steps required to recover using a backup control file and a backup SPFILE. The procedure is much the same as, and reiterates the importance of, mirroring your control file and ensuring that you configure your RMAN backups with AUTOBACKUP set to ON.

Finally, you saw the high-level steps required for recovering from the ultimate disaster: losing all datafiles, control files, and SPFILEs. The procedure is fairly straightforward and minimizes data loss, as long as your database is running in ARCHIVELOG mode. Many, if not all, of the steps required for performing disaster recovery were covered in separate sections earlier in the chapter.

TWO-MINUTE DRILL

Describe and Tune Instance Recovery

- ❑ Instance recovery, or crash recovery, is performed when a database is opened with one or more datafiles whose header contains an SCN different from the last SCN recorded in the control file.
- ❑ An OS memory issue, CPU problem, or other transient hardware failure that causes the Oracle instance to crash will trigger instance recovery when the instance is restarted.
- ❑ Instance recovery is automatically performed by Oracle upon database startup.
- ❑ The two distinct phases of instance recovery are rolling forward all changes and then rolling back uncommitted changes.
- ❑ The checkpoint position in a redo log file is right before the oldest data block not yet written to the database.
- ❑ An administrator can tune instance recovery to bring the database back online sooner at the expense of more DBW*n* activity during normal operations.
- ❑ The parameter FAST_START_MTTR_TARGET can be set to enable the MTTR advisor and automatically adjust other parameters to control the actual number of seconds it will take to finish instance recovery.

Perform Complete and Incomplete Recovery

- ❑ Use RMAN RESTORE and RECOVER for complete recovery from a critical and noncritical datafile loss.
- ❑ Datafiles from the SYSTEM and UNDO tablespaces are critical datafiles.
- ❑ When restoring and recovering a critical datafile, the database must be in MOUNT mode.
- ❑ You can completely recover any datafile if the database is in ARCHIVELOG mode.
- ❑ You use restore points to recover a database to an SCN or a time in the past.
- ❑ Use CREATE RESTORE POINT to create a restore point.
- ❑ You must open the database with RESETLOGS if you perform incomplete recovery.

- You can recover image copies with more recent incremental level 1 backups.
- RMAN automatically determines the best image copy to use if more than one is available.
- Use tags with an incrementally updated image copy strategy to ensure that the correct incremental backup updates the image copy.
- Using image copies skips the restore step and saves overall recovery time.
- Use the RMAN command SWITCH TO . . . COPY to switch to the most recent image copy for a datafile, tablespace, or database.
- RMAN automatically applies incremental backups and archived redo log files when you recover with an image copy.
- Use the dynamic performance views V$TABLESPACE and V$DATAFILE_HEADER to determine the tablespace and datafile number needing recovery.
- After switching to an image copy, you can switch back to an image copy at the original location when it becomes available.
- You use the SET NEWNAME command in RMAN to identify new locations for restored datafiles.
- After restoring one or more datafiles with RESTORE, you use the SWITCH command to update the control file and recovery catalog with the new datafile locations.
- You can use an RMAN autobackup to restore either an SPFILE or control file when all online copies are lost.
- RMAN restores the control file to all locations specified by the initialization parameter CONTROL_FILES.
- If the SPFILE is lost, RMAN uses a default SPFILE when you start the database with NOMOUNT.
- Use RESTORE SPFILE FROM AUTOBACKUP to restore the SPFILE.
- Use RESTORE CONTROLFILE FROM AUTOBACKUP to restore the control file.
- When restoring a control file from autobackup, you must open the database with RESETLOGS.
- You can optionally restore a copy of the control file to an alternate location.

Perform Recovery for SPFILEs, Password Files, Control Files, and Redo Log Files

- ❑ A redo log group can have six statuses: CURRENT, ACTIVE, INACTIVE, UNUSED, CLEARING, or CLEARING_CURRENT. The most common statuses are CURRENT, ACTIVE, and INACTIVE.
- ❑ You can use the dynamic performance view V$LOG to query the status of each redo log group.
- ❑ If one member of a log group becomes damaged or is lost, the LGWR (Log Writer) process continues to write to the undamaged member, and no data loss or interruption in service occurs.
- ❑ The dynamic performance view V$LOGFILE shows the status of each individual member of each log file group.
- ❑ If the status of a log file group member is INVALID in the view V$LOGFILE, it is damaged or unavailable and must be re-created.
- ❑ Losing a log file group with a status of INACTIVE will most likely not result in the loss of committed transactions as long as the other members of the log file group remain intact.
- ❑ Losing an inactive log file group that has not been archived will result in a gap in the archived redo log files and necessitates a full backup after recovering the log file group.
- ❑ Losing a redo log file group with a status of ACTIVE will not cause the loss of committed transactions if you can successfully perform ALTER SYSTEM CHECKPOINT. If the checkpoint fails, you must perform incomplete recovery.
- ❑ Losing a redo log file group with a status of CURRENT will crash the instance, and you must perform incomplete recovery.
- ❑ Losing a password file prevents DBAs from connecting to an open or closed instance with the SYSDBA, SYSOPER, or SYSASM privilege.
- ❑ You must use a password file if you are connecting remotely and the connection is not secure.
- ❑ Connecting with the SYSDBA or SYSASM privilege connects to the database as the SYS user. The SYSOPER privilege connects as PUBLIC.
- ❑ You use the **orapwd** command at an operating system prompt to re-create the password file.

- The default location for the password file is **$ORACLE_HOME/dbs** on Linux and **%ORACLE_HOME%\database** on Windows.
- The dynamic performance view V$PWFILE_USERS lists all the database users who have SYSDBA, SYSOPER, or SYSASM privileges.
- If you want to back up your control file while the database is open, you can do it with two different SQL commands: ALTER DATABASE BACKUP CONTROLFILE TO <*filename*> and ALTER DATABASE BACKUP CONTROLFILE TO TRACE.
- ALTER DATABASE BACKUP CONTROLFILE TO < *filename* > creates an exact binary copy of the control file at the specified location.
- ALTER DATABASE BACKUP CONTROLFILE TO TRACE creates an editable script that re-creates the control file in the directory **$ORACLE_BASE/diag/rdbms/<*database*>/<*instance*>/trace**.
- Losing all copies of the online control file does not lose any committed transactions if you have a recent backup copy of the control file and both the datafiles and online redo log files are intact.
- You do not have to open the database with RESETLOGS after restoring your control file if you manually create the replacement control file using CREATE CONTROLFILE or you use a version of the control file script that you created with ALTER DATABASE BACKUP CONTROLFILE TO TRACE.

Perform Recovery of Index and Read-Only Tablespaces and Tempfiles

- A tempfile can be recovered while the database is open.
- The impact of a lost tempfile is noticed when users attempt to sort large result sets.
- When a tempfile is lost, you can re-create it in the original location or specify a new location.
- If the database starts without tempfiles, it creates them in the location specified in the control file.

Restore a Database to a New Host

- ❑ Restoring a database to a new host is appropriate for disaster recovery testing or permanently moving the database to a new host.
- ❑ The DUPLICATE command is more appropriate if you want to make a permanent copy of the database with a new DBID.
- ❑ When connecting to the new database, do not connect to a recovery catalog.
- ❑ The RMAN recovery script uses SET NEWNAME to specify new locations for each datafile.
- ❑ Restore the database to the SCN of the last archived redo log file.
- ❑ You must open the new database with RESETLOGS.

SELF TEST

The following questions will help you measure your understanding of the material presented in this chapter. Read all the choices carefully because there might be more than one correct answer. Choose all correct answers for each question.

Describe and Tune Instance Recovery

1. Your database instance, running in ARCHIVELOG mode, crashes because of a power failure. All of the datafiles and redo log files are intact, but the latest SCN in the control file does not match the SCN in the headers of some datafiles. At what phase of instance recovery can users connect to the database and continue their work?

A. After all uncommitted transactions have been rolled back

B. The moment the instance starts, since all recovery steps can occur in the background

C. When both committed and uncommitted data from the online redo log files have been applied to the datafiles

D. After all previously committed data has been written to the datafiles

2. Which of the following conditions or factors affect the amount of time needed for instance recovery, also known as mean time to recovery (MTTR)? (Choose all that apply.)

A. Setting the value of the parameter FAST_START_MTTR_TARGET to 0

B. Setting the value of the parameter FAST_START_MTTR_TARGET to 3600

C. How close the checkpoint position is to the oldest block not yet written to the datafiles

D. The size of the largest datafile

E. How many datafile headers have SCNs that do not match the SCN in the control file

Perform Complete and Incomplete Recovery

3. What is the difference between a critical and a noncritical datafile in a recovery scenario?

A. To recover a critical datafile, only the tablespace containing the critical datafile must be offline.

B. To recover a noncritical datafile, both the SYSTEM tablespace and the tablespace containing the critical datafile must be offline.

C. To recover a critical datafile, the database must be in NOMOUNT mode. To recover a noncritical datafile, the database must be in MOUNT mode.

D. To recover a critical datafile, the database must be in MOUNT mode. To recover a noncritical datafile, the database can be open.

4. Which tablespaces contain critical datafiles that must be recovered when the database is offline?
   A. SYSTEM and SYSAUX
   B. SYSTEM and UNDO
   C. SYSTEM, SYSAUX, and UNDO
   D. SYSTEM and USERS
5. During complete recovery of a noncritical datafile, which of the following steps are not required? (Choose two answers.)
   A. Use the RMAN RESTORE command to load the missing datafiles from backup.
   B. Reopen the database with RESETLOGS.
   C. Shut down the database and reopen in MOUNT mode.
   D. Bring the tablespace containing the missing or damaged datafiles offline before the recovery operation and online after recovery is complete.
   E. Use the RMAN RECOVER command to apply committed transactions from archived and online redo log files.
6. Which of the following methods can you use to retrieve the current system change number (SCN)?
   A. Query the CURRENT_SCN column from V$DATAFILE_HEADER.
   B. Query the CURRENT_SCN column of the V$INSTANCE view.
   C. Query the LAST_SCN column of the V$DATABASE view.
   D. Query the CURRENT_SCN column of the V$DATABASE view.
   E. Start RMAN and connect to the target database; the current SCN and the DBID are displayed.
7. Which of the following CREATE RESTORE POINT commands will preserve the restore point past the time specified by the initialization parameter CONTROL_FILE_RECORD_KEEP_TIME?
   A. CREATE RESTORE POINT SAVE_IT_PAST KEEP
   B. CREATE RESTORE POINT SAVE_IT_PAST AS OF SCN 3988943
   C. CREATE RESTORE POINT SAVE_IT_NOW PRESERVE
   D. CREATE RESTORE POINT SAVE_IT_NOW UNTIL FOREVER
8. Which operating system environment variables should be set when you use RMAN time-based incomplete recovery? (Choose two answers.)
   A. ORACLE_SID
   B. NLS_LANG

C. ORACLE_BASE

D. NLS_DATE_FORMAT

E. NLS_TIME_FORMAT

9. You are implementing an incrementally updated backup strategy using the following RMAN script:

```
run {
        recover copy of database
           with tag 'inc_upd';
        backup incremental level 1
           for recover of copy
           with tag 'inc_upd'
           database;
    }
```

How many times do you need to run this script before the image copy is updated with an incremental level 1 backup?

A. Once

B. Twice

C. Three times

D. At least four times

10. The RMAN SWITCH command is equivalent to what SQL command?

A. ALTER SYSTEM RENAME FILE

B. ALTER DATABASE ARCHIVELOG

C. ALTER DATABASE OPEN RESETLOGS

D. ALTER SYSTEM SWITCH LOGFILE

11. You have these two commands within an RMAN RUN block:

```
set newname for datafile '/u01/oradata/dw/users04.dbf'
 to '/u06/oradata/dw/users04.dbf';
restore tablespace users;
```

What happens when the RESTORE command runs?

A. The command fails and the RUN block terminates because you need to run a SWITCH command first.

B. The control file is updated with the new location of the datafile.

C. The latest versions of the datafiles for the USERS tablespace are restored to the location **/u01/oradata/dw**.

D. The latest versions of the datafiles for the USERS tablespace are restored to the location **/u06/oradata/dw**.

12. Place the following commands in the correct order for restoring a control file from an RMAN autobackup:

1. RECOVER DATABASE
2. ALTER DATABASE OPEN RESETLOGS
3. STARTUP NOMOUNT
4. ALTER DATABASE MOUNT
5. RESTORE CONTROLFILE FROM AUTOBACKUP

A. 5, 3, 4, 1, 2

B. 3, 5, 4, 1, 2

C. 3, 5, 4, 2, 1

D. 5, 1, 3, 4, 2

13. When you run the RMAN RESTORE CONTROLFILE command, where does RMAN put the previous version of the control file? (Choose the best answer.)

A. To all available locations defined by the CONTROL_FILES initialization parameter

B. To the flash recovery area

C. To all locations defined by the CONTROL_FILES initialization parameter unless overridden with the TO '<*filename*>' clause

D. To the first location defined by the CONTROL_FILES initialization parameter

Perform Recovery for SPFILEs, Password Files, Control Files, and Redo Log Files

14. Which of the following is not a valid status for an online redo log group?

A. CURRENT

B. ACTIVE

C. INVALID

D. UNUSED

E. CLEARING

15. What is the difference between the V$LOG and V$LOGFILE views?

A. V$LOG contains the status of all archived redo log files, and V$LOGFILE contains the status of all online redo log files.

B. V$LOG contains the status of the online redo log group members, and V$LOGFILE contains the status of individual online redo log groups.

C. V$LOG contains the status of all online redo log files, and V$LOGFILE contains the status of all archived redo log files.

D. V$LOG contains the status of the online redo log groups, and V$LOGFILE contains the status of individual redo log group members.

16. Which methods can you use to recover a lost or damaged password file? (Choose all that apply.)
    A. Use the **orapwd** command at an operating system prompt to re-create the password file.
    B. Restore the password file from backup and apply any archived and online redo log files to bring its contents to the present time.
    C. Use the **orapwd** SQL command to re-create the password file.
    D. Restore the password file from an operating system backup.

17. Which of the following commands does not back up the current control file?
    A. SQL> ALTER DATABASE BACKUP CONTROLFILE TO TRACE;
    B. SQL> ALTER SYSTEM BACKUP CURRENT CONTROLFILE;
    C. RMAN> BACKUP CURRENT CONTROLFILE;
    D. SQL> ALTER DATABASE BACKUP CONTROLFILE TO '/U08/BACKUP/CTL.BAK';

18. You have lost all online control files. Specify the correct order for the following tasks:
    1. Restore the control file from backup or run CREATE CONTROLFILE.
    2. Start database recovery and specify the keywords BACKUP CONTROLFILE.
    3. Start up the database in MOUNT mode.
    4. Open the database with RESETLOGS.
    5. Shut down the database.

    A. 5, 1, 3, 2, 4
    B. 1, 5, 3, 2, 4
    C. 5, 1, 3, 4, 2
    D. 1, 5, 3, 4, 2

Perform Recovery of Index and Read-Only Tablespaces and Tempfiles

19. If you lose all of the tempfiles from your temporary tablespace, what is the most likely result noticed by your users?
    A. The database becomes unavailable and users cannot connect.
    B. The users can't perform SELECT statements.
    C. The users cannot add or delete rows in any table.
    D. The users can't use ORDER BY or GROUP BY in their queries.

20. Which is the best method for recovering a tempfile? (Choose the best answer.)
    A. Drop the TEMP tablespace and re-create it with a datafile in a new location.
    B. Add another tempfile to the TEMP tablespace and drop the corrupted or missing tempfile while the database is running.

C. Shut down the database, restore the tempfile from a backup, and recover it using archived and online redo log files.

D. Add another tempfile to the TEMP tablespace and drop the corrupted or missing tempfile after the database has been shut down and restarted in MOUNT mode.

Restore a Database to a New Host

21. Which of the following are valid reasons to restore backups of your database to a new host? (Choose all that apply.)

A. Creating a new node in a RAC environment

B. Testing your disaster recovery plan

C. Creating another copy of your database

D. When the DUPLICATE command is not available

E. Permanently moving your database to a new host

22. When restoring a database to a new host, what is the first command you should run as part of the restoration process?

A. STARTUP NOMOUNT

B. SET DBID

C. RESTORE SPFILE FROM AUTOBACKUP

D. RESTORE CONTROLFILE FROM AUTOBACKUP

SELF TEST ANSWERS

Describe and Tune Instance Recovery

1. ☑ **C.** The database is opened and available to users once all committed and uncommitted transactions have been written to the datafiles. After the database is open, all uncommitted transactions are rolled back.
   ☒ **A, B,** and **D** are incorrect. **A** is incorrect because the database is available to users before the uncommitted data is rolled back and removed from the datafiles. **B** is incorrect because the database cannot be open until both committed and uncommitted transactions are applied to the datafiles. The rollback of uncommitted transactions can occur in the background. **D** is incorrect because both committed and uncommitted transactions must be applied to the datafiles before the database can be opened and available to users.

2. ☑ **A** and **B. A** is correct because setting FAST_START_MTTR_TARGET to 0 disables the MTTR advisor and therefore affects the time it takes to perform instance recovery. **B** is correct because setting FAST_START_MTTR_TARGET to 3600 (the maximum value) means that the overhead of writing changed blocks to the datafiles is minimal but the instance recovery will likely take an hour.
   ☒ **C, D,** and **E** are incorrect. **C** is incorrect because the checkpoint position is always at the oldest block in the redo log files that has not yet been written to the datafiles. **D** is incorrect because the size of the redo log files, not the size of the datafiles, is a factor in determining the MTTR. **E** is incorrect because whether one or 100 datafile headers have SCNs that don't match the SCN in the control file, all records in the online redo log files will be applied to the datafiles, and therefore this has no significant influence on instance recovery time.

Perform Complete and Incomplete Recovery

3. ☑ **D.** When you restore and recover a critical datafile, the entire database must be shut down and reopened in MOUNT mode to open the control file and make the datafile locations available to RMAN.
   ☒ **A, B,** and **C** are incorrect. **A** is incorrect because the entire database must be offline when recovering a critical datafile. **B** is incorrect because recovering a noncritical datafile requires only the tablespace containing the missing or damaged datafile to be offline. **C** is incorrect because the database must be in MOUNT mode to recover a critical datafile and can be in OPEN mode to recover a noncritical datafile.

4. ☑ **B.** The SYSTEM and UNDO tablespaces contain critical datafiles and therefore require the database to be in MOUNT mode during the recovery process.
   ☒ **A, C,** and **D** are incorrect because the SYSAUX and USERS tablespaces do not contain critical datafiles.

5. ☑ **B** and **C.** The database does not need to be opened with RESETLOGS because you are not performing incomplete recovery. For a noncritical datafile, only the tablespace containing the missing or damaged datafile needs to be offline.
   ☒ **A, D,** and **E** are incorrect. These steps are all required.

6. ☑ **D.** V$DATABASE contains the most recent SCN in the CURRENT_SCN column.
   ☒ **A, B, C,** and **E** are incorrect. **A** and **B** are incorrect because the column CURRENT_SCN does not exist in either V$DATAFILE_HEADER or V$INSTANCE. **C** is incorrect because V$DATABASE does not have a column named LAST_SCN. **E** is incorrect because when RMAN starts, it shows only the DBID and not the current SCN.

7. ☑ **C.** The keyword PRESERVE keeps the restore point past the time specified by CONTROL_FILE_RECORD_KEEP_TIME.
   ☒ **A, B,** and **D** are incorrect. **A** is incorrect because the keyword KEEP is not valid for the command. **B** is incorrect because PRESERVE was not specified. **D** is incorrect because UNTIL FOREVER is not valid for the command.

8. ☑ **B** and **D.** Both NLS_LANG and NLS_DATE_FORMAT must be set so that RMAN will correctly interpret date strings provided during a recovery operation.
   ☒ **A, C,** and **E** are incorrect. ORACLE_SID and ORACLE_BASE are required to connect to the correct database and database software, but they are not directly related to RMAN time-based recovery. NLS_TIME_FORMAT is not a valid environment variable.

9. ☑ **C.** The first time the script runs, there is no level 0 image copy or a level 1 incremental backup. The second time the script runs, the level 0 image copy exists, but there is no incremental level 1 backup to apply to it. The third and successive time, the first incremental level 1 backup is applied to the image copy.
   ☒ **A, B,** and **D** are incorrect. They all specify the incorrect number of executions.

10. ☑ **A.** Both the RMAN SWITCH and the SQL ALTER SYSTEM RENAME FILE commands update the location of the datafile in both the control file and the recovery catalog.
   ☒ **B, C,** and **D** are incorrect. **B** is incorrect because this command puts the database into ARCHIVELOG mode. **C** is incorrect because the command is used only after incomplete recovery. **D** is incorrect because the command switches online redo log files, not datafile names.

11. ☑ **D.** The SET NEWNAME specifies the new location for the datafile, and RESTORE puts the backup version of the datafile at the new location.
   ☒ **A, B,** and **C** are incorrect **A** is incorrect because the datafile must be restored before the control file can be updated with SWITCH. **B** is incorrect because only SWITCH will update the control file with the new location. **C** is incorrect because the RESTORE command uses the new location specified with SET NEWNAME.

12. ☑ **B.** The specified order is correct. You must open the database with RESETLOGS since your restored control file has information about an older version of the database.
☒ **A, C,** and **D** are incorrect because they specify an incorrect sequence of commands.

13. ☑ **C.** The command restores the control file from autobackup to all locations defined by the initialization parameter CONTROL_FILES. If any of those locations are unavailable, change the value of CONTROL_FILES or use the TO '<*filename*>' option.
☒ **A, B,** and **D** are incorrect. **A** is incorrect because the command fails if any of the locations defined by CONTROL_FILES are not available. **B** is incorrect because the autobackup of the control file will most likely originate from the flash recovery area. **D** is incorrect because RMAN restores the control file to all locations defined by CONTROL_FILES.

Perform Recovery for SPFILEs, Password Files, Control Files, and Redo Log Files

14. ☑ **C.** The status INVALID is valid only for an online redo log group member, not for the entire group.
☒ **A, B, D,** and **E** are incorrect. They are valid statuses for an online redo log group.

15. ☑ **D.** V$LOG contains the status of redo log groups, including whether the group is currently being written to. V$LOGFILE contains the status of individual redo log group members.
☒ **A, B,** and **C** are incorrect. The views V$LOG and V$LOGFILE do not contain information about archived redo log files, although the view V$LOG has a column to indicate whether the redo log file group has been archived or not.

16. ☑ **A** and **D.** Either method can be used to recover the password file, but using the **orapwd** command requires that you re-create the privileged user accounts that need SYSDBA, SYSOPER, and SYSADM privileges.
☒ **B** and **C** are incorrect. **B** is incorrect because you do not apply redo log files to the password file. **C** is incorrect because **orapwd** is valid only at an operating system command prompt.

17. ☑ **B.** There is no such command.
☒ **A, C,** and **D** are incorrect. **A** is incorrect because it creates a text-based file containing two different CREATE CONTROLFILE commands, depending on the availability of your datafiles and online redo log files. **C** is incorrect because it is one of many ways that RMAN backs up the control file. **D** is incorrect because it creates a binary copy of the control file at the specified location.

18. ☑ **A.** The first step is to shut down the database (with ABORT), and the last step is to open the database with RESETLOGS (if you used a backup control file or you do not have current online redo logs or datafiles).
☒ **B, C,** and **D** are incorrect. All three of these sequences are out of order.

Perform Recovery of Index and Read-Only Tablespaces and Tempfiles

19. ☑ **D.** Temporary tablespaces provide sort space for queries that use ORDER BY and GROUP BY when the sort operation will not fit in memory. Other operations cause sorts as well: SELECT DISTINCT, index creations, and index rebuilds.

☒ **A, B,** and **C** are incorrect. **A** is incorrect because the database remains available for some queries and most DML activity even if the TEMP tablespace is unavailable. **B** is incorrect because users can still perform SELECT statements that don't need sorting or the sort operation will fit into memory. **C** is an incorrect answer because most DML activity does not require the TEMP tablespace.

20. ☑ **B.** Once the missing tempfile is dropped and a new one added, the TEMP tablespace is automatically available to users.

☒ **A, C,** and **D** are incorrect. **A** is incorrect because dropping the tablespace is not necessary, and you cannot drop the default temporary tablespace. **C** is incorrect because you cannot recover a temporary tablespace; there are no permanent objects in a temporary tablespace. **D** is incorrect because the database does not need to be shut down to recover a temporary tablespace.

Restore a Database to a New Host

21. ☑ **B** and **E.** Restoring your database to a new host is appropriate to test your disaster recovery plan or to move your database permanently to a new host since the procedure keeps the existing DBID.

☒ **A, C,** and **D** are incorrect. **A** is incorrect because you don't need to restore copies of datafiles for new nodes in a RAC environment; only a new instance is created. **C** is incorrect because the DBID remains the same on the new database, and this will cause conflicts in the recovery catalog. **D** is incorrect because the DUPLICATE command is always available in RMAN to let you make a second copy of your database along with the required changes to the DBID in the new database.

22. ☑ **B.** The DBID must be set first so that the correct datafiles, SPFILE, and control file are restored from the source database backup location.

☒ **A, C,** and **D** are incorrect. All of these steps are valid for restoring a database to a new host but must be run after the DBID is set.

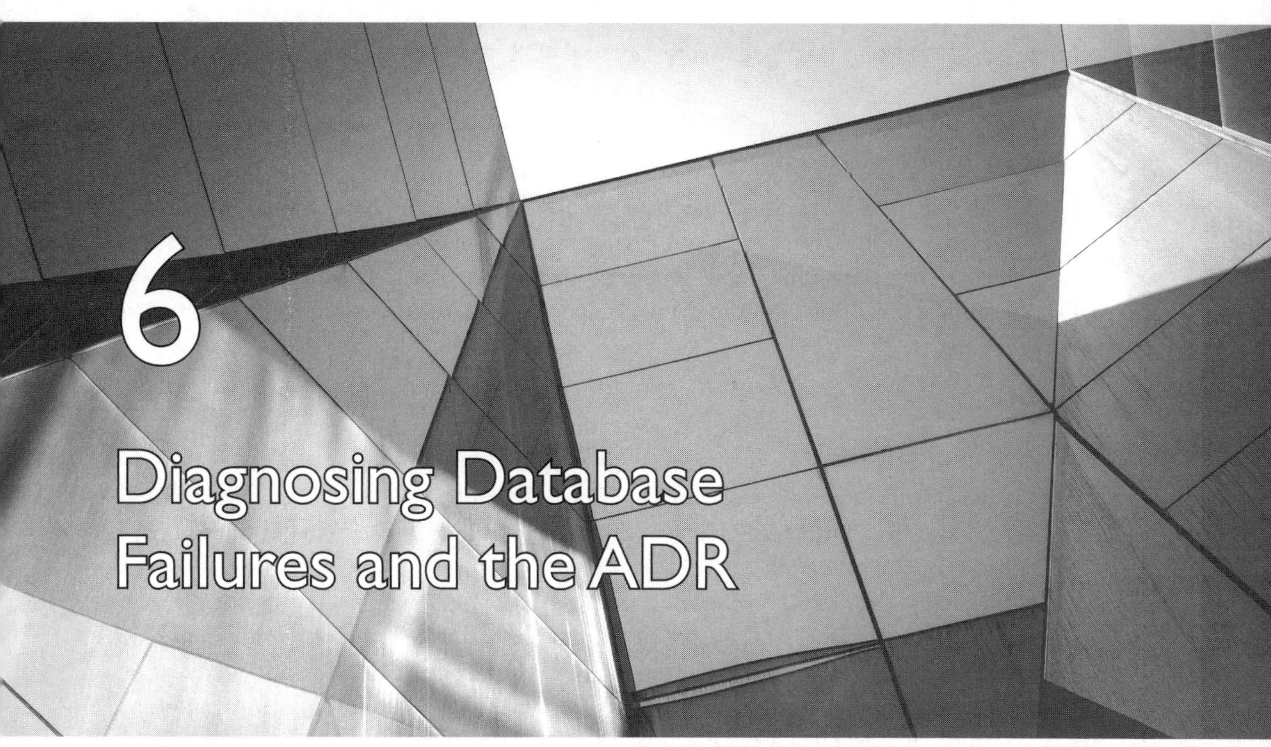

6

Diagnosing Database Failures and the ADR

CERTIFICATION OBJECTIVES

6.01	Describe the Automatic Diagnostic Workflow	✓	Two-Minute Drill
6.02	Handle Block Corruption	Q&A	Self Test

When you have to deal with database errors or even a database that is completely down, you don't want to spend extra time documenting one or more database error conditions for Oracle Support. This chapter first gives you a brief overview of how Oracle reports problems with the database and then shows how it categorizes errors into problems and incidents.

In addition, the Health Monitor framework provides both proactive and reactive tools to deal with database errors. The DBA can run a proactive health check manually using Enterprise Manager Cloud Control 12*c* (Cloud Control) or PL/SQL packages. In contrast, the Health Monitor can run diagnostic checks in response to critical database errors.

Finally, the chapter will switch from reporting, managing, and submitting service requests for database problems and incidents to recovering individual blocks after you have identified the problem. RMAN supports detection and recovery of individual blocks using the DB_BLOCK_CHECKING initialization parameter and the RMAN RECOVER . . . BLOCK command. RMAN also makes it easy to identify failures and implement repairs using the Data Recovery Advisor.

CERTIFICATION OBJECTIVE 6.01

Describe the Automatic Diagnostic Workflow

The key to the automated diagnostic repository (ADR) is the first word: *automatic*. ADR is an always-on facility that captures errors in trace and dump files the first and any successive times they occur (which is the reason for the *diagnostic* part of the Oracle feature name). The third part, *repository*, is a location on disk that stores the diagnostic information on disk and comes with a tool that makes it easy to query the repository even when the database is unavailable.

The following sections provide more details about the structure of the repository, how to retrieve information from the repository, and how to find the diagnostic information you're looking for in the repository using initialization parameters and data dictionary views. In addition, you'll see how easily and quickly you can package the diagnostic information from the ADR and send it to Oracle support for problem resolution.

Understanding the ADR

The ADR is a file-based repository of diagnostic and other noncritical information for all products in your environment. Each database instance and Automatic Storage Management (ASM) instance has its own directory structure called an *ADR home* within a top-level directory known as the *ADR base*. In a Real Application Cluster (RAC) environment, each instance has its own subdirectory, which not only makes it easy to view diagnostics for an individual instance but also makes it easy for the diagnostic tools to analyze data across instances for cluster-wide problems.

The ADR base directory is also known as the *ADR root directory*. The location for the ADR base is set depending on the values of initialization parameters and environment variables. If the initialization parameter DIAGNOSTIC_DEST is set, the ADR base directory is set to this value, and all other file locations are set relative to this location. If DIAGNOSTIC_DEST is not set, then DIAGNOSTIC_DEST is set to the environment variable ORACLE_BASE. If ORACLE_BASE is not set, DIAGNOSTIC_DEST is set to the value **$ORACLE_HOME/log**. Figure 6-1 shows the ADR directory structure for the COMPLREF database.

For the database in Figure 6-1, the initialization parameter DIAGNOSTIC_DEST is not set, so Oracle sets DIAGNOSTIC_DEST to the value of the environment variable ORACLE_BASE, which in this case is **/u01/app/oracle**.

```
[oracle@dw ~]$ echo $ORACLE_BASE
/u01/app/oracle
[oracle@dw ~]$ echo $ORACLE_HOME
/u01/app/oracle/product/12.1.0/dbhome_1
[oracle@dw ~]$
```

If ORACLE_BASE were not set, the location for the ADR would be **/u01/app/oracle/product/12.1.0/dbhome_1/log**.

You can retrieve the values for each diagnostic directory using the dynamic performance view V$DIAG_INFO, as in this example:

```
SQL> select inst_id,name,value from v$diag_info;
INST_ID NAME                  VALUE
------- -------------------- ------------------------------------
      1 Diag Enabled           TRUE
      1 ADR Base              /u01/app/oracle
      1 ADR Home              /u01/app/oracle/diag/rdbms/complref
                              /complref

      1 Diag Trace            /u01/app/oracle/diag/rdbms/complref
                              /complref/trace
```

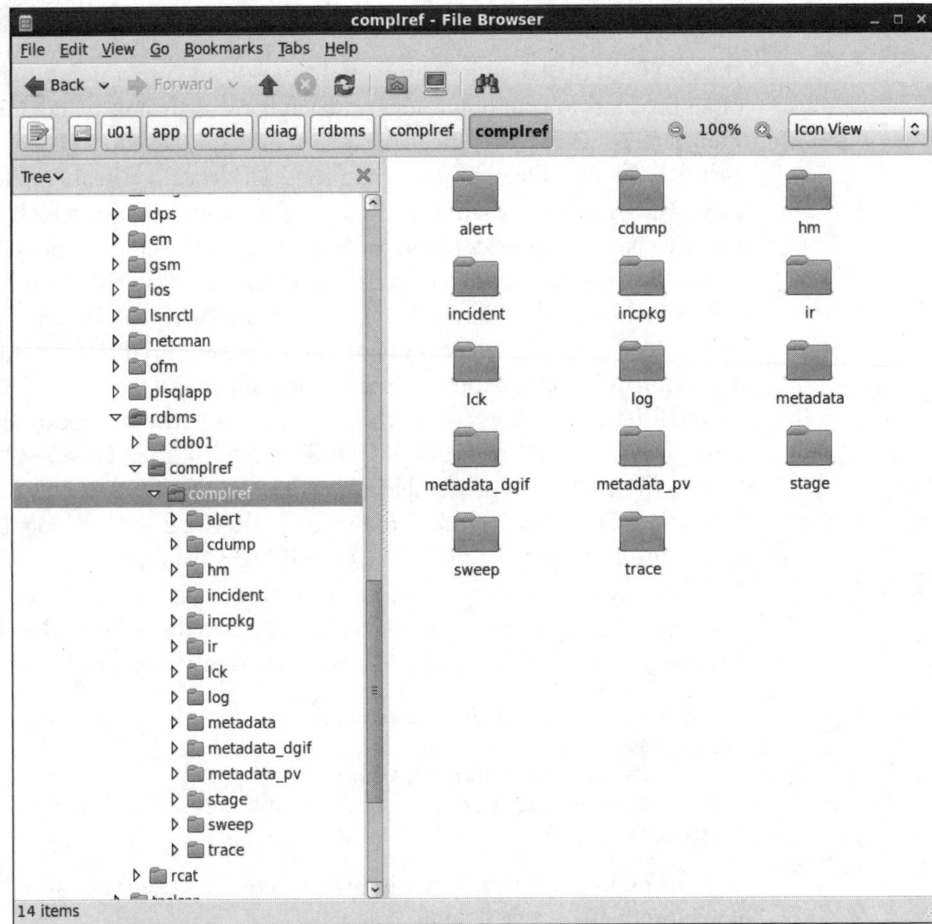

FIGURE 6-1 ADR directory structure for the COMPLREEF database

```
1 Diag Alert              /u01/app/oracle/diag/rdbms/complref
                          /complref/alert

1 Diag Incident           /u01/app/oracle/diag/rdbms/complref
                          /complref/incident

1 Diag Cdump              /u01/app/oracle/diag/rdbms/complref
                          /complref/cdump

1 Health Monitor          /u01/app/oracle/diag/rdbms/complref
                          /complref/hm
```

```
      1 Default Trace File      /u01/app/oracle/diag/rdbms/complref
                                /complref/trace/complref_ora_30559.
                                trc

      1 Active Problem Count    0
      1 Active Incident Count   0

11 rows selected.
```

Note the column INST_ID. In a RAC environment, this value differentiates the value of each directory by node. For example, if COMPLREF were the cluster name and the cluster contained the three instances COMPLREF1,COMPLREF2, and COMPLREF3, the value for the second instance's diagnostic trace directory would be as follows:

```
INST_ID NAME                      VALUE
-------- ------------------------ ------------------------------------
       2 Diag Trace                /u01/app/oracle/diag/rdbms/complref
                                     /complref2/trace
```

Compared to previous releases of Oracle, the diagnostic information is more partitioned. In other words, all nonincident traces are stored in the trace subdirectory, all core dumps are in the cdump directory, and all incident dumps are stored as individual directories within the incident subdirectory. Table 6-1 shows the ADR location for each type of diagnostic data.

Note the differentiation between trace and dump files. Trace files contain continuous output to diagnose a problem with a running process. A dump file is a one-time diagnostic output file resulting from an incident. Similarly, a core dump is a one-time platform-specific binary memory dump. Note also that there is no initialization parameter or environment variable named ADR_HOME. You can

TABLE 6-1 ADR Diagnostic Information Directory Locations

Diagnostic Data Type	Location Within the ADR
Foreground process trace files	ADR_HOME/trace
Background process trace files	ADR_HOME/trace
Alert log	ADR_HOME/alert (XML format) ADR_HOME/trace (plaintext format)
Core dumps	ADR_HOME/cdump
Incident dumps	ADR_HOME/incident/incdir_n
Health Monitor	ADR_HOME/hm

determine the value of ADR_HOME from the row in V$DIAG_INFO containing the name ADR Home:

```
1 ADR Home                    /u01/app/oracle/diag/rdbms/complref/complref
```

Using the ADRCI Tool

The ADR Command Interpreter (ADRCI) tool makes it easy to query the contents of the ADR. You can use the tool in command mode or create scripts to run in batch mode. You can use ADRCI even when the database is down—remember that the ADR is completely file system based. In addition to querying the contents of the ADR with ADRCI, you can also package incident and problem information into a compressed ZIP file that you can send to Oracle support.

Note that ADRCI does not require a login or any other authorization. The contents of the ADR are protected only by operating system permissions on the directory containing the ADR file structures. For a default installation of Oracle Database 12*c*, this means that the ADR has the same permissions as the ORACLE_BASE directory and its subdirectories. You can alter the permissions further if you want, but you must make sure the user owning the Oracle processes (usually the oracle user) has full read-write access to the ADR.

When you start ADRCI, you see the current ADR base directory. Type **help** for a list of commands.

```
[oracle@dw ~]$ adrci

ADRCI: Release 12.1.0.1.0 - Production on Fri Mar 7 07:31:29
2014

Copyright (c) 1982, 2013, Oracle and/or its affiliates.  All
rights reserved.

ADR base = "/u01/app/oracle"
adrci> help

 HELP [topic]
   Available Topics:
        CREATE REPORT
        ECHO
        EXIT
        HELP
        HOST
        IPS
        PURGE
        RUN
```

```
        SET BASE
        SET BROWSER
        SET CONTROL
        SET ECHO
        SET EDITOR
        SET HOMES | HOME | HOMEPATH
        SET TERMOUT
        SHOW ALERT
        SHOW BASE
        SHOW CONTROL
        SHOW HM_RUN
        SHOW HOMES | HOME | HOMEPATH
        SHOW INCDIR
        SHOW INCIDENT
        SHOW LOG
        SHOW PROBLEM
        SHOW REPORT
        SHOW TRACEFILE
        SPOOL

 There are other commands intended to be used directly by
Oracle, type
 "HELP EXTENDED" to see the list
adrci>
```

Even when there are no incidents or problems to view, you can perform more mundane tasks such as viewing the alert log from ADRCI.

```
adrci> show alert
Choose the home from which to view the alert log:
1: diag/rdbms/rcat/rcat
2: diag/rdbms/cdb01/cdb01
3: diag/rdbms/complref/complref
Q: to quit

Please select option: 3
Output the results to file: /tmp/alert_1768_14054_complref_1.ado
. . .
2014-03-06 22:00:00.221000 -06:00
Setting Resource Manager plan SCHEDULER[0x420F]:DEFAULT_
MAINTENANCE_PLAN via scheduler window
Setting Resource Manager plan DEFAULT_MAINTENANCE_PLAN via
parameter
Starting background process VKRM
VKRM started with pid=27, OS id=12750
. . .
Please select option: q
adrci>
```

Notice that the ADRCI tool tracks all ADR home directories within the ADR root directory. Therefore, you must select which database, ASM, or listener directory you want to view with ADRCI.

Of course, you can perform the same task from Cloud Control. At the bottom of the Cloud Control home page, click the Alert Log Contents link. Then, select the number of lines at the end of the alert log you want to see and click Go. You'll see the page shown in Figure 6-2.

Understanding Alerts, Problems, and Incidents

Although the alert log (either text format or XML format) contains all alerts for the instance, you see the alerts at the warning and critical levels on the Enterprise Manager (EM) home page. You can view specific incidents in the Incident Manager

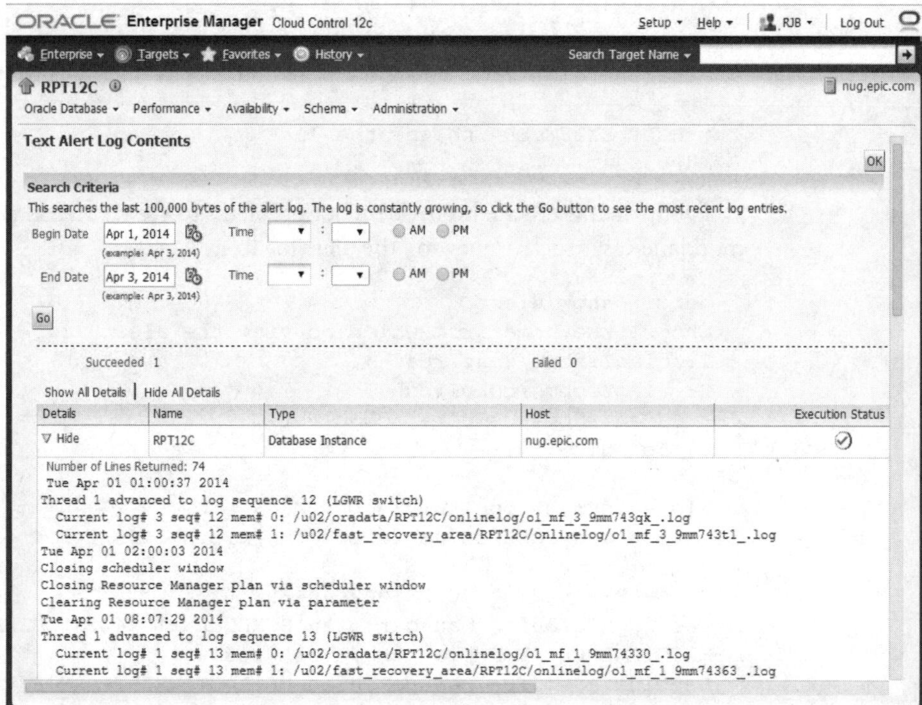

FIGURE 6-2 Viewing alert log contents from Cloud Control

in Cloud Control 12*c*. In Figure 6-3, you see several recent incidents. In the oldest incident (at the bottom), Cloud Control reported that a user was trying to access an object without the proper privileges. In the second-to-last incident, the database reported a data failure, usually attributed to a datafile being missing or corrupted. In the most recent incident, the database reports a user connected to the SYS user or another user with SYSDBA privileges.

A *problem*, defined by the Support Workbench framework, is a critical error in the database, such as the internal error ORA-00600 or some other serious event such as running out of memory in the shared pool or an operating system exception. An *incident* is a single occurrence of a problem. Each problem has a *problem key*, which is a text string that contains the error code and optionally other problem characteristics. A problem may have one or many incidents. Each incident is identified by a numeric incident ID and is stored in its own subdirectory of the ADR

FIGURE 6-3

Viewing error alerts in EM

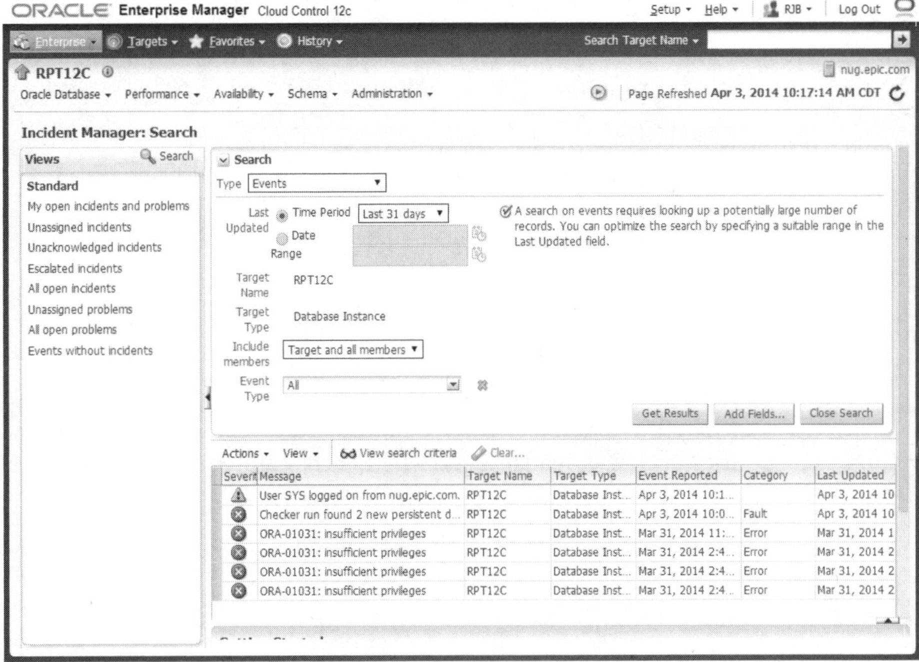

(**ADR_HOME/incident/incdir_*n***). When an incident occurs, the database performs the following steps:

1. Adds an entry to the alert log (both text and XML-based)
2. Sends an incident alert to EM
3. Sends an alert via e-mail to administrators (if configured)
4. Gathers trace files and other incident information
5. Tags all incident information with the incident ID
6. Creates an incident directory under ADR_HOME for the incident and stores incident information and trace files in the directory

Using the Health Monitor

You can use the Oracle Health Monitor framework to proactively or reactively assess the health of your database. Health Monitor checks the status of various database components, including the following:

- Datafiles
- Memory
- Transaction integrity
- Metadata
- Process usage

You can run health checks using Cloud Control via the Support Workbench, or you can manually run a health check using the DBMS_HM PL/SQL package. Some checks can be run only when the database is open. Other checks are available when the instance is running but the database is in NOMOUNT mode. You can list the checks available and whether they are available in offline or online mode by querying the dynamic performance view V$HM_CHECK.

```
SQL> select id, name, offline_capable from v$hm_check;

    ID NAME                                     OFF
------ ---------------------------------------- ---
     1 HM Test Check                            Y
     2 DB Structure Integrity Check             Y
    25 CF Block Integrity Check                 Y
     3 Data Block Integrity Check               Y
     4 Redo Integrity Check                     Y
     5 Logical Block Check                      N
```

```
    10 Transaction Integrity Check          N
    11 Undo Segment Integrity Check         N
    12 No Mount CF Check                    Y
    31 Mount CF Check                       Y
    13 CF Member Check                      Y
    14 All Datafiles Check                  Y
    15 Single Datafile Check                Y
    30 Tablespace Check Check               Y
    16 Log Group Check                      Y
    17 Log Group Member Check               Y
    18 Archived Log Check                   Y
    19 Redo Revalidation Check              Y
    20 IO Revalidation Check                Y
    21 Block IO Revalidation Check          Y
    34 Failover Check                       Y
    22 Txn Revalidation Check               N
    23 Failure Simulation Check             Y
    24 Dictionary Integrity Check           N
    26 ASM Mount Check                      Y
    27 ASM Allocation Check                 Y
    28 ASM Disk Visibility Check            Y
    29 ASM File Busy Check                  Y
    32 ASM Toomanyoff Check                 Y
    33 ASM Insufficient Disks Check         Y
    35 ASM Insufficient Mem Check           Y
    36 ASM DGFDM Check No DG Name           Y
    37 ASM DG Force Dismount Check          Y
    38 ASM Sync IO Fail Check               Y

34 rows selected.
SQL>
```

You can view the results of health checks from the ADRCI tool with the **show hm_run** command. In the following examples, you retrieve the results of a Health Monitor run first in text format, and then you generate a health monitor report in XML format:

```
adrci> show hm_run -p "run_id=36961"

**********************************************************
HM RUN RECORD 1607
**********************************************************
   RUN_ID                        36961
   RUN_NAME                      HM_RUN_36961
   CHECK_NAME                    DB Structure Integrity Check
   NAME_ID                       2
   MODE                          2
```

```
   START_TIME                     2014-02-25 09:37:20.403101 -05:00
   RESUME_TIME                    <NULL>
   END_TIME                       2014-02-25 09:37:20.658541 -05:00
   MODIFIED_TIME                  2014-02-25 09:37:20.658541 -05:00
   TIMEOUT                        0
   FLAGS                          0
   STATUS                         5
   SRC_INCIDENT_ID                0
   NUM_INCIDENTS                  0
   ERR_NUMBER                     0
   REPORT_FILE                    <NULL>

adrci> create report hm_run hm_run_36961
adrci> show report hm_run hm_run_36961
<?xml version="1.0" encoding="US-ASCII"?>
<HM-REPORT REPORT_ID="HM_RUN_36961">
    <TITLE>HM Report: HM_RUN_36961</TITLE>
    <RUN_INFO>
        <CHECK_NAME>DB Structure Integrity Check</CHECK_NAME>
        <RUN_ID>36961</RUN_ID>
        <RUN_NAME>HM_RUN_36961</RUN_NAME>
        <RUN_MODE>REACTIVE</RUN_MODE>
        <RUN_STATUS>COMPLETED</RUN_STATUS>
        <RUN_ERROR_NUM>0</RUN_ERROR_NUM>
        <SOURCE_INCIDENT_ID>0</SOURCE_INCIDENT_ID>
        <NUM_INCIDENTS_CREATED>0</NUM_INCIDENTS_CREATED>
        <RUN_START_TIME>2014-02-25 09:37:20.403101 -05:00</RUN_START_
TIME>
        <RUN_END_TIME>2014-02-25 09:37:20.658541 -05:00</RUN_END_TIME>
    </RUN_INFO>
    <RUN_PARAMETERS/>
    <RUN-FINDINGS/>
</HM-REPORT>
adrci>
```

CERTIFICATION OBJECTIVE 6.02

Handle Block Corruption

Many of the errors you will encounter will be related to bad blocks in your database datafiles, because of either media failures, server memory errors, or logical corruption caused by Oracle errors. Once you've identified these problems using the diagnostic methods provided earlier in this chapter, you can use the tools in the following sections to fix the problems.

As with nearly every Oracle feature, you can adjust the level of control and monitoring that Oracle performs; data block checking is no exception. Regardless of the settings you'll learn about shortly, Oracle always performs the following checks on a data block when it is read or written to a datafile:

- Block version (matches the version of the database)
- Data block address (DBA) in the cache is the same as the DBA value in the block buffer
- Block checksum is correct

You can repair a corrupt block by either recovering the block, dropping the object containing the bad block, or both. The following sections tell you more about block corruption, how to control the amount of overhead Oracle will use to ensure the integrity of blocks, and how to fix a corrupted block.

Understanding Block Corruption

When Oracle detects a corrupted block, it registers an ORA-01578 error in the alert log and on the EM home page. Included in the error message are the absolute file number and block number of the bad block. In addition, the session reading or writing the bad block sees the same error message. Here is an example of a block corruption error message:

```
ORA-01578: ORACLE data block corrupted (file # 6, block # 403)
ORA-01110: data file 6: '/u09/oradata/ord/oe_trans01.dbf'
```

Most often, corruption is caused by operating system or disk hardware failures such as faulty I/O hardware or firmware, operating system caching problems, memory or paging problems, or errors caused by disk repair utilities.

Using the DB_BLOCK_CHECKING Parameter

The initialization parameter DB_BLOCK_CHECKING controls how thoroughly Oracle checks the integrity of every data block that is read or written. The level of checking you enable depends on the level of failure tolerable in your environment (which is usually very low!) balanced against the overhead required to perform the continuous block checks. The possible values for DB_BLOCK_CHECKING are as follows:

- **OFF or FALSE** No block checking is performed.
- **LOW** Basic block checks are performed after blocks are changed in memory or read from disk, including interinstance block transfers in RAC environments.
- **MEDIUM** This includes all LOW checks plus block checking for all non-index-organized table blocks.
- **FULL or TRUE** This includes all LOW and MEDIUM checks plus checks for index blocks.

If you can tolerate the performance overhead, Oracle recommends using FULL. The default value is OFF, even though FULL block checking for the SYSTEM tablespace is always enabled. The overhead for block checking ranges from 1 percent to 10 percent but is closer to 10 percent in an OLTP environment.

Using Block Media Recovery

If you discover only a small handful of blocks to recover in a database from the aforementioned health checks or results discovered in the alert log, RMAN can perform *block media recovery* rather than a full datafile recovery. Block media recovery minimizes the time required to apply the redo logs (since only a small part of each redo log is needed, or possibly no redo logs are required!) and drastically reduces the amount of I/O required to recover only the block or blocks in question. While block media recovery is in progress, the affected datafiles can remain online and available to users.

In addition to the block verification performed by Oracle as defined by the DB_BLOCK_CHECKING initialization parameter, an RMAN BACKUP or BACKUP VALIDATE command can add corrupted blocks to the dynamic performance view V$DATABASE_BLOCK_CORRUPTION. In addition, the SQL commands ANALYZE TABLE and ANALYZE INDEX will detect corrupted blocks.

Block media recovery is available only from within the RMAN application.

You'll need to know the advantages and disadvantages of block media recovery; as you might expect, there are many more advantages than disadvantages. In addition to touting the benefits of RMAN block media recovery, the following sections cover the prerequisites for block media recovery are itemized and provide some real-world use cases.

Advantages of Block Media Recovery

Recovering one or a small number of blocks using RMAN has some obvious and some not-so-obvious advantages. First, recovering one block using a recent backup, together with archived and online redo log files, will almost certainly take much less time than restoring and recovering one or more datafiles. In addition, during block media recovery, the entire datafile remains online and available during the recovery process; only the blocks being recovered are unavailable. Therefore, only one table, index, or other database object remains unavailable during block media recovery.

When you use the RMAN RECOVER . . . BLOCK command, RMAN first searches the flashback logs for a good copy of the corrupted block (if Flashback Database is enabled). Otherwise, RMAN uses the latest level 0 or full backup, restores the bad blocks, and performs media recovery on the bad blocks using the redo stream. Note that RMAN cannot use incremental level 1 backups for block media recovery.

You can use the dynamic performance view V$DATABASE_BLOCK_CORRUPTION to view the bad blocks in the database. This view contains blocks that are both physically and logically corrupted. Here are the tools or commands that can populate this view when they find bad blocks:

- RMAN backup commands
- ANALYZE
- **dbv** operating system utility
- SQL queries that try to access a corrupted block

Prerequisites for Using Block Recovery

Before you can use block media recovery, your database must fulfill a few prerequisites. First, the target database must be in ARCHIVELOG mode. Unless your database is for testing or is a read-only database, your database should be in ARCHIVELOG mode for maximum recoverability anyway!

Second, the backups of datafiles with bad blocks must be full backups or level 0 incremental backups. RMAN cannot use level 1 incremental backups for block recovery. Thus, you must have all archived redo log files since the last full backup or level 0 incremental backup.

Alternatively, you can use flashback logs in the flash recovery area for retrieving uncorrupt versions of bad blocks. Therefore, for this recovery purpose, you can also have Flashback Database enabled. If an uncorrupt version of a bad block is available in the flash recovery area, RMAN will use that version of the block and perform media recovery on the block using archived and online redo log files. Unless the number of bad blocks is large, recovering a block from the flashback logs will certainly be faster than starting with a level 0 incremental or full backup.

Using the RMAN RECOVER . . . BLOCK Command

You can use the RMAN RECOVER . . . BLOCK command in response to an alert or other notification of a bad block. Typically, block corruption is reported in the following locations:

- Output from the RMAN LIST FAILURE, VALIDATE, or BACKUP . . . VALIDATE commands
- The V$DATABASE_BLOCK_CORRUPTION dynamic performance view
- Error messages during a SQL*Plus or other client session
- The alert log or user trace files
- Results from the SQL commands ANALYZE TABLE or ANALYZE INDEX
- Results from the DBVERIFY command-line utility (**dbv**)

To recover one or more data blocks, RMAN must know the datafile number and block number within the datafile. As mentioned previously, this information is available in a user trace file, as in the following example:

```
ORA-01578: ORACLE data block corrupted (file # 6, block # 403)
ORA-01110: data file 6: '/u09/oradata/ord/oe_trans01.dbf'
```

In addition, the block will appear in the view V$DATABASE_BLOCK_CORRUPTION; the columns FILE# and BLOCK# provide the information needed to execute the RECOVER command. The column CORRUPTION_TYPE identifies the type of corruption in the block, such as FRACTURED, CHECKSUM, or CORRUPT. Fixing the block is easily accomplished in RMAN.

```
RMAN> recover datafile 6 block 403;

Starting recover at 04-FEB-14
using channel ORA_DISK_1
```

```
starting media recovery
media recovery complete, elapsed time: 00:00:01

Finished recover at 04-FEB-14

RMAN>
```

A corrupted block must be restored completely. In other words, all redo operations up to the latest SCN against the data block must be applied before the block can be considered usable again.

If all bad blocks are recorded in V$DATABASE_BLOCK_CORRUPTION, you can easily recover all of them at once. Using the following command, RMAN will recover all physically corrupted blocks in V$DATABASE_BLOCK_CORRUPTION.

```
RMAN> recover corruption list;
```

After RMAN recovers the blocks, they are removed from V$DATABASE_BLOCK_CORRUPTION.

Using the Data Recovery Advisor

The Data Recovery Advisor is part of the Oracle advisor framework and automatically gathers information about a failure when an error is encountered. If you run the Data Recovery Advisor proactively, you are often able to detect and repair a failure before a user query or backup operation detects it. The Date Recovery Advisor can detect relatively small errors such as corrupted blocks. At the other end of the spectrum, it will detect errors that would otherwise prevent successful startup of the database, such as missing online redo log files. Your database may continue running for a short amount of time without online redo log files, but it will not start the next time you shut down and restart. Data Recovery Advisor will catch this error proactively.

Identifying Failures

As with most advisors and Oracle features, you can use either Cloud Control or command-line tools to run the Data Recovery Advisor, show the errors, and repair the failures.

Once the Data Recovery Advisor has identified a failure, you can review the details of the failure using the EM or RMAN interface. From RMAN, you can use the LIST FAILURE, ADVISE FAILURE, REPAIR FAILURE, and CHANGE FAILURE commands. Table 6-2 summarizes the purpose of these commands.

TABLE 6-2

RMAN Failure Advisory and Repair Commands

RMAN Command	Description
LIST FAILURE	Lists failures recorded by the Data Recovery Advisor
ADVISE FAILURE	Shows recommended repair option
REPAIR FAILURE	Repairs and closes failure using RMAN's recommendations
CHANGE FAILURE	Changes the status or closes a failure

The LIST FAILURE command has a number of options, depending on what types of errors you want to see:

- ***Failure#*** Lists an individual failure's details (by failure number).
- **ALL** Lists all failures.
- **CRITICAL** Lists failures that make the database unavailable.
- **HIGH** Lists serious failures that make parts of the database unavailable, such as a missing datafile.
- **LOW** Lists intermittent or lower-priority failures that can wait until more serious problems are fixed. For example, this can include corrupted blocks in infrequently used tablespaces.
- **CLOSED** Lists only closed failures.

For example, LIST FAILURE 2097 lists the details for a failure with an identifier of 2097. Also, LIST FAILURE ALL lists all open failures of any priority.

Implementing Repairs

Once the Data Recovery Advisor has identified a failure, you can use the RMAN ADVISE FAILURE command to recommend a repair option for the specified failure. RMAN will suggest a repair and create a script with the recommended repair. If the repair is acceptable (in terms of downtime or other factors), you can then run REPAIR FAILURE (within the same RMAN session) to perform the recommended action. After the repair action completes successfully, the failure is automatically closed.

You can also change the priority of a failure using CHANGE FAILURE. For example, a corrupted block will be recorded as a HIGH failure, but if it is in an infrequently used tablespace, then you can change its priority to LOW so that you see only other more serious failures in the LIST FAILURE command. However, you cannot change the priority of a CRITICAL failure. You can change the priority of a failure only from HIGH to LOW, or vice versa. Here is how you can change the priority of failure number 307 from HIGH to LOW:

```
RMAN> change failure 307 priority low;
```

Data Recovery Advisor Views

There are several dynamic performance views you can use to retrieve information about failures detected by the Data Recovery Advisor.

- **V$IR_FAILURE** Lists all failures, including closed failures
- V$**IR_MANUAL_CHECKLIST** Lists of manual advice
- **V$IR_REPAIR** Lists of repairs
- **V$IR_REPAIR_SET** Cross-references failure and advises on identifier numbers

For example, to retrieve the information for the failure with an ID of 37305, query V$IR_FAILURE as follows:

```
SQL> select failure_id, parent_id, description, status
  2  from v$ir_failure
  3  where failure_id = 37305;

FAILURE_ID  PARENT_ID DESCRIPTION                    STATUS
---------- ---------- ------------------------------ ------------
     37305       1345 Datafile 10: '/u05/oradata/xpo CLOSED
                      rt_dw.dbf' is corrupt

SQL>
```

CERTIFICATION SUMMARY

This chapter started with an overview of the Automatic Diagnostic Repository. ADR is an always-on facility that captures errors in trace and dump files the first and any successive times that they occur. It makes your life easier when an error occurs because it happens without DBA intervention. In addition to facilities within EM, you can use the ADRCI command-line tool to query the contents of ADR when either the database or EM (or both!) is down.

Once ADR has identified one or more problems, you can leverage the information in ADR by using the Support Workbench interface in EM. The tools available through the Support Workbench enable you to view details on problems and incidents, run health checks on your database (either reactively or proactively), generate additional diagnostic data for service requests, and run advisors to help you resolve the problem or incident. It also steps you through packaging all relevant information into a service request for Oracle support when you cannot solve the problem yourself. The Support Workbench makes it easy to analyze a problem and perform further analyses on the problem, potential causes, and solutions. You also learned the differences and similarities between alerts, problems, and incidents.

One of the more common problems you will encounter in your database is block corruption. You can control how thoroughly Oracle checks each data block as it is read and written using the DB_BLOCK_CHECKING initialization parameter. The trade-off is spending more CPU time on the front end to proactively detect problems versus relaxing the block checks and potentially discovering the problem later when you cannot afford the time to fix it.

The chapter closed with one of the RMAN-based repair tools, the Data Recovery Advisor. Using the RMAN command-line or EM interface, you can query all failures (open or closed) with a status of CRITICAL, HIGH, or LOW. Once a failure has been identified, you can use the advice from the Data Recovery Advisor (frequently in the form of an RMAN script) to repair the problem.

TWO-MINUTE DRILL

Describe the Automatic Diagnostic Workflow

- ADR is an always-on facility that captures errors in trace and dump files the first and any subsequent times they occur.
- ADR uses a location on disk to store the diagnostic information and comes with a tool that makes it easy to query the repository even when the database is unavailable.
- Each database instance or Automatic Storage Management instance has its own directory structure called an *ADR home* within a top-level directory known as the *ADR base*.
- The ADR base directory is also known as the *ADR root directory*.
- If the initialization parameter DIAGNOSTIC_DEST is set, the ADR base directory is set to this value, and all other file locations are set relative to this location.
- If DIAGNOSTIC_DEST is not set, then DIAGNOSTIC_DEST is set to the environment variable ORACLE_BASE.
- If ORACLE_BASE is not set, DIAGNOSTIC_DEST is set to the value **$ORACLE_HOME/log**.
- The ADR diagnostic information is partitioned. All nonincident traces are stored in the trace subdirectory, all core dumps are stored in the cdump directory, and all incident dumps are stored as individual directories within the incident subdirectory.
- The ADR Command Interpreter tool makes it easy to query the contents of the ADR. You can use ADRCI even when the database is down.
- ADRCI does not require a login or any other authorization. The contents of the ADR are protected only by operating system permissions on the directory containing the ADR file structures.
- A *problem*, as defined by the Support Workbench framework, is a critical error in the database. An example is the internal error ORA-00600 or some other serious event such as running out of memory in the shared pool or perhaps an operating system exception.
- An *incident* is a single occurrence of a problem.

- Each problem has a *problem key*, which is a text string that contains the error code and optionally other problem characteristics.
- Health Monitor checks the status of various database components, including datafiles, memory, transaction integrity, metadata, and process usage.
- You can run health checks using EM via the Support Workbench, or you can manually run a health check using the DBMS_HM PL/SQL package.

Handle Block Corruption

- When Oracle detects a corrupted block, it registers an ORA-01578 error in the alert log and on the EM home page.
- The initialization parameter DB_BLOCK_CHECKING controls how thoroughly Oracle checks the integrity of every data block that is read or written.
- If you discover only a small handful of blocks to recover in a database from the aforementioned health checks or results discovered in the alert log, then RMAN can perform *block media recovery* rather than a full datafile recovery.
- When you use the RMAN RECOVER . . . BLOCK command, RMAN first searches the flashback logs for a good copy of the corrupted block (if Flashback Database is enabled).
- You can use the dynamic performance view V$DATABASE_BLOCK_CORRUPTION to view the bad blocks in the database.
- The target database must be in ARCHIVELOG mode to use RMAN block recovery.
- Alternatively, you can use flashback logs in the flash recovery area for uncorrupt versions of bad blocks.
- The Data Recovery Advisor is part of the Oracle advisor framework and automatically gathers information about a failure when an error is encountered.
- Once the Data Recovery Advisor has identified a failure, you can review the details of the failure using the EM or RMAN interface.
- Once the Data Recovery Advisor has identified a failure, you can use the RMAN ADVISE FAILURE command to recommend a repair option for the specified failure.

SELF TEST

The following questions will help you measure your understanding of the material presented in this chapter. Read all the choices carefully because there might be more than one correct answer. Choose all correct answers for each question.

Describe the Automatic Diagnostic Workflow

1. The value of the initialization parameter DIAGNOSTIC_DEST is NULL, the environment variable ORACLE_HOME is set to **/u01/app/oracle/product/12.1.0/db_1**, and the value of the environment variable ORACLE_BASE is set to **/u01/app/oracle**. At startup, what value is assigned by Oracle to DIAGNOSTIC_DEST?

   A. /u01/app/oracle/diag

   B. /u01/app/oracle/log

   C. /u01/app/oracle/product/12.1.0/db_1/log

   D. /u01/app/oracle

2. Which of the following tasks can you accomplish using the ADRCI tool?

   A. Package incident information into a ZIP file to send to Oracle support

   B. View diagnostic data within ADR

   C. Perform a health check on the database while it is running

   D. Run recommended fixes from the most recent health check on the database

3. Which of the following file types are not identified in V$DIAG_INFO? (Choose the best answer.)

   A. Diagnostic trace files

   B. Diagnostic incident files

   C. Diagnostic problem files

   D. Active problem count

4. Which of the following advisors can you run from the EM Support Workbench Incident Details page? (Choose two answers.)

   A. The SQL Repair Advisor

   B. The Data Recovery Advisor

   C. The SQL Tuning Advisor

   D. The Disk Repair Advisor

Handle Block Corruption

5. Which of the following basic consistency checks are performed by Oracle when a block is written or read? (Choose all that apply.)
   A. Block checksum.
   B. Data block address in cache matches the address on disk.
   C. Block version.
   D. The data block is below the HWM when reading or updating a block.
6. What are some of the prerequisites for using block media recovery? (Choose all that apply.)
   A. Flashback Database must be enabled.
   B. The database must be in ARCHIVELOG mode.
   C. The last level 1 backup must be available.
   D. DB_BLOCK_CHECKING must be set to LOW, MEDIUM, or FULL.
   E. All archived redo logs since the last full backup must be available.
7. You can use the RMAN CHANGE FAILURE command to change the priority of which types of failures? (Choose all that apply.)
   A. OPEN
   B. HIGH
   C. CRITICAL
   D. LOW
   E. CLOSED

SELF TEST ANSWERS

Describe the Automatic Diagnostic Workflow

1. ☑ **D.** The ADR root directory (also known as the ADR base) is set by the parameter DIAGNOSTIC_DEST. If it is not set, Oracle sets DIAGNOSTIC_DEST to the environment variable ORACLE_BASE. If ORACLE_BASE is not set, then the ADR root directory is set to **$ORACLE_HOME/log.**
☒ **A, B,** and **C** are incorrect. All three locations are not assigned, given the values of DIAGNOSTIC_DEST, ORACLE_BASE, and ORACLE_HOME.

2. ☑ **A** and **B.** The ADRCI tool allows you to view diagnostic information in the ADR root directory in addition to packaging both problem and incident information for Oracle support.
☒ **C** and **D** are incorrect. The ADRCI tool cannot initiate health checks or run fixes recommended by other Oracle diagnostic tools.

3. ☑ **C.** The view V$DIAG_INFO does not specify a directory for problems, only incidents. Each incident is labeled with a text string representing the problem identifier.
☒ **A, B,** and **D** are incorrect. They are listed in V$DIAG_INFO with the operating system–specific path name.

4. ☑ **A** and **B.** You can run either the Data Recovery Advisor or the SQL Repair Advisor from the Incident Details page.
☒ **C** and **D** are incorrect. You cannot initiate the SQL Tuning Advisor from the EM Support Workbench. There is no such advisor as the Disk Repair Advisor.

Handle Block Corruption

5. ☑ **A, B,** and **C.** Oracle performs all of these checks regardless of the setting of DB_BLOCK_CHECKING.
☒ **D** is incorrect because Oracle does not check whether a block is below the high water mark (HWM) when updating or reading a block.

6. ☑ **A, B,** and **E.** To use RMAN's block recovery feature, the database must be in ARCHIVELOG mode, the backups of data files must be full backups or level 0 backups, and archived log files must be available since the last full or level 0 backup. In addition, if Flashback Database is enabled, then RMAN can look for uncorrupted versions of blocks in the flashback logs.
☒ **C** and **D** are incorrect. **C** is incorrect because RMAN cannot use level 1 backups for block recovery. **D** is incorrect because DB_BLOCK_CHECKING does not have to be enabled at all to use block recovery.

7. ☑ **B** and **D.** You can change the priority of a HIGH failure to LOW, and vice versa.
☒ **A, C,** and **E** are incorrect. **A** is incorrect because OPEN is not a failure status. **C** is incorrect because you cannot change the priority of a CRITICAL failure. **E** is incorrect because you cannot change the priority of a CLOSED failure.

7

Encrypting, Securing, Monitoring, and Tuning RMAN Backups

CERTIFICATION OBJECTIVES

7.01	Create RMAN-Encrypted Backups
7.02	Configure and Use Oracle Secure Backup
7.03	Tune RMAN Performance
✓	Two-Minute Drill
Q&A	Self Test

Security is at the forefront of every CIO's strategy. Oracle Database 12*c* provides two types of encrypted backups to ensure that enterprise data is not compromised or seen by the wrong person. The backup method you use (either via Oracle Advanced Security or Oracle Secure Backup) depends on the types of data you're backing up and its destination. As you've seen in previous chapters, RMAN can back up large datafiles as a multisection backup, leveraging multiple output devices (multiple channels either to disk or tape) to dramatically reduce the time it takes to back up the datafile, among other advantages. RMAN's alternative compression techniques and encryption methods further reduce backup size and make the backups unavailable to unauthorized parties by using standalone passwords or the database's encryption wallet.

Oracle Secure Backup, new to Oracle Database 12*c*, is based on a global client-server model where both Oracle databases and file systems can be encrypted and backed up via an enterprise tape library system while still using the familiar RMAN interface. You use the command-line tool **obtool** in addition to a web interface to manage Oracle Secure Backup.

Whether you use encryption, compression, or neither, performance of your RMAN backups is still a major concern. Not only do you want your backups to finish quickly, but you also want to ensure that your backups do not interfere with your daily batch and interactive activity. In a global 24/7 environment, you no longer have the luxury of shutting down the database on a daily or weekly basis to perform backups.

CERTIFICATION OBJECTIVE 7.01

Create RMAN-Encrypted Backups

To ensure the security and privacy of your backups, you can encrypt them in one of three ways: transparent encryption, password encryption, or dual mode encryption. By default, encryption is turned off:

```
CONFIGURE ENCRYPTION FOR DATABASE OFF; # default
CONFIGURE ENCRYPTION ALGORITHM 'AES128'; # default
```

In the following sections, you'll learn how to enable each type of encryption (transparent or password).

Configuring and Using Transparent Encryption

You can set transparent (wallet-based) encryption as the default RMAN encryption method using the CONFIGURE command as follows:

```
RMAN> configure encryption for database on;

new RMAN configuration parameters:
CONFIGURE ENCRYPTION FOR DATABASE ON;
new RMAN configuration parameters are successfully stored
starting full resync of recovery catalog
full resync complete

RMAN>
```

Keep in mind that your database wallet must be open as well. If it is not open, you might think that everything is going as planned—until the encryption process attempts to start. This is shown by the backup failure error message in the following output:

```
RMAN> backup as compressed backupset tablespace users;

Starting backup at 20-MAR-14
allocated channel: ORA_DISK_1
channel ORA_DISK_1: SID=137 device type=DISK
channel ORA_DISK_1: starting compressed full datafile backup set
channel ORA_DISK_1: specifying datafile(s) in backup set
input datafile file number=00006
     name=+DATA/COMPLREF/DATAFILE/users.259.821312559
channel ORA_DISK_1: starting piece 1 at 20-MAR-14
RMAN-00571: ===========================================================
=======
RMAN-00569: =============== ERROR MESSAGE STACK FOLLOWS
===============
RMAN-00571: ===========================================================
=======
RMAN-03009: failure of backup command on ORA_DISK_1 channel
     at 03/20/2014 21:39:32
ORA-19914: unable to encrypt backup
ORA-28365: wallet is not open

RMAN>
```

Setting up an encryption wallet for the instance is easy. Your **sqlnet.ora** file points to the location of the encryption wallet with an entry similar to the following:

```
ENCRYPTION_WALLET_LOCATION=
   (SOURCE=
      (METHOD=FILE)
         (METHOD_DATA=
           (DIRECTORY=/u01/app/oracle/product/12.1.0/dbhome_1/
                    network/admin/wallets)))
```

Within the **$ORACLE_HOME/network/admin/wallet** directory are the database encryption keys. Using an account with the SYSKM or ADMINISTER KEY MANAGEMENT system privilege, or via OS authentication as in this example, create the keystore for the **complref** database:

```
SQL> administer key management
  2  create keystore '/u01/app/oracle/product/12.1.0/dbhome_1/
          network/admin/wallet'
  3  identified by "fre#3dXX0";
```

Don't lose the contents of the files in the wallet directory—back it up. You won't be able to decrypt encrypted tablespaces or encrypted RMAN backups without it.

Opening the wallet at the SQL> prompt (and as of Oracle Database 12*c*, at the RMAN> prompt) and creating a master encryption key makes everything work a lot more smoothly:

```
SQL> connect / as sysdba
Connected.
SQL> administer key management
  2  set keystore open
  3  identified by "fre#3dXX0";

keystore altered.

SQL> administer key management
  2  set key identified by "fre#3dXX0"
  3  with backup using 'master_key_1';
keystore altered.
. . .
RMAN> backup as compressed backupset tablespace users;

Starting backup at 20-MAR-14
allocated channel: ORA_DISK_1
channel ORA_DISK_1: SID=254 device type=DISK
```

```
channel ORA_DISK_1: starting compressed full datafile backup set
channel ORA_DISK_1: specifying datafile(s) in backup set
input datafile file number=00006 name=+DATA/COMPLREF/DATAFILE/
users.259.821312559
channel ORA_DISK_1: starting piece 1 at 20-MAR-14
channel ORA_DISK_1: finished piece 1 at 20-MAR-14
piece handle=+RECOV/COMPLREF/BACKUPSET/2014_03_20
     /nnndf0_tag20140320t233149_0.273.842743911
     tag=TAG20140320T233149 comment=NONE
channel ORA_DISK_1: backup set complete, elapsed time: 00:00:01
Finished backup at 20-MAR-14

RMAN>
```

As you might expect, even if transparent encryption is not the default, you can turn it on just for the duration of a single backup. As in the previous example, the database wallet must be open. Here is an example:

```
RMAN> set encryption on;
executing command: SET encryption
RMAN> backup as compressed backupset tablespace sysaux;

Starting backup at 20-MAR-14
using channel ORA_DISK_1
channel ORA_DISK_1: starting compressed full datafile backup set
channel ORA_DISK_1: specifying datafile(s) in backup set
. . .
842743985 tag=TAG20140320T233305 comment=NONE
channel ORA_DISK_1: backup set complete, elapsed time: 00:01:25
Finished backup at 20-MAR-14
RMAN> set encryption off;
executing command: SET encryption
RMAN>
```

To restore or recover from an encrypted backup, the database wallet must be open, and either the encryption default must be ON or you must use SET ENCRYPTION ON before the recovery operation.

For password-based keystores, you had to specify WITH BACKUP in the earlier example when generating the master encryption key. A new master key need be generated only when you think that security has been compromised. Better yet, change it on a regular basis as a preventive measure.

If you need to restore an older copy of the keystore, you can recover old data only up to the point at which you changed the master encryption key.

Using Password Encryption

To enable password encryption for a specific backup, use the SET ENCRYPTION command as follows:

```
RMAN> set encryption identified by "F45$Xa98";

executing command: SET encryption

RMAN> backup as compressed backupset tablespace users;
. . .
```

on the job

Password encryption is inherently less secure and reliable than transparent (wallet-based) encryption because a password can be lost, forgotten, or intercepted easily. Use password encryption only when backups must be transportable to a different database.

When you want to restore this backup, either to the same database (if wallet-based encryption is off) or to a different database, you must specify the decryption password with SET DECRYPTION:

```
RMAN> set decryption identified by "F45$Xa98";
executing command: SET decryption
RMAN>
```

If you are recovering one or more tablespaces or the entire database from backups that have different passwords, you can conveniently specify all the passwords at once with SET DECRYPTION:

```
RMAN> set decryption identified by "F45$Xa98", "XX407$9!@";

executing command: SET decryption

RMAN>
```

RMAN will try each password in turn for every encrypted backup until it finds a match. RMAN will terminate with an error only if no passwords match any of the passwords in any of the backups.

Using Dual Mode Encryption

You can use both transparent encryption and password encryption at the same time. This is useful if your backup might be used to restore or recover within the same database, and on occasion it can be used to recover another database. When both methods are in effect, you can use either the password or the database wallet to restore the backup. When recovering to a remote database, you must specify the password before recovering, as follows:

```
RMAN> set encryption on identified by "F45$Xa98";

executing command: SET encryption

RMAN>
```

If you want to use only password-based encryption for a backup, add the ONLY clause to SET ENCRYPTION:

```
RMAN> set encryption on identified by "F45$Xa98" only;
```

As a result, even if ENCRYPTION defaults to ON (and therefore uses the wallet), all subsequent backups use password encryption only until you turn off password encryption or exit RMAN altogether.

CERTIFICATION OBJECTIVE 7.02

Configure and Use Oracle Secure Backup

Oracle Database 11*g* introduced multisection, compressed, and encrypted backups. Oracle Database 12*c* takes it several steps further: Not only have the compression options been enhanced, but the Oracle Secure Backup (OSB) option in Oracle Database 12*c* enhances the privacy of the data in your backup by encrypting backups using several new methods. In addition, the range of objects you can back up goes beyond just the database files.

Overview of Oracle Secure Backup

Oracle Secure Backup (OSB) backs up more than just the Oracle database and its components. It now backs up many other objects and files across the enterprise. OSB has its own catalog (much like RMAN has a recovery catalog feature) and can back up the same objects that RMAN can plus objects in external file systems. OSB also works with media servers such as tape libraries or other archive destinations.

The three main components in an OSB environment are as follows:

- **Administrative server** A server somewhere within the enterprise that has the OSB software installed. This could be installed on a database server but is usually on its own dedicated server.
- **Media server** A server that manages tiered storage such as big but slow disks, tape libraries, and optical media.
- **Client** The target for OSB backups. This can be an Oracle database or a file system on another server.

OSB can be leveraged in several ways: via Enterprise Manager Cloud Control 12*c*, seamlessly through RMAN via the existing SBT interface, using the OSB web tool, and using the command-line **obtool** utility.

Installing and Configuring Oracle Secure Backup

To install OSB, start by downloading the latest version of OSB, which as of this writing is 10.4.0.3.0. Designate a directory on the server where you want to install OSB (must be done with root access):

```
[root@oel63 ~]# mkdir /u01/app/oracle/osb
```

Next, download the latest version and use a ZIP utility to unpack the utilities:

```
[oracle@oel63 ~]$ ls Downloads
osb-10.4.0.3.0_linux.x64_release.zip
[oracle@oel63 ~]$ cd Downloads
[oracle@oel63 Downloads]$ unzip osb*.zip
. . .
inflating: osb-10.4.0.3.0_linux.x64_release/doc/doc.104/e21478/
toc.htm
inflating: osb-10.4.0.3.0_linux.x64_release/doc/doc.104/e21478/
apxa.htm
inflating: osb-10.4.0.3.0_linux.x64_release/doc/doc.104/e21478/
contents.js
```

Oracle Secure Backup does not follow the same release numbering scheme as Oracle Database. For Oracle Database 12*c* Release 1, the corresponding version of OSB is 10.4.

Start the installer by running the **setup** script:

```
[root@oel63 osb]# cd /home/oracle/Downloads/osb-10.4.0.3.0_linux.x64_release
[root@oel63 osb-10.4.0.3.0_linux.x64_release]# ls
cdtools  doc.tar      linux86_64    OSB.10.4.0.3.0_LINUX64.rel  welcome.html
doc      install.tar  obreadme.pdf  setup
[root@oel63 osb-10.4.0.3.0_linux.x64_release]# cd /u01/app/oracle/osb
[root@oel63 osb]# /home/oracle/Downloads/
                        osb-10.4.0.3.0_linux.x64_release/setup
Welcome to Oracle's setup program for Oracle Secure Backup.  This
program loads Oracle Secure Backup software from the CD-ROM to a
filesystem directory of your choosing.

This CD-ROM contains Oracle Secure Backup version 10.4.0.3.0_LINUX64.

Please wait a moment while I learn about this host... done.

Would you like to load the Oracle Secure Backup software into your
current directory /u01/app/oracle/osb?
(Oracle recommends using /usr/local/oracle/backup as the Oracle
Secure Backup home)
A 'yes' answer proceeds to use the current directory [yes]:


- - - - - - - - - - - - - - - - - - - - - - - - - - -
   1. linux86_64
      administrative server, media server, client

- - - - - - - - - - - - - - - - - - - - - - - - - - -
Loading Oracle Secure Backup installation tools... done.
Loading linux86_64 administrative server, media server, client... done.
. . .
   generating links for admin installation with Web server
   updating /etc/ld.so.conf
   checking Oracle Secure Backup's configuration file (/etc/obconfig)
   setting Oracle Secure Backup directory
         to /u01/app/oracle/osb in /etc/obconfig
   setting local database directory to /usr/etc/ob in /etc/obconfig
   setting temp directory to /usr/tmp in /etc/obconfig
   setting administrative directory
         to /u01/app/oracle/osb/admin in /etc/obconfig
   setting version to 10.4.0.3.0 in /etc/obconfig
   protecting the Oracle Secure Backup directory
   creating /etc/rc.d/init.d/observiced
   activating observiced via chkconfig
   initializing the administrative domain
. . .
```

Per Oracle recommendations, don't set up tape libraries or drives during installation.

```
Is oel63 connected to any tape libraries that you'd like to use with
Oracle Secure Backup [no]?

Is oel63 connected to any tape drives that you'd like to use with
Oracle Secure Backup [no]?
Installation summary:

    Installation  Host                OS        Driver     OS Move    Reboot
        Mode      Name                Name    Installed?  Required?  Required?

    admin         oel63               Linux    no          no         no

Oracle Secure Backup is now ready for your use.

[root@oel63 osb]#
```

OSB is now installed, and the **obtool** command is available. The user **admin** was created on installation, and its password was specified during installation.

```
[root@oel63 osb]# ./bin/obtool
Oracle Secure Backup 10.4.0.3.0
login: admin
Password:
ob>
```

Using RMAN with Oracle Secure Backup

RMAN (nor any other client that needs its data backed up) cannot automatically use OSB on the backup server and will not explicitly invoke the **obtool** command. Instead, RMAN will connect to OSB via the **sbt** interface. Here are the three requirements for using OSB by RMAN:

- RMAN must be pre-authorized on that host using the **obtool** command.
- The OS user identity of the Oracle instance must match the authorized user.
- The RMAN user must be assigned the pertinent OSB classes to perform Oracle backups and restores.

For example, here is how you would use **obtool** to create an OSB user called **pa_rman** on the host **oel63** to allow RMAN to perform backups under the OS user **oracle**:

```
ob> mkuser pa_rman --class oracle --preauth oel63:oracle+rman
```

From this point on, any RMAN job running under the **oracle** user on the server **oel63** can perform backups of any database objects accessible by the RMAN session.

Another important component of the RMAN to OSB integration is the object type *database backup storage selector*. These selectors are stored within the OSB administrative configuration and consist of the following:

- Database name (*=all) and ID
- Content type (archive log, full, incremental, autobackup)
- Copy number

When an RMAN backup begins, the database name, content type, and copy number are sent to OSB, which translates to a given storage selector that defines the devices and media families to use for the backup.

Miscellaneous obtool Commands

Dozens of **obtool** commands are available, but only a handful will be used on a daily basis. Most of these commands look and act like a Linux command with similar switches. In fact, many of these commands begin with **ls**!

Here's how to show OSB host information:

```
ob> lshost -l
oel63:
    Access mode:            OB
    IP names:               oel63
    Disable RDS:            not set (system default)
    TCP/IP buffer size:     not set (global policy)
    Algorithm:              aes192
    Encryption policy:      allowed
    Rekey frequency:        1 month
    Key type:               transparent
    In service:             yes
    Roles:                  admin,client
    Trusted host:           yes
    Certificate key size:   1024
    UUID:                   3131737a-9359-1031-b4f1-080027356346
ob>
```

Here's how to show detailed user information:

```
ob> lsuser -l
admin:
    Password:                  (set)
    User class:                admin
    Given name:                [none]
    UNIX name:                 root
    UNIX group:                root
    Windows domain/acct:       [none]
    NDMP server user:          no
    Email address:             [none]
    UUID:                      313f7aec-9359-1031-b4f1-080027356346
    Preauthorized access:      [none]
pa_rman:
    Password:                  (not set)
    User class:                oracle
    Given name:                [none]
    UNIX name:                 [none]
    UNIX group:                [none]
    Windows domain/acct:       [none]
    NDMP server user:          no
    Email address:             [none]
    UUID:                      c58b97a8-9363-1031-b781-080027356346
    Preauthorized access:
        Hostname:              oel63
        Username:              oracle
        Windows domain:        [all]
        RMAN enabled:          yes
        Cmdline enabled:       no
ob>
```

Here's how to list dataset backup contents:

```
ob> lsds
Top level dataset directory:
NEW_CLIENTS/
OSB-CATALOG-DS
ob>
```

CERTIFICATION OBJECTIVE 7.03

Tune RMAN Performance

Tuning RMAN backup and recovery operations is frequently an afterthought. If you run a full backup once a week and incremental backups daily, you might not think you need to optimize your backup and recovery operations because they take up only about four hours of your time every week. This logic seems to make sense, until any of the following events occur in your organization:

- Your company expands its offices worldwide, users will be accessing the database at all times of the day and night, and you don't want a backup operation reducing response time.
- New applications increase demand for the tape library system.
- Management demands improvements in the database recovery time to meet service level agreements (SLAs).

Optimizing your RMAN backup and recovery operations will mitigate the effects of these events. You need to understand the importance of tuning RMAN and be able to identify bottlenecks in the different phases of an RMAN backup.

First, you'll learn about the dynamic performance views you can use to monitor an RMAN backup in progress, such as V$SESSION and V$PROCESS. RMAN makes it easy to identify a specific backup job in V$SESSION.

Next, you'll dive into some tuning exercises, using techniques such as multiple channel allocation to improve the performance of your backup operations. You'll also learn where RMAN bottlenecks occur and how to measure a bottleneck with views such as V$BACKUP_SYNC_IO and V$BACKUP_ASYNC_IO. The RMAN BACKUP command offers you a lot of flexibility by letting you control the size of each backup piece, determine how many files to put into a backupset, and decrease the load on the system by defining a desired backup duration.

Monitoring RMAN Sessions and Jobs

At any given point in time, you may have multiple backup jobs running, each with one or more channels. Each channel utilizes one operating system process. If you want to identify which channel is using the most CPU or I/O resources at the operating system level, you can join the dynamic performance views V$SESSION and V$PROCESS to identify the operating system processes associated with each RMAN channel.

In addition to identifying the processes associated with each RMAN job, you can also determine the progress of a backup or restore operation. You can use the dynamic performance view V$SESSION_LONGOPS to identify how much work an RMAN session has completed and the estimated total amount of work.

Finally, RMAN provides troubleshooting information in a number of ways, above and beyond the command output at the RMAN> prompt, when something goes wrong. You can also enable enhanced debugging to help you and Oracle Support identify the cause of a serious RMAN problem.

In the following sections, you'll be introduced to the dynamic performance views V$SESSION, V$PROCESS, and V$SESSION_LONGOPS that can help you identify and monitor RMAN backup and restore jobs. Also, you'll learn where to look when a backup or restore job fails.

Using V$SESSION and V$PROCESS

The dynamic performance view V$PROCESS contains a row for each operating system process connected to the database instance. V$SESSION contains additional information about each session connected to the database, such as the current SQL command and the Oracle username executing the command. These sessions include RMAN sessions. As a result, you can monitor RMAN sessions using these views as well.

RMAN populates the column V$SESSION.CLIENT_INFO with the string **rman** and the name of the channel. Remember that each RMAN channel corresponds to a server process, and therefore V$SESSION will have one row for each channel.

To retrieve information from V$SESSION and V$PROCESS about current RMAN sessions, join the views V$SESSION and V$PROCESS on the PADDR and ADDR columns, as you will see in the first exercise.

EXERCISE 7-1

Monitor RMAN Channels

In this exercise, you'll start an RMAN job that uses two or more channels and retrieve the channel names from V$SESSION and V$PROCESS.

1. Create an RMAN job that backs up the USERS tablespace using two disk channels:

```
RMAN> run {
2>          allocate channel ch1 type disk;
3>          allocate channel ch2 type disk;
```

```
4>          backup as compressed backupset tablespace users;
5>        }

starting full resync of recovery catalog
full resync complete
released channel: ORA_DISK_1
allocated channel: ch1
channel ch1: SID=130 device type=DISK
starting full resync of recovery catalog
full resync complete

allocated channel: ch2
channel ch2: SID=126 device type=DISK
. . .
Finished Control File and SPFILE Autobackup at 20-MAR-14
released channel: ch1
released channel: ch2

RMAN>
```

2. While the RMAN job is running, join the views V$PROCESS and V$SESSION to retrieve the CLIENT_INFO column contents:

```
SQL> select sid, spid, client_info
  2  from v$process p join v$session s on (p.addr = s.paddr)
  3  where client_info like '%rman%'
  4  ;

       SID SPID                     CLIENT_INFO
---------- ------------------------ ------------------------
       126 25070                    rman channel=ch2
       130 7732                     rman channel=ch1

SQL>
```

Note that RMAN's user processes will still exist in V$SESSION until you exit RMAN or start another backup operation.

If you have multiple RMAN jobs running, some with two or more channels allocated, it might be difficult to identify which process corresponds to which RMAN backup or recovery operation. To facilitate the desired differentiation, you can use the SET COMMAND ID command within an RMAN RUN block, as in this example:

```
run {
     set command id to 'bkup users';
     backup tablespace users;
    }
```

When this RMAN job runs, the CLIENT_INFO column in V$SESSION contains the string **id=bkup users** to help you identify the session for each RMAN job.

EXERCISE 7-2

Monitor Multiple RMAN Jobs

In this exercise, you'll start two RMAN jobs and identify each job in V$SESSION and V$PROCESS using the SET COMMAND option in RMAN.

1. Create two RMAN jobs (in two different RMAN sessions) that back up the USERS and CHGTRK tablespaces and use the SET COMMAND option:

```
/* session 1 */
RMAN> run {
2>          set command id to 'bkup users';
3>          backup as compressed backupset tablespace users;
4>       }
. . .
/* session 2 */
RMAN> run {
2>          set command id to 'bkup chgtrk';
3>          backup as compressed backupset tablespace chgtrk;
4>       }
```

2. While the RMAN job is running, join the views V$PROCESS and V$SESSION to retrieve the CLIENT_INFO column contents:

```
SQL> select sid, spid, client_info
  2  from v$process p join v$session s on (p.addr = s.paddr)
  3  where client_info like '%id=%';

       SID SPID                     CLIENT_INFO
---------- ------------------------ ------------------------
       141 19708                    id=bkup users
        94 19714                    id=bkup chgtrk

SQL>
```

Using V$SESSION_LONGOPS

The dynamic performance view V$SESSION_LONGOPS isn't specific to RMAN either. Oracle records any operations that run for more than 6 seconds (in absolute time), including RMAN backup and recovery operations, statistics gathering, and long queries in V$SESSION_LONGOPS.

> **exam watch**
>
> ***The initialization parameter STATISTICS_LEVEL must be set to TYPICAL or ALL before the view V$SESSION_LONGOPS will contain information about long-running RMAN jobs. The default value for STATISTICS_LEVEL is TYPICAL.***

RMAN populates two different types of rows in V$SESSION_LONGOPS: detail rows and aggregate rows. Detail rows contain information about a single RMAN job step, such as creating a single backupset. Aggregate rows apply to all files referenced in a single RMAN command, such as BACKUP DATABASE. As you might expect, aggregate rows are updated less frequently than detail rows.

This example initiates a full database backup, and while the backup is running, both detail and aggregate rows for active RMAN jobs are shown:

```
SQL> select sid, serial#, opname, context, sofar, totalwork
     from v$session_longops
     where opname like 'RMAN%'
       and sofar <> totalwork
     ;

    SID    SERIAL# OPNAME                    CONTEXT      SOFAR  TOTALWORK
------- ---------- ------------------------ -------- ---------- ----------
    130      39804 RMAN: aggregate output          7      97557          0
     94      47546 RMAN: aggregate input           7     191692     331808
    155       1196 RMAN: full datafile backup      1     219980     331808
    155       1196 RMAN: full datafile backup      2     121172          0

SQL>
```

The SID and SERIAL# are the same columns you see in V$SESSION. The OPNAME column is a text description of the operation monitored in the row, and for RMAN, it contains the prefix RMAN:. The CONTEXT column contains a value of 7 for aggregate operations, 2 for backup output operations, and 1 for everything else.

The column SOFAR is, as you might expect, a measure of the progress of a step. Its value differs depending on the type of operation:

- For image copies, it is the number of blocks read.
- For backup input rows, it is the number of blocks read from the files being backed up.
- For backup output rows (backupset or image copy), it is the number of blocks written so far to the backup piece.
- For restore operations, it is the number of blocks processed so far to the destination files.
- For proxy copies (copy operations from a media manager to or from disk), it is the number of files that have been copied so far.

The column TOTALWORK has a similar definition, except that it estimates the total amount of work required during the step:

- For image copies, it is the total number of blocks in the file.
- For backup input rows, it is the total number of blocks to be read from all files in the step.
- For backup output rows, it is always zero because RMAN does not know how many blocks will be written into a backup piece until it is done.
- For restore operations, it is the total number of blocks in all files restored in a single job step or aggregate.
- For proxy copies, it is the total number of files to be copied in the job step.

To calculate the progress of an RMAN step as a percent complete, you can divide SOFAR by TOTALWORK as follows and add this expression to the SELECT statement:

```
round(sofar/totalwork*100,1)
```

Leveraging RMAN Error Logs and Messages

When something goes wrong, RMAN debugging information can be found in several places. The following sections show you where you can find debugging information. When you don't have enough information, you can turn on additional debugging output using the RMAN DEBUG command.

Identifying RMAN Message Output When disaster strikes your RMAN backup and recovery operations, you can find information in many locations, such as the following:

- **RMAN command output** The interactive output you see when you execute RMAN commands at the RMAN> prompt.
- **User-specified RMAN trace file** The output saved to a user-specified trace file when you use the RMAN . . . DEBUG TRACE command at the operating system prompt.
- **Alert log** The standard Oracle alert log location defined by the initialization parameter DIAGNOSTIC_DEST or USER_DUMP_DEST.
- **Oracle trace file** Detailed diagnostic output from Oracle errors generated during RMAN commands, located in DIAGNOSTIC_DEST or USER_DUMP_DEST.
- **Vendor trace files** The file **sbtio.log** or other vendor-assigned filenames containing media-management software errors in DIAGNOSTIC_DEST or USER_DUMP_DEST.

RMAN-specific error messages have a prefix with the format RMAN-*nnnn*, and this message can be preceded or followed by ORA-*nnnnn* messages or vendor-specific messages, depending on the type of error.

Using the RMAN DEBUG Command Turning on RMAN debugging generates a lot of output, so Oracle recommends you specify a file to contain debugging output. To turn on debugging, you use the **debug** option on the RMAN executable's command line. Add the **trace** option to specify a file for the debugging output. Here is an example:

```
[oracle@srv04 ~]$ rman target / catalog rman/rman@rcat \
>       debug trace dbg_rman.trc
```

When RMAN starts, debugging information is sent to the specified trace file. Within an RMAN session, you can turn on or turn off debugging using the DEBUG ON or DEBUG OFF command. For example, you might want to trace the errors when backing up one problematic datafile but not the others.

EXERCISE 7-3

Debug Part of an RMAN Session

In this exercise, you'll turn on RMAN debugging, back up the USERS and SYSAUX tablespaces, but debug only the backup of the CHGTRK tablespace.

1. Start RMAN with the **debug** option:

```
[oracle@oel63 ~]$ rman target / catalog rcat_owner/Rcat9095@rcat
                        debug trace rman_debug.txt

Recovery Manager: Release 12.1.0.1.0 -
      Production on Fri Mar 21 12:18:20 2014

Copyright (c) 1982, 2013, Oracle and/or its affiliates.
    All rights reserved.

RMAN-06005: connected to target database: COMPLREF (DBID=3854704461)
RMAN-06008: connected to recovery catalog database

RMAN>
```

2. Turn off debugging temporarily for the USERS tablespace, but turn it back on for the SYSAUX tablespace:

```
RMAN> run {
2>          debug off;
3>          backup tablespace users;
4>          debug on;
5>          backup tablespace sysaux;
6>         }

Debugging turned off

Starting backup at 21-MAR-14
allocated channel: ORA_DISK_1
channel ORA_DISK_1: SID=140 device type=DISK
. . .
RMAN-08540: channel ORA_DISK_1: backup set complete, elapsed
time: 00:00:35
RMAN-03091: Finished backup at 21-MAR-14

RMAN>
```

3. Verify the size of the trace file:

```
[oracle@oel63 ~]$ ls -l rman*txt
-rw-r--r-- 1 oracle oinstall 467370 Mar 21 12:29 rman_debug.txt
[oracle@oel63 ~]$
```

Note that even for a single tablespace backup, the trace file is larger than 450K bytes.

---

on the Job

Note that the DEBUG command at the RMAN> command line does not do anything unless you specify* debug *when starting the RMAN executable at the operating system command line.

CERTIFICATION OBJECTIVE 7.04

Tune RMAN Performance

You can tune RMAN operations in many ways. You can tune the overall throughput of a backup by using multiple RMAN channels and assigning datafiles to different channels. Each channel is assigned to a single process, so parallel processing can speed the backup process. Conversely, you can multiplex several backup files to the same backup piece. For a particular channel, you can use the MAXPIECESIZE and MAXOPENFILES parameters to maximize throughput to a specific output device. The BACKUP command uses these parameters in addition to FILESPERSET and BACKUP DURATION to optimize your backup operation. You can also use BACKUP DURATION to minimize the effect of the backup on response time if your database must be continuously available and you have to contend with stringent SLAs. Finally, you can also use database initialization parameters to optimize backup and recovery performance, especially for synchronous I/O operations.

If you understand how each tuning method works, you can keep the user response time fast, optimize your hardware and software environment, and potentially delay upgrades when budgets are tight (which is almost always). A throughput *bottleneck* will almost always exist somewhere in your environment. A bottleneck is the slowest step or task during an RMAN backup.

The next section reviews the basic steps that a channel performs during a backup operation. The techniques presented in the following sections will help you identify where the bottleneck is within the channel's tasks and how to minimize its impact on backup and recovery operations.

Identifying Backup and Restore Steps

RMAN backup performs its tasks within a channel in one of three main phases:

1. **Read phase** The channel reads data blocks into the input buffers.
2. **Copy phase** The channel copies blocks from the input buffers to the output buffers and performs additional processing, if necessary:
   - **Validation** Check blocks for corruption, which is not CPU-intensive.
   - **Compression** Use BZIP2 or ZLIB to compress the block, which is CPU-intensive.
   - **Encryption** Use an encryption algorithm (transparent, password-protected, or both) to secure the data, which is CPU-intensive.
3. **Write phase** The channel writes the blocks from the output buffers to the output device (disk or tape).

Using dynamic performance views, you can identify which phase of which channel operation is the bottleneck and address it accordingly.

In some scenarios, you may want to increase the backup time to ensure that the recovery time will be short. Creating image copies and recovering the image copies on a daily or hourly basis will add to the backup time but will dramatically reduce recovery time.

Parallelizing Backupsets

One of the simplest ways to improve RMAN performance is to allocate multiple channels (either disk or tape). The number of channels you allocate should be no larger than the number of physical devices; allocating two or more channels (and therefore processes) for a single physical device will not improve performance and may even decrease performance. If you're writing to a single Automatic Storage Management (ASM) disk group or a file system striped by the operating system, you can allocate more channels and improve throughput since the logical ASM disk group or striped file system maps to two or more physical disks. You can allocate up to 255 channels, and each channel can read up to 64 datafiles in parallel. Each channel writes to a separate backup copy or image copy.

If the number of datafiles in your database is relatively constant, you can allocate a fixed number of channels and assign each datafile to a specific channel. Here is an example:

```
run {
      allocate channel dc1 device type disk;
      allocate channel dc2 device type disk;
      allocate channel dc3 device type disk;
      backup incremental level 0
        (datafile 1,2,9    channel dc1)
        (datafile 3,8,7    channel dc2)
        (datafile 4,6,7    channel dc3)
        as compressed backupset;
    }
```

Note also that you can specify the path name for a datafile instead of the datafile number, as in this example:

```
(datafile '/u01/oradata/users02.dbf' channel dc2)
```

To automate this process further, you can use the CONFIGURE command to increase the parallelism for each device type. Here is the default RMAN configuration for disk device channels:

```
CONFIGURE DEVICE TYPE DISK PARALLELISM 1 BACKUP
      TYPE TO BACKUPSET; # default
```

Understanding RMAN Multiplexing

You can improve RMAN performance and throughput by *multiplexing* backup and recovery operations. Multiplexing enables RMAN to read from multiple files simultaneously and write the data blocks to the same backup piece.

You cannot multiplex image copies.

Using multiplexing as an RMAN tuning method is one way to reduce bottlenecks in backup and recovery operations. The level of multiplexing is primarily controlled by two parameters: FILESPERSET and MAXOPENFILES.

The FILESPERSET parameter of the RMAN BACKUP command determines the number of datafiles to put in each backupset. If a single channel backs up ten datafiles and the value of FILESPERSET is 4, RMAN will back up only four files per backupset. The parameter FILESPERSET defaults to 64.

The level of multiplexing (the number of input files that are read and written to the same backup piece) is the minimum of MAXOPENFILES and the number of files in each backupset. The default value for MAXOPENFILES is 8. Here is an equation that may make the calculation easier to understand:

```
multiplexing_level =
        min(MAXOPENFILES, min(FILESPERSET, files_per_channel))
```

TABLE 7-1 RMAN Datafile Buffer Sizing

Level of Multiplexing	Size of Input Disk Buffer
<= 4	16 buffers of 1MB each divided among all input files
5–8	A variable number of 512MB buffers to keep total buffer size under 16MB
> 8	Total of 4 buffers of 128KB for each (512KB) for each input file

This example backs up ten datafiles in one channel. The value for MAXOPENFILES is 12, and the value for FILESPERSET is at the default value of 64. Therefore, the multiplexing level is calculated as follows:

```
multiplexing_level = min(12, min(64, 10)) = 10
```

RMAN allocates a different number and size of disk I/O buffers depending on the level of multiplexing in your RMAN job. Once the level of multiplexing is derived by RMAN using the FILESPERSET and MAXOPENFILES parameters in the aforementioned equation, you can use the information in Table 7-1 to find out how many and what size buffers RMAN needs to perform the backup.

Oracle recommends that the value FILESPERSET should be 8 or less to optimize recovery performance. In other words, putting too many input files into a single backupset will slow down a recovery operation because the RESTORE or RECOVER command will still have to read a large number of unneeded blocks in the backupset when you recover a single datafile.

Tuning RMAN Channels

You can further tune your RMAN backup performance by tuning individual channels with the CONFIGURE CHANNEL and ALLOCATE CHANNEL commands. Each CHANNEL command accepts the following parameters:

- **MAXPIECESIZE** The maximum size of a backup piece
- **RATE** The number of bytes per second read by RMAN on the channel
- **MAXOPENFILES** The maximum number of input files that a channel can have open at a given time

The MAXPIECESIZE parameter is useful when you back up to disk and the underlying operating system limits the size of an individual disk file or when a tape media manager cannot split a backup piece across multiple tapes.

Note that the RATE parameter doesn't improve performance but throttles performance intentionally to limit the disk bandwidth available to a channel. This is useful when your RMAN backups must occur during periods of peak activity elsewhere in the database.

MAXOPENFILES was reviewed in the preceding section, but it is worth revisiting when you want to optimize the performance of an individual channel. For example, you can use MAXOPENFILES to limit RMAN's use of operating system file handles or buffers.

Tuning the BACKUP Command

Just like the CONFIGURE CHANNEL command, the BACKUP command has parameters that can help you improve performance or limit the computing resources that a channel uses for an RMAN backup. Here are the key tuning parameters for the BACKUP command:

- **MAXPIECESIZE** The maximum size of a backup piece per channel
- **FILESPERSET** The maximum number of files per backupset
- **MAXOPENFILES** The maximum number of input files that a channel can have open at a given time
- **BACKUP DURATION** Decrease or increase the time to complete the backup

You've seen the parameters MAXPIECESIZE, FILESPERSET, and MAXOPENFILES before. Note that MAXPIECESIZE and MAXOPENFILES have the same purpose as in the CHANNEL commands, except that they apply to all channels in the backup.

BACKUP DURATION specifies an amount of time to complete the backup. You can qualify this option with MINIMIZE TIME to run the backup as fast as possible or with MINIMIZE LOAD to use the entire time frame specified in the BACKUP DURATION window. In addition, you can use the PARTIAL option, as you might expect, to save a partial backup that was terminated because of time constraints. For example, to limit a full database backup to two hours, run it as fast as possible, and save a partial backup, use this command:

```
RMAN> backup duration 2:00 partial database;
```

If the backup does not complete in the specified time frame, the partial backup is still usable in a recovery scenario after a successive BACKUP command finishes the backup and you use the PARTIAL option.

Configuring LARGE_POOL_SIZE

You can adjust the value of the initialization parameter LARGE_POOL_SIZE to improve RMAN backup performance. If you do not set LARGE_POOL_SIZE, the RMAN server processes use memory from the shared pool. This may cause contention with many other processes that use the shared pool. If RMAN's request for memory from the shared pool cannot be fulfilled, RMAN uses memory from the Program Global Area (PGA), writes a message to the alert log, and uses synchronous I/O for this backup. But synchronous I/O can be inefficient; therefore, you can resize the value of the large pool for disk backups using this calculation:

```
additional_large_pool_size = #channels * 16MB
```

If you are backing up to tape, add memory to account for the size of the tape driver buffer (equivalent to the RMAN channel parameter BLKSIZE):

```
additional_large_pool_size = #channels * (16MB + (4 * tape_buffer_size))
```

Note also that RMAN will use memory from the large pool only if DBWR_IO_SLAVES is set to a value greater than zero.

CERTIFICATION SUMMARY

To enhance the security of your backups, RMAN can use either password-based or wallet-based encryption, or it can use both at the same time. Wallet-based encryption is the preferred method, but in cases where you must restore your datafiles to another database, providing a strong password keeps the backup secure until you are ready to restore it into a target database.

Oracle Secure Backup goes beyond just database backup on a single server to coordinating and storing backups of multiple databases and file systems across the enterprise. OSB authenticates and integrates RMAN clients and can back up Oracle databases to tape libraries on the administrative server through the existing RMAN **sbt** interface.

This chapter also provided a short but important list of tips to help you effectively tune your RMAN operations to maximize the throughput of your backup and recovery operations. First, you learned how to monitor the progress of RMAN jobs using the dynamic performance views V$SESSION, V$PROCESS, and V$SESSION_LONGOPS.

Other RMAN tuning methods include increasing the multiplexing level for one or more channels, tuning the BACKUP command with its command-line options, and configuring LARGE_POOL_SIZE for large RMAN memory buffer requests.

TWO-MINUTE DRILL

Create RMAN-Encrypted Backups

- Transparent encryption uses a database wallet to encrypt a backup, and the backup can be restored only to the source database.
- Password encryption uses a password to encrypt a backup, and the backup can be restored either to the source database or to another database.
- You can use both transparent encryption and password encryption on the same backup.
- Transparent encryption can be enabled for a single backup using the SET ENCRYPTION command.

Configure and Use Oracle Secure Backup

- Oracle Secure Backup is hosted on an administrative server and provides the interface between RMAN and media servers for both databases and file systems across the enterprise.
- An OSB storage selector consists of a database name, content type, and copy number.
- RMAN passes the storage selector to OSB and processes the backup job.
- OSB maintains its own backup catalog.
- Typical OSB **obtool** commands perform tasks such as showing registered hosts (**lshost**), devices (**lsdev**), backup datasets (**lsds**), and volumes (**lsvol**).

Tune RMAN Performance

- You can join V$SESSION with V$PROCESS to identify the operating system processes associated with each RMAN channel.
- The RMAN command SET COMMAND ID helps you to distinguish processes for different backup jobs in V$SESSION.
- Use V$SESSION_LONGOPS to monitor the status of RMAN jobs that run for more than 6 seconds.
- The view V$SESSION_LONGOPS contains both detail rows and aggregate rows for each RMAN job.

- You must set the initialization parameter STATISTICS_LEVEL to TYPICAL or ALL before RMAN will record job status information in V$SESSION_LONGOPS.
- RMAN debugging information appears in command-line output, RMAN-specific trace files, the alert log, Oracle trace files, and vendor-specific trace files.
- Add the **debug** option to the operating system command line to turn debugging on and optionally specify a file to contain the debugging output.
- Use the DEBUG ON or DEBUG OFF command to turn on or turn off RMAN debugging within an RMAN session.
- RMAN backup or recovery jobs perform tasks in three main phases: read, copy, and write.
- The RMAN copy phase is further broken down into three subphases: validation, compression, and encryption.
- Parallelization (allocating multiple channels) can improve backup performance.
- You can allocate up to 255 channels per RMAN session, and each channel can read up to 64 datafiles in parallel.
- Multiplexing is primarily controlled by the RMAN parameters FILESPERSET and MAXOPENFILES.
- You can calculate the level of multiplexing by using this formula: MIN(MAXOPENFILES, MIN(FILESPERSET, FILES_PER_CHANNEL)).
- You tune RMAN channels by using the MAXPIECESIZE, RATE, and MAXOPENFILES parameters.
- You tune the BACKUP command by using the MAXPIECESIZE, FILESPERSET, MAXOPENFILES, and BACKUP DURATION parameters.
- The BACKUP parameter BACKUP DURATION can be set to MINIMIZE TIME to perform the backup as quickly as possible or can be set to MINIMIZE LOAD to reduce the I/O demands on the database.
- You can configure the initialization parameter LARGE_POOL_SIZE to reduce contention on the shared pool for RMAN backups.

SELF TEST

The following questions will help you measure your understanding of the material presented in this chapter. Read all the choices carefully because there might be more than one correct answer. Choose all correct answers for each question.

Create RMAN-Encrypted Backups

1. You have a datafile from the smallfile tablespace USERS that has a size of 90MB, and you run the following RMAN command:

```
RMAN> backup tablespace users section size 40m;
```

   How many sections does this backup create?

   A. The command does not run because multisection backups apply only to bigfile tablespaces.

   B. Two sections of 45MB each.

   C. Two sections of 40MB each and one section of 10MB.

   D. The command does not run because you can back up the entire database only as a multisection backup.

2. Identify the true statement about the dynamic performance and data dictionary views related to multisection backups.

   A. The views V$BACKUP_SET and RC_BACKUP_SET have a column named MULTI_SECTION. The views V$BACKUP_DATAFILE and RC_BACKUP_DATAFILE have a column named SECTION_SIZE.

   B. The views V$BACKUP_SET and RC_BACKUP_SET have a column named SECTION_SIZE. The views V$BACKUP_DATAFILE and RC_BACKUP_DATAFILE have a column named MULTI_SECTION.

   C. The views V$BACKUP_SET and V$BACKUP_DATAFILE have a column named MULTI_SECTION. The views RC_BACKUP_SET and RC_BACKUP_DATAFILE have a column named SECTION_SIZE.

   D. The views V$BACKUP_SET and V$BACKUP_DATAFILE have a column named SECTION_SIZE. The views RC_BACKUP_SET and RC_BACKUP_DATAFILE have a column named MULTI_SECTION.

Configure and Use Oracle Secure Backup

3. Which of the following attributes or characteristics are passed by RMAN to OSB when performing a backup? Assume that the RMAN client has already been registered with OSB. (Choose all that apply.)
   A. Content type
   B. Unique hostname
   C. Database ID
   D. Database name
   E. Copy number
   F. Requested media group number
4. What RMAN retention policy should you use if the RMAN backups leverage OSB?
   A. RMAN inherits the OSB retention policy.
   B. RECOVERY WINDOW.
   C. COPIES.
   D. OSB inherits the RMAN retention policy.

Tune RMAN Performance

5. Which of the following two dynamic performance views can you use to identify the relationship between Oracle server sessions and RMAN channels?
   A. V$PROCESS and V$SESSION
   B. V$PROCESS and V$BACKUP_SESSION
   C. V$PROCESS and V$BACKUP_ASYNC_IO
   D. V$BACKUP_ASYNC_IO and V$SESSION
   E. V$BACKUP_SYNC_IO and V$BACKUP_ASYNC_IO
6. You create three RMAN sessions to back up three different tablespaces. Your third RMAN session runs this command:

```
run {
        set command id to 'user bkup';
        backup tablespace users;
    }
```

   What values does the column V$SESSION.CLIENT_INFO have for this command? (Choose all that apply.)
   A. rman channel=ORA_DISK_1, id=user bkup.
   B. id=user bkup, rman channel=ORA_DISK_1.
   C. id=user bkup, cmd=backup tablespace users.

D. id=user bkup.

E. The column CLIENT_INFO is in V$PROCESS, not V$SESSION.

7. Identify the location where RMAN message output and troubleshooting information can be found. (Choose all that apply.)

A. The Oracle server trace file

B. The RMAN trace file

C. The view V$PROCESS

D. The database alert log

E. RMAN command output

F. The vendor-specific file **sbtio.log**

G. The table SYS.AUDIT$

8. The initialization parameters in your database are set as follows:

```
BACKUP_TAPE_IO_SLAVES = TRUE
LARGE_POOL_SIZE = 50M
JAVA_POOL_SIZE = 75M
PGA_AGGREGATE_TARGET = 20M
```

Identify the correct statements regarding where RMAN allocates the memory buffers for tape backup.

A. RMAN uses the Java pool in the SGA.

B. RMAN uses the shared pool in the SGA.

C. RMAN allocates memory from the large pool in the PGA.

D. RMAN allocates memory from the large pool in the SGA.

9. Which of the following are bottlenecks that affect RMAN backup and recovery operations? (Choose all that apply.)

A. Reading data from the database

B. Writing data to disk

C. Writing data to tape

D. Validating data blocks

E. Using SGA memory buffers versus PGA memory buffers

10. Which RMAN parameter(s) control multiplexing to disk and tape? (Choose the best answer.)

A. FILESPERSET from the BACKUP command

B. FILESPERSET from the BACKUP command and MAXOPENFILES from the CONFIGURE command

C. FILESPERSET from the CONFIGURE command and MAXOPENFILES from the BACKUP command

D. MAXOPENFILES from the CONFIGURE command

SELF TEST ANSWERS

Create RMAN-Encrypted Backups

1. ☑ **C.** RMAN backs up the datafile in multiples of the section size, and any remainder resides in the last section.
☒ **A, B,** and **D** are incorrect. **A** is incorrect because you can use multisection backups for any type of tablespace. **B** is incorrect because RMAN does not round up the section size to create equal section sizes in the output. **D** is incorrect because you can back up either an individual tablespace or the entire database as a multisection backup.

2. ☑ **C.** SECTION_SIZE indicates the section size for the backup piece. MULTI_SECTION has a value of YES or NO to indicate whether the backup is a multisection backup.
☒ **A, B,** and **D** are incorrect. Each of these answers has an invalid combination of columns and their associated views.

Configure and Use Oracle Secure Backup

3. ☑ **A, C, D,** and **E.** When RMAN sends a backup request to OSB, you must specify the database name (or ID), the content type, and the copy number. Given this information, OSB will use the stored backup storage selector and send the backup to the appropriate backup devices and media family.
☒ **B** and **F** are incorrect. **B** is incorrect because the hostname is used to register the RMAN client with the OSB administration server but is not needed for each backup. **F** is incorrect because RMAN does not select the media group number; OSB does.

4. ☑ **B.** You should use a RECOVERY WINDOW retention policy when using RMAN with OSB. You will use a certain amount of disk space in the fast recovery area for meeting the recovery needs for a certain number of hours each day; longer recovery operations will also leverage tape backups managed by OSB. You will use an **obtool** command to create a media family for RMAN backups.
☒ **A, C,** and **D** are incorrect. **A** and **D** are incorrect because there is no inheritance of backup retention policies between RMAN and OSB. **C** is incorrect because you will not be able to leverage the contents of the fast recovery as much as you could with a recovery window-based policy.

Tune RMAN Performance

5. ☑ **A.** You join the views V$PROCESS and V$SESSION on the ADDR and PADDR columns and select rows where the beginning of the column CLIENT_INFO contains the string RMAN.
☒ **B, C, D,** and **E** are incorrect. **B** is incorrect because there is no such view V$BACKUP_SESSION. **C, D,** and **E** are incorrect because you use V$BACKUP_ASYNC_IO and

V$BACKUP_SYNC_IO to monitor the performance of RMAN jobs for asynchronous and synchronous I/O, respectively.

6. ☑ **B** and **D.** The view V$SESSION has two rows for each backup process, both of them with the value specified in the RMAN command SET COMMAND ID.
☒ **A**, **C**, and **E** are incorrect. **A** is incorrect because the values for CLIENT_INFO are in the incorrect order. **C** is incorrect because the actual RMAN command is not included in CLIENT_INFO. **E** is incorrect because CLIENT_INFO is, in fact, in the view V$SESSION.

7. ☑ **A, B, D, E,** and **F.** RMAN debugging information and other message output can be found in the Oracle server trace files, the RMAN trace file, the database alert log, output from the RMAN command itself, and the vendor-specific file **sbtio.log** (for tape libraries).
☒ **C** and **G** are incorrect. RMAN does not record any debugging or error information in the view V$PROCESS or in the table SYS.AUDIT$.

8. ☑ **D.** If you set BACKUP_TAPE_IO_SLAVES to TRUE, then RMAN allocates tape buffers from the shared pool unless the initialization parameter LARGE_POOL_SIZE is set, in which case RMAN allocates tape buffers from the large pool.
☒ **A, B,** and **C** are incorrect. The parameters JAVA_POOL_SIZE and PGA_AGGREGATE_TARGET have no effect on the location of the RMAN buffers.

9. ☑ **A, B, C,** and **D.** All of these options are potential bottlenecks.
☒ **E** is incorrect. The location of the RMAN data buffers is not a factor that can cause a bottleneck and reduce RMAN throughput.

10. ☑ **B.** Both FILESPERSET and MAXOPENFILES control the level of multiplexing during an RMAN backup operation.
☒ **A, C,** and **D** are incorrect. **A** is incorrect because MAXOPENFILES in the CONFIGURE command also controls the level of multiplexing, not just FILESPERSET. **C** is incorrect because FILESPERSET is not a valid option for the CONFIGURE command, and MAXOPENFILES is not a valid option for the BACKUP command. **D** is incorrect because MAXOPENFILES of the CONFIGURE command is not the only parameter that controls the level of multiplexing.

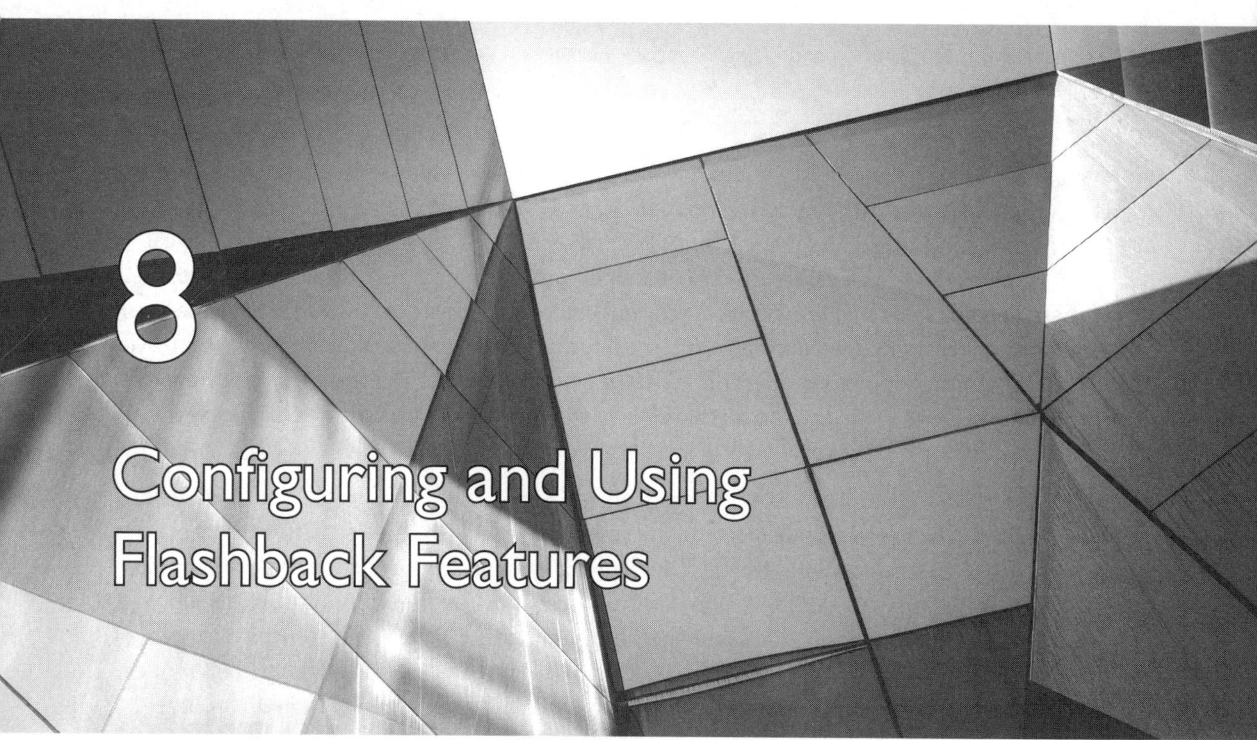

8

Configuring and Using Flashback Features

CERTIFICATION OBJECTIVES

8.01	Describe the Flashback Technologies	8.05	Describe and Use Flashback Data Archive
8.02	Use Flashback to Query Data	8.06	Perform Flashback Database
8.03	Perform Flashback Table Operations	✓	Two-Minute Drill
8.04	Perform Table Recovery from Backups	Q&A	Self Test

Disaster strikes when you least expect it, and Oracle's flashback features, which are part of Oracle's Flashback Technology suite, make it easy to recover from logical corruptions such as erroneously dropped tables or incorrect transactions. Most, if not all, of these recovery options are available to database users, freeing up the DBA for other tasks and potentially decreasing the recovery time. Flashback technology makes it easy for you to view the changes from the erroneous operations before you reverse the changes. You can view all data at a point in time, all changes to a row for a particular time period, or all changes within a specific transaction.

Oracle's flashback features are supported by one of three structures in the database: undo data, the flash recovery area, and the recycle bin. The *undo data* in the UNDO tablespace, in addition to supporting transaction rollback, supports most of the Flashback Table operations. *Flashback Data Archives* support queries of previous versions of table rows. Flashback Data Archives provide an area in one or more tablespaces outside of the UNDO tablespace to support a much longer retention period than an UNDO tablespace can. *Flashback logs*, which reside in the flash recovery area, make it easy to roll back your entire database to a previous time without performing a traditional restore and recovery operation. The *recycle bin* within each tablespace contains one or more versions of dropped tables and indexes, which can easily be restored by the user as long as there is no space pressure within the tablespace.

This chapter covers Flashback Drop after reviewing the role of the UNDO tablespace for other database features. Flashback Drop relies on a construct introduced in Oracle Database 10*g*, the recycle bin. The recycle bin is a data dictionary table that tracks one or more versions of dropped tables and allows you to recover any version of the table to its state immediately before it was dropped.

Next, you'll learn about flashback technologies at the table level. You can query a table to see what a row looked like at a particular time, and depending on how far back in time you need to go, Oracle will use either undo data or a Flashback Data Archive (FDA) if it is configured. You can also query the contents of a particular row as it changed during a specified time interval, or you can query changes to all rows for a particular database transaction.

Until Oracle Database 12*c*, your table recovery options were limited to recovering from the recycle bin, using the UNDO tablespace, or using a Flashback Data Archive for designated tables. But what if the table you want to recover is no longer in the recycle bin or the undo data required for table recovery has long since been purged from the UNDO tablespace? Or what if you did not realize how critical a table was and didn't have that table assigned to an FDA? You could restore and recover the database from a full backup, but the space and time requirements are usually prohibitive. As of Oracle Database 12*c*, you can perform a table recovery from an RMAN backup.

Finally, you'll learn how to use flashback technology at the database level with Flashback Database. Although you don't want to use a sledgehammer on a mosquito, you may have to roll back an entire database to an earlier point in time if the logical corruptions are widespread or the object dependencies make it difficult or impossible to use flashback technologies at the table level.

CERTIFICATION OBJECTIVE 8.01

Describe the Flashback Technologies

The Oracle Flashback technologies, formerly known as Total Recall, seem quite homogenous from a technology perspective until you look under the covers. These technologies are divided into two broad categories: analysis and recovery. First, you need to know what to fix and how to fix it; then, you need the tools to actually fix the logical errors!

Flashback Types and Dependencies

The Flashback error analysis tools include the following:

- **Flashback query** View committed data as of a point of time in the past given a timestamp or system change number (SCN).
- **Flashback Versions query** View all versions of a set of rows between two SCNs or timestamps.
- **Flashback Transaction query** View changes to a set of dependent objects for a given transaction ID number.

Once the logically incorrect data has been identified using one or more of the methods described, you can pick one or more of the following tools to fix the errors:

- **Flashback Transaction Backout** Roll back a specific transaction along with any dependent transactions.

- **Flashback Table** Rewind a single table to a point of time in the past without affecting the contents of any other tables.
- **Flashback Drop** Retrieve a table and its dependent objects (indexes, triggers, and so forth) from the recycle bin, if available.
- **Flashback Database** Rewind the entire database to a point in time in the past using flashback logs in the Fast Recovery Area (FRA).

Each of these technologies, for either identifying or fixing a logical data corruption, relies on a slightly different construct in the database. Table 8-1 lists the Flashback Technology type, the object level, and the database construct the technology depends on.

Configuring Flashback Parameters

To utilize flashback functionality fully, you need to configure your UNDO tablespace correctly. Your initialization parameters for the UNDO tablespace should look something like the following:

```
undo_management = auto
undo_tablespace = undotbs1
undo_retention = 1800
```

The UNDO_RETENTION parameter in this example specifies that the UNDO tablespace should retain undo data for at least 1,800 seconds (30 minutes) as long as enough space exists in the UNDO tablespace. Setting UNDO_MANAGEMENT to AUTO directs Oracle to subsequently adjust the undo retention based on the size of the UNDO tablespace. By default, unexpired undos will be overwritten

TABLE 8-1 Flashback Technologies and Dependencies

Flashback Type	Affected Object	Dependent On
Database	Database	Flashback logs
Drop	Table/index/constraint	Recycle bin
Table	N/A	Undo data
Query	N/A	Undo data
Version Query	N/A	Undo data
Transaction Query	Transaction query	Undo and redo from archived redo log files
Data Archive	Table/transaction	Tablespace

to ensure that DML operations will not fail due to a lack of available space in the UNDO tablespace.

exam watch

The UNDO_RETENTION parameter is ignored if your UNDO tablespace is a fixed size. In this case, Oracle automatically adjusts UNDO_RETENTION to give the best retention period based on the tablespace size and the current system load.

To ensure the success of flashback operations or long-running queries at the expense of DML activity, you must specify RETENTION GUARANTEE for the UNDO tablespace either when you create the tablespace or later with the ALTER TABLESPACE command, as in this example:

```
SQL> alter tablespace undotbs1 retention guarantee;

Tablespace altered.

SQL>
```

You can check the retention status of an UNDO tablespace by querying the data dictionary view DBA_TABLESPACES, as in this example:

```
SQL> select tablespace_name, retention
  2  from dba_tablespaces
  3  where contents = 'UNDO';

TABLESPACE_NAME                RETENTION
------------------------------ -----------
UNDOTBS1                       GUARANTEE

SQL>
```

When retention guarantee is enabled, the specified minimum undo retention period is guaranteed. As a result, DML activity can fail if long-running queries or flashback operations are using unexpired undo information.

If you need a much longer retention period for a subset of tables in the database, you should use Flashback Data Archive, which is covered later in this chapter.

CERTIFICATION OBJECTIVE 8.02

Use Flashback to Query Data

Flashback query makes it easy to see a row in a table at a particular time. In the following sections, you'll learn how to use Flashback Query to view one or more rows in a table at a time in the past. In addition, you'll see how to use flashback version query to view a single row's contents over a specified time range. Before you dive into any undo-dependent flashback features, however, you need to get familiar with the basic tablespace and initialization parameters that support flashback operations.

Using Flashback Query

Flashback Query allows you to query data in one or more tables in a SELECT query as of a time in the past. Any changes to data in a table generates undo (or optionally data in a Flashback Data Archive), which can give you a snapshot of the entire database down to the granularity of a transaction.

Flashback Query uses the AS OF clause to specify the previous point in time as a timestamp or system change number. In the following example, the user HR is cleaning up the EMPLOYEES table and deletes two employees who no longer work for the company:

```
SQL> delete from employees
  2  where employee_id in (195,196);
2 rows deleted.

SQL> commit;
Commit complete.

SQL>
```

Normally, the user HR will copy these rows to the EMPLOYEES_ARCHIVE table first, but she forgot to do that this time. The user HR doesn't need to put those rows back into the EMPLOYEES table, but she needs to put the two deleted rows into the archive table. Because the user HR knows she deleted the rows less than an hour ago, she can use a relative timestamp value with Flashback Query to retrieve the rows:

```
SQL>  insert into hr.employees_archive
  2      select * from hr.employees
  3         as of timestamp systimestamp - interval '60' minute
  4         where hr.employees.employee_id not in
  5              (select employee_id from hr.employees);
```

```
2 rows created.

SQL> commit;
Commit complete.

SQL>
```

You can use this to retrieve the employee records that existed an hour ago but do not exist now because you know that EMPLOYEE_ID is the primary key of the table. Note also that you didn't have to know which records were deleted. You essentially compare the table as it exists now to the table that existed an hour ago and then insert the records that no longer exist in the original table into the archive table.

on the job

It is preferable to use the SCN for flashback over a timestamp. SCNs are exact, whereas the timestamp values are stored only every 3 seconds to support flashback operations. As a result, enabling flashback using timestamps may be off by as much as 1.5 seconds.

Although you could use Flashback Table to get the entire table back and then archive and delete the affected rows, in this case it is much simpler to retrieve the deleted rows and insert them directly into the archive table.

Another variation of Flashback Table is to use Create Table As Select (CTAS) with the subquery being a Flashback Query:

```
SQL> delete from employees where employee_id in (195,196);
2 rows deleted.

SQL> commit;
Commit complete.

SQL> create table employees_deleted as
  2         select * from employees
  3            as of timestamp systimestamp - interval '60' minute
  4            where employees.employee_id not in
  5                   (select employee_id from employees);
Table created.

SQL> select employee_id, last_name from employees_deleted;

EMPLOYEE_ID LAST_NAME
----------- -------------------------
        195 Jones
        196 Walsh

2 rows selected.
```

This is known as an *out-of-place restore*, which means restoring the table or a subset of the table to a location that differs from the original. This has the advantage of letting you manipulate the missing rows, if necessary, before placing them back in the table. For example, after you review the out-of-place restore, an existing referential integrity constraint may require that you insert a row into a parent table before the restored row can be placed back into the child table.

One of the disadvantages of an out-of-place restore using CTAS is that neither constraints nor indexes are rebuilt automatically.

Using Flashback Version Query

Flashback Version Query is another flashback feature that relies on undo data and provides a finer level of detail than an AS OF query (a Flashback Query). Whereas the Flashback methods presented up to now bring back rows of a table (or an entire table for a particular point in time), Flashback Version Query will return the entire history of a row between two SCNs or timestamps.

For the examples in this and the next sections, the user HR makes a number of changes to the HR.EMPLOYEES and HR.DEPARTMENTS tables:

```
SQL> select dbms_flashback.get_system_change_number from dual;

GET_SYSTEM_CHANGE_NUMBER
------------------------
                27153780

SQL> update hr.employees set salary = salary*1.2 where employee_id=195;

1 row updated.

SQL> select dbms_flashback.get_system_change_number from dual;

GET_SYSTEM_CHANGE_NUMBER
------------------------
                27153831

SQL> delete from hr.employees where employee_id = 196;


1 row deleted.

SQL> select dbms_flashback.get_system_change_number from dual;

GET_SYSTEM_CHANGE_NUMBER
------------------------
                27153862
```

```
SQL> insert into hr.departments values (660,'Security', 100, 1700);

1 row created.

SQL> select dbms_flashback.get_system_change_number from dual;

GET_SYSTEM_CHANGE_NUMBER
------------------------
                27153917

SQL> update hr.employees set manager_id = 100 where employee_id = 195;

1 row updated.

SQL> commit;

Commit complete.

SQL> select dbms_flashback.get_system_change_number from dual;

GET_SYSTEM_CHANGE_NUMBER
------------------------
                27154008

SQL> update hr.employees set department_id = 660 where employee_id = 195;

1 row updated.

SQL> select dbms_flashback.get_system_change_number from dual;

GET_SYSTEM_CHANGE_NUMBER
------------------------
                27154044

SQL> commit;

Commit complete.

SQL> select dbms_flashback.get_system_change_number from dual;

GET_SYSTEM_CHANGE_NUMBER
------------------------
                27154069

SQL>
```

The next day, the primary HR account user is out of the office and the other HR department employees want to know which rows and tables were changed. Using Flashback Version Query, the user HR (or any account with the required privileges), can see not only the values of a column at a particular time but also the entire history of any changes between specified timestamps or SCNs.

A Flashback Version Query uses the VERSIONS BETWEEN clause to specify a range of SCNs or timestamps for analysis of a given table (in this case, the EMPLOYEES table). When VERSIONS BETWEEN is used in a Flashback Version Query, a number of pseudocolumns are available to help identify the SCN and timestamp of the modifications. Also, the transaction ID and the type of operation performed on the row are available. Table 8-2 shows the pseudocolumns available with Flashback Version Query.

The HR user runs a Flashback Version Query to see the changes to any key columns in HR.EMPLOYEES for the two employees with IDs 195 and 196:

```
SQL> select versions_startscn startscn, versions_endscn endscn,
          versions_xid xid, versions_operation oper,
          employee_id empid, last_name name, manager_id mgrid, salary sal
     from hr.employees
     versions between scn 27153780 and 27154069
     where employee_id in (195,196);

  STARTSCN     ENDSCN XID              OPER  EMPID NAME      MGRID    SAL
---------- ---------- ---------------- ---- ------ -------- ------ ------
  27154046            0500090092230000 U       195 Jones       100   3360
  27153964   27154046 0400000044230000 U       195 Jones       100   3360
             27153964                          195 Jones       123   2800
  27153964            0400000044230000 D       196 Walsh       124   3100
             27153964                          196 Walsh       124   3100

SQL>
```

TABLE 8-2 Flashback Version Query Pseudocolumns

Pseudocolumn	Description
VERSIONS_START{SCN | TIME}	The starting SCN or timestamp when the change was made to the row.
VERSION_END{SCN | TIME}	The ending SCN or timestamp when the change was no longer valid for the row. If this is NULL, either the row version is still current or the row was deleted.
VERSIONS_XID	The transaction ID of the transaction that created the row version.
VERSIONS_OPERATION	The operation performed on the row (I=Insert, D=Delete, U=Update).

The rows are presented with the most recent changes first. Alternatively, the user HR could have filtered the query by TIMESTAMP or displayed the TIMESTAMP values. If required later, either can be used in a Flashback Query or Flashback Table operation. From this output, you can see that one employee was deleted and that another employee received two pay adjustments instead of one. It's also worth noting that some of the transactions contain only one DML command and others have two. In the next section, you'll attempt to correct one or more of these problems using Flashback Transaction.

Some restrictions and caveats do apply when you use Flashback Version Query. First, you can't query these objects with the VERSIONS clause:

- External tables
- Fixed tables (internal Oracle X$ tables)
- Temporary tables
- Views

You would probably not consider querying most of these with the VERSIONS clause, except possibly views. As a result, you can use the VERSIONS clause as part of a view's definition.

Finally, you cannot use the VERSIONS clause across DDL statements that change the structure of the tables in the query. In other words, you can go back in time only up to the first transaction after the last DDL statement on the table, which of course includes creating the table itself!

CERTIFICATION OBJECTIVE 8.03

Perform Flashback Table Operations

Flashback Table actually refers to two different table recovery options. One version of Flashback Table recovers a table (and its associated indexes) from the recycle bin after an intentional or unintentional DROP TABLE command.

The other table recovery operation is a bit more granular: The table still exists, but it needs to be rewound to a point in time before some kind of logical error occurred such as the deletion and COMMIT of the wrong rows in a table. For this recovery operation to be successful, your UNDO tablespace must be sized correctly with an appropriate retention setting, as described at the beginning of the chapter.

Flashback Drop relies on a construct introduced in Oracle Database 10g, the recycle bin, which behaves much like the recycle bin on a Windows-based computer. If enough room is available in the tablespace, dropped objects can be restored to their original schema with all indexes, triggers, and constraints intact. The following sections explore every aspect of the recycle bin: how to configure it, how to restore dropped tables, how space is managed in the recycle bin, how to bypass the recycle bin, and how to access tables directly in the recycle bin.

Oracle's Flashback Table feature restores the state of rows in a table as of a point of time in the past. It also restores the table's indexes, triggers, and constraints while the database is online. This increases the overall availability of the database. In the following sections, you'll learn more about when to use Flashback Table and how to configure your environment for Flashback Table. You'll also see some real-world scenarios for which you might use Flashback Table.

In contrast, you may want to identify and repair DML operations on multiple tables on a transactional basis. Once you have identified any erroneous or incorrect changes to a table, you can use *Flashback Transaction Query* to identify any other changes that were made by the transaction containing the inappropriate changes. Once identified, all changes within the transaction can be reversed as a group, typically to maintain referential integrity or the business rules used to process the transaction in the first place.

Following the sections on Flashback Table, I'll provide the details for identifying the Structured Query Language (SQL) needed to reverse an entire transaction or part of the transaction. The data dictionary view FLASHBACK_TRANSACTION_QUERY has all the information you need to identify this SQL. You'll learn how to identify the SQL required using this view and look at how to use the Enterprise Manager (EM) interface to accomplish the same task.

Leveraging the Recycle Bin

If a table is dropped, either intentionally or unintentionally, the dropped table remains in the recycle bin until space pressure from new objects or new rows in a table requires the reuse of the space occupied by the dropped objects. The indexes associated with the dropped tables also remain in the recycle bin as long as the table is there. If there is enough space in the tablespace, there can be multiple versions of the dropped table.

In the following sections, you'll see how the recycle bin operates and how you can identify and retrieve objects in the recycle bin.

Understanding the Recycle Bin

In a nutshell, the recycle bin is a data dictionary table that keeps track of dropped objects. The objects themselves still exist in the same location within the tablespace, but they are renamed. They are still listed in data dictionary views such as USER_TABLES, albeit with new names. The recycle bin supports objects with the same original name. In other words, if you create an EMPLOYEES table three times and drop it three times, all three versions of the EMPLOYEES table will be available in the recycle bin as long as enough space is available in the tablespace.

Even though you can refer to all objects in the recycle bin collectively, each tablespace has its own local recycle bin. Thus, some newer dropped objects may be aged out of the USERS tablespace because of space pressure. However, older dropped objects can remain for a much longer time in the TRAINING tablespace if new objects are not created frequently in that tablespace.

The recycle bin is enabled by default. To turn the recycle bin on and off, you can use the RECYCLEBIN initialization parameter:

```
recyclebin = on
```

You can also enable or disable the recycle bin at the session level using ALTER SESSION:

```
SQL> alter session set recyclebin=off;
```

RECYCLEBIN is a dynamic initialization parameter, so you can change it using ALTER SYSTEM. The change will take effect immediately if you specify SCOPE=MEMORY or SCOPE=BOTH:

```
alter system set recyclebin=off scope=both;
```

Regardless of which method you use to disable the recycle bin, the objects that are already in the bin stay there unless you purge them or they are purged because of space pressure from new objects. Until you reenable the recycle bin, newly dropped objects will not be recoverable using the recycle bin.

When you drop an object with the recycle bin enabled, the space allocated to the dropped object and all associated objects (such as indexes) is immediately reflected in the data dictionary view DBA_FREE_SPACE. However, the space used by the objects still counts toward a user's quota until the object is explicitly removed from the recycle bin or is forced out by new objects in the tablespace. In addition, the table and its dependent objects are renamed to a system-assigned name using this format:

BIN$*unique_id*$*version*

The *unique_id* portion of the name is a 26-character globally unique name for the object. A table with the same name dropped in a different database will have a different *unique_id*. The *version* portion of the name is the version number of the dropped object, which is assigned by Oracle. The next time a table with the same name is dropped, both the *unique_id* and *version* are the same, but each will have different values for DROPTIME. You will learn how to select which version to recover later in this chapter.

Querying the Recycle Bin

To query the recycle bin, you can use the data dictionary view USER_RECYCLEBIN; RECYCLEBIN is a global synonym for USER_RECYCLEBIN. You can view purged objects for all users using the view DBA_RECYCLEBIN:

```
SQL> select owner, object_name, original_name,
  2     type, ts_name, droptime, can_undrop
  3  from dba_recyclebin;

OWNER         OBJECT_NAME                        ORIGINAL_NAME
------------ -------------------------------- ----------------------
TYPE       TS_NAME      DROPTIME            CAN_UNDROP
---------- ------------ ------------------- ----------
HR            BIN$UmhMiy3i2+zgQKjAYAI1cw==$0   JOB_HISTORY
TABLE      EXAMPLE      2014-05-02:16:38:48 YES

HR            BIN$UmhMiy3h2+zgQKjAYAI1cw==$0   JHIST_EMP_ID_ST_DATE_
PK
INDEX      EXAMPLE      2014-05-02:16:38:48 NO

HR            BIN$UmhMiy3g2+zgQKjAYAI1cw==$0   JHIST_DEPARTMENT_IX
INDEX      EXAMPLE      2014-05-02:16:38:47 NO

HR            BIN$UmhMiy3f2+zgQKjAYAI1cw==$0   JHIST_EMPLOYEE_IX
INDEX      EXAMPLE      2014-05-02:16:38:47 NO

HR            BIN$UmhMiy3e2+zgQKjAYAI1cw==$0   JHIST_JOB_IX
INDEX      EXAMPLE      2014-05-02:16:38:47 NO

BRETT         BIN$U/9fvJKUXOzgQKjAYAIWhw==$0   SYS_C0004004

INDEX      USERS        2014-05-10:10:17:59 NO

BRETT         BIN$U/9fvJKSXOzgQKjAYAIWhw==$0   FAVRE_2_JETS
TABLE      USERS        2014-05-10:10:16:39 YES
```

```
7 rows selected.

SQL>
```

Note the column CAN_UNDROP. At first glance, you might think that if the object is in the recycle bin, it can be recovered. Upon closer inspection, you can see that CAN_UNDROP is set to NO for objects such as indexes because you cannot undrop an index. You must undrop the table first, and any associated indexes will be automatically undropped.

The data dictionary view USER_RECYCLEBIN has the same columns as DBA_RECYCLEBIN, except that USER_RECYCLEBIN does not have the OWNER column. This is consistent with all other Oracle data dictionary views that have the USER_, DBA_, and ALL_ prefixes, although in this case no ALL_RECYCLEBIN data dictionary view exists.

EXERCISE 8-1

Move Objects to the Recycle Bin

In this exercise, you'll create and drop the same table twice and then query the recycle bin to identify the name of the table and its dependent objects in the recycle bin.

1. Create the table VAC_SCHED and insert a row into it:

```
SQL> create table vac_sched
  2  (
  3     emp_no     number,
  4     vac_no     number,
  5     start_date date,
  6     end_date   date,
  7   primary key(emp_no, vac_no)
  8  );

Table created.

SQL> insert into vac_sched values(4,17,'15-sep-13','30-sep-13');

1 row created.

SQL> commit;

Commit complete.

SQL>
```

2. Drop the table:

```
SQL> drop table vac_sched;

Table dropped.

SQL>
```

3. Create the table again and insert a row with different values from those in the row you inserted into the first version of the table:

```
SQL> create table vac_sched
  2  (
  3      emp_no     number,
  4      vac_no     number,
  5      start_date date,
  6      end_date   date,
  7   primary key(emp_no, vac_no)
  8  );

Table created.

SQL> insert into vac_sched values(58,2,'21-sep-13','25-sep-13');

1 row created.

SQL> commit;

Commit complete.

SQL>
```

4. Drop the table again:

```
SQL> drop table vac_sched;

Table dropped.

SQL>
```

5. Query the recycle bin and confirm that the table has two different system-assigned names in the recycle bin:

```
SQL> select object_name, original_name, type, droptime
  2  from recyclebin;

OBJECT_NAME                                           ORIGINAL_NAME
----------------------------------------------------- -------------
```

```
TYPE       DROPTIME
---------- -------------------
BIN$U/9fvJKbXOzgQKjAYAIWhw==$0                        VAC_SCHED
TABLE      2014-05-10:10:57:56

BIN$U/9fvJKaXOzgQKjAYAIWhw==$0                        SYS_C0013050
INDEX      2014-05-10:10:57:56

BIN$U/9fvJKXXOzgQKjAYAIWhw==$0                        SYS_C0013049
INDEX      2014-05-10:10:56:41

BIN$U/9fvJKYXOzgQKjAYAIWhw==$0                        VAC_SCHED
TABLE      2014-05-10:10:56:41

SQL>
```

Looking closely, you can see that the new names differ by one character in the eighth position of the unique_id portion of the name.

As you might expect, you can purge the entire contents of the recycle bin with the PURGE RECYCLEBIN command. If you have the appropriate privileges, you can purge the contents of the recycle bin for all users using the PURGE DBA_RECYCLEBIN command.

Restoring Tables from the Recycle Bin

To restore a table from the recycle bin, you use the FLASHBACK TABLE . . . TO BEFORE DROP command. If you specify the original table name in the command, the most recently dropped version of the table and its dependent objects are restored. If you want to restore a previous version of the same table, you must specify the name of the previous version in the recycle bin, as in this example:

```
SQL> flashback table "BIN$U/9fvJKcXOzgQKjAYAIWhw==$0" to before drop;

Flashback complete.

SQL>
```

Note that you will always have to put the recycle bin object name in double quotes because of the lowercase or special characters in the base-64 string representation of the dropped table.

If you attempt to restore a table that has been re-created since it was dropped, you will receive an error unless you use the RENAME TO clause to give the restored table a new name. Here is an example:

```
SQL> flashback table vac_sched to before drop
  2  rename to old_vac_sched;

Flashback complete.

SQL>
```

When you flashback a table using the RENAME option, the table acquires its original name, but the table's dependent objects do not. If you want to keep the original names for the indexes, triggers, and constraints, query the recycle bin before you flashback and rename the other objects after the table is restored.

EXERCISE 8-2

Restore a Table from the Recycle Bin, Keeping the Original Dependent Object Names

This exercise picks up where you left off in Exercise 8-1. Query the recycle bin for the VAC_SCHED table and its dependent objects, restore the most recent version of the table, and rename the dependent objects to their original names.

1. Query the recycle bin and identify the most recently dropped version of VAC_SCHED along with its dependent objects:

```
SQL> select object_name, original_name, type, droptime
  2  from recyclebin
  3  order by droptime desc;

OBJECT_NAME                                          ORIGINAL_NAME
---------------------------------------------------- -------------
TYPE       DROPTIME
---------- -------------------
BIN$U/9fvJKbXOzgQKjAYAIWhw==$0                       VAC_SCHED
TABLE      2014-05-10:10:57:56

BIN$U/9fvJKaXOzgQKjAYAIWhw==$0                       SYS_C0013050
INDEX      2014-05-10:10:57:56

BIN$U/9fvJKXXOzgQKjAYAIWhw==$0                       SYS_C0013049
INDEX      2014-05-10:10:56:41
```

```
BIN$U/9fvJKYXOzgQKjAYAIWhw==$0                          VAC_SCHED
TABLE       2014-05-10:10:56:41

SQL>
```

2. Restore the most recent version of the table:

```
SQL> flashback table vac_sched to before drop;

Flashback complete.

SQL>
```

3. Rename the primary key constraint's index to its original name (the index dropped at the same time as the table):

```
SQL> alter index "BIN$U/9fvJKaXOzgQKjAYAIWhw==$0" rename to
sys_c0013050;

Index altered.
SQL>
```

4. Query the data dictionary view USER_CONSTRAINTS to identify the name of the primary key constraint:

```
SQL> select table_name, constraint_name
  2  from user_constraints
  3  where table_name = 'VAC_SCHED';

TABLE_NAME                     CONSTRAINT_NAME
------------------------------ ------------------------------
VAC_SCHED                      BIN$U/9fvJKZXOzgQKjAYAIWhw==$0

SQL>
```

5. Rename the constraint to its original name, or at least to a more understandable name if the original name was system-generated:

```
SQL> alter table vac_sched
  2  rename constraint "BIN$U/9fvJKZXOzgQKjAYAIWhw==$0"
  3  to vac_sched_pk;

Table altered.

SQL>
```

Recycle Bin Space Reclamation

In the following sections, you'll learn more about how Oracle manages the space in the recycle bin, how you can manually manage the space, and how you can query the contents of the recycle bin. Both automated and manual recycle bin space management functions can be used.

Automatic Recycle Bin Space Reclamation The space in the recycle bin, and by extension the space in the tablespace containing the recycle bin, is managed automatically by Oracle. In other words, all dropped objects remain available for recovery in the recycle bin as long as new objects don't need the space occupied by dropped objects.

Older objects in the recycle bin are removed before new objects when free space is low; in the next section, you'll learn how to remove objects selectively from the recycle bin. If the tablespace is autoextensible (the tablespace has the AUTOEXTEND ON attribute), space from dropped objects is used first. If insufficient space is available for a new object, the tablespace autoextends.

Manual Recycle Bin Space Reclamation You can manually remove objects from the recycle bin by using the PURGE command. When you purge a table from the recycle bin, the table and all its dependent objects are removed as well. This makes sense because you would not have much use for a table's index once the table itself is gone!

When you purge a table from the recycle bin, you can use either the recycle bin name of the object or the original name of the object. If you specify the original table name, the oldest version of the table is purged first. Therefore, if you want to purge a more recent version of the table, use the recycle bin object name, as in this example:

```
SQL> show recyclebin;
ORIGINAL NAME    RECYCLEBIN NAME                OBJECT TYPE  DROP TIME
---------------- ------------------------------ ------------ -----------
SALES_Q4         BIN$U/9fvJKfXOzgQKjAYAIWhw==$0 TABLE        2014-05-10
                                                             :22:30:28
SALES_Q4         BIN$U/9fvJKeXOzgQKjAYAIWhw==$0 TABLE        2014-05-10
                                                             :22:28:10
VAC_SCHED        BIN$U/9fvJKYXOzgQKjAYAIWhw==$0 TABLE        2014-05-10
                                                             :10:56:41
SQL> purge table "BIN$U/9fvJKfXOzgQKjAYAIWhw==$0";

Table purged.

SQL>
```

You can also purge indexes in the recycle bin. This is useful if you want to keep tables in the recycle bin that otherwise might be aged out by new objects. If you need to recover a table from the recycle bin that no longer has its associated index, you can easily re-create the index after you have recovered the table itself.

If you need even finer-grained control of which objects you can purge from the recycle bin, you can purge recycle bin objects from a specific tablespace for the current user, as in this example:

```
SQL> purge tablespace users;

Tablespace purged.

SQL>
```

Furthermore, if you want to purge only objects owned by a particular user and you have the DROP ANY TABLE system privilege, you can drop all recycle bin objects for a specific user, as in this example:

```
SQL> purge tablespace web_orders user inet_us;

Tablespace purged.

SQL>
```

You can drop all objects from the recycle bin from all tablespaces if you have the SYSDBA privilege and you use the command PURGE DBA_RECYCLEBIN.

Bypassing the Recycle Bin

You can explicitly bypass the recycle bin when you drop a table by appending PURGE to the DROP TABLE command. This can be useful if you know that the table is temporary or has been erroneously created and you will never need to resurrect it. Remember also that a dropped table that remains in the recycle bin still counts toward a user's quota on the tablespace. Oracle's definition of *space pressure*, which drives removal of objects from the recycle bin, includes a user exhausting her disk quota in a tablespace. Therefore, using DROP TABLE . . . PURGE will prevent the removal of a user's other objects in the recycle bin even if enough free space exists in the tablespace.

Another operation that bypasses the recycle bin is the DROP TABLESPACE command. This makes a lot of sense when you consider that the objects in the recycle bin are still in the tablespace—just renamed. Note that you must include the INCLUDING CONTENTS clause if any non–recycle bin objects exist in the tablespace when you use the DROP TABLESPACE command.

Finally, if you issue the DROP USER . . . CASCADE command, all the user's objects are dropped from all tablespaces and not placed into the recycle bin. Any of the user's objects will be automatically purged if they are already in the recycle bin when you issue the DROP USER command.

Accessing Tables in the Recycle Bin

When an object resides in the recycle bin, you can still use a SELECT statement to access the dropped table. Also, the dropped table still appears in the data dictionary views DBA_TABLES, DBA_OBJECTS, and DBA_SEGMENTS. Other than the cryptic name of the table in the recycle bin, if the value of the column DROPPED in these views is set to YES, then you know the table is in the recycle bin.

Here is an example of accessing a table in the recycle bin:

```
SQL> show recyclebin
ORIGINAL NAME    RECYCLEBIN NAME                OBJECT TYPE  DROP TIME
---------------- ------------------------------ ------------ -----------
JOB_HISTORY      BIN$UmhMiy3i2+zgQKjAYAI1cw==$0 TABLE        2014-05-02
                                                             :16:38:48
OLD_EMPLOYEES    BIN$VCfmqQB0FfPgQKjAYAJKzg==$0 TABLE        2014-05-10
                                                             :23:50:57

SQL> describe "BIN$VCfmqQB0FfPgQKjAYAJKzg==$0"
 Name                                      Null?    Type
 ----------------------------------------- -------- --------------------
 EMPLOYEE_ID                                        NUMBER(6)
 FIRST_NAME                                         VARCHAR2(20)
 LAST_NAME                                 NOT NULL VARCHAR2(25)
 EMAIL                                     NOT NULL VARCHAR2(25)
 PHONE_NUMBER                                       VARCHAR2(20)
 HIRE_DATE                                 NOT NULL DATE
 JOB_ID                                    NOT NULL VARCHAR2(10)
 SALARY                                             NUMBER(8,2)
 COMMISSION_PCT                                     NUMBER(2,2)
 MANAGER_ID                                         NUMBER(6)
 DEPARTMENT_ID                                      NUMBER(4)

SQL> select last_name, first_name, email
  2  from "BIN$VCfmqQB0FfPgQKjAYAJKzg==$0"
  3  where rownum < 10;

LAST_NAME                 FIRST_NAME           EMAIL
------------------------- -------------------- -------------------------
King                      Steven               SKING
```

```
Kochhar                    Neena                    NKOCHHAR
De Haan                    Lex                      LDEHAAN
Hunold                     Alexander                AHUNOLD
Ernst                      Bruce                    BERNST
Austin                     David                    DAUSTIN
Pataballa                  Valli                    VPATABAL
Lorentz                    Diana                    DLORENTZ
Greenberg                  Nancy                    NGREENBE

9 rows selected.

SQL>
```

Note that you can also use the AS OF clause in a SELECT query on a table in the recycle bin for flashback queries, which was covered earlier in this chapter. No other Data Manipulation Language (DML) or Data Definition Language (DDL) operations are allowed on tables in the recycle bin unless you recover them with the FLASHBACK TABLE . . . TO BEFORE DROP command first.

Understanding Flashback Table

A table can be restored as of a timestamp or an SCN. Flashback Table is preferable to other Flashback methods if the scope of user errors is small and limited to one or few tables. It's also the most straightforward if you know that you want to restore the table to a point in the past unconditionally. For recovering the state of a larger number of tables, Flashback Database may be a better choice. Flashback Table cannot be used on a standby database and cannot reconstruct all DDL operations, such as adding and dropping columns. Since Flashback Table uses the UNDO tablespace, your window of recovery is relatively limited compared to other recovery methods, such as RMAN-based recovery or Flashback Database.

Flashback Table is performed in-place, while the database is online, rolling back changes to the table and all its dependent objects, such as indexes. If the table has other tables as dependent objects, you can specify more than one table in the FLASHBACK TABLE command. Whether you specify one or many tables in a Flashback Table operation, the operation is considered to be a single transaction. All changes are successful, or they are rolled back as in a traditional transaction.

Nonsystem users can perform the flashback as long as they have the appropriate privileges. You'll learn how to configure all aspects of using Flashback Table in the next section.

Configuring Flashback Table

To perform Flashback Table, a user must have the FLASHBACK ANY TABLE privilege or the FLASHBACK object privilege on a specific table:

```
SQL> grant flashback any table to m_phelps;

Grant succeeded.

SQL>
```

As is true with all schema objects, a user does not need additional privileges to flashback her own tables. However, to use Flashback Table on a table or tables, you must enable *row movement* on the table before performing the flashback operation. Row movement need not be in effect when the user error occurs. Row movement is also required to support Oracle's segment shrink functionality. This is because row movement will change the ROWID of a table row. Do not enable row movement if your applications depend on the ROWID being the same for a given row until the row is deleted.

Using Flashback Table

Before using Flashback Table, you must consider a few restrictions. First, even with the appropriate privileges, you cannot perform Flashback Table on system tables, fixed (X$) tables, or remote tables.

In addition, Flashback Table operations cannot span structural changes to the table (DDL operations), such as adding or dropping a column. This is true with all flashback features except for Flashback Database. However, you can flashback a table to a point in time before an index on the table was dropped, although the index will not be re-created during the Flashback Table operation.

Finally, any statistics gathered for the tables in the FLASHBACK TABLE command are not flashed back. As a result, it is a good practice to gather new statistics on the tables immediately after the Flashback Table operation is complete.

EXERCISE 8-3

Use Flashback Table on a Table

In this exercise, you will use Flashback Table to recover from accidental deletion of all rows from the EMPLOYEES table.

1. Enable row movement for several tables. You can safely enable row movement because none of your applications references your tables by ROWID:

```
SQL> alter table employees enable row movement;
Table altered.
SQL> alter table departments enable row movement;
Table altered.
SQL> alter table jobs enable row movement;
Table altered.
```

2. "Inadvertently" delete all the rows in the EMPLOYEES table:

```
SQL> delete from hr.employees
  2  /
107 rows deleted.

SQL> commit
  2  ;
Commit complete.
```

3. The HR user can bring back the entire table quickly without calling the DBA. This is because the UNDO tablespace is large enough and the HR user notices the problem within the retention period:

```
SQL> flashback table employees
  2       to timestamp systimestamp - interval '15' minute;
Flashback complete.

SQL> select count(*) from employees;
  COUNT(*)
----------
       107
```

If the accidental deletions were not noticed right away and changes were made to dependent tables in the meantime, you can include the dependent tables in the Flashback Table operation as well:

```
SQL>  flashback table employees, departments
  2        to timestamp systimestamp - interval '15' minute;
Flashback complete.
```

Understanding Flashback Transaction Query

Unlike a Flashback Version Query, a Flashback Transaction Query does not reference the table involved in DML transactions. Instead, you query the data dictionary view FLASHBACK_TRANSACTION_QUERY. Table 9-3 summarizes the columns of FLASHBACK_TRANSACTION_QUERY.

The table FLASHBACK_TRANSACTION_QUERY contains all changes to the database, including DDL operations. This makes sense because Oracle uses tables and indexes to manage the data dictionary and space allocation. Thus, a DDL operation shows up in FLASHBACK_TRANSACTION_QUERY as a series of space management and metadata maintenance operations.

Dropped tables and users show up in FLASHBACK_TRANSACTION_QUERY as well. However, they no longer exist, so object numbers show up instead of table names and user ID numbers replace the usernames.

Undo space is not unlimited; thus, you may have only partial transactions in FLASHBACK_TRANSACTION_QUERY. In this situation, the value of the OPERATION column contains UNKNOWN for any DML that is no longer in the UNDO tablespace for the selected transaction.

Flashback Transaction Query Prerequisites

Before you can use Flashback Transaction Query, you must enable additional logging to the redo log stream. The redo log stream is the same data that Log Miner uses, except with a different interface. The redo log stream data is in addition to the

TABLE 8-3

FLASHBACK_TRANSACTION_QUERY Columns

Column Name	Description
XID	Transaction ID number
START_SCN	SCN for the first DML in the transaction
START_TIMESTAMP	Timestamp of the first DML in the transaction
COMMIT_SCN	SCN when the transaction was committed
COMMIT_TIMESTAMP	Timestamp when the transaction was committed
LOGON_USER	User who owned the transaction
UNDO_CHANGE#	Undo SCN
OPERATION	DML operation performed: DELETE, INSERT, UPDATE, BEGIN, or UNKNOWN
TABLE_NAME	Table changed by DML
TABLE_OWNER	Owner of the table changed by DML
ROW_ID	ROWID of the row modified by DML
UNDO_SQL	SQL statement to undo the DML operation

information recorded in the UNDO tablespace. Both enhanced redo and undo information are required for Flashback Transaction Query.

First, enable logging of columns and primary key (PK) values referenced in DML changes, using these ALTER DATABASE commands:

```
SQL> alter database add supplemental log data;

Database altered.

SQL> alter database add supplemental log data (primary key) columns;

Database altered.

SQL>
```

Next, grant the appropriate permissions on the DBMS_FLASHBACK package, as well as give the SELECT ANY TRANSACTION privilege to the users who will be using Flashback Transaction Query:

```
SQL> grant execute on dbms_flashback to hr;

Grant succeeded.

SQL> grant select any transaction to hr;

Grant succeeded.

SQL>
```

Using Flashback Transaction Query

To investigate the changes that were made to the EMPLOYEES table, you can query the view FLASHBACK_TRANSACTION_QUERY with the oldest transaction from the Flashback Version Query shown earlier in this chapter:

```
SQL> select start_scn, commit_scn, logon_user,
  2       operation, table_name, undo_sql
  3  from flashback_transaction_query
  4  where xid = hextoraw('0400000044230000');

 START_SCN COMMIT_SCN LOGON_USER    OPERATION     TABLE_NAME
---------- ---------- ------------ ------------ ---------------
UNDO_SQL
----------------------------------------------------------------------
  27153828   27153964 HR            UPDATE        EMPLOYEES
update "HR"."EMPLOYEES" set "MANAGER_ID" = '123' where ROWID = 'AAARAIAA
```

```
FAAAABXABf';

  27153828    27153964 HR             INSERT        DEPARTMENTS
delete from "HR"."DEPARTMENTS" where ROWID = 'AAARADAAFAAAAA4AAA';

  27153828    27153964 HR             DELETE        EMPLOYEES
insert into "HR"."EMPLOYEES"("EMPLOYEE_ID","FIRST_NAME","LAST_NAME","EMA
IL","PHONE_NUMBER","HIRE_DATE","JOB_ID","SALARY","COMMISSION_PCT","MANAG
ER_ID","DEPARTMENT_ID") values ('196','Alana','Walsh','AWALSH','650.507.
9811',TO_DATE('24-APR-98', 'DD-MON-RR'),'SH_CLERK','3100',NULL,'124','50
');

  27153828    27153964 HR             UPDATE        EMPLOYEES
update "HR"."EMPLOYEES" set "SALARY" = '2800' where ROWID = 'AAARAIAAFAA
AABXABf';

  27153828    27153964 HR             BEGIN

SQL>
```

This confirms what you already expected—that another user in the HR department (using the same account, HR) made the deletion and salary update—pointing out the usefulness of assigning separate user accounts for each member of the HR department. The UNDO_SQL column contains the actual SQL code that can be used to reverse the effect of the transaction. Note, to the contrary, that in this example, this is the first transaction to occur between the SCNs of interest. If other transactions made further updates to the same columns, you might want to review the other updates before running the SQL code in the UNDO_SQL column.

CERTIFICATION OBJECTIVE 8.04

Perform Table Recovery from Backups

In Chapter 5, I covered tablespace point in time recovery (TSPITR) and how you could use an RMAN backup to recover only a single tablespace to a point in time or SCN right before logical corruptions had occurred on one or more tables within the tablespace. However, as important as recovering the single table is, you'll have to deal with all of the other objects in the tablespace that will also be rewound to a previous state.

As of Oracle Database 12*c*, you can use an RMAN backup to recover a single table. This method fills the gap between the TSPITR method (which is time consuming and must involve the DBA) and methods that are available to a database user such as Flashback Table using the UNDO tablespace and possibly a flashback data archive. Because the logical corruption of a table may have been discovered long after the UNDO data has expired and been purged from the UNDO tablespace, recovering a single table from an RMAN backup fills the gap between a full TSPITR and a Flashback Table or Flashback Drop operation.

Scenarios for Table Recovery from Backups

In addition to the time it takes to recover an entire tablespace versus a single table from a tablespace backup, there are several other reasons why you would use table recovery from backups (TRFB) instead of other flashback methods.

Using TSPITR may be a reasonable option if you have many tables in a tablespace that you need to recover, but what if the tablespace is not self-contained? In that scenario, you will have to recover more than one tablespace, which makes the TSPITR less attractive.

You may often rely on Flashback Drop to get back a table that might have been dropped even weeks ago but space pressure may have already purged it or the table was dropped while the recycle bin was turned off.

Finally, even if your UNDO tablespace and retention period is long, there may have been a recent structural change to the table, which will prevent any flashback operation using the UNDO tablespace.

Prerequisites and Limitations for Table Recovery from Backups

In addition to the limitations mentioned in the previous section, there are several other conditions that must be met to perform TRFB:

- The database must be in read-write mode.
- The database must be in ARCHIVELOG mode.
- COMPATIBLE must be set to 12.0 or higher.
- You cannot recover tables or table partitions from the SYS schema.
- You cannot recover objects from the SYSTEM or SYSAUX tablespace.
- Objects cannot be recovered to standby databases.

Using Table Recovery from Backups

Using TRFB is quite similar to TSPITR in many ways. In fact, you could argue that TRFB is more of an RMAN recovery method than a tool in your flashback toolkit. The key is the scope of the objects that you are recovering or rewinding to a previous point in time or SCN. Figure 8-1 shows the general steps and flow of the recovery operation.

Here are the steps you use in RMAN to recover a single table using TRFB:

1. Specify the RMAN parameters for the TRFB operation:
   a. Names of tables or table partitions to recover
   b. Point in time at which the objects need to be recovered to (timestamp or SCN)
   c. Whether the recovered objects must be imported into the target database
2. RMAN determines which backups will be used for the operation.
3. RMAN creates a temporary auxiliary instance.

FIGURE 8-1 Process flow for table recovery from backups

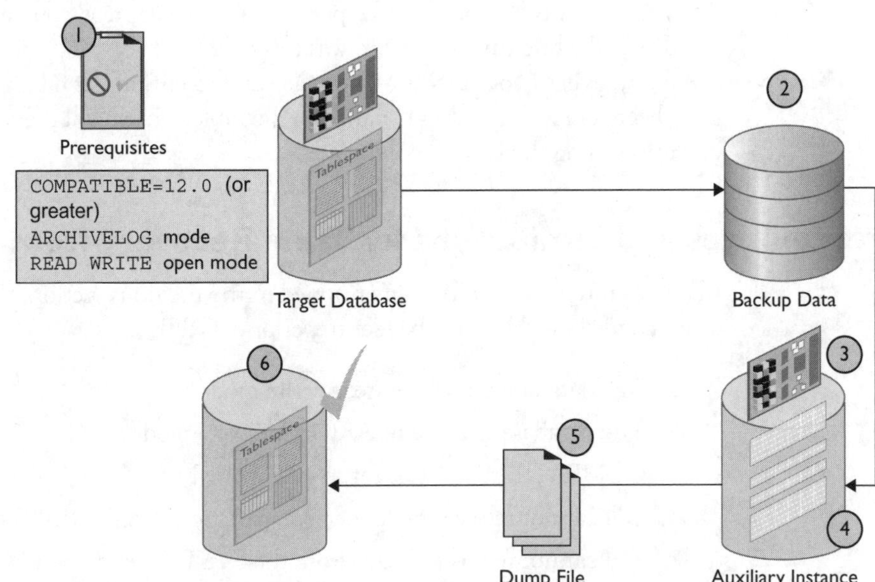

4. RMAN recovers the table or tables into a tablespace available to this auxiliary instance.
5. RMAN creates a Data Pump export dump file with the recovered objects.
6. If specified, RMAN will use Data Pump import to copy the objects into the target database.

As you may have noticed, this operation is somewhat automated compared to TSPITR, especially in versions of Oracle Database before 12*c*. This operation still must be performed by a DBA, however.

CERTIFICATION OBJECTIVE 8.05

Describe and Use Flashback Data Archive

Regulations such as Sarbanes-Oxley (2002) and the Health Insurance Portability and Accountability Act of 1996 (HIPAA) require strict control and tracking requirements for customer and patient data. Retaining an historical record of all changes to rows in critical tables is error prone and requires custom applications or database triggers to maintain repositories for the historical changes. Every time you create a new application or update a table in an application that requires historical tracking, you must make changes to your tracking application as well. You can use Flashback Data Archive to save historical changes automatically to all key tables for as long as regulatory agencies or your stakeholders require.

Understanding Flashback Data Archive

Flashback Data Archive is implemented natively in Oracle (as opposed to an application layer using triggers or a set of PL/SQL packages). In a nutshell, you create one or more repository areas (one of which can be the default), assign a default retention period for objects in the repository, and then mark the appropriate tables for tracking. It creates a *temporal history* of a table for a specified time window after which the data older than the cutoff date is purged.

A Flashback Data Archive acts much like an UNDO tablespace. However, a Flashback Data Archive records only UPDATE and DELETE statements and not INSERT statements. In addition, undo data is typically retained for a period of hours or days for all objects. Rows in Flashback Data Archives can span years or even decades. Flashback Data Archives have a much narrower focus as well, recording only historical changes to table rows. Oracle uses data in an UNDO tablespace for read-consistency in long-running transactions and to roll back uncommitted transactions.

exam watch

The exam will ask you about the physical and logical structures that support each flashback feature. Be sure you understand how UNDO tablespaces, online and archived redo logs, flashback logs, Flashback Data Archives, and the recycle bin support a particular flashback feature.

You can access data in a Flashback Data Archive just as you do with Flashback Query using the AS OF clause in a SELECT statement. Flashback Version Query and Flashback Transaction Query can also use the data in a Flashback Data Archive. In the following sections, you'll learn how to create a Flashback Data Archive, assign permissions to users and objects, and query historical data in a Flashback Data Archive.

Creating an Archive

You can create one or several Flashback Data Archives in existing tablespaces using the CREATE FLASHBACK ARCHIVE command. However, Oracle best practices recommend that you use dedicated tablespaces. All archives must have a default retention period using the RETENTION clause and can optionally be identified as the default archive using the DEFAULT keyword. The disk quota in an archive is limited by the disk space within the tablespace, unless you assign a maximum amount of disk space in the archive using the QUOTA keyword.

In this example, you first create a dedicated tablespace for your Flashback Data Archive:

```
SQL> create tablespace fbda1
  2  datafile '+data' size 10g;

Tablespace created.
SQL>
```

Next, you create three Flashback Data Archives: one for the ES department with no quota limit and a ten-year retention period, a second one for the finance department with a 500MB limit and a seven-year retention period, and a third for all other users in the USERS4 tablespace as the default with a 250MB limit and a two-year retention period:

```
SQL> create flashback archive fb_es
  2  tablespace fbda1 retention 10 year;

Flashback archive created.

SQL> create flashback archive fb_fi
  2  tablespace fbda1 quota 500m
  3  retention 7 year;

Flashback archive created.

SQL> create flashback archive default fb_dflt
  2  tablespace users4 quota 250m
  3  retention 2 year;

Flashback archive created.

SQL>
```

You cannot specify more than one tablespace in the CREATE FLASHBACK ARCHIVE command. You must use the ALTER FLASHBACK ARCHIVE command to add a tablespace, as you'll see later in this chapter in the section "Managing Flashback Data Archives."

Depending on your business requirements, you can enable and disable Flashback Data Archive on a table at will. For example, you might want to drop a column to a table being tracked by Flashback Data Archive. However, no DDL statements are allowed on tables being tracked using Flashback Data Archive except for adding columns. Once you disable Flashback Data Archive for a table, the historical data for the table is lost even if you immediately reenable it for the table.

Using Flashback Data Archive Data Dictionary Views

Two new data dictionary views support Flashback Data Archives: DBA_FLASHBACK_ARCHIVE and DBA_FLASHBACK_ARCHIVE_TS. DBA_FLASHBACK_ARCHIVE lists the archives, and DBA_FLASHBACK_ARCHIVE_TS displays the tablespace-to-archive mapping:

```
SQL> select flashback_archive_name, flashback_archive#,
  2       retention_in_days, status
  3  from dba_flashback_archive;

FLASHBACK_AR FLASHBACK_ARCHIVE# RETENTION_IN_DAYS STATUS
```

```
------------ ------------------ ---------------- -------
FB_ES                         1             3650
FB_FI                         2             2555
FB_DFLT                       3              730 DEFAULT

SQL> select * from dba_flashback_archive_ts;

FLASHBACK_AR FLASHBACK_ARCHIVE# TABLESPACE QUOTA_IN_M
------------ ------------------ ---------- ----------
FB_ES                         1 FBDA1
FB_FI                         2 FBDA1      500
FB_DFLT                       3 USERS4     250

SQL>
```

The view DBA_FLASHBACK_ARCHIVE_TABLES tracks the tables enabled for flashback archiving. I'll show you the contents of this view later in this chapter after you learn how to enable a table for flashback archiving.

Assigning Flashback Data Archive Permissions

A user must have the FLASHBACK ARCHIVE ADMINISTER system privilege to create or modify Flashback Data Archives and must have the FLASHBACK ARCHIVE object privilege to enable tracking on a table. Once enabled, a user doesn't need any specific permissions to use the AS OF clause in a SELECT statement other than the SELECT permission on the table itself.

The FLASHBACK ARCHIVE ADMINISTER privilege also includes privileges for adding and removing tablespaces from an archive, dropping an archive, and performing an ad hoc purge of history data.

Managing Flashback Data Archives

You can easily add another tablespace to an existing archive. Use the ALTER FLASHBACK ARCHIVE command like the following to add the USERS3 tablespace to the FB_DFLT archive with a quota of 400MB:

```
SQL> alter flashback archive fb_dflt
  2  add tablespace users3 quota 400m;

Flashback archive altered.

SQL>
```

You can purge archive data with the purge clause. In this example, you want to purge all rows in the FB_DFLT archive before January 1, 2010:

```
SQL> alter flashback archive fb_dflt
  2  purge before timestamp
  3  to_timestamp('2010-01-01 00:00:00', 'YYYY-MM-DD HH24:MI:SS');
```

Assigning a Table to a Flashback Data Archive

You assign a table to an archive either at table creation using the standard CREATE TABLE syntax with the addition of the FLASHBACK ARCHIVE clause or later with the ALTER TABLE command, as in this example:

```
SQL> alter table hr.employees flashback archive fb_es;

Table altered.
```

To create a new table and specify the FDA attribute, use the FLASHBACK ARCHIVE clause. In this example, you specify a non-default FDA:

```
create table chgtrk_hist
(fac_id         number,
 area_id        number,
 trk_req_dt     timestamp,
 trk_comm_txt   varchar2(100))
flashback archive f_arch;
```

Note that in the previous command that specified a particular archive for the HR.EMPLOYEES table, if you did not specify an archive, Oracle assigns FB_DFLT. You can review the tables that use Flashback Data Archive by querying the data dictionary view DBA_FLASHBACK_ARCHIVE_TABLES:

```
SQL> select * from dba_flashback_archive_tables;

TABLE_NAME             OWNER_NAME FLASHBACK_AR ARCHIVE_TABLE_NAME
---------------------- ---------- ------------ --------------------
EMPLOYEES              HR         FB_ES        SYS_FBA_HIST_70313

SQL>
```

Querying Flashback Data Archives

Querying the historical data for a table in a Flashback Data Archive is as easy as using the AS OF clause in a table when you are using DML activity stored in an UNDO tablespace. In fact, users will not know whether they are retrieving historical data from the UNDO tablespace or from a Flashback Data Archive.

In this scenario, much like in the scenarios earlier in this chapter, one of the employees in the HR department deletes an employee row in the EMPLOYEES table and forgets to archive it to the EMPLOYEE_HISTORY table first. With Flashback Data Archives enabled for the EMPLOYEES table, the HR employee can rely on the FB_ES archive to satisfy any queries on employees no longer in the EMPLOYEES table. This is a DELETE statement from three weeks ago:

```
SQL> delete from employees where employee_id = 169;

1 row deleted.

SQL> commit;

Commit complete.

SQL>
```

The HR employee needs to find the hire date for employee 169. She retrieves the historical information from the EMPLOYEES table with the AS OF clause specifying a time four weeks ago:

```
SQL> select employee_id, last_name, hire_date
  2  from employees
  3  as of timestamp (systimestamp - interval '28' day)
  4  where employee_id = 169;

EMPLOYEE_ID LAST_NAME                 HIRE_DATE
----------- ------------------------- ---------
        169 Bloom                     23-MAR-08

SQL>
```

It is completely transparent to the user whether Oracle is using an UNDO tablespace or a Flashback Data Archive for a query containing AS OF.

CERTIFICATION OBJECTIVE 8.06

Perform Flashback Database

As you might expect, Oracle's Flashback Database feature uses the FLASHBACK DATABASE command to return the database to a past time or SCN, providing a fast alternative to performing incomplete database recovery. In the following sections, you'll learn how to configure Flashback Database, you'll step through a simple example, and you'll learn how to monitor a Flashback Database. In addition, you'll review some of the finer points, such as how to exclude one or more tablespaces from a Flashback Database operation and how to use guaranteed restore points.

Understanding Flashback Database

You can use Flashback Database to bring your entire database quickly to a previous point in time. When you enable Flashback Database, the before images of modified blocks are saved in the flash recovery area as Flashback Database logs. When a logical corruption occurs that requires a recovery to a time in the past, the Flashback Database logs restore the data blocks before images, and then the archived and online redo logs roll forward to the desired flashback time. This process is typically much faster than performing a traditional restore and recovery operation because the database's datafiles do not need to be restored.

When Flashback Database is enabled, the before image data is saved in a buffer that is appropriately named the *flashback buffer*. Then it uses the Recovery Writer (RVWR) background process to save the before image information from the flashback buffer to the Flashback Database logs in the flash recovery area. The logs in the flash recovery area are reused in a circular fashion. How far back you can rewind the database depends on the amount of space in your flash recovery area and the guaranteed restore points you have configured. You'll learn more about guaranteed restore points later in this section.

Configuring Flashback Database

To use Flashback Database, you must configure the flash recovery area (see Chapter 2 for more information on configuring the flash recovery area using the parameters DB_RECOVERY_FILE_DEST and DB_RECOVERY_FILE_DEST_SIZE). Configuring the size of the flash recovery area correctly ensures that enough space exists for Flashback Database logs in addition to all the other information in the flash recovery area, such as archived redo log files and RMAN backups. You set the initialization parameter DB_FLASHBACK_RETENTION_TARGET to an upper limit (in minutes) for your usable recovery window. This parameter is a target and not a guarantee. You will use guaranteed restore points to ensure the retention of Flashback Database logs in the flash recovery area.

Here is the typical sequence of commands you will use to enable Flashback Database:

```
shutdown immediate;
startup mount exclusive;
alter database archivelog;
/* if you are not already in ARCHIVELOG mode */
alter system set db_flashback_retention_target=2880;
alter database flashback on;
alter database open;
```

In this example, the target retention time for flashback logs is 2,880 minutes (two days).

Using Flashback Database

The most straightforward scenario for using Flashback Database is to restore the entire database to a specific timestamp. However, many scenarios are not this clear. In the following sections, you'll learn how to use Flashback Database with an SCN or a guaranteed restore point. You'll also learn how to exclude one or more tablespaces from the Flashback Database operation, and you'll see some dynamic performance views that can help you monitor the ability to meet your retention target.

Performing Flashback Database

You can use the FLASHBACK DATABASE command from RMAN or from the SQL> prompt. Some subtle syntactical differences exist between the two versions. The RMAN version offers you some additional granularity options, such as flashing back to a particular log sequence number and thread (instance). Here's an example:

```
RMAN> flashback database to sequence=307 thread=2;
```

You'll use the SQL version of the FLASHBACK DATABASE command in the rest of this section. The basic syntax for the SQL FLASHBACK DATABASE command is as follows:

```
flashback [standby] database [database]
{ to {scn | timestamp} expr
| to before {scn | timestamp } expr
| to restore point expr
}
```

You can use either the TO SCN or TO TIMESTAMP clause to set the point to which the entire database should be flashed back, which is in addition to a guaranteed restore point. You can flash back TO BEFORE a critical point, such as a transaction that produced an unintended consequence for multiple tables. Use the ORA_ROWSCN pseudocolumn for a particular table row to see the SCNs of the most recent changes to the row:

```
SQL> select ora_rowscn, last_name, first_name
  2  from employees
  3  where employee_id = 102;

ORA_ROWSCN LAST_NAME                 FIRST_NAME
---------- ------------------------- --------------------
  27247532 De Haan                   Lex

SQL>
```

With the database open for more than an hour, verify that the flashback data is available and then flash it back—you will lose all transactions that occurred during that time:

```
shutdown;
startup mount exclusive;
flashback database to timestamp sysdate-(1/24);
```

When you execute the FLASHBACK DATABASE command, Oracle checks to make sure all required archived and online redo log files are available. If the logs are available, the online datafiles are reverted to the time, SCN, or guaranteed restore point specified.

If there is not enough data online in the archive logs and the flashback area, you will need to use traditional database recovery methods to recover the data. For example, you might need to use a file system recovery method followed by rolling the data forward.

Once the flashback has completed, you must open the database using the RESETLOGS option to have write access to the database:

```
alter database open resetlogs;
```

To turn off the flashback database option, execute the ALTER DATABASE FLASHBACK OFF command when the database is mounted but not open:

```
startup mount exclusive;
alter database flashback off;
alter database open;
```

Excluding Tablespaces from Flashback Database

By default, all tablespaces will participate in a Flashback Database operation unless you change the FLASHBACK attribute to OFF at the time the tablespace is created or later using the ALTER TABLESPACE command. Here's an example:

```
SQL> alter tablespace example flashback off;

Tablespace altered.

SQL>
```

To reenable Flashback Database on this tablespace, shut down and reopen the database in MOUNT mode; then use ALTER TABLESPACE EXAMPLE FLASHBACK ON, followed by ALTER DATABASE OPEN.

When you need to use Flashback Database, take all tablespaces offline with the FLASHBACK attribute set to OFF. When the database is back up, you can use other point-in-time recovery methods to recover the offline datafiles and eventually bring them back online.

Using Guaranteed Restore Points

A *guaranteed restore point* is similar to a regular restore point in that it can be used as an alias for an SCN during a recovery operation. A guaranteed restore point is different in that it is not aged out of the control file and must be explicitly dropped. Not surprisingly, guaranteed restore points are useful for Flashback Database operations. Creating a guaranteed restore point when you have flashback logging enabled ensures that flashback logs are retained in the flash recovery area so that the database can be rolled back to any point after the creation of the guaranteed restore point.

Here is an example of a guaranteed restore point created before a major application upgrade:

```
SQL> create restore point before_app_upgr
  2      guarantee flashback database;

Restore point created.

SQL>
```

Here is how you would use this guaranteed restore point:

```
SQL> flashback database to restore point before_app_upgr;
```

To use guaranteed restore points, you must also enable these prerequisites:

- The COMPATIBLE initialization parameter must be 10.2 or higher.
- The database must be running in ARCHIVELOG mode.
- You must have archived redo log files available starting from the time of the first guaranteed restore point.
- You must have a flash recovery area configured.

Keep in mind that guaranteed restore points will likely cause space pressure in the flash recovery area over time because Oracle will retain any flashback logs in the flash recovery area after the first guaranteed restore point.

Monitoring Flashback Database

You can use several dynamic performance views to monitor the space usage of the flash recovery area to ensure that you can meet the retention target for possible Flashback Database operations.

You can determine how far back you can flashback the database by querying the V$FLASHBACK_DATABASE_LOG view. The amount of flashback data retained in the database is controlled by the initialization parameter and the size of the flash recovery area. The following listing shows the available columns in V$FLASHBACK_DATABASE_LOG and sample contents:

```
SQL> describe V$FLASHBACK_DATABASE_LOG

Name                                      Null?    Type
----------------------------------------- -------- -------
OLDEST_FLASHBACK_SCN                               NUMBER
OLDEST_FLASHBACK_TIME                              DATE
RETENTION_TARGET                                   NUMBER
FLASHBACK_SIZE                                     NUMBER
ESTIMATED_FLASHBACK_SIZE                           NUMBER


SQL> select * from V$FLASHBACK_DATABASE_LOG;

OLDEST_FLASHBACK_SCN OLDEST_FL RETENTION_TARGET FLASHBACK_SIZE
-------------------- --------- ---------------- --------------
ESTIMATED_FLASHBACK_SIZE
------------------------
             5903482 12-AUG-13             1440        8192000
                95224008
```

You can verify the database's flashback status by querying V$DATABASE. The FLASHBACK_ON column will have a value of YES if the flashback has been enabled for the database:

```
SQL> select current_scn, flashback_on from V$DATABASE;

CURRENT_SCN FLA
----------- ---
    5910734 YES
```

Finally, you can use the view V$FLASHBACK_DATABASE_STAT to monitor the rate at which flashback data is generated on an hour-by-hour basis:

```
SQL> select to_char(begin_time,'dd-mon-yy hh24:mi') begin_time,
  2         to_char(end_time,'dd-mon-yy hh24:mi') end_time,
  3         flashback_data, db_data, redo_data,
  4         estimated_flashback_size est_fb_sz
  5  from v$flashback_database_stat;

BEGIN_TIME      END_TIME        FLASHBACK_DATA   DB_DATA  REDO_DATA EST_FB_SZ
--------------- --------------- -------------- --------- ---------- ---------
17-aug-13 16:28 17-aug-13 17:13       12738560  18407424    7079424  95224008

SQL>
```

FLASHBACK_DATA is the number of bytes of flashback data written during the interval. REDO_DATA is the number of bytes of redo written during the same period. DB_DATA is the number of bytes in all data blocks written. The column ESTIMATED_FLASHBACK_SIZE (abbreviated to EST_FB_SZ) contains the same value as ESTIMATED_FLASHBACK_SIZE in V$FLASHBACK_DATABASE_LOG.

CERTIFICATION SUMMARY

In the beginning of the chapter, you learned the basics of Flashback Query and how it can view one or more rows of a table at a time in the past. To use Flashback Query, you must first properly configure automatic undo management and then size the UNDO tablespace to accommodate undo retention of undo data as far back as needed. Undo retention must accommodate DML transactions, query read consistency, and support Flashback Query to the desired point of time in the past.

Flashback Transaction is similar to Flashback Query, except Flashback Transaction uses the data dictionary view FLASHBACK_TRANSACTION_QUERY to contain information about past transactions on one or more tables. To support Flashback Transaction, you must enable supplemental logging for all table columns and the primary key column, somewhat increasing the amount of data that the Log Writer (LGWR) process writes to the redo log files. Flashback Transaction leverages Log Miner technology to retrieve the details on previous transactions. Once you've identified the changes made within a transaction, you can use Enterprise Manager or the UNDO_SQL column in FLASHBACK_TRANSACTION_QUERY to reverse part or all of the transaction. This depends on your tolerance for atomicity and other subsequent transactions in the database.

Next, I reviewed Flashback Drop (one of the Flashback Table features) that uses a recycle bin construct supported in every tablespace. It behaves much like the recycle bin on a Windows-based computer. If enough room is available in the tablespace, dropped objects can be restored to their original schema with all indexes, triggers, and constraints intact. The recycle bin uses a data dictionary table that keeps track of dropped objects. You can restore one or more versions of a dropped table from the recycle bin as long as the recycle bin is enabled and space pressure in the tablespace has not purged the dropped table from the tablespace.

Flashback Table is another technology that lets you rewind the state of one table or a group of tables to a time in the past. Like many flashback features, Flashback Table relies on data in the UNDO tablespace and is subject to the configured retention policy.

The third table recovery option, new to Oracle Database 12*c*, allows you to recover a single table using an RMAN backup in a fraction of the time it would take to restore and recover an entire database to a previous point in time to copy the dropped table from the recovered database.

Flashback Data Archive (Temporal History) provides a way to preserve the history of selected tables over a much longer period of time than is supported by the UNDO tablespace. To configure and use Flashback Data Archive, you create one or more repository areas (one of which can be the default), assign a default retention period for objects in the repository, and then mark the appropriate tables for tracking. Once changes start recording in the Flashback Data Archive, you can use the familiar AS OF clause in the SELECT statement to view previous versions of rows in a table.

Finally, you learned how to configure and use Flashback Database to roll back the entire database to a time in the past. After you configure the flash recovery area to retain the before images of changed data blocks (flashback logs), you can recover the database to a specific timestamp or SCN as long as the required flashback logs are still in the flash recovery area. You can use guaranteed restore points to ensure that the database can be rolled back to the guaranteed restore point or any SCN or timestamp since you created the guaranteed restore point.

TWO-MINUTE DRILL

Describe the Flashback Technologies

- The investigative flashback features are Flashback Query, Flashback Version Query, and Flashback Transaction Query.
- To repair a logical error, you use one of these Flashback tools: Flashback Transaction Backout, Flashback Table, Flashback Drop, or Flashback Database.
- The key initialization parameters used to configure flashback features are UNDO_TABLESPACE, UNDO_MANAGEMENT, and UNDO_RETENTION.
- To perform any flashback repair operation, you must have the FLASHBACK system privilege.

Use Flashback to Query Data

- Flashback Query enables you to view one or more rows in a table at a time in the past.
- To ensure the success of flashback operations or long-running queries at the expense of DML activity, you must specify RETENTION GUARANTEE for the UNDO tablespace.
- You can check the retention status of an UNDO tablespace by querying the data dictionary view DBA_TABLESPACES.
- Flashback Query uses the AS OF clause to specify the previous point in time as a timestamp or SCN.
- Flashback Version Query, another flashback feature that relies on undo data, provides a finer level of detail than an AS OF query (a Flashback Query).
- Flashback Version Query uses the VERSIONS BETWEEN clause to specify a range of SCNs or timestamps for analysis of a given table.

Perform Flashback Table Operations

- Flashback Drop uses the recycle bin to recover dropped tables.
- The recycle bin is a data dictionary table that keeps track of dropped objects.

- ❑ You can restore the current or previous versions of dropped tables from the recycle bin.
- ❑ When you drop an object with the recycle bin enabled, the space allocated to the dropped object and all associated objects (such as indexes) is immediately reflected in the data dictionary view DBA_FREE_SPACE.
- ❑ When a table is dropped, the table and its dependent objects are renamed to a system-assigned name using the format BIN$unique_id$version.
- ❑ To query the recycle bin, you can use the data dictionary view USER_RECYCLEBIN. RECYCLEBIN is a global synonym for USER_RECYCLEBIN.
- ❑ The data dictionary view USER_RECYCLEBIN has the same columns as DBA_RECYCLEBIN, except that USER_RECYCLEBIN does not have the OWNER column.
- ❑ To restore a table from the recycle bin, you use the FLASHBACK TABLE . . . TO BEFORE DROP command.
- ❑ If you attempt to restore a table that has been re-created since it was dropped, you will receive an error unless you use the RENAME TO clause to give the restored table a new name.
- ❑ The space in the recycle bin, and by extension the space in the tablespace containing the recycle bin, is managed automatically by Oracle.
- ❑ All dropped objects remain available for recovery in the recycle bin as long as new objects don't need the space occupied by dropped objects.
- ❑ You can use the PURGE command to remove tables manually from the recycle bin.
- ❑ When an object resides in the recycle bin, you can still use a SELECT statement to access the dropped table. The dropped table still appears in the data dictionary views DBA_TABLES, DBA_OBJECTS, and DBA_SEGMENTS.
- ❑ Oracle's Flashback Table feature not only restores the state of rows in a table as of a point of time in the past but also restores the table's indexes, triggers, and constraints while the database is online.
- ❑ Flashback Table is preferable to other flashback methods if the scope of user errors is small and limited to one or few tables.
- ❑ Flashback Table is performed in place while the database is online, rolling back changes to the table and all its dependent objects, such as indexes.

- To perform Flashback Table, a user must have the FLASHBACK ANY TABLE privilege or the FLASHBACK object privilege on a specific table.
- To use Flashback Table on a table or tables, you must enable row movement on the table before performing the flashback operation, although row movement need not be in effect when the user error occurs.
- Flashback Table operations cannot span DDL operations, such as adding or dropping a column.
- The data dictionary view FLASHBACK_TRANSACTION_QUERY has all the information you need to identify the SQL required to reverse a transaction.
- Before you can use Flashback Transaction Query, you must enable additional logging to the redo log stream. This is the same data that Log Miner uses although using a different interface.
- You must grant permissions on the DBMS_FLASHBACK package, as well as the SELECT ANY TRANSACTION privilege to the users who will be using Flashback Transaction Query.
- The UNDO_SQL column of FLASHBACK_TRANSACTION_QUERY contains the actual SQL code that can be used to reverse the effect of the transaction.
- Enterprise Manager (EM) provides an easy-to-use GUI as the front end for the procedure DBMS_FLASHBACK.TRANSACTION_BACKOUT.
- The four transaction backout options are CASCADE, NOCASCADE, NOCASCADE_FORCE, and NONCONFLICT_ONLY.

Perform Table Recovery from Backups

- Individual tables can be recovered from an RMAN backup without recovering any other tables in the tablespace's datafiles.
- COMPATIBLE must be 12.0 or higher to recover tables from RMAN backups.
- ARCHIVELOG mode is required.
- You cannot recover tables from the SYSTEM or SYSAUX tablespace.
- Specify the timestamp or SCN for the point in time at which you want the table recovered along with the name of the table.

- ❑ A temporary auxiliary instance is created automatically to perform the table recovery.
- ❑ Data Pump moves the recovered table from the auxiliary instance to the target database.

Describe and User Flashback Data Archive

- ❑ A Flashback Data Archive retains historical data for one or more tables for a specified retention period.
- ❑ To enable a Flashback Data Archive, you create one or more repository areas (one of which can be the default), assign a default retention period for objects in the repository, and then mark the appropriate tables for tracking.
- ❑ A Flashback Data Archive acts much like an UNDO tablespace. However, a Flashback Data Archive records only UPDATE and DELETE statements but not INSERT statements.
- ❑ You can access data in a Flashback Data Archive just as you do with Flashback Query using the AS OF clause in a SELECT statement.
- ❑ You create one or several Flashback Data Archives in existing tablespaces using the CREATE FLASHBACK ARCHIVE command.
- ❑ The data dictionary views supporting Flashback Data Archives are DBA_FLASHBACK_ARCHIVE and DBA_FLASHBACK_ARCHIVE_TS.
- ❑ The view DBA_FLASHBACK_ARCHIVE_TABLES tracks the tables enabled for flashback archiving.
- ❑ A user must have the FLASHBACK ARCHIVE ADMINISTER system privilege to create or modify Flashback Data Archives.
- ❑ You assign a table to an archive either at table creation using the standard CREATE TABLE syntax with the addition of the FLASHBACK ARCHIVE clause, or later with the ALTER TABLE command.

Perform Flashback Database

- ❑ Flashback Database uses the FLASHBACK DATABASE command to return the database to a past time or SCN, providing a fast alternative to performing incomplete database recovery.
- ❑ When you enable Flashback Database, the before images of modified blocks are saved in the flash recovery area as Flashback Database logs.

- The logs in the flash recovery area are reused in a circular fashion.
- Configuring the size of the flash recovery area correctly ensures that enough space is available for Flashback Database logs in addition to all the other information in the flash recovery area.
- You set the initialization parameter DB_FLASHBACK_RETENTION_TARGET to an upper limit (in minutes) for your usable recovery window; this is a target, not a guarantee.
- You can use the FLASHBACK DATABASE command from RMAN or from the SQL> prompt.
- You can use either the TO SCN or TO TIMESTAMP clause to set the point to which the entire database should be flashed back, in addition to a guaranteed restore point.
- You can use the ORA_ROWSCN pseudocolumn for a given table row to see the SCNs of the most recent changes to a table's row.
- If not enough data exists in the archive logs and the flashback area, you will need to use traditional database recovery methods to recover the data.
- To turn off the flashback database option, execute the ALTER DATABASE FLASHBACK OFF command when the database is mounted but not open.
- By default, all tablespaces will participate in a Flashback Database operation unless you change the FLASHBACK attribute to OFF at the time the tablespace is created or later using the ALTER TABLESPACE command.
- A guaranteed restore point is similar to a regular restore point in that it can be used as an alias for an SCN during a recovery operation.
- A guaranteed restore point is different in that it is not aged out of the control file and must be explicitly dropped.
- Creating a guaranteed restore point when you have flashback logging enabled ensures that flashback logs are retained in the flash recovery area so that the database can be rolled back to any point after the creation of the guaranteed restore point.
- You can determine how far back you can flashback the database by querying the V$FLASHBACK_DATABASE_LOG view.
- You can use the view V$FLASHBACK_DATABASE_STAT to monitor the rate at which flashback data is generated on an hour-by-hour basis.

SELF TEST

The following questions will help you measure your understanding of the material presented in this chapter. Read all the choices carefully because there might be more than one correct answer. Choose all correct answers for each question.

Describe the Flashback Technologies

1. Which of the following flashback technologies use data from the current UNDO tablespace? (Choose all that apply.)
   A. Flashback Table
   B. Flashback Transaction Query
   C. Flashback Query
   D. Flashback Version Query
   E. Flashback Drop
   F. Flashback Database
   G. Flashback Data Archive

2. Which of the following parameters directly affect the behavior and proper functioning of Flashback Table? (Choose all that apply.)
   A. DB_RECOVERY_FILE_DEST
   B. UNDO_MANAGEMENT
   C. DB_RECOVERY_FILE_DEST_SIZE
   D. UNDO_TABLESPACE
   E. UNDO_RETENTION

Use Flashback to Query Data

3. When using the VERSIONS BETWEEN clause for Flashback Version Query, what can't you use to restrict the number of rows returned by the query?
   A. A timestamp
   B. An SCN
   C. A WHERE clause on any column in the table
   D. A guaranteed restore point

Perform Flashback Table Operations

4. Which of the following statements is true about the recycle bin?

A. When you drop an object, the space allocated by the object is not immediately reflected in DBA_FREE_SPACE and counts against the user's quota.

B. When you drop an object, the space allocated by the object is immediately reflected in DBA_FREE_SPACE and does not count against the user's quota.

C. When you drop an object, the space allocated by the object is immediately reflected in DBA_FREE_SPACE but still counts against the user's quota.

D. When you drop an object, the space allocated by the object is not immediately reflected in DBA_FREE_SPACE and does not count against the user's quota.

5. The column CAN_UNDROP is set to YES for an object in the view DBA_RECYCLEBIN. Which of the following is true for this object? (Choose all that apply.)

A. The object is a table.

B. The object can be undropped by the user who owns the object.

C. The object can be undropped only by a user with DBA privileges.

D. The object does not have any dependent objects in the recycle bin.

E. No existing object with the same name exists outside of the recycle bin.

6. Which of the following columns is not in the data dictionary view FLASHBACK_TRANSACTION_QUERY?

A. UNDO_SQL

B. XID

C. OPERATION

D. ORA_ROWSCN

7. What happens to the rows in FLASHBACK_TRANSACTION_QUERY when part of the transaction is no longer available in the UNDO tablespace?

A. The user ID number replaces the username in the LOGON_USER column.

B. The OPERATION column contains the value UNKNOWN.

C. The object number replaces the table name in the TABLE_NAME column.

D. The OPERATION column contains the value UNAVAILABLE.

E. All rows for the transaction are no longer available in FLASHBACK_TRANSACTION_QUERY.

8. What methods can you use in the AS OF clause of a Flashback Table operation to specify the time in the past to which you want to recover the table? (Choose all that apply.)
   A. A timestamp
   B. A filter condition in the WHERE clause
   C. An SCN
   D. A restore point
   E. A guaranteed restore point

9. You create the table VAC_SCHED on Monday with a primary key index; the SCN right after table creation was 5680123. On Wednesday, you drop the index. On Thursday, you accidentally delete most of the rows in the database. On Friday, you execute this command:

```
SQL> FLASHBACK TABLE VAC_SCHED TO SCN 5680123;
```

   You have set guaranteed undo retention to one week. What is the result of running this command?
   A. The table is recovered to SCN 5680123 without the index.
   B. The table is recovered using the data in the UNDO tablespace, and the index is re-created using the dropped index in the recycle bin.
   C. The table is recovered, and all rows deleted on Thursday are restored using archived and online redo log files.
   D. The command fails because FLASHBACK TABLE cannot recover a table before a change to a dependent object.

Perform Table Recovery from Backups

10. Which of the following conditions will prevent recovery of a table or table partition using table recovery from backups? (Choose all that apply.)
   A. The database is in read-only mode.
   B. COMPATIBLE is set to 12.1.
   C. You are recovering a table owned by SYS in the USERS tablespace.
   D. The table is partitioned, and the indexes are in a different partition.
   E. The database is in NOARCHIVELOG mode.

Describe and User Flashback Data Archive

11. Identify the true statement about Flashback Data Archives.

A. You can specify more than one default Flashback Data Archive.

B. If you do not specify a RETENTION clause for a Flashback Data Archive, you must specify it when assigning a table to the Flashback Data Archive.

C. The QUOTA parameter is required when creating a Flashback Data Archive to limit the amount of space used in the tablespace.

D. A Flashback Data Archive can exist in multiple tablespaces including UNDO tablespaces and temporary tablespaces.

12. Which of the following data dictionary views contains a list of the tables using a Flashback Data Archive?

A. DBA_FLASHBACK_ARCHIVE_TABLES

B. DBA_FLASHBACK_ARCHIVE

C. DBA_FLASHBACK_ARCHIVE_TS

D. DBA_FLASHBACK_DATA_ARCHIVE_TABLES

Perform Flashback Database

13. Which of the following initialization parameters is not required to configure Flashback Database operations?

A. DB_RECOVERY_FILE_DEST_SIZE

B. UNDO_RETENTION

C. DB_FLASHBACK_RETENTION_TARGET

D. DB_RECOVERY_FILE_DEST

14. What is the difference between a regular restore point and a guaranteed restore point? (Choose all that apply.)

A. A regular restore point does not require that a flash recovery area be configured.

B. A guaranteed restore point can be used only with Flashback Database.

C. A guaranteed restore point cannot be dropped.

D. A guaranteed restore point will never be aged out of the control file.

E. You must have flashback logging enabled to use guaranteed restore points.

SELF TEST ANSWERS

Describe the Flashback Technologies

1. ☑ **A, B, C,** and **D.** All of these technologies rely on the undo data in the UNDO tablespace.
☒ **E, F,** and **G** are incorrect. Flashback Drop relies on the recycle bin, Flashback Database relies on flashback logs in the flash recovery area, and Flashback Data Archive relies on history tables based on a permanent table in tablespaces designated for flashback data archives.

2. ☑ **B, D,** and **E.** For Flashback Query, Flashback Table, Flashback Transaction Query, and Flashback Version Query, you must have automatic undo management configured, an UNDO tablespace defined, and an undo retention value to specify how long undo data is retained in the UNDO tablespace.
☒ **A** and **C** are incorrect. The parameters DB_RECOVERY_FILE_DEST and DB_RECOVERY_FILE_DEST_SIZE are used to configure Flashback Data Archive retention, but not Flashback Query.

Use Flashback to Query Data

3. ☑ **D.** Guaranteed restore points are used only in recovery scenarios such as Flashback Database.
☒ **A, B,** and **C** are incorrect. All three can be used. You can restrict the results of a Flashback Version Query by SCN or timestamp. You can further filter the rows by using a WHERE clause on the table columns.

Perform Flashback Table Operations

4. ☑ **C.** A dropped object's space is immediately reflected in DBA_FREE_SPACE but still counts against the user's quota until it is purged from the recycle bin.
☒ **A, B,** and **D** are incorrect. All three reflect incorrect statements about free space management and quota management for objects in the recycle bin.

5. ☑ **A** and **B.** Table objects in the recycle bin can be undropped, and they can be undropped by the original owner or a user with DBA privileges.
☒ **C, D,** and **E** are incorrect. **C** is incorrect because an object in the recycle bin can be undropped by the owner or a user with DBA privileges; the view DBA_RECYCLEBIN has an OWNER column to indicate which user dropped the object. **D** is incorrect because a table in the recycle bin may or may not have dependent objects in the recycle bin. **E** is incorrect because there may or may not be an object with the same original name as an object in the recycle bin.

6. ☑ **D.** ORA_ROWSCN is a pseudocolumn that is available for all tables and contains the last SCN that modified or created the row.
   ☒ **A, B,** and **C** are incorrect. UNDO_SQL is the SQL you can use to reverse the change to the row, XID is the transaction ID, and OPERATION is the DML operation performed.

7. ☑ **B.** The OPERATION column in FLASHBACK_TRANSACTION_QUERY contains UNKNOWN for data no longer in the UNDO tablespace.
   ☒ **A, C, D,** and **E** are incorrect. **A** is incorrect because the user ID replaces the username in the LOGON_USER column when the user no longer exists. **C** is incorrect because the object number replaces the table name in the TABLE_NAME column when the table no longer exists. **D** is incorrect because the OPERATION column contains UNKNOWN, not UNAVAILABLE, when the information is no longer available in the UNDO tablespace. **E** is incorrect because part of a transaction might still be available in the UNDO tablespace.

8. ☑ **A, C, D,** and **E.** You can use the AS OF clause with the TIMESTAMP or SCN qualifier to specify a time to which you want to recover the table. In addition, you can specify a restore point or a guaranteed restore point for Flashback Table. Guaranteed restore points are also useful in Flashback Database operations to ensure that flashback logs are maintained in the flash recovery area at least as far back as the earliest guaranteed restore point.
   ☒ **B** is incorrect because you cannot use a WHERE clause to specify the time in the past for the FLASHBACK TABLE operation.

9. ☑ **A.** The table is recovered to its original state right after creation with no rows and without the index.
   ☒ **B, C,** and **D** are incorrect. **B** is incorrect because FLASHBACK TABLE does not leverage the recycle bin. **C** is incorrect because the table is recovered as of the SCN but not rolled forward. **D** is incorrect because a dropped index does not affect the recoverability of a table; however, a change to the structure of the table itself prevents a flashback operation to before the DDL change to the table.

Perform Table Recovery from Backups

10. ☑ **A, C,** and **E.** To successfully perform table recovery from backups (TRFB), the database must be in read-write mode, you cannot recover objects owned by SYS regardless of which tablespace they reside in, and the database must be in ARCHIVELOG mode. In addition, the COMPATIBLE parameter must be set to 12.0 or higher, and you cannot recover objects to the SYSTEM or SYSAUX tablespace.
    ☒ **B** and **D** are incorrect. The COMPATIBLE parameter must be at least 12.0, and the table to be recovered need not be contained in a single tablespace or group of tablespaces as would be required with traditional tablespace point in time recovery (TSPITR).

Describe and User Flashback Data Archive

11. ☑ **B.** You must either specify a default retention period for the Flashback Data Archive itself or specify a retention period when adding the table to the archive.
☒ **A, C,** and **D** are incorrect. **A** is incorrect because you can have several Flashback Data Archives. **C** is incorrect because the QUOTA parameter is needed only if you want to limit the amount of space used by the Flashback Data Archive in the tablespace; otherwise, it can grow to use all available space in the tablespace. **D** is incorrect because you can create Flashback Data Archives only in permanent, non-UNDO tablespaces.

12. ☑ **A.** DBA_FLASHBACK_ARCHIVE_TABLES contains a list of tables currently using a Flashback Data Archive.
☒ **B, C,** and **D** are incorrect. **B** is incorrect because DBA_FLASHBACK_ARCHIVE contains a list of the archives, but not the tables within. **C** is incorrect because DBA_FLASHBACK_ARCHIVE_TS contains the archive to tablespace mapping. **D** is incorrect because DBA_FLASHBACK_DATA_ARCHIVE_TABLES is not a valid data dictionary view.

Perform Flashback Database

13. ☑ **B.** The initialization parameter UNDO_RETENTION is required for other flashback features but not for Flashback Database.
☒ **A, C,** and **D** are incorrect. The parameters DB_RECOVERY_FILE_DEST_SIZE and DB_RECOVERY_FILE_DEST are required to define the location and size of the flash recovery area, and DB_FLASHBACK_RETENTION_TARGET is needed to define a desired upper limit for the Flashback Database recovery window.

14. ☑ **A** and **D.** A regular restore point does not require a flash recovery area, and it can be aged out of the control file; a guaranteed restore point will never be aged out of the control file unless it is explicitly dropped.
☒ **B, C,** and **E** are incorrect. **B** is incorrect because a guaranteed restore point can be referenced for other flashback features, not just Flashback Database. **C** is incorrect because you can explicitly drop any type of restore point. **E** is incorrect because you can define guaranteed restore points without flashback logging enabled; however, you must still have a flash recovery area enabled.

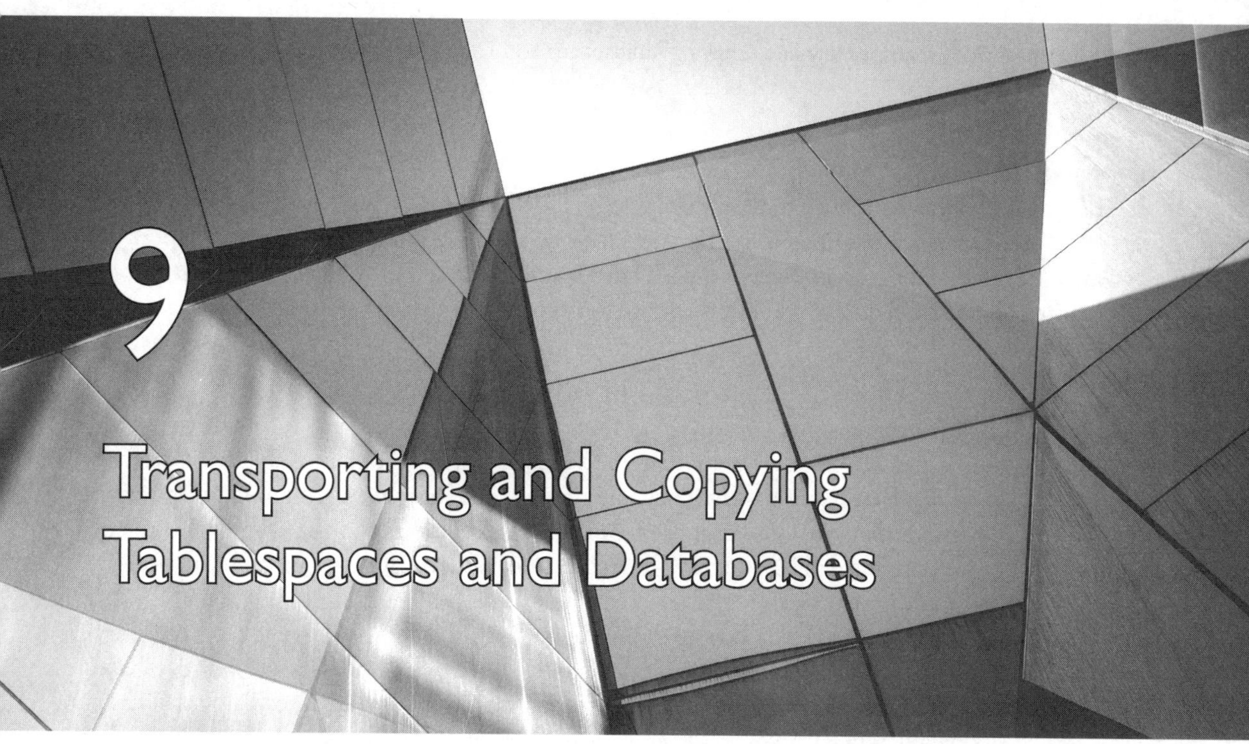

9 Transporting and Copying Tablespaces and Databases

CERTIFICATION OBJECTIVES

9.01	Describe and Use Transportable Tablespaces and Databases
9.02	Choose a Technique for Duplicating a Database
9.03	Create a Backup-Based Duplicate Database
9.04	Duplicate a Database Based on a Running Instance
✓	Two-Minute Drill
Q&A	Self Test

This chapter continues the journey into the world of RMAN and covers several additional features that will help you use your time more effectively and accomplish tasks in a shorter amount of time. These features make it easy to not only move tablespaces to and from a database but duplicate a database from either an RMAN backup or a running instance.

First, the chapter will cover another disk-related time-saving feature: transportable tablespaces. You can use this feature to quickly copy one or more tablespaces from one database to another without using the much more time-consuming export/import method from previous versions of Oracle. An extension to transportable tablespaces, transportable databases, makes it easy to create a new database and move all non-SYSTEM tablespaces to the new database.

Next, I'll show you how to duplicate a database. RMAN makes it easy to make a full copy or a subset of a target database. The copied database has a new database ID (DBID) and can thus coexist on the same network as the source database. The copied database can even be on the same host and can use the same RMAN catalog as the source database because it has its own DBID. A copy of a database has many uses, including testing of backup and recovery procedures.

If you must have your source database open on a continuous basis, you can even clone your database while it is open and available to users. Because you're copying from an open database, you don't need an intermediate RMAN backup, which can save a lot of time and disk space.

CERTIFICATION OBJECTIVE 9.01

Describe and Use Transportable Tablespaces and Databases

There are many ways to move data from one database to another, such as database links, Data Pump export/import, and transportable tablespaces. For large volumes of data, using transportable tablespaces is by far the fastest method. In a nutshell, you export just the metadata for the objects in the tablespace using Data Pump, copy the datafiles comprising the tablespace to the destination database, and import the tablespace's metadata into the destination database.

The following sections further investigate some of the restrictions of transportable tablespaces such as platform limitations. Even platforms with different hardware architectures are candidates for transportable tablespaces. In addition, you will learn how to transport a tablespace using both Enterprise Manager Cloud Control 12*c* (Cloud Control) and SQL commands. RMAN is required to transport a tablespace in some scenarios. Finally, a brief overview of how to transport an entire database will be given.

Configuring Transportable Tablespaces

Transporting tablespaces has many uses, such as quickly distributing data from a data warehouse to data marts in other databases or converting an entire database from one platform to another. When transporting between platforms, both the source and destination platforms must be on Oracle's list of supported platforms. Most likely, your source and destination platforms will be supported. For example, virtually all hardware platforms based on either 32-bit or 64-bit Intel architecture are supported, along with Solaris, Mac OS, and AIX on proprietary hardware.

The following sections step through the compatibility requirements as well as any additional steps you need to perform for some hardware platforms. Once the compatibility and configuration steps are complete, you will step through an example using both Cloud Control and SQL commands.

Determining Compatibility Requirements

Oracle Database feature compatibility is controlled by the COMPATIBLE initialization parameter, which enables or disables the use of certain features in the database. For the purposes of discussing transportable tablespaces, these are features that require a specific file format on disk. For example, if you want to upgrade to Oracle Database 12*c* from Oracle Database 11*g* R2, you may want to set COMPATIBLE to 11.2.0 for a short time. Thus, you can downgrade to version 11*g* R2 if you encounter problems in production, without requiring a restore and recover from backup because the datafile formats for version 12*c* are not usable on version 11*g* R2. Even though you may have tested the upgrade on a backup server, some problems with a new release do not appear until a week after you go live with the new release in production!

When you create a transportable tablespace set, Oracle determines the minimum compatibility level of the target database and stores this value in the metadata for the transportable tablespace set. Starting with Oracle Database 11*g*, you can always transport a tablespace to another database with the same or higher compatibility level, regardless of the target platform.

Regardless of the similarities or differences in hardware platforms between the source and target database, both databases must be using the same character set.

Table 9-1 shows the minimum compatibility settings for the source and target databases depending on the differences in block size and hardware platforms.

In other words, even if you are running Oracle Database 12*c* with COMPATIBLE set to 11.0.0, you can transport a tablespace from a database on a different platform that has COMPATIBLE set to 10.0.0.

Determining Endian Requirements

Oracle's transportable tablespace feature, although available for nearly every platform that Oracle Database runs on, requires an extra step depending on the underlying hardware platform. On Intel-based hardware, pairs of bytes in numeric or string values are reversed. For example, the value 2 is stored as 0x0200. This byte ordering is known as *little-endian* because the least significant byte is first. In contrast, a *big-endian* system stores bytes in order of most significant to least significant byte. Therefore, on a big-endian hardware platform, such as Sun SPARC, the value 2

TABLE 9-1 Minimum Compatibility Settings for Transportable Tablespace Scenarios

Operation Type	Source Database Minimum Compatibility Release Number	Target Database Minimum Compatibility Release Number
Transport using full transportable export/import	COMPATIBLE=12.0 (12*c* database) VERSION=12 (Data Pump export parameter)	COMPATIBLE=12.0
Transport on same platform using transportable tablespaces	COMPATIBLE=8.0	COMPATIBLE=8.0
Source database has different database block size than target database for transportable tablespaces	COMPATIBLE=9.0	COMPATIBLE=9.0
Source and target databases are on different platforms	COMPATIBLE=10.0	COMPATIBLE=10.0
Transporting tables between databases	COMPATIBLE=11.1.0.6	COMPATIBLE=11.1.0.6

is stored as 0x0002. Understandably, a conversion must be done on column data transported between platforms with different endian formats.

To determine the endian formats of all supported platforms, you can query the dynamic performance view V$TRANSPORTABLE_PLATFORM, as in this example:

```
SQL> select platform_id, platform_name, endian_format
  2  from v$transportable_platform;

PLATFORM_ID PLATFORM_NAME                                 ENDIAN_FORMAT
----------- --------------------------------------------- --------------
          1 Solaris[tm] OE (32-bit)                       Big
          2 Solaris[tm] OE (64-bit)                       Big
          7 Microsoft Windows IA (32-bit)                 Little
         10 Linux IA (32-bit)                             Little
          6 AIX-Based Systems (64-bit)                    Big
          3 HP-UX (64-bit)                                Big
          5 HP Tru64 UNIX                                 Little
          4 HP-UX IA (64-bit)                             Big
         11 Linux IA (64-bit)                             Little
         15 HP Open VMS                                   Little
          8 Microsoft Windows IA (64-bit)                 Little
          9 IBM zSeries Based Linux                       Big
         13 Linux x86 64-bit                              Little
         16 Apple Mac OS                                  Big
         12 Microsoft Windows x86 64-bit                  Little
         17 Solaris Operating System (x86)                Little
         18 IBM Power Based Linux                         Big
         19 HP IA Open VMS                                Little
         20 Solaris Operating System (x86-64)             Little
         21 Apple Mac OS (x86-64)                         Little

20 rows selected.

SQL>
```

This query also shows you all supported platforms for transportable tablespaces. If the value of ENDIAN_FORMAT is different, then you must use RMAN commands at the source or target database to convert the datafiles to the target database's endian format. The required RMAN commands will be discussed later in this chapter. To determine the endian format of your platform, you can join V$DATABASE to V$TRANSPORTABLE_PLATFORM:

```
SQL> select platform_name my_platform,
  2         endian_format my_endian_format
  3  from v$transportable_platform
  4     join v$database using(platform_name)
  5  ;

MY_PLATFORM                       MY_ENDIAN_FORM
--------------------------------- --------------
Linux x86 64-bit                  Little

SQL>
```

Transporting Tablespaces

Whether you use SQL commands or Cloud Control to transport a tablespace, the general steps are the same. EM does provide some automation to the process that streamlines the procedure and helps to avoid errors. However, as with most EM-based tools, EM does not cover every possible option available at the SQL> command line. Here are the steps:

1. Make the tablespace (or tablespaces) read-only on the source database.
2. Use Data Pump export to extract the tablespace metadata from the source database.
3. If the target does not have the same endian format, convert the tablespace contents.
4. Transfer the tablespace datafiles and metadata dump file from the source to the target.
5. Use Data Pump import to import tablespace metadata into the target tablespace.
6. Make the tablespace (or tablespaces) read-write on both the source and target databases.

The following two sections give you an overview of using EM to transport a tablespace and then provide the SQL version of the same operation.

Using Cloud Control to Transport a Tablespace

To transport a tablespace using Cloud Control, start at the database home page and navigate to Schema/Database Export Import/Transport Tablespaces; you'll see the page shown in Figure 9-1.

In this step, you'll generate a transportable tablespace set containing the tablespace MART_XFER in the RPT12C database and then transport it to the FINMART database. Ensure that the Generate radio button is selected and that you

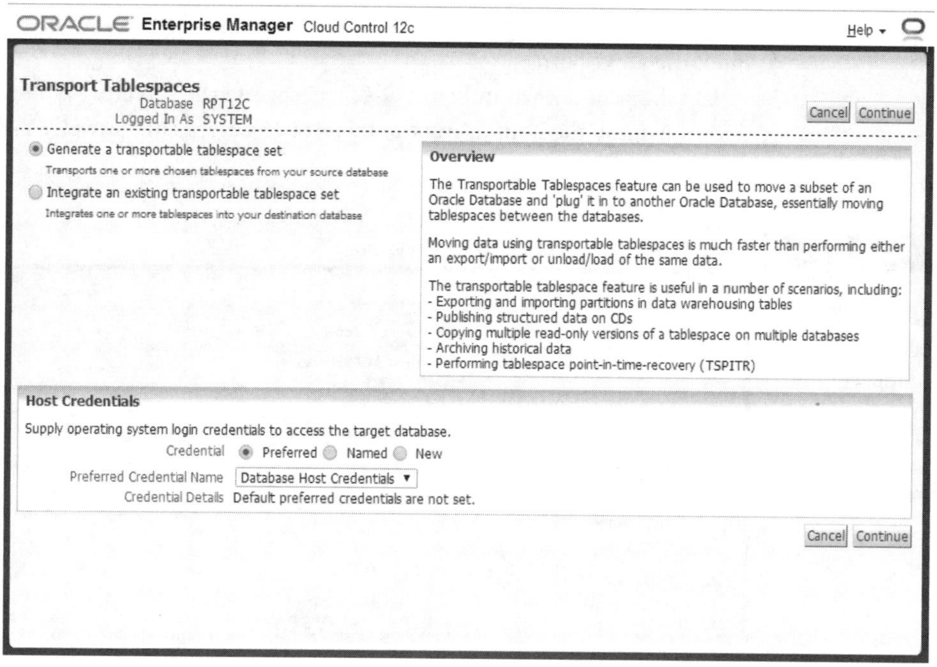

FIGURE 9-1 Transport Tablespaces start page

have provided the hostname credentials for the oracle user (the Linux Oracle user). Click the Continue button. On the page shown in Figure 9-2, add the MART_XFER tablespace to the list.

In addition, you can check that all objects in the tablespace are self-contained. In other words, there are no dependencies on objects in other tablespaces. You can take it a step further and check for the reverse condition in that there are no objects in other tablespaces dependent on the tablespace you are transporting.

When you click the Next button, Cloud Control checks for dependencies between the MART_XFER tablespace and other tablespaces in the database as well as confirming the target database's character sets. On the page shown in Figure 9-3, you specify the destination platform, which is the same for the source and target databases (in this case, both are Linux Intel Architecture 64-bit). If the target database has a different endian format, then Cloud Control (via RMAN) will convert the tablespace. Select the appropriate options for your environment and click the Next button.

On the page shown in Figure 9-4, you specify the directory where you want to save the dump file containing the tablespace's metadata, as well as a copy of the

FIGURE 9-2 Selecting tablespaces for transport

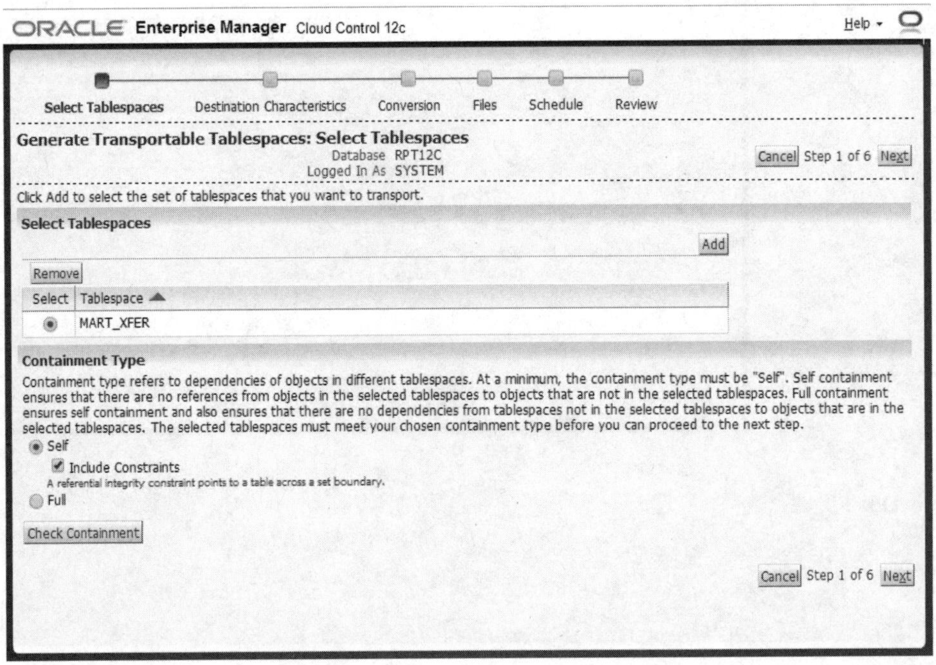

ORACLE Enterprise Manager Cloud Control 12c
Help

Select Tablespaces | Destination Characteristics | Conversion | Files | Schedule | Review

Generate Transportable Tablespaces: Select Tablespaces
Database RPT12C
Logged In As SYSTEM
Cancel Step 1 of 6 Next

Click Add to select the set of tablespaces that you want to transport.

Select Tablespaces
Add
Remove

Select	Tablespace
◉	MART_XFER

Containment Type
Containment type refers to dependencies of objects in different tablespaces. At a minimum, the containment type must be "Self". Self containment ensures that there are no references from objects in the selected tablespaces to objects that are not in the selected tablespaces. Full containment ensures self containment and also ensures that there are no dependencies from tablespaces not in the selected tablespaces to objects that are in the selected tablespaces. The selected tablespaces must meet your chosen containment type before you can proceed to the next step.
◉ Self
☑ Include Constraints
A referential integrity constraint points to a table across a set boundary.
○ Full
Check Containment

Cancel Step 1 of 6 Next

FIGURE 9-3

Specifying destination database characteristics

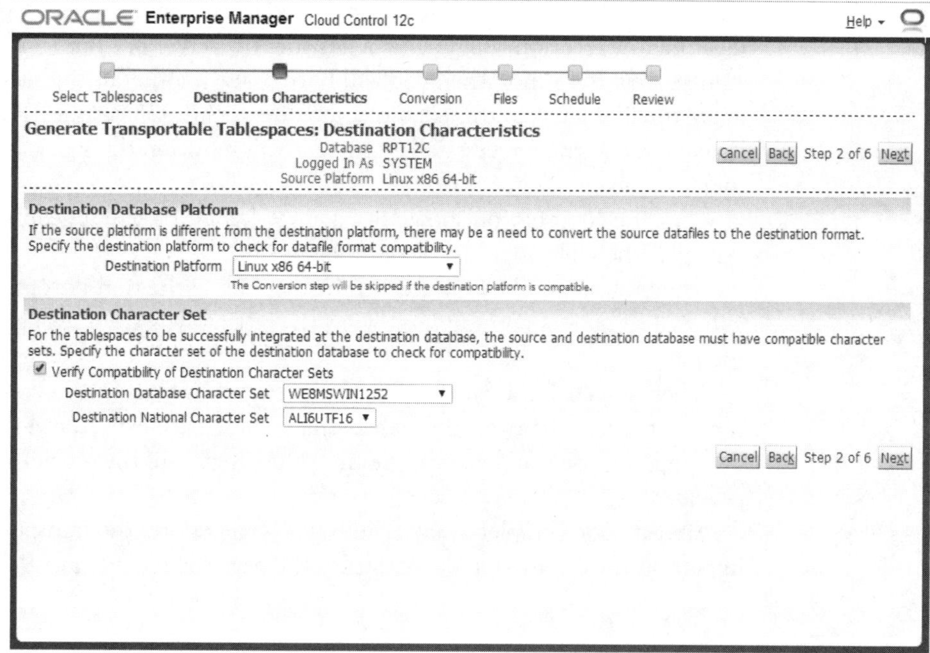

FIGURE 9-4

Specifying transportable tablespace dump file location

ORACLE Enterprise Manager Cloud Control 12c
Help

Select Tablespaces | Destination Characteristics | Conversion | **Files** | Schedule | Review

Generate Transportable Tablespaces: Files

Database RPT12C
Logged In As SYSTEM

Cancel | Finish | Back | Step 4 of 6 | Next

Dump File

Specify the location where the dump file associated with the transportable tablespace can be generated.

* Dump File Directory /u02/oradata/RPT12C/datafile/

* Dump File Name EXPDAT_GENERATETTS000041.DMP

Datafiles

A copy of the datafiles associated with the selected tablespaces is needed. Selected tablespaces will be made read-only as part of Generate Transportable Tablespaces operation.

(•) Copy Datafiles Automatically (Recommended)
The datafiles will be copied to the above specified dump file directory. This operation will require 100 MB of free disk space. The selected tablespaces will be made read-only for the duration of the job.

( ) Manually Copy Datafiles
You are responsible for copying the datafiles. Tablespaces remain in read-only mode after the job is completed to maintain datafile consistency with the dump file. You must manually put tablespaces back into read-write mode after copying datafiles.

Cancel | Finish | Back | Step 4 of 6 | Next

tablespace's datafile(s). This location should be accessible by the target database, meaning the location could be on a network file server or some similar shared storage area. If it is not, then you will have to use another utility such as FTP to move the files later. In this example, the directory **/u02/oradata/RPT12C/datafile** is accessible to the target database since it will reside on the same server as the source database.

Click the Next button shown in Figure 9-4, and you will schedule a job to transport the tablespace, as shown in Figure 9-5.

Figure 9-6 shows the final step in the first half of the transport process, which will give you the opportunity to review the settings you specified before you submit the job.

When you click the Submit Job button shown in Figure 9-6, Cloud Control submits the job to process the transportable tablespace export. EM generates a confirmation page, and you can monitor the progress of the job with the link provided.

After the job completes successfully, you can perform the transportable tablespace import on the destination database. On the page shown in Figure 9-7, you have

FIGURE 9-5 Scheduling transportable tablespace job

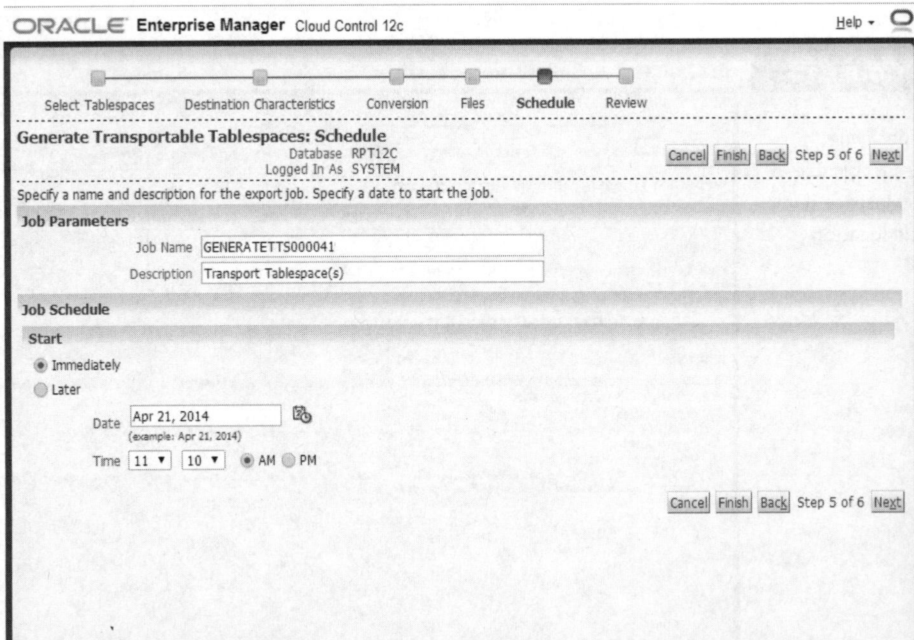

FIGURE 9-6

Reviewing transportable tablespace job settings

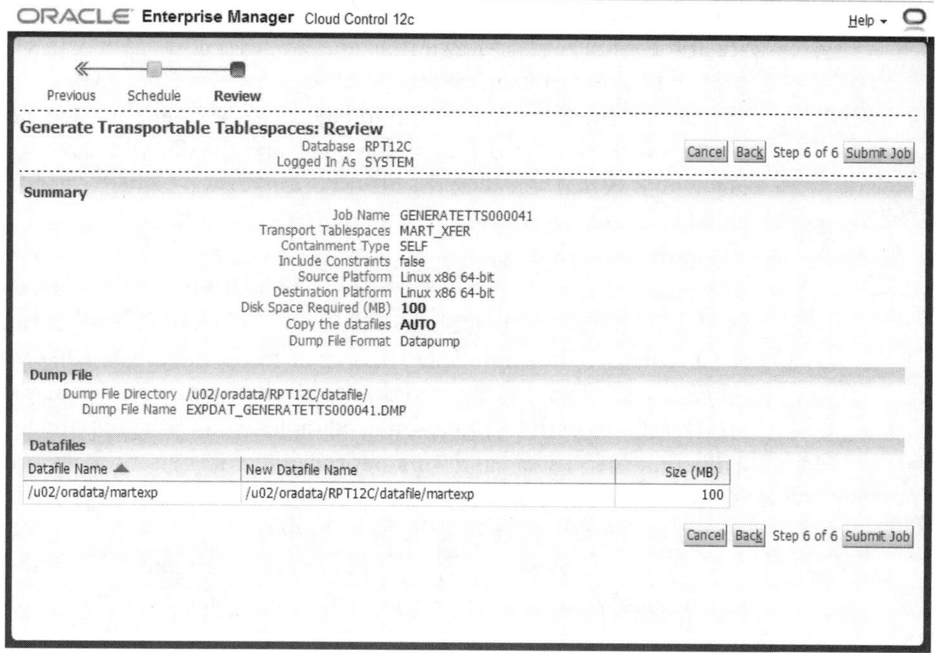

FIGURE 9-7

Transport Tablespaces import home page

ORACLE Enterprise Manager Cloud Control 12c
Help

Transport Tablespaces
Database finmart
Logged In As RJB
Cancel Continue

Generate a transportable tablespace set
Transports one or more chosen tablespaces from your source database

Integrate an existing transportable tablespace set
Integrates one or more tablespaces into your destination database

Overview

The Transportable Tablespaces feature can be used to move a subset of an Oracle Database and 'plug' it in to another Oracle Database, essentially moving tablespaces between the databases.

Moving data using transportable tablespaces is much faster than performing either an export/import or unload/load of the same data.

The transportable tablespace feature is useful in a number of scenarios, including:
- Exporting and importing partitions in data warehousing tables
- Publishing structured data on CDs
- Copying multiple read-only versions of a tablespace on multiple databases
- Archiving historical data
- Performing tablespace point-in-time-recovery (TSPITR)

Host Credentials

Supply operating system login credentials to access the target database.
Credential Preferred Named New
* UserName oracle
* Password ••••••
* Confirm Password ••••••
Save As NC_FINMART_2014-04-21-112551
Set As Preferred Credentials Database Host Credentials
Test Test Successful.
Cancel Continue

navigated within Cloud Control to the destination database FINMART, and you are at the same page as shown in Figure 9-2, except that you will specify Integrate (import) instead of Generate (export).

Clicking the Continue button in Figure 9-7, you see the page shown in Figure 9-8 where you can specify the dump file name and the datafile name you specified in Figure 9-4. When you click the Next button, Cloud Control reads the dump file and datafile(s).

On the next page, shown in Figure 9-9, you can change or accept the value EM chooses for the new datafile destination. In addition, you can leave the new datafile in place. After specifying the desired options, click the Next button.

On the page shown in Figure 9-10, you can optionally remap objects from one schema to another. In other words, if both the source and destination database have an HR schema with identically named tables, you can remap the imported objects to a different user instead and work out the differences after the import has completed.

After you click the Next button in Figure 9-10, you see the job scheduling page shown in Figure 9-11. Click the Next button.

On the page shown in Figure 9-12, you get one more opportunity to review the import job. When you are satisfied with the parameters, click Submit Job. You can

FIGURE 9-8 Transport tablespace dump file and datafile locations

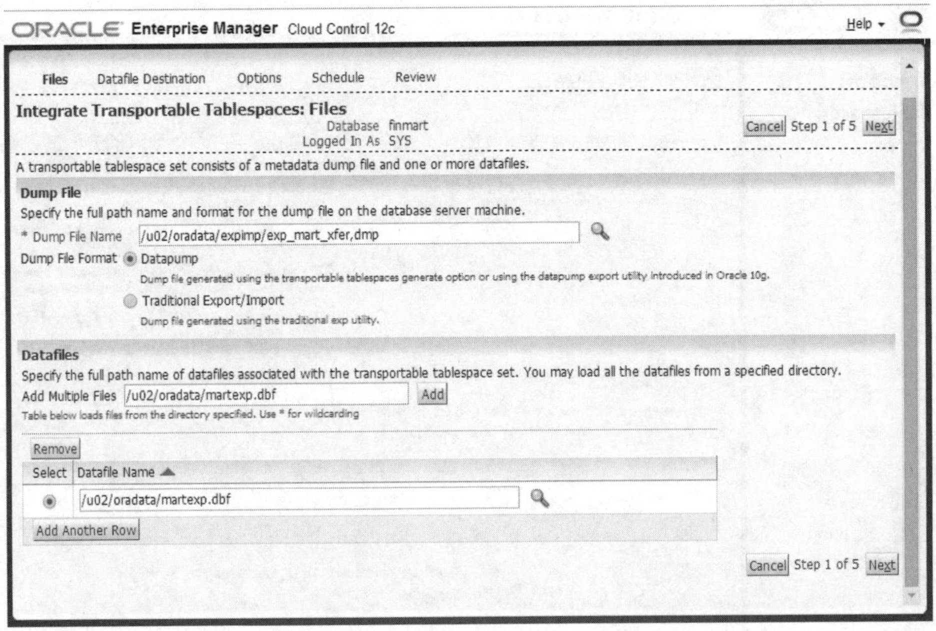

FIGURE 9-9

Specifying alternate location for imported tablespace

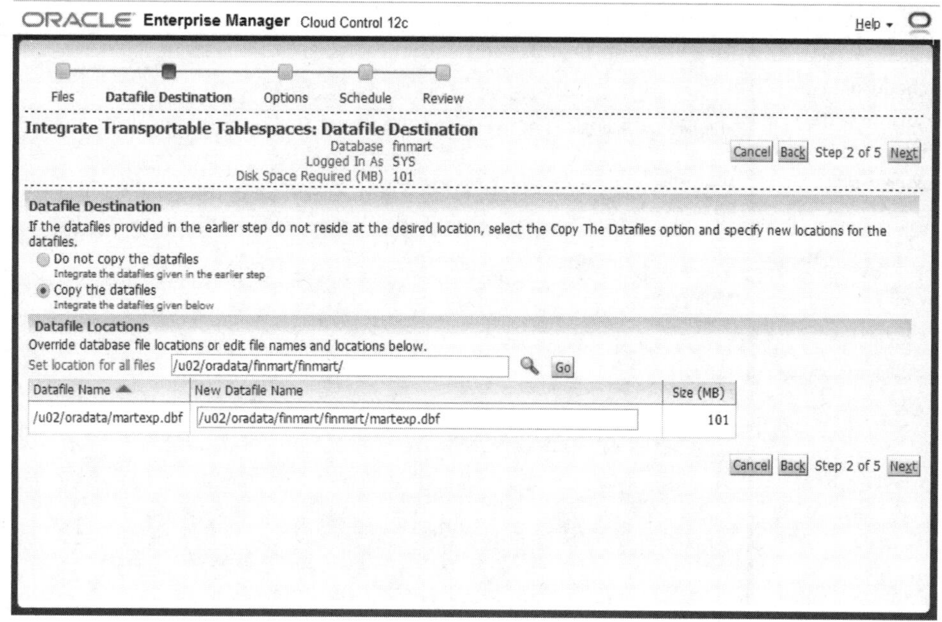

FIGURE 9-10

Specifying schema remapping during tablespace import

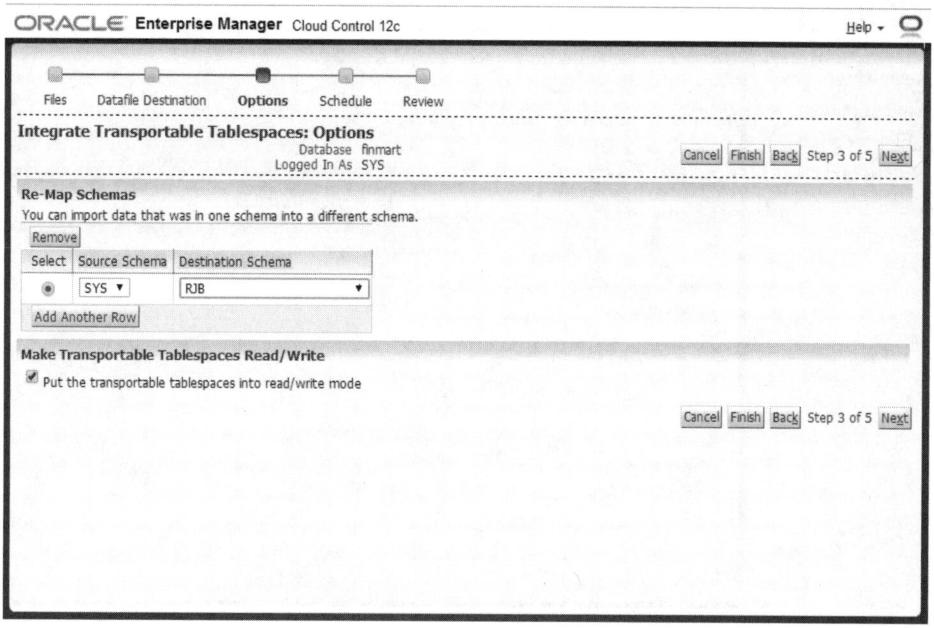

FIGURE 9-11 Scheduling transportable tablespace import processing

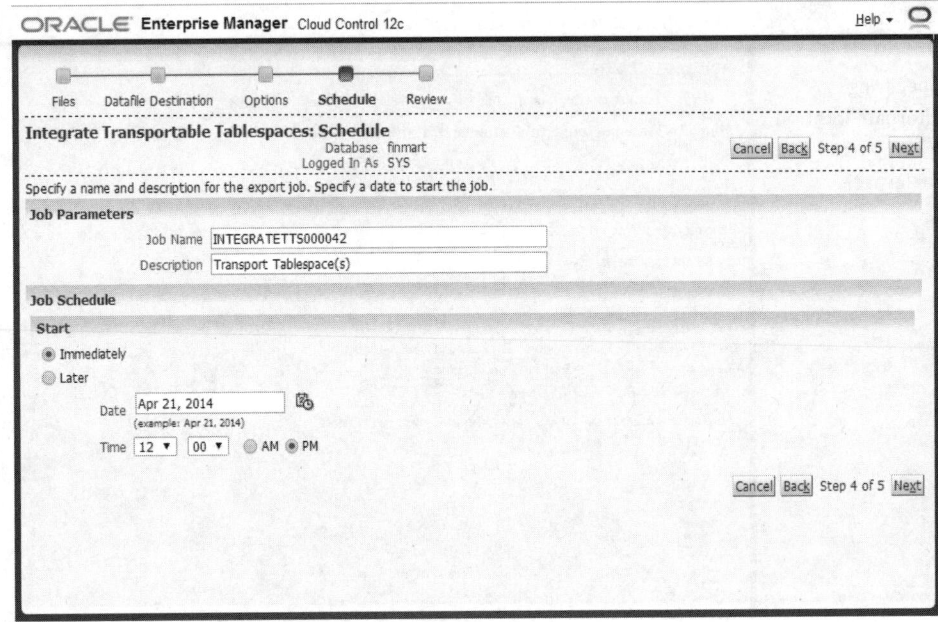

FIGURE 9-12 Reviewing transportable tablespace job parameters

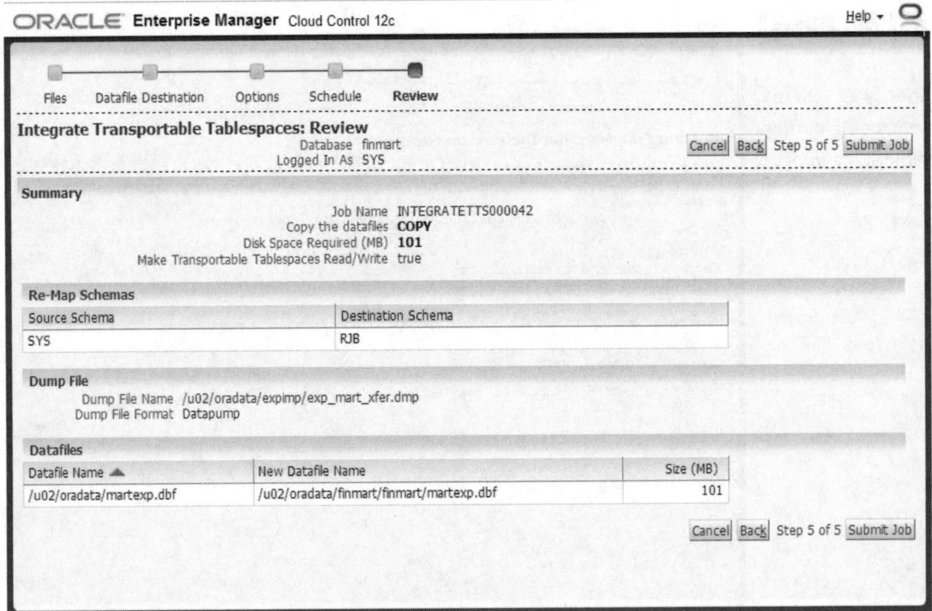

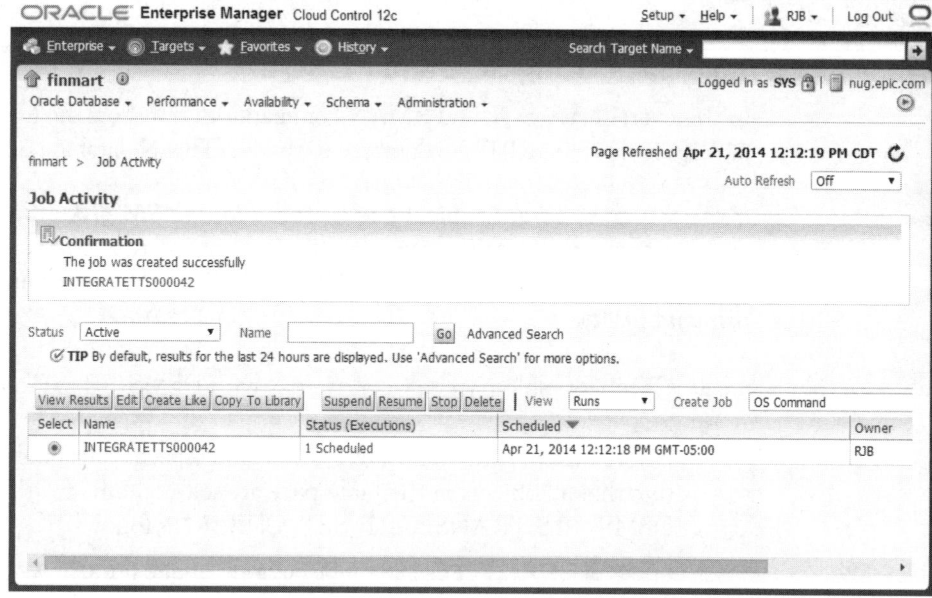

FIGURE 9-13 Monitoring transportable tablespace import job

monitor the progress of the tablespace import, as you can see in Figure 9-13. When the job completes, the tablespace MART_XFER is ready to use.

Using SQL Statements and Procedure Calls to Transport a Tablespace

You can, of course, use SQL commands and PL/SQL packages to perform the transportable tablespace operation. You use the **expdp** and **impdp** utilities and optionally the DBMS_FILE_TRANSFER PL/SQL package to copy tablespaces from one database to another. Here are the high-level steps:

1. Set up the directory objects on the source and target databases for the dump file sets and the tablespace datafiles (a one-time setup).
2. Check for tablespace self-consistency with DBMS_TTS.TRANSPORT_SET_CHECK.
3. Use **expdp** to create the metadata for the XPORT_DW tablespace.
4. Use your preferred method to copy the dump file set(s) and datafile(s) to the target database server (if on another server).
5. On the target database, use **impdp** to "plug in" the tablespace.

EXERCISE 9-1

Transport a Tablespace Using SQL and PL/SQL

In this exercise, use SQL and RMAN commands to transport the MART_XFER tablespace from the RPT12C database to the FINTRAN database on the same server.

on the job

If the source or target tablespace is stored in an ASM disk group, then to make a copy you must use ftp with the /sys/asm virtual directory in the XML DB repository, DBMS_FILE_TRANSFER, or the cp command in the asmcmd utility.

1. Check for tablespace self-consistency with DBMS_TTS.TRANSPORT_SET_CHECK.
   Before transporting the MART_XFER tablespace, you should check to make sure that all objects in the tablespace are self-contained with the procedure DBMS_TTS.TRANSPORT_SET_CHECK, as follows:

   ```
   SQL> exec dbms_tts.transport_set_check('MART_XFER', TRUE);
   PL/SQL procedure successfully completed.
   SQL> select * from transport_set_violations;
   no rows selected
   SQL>
   ```

   Not finding any rows in TRANSPORT_SET_VIOLATIONS means that the tablespace has no external dependent objects or any objects owned by SYS. This view is re-created every time you run DBMS_TTS.TRANSPORT_SET_CHECK.
2. Use a directory object and **expdp** to create the metadata for the MART_XFER tablespace.
   On the RPT12C database, you will run the **expdp** command to export the metadata associated with the XPORT_DW tablespace after making the XPORT_DW tablespace read-only:

   ```
   SQL> create directory exp_md as '/u02/oradata/expimp';
   Directory created.
   SQL> alter tablespace mart_xfer read only;
   Tablespace altered.
   SQL>
   ```

To run **expdp**, you open an operating system command prompt and perform the metadata export as follows:

```
[oracle@nug rman]$ expdp rjb dumpfile=exp_mart_xfer.dmp
directory=exp_md transport_tablespaces=mart_xfer

Export: Release 12.1.0.1.0 - Production on Mon Apr 21
08:59:03 2014

Copyright (c) 1982, 2013, Oracle and/or its affiliates.  All
rights reserved.
Password:

Connected to: Oracle Database 12c Enterprise Edition Release
12.1.0.1.0 - 64bit Production
With the Partitioning, OLAP, Advanced Analytics and Real
Application Testing options
Starting "RJB"."SYS_EXPORT_TRANSPORTABLE_01":  rjb/********
dumpfile=exp_mart_xfer.dmp directory=exp_md transport_
tablespaces=mart_xfer
Processing object type TRANSPORTABLE_EXPORT/PLUGTS_BLK
Processing object type TRANSPORTABLE_EXPORT/TABLE
Processing object type TRANSPORTABLE_EXPORT/TABLE_STATISTICS
Processing object type TRANSPORTABLE_EXPORT/STATISTICS/MARKER
Processing object type TRANSPORTABLE_EXPORT/POST_INSTANCE/
PLUGTS_BLK
Master table "RJB"."SYS_EXPORT_TRANSPORTABLE_01" successfully
loaded/unloaded
******************************************************************
*****************
Dump file set for RJB.SYS_EXPORT_TRANSPORTABLE_01 is:
  /u02/oradata/expimp/exp_mart_xfer.dmp
******************************************************************
*****************
Datafiles required for transportable tablespace MART_XFER:
  /u02/oradata/martexp
Job "RJB"."SYS_EXPORT_TRANSPORTABLE_01" successfully
completed at Mon Apr 21 08:59:34 2014 elapsed 0 00:00:28

[oracle@nug rman]$
```

3. Copy the datafile(s) for the MART_XFER tablespace to the location where the target database's datafiles reside:

```
[oracle@nug finmart]$ cp /u02/oradata/RPT12C/martexp.dbf \
   > /u02/oradata/finmart/finmart/martexp.dbf
```

4. On the target database, use **impdp** to "plug in" the tablespace.
   In the final step, you will create the directory object on the target database and run **impdp** on the target database to read the metadata file and "plug in" the tablespace datafile. Here is the output from this operation:

```
[oracle@nug finmart]$ cd /u02/oradata
[oracle@nug finmart]$ mkdir expimp
[oracle@nug finmart]$ sqlplus / as sysdba
SQL> create directory exp_md as '/u02/oradata/expimp';

Directory created.

SQL> quit
Disconnected from Oracle Database 12c Enterprise Edition
Release 12.1.0.1.0 - 64bit Production
With the Partitioning, OLAP, Advanced Analytics and Real
Application Testing options
[oracle@nug finmart]$ impdp rjb directory=exp_md
dumpfile=exp_mart_xfer.dmp transport_datafiles=/u02/oradata/
finmart/finmart/martexp.dbf

Import: Release 12.1.0.1.0 - Production on Mon Apr 21
09:07:59 2014

Copyright (c) 1982, 2013, Oracle and/or its affiliates.  All
rights reserved.
Password:

Connected to: Oracle Database 12c Enterprise Edition Release
12.1.0.1.0 - 64bit Production
With the Partitioning, OLAP, Advanced Analytics and Real
Application Testing options
Master table "RJB"."SYS_IMPORT_TRANSPORTABLE_01" successfully
loaded/unloaded
Starting "RJB"."SYS_IMPORT_TRANSPORTABLE_01":  rjb/********
directory=exp_md dumpfile=exp_mart_xfer.dmp transport_
datafiles=/u02/oradata/finmart/finmart/martexp.dbf
Processing object type TRANSPORTABLE_EXPORT/PLUGTS_BLK
Processing object type TRANSPORTABLE_EXPORT/TABLE
Processing object type TRANSPORTABLE_EXPORT/TABLE_STATISTICS
Processing object type TRANSPORTABLE_EXPORT/STATISTICS/MARKER
Processing object type TRANSPORTABLE_EXPORT/POST_INSTANCE/
PLUGTS_BLK
```

```
Job "RJB"."SYS_IMPORT_TRANSPORTABLE_01" successfully
completed at Mon Apr 21 09:08:13 2014 elapsed 0 00:00:04

[oracle@nug finmart]$

SQL*Plus: Release 12.1.0.1.0 Production on Mon Apr 21
09:09:17 2014

Copyright (c) 1982, 2013, Oracle.  All rights reserved.


Connected to:
Oracle Database 12c Enterprise Edition Release 12.1.0.1.0 -
64bit Production
With the Partitioning, OLAP, Advanced Analytics and Real
Application Testing options

SQL> select ts#,name from v$tablespace;

       TS# NAME
---------- ------------------------------
         0 SYSTEM
         1 SYSAUX
         2 UNDOTBS1
         4 USERS
         3 TEMP
         6 MART_XFER

6 rows selected.

SQL>

SQL> alter tablespace mart_xfer read write;

Tablespace altered.

SQL>
```

Note that you must change the tablespace from READ ONLY back to READ WRITE. When a tablespace is transported to another database, by default the copy of the tablespace is online but read-only. Also, don't forget to change the source tablespace back to READ WRITE after the completion of the tablespace transport if you made it read-only during a non-RMAN tablespace transport operation.

CERTIFICATION OBJECTIVE 9.02

Choose a Technique for Duplicating a Database

There are several methods you can use to duplicate a database on the same server or to a different server. The method you use depends on several factors, including the destination for the database copy, whether the target server is of the same OS and endian-ness, and the requirements for database availability.

Cross-Platform Data Transport

Transporting a subset of tablespaces or the entire database from one platform to another requires some downtime (taking them offline or READ ONLY). To transport these tablespaces, they must be put into READ ONLY mode to copy the datafiles that comprise the tablespaces. It's still quite fast because only the metadata is created with Data Pump export and loaded with Data Pump import. While the tablespaces are in READ ONLY mode, the datafiles themselves are copied to the destination database and will take much less time than doing a Data Pump export/import on the contents of the tablespaces themselves.

The catch, of course, is that both the source and target databases must be on the list of supported platforms, which can be identified using the view V$TRANSPORTABLE_PLATFORM view. You use V$DATABASE to identify the platform and endian-ness of your current database.

Using Image Copies for Data Transport

If you use image copies of a database's datafiles to transport tablespaces between databases with a different endian-ness, you must use the RMAN CONVERT command to swap pairs of bytes in every datafile of every tablespace being copied to a database on another platform. You can use the CONVERT command either on the source database or after the image copies are sent to the target database.

Using RMAN Backupsets for Database Transport

If you use RMAN backupsets for transporting a tablespace or database, there are several advantages. First, if you are running your database in ARCHIVELOG mode, you can take inconsistent backups of each tablespace while still in READ WRITE mode and therefore maintain high availability. After the initial level 0 backup, you take a series of level 1 incremental backups and apply them to the destination. The last, but very small, level 1 incremental backup will be done in READ ONLY mode thus minimizing the total amount of time that the tablespace is unavailable to users.

The other big advantage of using RMAN backupsets for database transport is that you probably have a combination of full and incremental backups already that can be used to transport a database. But wait, there's more: The RMAN backup will both compress the backup and can create a multisection backup reducing the amount of space required and the time to transport the backupsets to the destination database.

CERTIFICATION OBJECTIVE 9.03

Create a Backup-Based Duplicate Database

You can use several methods to create a duplicate database, but they all use RMAN, either directly or indirectly. You use existing RMAN backups for a backup-based duplicate database, and if you don't have too many customizations in the duplication process, you can use Enterprise Manager Cloud Control 12c to initiate the duplication process.

The following sections provide an in-depth example of cloning the reporting database (RPT12C) to a test database (TST12C) on the same host (**nug**).

Using RMAN to Create a Duplicate Database

Here are the general steps to follow to create a duplicate database on the same or another host:

1. Start the source database and open it as READ ONLY.
2. Run the RMAN command CONVERT specifying the location of the conversion script and the location of the database files for the new database.
3. Transport the files to another server if the destination server is not the same as the host.
4. Run the script **cnvt.sql** in RMAN to convert and prepare the transported database files.

5. Run the script **crdb.sql** in SQL*Plus to create the new database with the datafiles converted in step 4.

This process is much easier in Oracle Database 12*c* than in any previous release. Even in Oracle Database 11*g* you had to manually perform steps using an auxiliary instance along with several other RMAN and SQL*Plus commands.

First, create the directory to contain the database files exported from the target database:

```
[oracle@nug finmart]$ mkdir /u02/oradata/dbt
```

The second step is to shut down and open the source database as read-only:

```
[oracle@nug finmart]$ sqlplus / as sysdba

SQL*Plus: Release 12.1.0.1.0 Production on Mon Apr 21 09:38:26 2014
Copyright (c) 1982, 2013, Oracle.  All rights reserved.
Connected to:
Oracle Database 12c Enterprise Edition Release 12.1.0.1.0 - 64bit Production
With the Partitioning, OLAP, Advanced Analytics and Real Application Testing
options
SQL> shutdown immediate
Database closed.
Database dismounted.
ORACLE instance shut down.
SQL> startup mount
ORACLE instance started.

Total System Global Area 3.0398E+10 bytes
Fixed Size                  4272232 bytes
Variable Size            4227862424 bytes
Database Buffers         2.6105E+10 bytes
Redo Buffers               60723200 bytes
Database mounted.
SQL> alter database open read only;
Database altered.
SQL> quit
```

Third, run RMAN to create the scripts for the RMAN conversion steps and to create the new database RPTCLONE:

```
[oracle@nug finmart]$ rman target /
Recovery Manager: Release 12.1.0.1.0 -
     Production on Mon Apr 21 09:39:31 2014
Copyright (c) 1982, 2013, Oracle and/or its affiliates.  All rights reserved.
```

```
connected to target database: RPT12C (DBID=1783068274)
RMAN> convert database on target platform
2>        convert script 'cnvt_rpt.sql'
3>        transport script 'create_db.sql'
4>        new database 'rptclone'
5>        format '/u02/oradata/dbt';
Starting conversion at source at 21-APR-14
using target database control file instead of recovery catalog
allocated channel: ORA_DISK_1
channel ORA_DISK_1: SID=82 device type=DISK
allocated channel: ORA_DISK_2
channel ORA_DISK_2: SID=103 device type=DISK
allocated channel: ORA_DISK_3
. . .
Directory SYS.ORACLE_OCM_CONFIG_DIR found in the database
Directory SYS.ORACLE_OCM_CONFIG_DIR2 found in the database
Directory SYS.XMLDIR found in the database
Directory SYS.EXP_MD found in the database

User SYS with SYSDBA and SYSOPER privilege found in password file
User SYSDG with SYSDG privilege found in password file
User SYSBACKUP with SYSBACKUP privilege found in password file
User SYSKM with SYSKM privilege found in password file
channel ORA_DISK_2: starting to check datafiles
input datafile file number=00003 name=/u02/oradata/RPT12C/datafile/o1_mf_
sysaux_9mm70hz4_.dbf
. . .
channel ORA_DISK_6: starting to check datafiles
input datafile file number=00006 name=/u02/oradata/RPT12C/datafile/o1_mf_
users_9mm73b67_.dbf
channel ORA_DISK_6: datafile checking complete, elapsed time: 00:00:00
Edit init.ora file /u02/oradata/init_dbt.ora. This PFILE will be used to create
the database on the target platform
Run RMAN script /u02/oradata/cnvt_rpt.sql on target platform to convert
datafiles
Run SQL script /u02/oradata/create_db.sql on the target platform to create
database
To recompile all PL/SQL modules, run utlirp.sql and utlrp.sql on the target
platform
To change the internal database identifier, use DBNEWID Utility
Finished conversion at source at 21-APR-14
```

Most of the work is done at this point! Note the important sections of the output from the CONVERT command:

1. Edit **init.ora** file **/u02/oradata/init_dbt.ora**. This PFILE will be used to create the database on the target platform.
2. Run RMAN script **/u02/oradata/cnvt_rpt.sql** on the target platform to convert the datafiles.
3. Run SQL script **/u02/oradata/create_db.sql** on the target platform to create the database.
4. To recompile all PL/SQL modules, run **utlirp.sql** and **utlrp.sql** on the target platform.
5. To change the internal database identifier, use the **dbnewid** utility.

If you're on the same server or use an RMAN repository, you'll want to use the **dbnewid** command to change the database ID for the newly created database.

In summary, here is what the DUPLICATE command does, either directly or by building the appropriate commands in the RMAN and SQL scripts noted earlier:

- Creates a control file for the duplicate database
- Restores the target datafiles to the duplicate database or copies directly from the running database
- Performs incomplete recovery up to the last archived redo log file
- Shuts down and restarts the auxiliary instance
- Opens the auxiliary database with the RESETLOGS option
- Creates the online redo log files
- Generates a new DBID for the auxiliary database

Here are some other options available with the DUPLICATE command:

- **SKIP READONLY** Exclude read-only tablespaces from the copy operation.
- **SKIP TABLESPACE** Exclude specific tablespaces, except for SYSTEM and UNDO.
- **NOFILENAMECHECK** Don't check for duplicate filenames between the source and destination databases.
- **OPEN RESTRICTED** When the destination database is ready, open it immediately with the RESTRICTED SESSION option.

Using a Duplicate Database

A duplicate database can be used for many things, including the following:

- Testing backup and recovery procedures without disrupting the production database.
- Testing a database upgrade.
- Testing the effect of application upgrades on database performance.
- Generating reports that would otherwise have a detrimental effect on the response time for an online transaction processing (OLTP) production system.
- Exporting a table from a duplicate database that was inadvertently dropped from the production database and then importing it back into the production database; this assumes that the table is static or read-only. As of Oracle Database 12*c*, you can recover a single table from RMAN backups, but this method is preferable if you need more than just a few individual tables.

CERTIFICATION OBJECTIVE 9.04

Duplicate a Database Based on a Running Instance

As you might expect, you use the RMAN DUPLICATE command to copy a database to the same server or another server. You can specify that either the entire database be copied or just a subset. If the duplication process is based on a running instance, the target instance (auxiliary instance) receives a copy of the database from the source using the "push" method by running the RMAN DUPLICATE . . . FROM ACTIVE DATABASE command. The key here is that *no preexisting backups are required* for duplicating the database via a running instance. The running instance can be in either MOUNT or OPEN mode.

The "push" method is based on image copies; the "pull" method relies on backupsets and is available only in Oracle Database 12*c*. When you use one of these clauses in the DUPLICATE command, RMAN uses the "pull" method:

- USING BACKUPSET
- SECTION SIZE
- Encryption clause
- Compression clause

In the following sections, you'll use the following steps to create a duplicate database on another host:

1. Create a password file for the auxiliary instance.
2. Ensure network connectivity to the auxiliary instance.
3. Create an initialization parameter file for the auxiliary instance.
4. Start the auxiliary instance in NOMOUNT mode.
5. Start the source database in MOUNT or OPEN mode.
6. Create backups or copy existing backups and archived redo log files to a location accessible by the auxiliary instance unless you are using active database duplication.
7. Allocate auxiliary channels if necessary.
8. Run the RMAN DUPLICATE command.
9. Open the auxiliary instance.

Configure the Auxiliary Instance

Some preparation on the destination server is required before you perform the database duplication. First, you must create a password file for the auxiliary instance because you are going to duplicate from an active database instead of backups. You must also create a password file if your RMAN client runs on another host; however, the following scenario runs the RMAN executable on the same host as the destination database. Create the password file with the same SYS password as the source database's password file (the new database name is FINMART2):

```
[oracle@nug dbs]$ orapwd file=$ORACLE_HOME/dbs/orapwfinmart2
>     password=fin99test entries=10
```

Note that the default location for all database password files is **$ORACLE_HOME/dbs**.

Create an Initialization Parameter File

The next step is to create an initialization parameter file for the auxiliary instance. Only DB_NAME must be specified; all other parameters are optional, depending on whether you use Oracle Managed Files or you want to specify an alternative location for one or more file destinations. Table 9-2 lists the parameters you can specify in the auxiliary initialization file along with their descriptions and under what circumstances they are required.

TABLE 9-2 Initialization Parameters for the Auxiliary Instance

Initialization Parameter	Value(s)	Required?
DB_NAME	The name you specify in the DUPLICATE command, which must be unique among databases in the destination ORACLE_HOME.	Yes
CONTROL_FILES	All control file locations.	Yes, unless you use Oracle Managed Files (OMF)
DB_BLOCK_SIZE	The block size for the duplicate database. This size must match the source database.	Yes, if set in the source database
DB_FILE_NAME_CONVERT	Pairs of strings for converting datafile and tempfile names.	No
LOG_FILE_NAME_CONVERT	Pairs of strings to rename online redo log files.	No
DB_CREATE_FILE_DEST	Location for OMFs.	No
DB_CREATE_ONLINE_LOG_DEST_n	Location for Oracle-managed online redo log files.	No
DB_RECOVERY_FILE_DEST	Location of the flash recovery area.	No

Note that the DB_FILE_NAME_CONVERT parameter can be specified when you run the DUPLICATE command. Here is the initialization parameter file (**initfinmart2.ora**) for the auxiliary instance created in **$ORACLE_HOME/dbs**:

```
DB_NAME=finmart2
DB_BLOCK_SIZE=8192
CONTROL_FILES=(/u02/oradata/finmart2/control01.ctl,
               /u02/oradata/finmart2/control02.ctl,
               /u02/oradata/finmart2/control03.ctl)
DB_FILE_NAME_CONVERT=(/u02/oradata/finmart/finmart/,
                      /u02/oradata/finmart2/)
LOG_FILE_NAME_CONVERT=(/u02/oradata/finmart/finmart/,
                       /u02/oradata/finmart2/,
                       /u02/oradata/finmart/finmart/,
                       /u02/oradata/finmart2/)
```

Start the Auxiliary Instance in NOMOUNT Mode and Create an SPFILE

Using the initialization parameter file you just created, start the instance in NOMOUNT mode and create an SPFILE:

```
[oracle@nug dbs]$ export ORACLE_SID=finmart2
[oracle@nug dbs]$ sqlplus / as sysdba

SQL*Plus: Release 12.1.0.1.0 Production on Tue Apr 22 07:29:56 2014

Copyright (c) 1982, 2013, Oracle.  All rights reserved.

Connected to an idle instance.

SQL> startup nomount pfile='$ORACLE_HOME/dbs/initfinmart2.ora'
ORACLE instance started.

Total System Global Area  572100608 bytes
Fixed Size                  2290704 bytes
Variable Size             461376496 bytes
Database Buffers          100663296 bytes
Redo Buffers                7770112 bytes
SQL> create spfile from pfile;

File created.

SQL>
```

Note that you are setting the environment variable ORACLE_SID to the new instance name. This has the desired effect of creating any missing instance directories automatically, such as the diagnostic directory structure:

```
[oracle@nug finmart2]$ pwd
/u02/app/oracle/diag/rdbms/finmart2/finmart2
[oracle@nug finmart2]$ ls
alert  hm        incpkg  lck  metadata       metadata_pv  sweep
cdump  incident  ir      log  metadata_dgif  stage        trace
[oracle@nug finmart2]$
```

Note also that the newly created SPFILE resides in the default directory **$ORACLE_HOME/dbs** with other databases' SPFILEs and password files.

Start the Source Database in MOUNT or OPEN Mode

If the source database is not already open, start it in MOUNT or OPEN mode. If you do not want users to access the database during the duplication process, open it in MOUNT mode:

```
[oracle@nug ~]$ export ORACLE_SID=finmart
[oracle@nug ~]$ sqlplus / as sysdba

SQL*Plus: Release 12.1.0.1.0 Production on Tue Apr 22 07:33:43 2014

Copyright (c) 1982, 2013, Oracle.  All rights reserved.


Connected to:
Oracle Database 12c Enterprise Edition Release 12.1.0.1.0 - 64bit
Production
With the Partitioning, OLAP, Advanced Analytics and Real Application
Testing options

SQL> shutdown immediate
Database closed.
Database dismounted.
ORACLE instance shut down.
SQL> startup mount
ORACLE instance started.

Total System Global Area 1570009088 bytes
Fixed Size                  2288776 bytes
Variable Size             905970552 bytes
Database Buffers          654311424 bytes
Redo Buffers                7438336 bytes
Database mounted.
SQL>
```

Create Backups for the DUPLICATE Command

All datafile backups, including incremental backups and archived redo log files, must be available on a file system accessible by the auxiliary instance. In this scenario, you are performing an active database duplication; therefore, you do not have to create or copy backups for the operation since you're duplicating (copying) the database directly from the source to the target database.

Allocate Auxiliary Channels If Necessary

If you are using backups for the duplication process, you need to configure RMAN channels to be used on the auxiliary database instance. The channel on the auxiliary instance restores the backups, so you need to specify the ALLOCATE command in the RUN block, as in this example:

```
RMAN> run
      { allocate auxiliary channel aux0 device type disk;
        allocate auxiliary channel aux1 device type disk;
        . . .
        duplicate target database . . .
      }
```

Even if your device type is DISK, you can allocate multiple channels to enable parallel processing of the backups and therefore reduce the time it takes to perform the copy.

For the purposes of this scenario, the default DISK channel on the auxiliary instance is sufficient. So, you will not need to specify any additional channels for the DUPLICATE command.

Run the RMAN DUPLICATE Command

Here is the moment you've been waiting for: starting RMAN and performing the duplication process. Start the RMAN executable and connect to the source database:

```
[oracle@nug ~]$ rman

Recovery Manager: Release 12.1.0.1.0 - Production on Tue Apr 22 07:35:35 2014

Copyright (c) 1982, 2013, Oracle and/or its affiliates.  All rights reserved.

RMAN> connect target /

connected to target database: FINMART (DBID=2122736683, not open)

RMAN>
```

Next, connect to the auxiliary instance:

```
RMAN> connect auxiliary sys@finmart

auxiliary database Password:
connected to auxiliary database: FINMART2 (not mounted)

RMAN>
```

Of course, you can put all of the CONNECT statements on the RMAN command line:

```
[oracle@srv04 ~]$ rman target sys/pw1@finmart auxiliary sys/pw2@finmart2
```

Finally, run the DUPLICATE command with the ACTIVE DATABASE clause to perform the copy directly from the live datafiles:

```
RMAN> duplicate target database
2>       to finmart2
3>       from active database
4>    ;
```

RMAN conveniently creates a temporary script with all the appropriate SET NEWNAME commands and proceeds to copy the database:

```
Starting Duplicate Db at 18-APR-14
using target database control file instead of recovery catalog
allocated channel: ORA_AUX_DISK_1
channel ORA_AUX_DISK_1: SID=97 device type=DISK

contents of Memory Script:
{
   set newname for datafile  1 to
 "/u02/oradata/finmart2/system01.dbf";
   set newname for datafile  2 to
 "/u02/oradata/finmart2/sysaux01.dbf";
   set newname for datafile  3 to
 "/u02/oradata/finmart2/undotbs01.dbf";
   set newname for datafile  4 to
 "/u02/oradata/finmart2/users01.dbf";
   backup as copy reuse
   datafile  1 auxiliary format
 "/u02/oradata/finmart2/system01.dbf"   datafile
 2 auxiliary format
 "/u02/oradata/finmart2/sysaux01.dbf"   datafile
 3 auxiliary format
 "/u02/oradata/finmart2/undotbs01.dbf"   datafile
 4 auxiliary format
 "/u02/oradata/finmart2/users01.dbf"   datafile;
   sql 'alter system archive log current';
}
executing Memory Script

executing command: SET NEWNAME
executing command: SET NEWNAME
executing command: SET NEWNAME
executing command: SET NEWNAME
```

```
Starting backup at 18-APR-14
allocated channel: ORA_DISK_1
channel ORA_DISK_1: SID=116 device type=DISK
channel ORA_DISK_1: starting datafile copy
. . .
contents of Memory Script:
{
   Alter clone database open resetlogs;
}
executing Memory Script

database opened
Finished Duplicate Db at 18-APR-14

RMAN>
```

In summary, here is what the DUPLICATE command does:

1. Creates a control file for the duplicate database
2. Restores the target datafiles to the duplicate database or copies directly from the running database
3. Performs incomplete recovery up to the last archived redo log file
4. Shuts down and restarts the auxiliary instance
5. Opens the auxiliary database with the RESETLOGS option
6. Creates the online redo log files
7. Generates a new DBID for the auxiliary database

Here are some other options available with the DUPLICATE command:

- **SKIP READONLY** Exclude read-only tablespaces from the copy operation.
- **SKIP TABLESPACE** Exclude specific tablespaces, except for SYSTEM and UNDO.
- **NOFILENAMECHECK** Don't check for duplicate filenames between the source and destination databases.
- **OPEN RESTRICTED** When the destination database is ready, open it immediately with the RESTRICTED SESSION option.

CERTIFICATION SUMMARY

This chapter provided an in-depth overview of methods you can use to move very large objects from one database to another, specifically, entire tablespaces or the entire database. You can use one of two methods to copy or clone a database.

Transportable tablespaces help you move logically related objects to another database. In a fraction of the time it would take to restore and recover a backup of your database to another database, you can export the metadata for one or more tablespaces, copy the tablespaces to the new database, and then import the metadata to "plug in" the tablespace. Only a couple of caveats apply to transportable tablespaces: database compatibility level and platform endian formats. If the target platform has a different endian format, you must use RMAN either at the source database or at the target database to change the endian formats of the data by intelligently "flipping" pairs of bytes in the data blocks.

Duplicating a database using RMAN is mostly automated except for a few manual setup steps. These steps include tasks such as creating a password file, setting up network connectivity, and creating a text-based initialization parameter file with only a few required parameters, such as DB_NAME. Specifying other initialization parameters is dependent on whether you explicitly specify DB_BLOCK_SIZE in the source database and how much path name mapping you need to do to specify locations correctly for datafiles, control files, and online redo log files. Using Enterprise Manager Cloud Control 12*c* (Cloud Control) to duplicate a database is the easier method but may not provide the customization available using RMAN and SQL command-line commands.

TWO-MINUTE DRILL

Describe and Use Transportable Tablespaces and Databases

- ❑ When transporting between platforms, both the source and destination platforms must be on Oracle's list of supported platforms.
- ❑ Oracle Database feature compatibility is controlled by the COMPATIBLE initialization parameter.
- ❑ When you create a transportable tablespace set, Oracle determines the minimum compatibility level of the target database and stores this value in the metadata for the transportable tablespace set.
- ❑ A conversion process must be performed for data columns transported between platforms with different endian formats.
- ❑ To determine the endian formats of all supported platforms, you can query the dynamic performance view V$TRANSPORTABLE_PLATFORM.
- ❑ When transporting a tablespace, the source tablespace must be read-only during the copy process and changed to read-write after import to the target database.
- ❑ You use **expdp**, **impdp**, and the DBMS_FILE_TRANSFER PL/SQL package to copy metadata and the tablespace's datafiles from one database to another.

Choose a Technique for Duplicating a Database

- ❑ Cross-platform data transport requires tablespaces to be in READ ONLY mode to copy the tablespaces' datafiles to the target system.
- ❑ Only the metadata for a tablespace or entire database needs to be created for Data Pump export/import since the image copies themselves will be copied to the target database.
- ❑ Use RMAN backupsets for file transfer speed, compression, and minimal downtime of the source tablespace or database.

Create a Backup-Based Duplicate Database

- ❑ When you duplicate a database, the source database is copied to the duplicate database.
- ❑ The source database is also known as the target database.

- ❑ The duplicate database is also known as the auxiliary database.
- ❑ Preparing to create a duplicate database includes creating a password file, ensuring network connectivity, and creating an initialization parameter file for the auxiliary instance.
- ❑ At a minimum, you need to specify the DB_NAME value in the auxiliary instance's initialization parameter file. You must also specify DB_BLOCK_SIZE if it is set explicitly in the target database.
- ❑ The initialization parameter DB_FILE_NAME_CONVERT specifies the file system mapping for datafile and tempfile names.
- ❑ The initialization parameter LOG_FILE_NAME_CONVERT specifies the file system mapping for online redo log files.
- ❑ The initialization parameter CONTROL_FILES specifies the new names for all control files, unless you are using Oracle Managed Files because OMF will name files for you.
- ❑ The RMAN command for performing database duplication is DUPLICATE TARGET DATABASE.
- ❑ The duplicate database has a new DBID, even if it has the same database name as the source database.

Duplicate a Database Based on a Running Instance

- ❑ You use the RMAN DUPLICATE command to duplicate a database.
- ❑ You can use the "push" method to duplicate the database, which is based on image copies.
- ❑ The "pull" method relies on RMAN backupsets and is available only in Oracle Database 12*c*.
- ❑ You can specify FROM ACTIVE DATABASE in the DUPLICATE command to create the copy from an online database instead of from a database backup.

SELF TEST

The following questions will help you measure your understanding of the material presented in this chapter. Read all the choices carefully because there might be more than one correct answer. Choose all correct answers for each question.

Describe and Use Transportable Tablespaces and Databases

1. You are running Oracle Database 12*c* with the COMPATIBLE initialization parameter set to 12.0.0. What is the minimal compatibility level for transporting a tablespace from a database on a different platform?

A. 8.0

B. 10.0

C. 12.0

D. 11.0

E. All of the above

2. When transporting a tablespace, what is the purpose of DBMS_TTS.TRANSPORT_SET_CHECK? (Choose the best answer.)

A. It ensures that the COMPATIBILITY level is high enough for the transport operation.

B. It compares the endian level for the source and target databases and runs RMAN to convert the datafiles before transportation.

C. It validates that the metadata for the tablespace does not have any naming conflicts with the target database schemas.

D. It checks for tablespace self-consistency.

Choose a Technique for Duplicating a Database

3. You want to duplicate a database but minimize downtime for the source database and all its tablespaces. What is the best method to use for this type of database duplication?

A. Image copies

B. Data Pump export with FULL=Y

C. RMAN backupsets because then the downtime will be zero

D. RMAN backupsets because then the downtime will be close to zero

Create a Backup-Based Duplicate Database

4. Identify the correct statement regarding duplicate databases created with RMAN.

A. RMAN copies the source database to the target database, and both can have the same name.

B. RMAN creates an auxiliary instance for the duration of the copy operation and drops it after the copy operation is complete.

C. The auxiliary database is the same as the target database.

D. RMAN copies the database from the target to the duplicate database, and both can have the same name.

E. The source database must be shut down before you can start up the destination database.

5. To create a duplicate database, put the following steps in the correct order:

1. Start the auxiliary instance as NOMOUNT.
2. Allocate auxiliary channels if necessary.
3. Run the RMAN DUPLICATE command.
4. Create a password file for the auxiliary instance.
5. Ensure network connectivity to the auxiliary instance.
6. Open the auxiliary instance.
7. Start the source database in MOUNT or OPEN mode.
8. Create an initialization parameter file for the auxiliary instance.
9. Create backups or copy existing backups and archived log files to a common location accessible by the auxiliary instance.

A. 5, 4, 8, 1, 7, 9, 3, 2, 6

B. 4, 5, 8, 1, 7, 9, 2, 3, 6

C. 4, 5, 8, 1, 7, 9, 3, 2, 6

D. 5, 4, 1, 8, 7, 9, 2, 3, 6

6. Which of the following clauses is not valid for the RMAN DUPLICATE command?

A. SKIP OFFLINE

B. SKIP READONLY

C. SKIP TABLESPACE

D. NOFILENAMECHECK

E. OPEN RESTRICTED

Duplicate a Database Based on a Running Instance

7. Identify the true statement regarding the status of the source database and the auxiliary database instance when duplicating a database based on a running instance.
   A. The active database must be in MOUNT mode, and the auxiliary instance must be in MOUNT mode.
   B. The active database must be in MOUNT or OPEN mode, and the auxiliary instance must be in NOMOUNT mode.
   C. The active database must be in OPEN mode, and the auxiliary instance must be in NOMOUNT mode.
   D. The active database must be in NOMOUNT mode, and the auxiliary instance must be in MOUNT mode.

SELF TEST ANSWERS

Describe and Use Transportable Tablespaces and Databases

1. ☑ **B.** If the source and target databases are on different platforms, both the source and target must have a compatibility level of at least 10.0.
   ☒ **A, C, D,** and **E** are incorrect. For transporting between identical platforms, you need only COMPATIBLE=8.0. For transporting between databases with different block sizes, you need only COMPATIBLE=9.0.

2. ☑ **D.** DBMS_TTS.TRANSPORT_SET_CHECK checks to ensure that there are no objects in the tablespace to be transported that have dependencies on objects in other tablespaces in the source database.
   ☒ **A, B,** and **C** are incorrect because they are not valid uses for DBMS_TTS.TRANSPORT_SET_CHECK.

Choose a Technique for Duplicating a Database

3. ☑ **D.** Using RMAN for duplicating a database with backupsets has the advantage of keeping the tablespaces available as much as possible (in READ WRITE mode). Successive incremental backups will get smaller and smaller until the last backup in which you must make the tablespaces read-only to perform the last incremental backup to be applied to the target database.
   ☒ **A, B,** and **C** are incorrect. **A** is incorrect because image copies are a valid method for transporting a tablespace or database, but the tablespace's datafiles must be in READ ONLY mode to perform the image copy. **B** is incorrect because Data Pump can back up an entire database, but it is a logical backup, not a physical backup. **C** is incorrect because there will still be some unavailability of the tablespace to perform the last incremental backup to be applied to the target database's copy of the tablespace.

Create a Backup-Based Duplicate Database

4. ☑ **D.** You can keep the same name because RMAN creates a new DBID, and therefore you can use the same recovery catalog for both databases.
   ☒ **A, B, C,** and **E** are incorrect. **A** is incorrect because the target database is the same as the source database. **B** is incorrect because RMAN does not drop the auxiliary instance or database after the copy operation is complete. **C** is incorrect because the target database is the source database and the auxiliary database is the destination database. **E** is incorrect because both databases can be open at the same time, even on the same host and with the same recovery catalog.

5. ☑ **B.** These steps are in the correct order.
   ☒ **A, C,** and **D** are incorrect because they are in the wrong order.

6. ☑ **A.** The SKIP OFFLINE option is not valid for the DUPLICATE command.
   ☒ **B, C, D,** and **E** are incorrect. **B** is incorrect because the SKIP READONLY clause excludes read-only tablespaces. **C** is incorrect because SKIP TABLESPACE excludes one or more tablespaces from the copy operation; you cannot skip the SYSTEM or UNDO tablespaces. **D** is incorrect because NOFILENAMECHECK doesn't check for duplicate filenames between the source and destination. **E** is incorrect because OPEN RESTRICTED opens the destination database with the RESTRICTED SESSION option.

Duplicate a Database Based on a Running Instance

7. ☑ **B.** To duplicate a database based on a running instance, the source database can be in either MOUNT or OPEN mode; since the auxiliary database does not yet have even a control file, it must be opened in NOMOUNT mode.
   ☒ **A, C,** and **D** are incorrect. **A** is incorrect because the auxiliary instance does not have a control file right away, so it cannot be started in MOUNT mode. **C** is incorrect because the active database can also be in MOUNT mode. **D** is incorrect because the database can't be duplicated if the source database is in NOMOUNT mode, and the auxiliary instance can't be in MOUNT mode either!

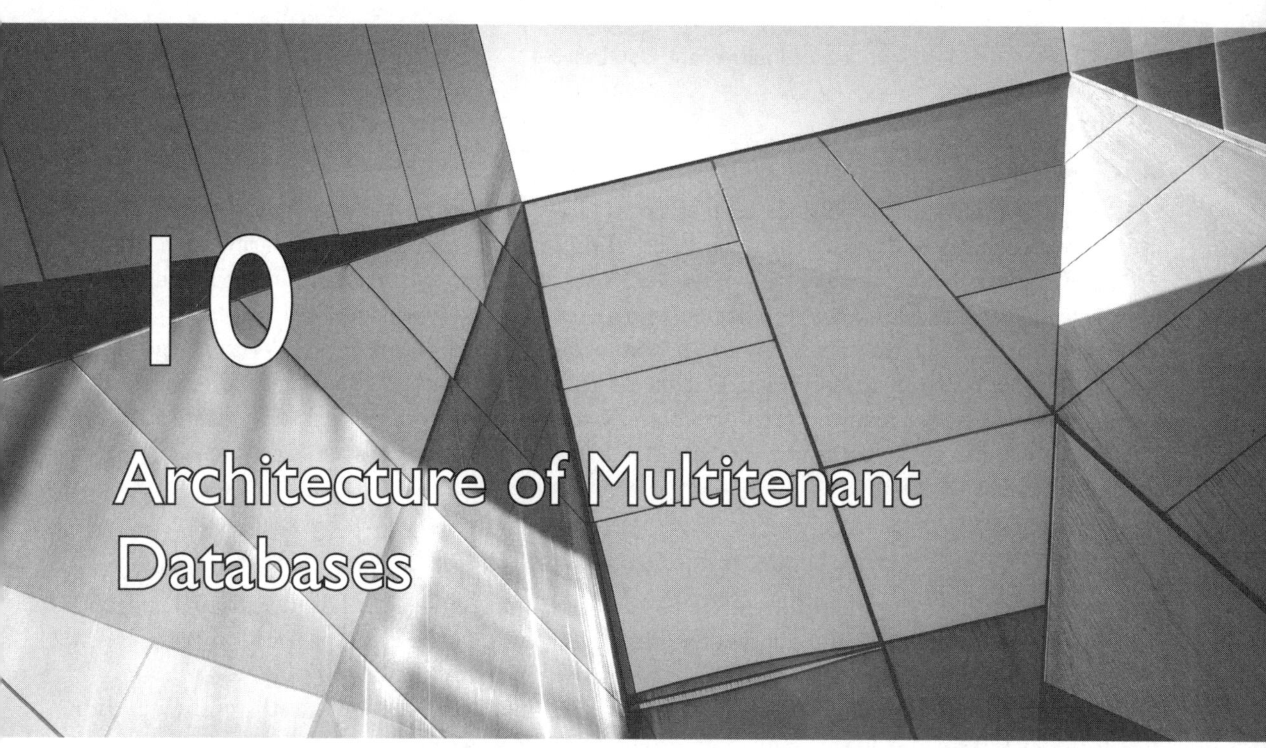

10 Architecture of Multitenant Databases

CERTIFICATION OBJECTIVES

10.01	Describe the Multitenant Architecture	✓	Two-Minute Drill
10.02	Explain Pluggable Database Provisioning	Q&A	Self Test

Using a database appliance such as Oracle Exadata helps database administrators consolidate dozens, if not hundreds, of databases in one cabinet. Managing each of these databases separately, however, is still a challenge from a resource management perspective. Instances for each of the databases may use their memory and CPU resources inefficiently, preventing even more databases from being deployed to the server. With pluggable databases (PDBs), introduced in Oracle Database 12*c*, you can leverage your database resources more efficiently because many different databases (each consisting of a collection of schemas) can coexist within a single container database (CDB). A CDB is also known as a *multitenant* container database.

Pluggable databases make database administration simpler for a DBA. Performance metrics are gathered for all PDBs as a whole. In addition, the DBA needs to manage only one SGA and not one for each PDB. Fewer database patches need to be applied as well: Only one CDB needs to be patched instead of having to patch each PDB within the CDB. With pluggable databases, hardware is used more efficiently, and the DBA can manage many more databases in the same amount of time.

Developers, network administrators, storage administrators, and database application users will rarely interact with a pluggable database or know they are using a pluggable database. One day the pluggable database may be plugged into container database CDB01 and the next day into container database CDB02, which is the point: A container database acts just like any other database except for the decreased maintenance effort for the DBA and the generally higher availability for database users. For a more in-depth analysis and additional use cases for pluggable databases and container databases, see my *Oracle Database 12*c *DBA Handbook*, published by McGraw-Hill/Professional.

Even though the complexity of a container database is higher than a traditional (pre-12*c*) database, the tools to manage container and pluggable databases keep up with the complexity. Enterprise Manager Cloud Control 12*c* Release 3 fully supports the monitoring of container and pluggable databases; Oracle SQL Developer version 4.0 and newer have a DBA module to perform most if not all of the operations you'll typically perform in a container database environment.

This chapter will cover two high-level topics; specifically, it will give an overview of the multitenant architecture and explain how pluggable databases are provisioned. Your first decision will be whether you want to create a multitenant container at all—in most cases, you will. It's easy to fix any mistakes you make by over-provisioning a container database: Just unplug it from the current container and plug it back into another container on the same or different server. In addition to moving a pluggable database to another container, I'll show you how to create a new one from a seed template and clone an existing pluggable database.

CERTIFICATION OBJECTIVE 10.01

Describe the Multitenant Architecture

In a multitenant environment, a database can be one of three types: a standalone database (non-CDB), a container database, or a pluggable database. In the following sections, I'll describe the multitenant architecture in greater detail along with the many advantages of using a multitenant environment.

Leveraging Multitenant Databases

Previous to Oracle Database 12*c*, the only type of database you could create was a non-CDB (as it's called now; the concept of a CDB or PDB had not yet been conceived then) either as a standalone database or as part of a cluster (Real Applications Cluster). Even if you ran multiple non-CDB instances on the same server, each instance would have its own memory structures (SGA, PGA, and so forth) and database files (storage structures).

Even with the efficient management of memory and disk space within each database, there is a duplication of memory structures and database objects. In addition, when upgrading a database version, at least one software upgrade must be performed on each server containing an application. With more efficient use of memory and disk via multitenant databases, more applications can be consolidated onto a much smaller number of servers or even one server.

In addition to consolidating multiple data dictionaries into a single container database, new databases can be provisioned quickly within the container by copying a subset of objects specific to the PDB. If you want to upgrade only one PDB to a new version of the database, you can unplug the database from the current CDB and plug it into a new CDB that is at the correct version in the time it takes to export and import the PDB's metadata.

Using pluggable databases makes efficient use of resources while still maintaining a separation of duties and application isolation.

exam watch

Be careful with the nomenclature used and the subtle differences in meaning among seemingly identical constructs. The multitenant architecture includes both the container database and the pluggable databases that run inside a container database. A non-CDB does not mean a pluggable database but instead a single traditional Oracle database regardless of version, sometimes referred to as a standalone database. Oracle's documentation may refer to a user container, which is the same as a PDB. A PDB can be either plugged in or unplugged and will always be a PDB.

Understanding Multitenant Configurations

Given the multitenant architecture of Oracle Database 12*c*, you can leverage CDBs and PDBs in a number of ways.

- **Multitenant configuration** A single CDB that contains zero, one, or more PDBs at any given time
- **Single-tenant configuration** A single CDB with a single PDB (licensing for the multitenant option is not required)
- **Non-CDB** Oracle 11*g* architecture (standalone database and instance)

Figure 10-1 shows a sample of a multitenant configuration with one CDB and one non-CDB instance. The CDB instance has three pluggable databases.

The following sections describe the three types of containers and databases: system containers (CDBs), user containers (PDBs), and standalone databases (non-CDBs).

System Container Database Architecture

Creating a system container (in other words, a CDB) is as easy as checking a radio button in the Database Configuration Assistant (DBCA). The resulting database is only the container for new databases that can be provisioned either by copying the seed database or by plugging in a database that was previously a tenant of this CDB or unplugged from a different CDB. Figure 10-2 shows a typical CDB configuration.

FIGURE 10-1

Multitenant architecture with a CDB and a non-CDB

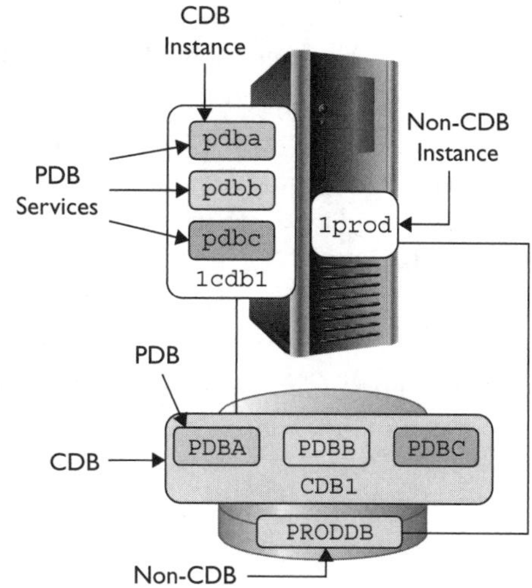

FIGURE 10-2

Typical container database

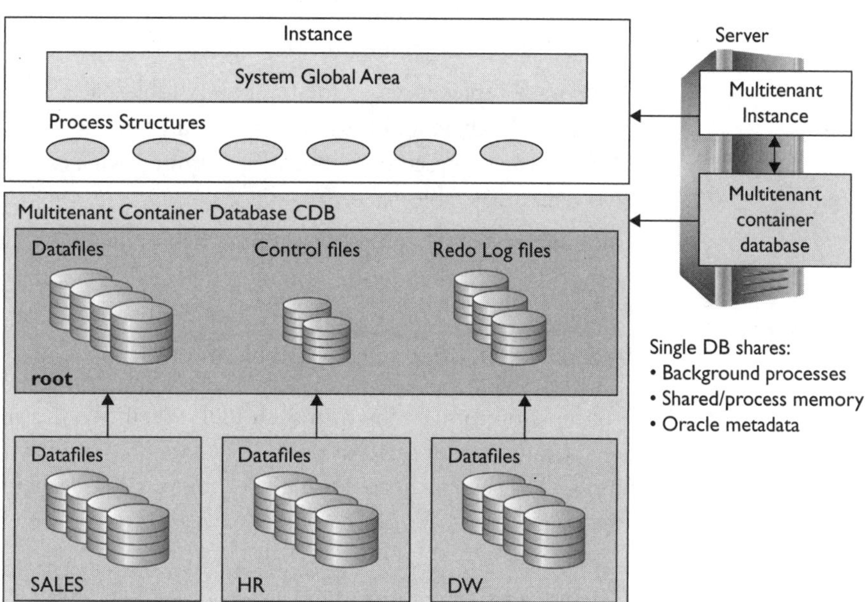

The single container database in Figure 10-2 has three pluggable databases: DW, SALES, and HR. All three PDBs share a single instance and its process structures. The root container has the control files and redo log files shared by all PDBs along with datafiles that contain system metadata common to all databases. The individual applications have their own datafiles isolated from all other PDBs within the container. A SYS user is owned by the root container and can manage the root container and all pluggable databases.

As noted earlier, a CDB has a single database instance and set of related datafiles regardless of the number of PDBs in the CDB. The definition and usage of tablespaces and objects in a non-CDB or pre-12*c* database are the same with the following exceptions and qualifications:

- **Redo log files** The redo log files are shared with the root container and all PDBs. Entries in the redo log files identify the source of the redo (which PDB or the root container). All user containers share the same ARCHIVELOG mode as well.
- **UNDO tablespace** All containers share the same UNDO tablespace.
- **Control files** The control files are shared. Datafiles added from any PDB are recorded in the common control file.
- **Temporary tablespaces** One temporary tablespace is required in the container database and is the initial default temporary tablespace for each PDB. However, based on application requirements, each PDB may have its own temporary tablespace.
- **Data dictionary** Each user container has its own data dictionary in its copy of the SYSTEM tablespace (common objects have pointers to the SYSTEM tablespace in the system container database) with its private metadata.
- **SYSAUX tablespace** Each PDB has its own copy of the SYSAUX tablespace.

Tablespaces can be created within each PDB specific to the application. Each tablespace's datafile is identified in the CDB's data dictionary with a container ID in the column CON_ID. Further information about container metadata is presented later in the chapter.

User Container Databases

User containers (in other words, PDBs) have SYSTEM tablespaces just like non-CDBs do but have links to the common metadata across the entire container. Only the user metadata specific to the PDB is stored in the PDB's SYSTEM tablespace. The object names are the same in a PDB as in a non-CDB or the CDB such as OBJ$, TAB$, and

SOURCE$. Thus, the PDB appears to an application as a standalone database. A DBA can be assigned to manage only that application with new roles and privileges created in Oracle Database 12*c* (discussed later in "Using CDB Security Features"). The DBA for an application in a PDB is also not aware that there may be one or many other PDBs sharing resources in the CDB.

Non-CDB Databases

Standalone (in other words, non-CDB) databases can still be created in Oracle Database 12*c* (with the Oracle Database 11*g* architecture). The system metadata and user metadata are stored in the same SYSTEM tablespace along with PL/SQL code and other user objects. A non-CDB can be converted to a PDB using the DBMS_PDB package. If a non-CDB database is at Oracle Database 11*g*, it must be upgraded to 12*c* first and then converted using DBMS_PDB. Other options for upgrading include Data Pump export/import or an ETL tool such as Oracle Data Integrator (ODI).

CERTIFICATION OBJECTIVE 10.02

Explain Pluggable Database Provisioning

In the previous section, I made the distinction between system containers (CDBs) and user containers (PDBs). The system container is also known as the *root* container. When a new CDB is created, a *seed* container is the template for a new PDB and makes it easy to create a new PDB within a CDB.

Understanding Root Containers

The root container within a CDB contains global Oracle metadata only. This metadata includes CDB users such as SYS, which is global to all current and future PDBs within the CDB. Once a new PDB is provisioned, all user data resides in datafiles owned by the PDB. No user data resides in the root container. The root container is named CDB$ROOT, and you'll see where this metadata is stored later in this chapter.

Leveraging Seed PDBs

When you create a new container database (CDB), one PDB is created: the seed PDB. It has the structure or template for a PDB that will contain the user data for a new application database. The seed database is named PDB$SEED. This provisioning operation is fast because it primarily consists of creating a couple of small tablespaces and empty tables for user metadata.

Using Intra-CDB Links

When databases are deployed as non-CDB databases in Oracle Database 11*g* or as a non-CDB in Oracle Database 12*c*, you often have reasons to share data between databases, whether the databases are on separate servers or even on the same server. In both Oracle Database 12*c* and many previous versions of Oracle, you use database links to access tables in other databases. You use database links to access tables from other PDBs within the same CDB as well. But since the objects in two PDBs reside within the same container, you are using a fast version of a database link under the covers. Remember that a PDB does not know where another PDB or non-CDB database resides, so the definition and use of a database link are the same regardless of where both databases reside.

Querying V$CONTAINERS

The system container's dynamic performance view V$CONTAINERS has just about everything you want to know about the user containers and the system container in your container database. In the following example, you view the available pluggable databases and then open the PDB DW_01 to make it available to users:

```
SQL> select con_id,name,open_mode,total_size
  2  from v$containers;

    CON_ID NAME                           OPEN_MODE  TOTAL_SIZE
---------- ------------------------------ ---------- ----------
         1 CDB$ROOT                       READ WRITE  975175680
         2 PDB$SEED                       READ ONLY   283115520
         3 CCREPOS                        MOUNTED             0
         4 DW_01                          MOUNTED             0
         5 QA_2014                        MOUNTED             0

SQL> alter pluggable database dw_01 open read write;

Pluggable database altered.
SQL> select con_id,name,open_mode,total_size
  2  from v$containers;

    CON_ID NAME                           OPEN_MODE  TOTAL_SIZE
---------- ------------------------------ ---------- ----------
```

```
         1 CDB$ROOT                       READ WRITE  975175680
         2 PDB$SEED                       READ ONLY   283115520
         3 CCREPOS                        MOUNTED             0
         4 DW_01                          READ WRITE  283115520
         5 QA_2014                        MOUNTED             0
SQL>
```

A system container (in other words, a CDB) has one and only one seed database and one root container; user containers are optional (but you will eventually have one or more). A CDB can contain up to 253 user containers (in other words, PDBs), which includes the seed database. Both the root container (CDB$ROOT) and the seed database (PDB$SEED) are displayed in V$CONTAINERS along with the PDBs.

Using CDB Security Features

The multitenant architecture necessarily requires new security objects and a new security hierarchy because you must be able to maintain the same separation of duties and application partitioning that existed when each application was stored in its own database.

To administer the entire container database and all of the PDBs within the system container, you need one "superuser" also known as the *container database administrator* (CDBA). Each PDB within a CDB has DBA privileges within the PDB and is known as the *pluggable database administrator* (PDBA). In a non-CDB, the DBA role works the same as in Oracle Database 11*g*.

Users (privileged or otherwise) are of two types in a multitenant environment: common or local. As the name implies, a common user has access to all PDBs within a CDB, and a local user has access only within a specific PDB. Privileges are granted the same way. Privileges can be granted across all containers or local to only one PDB.

The new data dictionary table CDB_USERS contains users who exist in the data dictionary table DBA_USERS across all PDBs. When you add a new common user to the CDB, the user also shows up in the DBA_USERS table in each PDB. As with all other features of multitenant features, the DBA_USERS table in each PDB contains only those users specific to that PDB and have the same characteristics as users created in non-CDB databases or pre-12*c* databases.

As you might expect, a common user can perform global operations such as starting up or shutting down the CDB as well as unplugging or plugging in a PDB. To unplug a database, you must first shut down the PDB and then issue the ALTER PLUGGABLE DATABASE command to create the XML metadata file so that the PDB can be plugged in later to the current or another CDB.

```
SQL> alter pluggable database dw_01
  2  unplug into '/u01/app/oracle/plugdata/dw_01.xml';

Pluggable database altered.

SQL>
```

In addition to new data dictionary views like CDB_USERS, a container database contains corollaries to other DBA_ views you would see in a non-CDB database such as CDB_TABLESPACES and CDB_PDBS.

```
SQL> select con_id,tablespace_name,status
  2  from cdb_tablespaces;

    CON_ID TABLESPACE_NAME                STATUS
---------- ------------------------------ ---------
         1 SYSTEM                         ONLINE
         1 SYSAUX                         ONLINE
         1 UNDOTBS1                       ONLINE
         1 TEMP                           ONLINE
         1 USERS                          ONLINE
         2 SYSTEM                         ONLINE
         2 SYSAUX                         ONLINE
         2 TEMP                           ONLINE
         5 SYSTEM                         ONLINE
         5 SYSAUX                         ONLINE
         5 TEMP                           ONLINE

11 rows selected.

SQL>
```

From a PDB local user's perspective, all of the DBA_ views behave just as they would in a non-CDB database.

CERTIFICATION SUMMARY

This chapter provided an overview of how a multitenant environment can provide benefits in your environment from both a management and cost savings point of view. All of your smaller databases may be able to exist on a single server in a multitenant architecture because of shared memory and disk resources.

With Oracle Database 12*c*, you have several options for using the multitenant architecture. You can create a database that has the same architecture as an Oracle

Database 11*g* database (a non-CDB database). You can easily convert a non-CDB to a PDB if the non-CDB was created as an Oracle 12*c* database. You can convert Oracle 11*g* databases to PDBs, but you must upgrade them to Oracle Database 12*c* first.

This chapter also reviewed the architecture of a multitenant database starting with the system container (the CDB). The CDB contains the Oracle metadata common to all PDBs, and it can have zero, one, or many PDBs, up to a total of 252 PDBs not including the seed PDB.

A pluggable database is also known as a user container and is a container for a single application that would traditionally run on a single database, and from the application perspective, it is running on a non-CDB. A PDB can easily be unplugged from one CDB and plugged into another. A PDB cannot be used while in an unplugged state. When a PDB is unplugged, an XML file is created that makes it easy (and fast) to plug it into another CDB. No datafiles are moved or deleted unless the PDB is explicitly dropped.

TWO-MINUTE DRILL

Describe the Multitenant Architecture

- ❑ The Oracle multitenant architecture helps use server resources more efficiently by sharing instance memory and processes as well as disk space.
- ❑ Multitenant databases can be managed at the SQL*Plus command line, from Cloud Control 12*c*, or from SQL Developer.
- ❑ Upgrading a multitenant container database upgrades all PDBs within the container.
- ❑ A CDB at any point in time can contain zero, one, or up to 252 user-defined PDBs.
- ❑ A CDB is a single instance regardless of the number of PDBs within the CDB.
- ❑ Across all PDBs within a CDB, the redo log files, undo tablespace, control files, and temporary tablespace are shared.
- ❑ An individual PDB may have its own copy of a temporary tablespace.
- ❑ Each PDB has its own copy of the SYSTEM tablespace with private metadata.
- ❑ The SYSTEM tablespace has pointers to common Oracle metadata stored in the SYSTEM tablespace within the CDB.
- ❑ In all container data dictionary tables, the CON_ID column identifies the container that owns the object or metadata.
- ❑ Non-CDBs can be converted to a PDB once they have been upgraded to Oracle Database 12*c*.

Explain Pluggable Database Provisioning

- ❑ The root container contains the root database CDB$ROOT and the seed database PDB$SEED.
- ❑ CDB users include the SYS user who is global to all PDBs.
- ❑ Table data can be shared between PDBs within a CDB by using an intra-CDB link.
- ❑ An intra-CDB link behaves just like a pre-12*c* database link and requires no application changes.

- ❑ The view V$CONTAINERS is visible only from the system container and contains metadata for all system and user containers within the CDB.
- ❑ The seed database PDB$SEED is always open and mounted as READ ONLY.
- ❑ You use ALTER PLUGGABLE DATABASE . . . CLOSE and ALTER PLUGGABLE DATABASE . . . OPEN to shut down and open a PDB.
- ❑ A PDB can be opened in MOUNT mode just like in a non-CDB.
- ❑ After a PDB has been changed to the MOUNTED state, it can be unplugged with the ALTER PLUGGABLE DATABASE . . . UNPLUG INTO . . . command.
- ❑ The data dictionary views DBA_ have corresponding views in the system container database with the CDB_ prefix.

SELF TEST

The following questions will help you measure your understanding of the material presented in this chapter. Read all the choices carefully because there might be more than one correct answer. Choose all correct answers for each question.

Describe the Multitenant Architecture

1. Which of the following is not a valid state (OPEN_MODE) for a system or user container?

A. READ WRITE

B. MOUNTED

C. READ ONLY

D. CLOSED

2. Identify the true statement about Oracle database versions and their compatibility with container databases.

A. Oracle databases created in 12*c* are automatically pluggable into an existing CDB.

B. Oracle 12*c* databases can be a non-CDB, a CDB (system container), or a PDB (user container).

C. Oracle 11*g* databases can be plugged into a container database if you create an XML file with Data Pump Export.

D. Oracle 11*g* databases can be easily upgraded to Oracle Database 12*c* by plugging it into a CDB created with Oracle Database 12*c* release 1 or newer.

E. A CDB created with Oracle Database 12*c* can be converted to a PDB by removing the PDB$SEED user container.

Explain Pluggable Database Provisioning

3. Which of the following database objects are always shared across all PDBs within a system container? (Choose all that apply.)

A. The temporary tablespace

B. The UNDO tablespace

C. The SYSTEM tablespace

D. Control files

E. Redo log files

4. You want to create a common user who can unplug PDBs or start up the CDB. Which of the following tasks will create the user with the required privileges?

A. Create a common user C##RJB in the root container.

B. Create a common user C##RJB in the root and grant the CDB_DBA role.

C. Create a common user C##RJB in the root and grant the SYSDBA role.

D. Create a common user C##RJB in the root and grant the UNPLUG_PDB and CDB_DBA roles.

E. Create a user in each PDB with the same name and grant the user the DBA role.

SELF TEST ANSWERS

Describe the Multitenant Architecture

1. ☑ **D.** When a pluggable database is shut down with the ALTER PLUGGABLE DATABASE . . . CLOSE command, the status in OPEN_MODE is MOUNTED.
   ☒ **A, B,** and **C** are incorrect. **A** is a valid state for the root container and for an opened pluggable database. **B** is valid for a PDB that is plugged in but not open. **C** is valid for the seed database PDB$SEED.

2. ☑ **B.** You can create an Oracle 12*c* database as either a standalone database (non-CDB), as a container database (CDB), or as a pluggable user container (PDB).
   ☒ **A, C, D,** and **E** are incorrect. **A** is incorrect because you have to use DBMS_PDB to create an XML file that must exist to plug a non-CDB into an existing CDB. **C** is incorrect because databases created under 11*g* must be upgraded to 12*c* before they can be plugged into a CDB. **D** is incorrect because you must go through a traditional upgrade process before becoming pluggable. **E** is incorrect because once a database is created as a CDB, it is always a CDB (system container).

Explain Pluggable Database Provisioning

3. ☑ **B, D,** and **E.** The UNDO tablespace, control files, and redo log files are always shared across all PDBs in a CDB.
   ☒ **A** and **C** are incorrect. **A** is incorrect because there is a common temporary tablespace that can be used by all PDBs, but any PDB can have its own temporary tablespace. **C** is incorrect because there is a SYSTEM tablespace in each PDB, and it contains the metadata and other objects specific to the PDB.

4. ☑ **C.** To unplug a PDB or start up a CDB, you must use a common user with the SYSDBA role on the root container.
   ☒ **A, B, D,** and **E** are incorrect. **A** is incorrect because a common user must have CONNECT privileges along with the SYSDBA role for the root container. **B** is incorrect because the CDB_DBA role does not have enough privileges to unplug a PDB or start up a CDB. **D** is incorrect because there is no such role UNPLUG_PDB. **E** is incorrect because creating a user for each PDB is not necessary; create a common user instead for all current and future PDBs.

11

Creating Multitenant Container Databases and Pluggable Databases

CERTIFICATION OBJECTIVES

11.01 Configure and Create a CDB

11.02 Create a PDB Using Different Methods

11.03 Unplug and Drop a PDB

11.04 Migrate Pre-12.1 Non-CDB Database to CDB

✓ Two-Minute Drill

Q&A Self Test

In Chapter 10, I covered the basics of Oracle's multitenant architecture. This included the different types of containers available: the root container (container database, or CDB) that at a minimum comprises the root database and a seed database and zero or more pluggable databases (PDBs). Oracle 12*c* databases can be standalone databases as well and converted to pluggable databases. I also distinguished between common and local users; common users have privileges across all pluggable databases within a container, and local users see the pluggable database as a standalone database (non-CDB). In a multitenant environment, the traditional USER_, ALL_, and DBA_ data dictionary views are supplemented with CDB_ views that are visible across the entire container to common users.

In this chapter, I'll expand on some of these concepts and demonstrate the mechanics of creating a new container database using several different tools. Once the container database is in place, you can create a new pluggable database by cloning the seed database (PDB$SEED).

Databases created in Oracle 11*g* are not left out, though. You can either upgrade the pre-12*c* database to 12.1 and then plug it into an existing CDB or use Data Pump export (**expdp**) on the 11*g* database and then use Data Pump import (**impdp**) on a new pluggable database.

Last, but not least, having accurate and easy-to-manage diagnostic information for your CDB and PDBs is more important than ever. The ADR has the same structure as in previous releases, and the CDB and the PDBs within the CDB have their own subdirectories under the ADR Base directory.

CERTIFICATION OBJECTIVE 11.01

Configure and Create a CDB

Creating a multitenant container database has many uses and many configurations. Compared to previous versions of Oracle Database, the flexibility of grouping or consolidating databases using the multitenant architecture (compared to using RAC or multiple non-CDB databases on the same server) has increased dramatically while at the same time not increasing the complexity of managing multiple databases within a CDB. In fact, managing multiple PDBs within a CDB not only makes more efficient use of memory and CPU resources but makes it easier to manage multiple databases. As mentioned in previous chapters, you'll be able to do things like perform upgrades on the container database, which in turn automatically upgrades the pluggable databases that reside in the container database.

Container databases can be used by developers, by testers, and of course in a production environment. For a new application, you can clone an existing database or create a new database using the seed database in a fraction of the time it takes to create a new standalone database. For testing applications in new hardware and software environments, you can easily unplug a database from one CDB and plug it into another CDB on the same or different server.

In the following sections, I'll show you how to create a new CDB using either SQL*Plus or the Database Configuration Assistant (DBCA). To view and manage the diagnostic information in a multitenant environment, I'll review how the Automatic Diagnostic Repository (ADR) is structured. To close out this section, you'll get a recap of the new data dictionary views available at the container level that expands on the material presented in Chapter 10.

Creating a CDB Using Different Methods

As with many Oracle features, you have many tools at your disposal to create and maintain objects, which in this case means CDBs and PDBs. What tool you use depends on the level of control you need when creating these objects as well as whether you need to script the operation in a batch environment. Table 11-1 shows the tools you can use to perform various operations on CDBs and PDBs.

To create a new CDB, you have three options: SQL*Plus, the Database Configuration Assistant, and the Oracle Universal Installer (OUI). Enterprise Manager Database Express (EMDE) cannot create a CDB or browse the CDB or

TABLE 11-1 CDB- and PDB-Compatible Oracle Tools

Operation/ Tool	SQL*Plus	OUI	DBCA	EM Cloud Control 12c	SQL Developer	DBUA	EMDE
Create new CDB or PDB	✔	✔	✔	✔ (PDB only)	✔ (PDB only)		
Browse CDB or PDB	✔			✔	✔		✔ (PDB only)
Upgrade 12.1 non-CDB to CDB	✔					✔	

PDB architecture. However, EMDE can view any PDB as if it were a standalone database (non-CDB).

Using SQL*Plus to Create a CDB

Using SQL*Plus to create a CDB is similar in many ways to creating a new standalone database instance. The differences are apparent when you use some of the new keywords available with the CREATE DATABASE command such as ENABLE PLUGGABLE DATABASE and SEED FILE_NAME_CONVERT. Once the initial CDB is created, you run the same postcreation scripts as you would in an Oracle 11*g* database or non-CDB 12*c* database.

The steps to create the CDB are as follows:

1. Create an **init.ora** file with the typical parameters for any instance such as DB_NAME, CONTROL_FILES, and DB_BLOCK_SIZE plus the new parameter ENABLE_PLUGGABLE_DATABASE.
2. Set the ORACLE_SID environment variable.
3. Create the CDB using the CREATE DATABASE command with the ENABLE PLUGGABLE DATABASE keywords.
4. Set a special session parameter to indicate that this is a new CDB:

   ```
   alter session set "_oracle_script"=true;
   ```

5. Close and open the seed PDB.
6. Run the postcreation scripts, including the following:

   ```
   ?/rdbms/admin/catalog.sql
   ?/rdbms/admin/catblock.sql
   ?/rdbms/admin/catproc.sql
   ?/rdbms/admin/catoctk.sql
   ?/rdbms/admin/owminst.plb
   ?/sqlplus/admin/pupbld.sql
   ```

EXERCISE 11-1

Creating a New Container Database (CDB) Using SQL Commands

In this exercise, you'll create a new CDB and place its datafiles, control files, and redo log files within an existing ASM disk group. After the CDB database exists, then create an SPFILE in the ASM disk group.

1. Create the **init.ora** file with the parameters required to start an instance named **cdb02** and create control files:

```
[oracle@tettnang dbs]$ cd $ORACLE_HOME/dbs
[oracle@tettnang dbs]$ ls
hc_cdb01.dat     hc_RPTQA14.dat  init.ora          lkCDB01
orapwcdb01
hc_rptqa12c.dat  initcdb01.ora   initrptqa12c.ora  lkRPTQA12C
orapwrptqa12c
[oracle@tettnang dbs]$ cat > initcdb02.ora
db_name='cdb02'
db_create_file_dest='+data'
db_block_size=8192
enable_pluggable_database=true
control_files=(control1,control2,control3)
processes=500
compatible='12.0.0'
[oracle@tettnang dbs]$
```

Notice that you set DB_CREATE_FILE_DEST to +DATA. This enables Oracle Managed Files (OMF) to automatically place all database objects in a standard file directory layout that's easy to navigate. This applies to file systems as well as ASM disk groups. If you want to use a file system location as the base for all database objects, the parameter might look like this:

```
db_create_file_dest='/u01/app/oradata'
```

2. Create the ORACLE_SID environment variable. Oracle best practices dictate that the container's instance name should be the same as the database name:

```
export ORACLE_SID=cdb02
[oracle@tettnang dbs]$
```

3. Start the instance in NOMOUNT mode:

```
[oracle@tettnang dbs]$ sqlplus / as sysdba

SQL*Plus: Release 12.1.0.1.0 Production on Tue May 27
09:33:37 2014

Copyright (c) 1982, 2013, Oracle.  All rights reserved.

Connected to an idle instance.
```

```
SQL> startup nomount
ORACLE instance started.

Total System Global Area  292319232 bytes
Fixed Size                  2287528 bytes
Variable Size             234883160 bytes
Database Buffers           50331648 bytes
Redo Buffers                4816896 bytes
SQL>
```

4. Create the database. The new parameters are highlighted:

```
-- create a new container database
SQL>
create database cdb02
   user sys identified by abc123
   user system identified by xyz789
   logfile group 1 size 100m,
           group 2 size 100m,
           group 3 size 100m
   maxdatafiles 2000
   character set al32utf8
   national character set al16utf16
   extent management local
   datafile '+DATA' size 1g
      autoextend on next 500m maxsize unlimited
sysaux datafile '+DATA' size 500m
   autoextend on next 250m maxsize unlimited
default tablespace users datafile '+DATA' size 500m
   autoextend on next 250m maxsize unlimited
default temporary tablespace temp01 tempfile '+DATA' size
250m
   autoextend on next 250m maxsize unlimited
undo tablespace undotbs01 datafile '+DATA' size 250m
   autoextend on next 250m maxsize unlimited
enable pluggable database
   seed file_name_convert = ('+DATA','+DATA')
   system datafiles size 250m autoextend on next 100m maxsize
unlimited
   sysaux datafiles size 100m autoextend on next 50m maxsize
unlimited
   user_data tablespace usertbs1 datafile '+DATA' size 250m
      autoextend on maxsize unlimited;

Database created.
SQL>
```

5. Set session parameters and close/open the seed database (which is required for proper initialization of the seed database):

```
SQL> alter session set "_oracle_script"=true;
Session altered.
SQL> alter pluggable database pdb$seed close;
Pluggable database altered.
SQL> alter pluggable database pdb$seed open;
Pluggable database altered.
SQL>
```

6. Run postinstall scripts:

```
SQL> @?/rdbms/admin/catalog.sql
. . .
PL/SQL procedure successfully completed.


TIMESTAMP
------------------------------------------------------------
COMP_TIMESTAMP CATALOG    2014-05-27 10:56:39

Session altered.

Session altered.

SQL>
```

7. Create an SPFILE to replace the **init.ora** file:

```
SQL> create spfile='+DATA/CDB02/spfilecdb02.ora' from pfile;
File created.
SQL> exit
[oracle@tettnang dbs]$ cat > initcdb02.ora
SPFILE='+DATA/cdb02/spfilecdb02.ora'
[oracle@tettnang dbs]$ sqlplus / as sysdba

SQL*Plus: Release 12.1.0.1.0 Production on Tue May 27 11:04:49 2014

Copyright (c) 1982, 2013, Oracle.  All rights reserved.
. . .
SQL> shutdown immediate
Database closed.
Database dismounted.
ORACLE instance shut down.
SQL> quit
```

```
[oracle@tettnang dbs]$ export ORACLE_SID=cdb02
[oracle@tettnang dbs]$ sqlplus / as sysdba
SQL*Plus: Release 12.1.0.1.0 Production on Tue May 27 11:09:29 2014
Copyright (c) 1982, 2013, Oracle.  All rights reserved.
Connected to an idle instance.
SQL> startup upgrade
ORACLE instance started.
Total System Global Area  292319232 bytes
Fixed Size                  2287528 bytes
Variable Size             234883160 bytes
Database Buffers           50331648 bytes
Redo Buffers                4816896 bytes
Database mounted.
Database opened.
SQL> show parameter spfile

NAME                         TYPE        VALUE
---------------------------- ----------- ------------------------------
spfile                       string      +DATA/cdb02/spfilecdb02.ora
SQL>
```

That's it! You can now create new PDBs or plug in existing PDBs to the new CDB02 container database.

Using SQL*Plus to create a new container database is the ultimate in control, but as you can see, it can be quite convoluted. Unless you want to create many databases at once with slight changes in parameters or the same set of databases on several servers, using DBCA (discussed in the next section) might be an easier and less error-prone method for creating a CDB.

Using DBCA to Create a CDB

The Database Creation Assistant tool is likely the tool you'll use to create a new container database. In fact, it gives you the options to create a non-CDB database (much like a pre-12.1 database), just a container database, or a container database with a new pluggable database. In Figure 11-1, I am using the "express" method to create a new container database called CDB58, which will reside in the existing ASM disk group +DATA. The recovery files will reside in +RECOV. An initial pluggable database called RPTQA10 will be created along with the container.

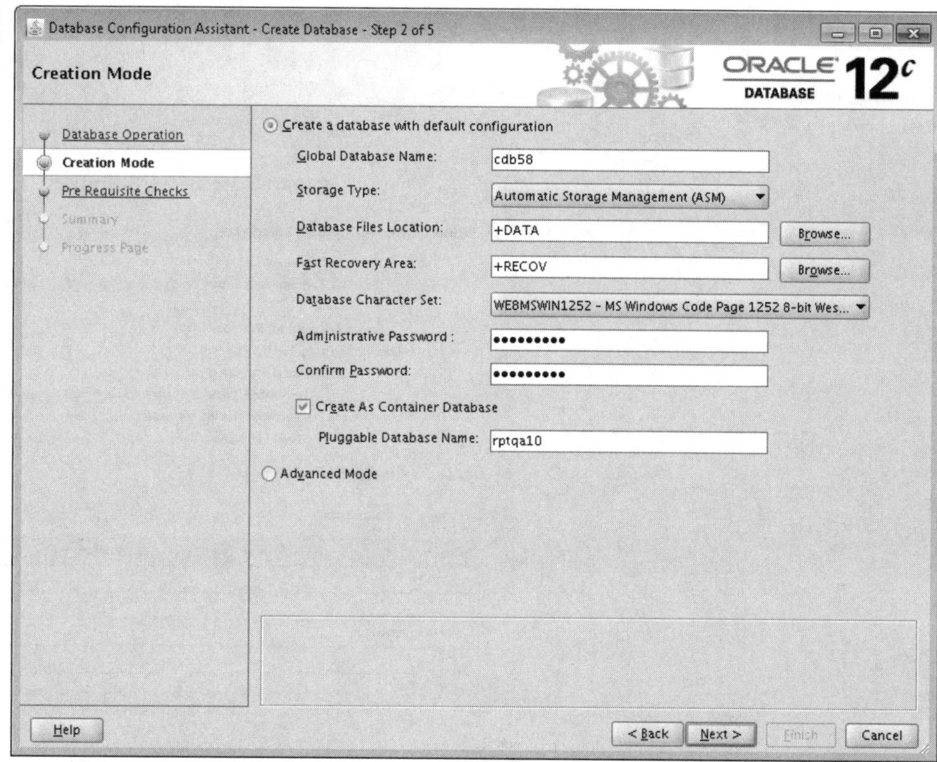

FIGURE 11-1 Creating a container database using DBCA

In the next window, you can review the summary of the container database to be created. Note in Figure 11-2 that creating a container database creates a pluggable database as well.

The Progress page in Figure 11-3 shows the progress of creating the container database and the initial pluggable database.

Once the installation completes, you can see the container database listed in **/etc/oratab**:

```
#
# Multiple entries with the same $ORACLE_SID are not allowed.
#
#
+ASM:/u01/app/product/12.1.0/grid:N:     # line added by Agent
complref:/u01/app/product/12.1.0/database:N:     # line added by Agent
cdb58:/u01/app/product/12.1.0/database:N:     # line added by Agent
```

FIGURE 11-2

Create Database – Summary page

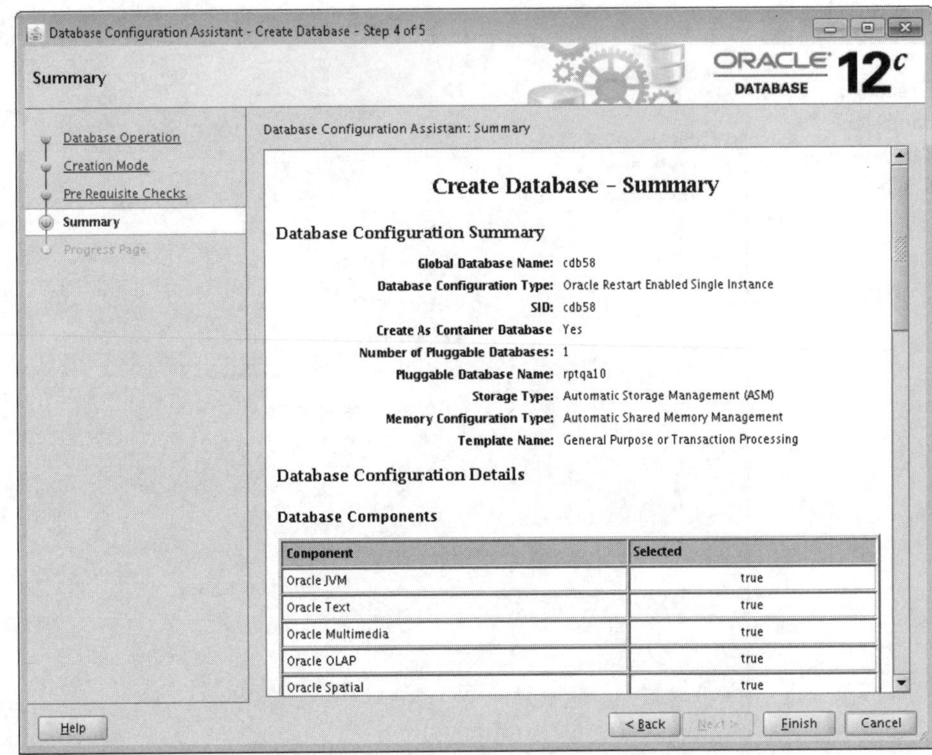

But where is the initial pluggable database? For clues, you can check the listener.

```
[oracle@oel63 ~]$ lsnrctl status
LSNRCTL for Linux: Version 12.1.0.1.0 - Production on 27-MAY-2013 20:47:02
. . .
Service "cdb58" has 1 instance(s).
  Instance "cdb58", status READY, has 1 handler(s) for this service...
. . .
Service "complrefXDB" has 1 instance(s).
  Instance "complref", status READY, has 1 handler(s) for this service...
Service "rptqa10" has 1 instance(s).
  Instance "cdb58", status READY, has 1 handler(s) for this service...
The command completed successfully
[oracle@oel63 ~]$
```

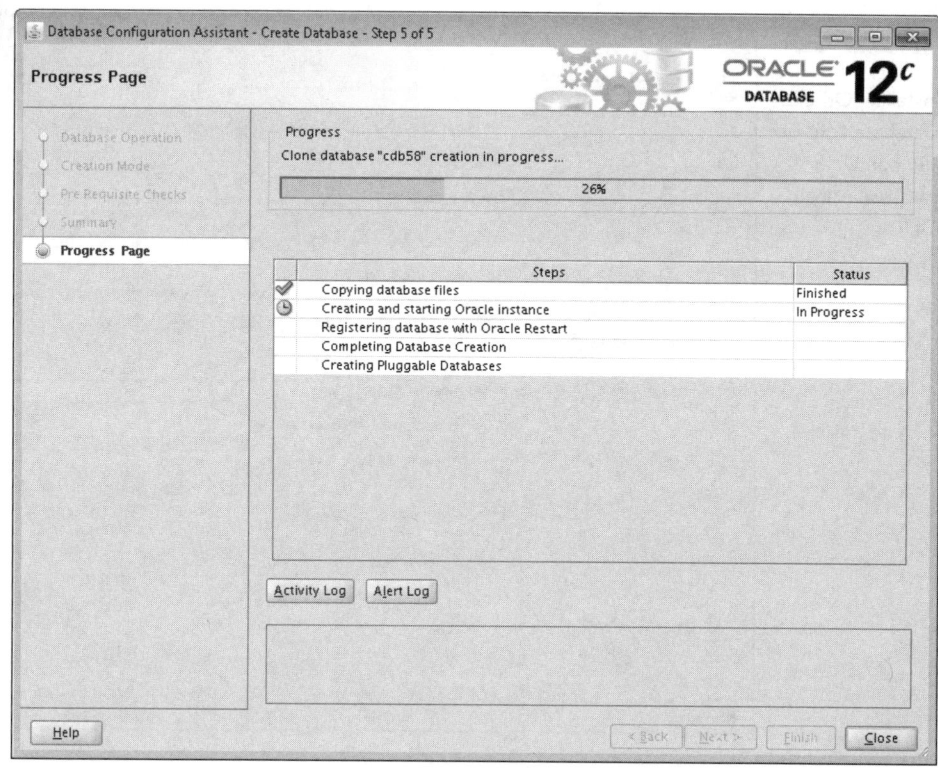

FIGURE 11-3 Container database Progress page

The listener hands off any requests for service **rptqa10** to the pluggable database with the same name in the container database CDB58.

Using OUI to Create a CDB

Using the Oracle Universal Installer is much like one-stop shopping. You can install the Oracle database files, create a new container database, and create a new pluggable database all in one session. Since you'll likely install the database software only once on a server, using OUI to create a new container or pluggable database happens only once per server. In Figure 11-4, I am launching OUI to install the database software and to create a container database named CDB99 and a single pluggable database called QAMOBILE. By default, OUI will use ASM for database files if an ASM disk group is available on the server.

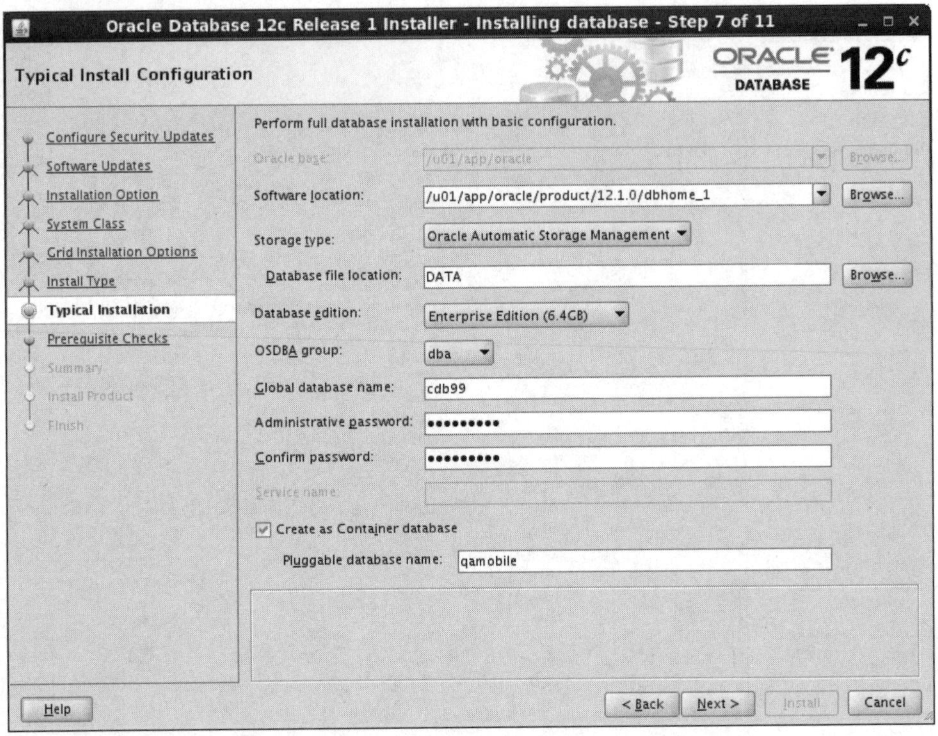

FIGURE 11-4 Installing Oracle Database software and container database using OUI

Understanding New Data Dictionary Views: The Sequel

In Chapter 10, I presented a brief overview of the new data dictionary views available in a multitenant environment. Remember that from the perspective of a local user, there is no distinction between a non-CDB and a PDB. The local user still sees the container-related dynamic performance views and data dictionary views, but the rows returned are filtered based on the privileges and scope of the database user.

For example, a common user with DBA privileges (particularly the SELECT ANY DICTIONARY system privilege) can see all PDBs in the CDB:

```
[oracle@oel63 ~]$ sqlplus c##rjb/rjb@oel63/cdb01
SQL*Plus: Release 12.1.0.1.0 Production on Tue May 27 23:46:10 2014
Copyright (c) 1982, 2013, Oracle.  All rights reserved.
Last Successful login time: Tue May 27 2014 23:15:45 -05:00
Connected to:
Oracle Database 12c Enterprise Edition Release 12.1.0.1.0 - 64bit Production
With the Partitioning, Automatic Storage Management, OLAP, Advanced Analytics
```

```
and Real Application Testing options
SQL> select pdb_id,pdb_name from cdb_pdbs;

    PDB_ID PDB_NAME
---------- ------------------------
         3 QATEST1
         2 PDB$SEED
         4 QATEST2

SQL>
```

A nonprivileged common user won't even see that data dictionary view:

```
SQL> connect c##klh
Enter password:
Connected.
SQL> select pdb_id,pdb_name from cdb_pdbs;
select pdb_id,pdb_name from cdb_pdbs
                            *
ERROR at line 1:
ORA-00942: table or view does not exist

SQL>
```

Local users, even with DBA privileges, will see data dictionary views like CDB_PDBS but won't see any PDBs:

```
[oracle@oel63 ~]$ sqlplus rjb/rjb@oel63/qatest1

SQL*Plus: Release 12.1.0.1.0 Production on Tue May 27 23:53:19 2014

Copyright (c) 1982, 2013, Oracle.  All rights reserved.

Last Successful login time: Tue May 27 2014 23:37:44 -05:00

Connected to:
Oracle Database 12c Enterprise Edition Release 12.1.0.1.0 - 64bit Production
With the Partitioning, Automatic Storage Management, OLAP, Advanced Analytics
and Real Application Testing options

SQL> select pdb_id,pdb_name from cdb_pdbs;

no rows selected

SQL>
```

In previous versions of Oracle Database, the USER_ views show objects owned by the user accessing the view, the ALL_ views show objects accessible to the user accessing the view, and the DBA_ views show all objects in the database and are accessible to users with the SELECT ANY DICTIONARY system privilege, which is usually granted via the DBA role. Whether the database is a non-CDB, a CDB, or a PDB, the DBA_ views show the objects relative to where the view is accessed. For example, in a PDB, the DBA_TABLESPACES view shows tablespaces that exist only in that PDB.

If you are in the root container, DBA_USERS shows only common users, since in the root container only common users exist. In a PDB, DBA_USERS shows both common and local users.

For databases created in Oracle Database 12c, the CDB_ data dictionary views show object information across all PDBs and even exists for non-CDBs. For local users and non-CDBs, the CDB_ views show the same information as the equivalent DBA_ view: the visibility does not go past the PDB or non-CDB even if the local user has the DBA role. Here are some CDB_ data dictionary views, including the new data dictionary view CDB_PDBS:

- **CDB_PDBS** All PDBs within the CDB
- **CDB_TABLESPACES** All tablespaces within the CDB
- **CDB_DATA_FILES** All datafiles within the CDB
- **CDB_USERS** All users within the CDB (common and local)

Figure 11-5 shows the hierarchy of data dictionary views in a multitenant environment. At the CDB_ view level, the main difference in the structure of the table is the new column CON_ID, which is the container ID that owns the objects. The root container and the seed container are, of course, containers as well and have their own CON_ID.

FIGURE 11-5 Multitenant data dictionary view hierarchy

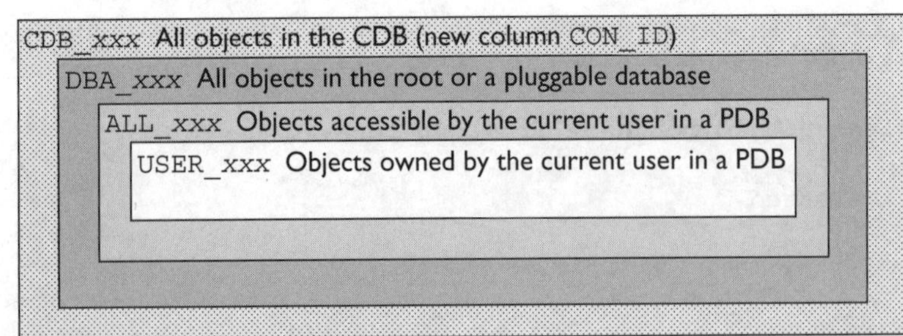

Note that even common users (prefixed with C##) cannot access the CDB_ views unless they have the SELECT ANY DICTIONARY system privilege or that privilege granted via a role such as the DBA role.

CERTIFICATION OBJECTIVE 11.02

Create a PDB Using Different Methods

Once you have the container database created, you can add a new PDB whether or not you created a new PDB when you created the CDB. There are four methods: creating a PDB by cloning the seed PDB, cloning an existing PDB, plugging in a previously unplugged PDB, or plugging in a non-CDB.

Using PDB$SEED to Create a New PDB

Every container database has a read-only seed database container called PDB$SEED used for quickly creating a new pluggable database. When you create a new PDB from PDB$SEED, the following things happen, regardless of whether you use SQL*Plus, SQL Developer, or Enterprise Manager Cloud Control 12*c*. Each of these steps is performed with a CREATE PLUGGABLE DATABASE statement, either manually or via DBCA:

- Datafiles in PDB$SEED are copied to the new PDB.
- Local versions of the SYSTEM and SYSAUX tablespaces are created.
- Local metadata catalog is initialized (with pointers to common read-only objects in the root container).
- The common users SYS and SYSTEM are created.
- A local user is created and is granted the local PDB_DBA role.
- A new default service for the PDB is created and is registered with the listener.

Given the relatively small amount of data creation and movement in those steps, the creation of the PDB is very fast.

EXERCISE 11-2

Create a New Pluggable Database Using PDB$SEED

In this exercise, you'll use SQL*Plus to create and configure a new PDB named TOOL.

1. Connect as a common user with the SYSDBA privilege or a common user with the CREATE PLUGGABLE DATABASE privilege and then confirm that OMF will be used with an ASM disk group:

```
[oracle@tettnang ~]$ sqlplus / as sysdba

SQL*Plus: Release 12.1.0.1.0 Production on Wed May 28
09:25:34 2014

Copyright (c) 1982, 2013, Oracle.  All rights reserved.


Connected to:
Oracle Database 12c Enterprise Edition Release 12.1.0.1.0 -
64bit Production
With the Partitioning, Automatic Storage Management, OLAP,
Advanced Analytics
and Real Application Testing options

SQL> show parameter db_create_file

NAME                                 TYPE        VALUE
------------------------------------ ----------- ------------------
db_create_file_dest                  string      +DATA
SQL>
```

2. Use CREATE DATABASE to create the TOOL pluggable database:

```
SQL> create pluggable database tool
  2     admin user hammer identified by thyme101
  3     roles=(connect);

Pluggable database created.

SQL>
```

Confirming the PDB_ID of the new PDB:

```
SQL> select pdb_id,pdb_name,status
  2  from cdb_pdbs;

    PDB_ID PDB_NAME                                 STATUS
---------- ---------------------------------------- -------------
         3 CCREPOS                                  NORMAL
         2 PDB$SEED                                 NORMAL
         4 TOOL                                     NEW
         5 QA_2014                                  NORMAL

SQL>
```

3. Open the new PDB as READ WRITE to change the STATUS of the PDB to NORMAL:

```
SQL> alter pluggable database tool open read write;

Pluggable database altered.

SQL>
```

Cloning a PDB to Create a New PDB

If you need a new database that's similar to one that already exists, you can clone an existing database within the CDB. The new PDB will be identical to the source except for the PDB name and the DBID. In this example, you'll use the DBA features of SQL Developer to clone the PDB. No worries about what's going on under the covers; each step of the way you can see the DDL that SQL Developer runs to create the clone.

Before cloning an existing PDB, you must close it and reopen it in READ ONLY mode:

```
SQL> alter pluggable database qa_2014 close;

Pluggable database altered.
SQL> alter pluggable database qa_2014 open read only;

Pluggable database altered.

SQL>
```

You can browse the DBA connections for the container database CDB01 and its PDBs. Right-click the QA_2014 PDB and select Clone Pluggable Database, as shown in Figure 11-6.

In the dialog box that opens, as shown in Figure 11-7, change the database name to QA_2015. All other features and options of QA_2014 are retained for QA_2015.

The SQL tab shows the command that SQL Developer will run to clone the database:

```
CREATE PLUGGABLE DATABASE QA_2015 FROM QA_2014
 STORAGE UNLIMITED
 FILE_NAME_CONVERT=NONE;
```

Once you click the Apply button, the cloning operation proceeds and creates the new PDB. As with the SQL*Plus method of creating a new PDB, you have to open the new PDB as READ WRITE.

```
SQL> alter pluggable database qa_2015 open read write;

Pluggable database altered.

SQL>
```

FIGURE 11-6

Selecting a database to clone in SQL Developer

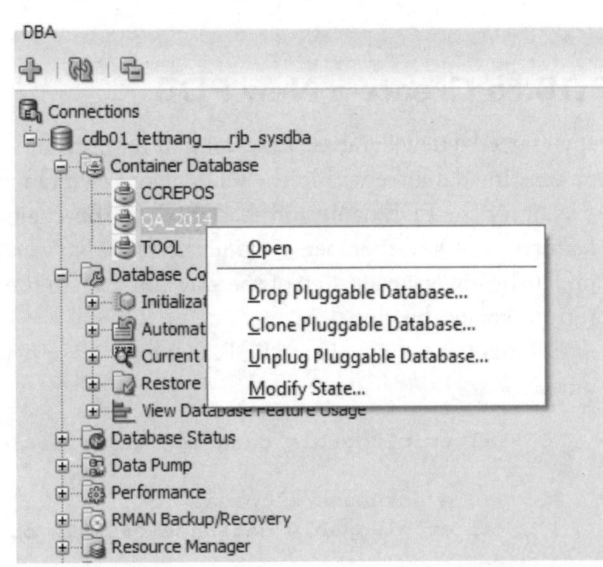

FIGURE 11-7 Specifying PDB clone characteristics

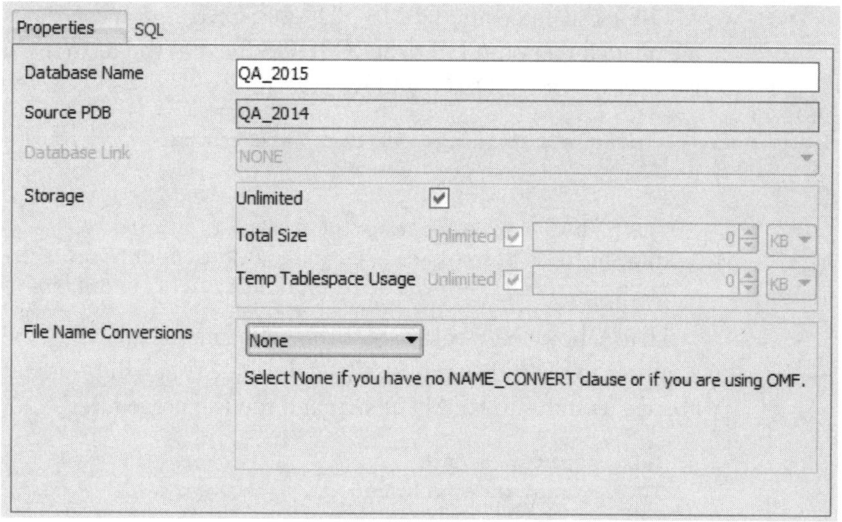

Properties SQL

Database Name QA_2015

Source PDB QA_2014

Database Link NONE

Storage Unlimited

Total Size Unlimited 0 KB

Temp Tablespace Usage Unlimited 0 KB

File Name Conversions None

Select None if you have no NAME_CONVERT clause or if you are using OMF.

Finally, you need to open the QA_2014 database as READ WRITE again since it was set to READ ONLY for the clone operation.

```
SQL> alter pluggable database qa_2014 close;

Pluggable database altered.

SQL> alter pluggable database qa_2014 open read write;

Pluggable database altered.

SQL>
```

Plug a Non-CDB into a CDB

You may have a standalone (non-CDB) 12*c* database that you'd like to consolidate into an existing CDB. If you have a pre-12*c* database, you must upgrade it to 12*c* first or use an alternate method to move that database (see the "Unplug a PDB Using Different Methods" section of this chapter). For an existing non-CDB 12*c* database, it's a straightforward process involving the PL/SQL procedure DBMS_PDB.DESCRIBE.

Using the procedure DBMS_PDB.DESCRIBE, you can quickly export the metadata for a non-CDB to an XML OS file. On the **tettnang** server, there are three instances: ASM, CDB01, and RPTQA12C:

```
[oracle@tettnang ~]$ cat /etc/oratab
. . .
#
+ASM:/u01/app/oracle/product/12.1.0/grid:N:
cdb01:/u01/app/oracle/product/12.1.0/dbhome_1:N:
rptqa12c:/u01/app/oracle/product/12.1.0/dbhome_1:N:
```

Here is how you would export the metadata for the RPTQA12C database. Connect to the target database (the database that will be assimilated into CDB01), change its status to READ ONLY, and run the procedure:

```
SQL> startup mount
ORACLE instance started.

Total System Global Area 2622255104 bytes
Fixed Size                  2685024 bytes
Variable Size            1644169120 bytes
Database Buffers          956301312 bytes
Redo Buffers               19099648 bytes
Database mounted.
SQL> alter database open read only;

Database altered.

SQL> exec dbms_pdb.describe('/tmp/rptqa12c.xml');

PL/SQL procedure successfully completed.

SQL>
```

The XML looks like this:

```
<?xml version="1.0" encoding="UTF-8"?>
<PDB>
  <pdbname>rptqa12c</pdbname>
  <cid>0</cid>
  <byteorder>1</byteorder>
  <vsn>202375168</vsn>
  <dbid>1288637549</dbid>
  <cdbid>1288637549</cdbid>
  <guid>F754FCD8744A55AAE043E3A0080A3B17</guid>
```

```
    <uscnbas>3905844</uscnbas>
    <uscnwrp>0</uscnwrp>
    <rdba>4194824</rdba>
    <tablespace>
      <name>SYSTEM</name>
      <type>0</type>
      <tsn>0</tsn>
      <status>1</status>
      <issft>0</issft>
      <file>
        <path>+DATA/RPTQA12C/DATAFILE/system.261.845207525</path>
. . .
      </options>
      <olsoid>0</olsoid>
      <dv>0</dv>
      <ncdb2pdb>1</ncdb2pdb>
      <APEX>4.2.0.00.27:1</APEX>
      <parameters>
        <parameter>processes=300</parameter>
        <parameter>shared_pool_size=805306368</parameter>
        <parameter>sga_target=2634022912</parameter>
        <parameter>db_block_size=8192</parameter>
        <parameter>compatible=12.1.0.0.0</parameter>
        <parameter>shared_servers=0</parameter>
        <parameter>open_cursors=300</parameter>
        <parameter>star_transformation_enabled=TRUE</parameter>
        <parameter>pga_aggregate_target=524288000</parameter>
      </parameters>
      <tzvers>
        <tzver>primary version:18</tzver>
        <tzver>secondary version:0</tzver>
      </tzvers>
      <walletkey>0</walletkey>
    </optional>
  </PDB>
```


Next, connect to the container database CDB01 and import the XML for RPTQA12C:

```
[oracle@tettnang ~]$ . oraenv
ORACLE_SID = [rptqa12c] ? cdb01
The Oracle base remains unchanged with value /u01/app/oracle
[oracle@tettnang ~]$ sqlplus / as sysdba

SQL*Plus: Release 12.1.0.1.0 Production on Wed May 28 12:40:34 2014

Copyright (c) 1982, 2013, Oracle.  All rights reserved.
```

```
Connected to:
Oracle Database 12c Enterprise Edition Release 12.1.0.1.0 - 64bit Production
With the Partitioning, Automatic Storage Management, OLAP, Advanced Analytics
and Real Application Testing options

SQL> create pluggable database rptqa12c using '/tmp/rptqa12c.xml';

Pluggable database created.

SQL>
```

The plugging operation may take as little as a minute or two if the datafiles for the non-CDB database are in the same ASM disk group as the destination CDB. Some final cleanup and configuration is needed before the plugged-in database can be used. The script **noncdb_to_pdb.sql** cleans up unnecessary metadata not needed in a multitenant environment. In addition, you must open the newly plugged-in database just as you would with a clone operation:

```
SQL> alter session set container=rptqa12c;
SQL> @$ORACLE_HOME/rdbms/admin/noncdb_to_pdb.sql
. . .
  6       IF (sqlcode <> -900) THEN
  7         RAISE;
  8       END IF;
  9     END;
 10   END;
 11   /

PL/SQL procedure successfully completed.

SQL>
SQL> WHENEVER SQLERROR CONTINUE;
SQL> SQL> alter pluggable database rptqa12c open read write;

Pluggable database altered.

SQL>
```

Plug an Unplugged PDB into a CDB

You may have several unplugged databases at any given time. Usually, you're in the process of migrating a PDB from one container to another on the same or a different server. In any case, an unplugged database can't be opened outside of a CDB, so you'll likely plug an unplugged database (PDB) back into a CDB. In this example, the PDB CCREPOS is currently unplugged and has its XML file located in **/tmp/ccrepos.xml** on the server. The steps to plug a currently unplugged PDB into a CDB are both straightforward and finish quickly just as most multitenant operations do! All you have to do is run one command to plug it in and another command to open it. Connect as a common user with the ALTER PLUGGABLE DATABASE privilege as follows (connecting as SYSDBA to CDB01 with OS authentication works great):

```
SQL> create pluggable database ccrepos using '/tmp/ccrepos.xml' nocopy;

Pluggable database created.

SQL> alter pluggable database ccrepos open read write;

Pluggable database altered.

SQL>
```

Note that a PDB must be dropped, and not just unplugged, from a CDB before it can be plugged back in. Using the NOCOPY option saves time if the PDB's datafiles are already in the correct location.

CERTIFICATION OBJECTIVE 11.03

Unplug and Drop a PDB

Since a PDB is by nature highly mobile, it's likely that you'll move it to another CDB on the same or another server. You may just unplug it to make it unavailable to users (and prevent common users from opening it inadvertently). You may also unplug it to drop it completely. There are a few different ways to unplug and then drop a PDB.

Unplug a PDB Using Different Methods

You can unplug a PDB using both SQL*Plus and SQL Developer. Both methods are just about as easy and are just as fast. Which one you use depends on your comfort level and which tool you happen to have open at the time.

Unplug a PDB Using SQL*Plus

When you unplug a PDB from a CDB, you make the PDB unavailable to users, but its status remains UNPLUGGED. To drop the PDB from the CDB, see the section "Dropping a PDB." Before you can unplug a PDB, you must first close it. When you unplug it, you specify the location of an XML file for the PDB's metadata. This metadata will ensure that the PDB will be pluggable later, either into the same or another CDB:

```
SQL> alter pluggable database ccrepos close;

Pluggable database altered.

SQL> alter pluggable database ccrepos unplug into '/tmp/ccrepos.xml';

Pluggable database altered.

SQL>
```

Unplug a PDB Using SQL Developer

Using SQL Developer to unplug a PDB is even easier than using SQL*Plus. From the CDB's connection in the DBA window, expand the Container Database branch and right-click the PDB to be unplugged. Select Unplug Pluggable Database from the context menu, as in Figure 11-8.

FIGURE 11-8 Unplugging a PDB from SQL Developer

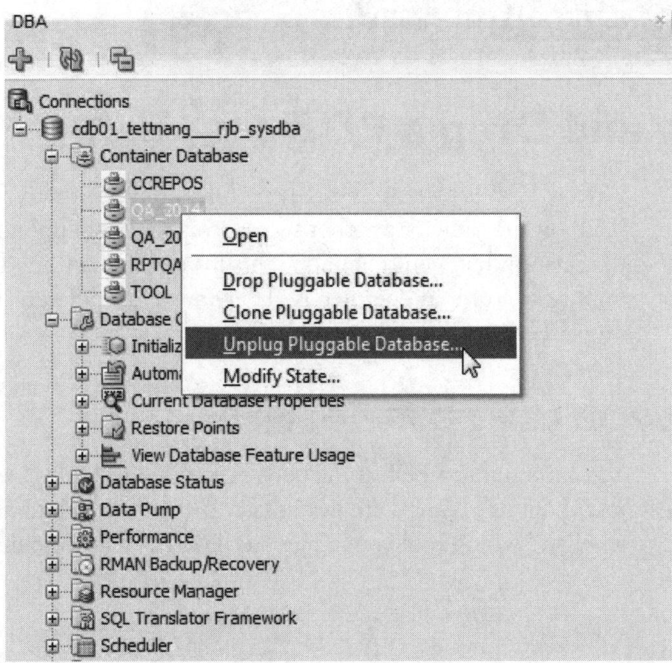

FIGURE 11-9

Specifying the location for the unplugged PDB's XML file

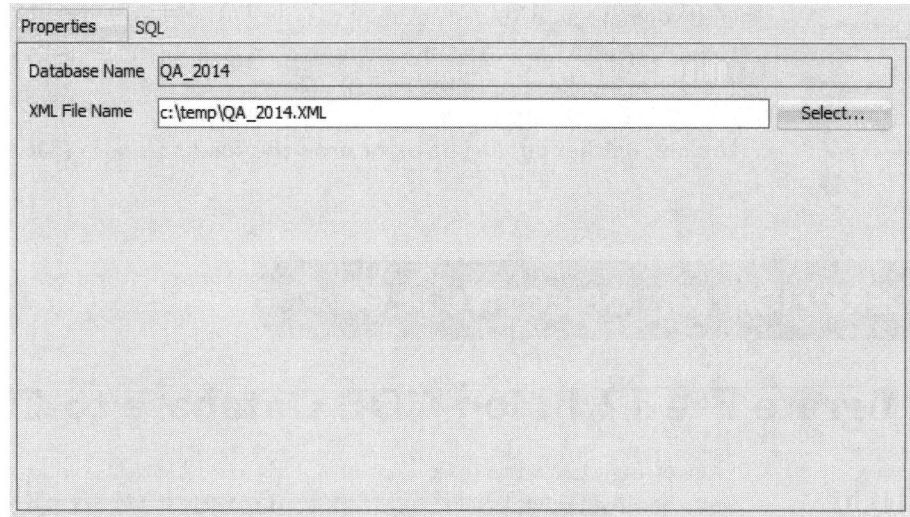

The Unplug dialog box gives you the opportunity to specify the name and location of the XML file containing the PDB's metadata, as you can see in Figure 11-9.

Dropping a PDB

As with most CDB and PDB operations, you can use both SQL*Plus and SQL Developer to drop a PDB. In addition, you can use DBCA and Enterprise Manager Cloud Control 12*c* to drop a PDB. When you drop a PDB, all references to the PDB are removed from the CDB's control file. By default, the datafiles are retained; therefore, if you had previously unplugged that PDB, you can use the XML file to plug that PDB back into the same or another CDB. In this example, you will drop the QA_2014 PDB along with its datafiles. It will no longer be available to plug into another database even if you still have the XML metadata.

```
SQL> alter pluggable database qa_2014 close;

Pluggable database altered.

SQL> drop pluggable database qa_2014 including datafiles;

Pluggable database dropped.

SQL>
```

If you have an RMAN backup of the QA_2014 PDB, you could restore it from there. Otherwise, if you want to remove all remaining traces of QA_2014, you'll have to manually remove the backups of QA_2014 using RMAN.

You can neither unplug, open, or drop the seed database PDB$SEED.

CERTIFICATION OBJECTIVE 11.04

Migrate Pre-12.1 Non-CDB Database to CDB

Converting Oracle Database 12*c* non-CDBs to a PDB is fast and straightforward, but what if your database is a previous version such as 11*g* or even 10*g*? You have a few options available depending on whether you want to keep the original database intact for some length of time.

Using the Upgrade Method to Migrate a Non-CDB

If your application is not sensitive or dependent on the version of the database (which you should have verified by now), then your cleanest option is to upgrade the non-CDB in place up to version 12*c* (12.1.0.1 or later), and then plug it in to the CDB using the methods mentioned earlier in this chapter. The biggest advantage to this method is that you don't need to allocate any extra space for the migration as you would for the other two methods.

Using the Data Pump Method to Migrate a Non-CDB

To use the Data Pump method, you'll use Data Pump export/import as you would in a non-CDB environment. Create a new PDB from the seed database in the CDB and adjust the initialization parameters to be comparable to those in the existing database.

One of the advantages with this method is that you can leave the current non-CDB in place to ensure compatibility with Oracle Database 12*c* before dropping the original database.

Using the Database Link Method to Migrate a Non-CDB

Using database links, you create a new PDB from the seed database and copy over the application's tables using database links. This is the most labor-intensive option but is probably the easiest if the number of tables in an application is small. A table migration would look like this:

```
SQL> insert into hr.employee_hist select * from employee_hist@HR11gDB;
```

CERTIFICATION SUMMARY

Creating and managing multitenant databases is one of the most important and versatile features available in Oracle Database 12*c*. Not only does it make moving databases from one server's container database to another almost trivial, it makes better use of all server resources including CPU, memory, and disk space. Since all PDBs reside in one or a small number of CDBs on a server, there is significantly less wasted or unused memory and disk space compared to each PDB being a non-CDB database with its own allocation of disk space and memory.

As with many Oracle features and capabilities, you're able to use many different tools to accomplish the same task. Most of the basic tasks such as creating or dropping a CDB or PDB are available in several tools. Which tool you use depends a lot on your level of expertise and permissions in the database environment. You can almost always count on SQL*Plus to perform all of your multitenant operations, especially since the other tools rely on SQL*Plus commands to execute the operation. In addition, SQL*Plus is a good method for environments where you have to create, unplug, or drop a large number of pluggable databases at once or on a regular basis, such as in a training environment.

Given that a pluggable database, by definition, can be plugged into a container database and later unplugged and moved to another container database, the unplug and plug operations must be fast and easy. For any unplug or plug operation, you need to have the metadata information for the pluggable database available. This metadata is created as an XML file that is easy to move to another server as you plug in a database that was unplugged from another CDB. This XML can also be created for a non-CDB 12.1 database that will be plugged into a CDB for the first time. The new package DBMS_PDB contains a procedure to create this XML file from a non-CDB database, and it is used much like the XML file created for an unplugged database when you want to plug it into a different CDB.

There are still thousands if not hundreds of thousands of Oracle Database 10*g* and 11*g* databases that cannot immediately take advantage of the Oracle Database 12*c* multitenant architecture. Several migration methods are available, however, ranging from using database links to using Data Pump export/import to upgrading an older database to 12.1.0.1 or newer in place and plugging it into a CDB.

TWO-MINUTE DRILL

Configure and Create a CDB

- Container databases facilitate database consolidation, resource savings, and ease of migration to other servers and CDBs.
- Every CDB is created with a seed database and a root container.
- New CDBs can be created using SQL*Plus, DBCA, OUI, Cloud Control, and SQL Developer.
- To create a new CDB, you must use the ENABLE PLUGGABLE DATABASE clause of the CREATE DATABASE statement.
- If you are not using OMF (ideally with ASM), you must use the SEED FILE_NAME_CONVERT clause to specify the location and names for the database files and seed database for the new CDB.
- Creating a CDB using CREATE DATABASE requires that you run a number of PL/SQL procedures in the **?/rdbms/admin** directory to enable other Oracle features and create data dictionary objects.
- You can use the Oracle Universal Installer to install the database software, create a new container database, and optionally create a new pluggable database in the same session.
- Multitenant database users are divided into two classes: common users and local users.
- Common users must be prefixed with C##.
- The data dictionary views USER_, ALL_, and DBA_ behave exactly like they do in a non-CDB environment.
- Data dictionary views beginning with CDB_ contain metadata for objects across all pluggable databases and the root container and are differentiated by the CON_ID column.

Create a PDB Using Different Methods

- Creating a new PDB clones the PDB$SEED database within the same container.
- The new PDB has its own metadata catalog, local versions of SYSTEM and SYSAUX, and common users SYS and SYSTEM.
- After starting the new PDB, the new default service name is registered with the listener.

- Cloning an existing PDB within the same or another CDB requires that the PDB to be cloned be shut down for the clone operation.
- After cloning, both the original and cloned database must be opened as READ WRITE to make it available to users.
- Plugging a non-CDB that is at version 12.1.0.1 or newer requires an XML file to be created with DBMS_PDB.DESCRIBE.
- The non-CDB database to be plugged in must be shut down and opened as READ ONLY for the plugging operation.
- After plugging in a non-CDB, you must run the **noncdb_to_pdb.sql** script to remove duplicate metadata and create other system objects required in a multitenant environment.

Unplug and Drop a PDB

- Unplugging a PDB requires you to create the metadata XML file so that it can be plugged into the same or another CDB later.
- After unplugging a database, its status in the container becomes UNPLUGGED, and the database is no longer available to users.
- Dropping a PDB from a CDB completely removes the metadata for the PDB from the container's data dictionary. In addition, all references to that PDB are removed from the control files.
- By default, the PDB's datafiles are not dropped unless you use the INCLUDING DATAFILES clause.
- The pluggable database (template) PDB$SEED can be neither unplugged nor dropped from its container.

Migrate Pre-12.1 Non-CDB Database to CDB

- The upgrade method requires that the non-CDB be upgraded to Oracle Database version 12.1.0.1 or newer before it can be plugged into a CDB.
- Oracle Data Pump export/import is another method for migrating an older database to a PDB.
- Before using Data Pump to migrate a database, create a new PDB in the target container.
- Using database links is another method to migrate a database to a multitenant environment. This method is viable if the number of tables is small and the tables themselves are small.

SELF TEST

The following questions will help you measure your understanding of the material presented in this chapter. Read all the choices carefully because there might be more than one correct answer. Choose all correct answers for each question.

Configure and Create a CDB

1. Which of the following clauses are required in the CREATE DATABASE command to create a container database? (Choose all that apply.)
   A. ENABLE PLUGGABLE DATABASE
   B. CHARACTER SET
   C. SEED FILE_NAME_CONVERT
   D. ENABLE CONTAINER DATABASE

Create a PDB Using Different Methods

2. A new user is created as follows:

```
SQL> grant connect,resource
  2>   to c##bob identified by bob container=all;
Grant succeeded.
SQL> connect c##bob/bob;
Connected.
SQL> select pdb_id,pdb_name,con_id from cdb_pdbs;
no rows selected
```

   Since C## is a common user, why aren't any rows seen in CDB_PDBS?
   A. When the container was created, the DBA forgot to run the appropriate setup scripts from **?/rdbms/admin**.
   B. The user C##BOB does not have the SELECT ANY DICTIONARY system privilege.
   C. You can see only the information from the CDB_ views in the root container.
   D. Only common or local users with the DBA role can see the CDB_ views.

Unplug and Drop a PDB

3. To unplug a database, which of the following conditions must be true? (Choose all that apply.)
   A. The database must be exported with Data Pump before dropping a PDB.
   B. There must be a full RMAN backup of the container.
   C. The PDB must be shut down.
   D. You must create an XML file with the metadata for the PDB.

Migrate Pre-12.1 Non-CDB Database to CDB

4. Which of the following methods are viable options for migrating a pre-12.1 database to a PDB within an existing CDB? (Choose all that apply.)

A. Upgrade the pre-12.1 database in place to version 12.1.0.1 or newer and plug it into an existing CDB.

B. For Oracle Database versions 11*g* and 10*g*, you can use the DBMS_PDB.DESCRIBE PL/SQL procedure to create the XML file that will allow you to migrate the database to a CDB environment.

C. Leave the existing database in place and perform a logical migration of the data using Data Pump export/import into a new PDB.

D. Leave the existing database in place and perform a logical migration of the data using database links between the existing database and a new PDB.

SELF TEST ANSWERS

Configure and Create a CDB

1. ☑ **A.** For creating a container database, the only required clause is ENABLE PLUGGABLE DATABASE. If you are not using OMF and you do not have the parameter DB_CREATE_FILE_DEST set (for example, to an ASM disk group), then you need to use the optional SEED FILE_NAME_CONVERT to specify where the seed database (PDB$SEED) files will reside.
☒ **B, C,** and **D** are incorrect. **B** is incorrect because the database character set is not related to whether the database is a CDB. **C** is incorrect because SEED FILE_NAME_CONVERT is required only if you are not using OMF for your database files. **D** is incorrect because there is no such clause ENABLE CONTAINER DATABASE in the CREATE DATABASE command.

Create a PDB Using Different Methods

2. ☑ **C.** For common users the CDB_ views are available. However, the CDB_ views return no rows if the current container is not the root container.
☒ **A, B,** and **D** are incorrect. **A** is incorrect because the CDB_ views and permissions are not created with these scripts although they should all be run right after the database is created. **B** is incorrect because that privilege is not required to access the CDB_ data dictionary views. **D** is incorrect because you don't need the DBA role to see the contents of the CDB_ data dictionary views.

Unplug and Drop a PDB

3. ☑ **C** and **D.** To unplug a PDB from a CDB, it must first be shut down with the ALTER PLUGGABLE DATABASE . . . CLOSE command; you must also create the XML metadata file with DBMS_PDB.DESCRIBE so that the PDB can be plugged in later to this or another CDB in the future.
☒ **A** and **B** are incorrect. Neither a Data Pump export nor an RMAN backup of the PDB is required to unplug a PDB. When a PDB is unplugged, its datafiles are not dropped unless you explicitly drop the PDB and specify the INCLUDING DATAFILES clause.

Migrate Pre-12.1 Non-CDB Database to CDB

4. ☑ **A, C,** and **D.** If you upgrade the database to version 12.1.0.1 or newer, you can run DBMS_PDB.DESCRIBE to create the XML file and plug the database into an existing CDB. Both Data Pump and database links are viable options for database migration in particular because both methods leave the original database intact at its original version.
☒ **B** is incorrect. You cannot directly plug a pre-12.1 Oracle Database into a CDB using this method since the DBMS_PDB package exists only in Oracle Database 12*c* container databases.

CERTIFICATION OBJECTIVES

12.01	Establish Connections to CDBs and PDBs
12.02	Start Up and Shut Down a CDB and Open and Close PDBs
12.03	Evaluate the Impact of Parameter Value Changes
12.04	Manage Permanent and Temporary Tablespaces in a CDB and PDBs
12.05	Manage Common and Local Users
12.06	Manage Common and Local Privileges
12.07	Manage Common and Local Roles
12.08	Enable Common Users to Access Data in Specific PDBs
✓	Two-Minute Drill
Q&A	Self Test

This is one of the most important chapters of the book. The concepts in this chapter—namely, how to connect to a CDB or PDB, manage permanent and temporary tablespaces, and ensure that each PDB within a CDB has the right level of security for both the local and common users—comprise the tasks you'll be performing on a daily basis.

The first part of the chapter sounds a lot like an introductory Oracle database administration course. You will find out how to set up the connections to a database, start up and shut down a database, and set the parameters for a database. The difference is that you're doing those things for the container (CDB) as a whole and differently for each PDB within the CDB. You'll find out that some database parameters apply only at the CDB level, whereas other parameters can be set at the PDB level. Once you start up a CDB, you can have each PDB in a different state. Some PDBs will remain in the MOUNT state while the rest can be OPEN as READ ONLY or READ WRITE.

Managing permanent and temporary tablespaces in a multitenant environment is similar to managing those tablespace types in a non-CDB environment. The SYSTEM and SYSAUX tablespaces exist only in the CDB (CDB$ROOT), but otherwise the CDB and each PDB can have its own permanent tablespaces. For temporary tablespaces, every PDB can use the temporary tablespace in the CDB. However, if a particular PDB has specific temporary tablespace requirements that might not operate efficiently with the CDB's shared temporary tablespace, then that PDB can have its own temporary tablespace.

Last, but certainly not least, a DBA in a multitenant environment must understand the distinction between common and local users along with the roles and privileges assigned to each. Much like an application user has no knowledge of whether a database is a PDB or a non-CDB, a DBA can have a local user account in a PDB and manage that PDB with no privileges or visibility outside of the PDB.

CERTIFICATION OBJECTIVE 12.01

Establish Connections to CDBs and PDBs

You connect to a PDB or CDB much like you connect to a non-CDB. You can connect to a CDB via OS authentication and the common user SYS. Otherwise, you will connect to either a CDB or one of the PDBs within the CDB using a service name. The service name is referenced either using an EasyConnect string or within a **tnsnames.ora** entry. This method is the same whether you are using SQL*Plus or SQL Developer.

By default, a service name is created for each new, cloned, or plugged-in PDB. If that is not sufficient in your environment, you'll use the DBMS_SERVICE package to create additional services for the PDB.

Understanding CDB and PDB Service Names

In a non-CDB environment, a database instance is associated with at least one service managed by at least one listener. One listener can manage a combination of non-CDB and PDB services. The database server **oel63** has two databases: DBAHANDBOOK and CDB01. As you might suspect, the database CDB01 is a multitenant database, and DBAHANDBOOK is a non-CDB, but they are both Oracle Database version 12*c* and are managed by a single listener called LISTENER:

```
[oracle@oel63 ~]$ lsnrctl status

LSNRCTL for Linux: Version 12.1.0.1.0 - Production on 02-JUL-2014 22:47:35

Copyright (c) 1991, 2013, Oracle.  All rights reserved.
. . .
Services Summary...
Service "+ASM" has 1 instance(s).
  Instance "+ASM", status READY, has 1 handler(s) for this service...
Service "cdb01" has 1 instance(s).
  Instance "cdb01", status READY, has 1 handler(s) for this service...
Service "cdb01XDB" has 1 instance(s).
  Instance "cdb01", status READY, has 1 handler(s) for this service...
Service "dbahandbook" has 1 instance(s).
  Instance "dbahandbook", status READY, has 1 handler(s) for this service...
Service "dbahandbookXDB" has 1 instance(s).
  Instance "dbahandbook", status READY, has 1 handler(s) for this service...
Service "dw17" has 1 instance(s).
  Instance "cdb01", status READY, has 1 handler(s) for this service...
Service "qatest1" has 1 instance(s).
  Instance "cdb01", status READY, has 1 handler(s) for this service...
The command completed successfully
[oracle@oel63 ~]$
```

The container database CDB01 has two PDBs, DW17 and QATEST1, and the same listener manages connections for both PDBs.

Every container in a CDB has its own service name. The CDB itself has the default service name that's the same as the container name plus the domain, if any. For each PDB created or cloned, a new service is created and managed by the default listener unless otherwise specified. As you might expect, the only exception to this rule is the seed container (PDB$SEED). Since it is read-only and used only to create new PDBs, there is no reason to create a service and connect to it.

In addition to using the service name to connect to the CDB or any PDBs contained within, you can use OS authentication and connect as SYSDBA just as you would with a non-CDB. You'll be connected as the SYS user—a common user with privileges to maintain all PDBs within the CDB.

The transparency of a PDB and how it appears as a non-CDB to nonprivileged users extends to how you connect using entries in **tnsnames.ora** or using Oracle EasyConnect. As you may recall, the format for an EasyConnect connect string is as follows:

```
<username>/<password>@<hostname>:<port_number>/<service_name>
```

Therefore, for connecting to the user RJB in the PDB named DW17 in the CDB named CDB01 on the server **oel63**, you would use the following when starting SQL*Plus:

```
[oracle@oel63 ~]$ sqlplus rjb/rjb@oel63:1521/dw17

SQL*Plus: Release 12.1.0.1.0 Production on Thu Jul 3 21:56:44 2014

Copyright (c) 1982, 2013, Oracle.  All rights reserved.


Connected to:
Oracle Database 12c Enterprise Edition Release 12.1.0.1.0 - 64bit Production
With the Partitioning, Automatic Storage Management, OLAP, Advanced Analytics
and Real Application Testing options

SQL>
```

Notice that no reference to CDB01 is necessary. The PDB's service name masks the existence of the CDB or any other PDBs in the CDB.

Connecting to a CDB or PDB Using SQL Developer

Connecting to the root container or any PDB within a container using SQL Developer is just as easy. You use the username (common or local), server name, port, and service name. In other words, this is EasyConnect format. Figure 12-1 shows several connections to CDB01 plus a connection to a non-CDB.

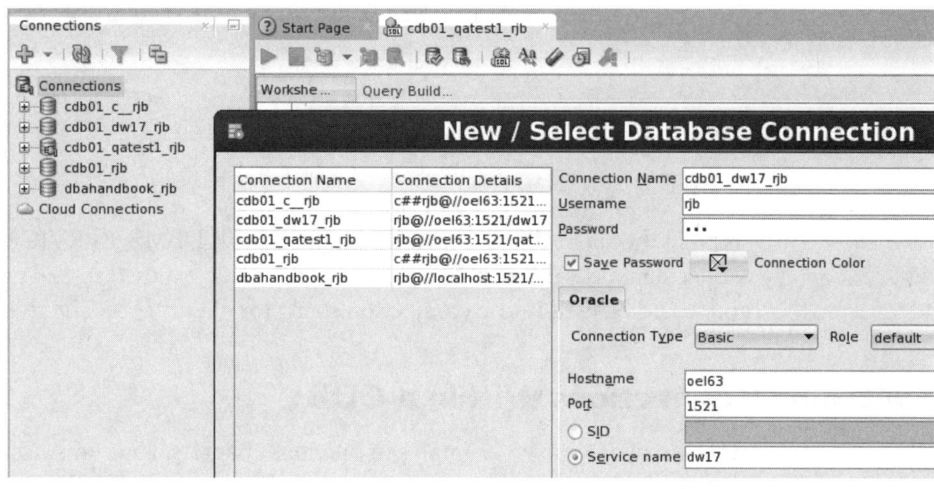

FIGURE 12-1 Connecting to CDBs and PDBs in SQL Developer

Creating Services for CDBs or PDBs

If you're using a standalone server environment with Oracle Restart or a clustered environment using Oracle Clusterware, you'll automatically get a new service created with every new or cloned PDB or non-CDB (database instance). If you want additional services for a PDB, use the **srvctl** command like this:

```
[oracle@oel63 ~]$ srvctl add service -db cdb01 -service dwsvc2 -pdb dw17
[oracle@oel63 ~]$ srvctl start service -db cdb01 -service dwsvc2
[oracle@oel63 ~]$ lsnrctl status
. . .
Service "dwsvc2" has 1 instance(s).
  Instance "cdb01", status READY, has 1 handler(s) for this service...
. . .
[oracle@oel63 ~]$
```

In a nonrestart or nonclustered environment, you can use the DBMS_SERVICE package to create and start the service. To create the same new service as in the previous example with **srvctl** but instead using DBMS_SERVICE, you would do the following:

```
SQL> begin
  2      dbms_service.create_service(
  3         service_name => 'dwsvc2',
  4         network_name => 'dwsvcnew');
```

```
      dbms_service.start_service(service_name => 'dwsvc2');
  end;
  /

PL/SQL procedure successfully completed.

SQL>
```

Note the slight difference in the example with DBMS_SERVICE: The actual service name is still **dwsvc2**, but the service name exposed to end users is **dwsvcnew** and would be used in the connection string for clients accessing this service.

Switching Connections Within a CDB

As you may infer from examples in previous chapters, you can switch containers within a session if you either are a common user with the SET CONTAINER system privilege or have a local user in each container and you connect using the service name.

```
[oracle@oel63 ~]$ sqlplus / as sysdba

SQL*Plus: Release 12.1.0.1.0 Production on Sat Jul 5 22:09:41 2014

Copyright (c) 1982, 2013, Oracle.  All rights reserved.


Connected to:
Oracle Database 12c Enterprise Edition Release 12.1.0.1.0 - 64bit Production
With the Partitioning, Automatic Storage Management, OLAP, Advanced Analytics
and Real Application Testing options

SQL> show con_name

CON_NAME
------------------------------
CDB$ROOT
SQL> alter session set container=qatest1;

Session altered.

SQL> show con_name

CON_NAME
------------------------------
QATEST1
SQL> connect rjb/rjb@oel63/dw17
```

```
Connected.
SQL> show con_name

CON_NAME
------------------------------
DW17
SQL>
```

You can have a pending transaction in the first container, switch to a new container, and then switch back to the first container, and you still have the option to COMMIT or ROLLBACK the pending transaction.

Common users who have the SET CONTAINER system privilege or local users who switch containers using CONNECT local_user@PDB_NAME do not automatically commit pending transactions when switching containers.

CERTIFICATION OBJECTIVE 12.02

Start Up and Shut Down a CDB and Open and Close PDBs

Starting up and shutting down a CDB or opening and closing a PDB will seem familiar to any Oracle DBA who starts up and shuts down a non-CDB. The point that is often missed is that a CDB is ultimately a single database instance, and each PDB shares the resources of the CDB's instance. This is to be expected since each PDB is logically partitioned from each other PDB using the CON_ID column in every table that is in common with the root and all PDBs. This logical partitioning extends to user accounts and security as well; thus, it appears to noncommon users that the PDB has its own dedicated instance.

on the job

As you might expect, in a clustered (RAC) environment a CDB has one instance on each node of the cluster.

Since the CDB is a database instance, anything running within the CDB is shut down or disconnected when the CDB is shut down. This means that a PDB is not open for users until the CDB has been started and explicitly opened (either manually by the DBA or via a trigger), and similarly, the PDB is closed when the CDB instance is shut down.

In the following sections, I'll show you how CDBs and PDBs are started up and shut down as well as how to automate the process. You'll also want to know how to change parameters that are specific to a PDB as well as database objects such as temporary tablespaces that can be created specifically for a PDB if the default global temporary tablespace does not meet the needs of the PDB's application.

CDB Instance Startup

The CDB instance is most like a traditional non-CDB instance. Figure 12-2 shows the five possible states for CDBs and PDBs in a multitenant environment.

From the shutdown state, you can perform a STARTUP NOMOUNT (connecting AS SYSDBA using OS authentication) to start a CDB instance by opening the SPFILE, creating the processes and memory structures, but not yet opening the control file:

```
SQL> startup nomount
ORACLE instance started.

Total System Global Area 2622255104 bytes
Fixed Size                  2291808 bytes
Variable Size            1140852640 bytes
```

FIGURE 12-2 CDB and PDB states

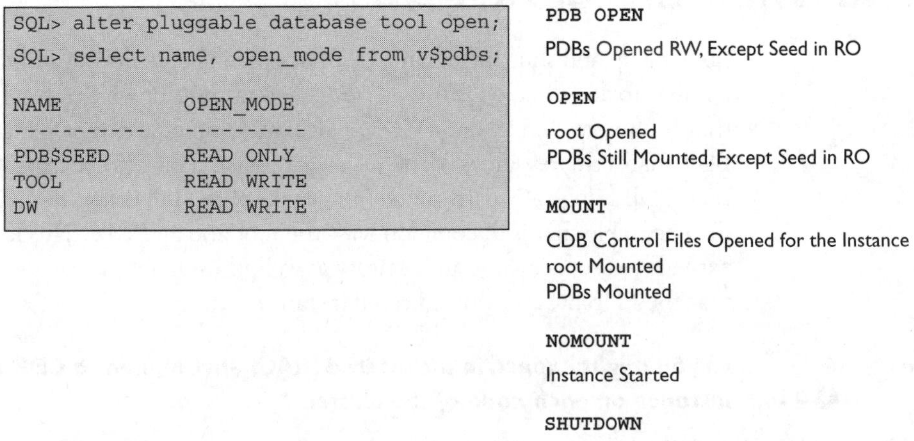

```
SQL> alter pluggable database tool open;
SQL> select name, open_mode from v$pdbs;

NAME          OPEN_MODE
-----------   ----------
PDB$SEED      READ ONLY
TOOL          READ WRITE
DW            READ WRITE
```

PDB OPEN
PDBs Opened RW, Except Seed in RO

OPEN
root Opened
PDBs Still Mounted, Except Seed in RO

MOUNT
CDB Control Files Opened for the Instance
root Mounted
PDBs Mounted

NOMOUNT
Instance Started

SHUTDOWN

```
Database Buffers     1459617792 bytes
Redo Buffers                 19492864 bytes
SQL> select con_id,name,open_mode from v$pdbs;

no rows selected

SQL>
```

At this point in the startup process, the instance has no information about the PDBs within the CDB yet. You would typically perform a STARTUP NOMOUNT when you need to re-create or restore a missing control file for the CDB instance.

A lot of things happen when you move a CDB to the MOUNT state, as you can see in Figure 12-2. Not only are the CDB's control files opened for the instance, but both the CDB$ROOT and all PDBs are changed to the MOUNT state:

```
SQL> alter database mount;

Database altered.

SQL> select con_id,name,open_mode from v$pdbs;

    CON_ID NAME                           OPEN_MODE
---------- ------------------------------ ----------
         2 PDB$SEED                       MOUNTED
         3 QATEST1                        MOUNTED
         5 DW17                           MOUNTED

SQL>
```

If any datafile operations are necessary (restore and recover, for example), this is where you would perform those, especially if those operations are required on the SYSTEM tablespace. The final step to make the root container available for opening PDBs is to change the CDB's state to OPEN. After CDB$ROOT is OPEN, it's available for read and write operations. The PDBs are still mounted with the seed database PDB$SEED mounted as READ ONLY:

```
SQL> alter database cdb01 open;

Database altered.

SQL> select con_id,name,open_mode from v$pdbs;

    CON_ID NAME           OPEN_MODE
---------- -------------- ----------
```

```
         2 PDB$SEED      READ ONLY
         3 QATEST1       MOUNTED
         5 DW17          READ WRITE

SQL>
```

Because I created a second service for the PDB named DW17 earlier in the chapter and Oracle Restart is installed in this environment, DW17 is automatically opened in READ WRITE mode. The seed database PDB$SEED is always opened READ ONLY.

Once the CDB is opened (in other words, the root's datafiles are available along with the global temporary tablespace and the online redo log files), the PDBs are mounted but not yet open and available to users. Unless a PDB is opened with a trigger or via Oracle Restart, it remains in the MOUNTED state.

At this point, the CDB instance behaves much like a non-CDB instance. In the next section, you'll see how individual PDBs are opened and closed.

Open and Close a PDB

Once you have the root (CDB$ROOT) container of a CDB open, you can perform all desired operations on the PDBs within the CDB, including but not limited to cloning PDBs, creating a new PDB from the seed, unplugging a PDB, or plugging in a previously unplugged PDB. Remember that the seed container, PDB$SEED, is always open when CDB$ROOT is open but with an OPEN_MODE of READ ONLY.

There are quite a few options when you want to open or close a PDB. You can use ALTER PLUGGABLE DATABASE when connected as SYSDBA or SYSOPER, or if you're connected as SYSDBA within a PDB, you can use the same commands without having to specify the PDB name. In addition, you can selectively open or close one or more PDBs with the ALL or EXCEPT ALL option.

Using the ALTER PLUGGABLE DATABASE Command

You can open or close a PDB from any container by specifying the PDB name; alternatively, you can change the session context to a specific PDB and perform multiple operations on that PDB without qualifying it, as in these examples. Regardless of the current container, you can open and close any PDB by explicitly specifying the PDB name:

```
SQL> select con_id,name,open_mode from v$pdbs;

    CON_ID NAME                           OPEN_MODE
```

```
---------- ------------------------------ ----------
         2 PDB$SEED                       READ ONLY
         3 QATEST1                        MOUNTED
         5 DW17                           READ WRITE

SQL> alter pluggable database dw17 close;

Pluggable database altered.

SQL> alter pluggable database dw17 open read only;

Pluggable database altered.

SQL> alter pluggable database qatest1 open;

Pluggable database altered.

SQL>
```

Alternatively, you can set the default PDB name at the session level:

```
SQL> alter session set container=dw17;

Session altered.

SQL> alter pluggable database close;

Pluggable database altered.

SQL> alter pluggable database open read write;

Pluggable database altered.

SQL>
```

To set the default container back to the root container, use CONTAINER=CDB$ROOT in the ALTER SESSION command.

Selectively Opening or Closing PDBs

Even if you configure the PDBs in your CDB to open automatically with triggers, what if you have dozens of PDBs in your CDB and you want to open all of them except for one? You can use ALL EXCEPT to accomplish this in one command:

```
SQL> select con_id,name,open_mode from v$pdbs;

    CON_ID NAME                           OPEN_MODE
---------- ------------------------------ ----------
```

```
         2 PDB$SEED                       READ ONLY
         3 QATEST1                        MOUNTED
         4 DEV2015                        MOUNTED
         5 DW17                           MOUNTED

SQL> alter pluggable database all except qatest1 open;

Pluggable database altered.

SQL> select con_id,name,open_mode from v$pdbs;

    CON_ID NAME                           OPEN_MODE
---------- ------------------------------ ----------
         2 PDB$SEED                       READ ONLY
         3 QATEST1                        MOUNTED
         4 DEV2015                        READ WRITE
         5 DW17                           READ WRITE

SQL>
```

If you want to close all PDBs at once, just use ALL:

```
SQL> alter pluggable database all close;

Pluggable database altered.

SQL> select con_id,name,open_mode from v$pdbs;

    CON_ID NAME                           OPEN_MODE
---------- ------------------------------ ----------
         2 PDB$SEED                       READ ONLY
         3 QATEST1                        MOUNTED
         4 DEV2015                        MOUNTED
         5 DW17                           MOUNTED

SQL>
```

For a specific PDB, you can use either SHUTDOWN or SHUTDOWN IMMEDIATE. There is no PDB equivalent to the TRANSACTIONAL or ABORT options for a PDB or a non-CDB instance.

Opening or closing all PDBs leaves the root container in its current state and as noted earlier the seed container PDB$SEED is always READ ONLY and is in the MOUNT state only when the CDB is in the MOUNT state.

When you close one or more PDBs, you can add the IMMEDIATE keyword to roll back any pending transactions within the PDB. If you leave off the IMMEDIATE keyword, the PDB is not shut down until all pending transactions have been either committed or rolled back just as in a non-CDB database instance and all user sessions are disconnected by the user. If your session context is in a specific PDB, you can also use the SHUTDOWN IMMEDIATE statement to close the PDB, but note that this does not affect any other PDBs and that the root container's instance is still running.

CDB Instance Shutdown

When you are connected to the root container, you can shut down the CDB instance and close all PDBs with one command, much like you would shut down a non-CDB database instance:

```
SQL> shutdown immediate
Database closed.
Database dismounted.
ORACLE instance shut down.
SQL>
```

When specifying IMMEDIATE, the CDB instance does not wait for a COMMIT or ROLLBACK of pending transactions, and all user sessions to any PDB are disconnected. Using TRANSACTIONAL waits for all pending transactions to complete and then disconnects all sessions before terminating the instance.

As described in the previous section, you can use the same command to shut down a specific PDB, but only that PDB's datafiles are closed, and its services will no longer accept connection requests until it is opened again.

Automating PDB Startup

There are new options available in database event triggers for a multitenant environment. One of these triggers is persistent, while two others are not; the reason for this will be clear shortly.

By default, after a CDB instance starts, all PDBs within the CDB are in MOUNT mode. If your PDB is not automatically opened by any other method (such as Oracle Restart), you can create a database trigger to start up all PDBs or just a few or just one. In the container database CDB01, the pluggable database DW17 starts up automatically via Oracle Restart; for the DEV2015 pluggable database, you'll create a trigger to change its status to OPEN READ WRITE when the container database is open, as shown here:

```
SQL> select con_id,name,open_mode from v$pdbs;

    CON_ID NAME                           OPEN_MODE
```

```
---------- ------------------------------ ----------
         2 PDB$SEED                       READ ONLY
         3 QATEST1                        MOUNTED
         4 DEV2015                        MOUNTED
         5 DW17                           READ WRITE

SQL> create trigger open_dev
       after startup on database
     begin
       execute immediate 'alter pluggable database dev2015 open';
     end;
     /

Trigger created.

SQL>
```

Next, shut down and restart the container CDB01 and see what happens:

```
SQL> shutdown immediate
Database closed.
Database dismounted.
ORACLE instance shut down.
SQL> startup
ORACLE instance started.

Total System Global Area 2622255104 bytes
Fixed Size                 291808 bytes
Variable Size              1140852640 bytes
Database Buffers   1459617792 bytes
Redo Buffers                 19492864 bytes
Database mounted.
Database opened.
SQL> select con_id,name,open_mode from v$pdbs;

    CON_ID NAME                           OPEN_MODE
---------- ------------------------------ ----------
         2 PDB$SEED                       READ ONLY
         3 QATEST1                        MOUNTED
         4 DEV2015                        READ WRITE
         5 DW17                           READ WRITE

SQL>
```

The AFTER STARTUP ON DATABASE trigger is persistent unless you drop or disable it. Two new database event triggers for Oracle Database 12*c*, AFTER

CLONE and BEFORE UNPLUG, are more dynamic. Both of those triggers must be specified with ON PLUGGABLE DATABASE; otherwise, the trigger will be invalid and not fire.

You would use a trigger such as AFTER CLONE for a PDB that you'll frequently clone in a testing or development environment. The trigger itself exists in the source PDB and will persist unless you explicitly drop it. However, when you create a new PDB by cloning the existing PDB that contains this trigger, you can perform one-time initialization tasks in the cloned PDB right after it is cloned. Once those tasks are completed, the trigger is deleted so that any clones of the already cloned database won't perform those initialization tasks.

Changing PDB Status

In a non-CDB environment, you often have reason to restrict access to a database for either maintenance tasks or to prepare it for a transportable tablespace or database operation. This is also true in a CDB environment. Previously in this chapter, you saw how to open a PDB as READ ONLY. For any PDB that you want restricted to users with SYSDBA privileges (granted to either a global user or a local user), you use the RESTRICTED clause just as you would in a non-CDB environment:

```
SQL> alter pluggable database qatest1 close;

Pluggable database altered.

SQL> alter pluggable database qatest1 open restricted;

Pluggable database altered.

SQL> select con_id,name,open_mode from v$pdbs;

    CON_ID NAME                           OPEN_MODE
---------- ------------------------------ ----------
         2 PDB$SEED                       READ ONLY
         3 QATEST1                        RESTRICTED
         4 DEV2015                        READ WRITE
         5 DW17                           READ WRITE

SQL>
```

To turn off RESTRICTED mode, you close and reopen the PDB without the RESTRICTED keyword.

There are several operations you can perform on a PDB that do not require restarting the PDB in RESTRICTED mode.

- Take PDB datafiles offline or bring them back online
- Change the PDB's default tablespace
- Change the PDB's default temporary tablespace (local tablespace)
- Change the maximum size of a PDB:
  `alter pluggable database storage (maxsize 50g);`
- Change the name of a PDB

These dynamic settings help to maximize the availability of a PDB and allow you to make changes to a PDB much more quickly than the same changes you would make to a non-CDB that would require shutting down and restarting the database.

CERTIFICATION OBJECTIVE 12.03

Evaluate the Impact of Parameter Value Changes

Although the application developer or database user of a PDB will not see any difference in how a PDB operates compared to a non-CDB, some of the differences require careful consideration by the global and local DBAs. A subset of parameters can be changed at the PDB level, but for the most part, a PDB inherits the parameter settings of the CDB. In addition, some ALTER SYSTEM commands behave slightly differently depending on the context in which they are run by the DBA.

Understanding the Scope of Parameter Changes

Because a CDB is a database instance and PDBs share this instance, some of the CDB's parameters (stored in an SPFILE, of course) apply to the CDB and all PDBs and cannot be changed for any given PDB. You can identify the parameters that can be changed at the PDB level by looking at the ISPDB_MODIFIABLE column of V$PARAMETER. The data dictionary view PDB_SPFILE$ shows the nondefault values for specific parameters across all PDBs:

```
SQL> select pdb_uid,name,value$
  2  from pdb_spfile$
  3  where name='star_transformation_enabled';
```

```
   PDB_UID NAME                              VALUE$
---------- ------------------------------ --------------
2557165657 star_transformation_enabled    'FALSE'
3994587631 star_transformation_enabled    'TRUE'

SQL>
```

The settings local to a PDB stay with the PDB even when the PDB has been cloned or unplugged.

Using ALTER SYSTEM in a Multitenant Environment

Many of the ALTER SYSTEM commands you would use in a non-CDB environment work as you'd expect in a multitenant environment with a few caveats and exceptions. Some of the ALTER SYSTEM commands affect only the PDB or the CDB in which they are run. In contrast, some ALTER SYSTEM commands can be run only in the root container.

Using PDB-Specific ALTER SYSTEM Commands

Within a PDB (as a local DBA or a global DBA with a PDB as the current container), the following ALTER SYSTEM commands affect objects, parameters, or sessions specific to the PDB with no effect on any other PDBs or the root container:

- ALTER SYSTEM FLUSH SHARED_POOL
- ALTER SYSTEM FLUSH BUFFER_CACHE
- ALTER SYSTEM ENABLE RESTRICTED SESSION
- ALTER SYSTEM KILL SESSION
- ALTER SYSTEM SET <*parameter*>

As you might expect, if flushing the shared pool in a PDB affected the shared pool of any other PDB, the side effects would be dramatic and unacceptable!

Understanding ALTER SYSTEM Commands with Side Effects in a PDB

There are a few ALTER SYSTEM commands that you can run at the PDB level but affect the entire CDB. For example, running ALTER SYSTEM CHECKPOINT affects datafiles across the entire container unless the datafiles belong to a PDB that is opened as READ ONLY or are OFFLINE.

Using CDB-Specific ALTER SYSTEM Commands

Some ALTER SYSTEM commands are valid only for the entire container *and* must be run by a common user with SYSDBA privileges in the root container. For example, running ALTER SYSTEM SWITCH LOGFILE switches to the next online redo log file group. Since the online redo log files are common to all containers, this is the expected behavior.

CERTIFICATION OBJECTIVE 12.04

Manage Permanent and Temporary Tablespaces in CDB and PDBs

In a multitenant environment, tablespaces and the datafiles that comprise them belong to either the root container or one of the PDBs within the CDB. Of course, some objects are shared across all PDBs, and these objects are stored in the root container's tablespaces and shared with the PDB via database links. There are some syntax changes to the CREATE DATABASE command as well as behavior changes to the CREATE TABLESPACE and other tablespace-related commands within a PDB.

Using CREATE DATABASE

The CREATE DATABASE statement for a CDB is nearly identical to that for a non-CDB with a couple of exceptions. Oracle recommends that you use the Database Creation Assistant (DBCA) to create a new CDB, but if you must use a CREATE DATABASE command (for example, to create dozens of CDBs in a script), you will use the USER_DATA TABLESPACE clause to specify a default tablespace for user objects for all PDBs created in this CDB. This tablespace is *not* used in the root container.

Using CREATE TABLESPACE

Creating a new tablespace in a CDB (root) container with CREATE TABLESPACE looks the same as creating a tablespace in any PDB. If you are connected to CDB$ROOT, then the tablespace is visible and usable only in the root container; similarly, a tablespace created when connected to a PDB is visible only to that PDB and cannot be used by any other PDB unless connected with a database link.

For ease of management, Oracle recommends using separate directories to store datafiles for each PDB and the CDB. Even better, if you use Automatic Storage Management (ASM), you'll automatically get your datafiles and other database objects segregated into separate directories by container ID. Here is how the datafiles for the container database CDB01 are stored in an ASM disk group:

```
SQL> select con_id,name,open_mode from v$pdbs;

    CON_ID NAME                           OPEN_MODE
---------- ------------------------------ ----------
         2 PDB$SEED                       READ ONLY
         3 QATEST1                        READ WRITE
         4 DEV2015                        READ WRITE
         5 DW17                           READ WRITE

SQL> quit
Disconnected from Oracle Database 12c Enterprise Edition Release
12.1.0.1.0 - 64bit Production
With the Partitioning, Automatic Storage Management, OLAP, Advanced
Analytics
and Real Application Testing options
[oracle@oel63 ~]$ . oraenv
ORACLE_SID = [cdb01] ? +ASM
The Oracle base has been changed from /u01/app/oracle to /u01/app
[oracle@oel63 ~]$ asmcmd
ASMCMD> ls
DATA/
RECOV/
ASMCMD> cd data
ASMCMD> ls
ASM/
CDB01/
DBAHANDBOOK/
orapwasm
ASMCMD> cd cdb01
ASMCMD> ls
CONTROLFILE/
DATAFILE/
DD7C48AA5A4404A2E04325AAE80A403C/
EA128C7783417731E0434702A8C08F56/
EA129627ACA47C9DE0434702A8C0836F/
FAE6382E325C40D8E0434702A8C03802/
FD8E768DE1094F9AE0434702A8C03E94/
ONLINELOG/
PARAMETERFILE/
```

```
TEMPFILE/
spfilecdb01.ora
ASMCMD> cd datafile
ASMCMD> ls
SYSAUX.272.830282801
SYSTEM.273.830282857
UNDOTBS1.275.830282923
USERS.274.830282921
ASMCMD>
```

The container's datafiles are stored in the DATAFILE subdirectory; each of the PDBs has its own set of datafiles in one of those subdirectories with the long string of hexadecimal digits. You use Oracle Managed Files (OMF) with ASM in this scenario; you don't need to know or care what those hexadecimal characters are since the locations of the datafiles are managed automatically.

Changing the Default Tablespace in a PDB

Changing the default tablespace in a CDB or PDB is identical to changing the default tablespace in a non-CDB. For both CDBs and PDBs, you use the ALTER DATABASE DEFAULT TABLESPACE command. If you're changing the default tablespace for a PDB, you should add the PLUGGABLE keyword because the ALTER DATABASE command within a PDB will be deprecated in a future release. In this example, you set the container to QATEST1, create a new tablespace within QATEST1, and change the default tablespace to be the tablespace you just created:

```
SQL> alter session set container=qatest1;

Session altered.

SQL> create tablespace qa_dflt datafile size 100m
  2       autoextend on next 100m maxsize 1g;

Tablespace created.

SQL> alter pluggable database
  2       default tablespace qa_dflt;

Pluggable database altered.

SQL>
```

Going forward, any new local users within QATEST1 that don't have a specific default permanent tablespace will use the tablespace QA_DFLT.

Using Local Temporary Tablespaces

For any CDB, you can have one default temporary tablespace or temporary tablespace group defined at the CDB level that can be used for all PDBs as their temporary tablespace. You can, however, create a temporary tablespace for a PDB that is used only by that PDB. In this example, you create a new temporary tablespace called QA_DFLT_TEMP in the PDB QATEST1 and make it the default temporary tablespace for QATEST1:

```
SQL> create temporary tablespace qa_dflt_temp
  2  tempfile size 100m autoextend on
  3  next 100m maxsize 500m;

Tablespace created.

SQL> alter pluggable database
  2  default temporary tablespace qa_dflt_temp;

Pluggable database altered.

SQL>
```

A temporary tablespace created within a PDB stays with that PDB when it's unplugged and plugged back into the same or a different CDB. If a user is not assigned a specific temporary tablespace, then that user is assigned the default temporary tablespace for the PDB. If there is no default temporary tablespace for the PDB, then the default temporary tablespace for the CDB applies.

CERTIFICATION OBJECTIVE 12.05

Manage Common and Local Users

In a multitenant environment, there are two types of users: *common* users and *local* users. A common user in a CDB (root container) has visibility and an account available in the root container and automatically in each PDB within the CDB. Common users start with C##, which makes it easy to distinguish a common user from a local user in each PDB.

Creating a local user is exactly like creating a user in a non-CDB. You can create a local user either with a common user or with another local user with the CREATE USER privileges:

```
SQL> alter session set container=qatest1;

Session altered.

SQL> create user qa_fnd1 identified by qa901;

User created.

SQL> grant create session to qa_fnd1;

Grant succeeded.

SQL> connect qa_fnd1/qa901@oel63:1521/qatest1
Connected.
SQL>
```

The root container (CDB$ROOT) cannot have local users, only common users. Common users have the same identity and password in the root container and every PDB, both current and future. Having a common user account doesn't automatically mean you have the same privileges across every PDB including the root container. The accounts SYS and SYSTEM are common users who can set any PDB as their default container. For new common users, the username must begin with C## or c##, although creating a username with lowercase letters by using double quotation marks around the username is highly discouraged.

When you create a common user with the CREATE USER command, you typically add CONTAINER=ALL to the command, as in this example:

```
SQL> create user c##secadmin identified by sec404 container=all;

User created.

SQL> grant dba to c##secadmin;

Grant succeeded.

SQL>
```

If you are connected to the root container and have the CREATE USER privilege, the CONTAINER=ALL clause is optional. The same applies to a local user and the CONTAINER=CURRENT clause. The C##SECADMIN user now has

DBA privileges in the root container. This user has an account set up in each PDB but no privileges in any PDB unless explicitly assigned:

```
SQL> connect c##secadmin/sec404@oel63:1521/cdb01
Connected.
SQL> alter session set container=qatest1;
ERROR:
ORA-01031: insufficient privileges


SQL>
```

To allow the user C##SECADMIN to at least connect to the QATEST1 database, grant the appropriate privileges as follows:

```
SQL> grant create session, set container to c##secadmin;

Grant succeeded.

SQL> connect c##secadmin/sec404@oel63:1521/cdb01
Connected.
SQL> alter session set container=qatest1;

Session altered.

SQL>
```

When using CREATE USER, you can optionally specify the default tablespace, the default temporary tablespace, and the profile. These three attributes must exist in each PDB; otherwise, those values will be set to the PDB defaults for those items.

What if a common user is created while one of the PDBs is currently not OPEN, in RESTRICTED mode, or in READ ONLY mode? The new common user's attributes are synced the next time the other PDBs are opened.

CERTIFICATION OBJECTIVE 12.06

Manage Common and Local Privileges

Common and local privileges apply to common and local users. If a privilege is granted across all containers to a common user, it's a common privilege. Similarly, a privilege granted in the context of a single PDB is a local privilege regardless of whether the user is local or common.

In the previous section, the user C##SECADMIN, a common user, was granted the CREATE SESSION privilege but only on the QATEST1 container. If C##SECADMIN needs access to all PDBs by default, use the CONTAINER=ALL keyword to grant that privilege across all current and new PDBs in the CDB:

```
SQL> connect / as sysdba
Connected.
SQL> show con_id

CON_ID
----------------
1
SQL> grant create session to c##secadmin container=all;

Grant succeeded.

SQL> connect c##secadmin/sec404@oel63:1521/dw17
Connected.
SQL>
```

From a security perspective, you can grant common users privileges in the root container but no other containers. Remember that only common users can connect to the root container regardless of the privileges granted; for a common user to connect to the root container, the user will need the CREATE SESSION privilege in the context of the root container, as you can see in this example:

```
SQL> connect / as sysdba
Connected.
SQL> alter session set container=cdb$root;

Session altered.

SQL> create user c##rootadm identified by adm580;

User created.

SQL> connect c##rootadm/adm580@oel63:1521/cdb01
ERROR:
ORA-01045: user C##ROOTADM lacks CREATE SESSION privilege; logon denied


Warning: You are no longer connected to ORACLE.
SQL>
```

To fix this issue for C##ROOTADM, you need to grant the CREATE SESSION privilege in the context of the root container:

```
SQL> grant create session to c##rootadm container=current;

Grant succeeded.

SQL> connect c##rootadm/adm580@oel63:1521/cdb01
Connected.
SQL>
```

You revoke privileges from users and roles using the REVOKE command as in previous releases and non-CDBs. The key difference using GRANT and REVOKE in a multitenant environment is the addition of the CONTAINER clause where you specify the context of the GRANT or REVOKE. Here are some examples of the CONTAINER clause:

- CONTAINER=QATEST1 (privileges valid only in the PDB QATEST1)
- CONTAINER=ALL (privileges valid across all PDBs, current and future)
- CONTAINER=CURRENT (privileges granted or revoked in the current container)

To grant a privilege with CONTAINER=ALL, the grantor must have the SET CONTAINER privilege along with the GRANT ANY PRIVILEGE system privilege.

CERTIFICATION OBJECTIVE 12.07

Manage Common and Local Roles

Roles, just like system and object privileges, work much the same in a multitenant environment as they do in a non-CDB environment. Common roles use the same conventions as common users and start with C##; a common role can have the same privileges across all containers or specific privileges or no privileges in a subset of containers. You use the CONTAINER clause to specify the context of the role:

```
SQL> connect / as sysdba
Connected.
SQL> create role c##mv container=all;
```

```
Role created.

SQL> alter session set container=dw17;

Session altered.

SQL> create user dw_repl identified by dw909;

User created.

SQL> grant c##mv to dw_repl;

Grant succeeded.

SQL>
```

Note in the example that a common role (C##MV) was granted to a local user (DW_REPL) in DW17. The user DW_REPL inherits all the privileges in the role C##MV but only in the DW17 PDB. The reverse is also possible: A common user (such as C##RJB) can be granted a local role (such as LOCAL_ADM) in a specific PDB (such as QATEST1), and therefore the privileges granted via LOCAL_ADM are available only in QATEST1 for C##RJB.

CERTIFICATION OBJECTIVE 12.08

Enable Common Users to Access Data in Specific PDBs

Just as in a non-CDB environment, you may want to share objects with users in other PDBs. By default, any tables created by a common or local user are nonshared and are accessible only in the PDB where they were created.

Shared tables, on the other hand, have some restrictions. Only Oracle-supplied common users (such as SYS or SYSTEM) can create shared tables; common users that the DBA creates (even with DBA privileges such as CREATE USER, DROP ANY TABLE, and so forth) cannot create shared tables.

The two types of shared objects are "links": Object Links and Metadata Links. Object Links connect every PDB to a table in the root container, and each PDB sees the same rows. A good example of this is AWR data in tables like DBA_HIST_ACTIVE_SESS_HISTORY, which has the column CON_ID so you can identify which container the row in DBA_HIST_ACTIVE_SESSION_HISTORY applies to.

In contrast, Metadata Links allow access to tables in the root container plus their own private copies of the data. Most of the DBA_xxx views use this method. For example, looking at the DBA_USERS view in the PDB QATEST1, there is no CON_ID column from the PDB perspective:

```
SQL> select username, common from dba_users;

USERNAME                       COMMON
------------------------------ ----------
C##KLH                         YES
PDBADMIN                       NO
AUDSYS                         YES
GSMUSER                        YES
SPATIAL_WFS_ADMIN_USR          YES
C##RJB                         YES
SPATIAL_CSW_ADMIN_USR          YES
APEX_PUBLIC_USER               YES
RJB                            NO
SYSDG                          YES
DIP                            YES
QA_FND1                        NO
```

However, from the same table in the root container, you can look at CDB_USERS and see the local and common users across all containers:

```
SQL> select con_id,username,common from cdb_users
  2  order by username,con_id;

    CON_ID USERNAME                       COMMON
---------- ------------------------------ ----------
         1 ANONYMOUS                      YES
. . .
         5 AUDSYS                         YES
         1 C##KLH                         YES
         3 C##KLH                         YES
         4 C##KLH                         YES
         5 C##KLH                         YES
         1 C##RJB                         YES
         3 C##RJB                         YES
         4 C##RJB                         YES
         5 C##RJB                         YES
         1 C##ROOTADM                     YES
```

```
         3 C##ROOTADM                   YES
. . .
         4 DVSYS                        YES
         5 DVSYS                        YES
         5 DW_REPL                      NO
         1 FLOWS_FILES                  YES
         2 FLOWS_FILES                  YES
. . .
         5 OUTLN                        YES
         3 PDBADMIN                     NO
         3 QAFRED                       NO
         3 QA_FND1                      NO
         3 RJB                          NO
         4 RJB                          NO
         5 RJB                          NO
         1 SI_INFORMTN_SCHEMA           YES
         2 SI_INFORMTN_SCHEMA           YES
. . .
198 rows selected.

SQL>
```

The common users such as C##RJB exist for every PDB (other than the seed database). Users such as QAFRED exist only in the PDB with CON_ID=3 (QATEST1). Note also that the common users you create must start with C##; Oracle-supplied common users do not need this prefix.

By default, common users cannot see information about specific PDBs. This follows the principle of least privilege required to accomplish a task; a common user won't automatically be able to connect to a specific PDB nor see metadata about any PDB unless explicitly granted.

To leverage the granularity of data dictionary views by common users, you'll use the ALTER USER command to specify a common user, what container data they can access, and what container they can access it from. For example, you may want only the common user C##RJB to see rows in V$SESSION for the PDB DW17 when connected to the PDB QATEST1. You would use the following command to accomplish this:

```
SQL> alter user c##rjb
  2      set container_data=(cdb$root,dw17)
  3      for v$session container=current;

User altered.

SQL>
```

To view the list of users and the container objects accessible to them, look in DBA_CONTAINER_DATA:

```
SQL> select username,owner,object_name,
  2      all_containers,container_name
  3  from dba_container_data
  4  where username='C##RJB';

USERNAME     OWNER        OBJECT_NAME       A CONTAINER_NAME
------------ ------------ ---------------- - --------------------
-----
C##RJB            SYS        V$SESSION     N DW17
C##RJB            SYS        V$SESSION     N CDB$ROOT

SQL>
```

The common user C##RJB will be able to see only rows in V$SESSION for the container DW17.

CERTIFICATION SUMMARY

This chapter covered many topics in three areas: container connectivity, storage management, and security. Most of the information you already knew in those subject areas applies to a multitenant environment.

Connectivity to a root container (CDB) or a pluggable database (PDB) is via service names managed by the Oracle listener. You can connect to these services using the same methods as a non-CDB including Oracle EasyConnect and entries in a client **tnsnames.ora** file.

Starting up/shutting down a CDB and its PDBs shows the dependencies between the PDB and its container: The CDB is an Oracle instance just as a non-CDB has an Oracle instance. Each PDB in a CDB shares the instance with the root container. When you start a CDB, you go through the same basic steps as a non-CDB. From a shutdown state, you can open a CDB in NOMOUNT mode and then MOUNT and OPEN. Once a CDB is mounted, all PDBs are in a MOUNT state as well. Once the container is open, you can manually open each PDB or set up a trigger to open them automatically.

Storage for the CDB and PDB is managed similarly to a non-CDB. The root container has the SYSTEM and SYSAUX tablespaces, and each PDB shares data specific to its environment. Each PDB can have its own set of application tablespaces whose total size is within the limit specified for the PDB. Other database objects, such as temporary tablespaces, can be shared among all PDBs, but for a particular application, a PDB can have its own temporary tablespaces if the global temporary tablespace is not sufficient to meet the needs of the application. Other database objects, such as the online redo log files, are only at the root container level since they reflect the container's instance activity. All PDBs and the root container share a single database instance!

Security is a concern in any database environment and is even more critical in a multitenant environment because of the shared nature of the database instance and some datafiles with each PDB. Once connected to a PDB, there should be no access or awareness of any other PDBs in the same container. Oracle Database 12*c* ensures the security of a multitenant environment by using two types of users: common and local. For ease of maintenance across all PDBs, common users have the same user account and password for all PDBs in a container. However, the privileges available for a common user may vary widely depending on the application in each PDB. Local users are managed in the same way as in a non-CDB or pre-12*c* environment. Common and local roles and privileges add another level of granularity to security in a multitenant environment to ensure compliance with corporate policy and privacy requirements.

TWO-MINUTE DRILL

Establish Connections to CDBs and PDBs

- ❑ You can connect to the root container as SYSDBA with OS authentication.
- ❑ Each PDB has at least one service managed by a server listener.
- ❑ For clustered Oracle databases, the **srvctl** utility can create new services for existing PDBs.
- ❑ Additional services can be created manually using DBMS_SERVICE.
- ❑ Connections to PDBs can use EasyConnect or **tnsnames.ora** entries.
- ❑ SQL Developer can easily connect to a CDB or PDB using either EasyConnect or **tnsnames.ora**.
- ❑ A new PDB service created with Oracle Restart will automatically open a PDB when the CDB opens.
- ❑ To switch between PDBs and the CDB within a SQL*Plus session, use ALTER SESSION SET CONTAINER=. . ..

Start Up and Shut Down a CDB and Open and Close PDBs

- ❑ A container database (root container) starts up and shuts down in much the same way as a non-CDB.
- ❑ A CDB moves from the shutdown state to NOMOUNT, MOUNT, and OPEN if necessary.
- ❑ When the container database is in the OPEN state, all PDBs are initially in the MOUNT state unless automatically started via a trigger or Oracle Restart.
- ❑ The seed container PDB$SEED stays in the MOUNT and READ ONLY states even when all other PDBs are open and cannot be set to READ WRITE.
- ❑ To change the state of a PDB from READ WRITE to READ ONLY, you need to close the PDB first and open it with the READ ONLY option.
- ❑ For a local user with DBA privileges, a PDB can be shut down with the SHUTDOWN or SHUTDOWN IMMEDIATE command.
- ❑ A PDB has no equivalent to the SHUTDOWN ABORT or SHUTDOWN TRANSACTIONAL command.
- ❑ You use the SHUTDOWN, SHUTDOWN IMMEDIATE, TRANSACTIONAL, or SHUTDOWN ABORT command to shut down the entire container and the instance.

- An AFTER STARTUP ON DATABASE trigger can automatically start one or more PDBs when the CDB is opened.
- PDBs support both the AFTER CLONE and BEFORE UNPLUG triggers, but these triggers are dropped after being executed once for the PDB target.
- RESTRICTED mode for a PDB is used just as in a non-CDB.

Evaluate the Impact of Parameter Value Changes

- The data dictionary view PDB_SPFILE$ contains the contents of the PDB instance's SPFILE with the PDB_UID column identifying parameters specific to a PDB.
- Several ALTER SYSTEM commands, run by user with DBA privileges in a PDB, operate only on the PDB such as flushing the shared pool, flushing the buffer cache, killing sessions, and setting parameters specific to the PDB.
- ALTER SYSTEM CHECKPOINT in a PDB performs a checkpoint on the container database and therefore across all PDBs.

Manage Permanent and Temporary Tablespaces in CDB and PDBs

- The CREATE DATABASE command for a CDB includes the USER_DATA TABLESPACE clause to specify a default permanent tablespace for all users across all PDBs.
- The CREATE TABLESPACE command creates a tablespace whose visibility is limited to the container in which it was created, either the CDB or any of the PDBs.
- Using ASM and OMF for tablespaces in a multitenant environment automatically keeps datafiles for each PDB in a separate directory for ease of maintenance.
- To change the default tablespace within a PDB, add the PLUGGABLE keyword.
- Changing the default tablespace in the root container uses the standard ALTER DATABASE DEFAULT TABLESPACE command.
- Each PDB can have its own temporary tablespace or temporary tablespace group.
- Temporary tablespaces created in a PDB persist with that PDB even when it is unplugged and plugged in elsewhere.

Manage Common and Local Users

- The two types of users in a multitenant environment are common and local.
- Common users not created during an Oracle installation must begin with C##.

- ❑ The root container cannot have local users, only common users.
- ❑ Use CONTAINER=ALL when creating a common user and the root container is not the default container.
- ❑ Common users have no privileges in any container until explicitly granted.

Manage Common and Local Privileges

- ❑ Common users need the CREATE SESSION privilege to connect to any container, including CDB$ROOT.
- ❑ The GRANT and REVOKE commands work as in a non-CDB environment with the addition of the CONTAINER clause.
- ❑ The CONTAINER clause can specify a specific container, all containers (ALL), or the currently connected container (CURRENT).

Manage Common and Local Roles

- ❑ Common roles begin with C##.
- ❑ Common roles can have different privileges in each PDB.
- ❑ The CONTAINER clause specifies the scope of the changes to the role with GRANT or REVOKE.

Enable Common Users to Access Data in Specific PDBs

- ❑ Only Oracle-supplied common users can create shared tables.
- ❑ The two shared object types are Object Links and Metadata Links.
- ❑ Object links connect to shared tables and have a CON_ID column that can filter results.
- ❑ The CDB_USERS data dictionary view has the same columns as DBA_USERS with the addition of the CON_ID column.
- ❑ Metadata Links contain shared data and local data.
- ❑ You can use ALTER USER with the SET CONTAINER_DATA keywords to restrict a common user's access to some V$ views by container.
- ❑ The data dictionary table DBA_CONTAINER_DATA shows the common users, the owner of a system object, and the common user's access to that object.

SELF TEST

The following questions will help you measure your understanding of the material presented in this chapter. Read all the choices carefully because there might be more than one correct answer. Choose all correct answers for each question.

Establish Connections to CDBs and PDBs

1. Which of the following methods can you use to create a service for a new PDB or add another service to an existing PDB? Choose all that apply.
   A. A new service is created when the PDB is created or cloned; only one service is allowed per PDB.
   B. Use the **srvctl add service** command for an existing PDB.
   C. Use the DBMS_SERVICE package.
   D. Add a new listener to the configuration and add services with **lsnrctl**.

Start Up and Shut Down a CDB and Open and Close PDBs

2. You execute the following commands for container CDB01:

```
SQL> shutdown immediate;
SQL> startup mount;
SQL> alter database open;
```

   What is the state of the CDB and its PDBs?
   A. All PDBs remain in a MOUNT state including the root container.
   B. After STARTUP MOUNT, all PDBs are opened as READ WRITE but still in the MOUNT state.
   C. Only the root container is OPEN, and each PDB must be opened with a STARTUP command from the root container.
   D. The PDBs are opened if a trigger is defined or you use Oracle restart; the root container is opened in RESTRICTED mode.
   E. The root container is open, the seed database is mounted READ ONLY, and any PDBs with a trigger are opened.

Evaluate the Impact of Parameter Value Changes

3. What is the best way to find out whether an initialization parameter is modifiable at the PDB level?
   A. Change the session context to a specific PDB and use ALTER SYSTEM SET . . . .
   B. The TYPE column in V$PARAMETER will be PDB.
   C. Check the column ISPDB_MODIFIABLE in V$PARAMETER.
   D. Check the column ISCDB_MODIFIABLE in V$PARAMETER.

Manage Permanent and Temporary Tablespaces in CDB and PDBs

4. What is the minimum and maximum number of temporary tablespaces that can exist in a CDB?
   A. One; unlimited
   B. Exactly one for the root container and one for each PDB
   C. One; one
   D. Zero; one for each container

Manage Common and Local Users

5. Identify the true statements regarding common users. (Choose all that apply.)
   A. A common user can create a common or local user with the appropriate privileges.
   B. All common users must begin with C## or c##.
   C. A local user can create a common user if the local user is in the root container.
   D. A common user must have the same password in each container.

Manage Common and Local Privileges

6. Which of the following GRANT commands will give the common user C##RWR the ability to access any table across all PDBs and the root container?
   A. grant select any table to c##rwr container=current;
   B. grant select any table to c##rwr container=all;
   C. grant select any table to c##rwr;
   D. grant select any table to c##rwr container=cdb$root;

Manage Common and Local Roles

7. Which of the following statements is not true regarding local and common roles?
   A. Common roles can be granted to local roles.
   B. Local roles can be granted to common roles.
   C. Common roles can be granted only to common users.
   D. Local roles can be granted to local or common users.

Enable Common Users to Access Data in Specific PDBs

8. You have restricted the common user C##RJB to see the contents of V$SESSION only in the WHSE container (PDB). In which table would you look to confirm that C##RJB is limited to WHSE for V$SESSION data?
   A. V$SESSION, check the CON_ID column in C##RJB's session
   B. PDB_CONTAINER_DATA
   C. CONTAINER_DATA
   D. CDB_CONTAINER_DATA

SELF TEST ANSWERS

Establish Connections to CDBs and PDBs

1. ☑ **B** and **C.** A listener service is automatically added when you create, clone, or plug in a PDB, but if you want an additional listener for a PDB, you can either use the **srvctl** command in an Oracle Restart or clustered environment or use the DBMS_SERVICE package with calls to CREATE_SERVICE and START_SERVICE to create and start the service.
   ☒ **A** and **D** are incorrect. **A** is incorrect because even though a service is automatically created when a PDB is created, cloned, or plugged in, you can have more than one service per PDB. **D** is incorrect because all services can share the default listener if desired.

Start Up and Shut Down a CDB and Open and Close PDBs

2. ☑ **E.** When a CDB is in the OPEN state, the root container is available for connections, and the seed database is open but as READ ONLY. Any PDBs that have a trigger defined or are managed with Oracle Restart are opened automatically.
   ☒ **A, B, C,** and **D** are incorrect. **A** is incorrect because once the CDB is OPEN, the root container is open for READ WRITE, the seed database is open for READ ONLY, and all PDBs with a trigger or Oracle Restart service are opened as well. **B** is incorrect because the seed PDB is READ ONLY. **C** is incorrect because even if no PDBs are automatically opened, you can open them from the root container with the ALTER PLUGGABLE DATABASE command one at a time or all at once. You can use the STARTUP command to open a PDB only if you set the session parameter CONTAINER to the name of the PDB. **D** is incorrect because the root container must be explicitly opened in RESTRICTED mode when required.

Evaluate the Impact of Parameter Value Changes

3. ☑ **C.** The column ISPDB_MODIFIABLE is TRUE in V$PARAMETER if you can change this parameter for a single PDB.
   ☒ **A, B,** and **D** are incorrect. **A** is incorrect because even though you'll find out whether the parameter is modifiable, it is much easier to look in V$PARAMETER. **B** is incorrect because the TYPE column in V$PARAMETER indicates the data type of the parameter value. **D** is incorrect because there is no such column ISCDB_MODIFIABLE in V$PARAMETER.

Manage Permanent and Temporary Tablespaces in CDB and PDBs

4. ☑ **A.** There is always one temporary tablespace in the root container that can be shared by any PDB. Each PDB can have its own temporary tablespace and use it for the default.

☒ **B, C,** and **D** are incorrect. **B** is incorrect because any container database can have as many temporary tablespaces as is practical, but only one can be the default at any given time. **C** is incorrect because in addition to the root container, each PDB can have its own temporary tablespaces. **D** is incorrect because there must be at least one temporary tablespace in the root container to share with all PDBs.

Manage Common and Local Users

5. ☑ **A, B,** and **D.** A common user with the CREATE USER privilege in the root container can create other common users with CONTAINER=ALL or local users with CONTAINER=CURRENT. All common users (except for those supplied during an Oracle installation such as SYS and SYSTEM) must begin with C## or c##. Although a common user can have different privileges in a different container, the password is the same regardless of the current container.
☒ **C** is incorrect. You cannot create a local user in the root container.

Manage Common and Local Privileges

6. ☑ **B.** The GRANT statement must include the CONTAINER=ALL and be run by a privileged user with the GRANT ANY PRIVILEGE system privilege.
☒ **A, C,** and **D** are incorrect. **A** is incorrect because specifying CONTAINER=CURRENT gives privileges only to C##RWR in the current container. **C** is incorrect because without a CONTAINER keyword, the privilege is granted locally. **D** is incorrect because the values for CONTAINER must be either CURRENT or ALL; you cannot specify a PDB or root container name.

Manage Common and Local Roles

7. ☑ **C.** Common roles can be granted to either common or local users.
☒ **A, B,** and **D** are incorrect. They are all valid role assignments, either local or common, to either local or common users or roles.

Enable Common Users to Access Data in Specific PDBs

8. ☑ **D.** The data dictionary view CDB_CONTAINER_DATA contains the usernames, the objects they will access, and which containers' rows they can access.
☒ **A, B,** and **C** are incorrect. **A** is incorrect because V$SESSION has no columns indicating which user can access specific rows in the view. **B** is incorrect because there is no such view PDB_CONTAINER_DATA. **C** is incorrect because CONTAINER_DATA is not a data dictionary view; instead, it is part of the clause you use in the ALTER USER command to specify which containers a common user can access for a particular object.

13

Backup and Recovery of CDBs and PDBs

CERTIFICATION OBJECTIVES

13.01	Perform Backups of a CDB and PDBs	13.04	Duplicate PDBs Using RMAN
13.02	Recover PDB from PDB Datafiles Loss	✓	Two-Minute Drill
13.03	Use Data Recovery Advisor	Q&A	Self Test

In a multitenant environment, you still need to perform backups and recoveries, but you'll use the same tools and be able to back up more databases in less time than in a non-CDB environment. As in any database environment, you need to back up and recover a CDB or PDB. The methods you use to back up the entire CDB or just a PDB are slightly different and as you'd expect have different impacts.

Next, I'll cover the recovery options for a CDB or PDB. Using ARCHIVELOG mode enhances the recoverability of a database, but in a multitenant environment you can enable ARCHIVELOG mode only at the CDB level since the redo log files are only at the CDB level. Otherwise, you can still back up your database in much the same way as in a non-CDB environment. You can back up the entire CDB, a single PDB, a tablespace, a datafile, or even a single block anywhere in the container.

The Data Recovery Advisor works much the same way as it did in previous releases of Oracle Database: When a failure occurs, the Data Recovery Advisor gathers failure information into the Automatic Diagnostic Repository (ADR). The Data Recovery Advisor also has proactive features to check for failures before they are detected by a user session.

Finally, you can duplicate a PDB using RMAN. Using RMAN gives you more flexibility when copying a PDB compared to the CREATE PLUGGABLE DATABASE . . . FROM . . . option. For example, you can use the RMAN DUPLICATE command to copy all PDBs within its CDB to a new CDB with the same PDBs plus the root and seed databases.

CERTIFICATION OBJECTIVE 13.01

Perform Backups of a CDB and PDBs

For multitenant databases, the RMAN syntax has been modified, and new clauses have been added. At the OS level, the environment variable ORACLE_SID was previously set at the instance level, but now that all databases within a CDB are running in the same database instance, you must connect to a single PDB with RMAN using the service name and not the instance name. Here's an example:

```
[oracle@tettnang ~]$ echo $ORACLE_SID
cdb01
[oracle@tettnang ~]$ rman target rjb/rjb@tettnang/tool
```

```
Recovery Manager: Release 12.1.0.1.0 - Production on Tue Jun 3 07:50:06 2014
Copyright (c) 1982, 2013, Oracle and/or its affiliates.  All rights reserved.
connected to target database: CDB01 (DBID=1382179355)
RMAN>
```

As in previous releases, you can connect to the CDB with RMAN using the syntax you're familiar with:

```
[oracle@tettnang ~]$ rman target /
Recovery Manager: Release 12.1.0.1.0 - Production on Tue Jun 3 07:52:33 2014
Copyright (c) 1982, 2013, Oracle and/or its affiliates.  All rights reserved.
connected to target database: CDB01 (DBID=1382179355)
RMAN>
```

Note, however, that the target database is displayed as CDB01 in both cases. How else would you know that you're connected to a specific PDB instead of the CDB? To find out, just use the REPORT SCHEMA command:

```
 [oracle@tettnang ~]$ rman target /
Recovery Manager: Release 12.1.0.1.0 - Production on Tue Jun 3
10:00:38 2014
Copyright (c) 1982, 2013, Oracle and/or its affiliates.  All
rights reserved.
connected to target database: CDB01 (DBID=1382179355)
RMAN> report schema;

using target database control file instead of recovery catalog
Report of database schema for database with db_unique_name CDB01

List of Permanent Datafiles
===========================
File Size(MB) Tablespace           RB segs Datafile Name
---- -------- -------------------- ------- --------------------
1    790      SYSTEM               ***     +DATA/CDB01/DATAFILE/
system.268.845194003
3    1460     SYSAUX               ***     +DATA/CDB01/DATAFILE/
sysaux.267.845193957
4    735      UNDOTBS1             ***
      +DATA/CDB01/DATAFILE/undotbs1.270.845194049
5    250      PDB$SEED:SYSTEM      ***
   +DATA/CDB01/DD7C48AA5A4404A2E04325AAE80A403C/DATAFILE/
```

```
system.277.845194085
6    5        USERS                ***
   +DATA/CDB01/DATAFILE/users.269.845194049
7    590      PDB$SEED:SYSAUX      ***
   +DATA/CDB01/DD7C48AA5A4404A2E04325AAE80A403C/DATAFILE/
sysaux.276.845194085
18   260      TOOL:SYSTEM          ***
   +DATA/CDB01/FA782A61F8447D03E043E3A0080A9E54/DATAFILE/
system.286.848743627
19   620      TOOL:SYSAUX          ***
   +DATA/CDB01/FA782A61F8447D03E043E3A0080A9E54/DATAFILE/
sysaux.303.848743627
20   260      QA_2015:SYSTEM       ***
   +DATA/CDB01/FA787E0038B26FFBE043E3A0080A1A75/DATAFILE/
system.298.848745309
21   610      QA_2015:SYSAUX       ***
   +DATA/CDB01/FA787E0038B26FFBE043E3A0080A1A75/DATAFILE/
sysaux.292.848745309
22   800      RPTQA12C:SYSTEM      ***
   +DATA/CDB01/F754FCD8744A55AAE043E3A0080A3B17/DATAFILE/
system.290.848752939
23   1340     RPTQA12C:SYSAUX      ***
   +DATA/CDB01/F754FCD8744A55AAE043E3A0080A3B17/DATAFILE/
sysaux.302.848752939
24   5        RPTQA12C:USERS       ***
   +DATA/CDB01/F754FCD8744A55AAE043E3A0080A3B17/DATAFILE/
users.301.848752939
25   260      CCREPOS:SYSTEM       ***
   +DATA/CDB01/F751E0E9988D6064E043E3A0080A6DC5/DATAFILE/
system.280.845194249
26   620      CCREPOS:SYSAUX       ***
   +DATA/CDB01/F751E0E9988D6064E043E3A0080A6DC5/DATAFILE/
sysaux.281.845194249
27   5        CCREPOS:USERS        ***
   +DATA/CDB01/F751E0E9988D6064E043E3A0080A6DC5/DATAFILE/
users.283.845194257
28   100      UNDOTBS1             ***
   +DATA/CDB01/DATAFILE/undotbs1.263.848922747
29   100      TOOL:PROCREPO        ***
   +DATA/CDB01/FA782A61F8447D03E043E3A0080A9E54/DATAFILE/
procrepo.257.849257047

List of Temporary Files
=======================
File Size(MB) Tablespace           Maxsize(MB) Tempfile Name
---- -------- -------------------- ----------- ----------------
```

```
1     521       TEMP                  32767
       +DATA/CDB01/TEMPFILE/temp.275.845194083
2     20        PDB$SEED:TEMP         32767
      +DATA/CDB01/DD7C48AA5A4404A2E04325AAE80A403C/DATAFILE/
pdbseed_temp01.dbf
3     20        CCREPOS:TEMP          32767
      +DATA/CDB01/F751E0E9988D6064E043E3A0080A6DC5/TEMPFILE/
temp.282.848755025
4     20        TOOL:TEMP             32767
      +DATA/CDB01/FA782A61F8447D03E043E3A0080A9E54/TEMPFILE/
temp.299.848743629
6     20        QA_2015:TEMP          32767
      +DATA/CDB01/FA787E0038B26FFBE043E3A0080A1A75/TEMPFILE/
temp.291.848745313
7     60        RPTQA12C:TEMP         32767
      +DATA/CDB01/F754FCD8744A55AAE043E3A0080A3B17/TEMPFILE/
temp.300.848752943
8     100       TEMP                  1000
      +DATA/CDB01/TEMPFILE/temp.258.848922745

RMAN> quit


Recovery Manager complete.
```

Note that connecting to the CDB shows all tablespaces including those of the seed and root containers. Connecting to an individual PDB returns different (but expected) results for the REPORT SCHEMA command:

```
[oracle@tettnang ~]$ rman target rjb/rjb@tettnang/tool

Recovery Manager: Release 12.1.0.1.0 - Production on Tue Jun 3
10:00:50 2014

Copyright (c) 1982, 2013, Oracle and/or its affiliates.  All
rights reserved.

connected to target database: CDB01 (DBID=1382179355)

RMAN> report schema;

using target database control file instead of recovery catalog
Report of database schema for database with db_unique_name CDB01

List of Permanent Datafiles
===========================
```

```
File Size(MB) Tablespace           RB segs Datafile Name
---- -------- -------------------- ------- ---------------------
18   260      SYSTEM               ***     +DATA/CDB01/
FA782A61F8447D03E043E3A0080A9E54/DATAFILE/system.286.848743627
19   620      SYSAUX               ***     +DATA/CDB01/
FA782A61F8447D03E043E3A0080A9E54/DATAFILE/sysaux.303.848743627
29   100      PROCREPO             ***     +DATA/CDB01/
FA782A61F8447D03E043E3A0080A9E54/DATAFILE/procrepo.257.849257047

List of Temporary Files
=======================
File Size(MB) Tablespace           Maxsize(MB) Tempfile Name
---- -------- -------------------- ----------- -----------------
4    20       TEMP                 32767       +DATA/CDB01/
FA782A61F8447D03E043E3A0080A9E54/TEMPFILE/temp.299.848743629

RMAN>
```

The RMAN BACKUP, RESTORE, and RECOVER commands have been enhanced to include the PLUGGABLE keyword when operating on one or more pluggable databases:

```
RMAN> backup pluggable database rptqa12c;
```

In addition, you can qualify a tablespace backup with a PDB name to back up one specific tablespace within a PDB:

```
[oracle@tettnang ~]$ rman target /

Recovery Manager: Release 12.1.0.1.0 - Production on Tue Jun 3
08:44:15 2014

Copyright (c) 1982, 2013, Oracle and/or its affiliates.  All
rights reserved.

connected to target database: CDB01 (DBID=1382179355)

RMAN> backup tablespace tool:procrepo;

Starting backup at 03-JUN-14
using target database control file instead of recovery catalog
allocated channel: ORA_DISK_1
channel ORA_DISK_1: SID=258 device type=DISK
channel ORA_DISK_1: starting full datafile backup set
```

```
channel ORA_DISK_1: specifying datafile(s) in backup set
input datafile file number=00029 name=+DATA/CDB01/
FA782A61F8447D03E043E3A0080A9E54/DATAFILE/procrepo.257.849257047
channel ORA_DISK_1: starting piece 1 at 03-JUN-14
channel ORA_DISK_1: finished piece 1 at 03-JUN-14
piece handle=+RECOV/CDB01/FA782A61F8447D03E043E3A0080A9E54/
BACKUPSET/2014_06_03/nnndf0_tag20140603t084425_0.256.849257065
tag=TAG20140603T084425 comment=NONE
channel ORA_DISK_1: backup set complete, elapsed time: 00:00:01
Finished backup at 03-JUN-14

Starting Control File and SPFILE Autobackup at 03-JUN-14
piece handle=+RECOV/CDB01/AUTOBACKUP/2014_06_03
/s_849257066.257.849257067 comment=NONE
Finished Control File and SPFILE Autobackup at 03-JUN-14

RMAN>
```

Without any qualification, when connected to the CDB, any RMAN commands operate on the root container and all PDBs. To back up just the root container, use the name CDB$ROOT, which as you know from Chapter 11 is the name of the root container within the CDB.

Backing Up CDBs

As mentioned in the previous section, you can back up the entire CDB as a full backup, a single PDB within the CDB, or individual tablespaces in any of the PDBs or root container. To run RMAN and back up a container, the user must have a common account with either the SYSDBA or SYSBACKUP privilege in the root container. To accommodate separation of duties, Oracle recommends assigning only the SYSBACKUP privilege to a database user who is responsible only for database backups and recovery.

Since a CDB is most similar to a pre-12*c* database (non-CDB), your backups will look similar to RMAN backups you created in Oracle Database 11*g*. You can create backupsets or image copies along with the control file, SPFILE, and optionally the archived redo log files.

Backing up the CDB (and all PDBs) with the container open requires ARCHIVELOG mode as in previous releases; if the CDB is in NOARCHIVELOG mode, then the container must be open in MOUNT mode (and therefore no PDBs are open as well). Here is an example:

```
[oracle@tettnang ~]$ rman target /

Recovery Manager: Release 12.1.0.1.0 - Production on Tue Jun 3
12:13:26 2014

Copyright (c) 1982, 2013, Oracle and/or its affiliates.  All
rights reserved.

connected to target database: CDB01 (DBID=1382179355)

RMAN> backup database;

Starting backup at 03-JUN-14
using target database control file instead of recovery catalog
allocated channel: ORA_DISK_1
channel ORA_DISK_1: SID=6 device type=DISK
allocated channel: ORA_DISK_2
channel ORA_DISK_2: SID=1021 device type=DISK
allocated channel: ORA_DISK_3
channel ORA_DISK_3: SID=1281 device type=DISK
allocated channel: ORA_DISK_4
channel ORA_DISK_4: SID=1025 device type=DISK
channel ORA_DISK_1: starting compressed full datafile backup set
channel ORA_DISK_1: specifying datafile(s) in backup set
input datafile file number=00003 name=+DATA/CDB01/DATAFILE/
sysaux.267.845193957
channel ORA_DISK_1: starting piece 1 at 03-JUN-14
channel ORA_DISK_2: starting compressed full datafile backup set
channel ORA_DISK_2: specifying datafile(s) in backup set
input datafile file number=00023 name=+DATA/CDB01/
F754FCD8744A55AAE043E3A0080A3B17/DATAFILE/sysaux.302.848752939
channel ORA_DISK_2: starting piece 1 at 03-JUN-14
channel ORA_DISK_3: starting compressed full datafile backup set
channel ORA_DISK_3: specifying datafile(s) in backup set
input datafile file number=00004 name=+DATA/CDB01/DATAFILE/
undotbs1.270.845194049
input datafile file number=00028 name=+DATA/CDB01/DATAFILE/
undotbs1.263.848922747
. . .
channel ORA_DISK_2: backup set complete, elapsed time: 00:00:00
channel ORA_DISK_3: finished piece 1 at 03-JUN-14
piece handle=+RECOV/CDB01/F751E0E9988D6064E043E3A0080A6DC5/
```

```
BACKUPSET/2014_06_03/nnndf0_tag20140603t121337_0.280.849269683
tag=TAG20140603T121337 comment=NONE
channel ORA_DISK_3: backup set complete, elapsed time: 00:00:01
Finished backup at 03-JUN-14

Starting Control File and SPFILE Autobackup at 03-JUN-14
piece handle=+RECOV/CDB01/AUTOBACKUP/2014_06_03
/s_849269683.281.849269683 comment=NONE
Finished Control File and SPFILE Autobackup at 03-JUN-14

RMAN>
```

Note the references to tablespaces and datafiles like this:

```
name=+DATA/CDB01/F754FCD8744A55AAE043E3A0080A3B17/
        DATAFILE/sysaux.302.848752939
```

It's the datafile for the SYSAUX tablespace in one of the PDBs. To find out which one, you can look in the dynamic performance view V$PDBS at the column GUID. The globally unique identifier (GUID) value is a unique and long hexadecimal string that uniquely identifies the container even when it's unplugged from one CDB and plugged back into another.

```
SQL> select con_id,dbid,guid,name from v$pdbs;

  CON_ID       DBID GUID                             NAME
-------- ---------- -------------------------------- -----------
       2 4087805696 F751D8C27D475B57E043E3A0080A2A47 PDB$SEED
       3 1248256969 F751E0E9988D6064E043E3A0080A6DC5 CCREPOS
       4 1258510409 FA782A61F8447D03E043E3A0080A9E54 TOOL
       6 2577431197 FA787E0038B26FFBE043E3A0080A1A75 QA_2015
       7 1288637549 F754FCD8744A55AAE043E3A0080A3B17 RPTQA12C

SQL>
```

In this case, the SYSAUX datafile belongs to the RPTQA12C PDB.

If you want to perform a *partial CDB backup*, you connect to the container (CDB) with RMAN and back up one or more containers in a single command along with the root container using the PLUGGABLE DATABASE clause, as in this example:

```
RMAN> backup pluggable database tool,rptqa12c,"CDB$ROOT";
```

In a recovery scenario, you can restore and recover the TOOL PDB separately from the RPTQA12C PDB or just the root container.

Backing Up PDBs

Backing up a PDB is also similar to backing up a non-CDB in Oracle Database 12*c* or previous releases. Note that backing up a PDB is identical to backing up part of a CDB but without the root container (CDB$ROOT). For separation of duties, you can have a user with SYSBACKUP privileges in only one PDB. They will connect only to the PDB and then back it up as if it were a non-CDB. This example shows a backup administrator connecting to only the CCREPOS PDB as a local user and performing a full RMAN backup:

```
[oracle@tettnang ~]$ rman target rjb/rjb@tettnang/ccrepos

Recovery Manager: Release 12.1.0.1.0 - Production on Tue Jun 3
21:00:27 2014

Copyright (c) 1982, 2013, Oracle and/or its affiliates.  All
rights reserved.

connected to target database: CDB01 (DBID=1382179355)

RMAN> backup database;

Starting backup at 03-JUN-14
using target database control file instead of recovery catalog
allocated channel: ORA_DISK_1
channel ORA_DISK_1: SID=1027 device type=DISK
allocated channel: ORA_DISK_2
channel ORA_DISK_2: SID=1283 device type=DISK
allocated channel: ORA_DISK_3
channel ORA_DISK_3: SID=1028 device type=DISK
allocated channel: ORA_DISK_4
channel ORA_DISK_4: SID=13 device type=DISK
channel ORA_DISK_1: starting compressed full datafile backup set
channel ORA_DISK_1: specifying datafile(s) in backup set
input datafile file number=00026 name=+DATA/CDB01/
F751E0E9988D6064E043E3A0080A6DC5/DATAFILE/sysaux.281.845194249
channel ORA_DISK_1: starting piece 1 at 03-JUN-14
channel ORA_DISK_2: starting compressed full datafile backup set
channel ORA_DISK_2: specifying datafile(s) in backup set
input datafile file number=00025 name=+DATA/CDB01/
F751E0E9988D6064E043E3A0080A6DC5/DATAFILE/system.280.845194249
channel ORA_DISK_2: starting piece 1 at 03-JUN-14
channel ORA_DISK_3: starting compressed full datafile backup set
channel ORA_DISK_3: specifying datafile(s) in backup set
```

```
input datafile file number=00027 name=+DATA/CDB01/
F751E0E9988D6064E043E3A0080A6DC5/DATAFILE/users.283.845194257
channel ORA_DISK_3: starting piece 1 at 03-JUN-14
channel ORA_DISK_3: finished piece 1 at 03-JUN-14
piece handle=+RECOV/CDB01/F751E0E9988D6064E043E3A0080A6DC5/
BACKUPSET/2014_06_03/nnndf0_tag20140603t210035_0.284.849301235
tag=TAG20140603T210035 comment=NONE
channel ORA_DISK_3: backup set complete, elapsed time: 00:00:01
channel ORA_DISK_2: finished piece 1 at 03-JUN-14
piece handle=+RECOV/CDB01/F751E0E9988D6064E043E3A0080A6DC5/
BACKUPSET/2014_06_03/nnndf0_tag20140603t210035_0.285.849301235
tag=TAG20140603T210035 comment=NONE
channel ORA_DISK_2: backup set complete, elapsed time: 00:00:07
channel ORA_DISK_1: finished piece 1 at 03-JUN-14
piece handle=+RECOV/CDB01/F751E0E9988D6064E043E3A0080A6DC5/
BACKUPSET/2014_06_03/nnndf0_tag20140603t210035_0.283.849301235
tag=TAG20140603T210035 comment=NONE
channel ORA_DISK_1: backup set complete, elapsed time: 00:00:25
Finished backup at 03-JUN-14

Starting Control File and SPFILE Autobackup at 03-JUN-14
piece handle=+RECOV/CDB01/F751E0E9988D6064E043E3A0080A6DC5/AUTOB
ACKUP/2014_06_03/s_849301260.286.849301261 comment=NONE
Finished Control File and SPFILE Autobackup at 03-JUN-14

RMAN>
```

Note that you do not need to specify the PLUGGABLE keyword since you're doing the backup from the perspective of a single PDB. Even though you're backing up a single PDB, the control file and SPFILE are included in the full backup despite that the control file and SPFILE are shared across the entire container for all PDBs.

CERTIFICATION OBJECTIVE 13.02

Recover PDB from PDB Datafiles Loss

As with non-CDB databases, both PDBs and a CDB can suffer from instance failure or media failure requiring some kind of recovery operation. The recovery can occur at the CDB level, the PDB level, a tablespace within a PDB, a datafile, or even an individual block. The one major difference is instance recovery: Since all PDBs and the CDB share a single instance, crash recovery for the instance occurs only at the CDB level since all PDBs go down with the CDB. Similarly, any objects that are global and exist at the CDB level, such as the control files, redo log files, or datafiles from the root's SYSTEM or UNDO tablespaces, require media recovery at the CDB level only.

In the following sections, I'll review the types of media failure and how to recover from them. Many of the scenarios have the same recovery solution as a non-CDB and in the case of a single PDB, the recovery of that PDB can occur with little or no disruption to other PDBs that may be open at the time.

Tempfile Recovery

As you recall from Chapter 11, a temporary tablespace (with one or more tempfiles) exists at the CDB level, but each PDB can have its own temporary tablespace if the application has different requirements. If a PDB's DML or SELECT statements require the TEMP tablespace at the CDB level and it is suddenly lost because of media failure, the statement will fail. In this example, one of the ASM administrators accidentally deletes one of the tempfiles belonging to the CDB:

```
[oracle@tettnang ~]$ asmcmd
ASMCMD> cd +data/cdb01/tempfile
ASMCMD> ls -l
Type      Redund  Striped  Time             Sys  Name
TEMPFILE  UNPROT  COARSE   JUN 03 08:00:00  Y
TEMP.258.848922745
TEMPFILE  UNPROT  COARSE   JUN 03 08:00:00  Y
TEMP.275.845194083
ASMCMD> rm TEMP.258.848922745
ASMCMD> quit
[oracle@tettnang ~]$
```

The easy but Draconian solution to fix the problem would be to restart the entire CDB. Instead, you can just add another tempfile to the TEMP tablespace and drop the one that no longer exists:

```
SQL> alter tablespace temp add tempfile '+DATA'
  2      size 100m autoextend on next 100m maxsize 2g;

Tablespace altered.
```

```
SQL> alter tablespace temp drop tempfile
  2     '+DATA/CDB01/TEMPFILE/temp.258.848922745';

Tablespace altered.

SQL>
```

As with non-CDBs, if a temporary tablespace (at either the CDB or PDB level) is missing at container startup, it is re-created automatically.

Recovering from Control File Loss

Losing one or all control files is just as serious as losing a control file in a non-CDB. Oracle best practices dictate that you have at least three copies of the control file available. If you lose all copies of the control file, you can get them from the latest RMAN autobackup. In this example, the copy of the control file in the +RECOV disk group is missing, and the CDB will not start; as a result, none of the PDBs can start.

```
[oracle@tettnang ~]$ . oraenv
ORACLE_SID = [+ASM] ? cdb01
The Oracle base remains unchanged with value /u01/app/oracle
[oracle@tettnang ~]$ sqlplus / as sysdba

SQL*Plus: Release 12.1.0.1.0 Production on Tue Jun 3 23:03:52 2014

Copyright (c) 1982, 2013, Oracle.  All rights reserved.

Connected to an idle instance.

SQL> startup
ORACLE instance started.

Total System Global Area 5027385344 bytes
Fixed Size                  2691952 bytes
Variable Size            1241517200 bytes
Database Buffers         3774873600 bytes
Redo Buffers                8302592 bytes
ORA-00205: error in identifying control file, check alert log for more
info


SQL>
```

Shut down the instance and recover the control file from the last RMAN backup:

```
SQL> shutdown immediate
ORA-01507: database not mounted


ORACLE instance shut down.
SQL> quit
Disconnected from Oracle Database 12c Enterprise Edition Release
12.1.0.1.0 - 64bit Production
With the Partitioning, OLAP, Advanced Analytics and Real
Application Testing options
[oracle@tettnang ~]$ rman target /

Recovery Manager: Release 12.1.0.1.0 - Production on Tue Jun 3
23:07:30 2014

Copyright (c) 1982, 2013, Oracle and/or its affiliates.  All
rights reserved.

connected to target database (not started)

RMAN> startup nomount;

Oracle instance started

Total System Global Area    5027385344 bytes

Fixed Size                     2691952 bytes
Variable Size               1241517200 bytes
Database Buffers            3774873600 bytes
Redo Buffers                   8302592 bytes

RMAN> restore controlfile from autobackup;

Starting restore at 03-JUN-14
using target database control file instead of recovery catalog
allocated channel: ORA_DISK_1
channel ORA_DISK_1: SID=1021 device type=DISK

recovery area destination: +RECOV
database name (or database unique name) used for search: CDB01
channel ORA_DISK_1: AUTOBACKUP +RECOV/CDB01/AUTOBACKUP/2014_06_0
3/s_849308463.289.849308463 found in the recovery area
AUTOBACKUP search with format "%F" not attempted because DBID
```

```
was not set
channel ORA_DISK_1: restoring control file from AUTOBACKUP
+RECOV/CDB01/AUTOBACKUP/2014_06_03/s_849308463.289.849308463
channel ORA_DISK_1: control file restore from AUTOBACKUP
complete
output file name=+DATA/CDB01/CONTROLFILE/current.271.849308871
output file name=+RECOV/CDB01/CONTROLFILE/current.260.845194075
Finished restore at 03-JUN-14

RMAN>
```

Even though only one copy of the control file was lost, the RMAN recovery operation restores both copies; the remaining control file is almost certainly out of sync with the autobackup version:

```
RMAN> alter database mount;

Statement processed
released channel: ORA_DISK_1

RMAN> recover database;

Starting recover at 03-JUN-14
Starting implicit crosscheck backup at 03-JUN-14
allocated channel: ORA_DISK_1
channel ORA_DISK_1: SID=1021 device type=DISK
allocated channel: ORA_DISK_2
channel ORA_DISK_2: SID=260 device type=DISK
allocated channel: ORA_DISK_3
channel ORA_DISK_3: SID=514 device type=DISK
allocated channel: ORA_DISK_4
channel ORA_DISK_4: SID=769 device type=DISK
Crosschecked 25 objects
Finished implicit crosscheck backup at 03-JUN-14

Starting implicit crosscheck copy at 03-JUN-14
using channel ORA_DISK_1
using channel ORA_DISK_2
using channel ORA_DISK_3
using channel ORA_DISK_4
Finished implicit crosscheck copy at 03-JUN-14

searching for all files in the recovery area
cataloging files...
cataloging done
```

```
List of Cataloged Files
=======================
File Name: +RECOV/CDB01/AUTOBACKUP/2014_06_03
/s_849308463.289.849308463

using channel ORA_DISK_1
using channel ORA_DISK_2
using channel ORA_DISK_3
using channel ORA_DISK_4

starting media recovery

archived log for thread 1 with sequence 215 is already on disk
as file +DATA/CDB01/ONLINELOG/group_2.273.845194077
archived log file name=+DATA/CDB01/ONLINELOG/
group_2.273.845194077 thread=1 sequence=215
media recovery complete, elapsed time: 00:00:00
Finished recover at 03-JUN-14

RMAN> alter database open resetlogs;

Statement processed

RMAN> alter pluggable database all open;

Statement processed

RMAN>
```

Data loss will not occur unless you have objects defined in the recovered control file that were created after the last RMAN autobackup of the control file.

Recovering from Redo Log File Loss

Redo log files are only at the CDB level and therefore are recovered in much the same way as in a non-CDB. Redo log files should be multiplexed with at least two copies. If one copy of a redo log group is lost or corrupted, the database writes to the remaining log group members, and an alert is issued. No database recovery is required, but the missing or corrupted redo log group member should be replaced as soon as possible to avoid possible data loss.

If all members of a redo log file group go missing or become corrupted, the database shuts down, and media recovery will likely be required since there are committed transactions in the lost redo log file group that have not yet been written to the datafiles. If the entire log file group was on a disk that was temporarily offline, just changing the status of the log file group to ONLINE will trigger an automatic instance recovery, and no data should be lost.

Recovering from Root Datafile Loss

Losing the critical SYSTEM or UNDO tablespace datafiles is just as serious as losing them in a non-CDB. If the instance does not shut down automatically, you'll have to shut down the CDB and perform media recovery. The media recovery will also affect any PDBs that were open at the time of datafile loss or corruption.

The recovery process is the same as in a non-CDB for the loss of SYSTEM or UNDO. Losing a noncritical tablespace (such as SYSAUX or another root tablespace like SYSAUX) does allow the CDB to remain open along with all PDBs while you perform media recovery.

Recovering the SYSTEM or UNDO Tablespace

The datafile(s) for the CDB's SYSTEM tablespace is accidentally deleted while the CDB is down. Starting it up gives the expectedly ominous message:

```
[oracle@tettnang ~]$ . oraenv
ORACLE_SID = [+ASM] ? cdb01
The Oracle base remains unchanged with value /u01/app/oracle
[oracle@tettnang ~]$ sqlplus / as sysdba

SQL*Plus: Release 12.1.0.1.0 Production on Wed Jun 4 07:37:25 2014

Copyright (c) 1982, 2013, Oracle.  All rights reserved.

Connected to an idle instance.

SQL> startup
ORACLE instance started.

Total System Global Area 5027385344 bytes
Fixed Size                  2691952 bytes
Variable Size            1241517200 bytes
Database Buffers         3774873600 bytes
Redo Buffers                8302592 bytes
Database mounted.
ORA-01157: cannot identify/lock data file 1 - see DBWR trace file
```

```
ORA-01110: data file 1: '+DATA/CDB01/DATAFILE/system.268.845194003'

SQL>
```

Since you're in ARCHIVELOG mode and you did a recent full backup, you can restore and recover the CDB's SYSTEM tablespace up to the point in time when the CDB was shut down last. Stop the instance and initiate recovery as you would with a non-CDB:

```
SQL> shutdown immediate
ORA-01109: database not open


Database dismounted.
ORACLE instance shut down.
SQL> quit
Disconnected from Oracle Database 12c Enterprise Edition Release
12.1.0.1.0 - 64bit Production
With the Partitioning, Automatic Storage Management, OLAP,
Advanced Analytics
and Real Application Testing options
[oracle@tettnang ~]$ rman target /

Recovery Manager: Release 12.1.0.1.0 - Production on Wed Jun 4
07:39:44 2014

Copyright (c) 1982, 2013, Oracle and/or its affiliates.  All
rights reserved.

connected to target database (not started)

RMAN> startup mount

Oracle instance started
database mounted

Total System Global Area    5027385344 bytes

Fixed Size                     2691952 bytes
Variable Size               1241517200 bytes
Database Buffers            3774873600 bytes
Redo Buffers                   8302592 bytes

RMAN> restore tablespace system;
```

```
Starting restore at 04-JUN-14
using target database control file instead of recovery catalog
allocated channel: ORA_DISK_1
. . .
channel ORA_DISK_1: restoring datafile 00001 to +DATA/CDB01/
DATAFILE/system.268.845194003
channel ORA_DISK_1: reading from backup piece +RECOV/CDB01/
BACKUPSET/2014_06_04/nnndf0_tag20140604t073433_0.302.849339275
channel ORA_DISK_1: piece handle=+RECOV/CDB01/
BACKUPSET/2014_06_04/nnndf0_tag20140604t073433_0.302.849339275
tag=TAG20140604T073433
channel ORA_DISK_1: restored backup piece 1
channel ORA_DISK_1: restore complete, elapsed time: 00:00:25
Finished restore at 04-JUN-14

RMAN> recover tablespace system;

Starting recover at 04-JUN-14
using channel ORA_DISK_1
using channel ORA_DISK_2
using channel ORA_DISK_3
using channel ORA_DISK_4

starting media recovery
media recovery complete, elapsed time: 00:00:00

Finished recover at 04-JUN-14

RMAN> alter database open;

Statement processed

RMAN> alter pluggable database all open;

Statement processed

RMAN>
```

Note that in Oracle Database 12*c*, nearly all commands you would run in SQL*Plus are now available in RMAN without having to qualify them with the SQL keyword.

Recovering the SYSAUX or Other Root Tablespace

Restoring and recovering a missing noncritical root container tablespace other than SYSTEM or UNDO (such as SYSAUX) is even easier; there is no need to shut down the database (if it's not down already). You merely have to take the tablespace with the missing datafiles offline, perform a tablespace restore and recovery, and then bring the tablespace online. All PDBs and the root container can remain online during this operation since root-specific tablespaces other than SYSTEM, TEMP, and UNDO are not shared with any PDB (other than TEMP if the PDB does not have its own TEMP tablespace). The series of commands looks something like this:

```
RMAN> alter tablespace sysaux offline immediate;
RMAN> restore tablespace sysaux;
RMAN> recover tablespace sysaux;
RMAN> alter tablespace sysaux online;
```

Recovering from PDB Datafiles

Since all PDBs operate independently as if they were a non-CDB, any failures or datafile loss in a PDB has no effect on the root container or other PDBs unless the datafiles in the PDB's SYSTEM tablespace are lost or damaged. Otherwise, restoring/recovering datafiles in a PDB is much the same as restoring and recovering datafiles in a CDB or non-CDB.

PDB SYSTEM Datafile Loss

The loss of the SYSTEM tablespace in an open PDB is one of the few cases where the entire CDB must be shut down to recover the PDB's SYSTEM tablespace. Otherwise, if the PDB is closed and won't open because of a damaged or missing SYSTEM datafile, the CDB and other PDBs can remain open during the PDB's restore and recover operation.

In this example, the SYSTEM datafile for the PDB CCREPOS is accidentally dropped while CCREPOS is closed. Trying to open CCREPOS fails as expected:

```
SQL> alter pluggable database ccrepos open;
alter pluggable database ccrepos open
*
ERROR at line 1:
ORA-01157: cannot identify/lock data file 30 - see DBWR trace file
ORA-01110: data file 30:
'+DATA/CDB01/FB03AEEBB6F60995E043E3A0080AEE85/DATAFILE/
system.258.849342981'
SQL>
```

Next, start RMAN and initiate a recovery on the SYSTEM tablespace. Be sure to qualify the tablespace name with the PDB name in the RESTORE command:

```
RMAN> restore tablespace ccrepos:system;

Starting restore at 04-JUN-14
using target database control file instead of recovery catalog
allocated channel: ORA_DISK_1
channel ORA_DISK_1: SID=774 device type=DISK
allocated channel: ORA_DISK_2
channel ORA_DISK_2: SID=1028 device type=DISK
allocated channel: ORA_DISK_3
channel ORA_DISK_3: SID=1279 device type=DISK
allocated channel: ORA_DISK_4
channel ORA_DISK_4: SID=9 device type=DISK

channel ORA_DISK_1: starting datafile backup set restore
channel ORA_DISK_1: specifying datafile(s) to restore from
backup set
channel ORA_DISK_1: restoring datafile 00030 to +DATA/CDB01/
FB03AEEBB6F60995E043E3A0080AEE85/DATAFILE/system.258.849342981
channel ORA_DISK_1: reading from backup piece +RECOV/CDB01/
FB03AEEBB6F60995E043E3A0080AEE85/BACKUPSET/2014_06_04/nnndf0_tag
20140604t084003_0.316.849343205
channel ORA_DISK_1: piece handle=+RECOV/CDB01/
FB03AEEBB6F60995E043E3A0080AEE85/BACKUPSET/2014_06_04/nnndf0_tag
20140604t084003_0.316.849343205 tag=TAG20140604T084003
channel ORA_DISK_1: restored backup piece 1
channel ORA_DISK_1: restore complete, elapsed time: 00:00:07
Finished restore at 04-JUN-14

RMAN> recover tablespace ccrepos:system;

Starting recover at 04-JUN-14
using channel ORA_DISK_1
using channel ORA_DISK_2
using channel ORA_DISK_3
using channel ORA_DISK_4

starting media recovery
media recovery complete, elapsed time: 00:00:00

Finished recover at 04-JUN-14
```

```
RMAN> alter pluggable database ccrepos open;

Statement processed

RMAN>
```

PDB Non-SYSTEM Datafile Loss

Recovering a non-SYSTEM datafile in a PDB uses the same steps as recovering a non-SYSTEM datafile or tablespace in a CDB: offline the tablespace and then restore and recover. The only difference is that you qualify the tablespace name with the PDB name, like this:

```
RMAN> restore tablespace tool:fishinv;
RMAN> recover tablespace tool:fishinv;
. . .
SQL> connect rjb/rjb@tettnang/tool
SQL> alter tablespace fishinv online;
```

CERTIFICATION OBJECTIVE 13.03

Use Data Recovery Advisor

The Data Recovery Advisor (DRA) can both proactively and reactively analyze failures. In both scenarios, it will not automatically fix problems it finds but instead provide one or more possible fixes and give you the option and the commands to perform the fix. As of Oracle Database 12c release 1 (12.1.0.1), only non-CDBs and single-instance CDBs are supported (non-RAC environments).

In previous releases of Oracle RMAN, you could perform proactive checks of the database's datafiles with the VALIDATE command. In a CDB environment, the VALIDATE command has been enhanced to analyze individual PDBs or the entire CDB.

Data Failures

In one of the scenarios presented earlier, the SYSTEM tablespace's datafiles of the CCREPOS PDB were lost. You might come to that conclusion after viewing the alert log or more likely after a user submits a help-desk ticket saying they can't get into the CCREPOS database. You suspect that there might be more failures, so you start RMAN and use the DRA commands LIST FAILURE, ADVISE FAILURE, and REPAIR FAILURE to fix one or more issues.

To view and repair any issues with the CDB containing the CCREPOS PDB, start RMAN from the root container and run the LIST FAILURE DETAIL command:

```
RMAN> list failure detail;

using target database control file instead of recovery catalog
Database Role: PRIMARY

List of Database Failures
=========================

Failure ID Priority Status    Time Detected Summary
---------- -------- --------- ------------- -------
1562       CRITICAL OPEN      04-JUN-14     System datafile
30: '+DATA/CDB01/FB03AEEBB6F60995E043E3A0080AEE85/DATAFILE/
system.258.849343395' is missing
  Impact: Database cannot be opened

Failure ID Priority Status    Time Detected Summary
---------- -------- --------- ------------- -------
1542       CRITICAL OPEN      04-JUN-14     System datafile
30: '+DATA/CDB01/FB03AEEBB6F60995E043E3A0080AEE85/DATAFILE/
system.258.849342981' is missing
  Impact: Database cannot be opened

RMAN>
```

It looks like the SYSTEM datafile was lost once already (and recovered) earlier in the chapter! But the failure was not cleared from RMAN, so use CHANGE FAILURE to clear the earlier event:

```
RMAN> change failure 1542 closed;

Database Role: PRIMARY

List of Database Failures
=========================

Failure ID Priority Status    Time Detected Summary
---------- -------- --------- ------------- -------
1542       CRITICAL OPEN      04-JUN-14     System datafile
```

```
30: '+DATA/CDB01/FB03AEEBB6F60995E043E3A0080AEE85/DATAFILE/
system.258.849342981' is missing

Do you really want to change the above failures (enter YES or
NO)? yes
closed 1 failures

RMAN>
```

Next, let's see what RMAN recommends to fix the problem:

```
RMAN> advise failure 1562;

Database Role: PRIMARY

List of Database Failures
=========================

Failure ID Priority Status    Time Detected Summary
---------- -------- --------- ------------- -------
1562       CRITICAL OPEN      04-JUN-14     System datafile
30: '+DATA/CDB01/FB03AEEBB6F60995E043E3A0080AEE85/DATAFILE/
system.258.849343395' is missing

analyzing automatic repair options; this may take some time
allocated channel: ORA_DISK_1
channel ORA_DISK_1: SID=774 device type=DISK
allocated channel: ORA_DISK_2
channel ORA_DISK_2: SID=1028 device type=DISK
allocated channel: ORA_DISK_3
channel ORA_DISK_3: SID=1276 device type=DISK
allocated channel: ORA_DISK_4
channel ORA_DISK_4: SID=10 device type=DISK
analyzing automatic repair options complete

Mandatory Manual Actions
========================
no manual actions available

Optional Manual Actions
=======================
1. If file +DATA/CDB01/FB03AEEBB6F60995E043E3A0080AEE85/
DATAFILE/system.258.849343395 was unintentionally renamed or
moved, restore it
2. Automatic repairs may be available if you shut down the
```

```
database and restart it in mount mode

Automated Repair Options
========================
Option Repair Description
------ ------------------
1      Restore and recover datafile 30
  Strategy: The repair includes complete media recovery with no
data loss
  Repair script: /u01/app/oracle/diag/rdbms/cdb01/cdb01/hm/
reco_461168804.hm

RMAN>
```

The repair script generated by RMAN is as follows:

```
# restore and recover datafile
sql 'CCREPOS' 'alter database datafile 30 offline';
restore ( datafile 30 );
recover datafile 30;
sql 'CCREPOS' 'alter database datafile 30 online';
```

The script is generated to run as is in RMAN. Knowing that the CCREPOS PDB is closed, however, means you can skip the first and last commands and just run the RESTORE and RECOVER:

```
RMAN> restore (datafile 30);

Starting restore at 04-JUN-14
using channel ORA_DISK_1
using channel ORA_DISK_2
using channel ORA_DISK_3
using channel ORA_DISK_4

channel ORA_DISK_1: starting datafile backup set restore
channel ORA_DISK_1: specifying datafile(s) to restore from
backup set
channel ORA_DISK_1: restoring datafile 00030 to +DATA/CDB01/
FB03AEEBB6F60995E043E3A0080AEE85/DATAFILE/system.258.849343395
channel ORA_DISK_1: reading from backup piece +RECOV/CDB01/
FB03AEEBB6F60995E043E3A0080AEE85/BACKUPSET/2014_06_04/nnndf0_tag
20140604t084003_0.316.849343205
channel ORA_DISK_1: piece handle=+RECOV/CDB01/
FB03AEEBB6F60995E043E3A0080AEE85/BACKUPSET/2014_06_04/nnndf0_tag
20140604t084003_0.316.849343205 tag=TAG20140604T084003
channel ORA_DISK_1: restored backup piece 1
```

```
channel ORA_DISK_1: restore complete, elapsed time: 00:00:07
Finished restore at 04-JUN-14

RMAN> recover datafile 30;

Starting recover at 04-JUN-14
using channel ORA_DISK_1
using channel ORA_DISK_2
using channel ORA_DISK_3
using channel ORA_DISK_4

starting media recovery
media recovery complete, elapsed time: 00:00:01

Finished recover at 04-JUN-14

RMAN>
```

Finally, open the PDB and see whether all is well:

```
RMAN> alter pluggable database ccrepos open;
Statement processed
RMAN>
```

Since CCREPOS starts fine now, you can clear the failure in RMAN:

```
RMAN> change failure 1562 closed;

Database Role: PRIMARY

List of Database Failures
=========================

Failure ID Priority Status    Time Detected Summary
---------- -------- --------- ------------- -------
1562       CRITICAL OPEN      04-JUN-14     System datafile
30: '+DATA/CDB01/FB03AEEBB6F60995E043E3A0080AEE85/DATAFILE/
system.258.849343395' is missing

Do you really want to change the above failures (enter YES or
NO)? yes
closed 1 failures

RMAN>
```

PITR Scenarios

There are occasions where you want to roll the entire database back to a point in time before a logical corruption occurred. If the flashback retention is not sufficient to rewind back as far as you would like, then you will have to resort to restoring the entire database and applying incremental backups and archived redo logs to a point in time right before the logical corruption occurred (for example, dropping several large tables or updating hundreds of tables with the wrong date).

Therefore, point in time recovery (PITR) is a good solution for a PDB tablespace or the entire PDB. As you might expect, all other PDBs and the CDB are unaffected when performing PITR for a PDB. As with a non-CDB PITR, when you perform an incomplete recovery, you have to open the PDB with RESETLOGS. For a tablespace within the PDB, the PDB remains open for the duration of the tablespace PITR recovery.

In the PDB named TOOL, you have a series of routine transactions and a logically consistent database as of SCN 4759498:

```
SQL> select current_scn from v$database;

CURRENT_SCN
-----------
    4759498
SQL>
```

Later in the day, at SCN= 4767859, all of the rows in the table BIG_IMPORT are accidentally deleted, and neither the flashback data for that table or UNDO data is available. The only viable option is to recover the tablespace USERS to SCN=4759498 using PITR.

```
RMAN>  recover tablespace tool:users until scn 4759498
2>          auxiliary destination '+RECOV';
. . .
SQL> alter tablespace tool:users online;
```

If this PDB did not use a flash recovery area, the AUXILIARY DESTINATION clause would specify the location to hold temporary files for the auxiliary instance including the datafiles, control files, and online log files.

Using Flashback CDB

If you do have enough space for flashback logs for a specific recovery window across all PDBs in a CDB, then using Flashback CDB is another good option for recovery when doing a full CDB restore and recovery operation would take significantly longer. Even if you have plenty of disk space for flashback logs, the flashback operation is across all PDBs and the CDB. If an individual PDB needs to be flashed back, you would instead use PDB PITR and leave the rest of the PDBs and CDB at their current SCN.

To configure the Fast Recovery Area, enable ARCHIVELOG mode, set your flashback retention target, and turn on flashback:

```
SQL> alter system  set db_flashback_retention_target=4000;

System altered.

SQL> alter database flashback on;

Database altered.

SQL>
```

One other caveat to using Flashback CDB is that you won't be able to flashback the CDB to a point in time earlier than any PDB that has been rewound with database PITR.

Identifying Block Corruption

The RMAN VALIDATE command works in a CDB environment much like it did in previous releases of Oracle with the expected granularity in Oracle Database 12*c* to validate individual PDBs, the root container, or the entire CDB. Connecting to the root container in RMAN, you can use the VALIDATE command as in this example to check the existence of all datafiles in the TOOL and CCREPOS PDBs as well as for any block corruptions:

```
[oracle@tettnang ~]$ rman target /

Recovery Manager: Release 12.1.0.1.0 - Production on Wed Jun 4
21:09:02 2014

Copyright (c) 1982, 2013, Oracle and/or its affiliates.  All
rights reserved.

connected to target database: CDB01 (DBID=1382179355)

RMAN> validate pluggable database tool,ccrepos;
```

```
Starting validate at 04-JUN-14
using target database control file instead of recovery catalog
allocated channel: ORA_DISK_1
channel ORA_DISK_1: SID=1276 device type=DISK
allocated channel: ORA_DISK_2
channel ORA_DISK_2: SID=517 device type=DISK
allocated channel: ORA_DISK_3
channel ORA_DISK_3: SID=1277 device type=DISK
allocated channel: ORA_DISK_4
channel ORA_DISK_4: SID=1025 device type=DISK
channel ORA_DISK_1: starting validation of datafile
channel ORA_DISK_1: specifying datafile(s) for validation
input datafile file number=00033 name=+DATA/CDB01/
FA782A61F8447D03E043E3A0080A9E54/DATAFILE/users.283.849369565
. . .
channel ORA_DISK_3: validation complete, elapsed time: 00:00:01
List of Datafiles
=================
File Status Marked Corrupt Empty Blocks Blocks Examined High SCN
---- ------ -------------- ------------ --------------- --------
31   OK     0              20112        80685           4769786
  File Name: +DATA/CDB01/FB03AEEBB6F60995E043E3A0080AEE85/
DATAFILE/sysaux.282.849342981
  Block Type Blocks Failing Blocks Processed
  ---------- -------------- ----------------
  Data       0              14367
  Index      0              7673
  Other      0              38488

Finished validate at 04-JUN-14

RMAN>
```

CERTIFICATION OBJECTIVE 13.04

Duplicate PDBs Using RMAN

In Chapter 11, I showed you how to clone a PDB using the CREATE PLUGGABLE DATABASE . . . FROM command. RMAN gives you more flexibility and scalability when duplicating one or more PDBs within a CDB or the entire CDB.

As in any RMAN DUPLICATE operation, you must create an auxiliary instance for the destination CDB and PDBs. Even when duplicating a PDB, the auxiliary instance must be started with the initialization parameter ENABLE_PLUGGABLE_DATABASE=TRUE, and therefore the target is a complete CDB with the root container (CDB$ROOT) and the seed database (PDB$SEED).

To duplicate a single PDB called TOOL to a new CDB called NINE, the RMAN DUPLICATE command would look like this:

```
RMAN> duplicate database to nine pluggable database tool;
```

If you want to copy two or more pluggable databases, you just add them to the end of the DUPLICATE command:

```
RMAN> duplicate database to nine pluggable database qa_2015,tool;
```

Exclusions are allowed in the DUPLICATE command. If you wanted to clone an entire CDB but without the CCREPOS PDB, do this:

```
RMAN> duplicate database to nine skip pluggable database ccrepos;
```

Finally, you can duplicate not only pluggable databases but also individual tablespaces to a new CDB:

```
RMAN> duplicate database to nine
2>          pluggable databases qa_2015,ccrepos tablespace tool:users;
```

CERTIFICATION SUMMARY

Multitenant architecture, consisting of a container database with one or more pluggable databases, expands the options you have for hosting multiple databases on a single server or multiple servers in a clustered (RAC) environment. The capabilities of container databases need the management tools to effectively monitor and maintain databases in a multitenant environment, and therefore many of the existing SQL commands and RMAN commands have been enhanced to support a multitenant environment.

After you create your first CDB, the first thought on your mind probably is, "How do I back this up?" The existing BACKUP command operates as you'd expect in a non-CDB environment and backs up the entire CDB and all of its PDBs (including the seed container) as if it were a single database, which it is to some extent because all PDBs within a CDB share the same instance. Some PDBs within a CDB may have higher activity levels or more DML activity and therefore will need to be backed up more often. RMAN easily accommodates this by qualifying the BACKUP command with the PLUGGABLE keyword. Individual tablespaces can be backed up from one or more PDBs by prefixing the tablespace name with the PDB name.

Once you have a full backup completed with incremental backups and multiple copies of the archived redo log files being generated on a continuous basis, the second thought that pops into your head probably is, "How do I recover the CDB or any of the PDBs if disaster strikes?" There are similar enhancements to the RMAN RECOVER command. Individual datafiles or an entire PDB tablespace can be recovered using RMAN while the CDB and other PDBs remain online and available to other users. Even the PDB being recovered can remain open if the SYSTEM or TEMP tablespace is not the target of the recovery operation.

Sometimes database errors and their source are not obvious, even when you get a phone call from a database user who can't run any queries. In that case, you can use the Data Recovery Advisor from RMAN or from Oracle Database Cloud Control 12*c* to display any outstanding errors with any component of the CDB. After viewing the error, DRA can give advice on how to fix the error and most likely offer a script that you can use to perform the repair.

Finally, instead of waiting for errors to occur and users to call you, RMAN provides an enhanced version of the VALIDATE command to check the entire CDB or individual PDBs for missing datafiles or corrupted blocks. Repairs can be initiated and problems fixed even before the users discover there is a problem.

TWO-MINUTE DRILL

Perform Backups of a CDB and PDBs

- RMAN includes the new clause PLUGGABLE to back up and recover a PDB.
- You can back up the root container as a PDB with the name CDB$ROOT.
- The REPORT SCHEMA command shows each tablespace and datafile within a CDB or PDB depending on how you connected to RMAN.
- The PLUGGABLE keyword is available in other RMAN commands such as DUPLICATE, SWITCH, and DELETE.
- To back up a CDB, you must connect with a user who has SYSDBA or SYSBACKUP privileges.
- You can back up an individual PDB as the container owner with SYSDBA privileges or as a local (noncommon) user with SYSDBA or SYSBACKUP privileges.

Recover PDB from PDB Datafiles Loss

- Instance recovery occurs only at the CDB level.
- Missing temporary datafiles (tempfiles) are re-created automatically at container open.
- Flashback Database is available only at the CDB level.
- PDB PITR recovery works similarly to a tablespace recovery in a non-CDB.
- Tablespace PITR is available for any tablespace other than SYSTEM, UNDO, and SYSAUX.
- Control file loss is handled the same way as a non-CDB: Either replace the missing or damaged control file with a multiplexed copy or restore from an RMAN autobackup.
- Recovery of the root SYSAUX datafile can occur with the CDB and all PDBs online.

Use Data Recovery Advisor

- The Data Recovery Advisor supports single-instance CDBs and non-CDBs but not clustered (RAC) databases.
- You use the LIST FAILURE command to see any outstanding data failures within RMAN.
- ADVISE FAILURE shows one or more options to repair the database error.
- REPAIR FAILURE PREVIEW shows you the steps RMAN will take to repair the corrupt or lost datafiles.
- REPAIR FAILURE implements one of the recommendations provided with ADVISE FAILURE.
- Media failure can be repaired using PITR at either the PDB or PDB tablespace level.
- Flashback CDB rewinds both the CDB and all PDBs within the CDB.
- You cannot flashback a CDB to an SCN before any PDB's database point in time recovery (DBPITR).

Duplicate PDBs Using RMAN

- You use the RMAN command DUPLICATE with new clauses that specify one or more PDBs to duplicate.
- Using the SKIP keyword, you can duplicate all PDBs within a CDB except for the specified PDBs.
- The TABLESPACE keyword with a qualified tablespace name will duplicate a single tablespace along with any other complete PDBs in a single DUPLICATE command.

SELF TEST

The following questions will help you measure your understanding of the material presented in this chapter. Read all the choices carefully because there might be more than one correct answer. Choose all correct answers for each question.

Perform Backups of a CDB and PDBs

1. Which of the following are true about multitenant (CDB and PDB) backups? (Choose all that apply.)

A. You can back up just the root container of a CDB.

B. Tablespace backups can include multiple tablespaces from different PDBs.

C. PDBs can be backed up individually only by connecting to the target PDB in RMAN.

D. RMAN allows you to enforce division of responsibility by connecting to an individual container.

Recover PDB from PDB Datafiles Loss

2. RMAN is configured for autobackup of the control file and SPFILE. You perform a whole PDB backup with RMAN like this:

```
RMAN> connect target /
RMAN> backup pluggable database ccrepos;
```

Shortly afterward, you lose all copies of the control file. What are your options for recovering the control file?

A. Shut down the CDB instance if it is not down already, recover the CDB, and open it with RESETLOGS.

B. Shut down the CDB instance if it is not down already, restore the control file from the latest backup, recover the CDB, and open it with RESETLOGS.

C. Shut down the CDB instance if it is not down already, recover the PDB CCREPOS, copy the latest control file from the Fast Recovery Area, and open it with RESETLOGS.

D. Restore the entire CDB, recover the CDB, and open it with RESETLOGS.

3. Your container database (CDB) is in NOARCHIVELOG mode. Which of the following is true regarding the recoverability of any hosted databases (CDB or PDB)?

A. The container (root) must be shut down to perform any recovery operations.

B. The loss of a datafile requires restore of the datafile only if the tablespace containing that datafile is read-only.

C. Losing a datafile local to a PDB requires only that the PDB be shut down for a recovery.

D. NOARCHIVELOG should be set only at the PDB level.

Use Data Recovery Advisor

4. Which of the following database configurations are supported by the RMAN Data Recovery Advisor (DRA)? (Choose all that apply.)

A. Non-CDBs

B. Single-instance CDB

C. Single-instance PDB

D. NOARCHIVELOG databases or CDBs

E. RAC or RAC One

F. Data Guard Failover to Standby

Duplicate PDBs Using RMAN

5. Identify the RMAN DUPLICATE command that is syntactically incorrect.

A. duplicate database to cdb03 pluggable database ccrepos, qa_2012;

B. duplicate database to pdb90 skip pluggable database ccrepos;

C. duplicate pluggable database cdb01 to cdb02;

D. duplicate database to cdb02 tablespace tool:users;

SELF TEST ANSWERS

Perform Backups of a CDB and PDBs

1. ☑ **A, B,** and **D.** You can back up just the root container of a CDB by specifying PDB$ROOT as the container name. The BACKUP command supports various combinations of containers and tablespaces in the BACKUP command. In addition, creating local users with SYSBACKUP privileges in a PDB helps to enforce division or responsibility in an organization.
   ☒ **C** is incorrect because you can back up a PDB either by connecting to the root container as a common user with SYSDBA or SYSBACKUP privileges or by a local user with either SYSDBA or SYSBACKUP privileges in the PDB.

Recover PDB from PDB Datafiles Loss

2. ☑ **B.** Once the control file is lost, the CDB instance will crash and bring down every PDB with it. Start up the CDB in MOUNT mode, restore the control file (it will be the copy created with autobackup of the CCREPOS PDB), and open the database with RESETLOGS. Once the CDB is up, open any PDBs that were open at the time of the crash.
   ☒ **A, C,** and **D** are incorrect. **A** is incorrect because you need to explicitly restore the control file from the most recent backup. **C** is incorrect because neither the CCREPOS PDB nor any other PDB needs recovery; only the control file needs to be restored. **D** is incorrect because the entire CDB does not need to be restored. Only the control files are missing.
3. ☑ **A.** In NOARCHIVELOG mode, the CDB and as a result all of its PDBs must be shut down to perform a recovery operation on either the root or a PDB.
   ☒ **B, C,** and **D** are incorrect. The loss of any datafile in a CDB in NOARCHIVELOG mode requires the restore and recovery of all control files as well as the datafiles for the root container and all PDBs. NOARCHIVELOG mode can be set only at the CDB level.

Use Data Recovery Advisor

4. ☑ **A, B, C, D,** and **F.** Any non-CDB or CDB is supported by the Data Recovery Advisor as well as databases in NOARCHIVELOG mode or the primary database in a standby environment. If a CDB is in NOARCHIVELOG mode, the DRA will require that all recovery options start with the database in MOUNT mode.
   ☒ **E** is incorrect because RAC (multi-instance) environments are not supported by DRA as of Oracle Database 12*c* release 1 (12.1.0.1).

Duplicate PDBs Using RMAN

5. ☑ **C.** Using the RMAN DUPLICATE command does not require the PLUGGABLE keyword unless you are specifying the list of PDBs to duplicate.
☒ **A, B,** and **D** are incorrect. The DUPLICATE command has the flexibility to copy more than PDB at a time as well as exclude one or more with the SKIP keyword. DUPLICATE also makes it easy to make a copy of a single tablespace to a new PDB.

14

Managing Performance

CERTIFICATION OBJECTIVES

14.01	Monitor Operations and Performance in a CDB and PDBs	14.03	Perform Database Replay
14.02	Manage Allocation of Resources Between PDBs and Within a PDB	✓	Two-Minute Drill
		Q&A	Self Test

As you might expect, tuning a multitenant container database (the container itself or one of the pluggable database), is much like tuning a non-CDB in that you're tuning a single instance with many different applications (pluggable databases) sharing and competing for the same server resources. This is in line with the multitenant database architecture in that there are minimal or no difference between a CDB and a non-CDB from a usage, compatibility, and tuning perspective.

The keys to performance tuning a pluggable database are monitoring and resource allocation. Not only must you tune individual SQL statements within a PDB, but you also must decide what percentage of the server's resources a PDB can have if all PDBs are active. Many of the same tools you use for a non-CDB database are also used for a CDB, such as the SQL Tuning Advisor as well as the familiar AWR, ASH, and ADDM reports. The big difference in a CDB environment is that tuning SQL statements happens at the PDB level, whereas the AWR, ASH, and ADDM reports are at the instance (CDB) level.

As you may recall from Chapter 12, some initialization parameters can also be set at the PDB level if the default value at the CDB level is not appropriate. I'll show you how to change some of these parameters at the PDB level in a tuning scenario.

Finally, you'll use a variation of another familiar toolset to see how well separate databases behave in a single container: Consolidated Database Replay. To find the right settings at the CDB level, you use an iterative process to make your best first guess at a combined resource requirement for each PDB, allocate the resources among the PDBs using Resource Manager, and then run the combined workload.

CERTIFICATION OBJECTIVE 14.01

Monitor Operations and Performance in a CDB and PDBs

Even though there is database activity at the CDB level, the bulk of the activity should be occurring in each PDB from a logical perspective. Remember that from an instance perspective it's still one database instance. Therefore, the standard Oracle tuning methodologies still apply to a CDB environment.

At the CDB level, you want to optimize the amount of memory you need to host one or more PDBs; that's the reason you're using a multitenant environment in the first place! In the following sections, I'll review the standard tuning methodologies as well as how you can change initialization parameters at the PDB level. Using performance reports such as the ASH, ADDM, and AWR reports help you identify performance issues for the CDB, and using the SQL Tuning Advisor will help you optimize your SQL activity within each PDB.

Tuning Methodology

The standard Oracle tuning methodology developed and refined over the last several releases of Oracle Database still apply to multitenant environments. The overall steps are as follows:

1. Identify the tuning goal:
   a. Reduce elapsed time for individual queries.
   b. Increase the number of users without buying new hardware.
   c. Optimize memory usage.
   d. Reduce disk space usage (compression, normalization).
2. Determine the cause of the bottleneck (OS, network, I/O); usually it's one cause.
3. Tune the application from the top down:
   a. Review the application design.
   b. Modify the database design (denormalization, materialized views, data warehouse).
   c. Tune the SQL code.
   d. Tune the instance.
4. Use database analysis tools once you finish step 3:
   a. Collect statistics at the instance and OS levels.
   b. Use the AWR report to identify wait events and poorly performing SQL.
   c. Use the SQL Tuning Advisor, memory advisors, and other advisors to tune and reduce elapsed time, CPU, and I/O.
5. After tuning one or more components, start again at step 2 if the tuning goal has not yet been met.

The biggest focus of any tuning effort is identifying when to stop tuning. In other words, you need to identify the goal for a tuning effort after several users complain that "the database is slow." Identifying the performance issue, reevaluating the SLAs in place, and monitoring database growth and the user base are important factors in deciding how much time you want to spend tuning a database (CDB or non-CDB) before you reach the decision that you need faster hardware, a faster network, or a new database design.

Sizing the CDB

Adjusting parameters at the CDB is much like tuning a single instance in a non-CDB environment that has several applications with different resource and availability requirements. It's worth mentioning again that a CDB *is* a single database instance, but with the added features of the multitenant environment, you have much more control over resource consumption among the several applications (each in their own PDB) in addition to the strong isolation between the applications from a security perspective.

Tuning CDB Memory and CPU Resources

Tuning the memory in a CDB means you're changing the same memory areas as in a non-CDB:

- Buffer cache (SGA)
- Shared pool (SGA)
- Program Global Area (PGA)

When you calculate the memory requirements for a CDB, your first estimate can be the sum of all corresponding memory requirements for each non-CDB that will become a PDB. Of course, you will eventually want to reduce the total memory footprint for the CDB based on a number of factors. For example, not all PDBs will be active at the same time; therefore, you will likely not need as much total memory allocated to the CDB.

Using Enterprise Manager Cloud Control 12*c* is a good way to see resource usage across the CDB. In Figure 14-1, the container CDB01 has three PDBs active and two inactive.

The total memory allocated for the CDB is approximately 5GB. Three non-CDB databases would likely use 5GB or more each; all five PDBs in CDB01 may perform just fine in a total of 5GB.

FIGURE 14-1

Viewing PDB resource usage within a CDB using Cloud Control 12*c*

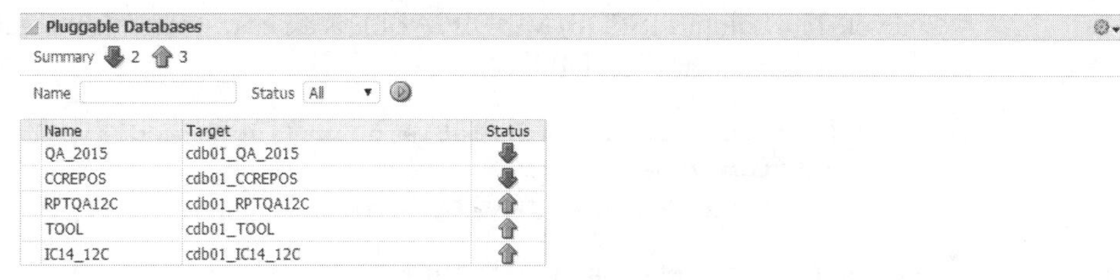

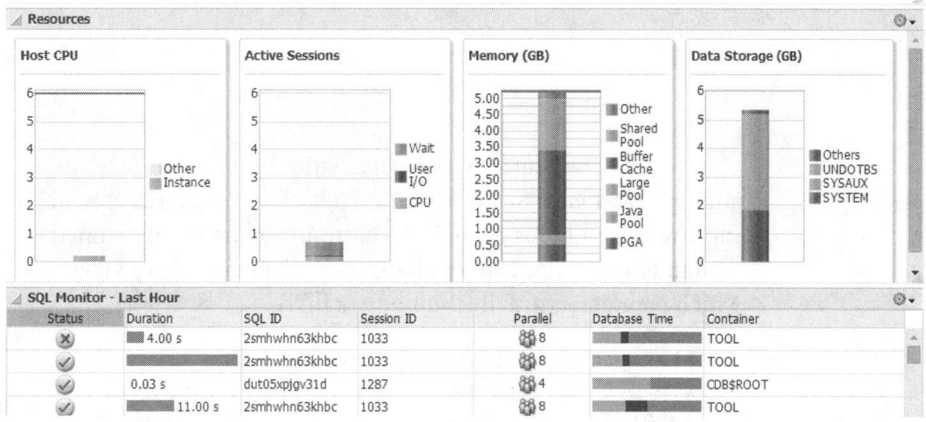

There are a few different approaches to resource allocation among PDBs within a CDB:

- **None** Let each PDB use all resources of the CDB if no other PDB is active; when multiple PDBs need resources, they are divided equally.
- **Minimum** Each PDB gets a minimum guaranteed resource allocation.
- **Minimum/maximum** Each PDB gets both a minimum guaranteed resource allocation and a maximum.

Resource usage allocation in a CDB is measured in *shares*. By default, all PDBs can consume all resources allocated to the CDB. I cover more details on how shares are allocated and calculated later in the chapter.

Modifying Initialization Parameters

As you found out in Chapter 11, there is only one SPFILE per CDB instance. All database parameters are stored in the CDB's SPFILE, but 171 of those parameters (out of a total of 367 for Oracle Database 12*c* 12.1.0.1) can be changed at the PDB level. The column ISPDB_MODIFIABLE is an easy way to see which parameters you can change at the PDB level:

```
SQL> select ispdb_modifiable,count(ispdb_modifiable)
  2  from v$parameter
  3  group by ispdb_modifiable;

ISPDB COUNT(ISPDB_MODIFIABLE)
----- -----------------------
TRUE                      171
FALSE                     196

SQL>
```

When you unplug a PDB, its customized parameters stay with the unplugged PDB and are set when that PDB is plugged back in regardless of which PDB it is plugged into. When a PDB is cloned, the custom parameters are cloned as well. At the container level, you can also look at the data dictionary view PDB_SPFILE$ to see which parameters are different across PDBs:

```
select pdb_uid,pdb_name,name,value$
from pdb_spfile$ ps
   join cdb_pdbs cp
      on ps.pdb_uid=cp.con_uid;

   PDB_UID PDB_NAME           NAME                           VALUE$
---------- -----------        ------------------------       ------
1258510409 TOOL               sessions                       200
1288637549 RPTQA12C           cursor_sharing
'FORCE'
1288637549 RPTQA12C           star_transformation_enabled    TRUE
1288637549 RPTQA12C           open_cursors                   300
```

In the TOOL PDB, the SESSIONS parameter is different from the default (at the CDB level); the RPTQA12C PDB has three nondefault parameters set.

Using Memory Advisors

The buffer cache in a CDB, shared across all PDBs, behaves much like the buffer cache in a non-CDB: The same LRU algorithms are used to determine when and if a block should stay in the buffer cache. Because the buffer cache is shared, the PDB's container ID (CON_ID) is also stored in each block. The same container ID is stored in the other SGA and PGA memory areas such as the shared pool in the SGA and the global PGA. The memory advisors from previous versions of Oracle Database work in much the same way in a multitenant environment; sizing recommendations are at the CDB (instance) level. Individual memory parameters that can be adjusted at the PDB are limited to SORT_AREA_SIZE and SORT_AREA_RETAINED_SIZE.

In Figure 14-2, is the output from the SGA Memory Advisor is launched from Cloud Control 12*c*.

Even with several PDBs in the CDB01 container, it appears that the total memory for the CDB can be reduced by at least 1GB and still retain good performance for all PDBs.

To accommodate a potentially larger number of sessions in a CDB, the parameter PGA_AGGREGATE_LIMIT was added to place a hard limit on the amount of PGA memory used. The existing parameter PGA_AGGREGATE_TARGET was useful in previous releases as a soft limit but only for tunable memory. Several sessions using untunable memory (such as PL/SQL applications that allocate large memory arrays) could potentially use up all available PGA memory, causing swap activity at the OS level and affecting performance across all instances on the server. Thus, the parameter PGA_AGGREGATE_LIMIT was added to abort PGA memory requests by one or more nonsystem connections to get under this limit.

FIGURE 14-2

CDB SGA Memory Advisor in Cloud Control 12*c*

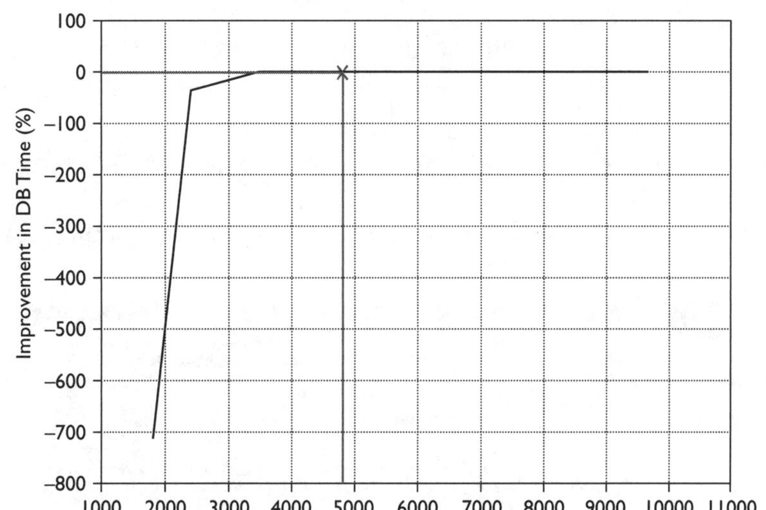

Leveraging AWR Reports

As with all previously described Oracle tuning tools, AWR snapshots include a container ID number, and that container ID is reflected in any AWR report. Figure 14-3 shows an excerpt of the SQL statements executed during the three-hour window specified for the AWR report.

The SQL statements run during this window were from two PDBs and the root container. As in a non-CDB environment, your tuning effort will focus first on the statements with the longest elapsed time along with statements whose total time across multiple executions is at the top of the list.

Using the SQL Tuning Advisor

When you run the SQL Tuning Advisor against one or more SQL statements, such as those in Figure 14-3, the advisor runs only in the context of a single PDB. In other words, the recommendations are based only on the performance and resource usage within the PDB. Even if the same SQL statement is run in multiple PDBs, the schema names, statistics, data volumes, and initialization parameters can and will likely be different between PDBs. Therefore, if any recommendations are implemented, they are applied in only a single PDB.

Other new and enhanced SQL Tuning features in Oracle Database 12*c* can be used for CDBs and non-CDBs:

- Adaptive SQL plan management
- Automatic SQL plan baseline evolution
- SQL management base
- SQL plan directives
- Improved statistics gathering performance

The usage of these tools is beyond the scope of this book and the OCP exam.

FIGURE 14-3 AWR report in a multitenant environment

Elapsed Time (s)	Executions	Elapsed Time per Exec (s)	%Total	%CPU	%IO	SQL Id	SQL Module	PDB Name	SQL Text
46.45	3	15.48	21.54	27.70	9.92	2smhwhn63khbc	SQL*Plus	TOOL	insert /*+ parallel(8) */ int...
33.03	165	0.20	15.31	95.94	2.03	dt2babdaankpg	EM Realtime Connection		select dbms_report.get_report(...
22.73	165	0.14	10.54	96.82	2.65	6fwy90bgdvdfn	EM Realtime Connection		with base_metrics as (select...
19.88	2	9.94	9.22	95.55	2.82	gsbdfku007tup	Admin Connection		select output from table(dbms_...
15.23	240	0.06	7.06	98.61	0.00	5yv7yvjgixugg			select TIME_WAITED_MICRO from ...
14.36	117	0.12	6.66	90.79	2.91	fhf8upax5cxsz	MMON_SLAVE		BEGIN sys.dbms_auto_report_int...
12.64	117	0.11	5.86	91.75	3.16	0w26sk6t6gq98	MMON_SLAVE		SELECT XMLTYPE(DBMS_REPORT.GET...
8.63	117	0.07	4.00	88.42	4.47	7r24h5ucyjggz	MMON_SLAVE		WITH MONITOR_DATA AS (SELECT I...
7.66	4	1.91	3.55	32.30	10.03	8fypn587m9tc5	SQL*Plus	TOOL	insert into temp_objects selec...
7.54	165	0.05	3.49	99.35	0.00	01w7zgb118hpb	EM Realtime Connection		select xmlelement("references...
6.19	1,437	0.00	2.87	96.95	0.28	fng8p3fj3r5as			select /*+ no_monitor */ job, ...
5.07	78	0.07	2.35	98.94	0.00	5m2z5vch05wap	EM Realtime Connection		select end_time endTime, round...
4.44	49	0.09	2.06	98.51	0.14	g57kbmvd1ggfk	EM Realtime Connection		select dbms_sqltune.report_sql...
3.97	6	0.66	1.84	21.87	62.07	4t8wz8471kxf2	EM Realtime Connection	RPTQA12C	WITH F AS (select tablespace_n...
3.62	2	1.81	1.68	73.18	26.94	a3a61zmn8t5k4	SQL*Plus	TOOL	select owner, status, count(ob...
3.57	6	0.60	1.66	98.86	0.10	2vwhap18bjf9h	ClarityDataTransferService.exe	RPTQA12C	SELECT DISTINCT CC.COLUMN_NAME...

CERTIFICATION OBJECTIVE 14.02

Manage Allocation of Resources Between PDBs and Within a PDB

In the previous section, I introduced the concept of resource sharing within a CDB by using shares. I'll expand on that concept by showing how you can allocate shares among PDBs within a CDB. In addition, I'll talk about resource management within a PDB, which is much like how Resource Manager operates in a non-CDB environment and previous versions of Oracle Database.

Once a portion of resources is allocated to a PDB, Resource Manager will prioritize resource requests by users. In both cases, you'll use the DBMS_RESOURCE_MANAGER package to create and deploy resource allocations.

Using Shares to Manage Inter-PDB Resources

Each PDB that's plugged into a CDB competes for the resources of a CDB—primarily CPU, parallel servers, and, in the case of Oracle Exadata, I/O. How much of each resource a PDB gets depends on how many *shares* that PDB was assigned when it was created.

Neither consumer groups (using Resource Manager) nor shares can be defined for the root container.

By default, each PDB gets one share unless otherwise specified. When a new PDB is added or an existing PDB is unplugged, the number of shares each PDB has remains the same. Table 14-1 shows a CDB with four PDBs: HR, BI, REPOS, and TOOL. The BI PDB has three shares, and the rest have one each, the default.

TABLE 14-1

PDBs and Share Allocation for Four PDBs

PDB Name	Shares	CPU Percent (Maximum)
HR	1	16.67 percent
BI	3	50 percent
REPOS	1	16.67 percent
TOOL	1	16.67 percent

TABLE 14-2 PDBs and Share Allocation for Five PDBs After Adding a New One

PDB Name	Shares	CPU Percent (Maximum)
HR	1	14.29 percent
BI	3	42.86 percent
REPOS	1	14.29 percent
TOOL	1	14.29 percent
NCAL	1	14.29 percent

The TOOL database, for example, is guaranteed 16.67 percent of the server's CPU resources if needed. If one or more of the other PDBs are not active, TOOL can use its default allocation if there is no activity in the other PDBs.

In Table 14-2, you create a PDB called NCAL and don't specify the number of shares, so it defaults to 1.

The minimum CPU guaranteed for each PDB is automatically recalculated based on the new total number of shares. Each PDB with one share now gets 14.29 percent of the CPU resources, and the CPU resources available (at a minimum) for the BI PDB is now 42.86 percent.

Creating and Modifying Resource Manager Plans

To further refine the resource consumption, you can set limits within each PDB using Resource Manager. From the perspective of the PDB, all resources are controlled by directives created using DBMS_RESOURCE_MANAGER. The amount of CPU, Exadata I/O, and concurrent parallel servers used by the PDB default to 100 percent but can be adjusted down to 0 percent depending on the time of day or other circumstances.

The resource plan itself is created at the CDB level, and you create directives for each PDB within the CDB. You can also specify a set of default directives for those PDBs that do not have an explicit set of directives.

Identifying Parameters to Limit PDB Resource Usage

As part of the utilization plan for each PDB, there are two key limits you can control: the utilization limit for CPU, Exadata I/Os, and parallel servers as well as a parallel server limit. These plan directive limits are UTILIZATION_LIMIT and PARALLEL_SERVER_LIMIT, respectively.

The resource directive UTILIZATION_LIMIT defines the percentage of CPU, I/Os, and parallel servers available to a PDB. If UTILIZATION_LIMIT is set at 30, then the PDB can use no more than 30 percent of the resources available to the CDB.

To further refine the resource limits, you can use PARALLEL_SERVER_LIMIT to define the maximum percentage of the CDB's PARALLEL_SERVERS_TARGET value; this value overrides the UTILIZATION_LIMIT directive but only for parallel resources. The default is 100 percent.

Creating the CDB Resource Plan

The steps for creating a CDB resource plan are similar to creating a resource plan in a non-CDB, but with additional steps for each PDB. You create and manage the resource plan from the root container only. Table 14-3 lists the steps and corresponding DBMS_RESOURCE_MANAGER calls needed to create and configure the CDB resource plan.

Other key procedures in DBMS_RESOURCE_MANAGER include UPDATE_CDB_PLAN to change the characteristics of the CDB resource plan and DELETE_CDB_PLAN to delete the resource plan and all of its directives. To update and delete individual CDB plan directives, use UPDATE_CDB_PLAN_DIRECTIVE and DELETE_CDB_PLAN_DIRECTIVE.

TABLE 14-3 Steps to Create a Resource Plan with DBMS_RESOURCE_MANAGER Calls

Step	Description	DBMS_RESOURCE_MANAGER Procedure
1	Create a pending area.	CREATE_PENDING_AREA
2	Create a CDB resource plan.	CREATE_CDB_PLAN
3	Create PDB directives.	CREATE_CDB_PLAN_DIRECTIVE
4	Update default PDB directives.	UPDATE_CDB_DEFAULT_DIRECTIVE
5	Update default autotask directives.	UPDATE_CDB_AUTOTASK_DIRECTIVE
6	Validate the pending area.	VALIDATE_PENDING_AREA
7	Submit the pending area.	SUBMIT_PENDING_AREA

EXERCISE 14-1

Creating a CDB resource plan with PDB directives

In this exercise, you'll create a CDB resource plan for the CDB01 container and define plan directives for two of the PDBs in the CDB.

1. Create a pending area for the CDB plan:

```
SQL> connect / as sysdba
Connected.
SQL> exec dbms_resource_manager.create_pending_area();

PL/SQL procedure successfully completed.
```

2. Create a resource plan that manages the TOOL and CCREPOS PDBs to minimize CPU and other resource usage:

```
SQL> begin
       dbms_resource_manager.create_cdb_plan(
          plan       => 'low_prio_apps',
          comment    => 'TOOL and repository database low
priority');
     end;
     /

PL/SQL procedure successfully completed.
SQL>
```

3. Create a plan directive that gives both the TOOL and CCREPOS PDBs one share. The utilization limit for TOOL should be 50 percent, and for CCREPOS it will be 75 percent:

```
SQL> begin
       dbms_resource_manager.create_cdb_plan_directive(
          plan => 'low_prio_apps',
          pluggable_database => 'tool',
          shares => 1,
          utilization_limit => 50,
          parallel_server_limit => 50);
     end;
     /

PL/SQL procedure successfully completed.

SQL> begin
       dbms_resource_manager.create_cdb_plan_directive(
           plan => 'low_prio_apps',
```

```
        pluggable_database => 'ccrepos',
        shares => 1,
        utilization_limit => 75,
        parallel_server_limit => 75);
end;
/

PL/SQL procedure successfully completed.

SQL>
```

4. Validate and submit the pending area:

```
SQL> exec dbms_resource_manager.validate_pending_area();

PL/SQL procedure successfully completed.

SQL> exec dbms_resource_manager.submit_pending_area();

PL/SQL procedure successfully completed.

SQL>
```

5. Finally, make this resource manager plan the current plan:

```
SQL> alter system set resource_manager_plan='low_prio_apps';
System altered.
SQL>
```

Viewing Resource Plan Directives

In Oracle Database 12*c*, you have a data dictionary view called DBA_CDB_RSRC_PLAN_DIRECTIVES to see all of the current resource plans. Querying that view, you can see the resource plans you just created for TOOL and CCREPOS.

```
SQL> select plan, pluggable_database, shares,
       utilization_limit, parallel_server_limit
  from dba_cdb_rsrc_plan_directives
  order by plan,pluggable_database;

PLAN                      PLUGGABLE_DATABASE SHARES UTILIZA PARALLEL_
------------------------- ------------------ ------ ------- ---------
DEFAULT_CDB_PLAN          ORA$AUTOTASK                   90       100
DEFAULT_CDB_PLAN          ORA$DEFAULT_PDB_DI      1     100       100
                          RECTIVE
```

```
DEFAULT_MAINTENANCE_PLAN  ORA$AUTOTASK                   90       100
DEFAULT_MAINTENANCE_PLAN  ORA$DEFAULT_PDB_DI       1    100       100
                          RECTIVE

LOW_PRIO_APPS             CCREPOS                  1     75        75
LOW_PRIO_APPS             ORA$AUTOTASK                   90       100
LOW_PRIO_APPS             ORA$DEFAULT_PDB_DI       1    100       100
                          RECTIVE
LOW_PRIO_APPS             TOOL                     1     50        50
ORA$INTERNAL_CDB_PLAN     ORA$AUTOTASK
ORA$INTERNAL_CDB_PLAN     ORA$DEFAULT_PDB_DI
                          RECTIVE
ORA$QOS_CDB_PLAN          ORA$AUTOTASK                   90       100
ORA$QOS_CDB_PLAN          ORA$DEFAULT_PDB_DI       1    100       100
                          RECTIVE
```

In previous releases of Oracle Database and for non-CDBs in Oracle Database 12*c*, the corresponding data dictionary view is DBA_RSRC_PLAN_DIRECTIVES.

Managing Resources Within a PDB

Resource plans can manage workloads within a PDB as well. These resource plans manage workloads just as they do in a non-CDB and not surprisingly are called PDB resource plans. There are a few restrictions and differences with PDB plans. Table 14-4 shows the parameter and feature differences between non-CDB and PDB resource plans.

TABLE 14-4 Differences Between Non-CDB and PDB Resource Plans

Resource Plan Feature	Non-CDB	PDB
Multilevel plans	Yes	No
Consumer groups	Maximum: 32	Maximum: 8
Subplans	Yes	No
CREATE_PLAN_DIRECTIVE parameter	N/A	SHARE
CREATE_PLAN_DIRECTIVE parameter	MAX_UTILIZATION_LIMIT	UTILIZATION_LIMIT
CREATE_PLAN_DIRECTIVE parameter	PARALLEL_TARGET_PERCENTAGE	PARALLEL_SERVER_LIMIT

Regardless of the container type, you still view resource plans using the V$RSRC_PLAN dynamic performance view. To find the active CDB resource plan, select the row in V$RSRC_PLAN with CON_ID=1.

Migrating Non-CDB Resource Plans

You will likely convert and plug in many non-CDBs as new PDBs. This process is straightforward, and all of your applications should work as expected. If the non-CDB has a resource plan, it will be converted as well, as long as it meets these conditions:

- There are no more than eight consumer groups.
- There are no subplans.
- All resource allocations are on level 1.

In other words, the migrated resource plan must be compatible with a new PDB resource plan that follows the rules in the previous section. If the plan violates any of these conditions, the plan is converted during the plug-in operation to a plan that is compatible with a PDB. This plan may be unsuitable; you can drop, modify, or create a new resource plan. The original plan is saved in DBA_RSRC_PLAN_DIRECTIVES with the STATUS column having a value of LEGACY.

CERTIFICATION OBJECTIVE 14.03

Perform Database Replay

The Database Replay functionality from previous Oracle Database releases has also been enhanced in Oracle Database 12*c* to include simultaneous workload replays as a planning tool for estimating how multiple non-CDBs will perform in a CDB environment. You can take production workloads from *multiple* servers in a non-CDB environment and play them back in various configurations on a single new server to simulate how well they would coexist in a multitenant environment.

Analyze the Source Database Workloads

When you capture workloads for potential multitenant deployment, the workloads are typically in different business units and locations; the peak load for each application is likely at different times of the day, which makes these applications ideal candidates for consolidation. Figure 14-4 shows a typical set of workloads from applications currently on different servers.

You can also analyze existing PDBs and capture workloads to see how they would perform as a PDB of another CDB on a different server. The general steps you'll follow as part of this analysis phase are as follows:

1. Capture the workload of an existing non-CDB or PDB.
2. Optionally export the AWR snapshots for the database.
3. Restore the candidate database onto the target system.
4. Make changes to the imported candidate database as needed, such as upgrading to Oracle Database 12*c*.
5. Copy the generated workload files to the target system.
6. Process the workload as a one-time prerequisite step.
7. Repeat steps 1–6 for all other candidate databases.
8. Configure the target system for replay (such as the workload replay client processes).
9. Replay the workloads for all PDBs within the single CDB on the target system.

Capture Source Database Workloads

On the source database server, you'll capture the workload for a typical 8-hour or 24-hour period. You'll want all captured workloads to cover the same time period.

FIGURE 14-4

Candidate workloads for multitenant consolidation

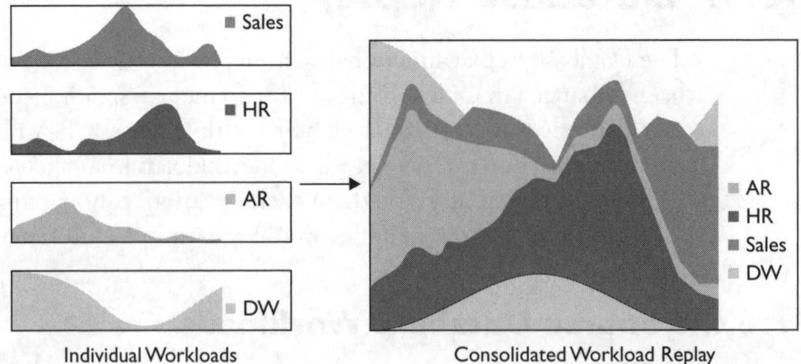

To optimize the performance of the replay test, you can optionally export AWR snapshots, SQL profiles, and SQL tuning sets.

Process Workloads on Target System

After you import the candidate database into a PDB of the new CDB, you import the workload generated on the source server. You preprocess the workload files in preparation for the replay, which needs to happen only once for each imported workload. It's recommended that you replay each imported workload individually to ensure that there are no extreme variations in performance compared to that database's performance on the original server.

Replay Workloads on Target CDB

After all PDBs have been created and preprocessed, remap any connections that might refer to objects that don't exist on the target system. Create a replay schedule that will replay each workload at the same time and rate that it does on the source system. You can create multiple schedules to see how workloads can be shifted to optimize the CDB's overall performance.

Verify Replay Results

After the replay session is complete, you review the reports generated by Consolidated Database Replay to see, for example, if the response time and overall SLA of the databases on their original servers can be met by this consolidation platform. If there are severe regressions, then you can use the tuning methodologies discussed earlier in this chapter and run the replay again. Even after tuning, you may find that the server needs more CPUs or memory. Ideally, you'll find out that each database runs just as fast or faster than it did on the original server!

CERTIFICATION SUMMARY

Performance tuning in a multitenant environment is even more important than in a non-CDB environment. One of the primary reasons for having a multitenant environment is to optimize your CPU, memory, disk, and I/O by sharing those resources across multiple pluggable databases (PDBs).

When you tune your applications in a multitenant environment, the tuning methodology is the same as in a non-CDB environment. Most of the gains in performance are achieved by a sound application and database design, and that should be reviewed first. In conjunction with OS and hardware tuning, you can use the familiar SQL tuning tools such as the memory advisors and AWR reports to identify and fix performance issues at the CDB level. Even though an AWR report runs at the CDB level, each SQL statement in the report is identified by a container ID (CON_ID), and the SQL Tuning Advisor is run at the PDB level.

As a starting point for creating a CDB to consolidate multiple non-CDBs, estimate memory requirements by adding together the memory requirements of each individual non-CDB. The total memory actually required for the CDB will almost certainly be less because the PDBs may not compete for the same resources at the same time.

Many initialization parameters are modifiable at the PDB level. These parameters stay with the PDB during unplug and plug operations. New parameters such as PGA_AGGREGATE_LIMIT help to manage the resource allocation among PDBs by preventing one PDB's application from having an adverse effect on other PDBs by using too much PGA memory.

Resource management is more important than ever in a multitenant environment. One way resource management is implemented in a multitenant environment is by using shares. The number of shares a PDB has in a container relative to the total number of shares across all PDBs determines the percentage of resources available to that PDB. By default, each PDB has one share; you change the number of shares using Resource Manager.

In addition to shares, Resource Manager has two new resource directives to manage PDB resource usage: UTILIZATION_LIMIT and PARALLEL_SERVERS_TARGET. You can manage resource allocation at the CDB level too, much like you'd manage resources in a non-CDB.

Finally, I talked about the Database Replay feature of Oracle Database 12c, renamed to Consolidated Database Replay. As the name implies, the Database Replay feature in previous releases has been enhanced to support load testing in a multitenant environment. Its primary purpose is to see how well a new multitenant environment on a new server will support the consolidation of workloads from several non-CDB databases. In addition, it helps you plan for future hardware expansion by testing peak load capacity. For example, what if all PDBs are active at once and suddenly require 25 percent more resources than average?

TWO-MINUTE DRILL

Monitor Operations and Performance in a CDB and PDBs

- ❑ A CDB and its PDBs are tuned as a single instance since, well, a CDB is a single instance.
- ❑ CDB tuning methodologies are identical to well-established tuning methodologies for non-CDB environments.
- ❑ When consolidating multiple non-CDBs into a single CDB, start by adding together the resource usage of each non-CDB as a starting point.
- ❑ Three general methodologies are used for allocating resources within a CDB: none, minimum, and minimum/maximum.
- ❑ Resource usage allocations are measured in shares.
- ❑ Parameters that can be changed within a PDB are identified by the column ISPDB_MODIFIABLE in V$PARAMETER.
- ❑ The buffer cache in the CDB's instance is shared by all PDBs, and each block in the buffer cache has a container ID.
- ❑ The new parameter PGA_AGGREGATE_LIMIT is a hard limit on total PGA usage across all PDBs.

Manage Allocation of Resources Between PDBs and Within a PDB

- ❑ You use DBMS_RESOURCE_MANAGER to create resource allocations both at the CDB and PDB levels.
- ❑ A share is the basic unit of minimum resource required for the PDB and defaults to 1.
- ❑ The minimum amount of resources for a PDB is a percentage calculated by its share value divided by the total number of shares across all PDBs in the CDB.
- ❑ Adding new PDBs to a CDB does not change the share value of other PDBs; however. the percentage of resources allocated for other PDBs will decrease proportionally.
- ❑ Using Resource Manager, you cannot define consumer groups or shares at the CDB level.
- ❑ The utilization limit for CPU, Exadata I/O, and parallel servers is defined by the UTILIZATION_LIMIT directive in a PDB resource plan.
- ❑ The parallel server limit in a PDB can be set in a resource plan using the PARALLEL_SERVER_LIMIT directive.

- At a minimum, you use the procedures CREATE_PENDING_AREA, CREATE_CDB_PLAN, CREATE_CDB_PLAN_DIRECTIVE, VALIDATE_PENDING_AREA, and SUBMIT_PENDING_AREA to create a CDB resource plan.
- For CDB resource plans, you can optionally use the UPDATE_CDB_DEFAULT_DIRECTIVE and UPDATE_CDB_AUTOTASK_DIRECTIVE parameters to update the defaults for new or existing PDB resource plans.
- The data dictionary view DBA_CDB_RSRC_PLAN_DIRECTIVES contains all current resource plans.
- PDB resource plans are limited to one level and eight consumer groups and cannot have subplans.
- You can find the active CDB resource plan by querying V$RSRC_PLAN with a CON_ID of 1.
- When you plug in a non-CDB as a new PDB, all existing resource plans are migrated as is unless the plan has more than eight consumer groups, has subplans, or is multilevel.
- Imported resource plans from a non-PDB are converted if they violate the resource plan restrictions for a PDB.
- A noncompliant resource plan for an imported non-CDB is saved in DBA_RSRC_PLAN_DIRECTIVES with STATUS='LEGACY'.

Perform Database Replay

- Consolidated Database Replay uses Oracle Database Replay to measure performance of multiple databases in a new server environment.
- The first step in the analysis phase for Database Replay is to identify candidate databases for consolidation into a CDB on a new server.
- For each source database, capture workload data for replay.
- Optionally, you can export AWR snapshots and SQL profiles to optimize performance in the target CDB.
- You need to preprocess each imported workload only once on the target CDB.
- Replay the consolidated workloads multiple times with tuning steps for major performance regression.
- All databases must be flashed back or restored between each replay step.

SELF TEST

The following questions will help you measure your understanding of the material presented in this chapter. Read all the choices carefully because there might be more than one correct answer. Choose all correct answers for each question.

Monitor Operations and Performance in a CDB and PDBs

1. Identify the true statements about initialization parameters in a multitenant environment. (Choose all that apply.)
   A. A subset of parameters set at the container level can be overridden at the PDB level.
   B. Pluggable databases can have parameters that are not set at the container level.
   C. Unplugging a PDB and plugging it back into the same container preserves the customized parameters set in the PDB.
   D. Unplugging a PDB and plugging it into a different container preserves the customized parameters set in the PDB.
2. Which of the following is true about allocating resources between PDBs in a CDB?
   A. Using a minimal allocation plan, the shares allocated to a PDB prevent other PDBs from using those shares even if the PDB is not busy.
   B. Using no resource plan in a CDB environment is the default and lets PDBs compete equally for all resources.
   C. In a minimum/maximum allocation scheme, a PDB can still go over the maximum if no other PDBs are busy.
   D. The "share" amount is the percentage of overall resources that a PDB can use within the CDB.
   E. The tiered allocation plan gives some users in one PDB a higher priority than users in another PDB.

Manage Allocation of Resources Between PDBs and Within a PDB

3. You are importing (plugging in) a non-CDB into a new PDB in an existing container, and the non-CDB has several resource plans. Which of the following conditions will invalidate the imported resource plan? (Choose all that apply.)
   A. The original plan has 12 consumer groups.
   B. The resource allocations are only on the first level.
   C. The imported resource plan has the same name as an existing resource plan.

D. The imported resource plan already has a status of LEGACY.

E. The resource plan directive PARALLEL_SERVER_LIMIT is higher than the value of the CDB initialization parameter PARALLEL_MAX_SERVERS.

F. The number of shares in the original resource plan is more than the total shares of all PDBs already in the container.

4. When you create a new CDB resource manager plan with DBMS_RESOURCE_MANAGER, what is the difference between the procedures UPDATE_CDB_DEFAULT_DIRECTIVE and UPDATE_CDB_AUTOTASK_DIRECTIVE?

A. UPDATE_CDB_AUTOTASK_DIRECTIVE applies only to maintenance operations in PDBs, and UPDATE_CDB_DEFAULT_DIRECTIVE sets the default values for shares, CPU, and parallelism in the PDBs.

B. UPDATE_CDB_AUTOTASK_DIRECTIVE applies only to maintenance operations in the CDB, and UPDATE_CDB_DEFAULT_DIRECTIVE changes the values for all PDBs for shares, CPU, and parallelism in the PDBs.

C. UPDATE_CDB_AUTOTASK_DIRECTIVE applies only to maintenance operations in the CDB, and UPDATE_CDB_DEFAULT_DIRECTIVE sets the default values for shares, CPU, and parallelism in the PDBs.

D. UPDATE_CDB_AUTOTASK_DIRECTIVE applies only to maintenance operations in non-CDBs, and UPDATE_CDB_DEFAULT_DIRECTIVE sets the default values for shares, CPU, and parallelism in the PDBs.

Perform Database Replay

5. Which of the following steps are optional when exporting or importing the workload for a database that is a candidate for multitenant consolidation?

A. Exporting AWR snapshots from every candidate database

B. Exporting SQL tuning sets from the candidate database

C. Capturing and exporting the workload for a candidate database

D. Creating a replay schedule

E. Creating a PDB for each database application

SELF TEST ANSWERS

Monitor Operations and Performance in a CDB and PDBs

1. ☑ **A, C,** and **D.** When you create a PDB, it automatically inherits all of the parameters at the CDB level. A subset of parameters can be set at the PDB level. These parameter values persist even if the PDB is unplugged and plugged back into the same or another container.
☒ **B** is incorrect because there are no parameters at the PDB level that do not exist at the CDB level.

2. ☑ **B.** The default resource allocation in a CDB is none. One PDB can use all CDB resources.
☒ **A, C, D,** and **E** are incorrect. **A** is incorrect because a PDB can use all remaining resources in a CDB even if another PDB with a higher number of shares is not active. **C** is incorrect because a PDB cannot exceed the maximum number of shares even if no other PDBs are busy. **D** is incorrect because shares are relative resource quantities and not percentages. **E** is incorrect because there is no such tiered resource allocation plan across PDBs in a multitenant environment, although the Resource Manager can control resource usage between users in a single PDB.

Manage Allocation of Resources Between PDBs and Within a PDB

3. ☑ **A.** When importing a non-CDB and plugging it into a PDB of an existing container (CDB), any existing resource manager plans must have no more than eight consumer groups, must all be at level 1, and have no subplans.
☒ **B, C, D, E,** and **F** are incorrect. **B** is incorrect because existing resource plans will import just fine with only one level. **C** is incorrect because the resource plans are qualified with the PDB name, and thus there is no name conflict. **D** is incorrect because a non-CDB's resource plan will never have a STATUS of LEGACY since only PDBs can have imported resource plans with that status. **E** is incorrect because an existing non-CDB resource plan will not have a plan directive of PARALLEL_SERVER_LIMIT, which is valid only in a multitenant environment. **F** is incorrect because a non-CDB will not have a resource plan with a share directive.

4. ☑ **C.** UPDATE_CDB_AUTOTASK_DIRECTIVE sets resource manager directives for automated maintenance tasks in the CDB. UPDATE_CDB_DEFAULT_DIRECTIVE sets the default values for directives in PDBs that do not specify these directives: SHARES, UTILIZATION_LIMIT, and PARALLEL_SERVER_LIMIT. Both of these procedures are optional when creating a new resource manager plan.
☒ **A, B,** and **D** are incorrect. **A** is incorrect because maintenance operations occur only at the CDB level. **B** is incorrect because UPDATE_CDB_DEFAULT_DIRECTIVE does not change any existing PDB resource plan directives. **D** is incorrect because these directives are not valid in a non-CDB.

Perform Database Replay

5. ☑ **A** and **B**. You do not need to export AWR snapshots and SQL tuning sets from the source databases, but they would be helpful when tuning the combined workloads in the target CDB.
   ☒ **C, D,** and **E** are incorrect. **C** is incorrect because you cannot use Consolidated Database Replay on a target server without a workload capture. **D** is incorrect because you won't be able to replay the workloads side-by-side in the new CDB without the configured schedule. **E** is incorrect because each candidate database must be converted (if necessary) and plugged into the new CDB as a PDB to test the consolidated workload.

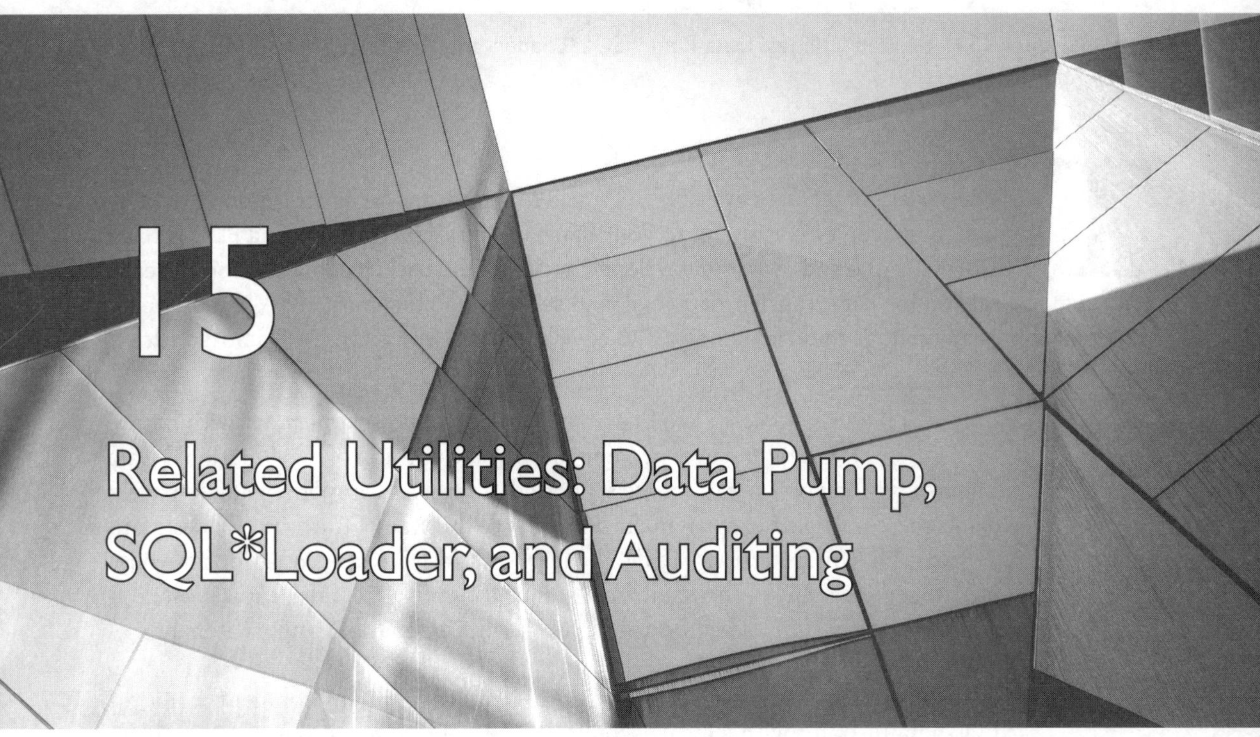

15 Related Utilities: Data Pump, SQL*Loader, and Auditing

CERTIFICATION OBJECTIVES

15.01	Use Data Pump	✓	Two-Minute Drill
15.02	Use SQL*Loader	Q&A	Self Test
15.03	Audit Operations		

The wide variety of features available in Oracle's multitenant architecture don't exist in a vacuum; they won't be as useful to your database infrastructure unless a PDB is truly transparent to the end user, the developer, and even the backup administrators. Therefore, the tools you rely on for data transfer, data load, and security auditing must work just as well in a multitenant environment as they did in non-CDB environments before Oracle Database 12*c*.

First, I'll review Oracle Data Pump and how it seamlessly integrates with both PDBs and non-CDBs and every combination you can think of. Conventional Data Pump export/import operations are supported, as well as transportable tablespace, full database, and schema export/import regardless of the type of the source or destination.

Next, I'll demonstrate how SQL*Loader works as you'd expect as long as you use the service name of the database instance. Both SQL*Loader Express Mode and a pre-12*c* SQL*Loader control file work without change in a multitenant environment.

Finally, I'll review how auditing works in a multitenant environment. For a PDB administrator with a local account, the AUDIT commands work much like before. In a multitenant environment, however, you have the added ability to define auditing actions at the CDB (root) level.

CERTIFICATION OBJECTIVE 15.01

Use Data Pump

Oracle Data Pump has been a great way to transfer tables, indexes, and entire tablespaces between databases since Oracle Database 10*g*. In Oracle Database 12*c*, Data Pump fully supports import and export to and from previous versions of Oracle Database (non-CDBs) and Oracle Database 12*c* non-CDBs and PDBs. Since Data Pump is a logical export and import tool, the only operation not supported in a multitenant environment is import into or export from a container database (CDB$ROOT).

In the following sections, you'll explore many of these combinations, including full database transport over the network. The key to using Data Pump in a multitenant environment is to use the PDB service name as the source or target of the Data Pump operation. In this way, the type of database (non-CDB or PDB) is not a factor in the operation. Figure 15-1 shows several of the scenarios you can use Data Pump for in a multitenant environment.

FIGURE 15-1 Oracle Data Pump scenarios in a multitenant environment

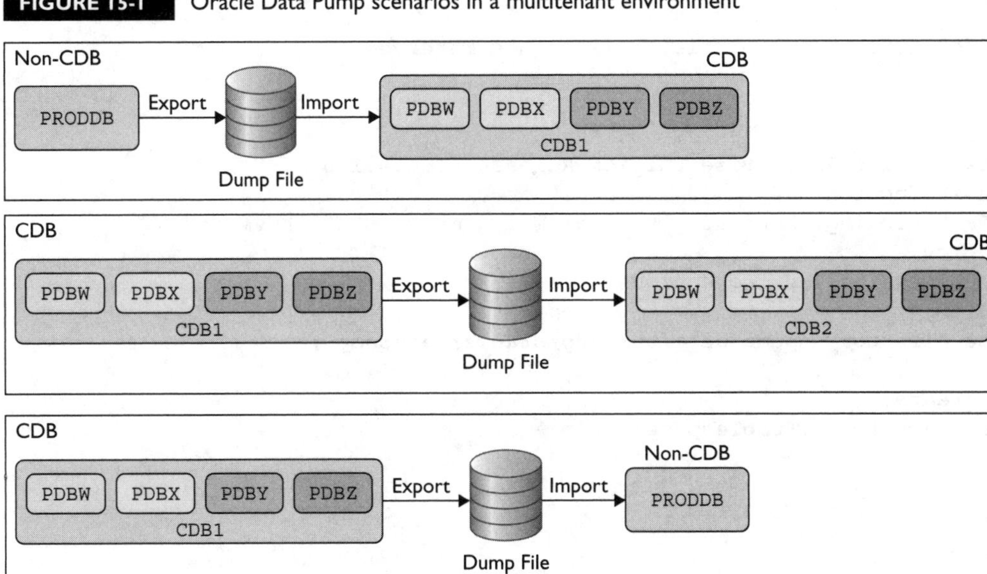

Export from Non-CDB and Import into PDB

Using Data Pump export from a non-CDB to a PDB is an easy way to convert a non-CDB from Oracle Database 11*g* or earlier to a PDB in Oracle Database 12*c* without upgrading the non-CDB to Oracle Database 12*c* and then converting the database to a PDB. If the target PDB does not exist, you must create it first. In this example, you have a non-CDB called HR, and you want to migrate the users and tablespaces to a PDB in the container CDB01.

The basic steps are as follows:

1. Create the Oracle and OS directory for the Data Pump dump file.
2. Export the database.
3. Create the target PDB if it does not already exist.
4. Import the database from the dump file into the PDB.

```
[oracle@tettnang oracle]$ cd /u01/app/oracle
[oracle@tettnang oracle]$ mkdir datapump
[oracle@tettnang oracle]$ cd
[oracle@tettnang ~]$ . oraenv
ORACLE_SID = [cdb01] ? hr
The Oracle base remains unchanged with value /u01/app/oracle
[oracle@tettnang ~]$ sqlplus / as sysdba
```

```
SQL*Plus: Release 12.1.0.1.0 Production on Tue Jun 24 07:44:25 2014

Copyright (c) 1982, 2013, Oracle.  All rights reserved.


Connected to:
Oracle Database 12c Enterprise Edition Release 12.1.0.1.0 -
     64bit Production
With the Partitioning, Automatic Storage Management, OLAP, Advanced
     Analytics
and Real Application Testing options

SQL> create directory dpump as '/u01/app/oracle/datapump';

Directory created.
SQL> select name from v$tablespace;

NAME
------------------------------
SYSTEM
SYSAUX
UNDOTBS1
USERS
TEMP
ACCT_PAY
ACCT_REC

7 rows selected.

SQL> quit
Disconnected from Oracle Database 12c Enterprise Edition
     Release 12.1.0.1.0 - 64bit Production
With the Partitioning, Automatic Storage Management, OLAP, Advanced
     Analyticsand Real Application Testing options
[oracle@tettnang ~]$ expdp rjb@hr full=y directory=dpump dumpfile=hr_exp.dmp

Export: Release 12.1.0.1.0 - Production on Tue Jun 24 07:47:08 2014

Copyright (c) 1982, 2013, Oracle and/or its affiliates.  All rights reserved.
Password:

Connected to: Oracle Database 12c Enterprise Edition
     Release 12.1.0.1.0 - 64bit Production
With the Partitioning, Automatic Storage Management, OLAP, Advanced
Analytics and Real Application Testing options
Starting "RJB"."SYS_EXPORT_FULL_01":  rjb/********@hr full=y
     directory=dpump dumpfile=hr_exp.dmp
```

```
Estimate in progress using BLOCKS method...
Processing object type DATABASE_EXPORT/EARLY_OPTIONS/VIEWS_AS_TABLES/TABLE_DATA
Processing object type DATABASE_EXPORT/NORMAL_OPTIONS/TABLE_DATA
Processing object type DATABASE_EXPORT/NORMAL_OPTIONS/VIEWS_AS_TABLES/TABLE_DATA
Processing object type DATABASE_EXPORT/SCHEMA/TABLE/TABLE_DATA
Total estimation using BLOCKS method: 4.890 MB
Processing object type DATABASE_EXPORT/PRE_SYSTEM_IMPCALLOUT/MARKER
Processing object type DATABASE_EXPORT/PRE_INSTANCE_IMPCALLOUT/MARKER
Processing object type DATABASE_EXPORT/TABLESPACE
Processing object type DATABASE_EXPORT/PROFILE
. . .
. . exported "SYS"."NACL$_WALLET_EXP"                          0 KB       0 rows
. . exported "SYSTEM"."SCHEDULER_JOB_ARGS"                     0 KB       0 rows
. . exported "SCOTT"."DEPT"                                6.007 KB       4 rows
. . exported "SCOTT"."EMP"                                 8.757 KB      14 rows
. . exported "SCOTT"."SALGRADE"                            5.937 KB       5 rows
. . exported "SCOTT"."BONUS"                                   0 KB       0 rows
Master table "RJB"."SYS_EXPORT_FULL_01" successfully loaded/unloaded
******************************************************************************
Dump file set for RJB.SYS_EXPORT_FULL_01 is:
  /u01/app/oracle/datapump/hr_exp.dmp
Job "RJB"."SYS_EXPORT_FULL_01" successfully completed at
     Tue Jun 24 07:49:10 2014 elapsed 0 00:01:55

[oracle@tettnang ~]$ . oraenv
ORACLE_SID = [hr] ? cdb01
The Oracle base remains unchanged with value /u01/app/oracle
[oracle@tettnang ~]$ sqlplus / as sysdba

SQL*Plus: Release 12.1.0.1.0 Production on Tue Jun 24 07:51:28 2014

Copyright (c) 1982, 2013, Oracle.  All rights reserved.


Connected to:
Oracle Database 12c Enterprise Edition Release 12.1.0.1.0 - 64bit Production
With the Partitioning, Automatic Storage Management, OLAP, Advanced Analytics
and Real Application Testing options

SQL> create pluggable database hr admin user hr_admin
  2       identified by hr_admin49 roles=(connect);

Pluggable database created.

SQL> alter session set container=hr;
```

```
Session altered.

SQL> alter pluggable database hr open;

Pluggable database altered.

SQL> create directory dpump as '/u01/app/oracle/datapump';

Directory created.
SQL> quit

[oracle@tettnang ~]$ impdp rjb@hr full=y directory=dpump dumpfile=hr_exp.dmp

Import: Release 12.1.0.1.0 - Production on Tue Jun 24 08:05:10 2014

Copyright (c) 1982, 2013, Oracle and/or its affiliates.  All rights reserved.
Password:

Connected to: Oracle Database 12c Enterprise Edition
    Release 12.1.0.1.0 - 64bit Production
With the Partitioning, Automatic Storage Management, OLAP,
    Advanced Analytics and Real Application Testing options
Master table "RJB"."SYS_IMPORT_FULL_01" successfully loaded/unloaded
Starting "RJB"."SYS_IMPORT_FULL_01":  rjb/********@hr full=y
    directory=dpump dumpfile=hr_exp.dmp
Processing object type DATABASE_EXPORT/PRE_SYSTEM_IMPCALLOUT/MARKER
Processing object type DATABASE_EXPORT/PRE_INSTANCE_IMPCALLOUT/MARKER
Processing object type DATABASE_EXPORT/TABLESPACE
. . .
Processing object type DATABASE_EXPORT/AUDIT_UNIFIED/AUDIT_POLICY_ENABLE
Processing object type DATABASE_EXPORT/AUDIT
Processing object type DATABASE_EXPORT/POST_SYSTEM_IMPCALLOUT/MARKER
Job "RJB"."SYS_IMPORT_FULL_01" completed with 21 error(s) at Tue Jun 24 08:06:41
2014 elapsed 0 00:01:16

[oracle@tettnang ~]$
```

During the import, any tablespaces that already exist will not be re-created, as in any Data Pump job. To verify that the new tablespaces were created, execute the following query:

```
[oracle@tettnang ~]$ sqlplus rjb@hr

SQL*Plus: Release 12.1.0.1.0 Production on Tue Jun 24 08:10:03 2014

Copyright (c) 1982, 2013, Oracle.  All rights reserved.
```

```
Enter password:
Last Successful login time: Tue Jun 24 2014 08:05:19 -05:00

Connected to:
Oracle Database 12c Enterprise Edition Release 12.1.0.1.0 - 64bit Production
With the Partitioning, Automatic Storage Management, OLAP, Advanced Analytics
and Real Application Testing options

SQL> select name from v$tablespace;

NAME
------------------------------
UNDOTBS1
SYSTEM
SYSAUX
TEMP
USERS
ACCT_PAY
ACCT_REC

7 rows selected.

SQL>
```

In the target PDB, all users from the non-CDB are re-created as local users in the new PDB.

Export and Import Between PDBs

Exporting from an existing PDB to a new PDB, either in the same container or in a new container, follows most of the same steps as in the previous section. If the target PDB does not exist, you create it ahead of time in the target CDB. For both the source and target PDBs, you need to create a directory object for the dump file. The directory object must be at the PDB, not CDB, level because the new PDB will not have visibility to that directory object; as you'd expect, the same directory name can exist at the CDB level and in every PDB.

When you export from an existing PDB, you may have common users who own objects in the source PDB. That user and their objects won't be imported successfully into a new target PDB because the Data Pump import is at the PDB level and you can't create local users in a PDB with the C## prefix as part of Data Pump import.

For example, if an existing PDB's common user C##RJB owns objects, the import to a new PDB in a different CDB without the common user C##RJB will fail with this error message:

```
ORA-65094: invalid local user or role name
```

To fix this issue, you can do one of two things. The first option is to create the same common user in the target CDB before starting the Data Pump import. If you don't want to have the same common user in the target CDB, use the REMAP_SCHEMA option on the **impdp** command line to create a local user who will temporarily or permanently own the objects from the common user in the source PDB:

```
impdp rjb@hr full=y directory= . . . remap_schema=c##rjb:jan_d
```

On a similar note, if you have tablespace name conflicts and you don't want the source PDB's objects to end up in the tablespace with the same name, use the REMAP_TABLESPACE option.

Export from PDB and Import into Non-CDB

An export from an existing PDB to a non-PDB operates as expected, and you can perform all types of export operations: full, conventional, schema, and transportable. The only exception is as you'd expect: You cannot import a common user's objects into a non-CDB, and you'll get the same error message as if you were trying to import another PDB's common users into a new PDB. The workaround is the same: Use the REMAP_SCHEMA option.

If you are importing into an Oracle 11*g* non-CDB, however, you *will* get the common users' schemas and objects imported successfully. The # character is valid in schema names; therefore, you can create the user C##RJB in an Oracle 11*g* database, and it will be treated no differently than any other user in that database since the multitenant option exists only in Oracle Database 12*c* and newer.

Full Transportable Export and Import

As you recall, one of the new features of Oracle Database 12*c* is full transportable export and import. This operation is more like a transportable tablespace operation than a Data Pump operation: The **expdp** command creates only the metadata for the database, and the actual datafiles are copied or moved as is to the target destination.

In a multitenant environment, you can leverage full transportable export/import both to move tablespaces quickly and to avoid upgrading an existing database in place; instead, you use an existing PDB or create a new PDB and transport the datafiles from an 11.2.0.3 database (or newer) to the PDB.

Of course, since full transportable export/import would normally include the SYSTEM and SYSAUX tablespaces, those are not included in a transportable import operation if the target is a PDB.

Transporting a Database Over the Network

When using transportable export/import over the network to transport a database into a PDB, you follow these steps:

1. Create the new PDB in the target container.
2. Create a database link in the target PDB to the source database with the appropriate permissions granted to the user defined in the database link.
3. Change the status of the nonsystem tablespaces (SYSTEM and SYSAUX) in the source database to READ ONLY.
4. Copy the datafiles from the source location to the target location accessible to the new PDB.
5. Convert the datafiles if necessary (for endian conversion).
6. Import into the target database.

   Change the source database's tablespaces back to READ WRITE.

   Your **impdp** operation will look something like this:

```
impdp rjb@hr full=y network_link=remote_hrdb
transportable=always
      transport_datafiles=. . . version=12
```

In Oracle Database 11*g* Data Pump, you could perform import/export over the network as well, and the same applies to Oracle Database 12*c* Data Pump in a multitenant scenario. No dump file is required, saving both time and disk space. Only the metadata file for the source database is created on the file system.

CERTIFICATION OBJECTIVE 15.02

Use SQL*Loader

Using SQL*Loader in a multitenant environment is just as easy as using SQL*Loader in a non-CDB environment. Once again, the key to ensuring success is to specify the service name of the new or existing PDB when loading data into one or more tables.

As of Oracle Database 12*c*, you have the option to use SQL*Loader *Express Mode*. Express Mode lets you load a flat file with typical delimiters into a database table without having to create a control file.

In the following example, you'll use SQL*Loader Express Mode to create a new table NEW_EMP from a delimited text file in a PDB and create it in the HR schema. Here is the definition of the NEW_EMP table and the text file **new_emp.dat** that you want to load into the table:

```
SQL> create table new_emp
  2      (id        number,
  3       lastname varchar2(30),
  4       firstname varchar2(30),
  5       zipcode  number);

Table created.
SQL>

301,Doe,John,60010
302,Deer,Jane,50505
310,Xavier,Zack,53593
```

The command-line format for SQL*Loader Express Mode is minimal unless you want to override any options:

```
[oracle@tettnang ~]$ sqlldr rjb@hr table=hr.new_emp
Password:

SQL*Loader: Release 12.1.0.1.0 - Production on Tue Jun 24 10:46:14 2014

Copyright (c) 1982, 2013, Oracle and/or its affiliates.  All rights
reserved.

Express Mode Load, Table: HR.NEW_EMP
Path used:      External Table, DEGREE_OF_PARALLELISM=AUTO

Table HR.NEW_EMP:
  3 Rows successfully loaded.
```

```
Check the log files:
  hr.log
  hr_%p.log_xt
for more information about the load.
[oracle@tettnang ~]$
```

After the SQL*Loader operation is complete, you can look at the file **hr.log** to see the actual control file and INSERT statement that SQL*Loader used to populate the table:

```
. . .
Generated control file for possible reuse:
OPTIONS(EXTERNAL_TABLE=EXECUTE, TRIM=LRTRIM)
LOAD DATA
INFILE '(null)'
APPEND
INTO TABLE HR.NEW_EMP
FIELDS TERMINATED BY ","
(
  ID,
  LASTNAME,
  FIRSTNAME,
  ZIPCODE
)
End of generated control file for possible reuse.
. . .
CREATE TABLE "SYS_SQLLDR_X_EXT_NEW_EMP"
(
  "ID" NUMBER,
  "LASTNAME" VARCHAR2(30),
  "FIRSTNAME" VARCHAR2(30),
  "ZIPCODE" NUMBER
)
ORGANIZATION external
(
  TYPE oracle_loader
  DEFAULT DIRECTORY SYS_SQLLDR_XT_TMPDIR_00000
  ACCESS PARAMETERS
  (
    RECORDS DELIMITED BY NEWLINE CHARACTERSET US7ASCII
    BADFILE 'SYS_SQLLDR_XT_TMPDIR_00000':'new_emp.bad'
    LOGFILE 'hr_%p.log_xt'
    READSIZE 1048576
    FIELDS TERMINATED BY "," LRTRIM
    REJECT ROWS WITH ALL NULL FIELDS
    (
      "ID" CHAR(255),
```

```
        "LASTNAME" CHAR(255),
        "FIRSTNAME" CHAR(255),
        "ZIPCODE" CHAR(255)
    )
  )
  location
  (
    'new_emp.dat'
  )
)REJECT LIMIT UNLIMITED

executing INSERT statement to load database table HR.NEW_EMP

INSERT /*+ append parallel(auto) */ INTO HR.NEW_EMP
(
  ID,
  LASTNAME,
  FIRSTNAME,
  ZIPCODE
)
SELECT
  "ID",
  "LASTNAME",
  "FIRSTNAME",
  "ZIPCODE"
FROM "SYS_SQLLDR_X_EXT_NEW_EMP"

dropping external table "SYS_SQLLDR_X_EXT_NEW_EMP"

Table HR.NEW_EMP:
  3 Rows successfully loaded.
```

CERTIFICATION OBJECTIVE 15.03

Audit Operations

Auditing actions in a multitenant environment are two-tiered much like resource management. Setting up audit policies at the CDB level applies to all PDBs; for specific PDBs, you can set up policies that apply only to that PDB. To create auditing policies in a multitenant environment, you must have the AUDIT_ADMIN or DBA role to use the CREATE AUDIT POLICY command. Once the policies have been created, you enable or disable auditing using the AUDIT or NOAUDIT command as you would in previous versions of Oracle Database.

Creating the Audit Policy

The audit policy itself can be created at the CDB level or on individual PDBs. You can specify three options with the CREATE AUDIT POLICY command:

- **Privilege** Audits events that use the specified system privileges
- **Action** Audits DDL actions such as CREATE TABLE or DROP INDEX
- **Role** Audits the use of any system or object privileges granted to the specified role

You can mix and match! One audit policy can trigger an audit only when a specific system privilege is invoked, and another can encompass all three options, as in this example at the CDB level:

```
[oracle@tettnang ~]$ sqlplus / as sysdba

SQL*Plus: Release 12.1.0.1.0 Production on Tue Jun 24 11:26:31
2014

Copyright (c) 1982, 2013, Oracle.  All rights reserved.


Connected to:
Oracle Database 12c Enterprise Edition Release 12.1.0.1.0 -
64bit Production
With the Partitioning, Automatic Storage Management, OLAP,
Advanced Analytics
and Real Application Testing options

SQL> create audit policy cdb_global_privact
  2     privileges alter tablespace
  3     actions drop index, drop sequence
  4     roles dba;

Audit policy created.

SQL>
```

Since this policy was created at the CDB level, it therefore applies to all PDBs. It only exists and does not perform any logging right away; you have to enable it first, and you'll see how to do that in the next section.

You can also fine-tune the audit policy to log an audit record for every statement, per session, or per instance (in a RAC environment). This can help keep the number of audit rows low when you're not concerned if a user creates one or one thousand tables within the same session, for example. You use the WHEN *audit_condition* EVALUATE PER clause to specify how often an auditable action is recorded for a particular session, as in this example where the user HR triggers a single audit event per session whenever the HR user creates a table, regardless of how many tables HR creates in one session:

```
SQL> create audit policy audit_hr_new_tables
  2      actions create table
  3      when 'sys_context(''USERENV'',''SESSION_USER'')=''HR'''
  4      evaluate per session;

Audit policy created.

SQL>
```

Enabling the Audit Policy

Once the audit policy is in place, you must enable it. You can enable it for all users, a list of users, or a single user. In a multitenant environment, you can apply the audit policy globally or for one or more PDBs. In this example, you enable the CDB_GLOBAL_PRIVACT audit policy just for the RJB user in the HR PDB:

```
SQL>  audit policy cdb_global_privact by rjb;
Audit succeeded.
SQL>
```

Turning off any audit policy is as easy as you'd expect by using the NOAUDIT POLICY command:

```
SQL> noaudit policy cdb_global_privact;
Noaudit succeeded.
SQL>
```

Viewing Audit Policies

Having a flexible and robust audit policy infrastructure doesn't help unless you can review not only the policies themselves but also the events that trigger the policies. Use the data dictionary table AUDIT_UNIFIED_POLICIES at either the CDB or PDB level to review the policies that exist (but are not necessarily enabled):

```
SQL> select policy_name,audit_option
  2  from audit_unified_policies
  3  where policy_name like 'CDB%' or policy_name like 'AUDIT_HR%';

POLICY_NAME                    AUDIT_OPTION
------------------------------ ----------------------------------------
CDB_GLOBAL_PRIVACT             ALTER TABLESPACE
CDB_GLOBAL_PRIVACT             DROP INDEX
CDB_GLOBAL_PRIVACT             DROP SEQUENCE
AUDIT_HR_NEW_TABLES            CREATE TABLE
CDB_GLOBAL_PRIVACT             DBA

SQL>
```

To actually see which policies are currently enabled, use the view AUDIT_UNIFIED_ENABLED_POLICIES, as in this example:

```
SQL> alter session set container=hr;

Session altered.

SQL> select user_name,policy_name,enabled_opt,success,failure
  2  from audit_unified_enabled_policies;

USER_NAME       POLICY_NAME                    ENABLED_ SUC FAI
--------------- ------------------------------ -------- --- ---
RJB             CDB_GLOBAL_PRIVACT             BY       YES YES
ALL USERS       ORA_SECURECONFIG               BY       YES YES

SQL>
```

Note that in the HR container, the policy CDB_GLOBAL_PRIVACT is enabled for the RJB user. The SUCCESS and FAILURE columns indicate whether the auditing occurs upon success of the executed command or upon failure, respectively.

Viewing Audited Events

Finally, to view audit records in the HR container, use the data dictionary view UNIFIED_AUDIT_TRAIL:

```
SQL> select dbusername,unified_audit_policies,
  2      action_name,event_timestamp
  3  from UNIFIED_AUDIT_TRAIL
  4  where event_timestamp > systimestamp-(1/24);

DBUSERNAME   UNIFIED_AUDIT_PO ACTION_NAME         EVENT_TIMESTAMP
------------ ---------------- ------------------- -------------------------
SYS                           CREATE AUDIT POLICY 24-JUN-14 05.46.06.036264 AM
SYS                           AUDIT               24-JUN-14 05.45.18.451898 AM
SYS                           NOAUDIT             24-JUN-14 05.07.17.775524 AM
HR           ORA_SECURECONFIG LOGON               24-JUN-14 05.47.42.119372 AM
HR           ORA_SECURECONFIG LOGOFF              24-JUN-14 05.49.54.046880 AM

SQL>
```

During the last hour, the SYS user created, turned on, and then turned off an audit policy. The HR user logged on and logged off with no other auditable events occurring.

The view UNIFIED_AUDIT_TRAIL contains rows specifically for the current container, even the root container (CDB$ROOT). If you want to see audit records across all containers including the root container, use the view CDB_UNIFIED_AUDIT_TRAIL instead.

CERTIFICATION SUMMARY

In an Oracle 12*c* multitenant environment, there are many familiar tools from previous versions of Oracle Database that work transparently regardless of whether the database is a CDB, PDB, or non-CDB. Many of these tools have been enhanced in a multitenant environment to make management easy and to make the availability of the database even higher.

Data Pump export/import supports nearly all combinations of non-CDBs and PDBs as the source and the target. You can export from a non-CDB and import into a PDB as a way to upgrade a database to 12.1.0.1 and move the database to a multitenant environment at the same time. You can move non-CDBs from previous versions of Oracle to non-CDBs in Oracle Database 12.1.0.1 as long as the source database version is 11.2.0.3 or newer. PDBs can be exported and imported to another

PDB within the same container or to another container. For each of these options, you can export and import a single tablespace, a schema, a full logical export, or a full database in transportable mode. Using transportable mode is extremely fast primarily because you're creating the metadata of only the source database and either moving or copying the datafiles from the source database to the non-CDB or new PDB. For scenarios when the only method to copy files is over the network, you can create a database link to the source database and perform a full transportable export without a dump file.

The SQL*Loader tool works the same as before as long as you use the service name when connecting to the database. Additional features in SQL*Loader make it easy to load a text file with table data into an existing PDB table or into a non-CDB without using a control file.

Security is always the utmost concern for a DBA. Auditing user events and actions is even more critical in a multitenant environment. Not only do you want to audit events across all containers including the root container, but you may want to have more targeted auditing at the PDB level. The enhanced auditing capabilities using the CREATE AUDIT POLICY command and the familiar AUDIT command make this easy in a multitenant environment.

TWO-MINUTE DRILL

Use Data Pump

- Data Pump is primarily a logical export/import tool with the exception of transportable tablespaces and full transportable exports.
- Using the database instance's service name is the key to shielding the export/import process from the details of the CDB.
- Data Pump export/import supports non-CDB to PDB, PDB to PDB, and 11.2.0.3/4 export to non-CDB or PDB import.
- You can export and import schemas, tablespaces, full databases, transportable tablespaces, and transportable databases.
- The source database needs a directory object created for the Data Pump export; Data Pump import will create a temporary directory object if not specified.
- Full transportable export/import from a non-CDB to a PDB copies all tablespaces except for SYSTEM and SYSAUX.
- Existing tablespaces will not be dropped and re-created in a Data Pump import.
- For common users with objects in a Data Pump export from a non-CDB or PDB in Oracle Database 12.1.0.1, the **impdp** command line must include an REMAP_SCHEMA clause to ensure that schemas starting with C## will be imported into the target database.
- Full transportable export/import over the network requires a database link from the target database to the source database.
- During a network export, there is no dump file, but a metadata file containing the database's DDL must be created for use by the import process.

Use SQL*Loader

- SQL*Loader works like in previous versions of Oracle Database when you use the database's service name.
- SQL*Loader Express Mode can load a comma-delimited text file into an existing table without a control file.

- ❑ The output of an SQL*Loader Express Mode session includes the control file (if needed later), the INSERT command used to load the data, and the table definition re-created as an external table definition.

Audit Operations

- ❑ Audit policies have three basic options: privileges, actions, and roles.
- ❑ A single audit policy can have any combination of privileges, actions, or roles.
- ❑ The WHEN . . . EVALUATE PER clause can fine-tune the audit trigger to limit audit records to a session, user, or instance.
- ❑ Audit policies can be global (at the CDB level) or specific to one PDB (local).
- ❑ After creating the audit policy, you can enable and disable it with the AUDIT POLICY and NOAUDIT POLICY commands.
- ❑ Use the data dictionary view AUDIT_UNIFIED_POLICIES to view policies and their contents.
- ❑ Use the data dictionary view AUDIT_UNIFIED_ENABLED_POLICIES to see policies and their status at either the CDB or PDB level.
- ❑ The UNIFIED_AUDIT_TRAIL view shows one row for each policy triggered by a single user.
- ❑ The CDB_UNIFIED_AUDIT_TRAIL view shows audit actions across the CDB and all PDBs.

SELF TEST

The following questions will help you measure your understanding of the material presented in this chapter. Read all the choices carefully because there might be more than one correct answer. Choose all correct answers for each question.

Use Data Pump

1. Which of the following operations are supported with Oracle Database 12*c* Data Pump export/import in a multitenant environment? (Choose all that apply.)
   A. You must always upgrade a pre-12.1.0.1 database to version 12.1.0.1 before performing an export and importing to a 12.1.0.1 non-CDB.
   B. An Oracle 11.2.0.4 database can be exported and imported into an Oracle 12.1.0.1 PDB as a full transportable database operation.
   C. Only PDBs can be exported and imported into another PDB.
   D. Only PDBs can be exported and imported into the root container (CDB$ROOT).
   E. Only non-CDBs can be imported into another non-CDB.
   F. You can export a PDB and import it into a different PDB within the same CDB.

Use SQL*Loader

2. Your SQL*Loader Express Mode job runs, is able to find the destination table, but fails with zero rows loaded. Which of the following is a possible cause?
   A. The service name was not specified in the **sqlldr** command.
   B. The **sqlldr** job cannot write to the default directory to create the log file containing the control file.
   C. There are no parallel slaves available to load the table in APPEND mode.
   D. The delimiter in the text file is a colon, but the default is a comma.

Audit Operations

3. You are creating an audit policy that will audit all users who might create indexes in another schema. Which options within CREATE AUDIT POLICY will work the best to efficiently audit this user action?
   A. PRIVILEGES CREATE ANY INDEX
   B. ACTIONS DROP TABLE
   C. ROLES DBA
   D. PRIVILEGES CREATE ANY INDEX, DROP ANY INDEX, ALTER ANY INDEX
   E. ACTIONS CREATE ANY INDEX

SELF TEST ANSWERS

Use Data Pump

1. ☑ **B** and **F**. You can perform an export of any type (schema, tablespace, full transportable) from any database version 11.2.0.3 or newer and import it into a PDB. Also, you can use Data Pump export/import with the full transportable option to copy a PDB within the same CDB.
   ☒ **A, C, D,** and **E** are incorrect. **A** is incorrect because you do not need to upgrade a database before using Data Pump export/import as long as the version of Oracle Database is 11.2.0.3 or newer. **C** is incorrect because you can always import a non-CDB into a new PDB as long as you use the service name when connecting to the PDB. **D** is incorrect because you cannot use Data Pump import into the root container of a CDB. **E** is incorrect because non-CDBs can be imported into another non-CDB or a PDB as long as the source database version is 11.2.0.3 or newer.

Use SQL*Loader

2. ☑ **D.** If you specify only the target PDB (with the service name) and the target table name in the **sqlldr** command line, the default temporary control file generated uses a comma (,) as the field delimiter in each line of the input datafile. If your delimiter is anything else, you'll have to add the TERMINATED_BY parameter on the command line.
   ☒ **A, B,** and **C** are incorrect. **A** is incorrect because SQL*Loader wouldn't be able to locate the table without specifying the service name and username on the **sqlldr** command line. **B** is incorrect because **sqlldr** would terminate immediately if the default file system was not writable for log files. **C** is incorrect because SQL*Loader does not have to run in APPEND or PARALLEL mode regardless of whether you're using SQL*Loader Express Mode.

Audit Operations

3. ☑ **A.** Using the PRIVILEGES CREATE ANY INDEX clause in CREATE AUDIT POLICY will ensure that only actions by users who create indexes in other schemas will be recorded in the audit trail.
   ☒ **B, C, D,** and **E** are incorrect. **B** is incorrect because dropping a table has nothing to do with creating indexes on tables in other schemas. **C** is incorrect because even though the DBA role contains the CREATE ANY INDEX system privilege, there are dozens of other privileges in the DBA role that do not need to be audited in this scenario. **D** is incorrect because only creating the index needs to be audited. **E** is incorrect because CREATE ANY INDEX is not an action; it's a system privilege.

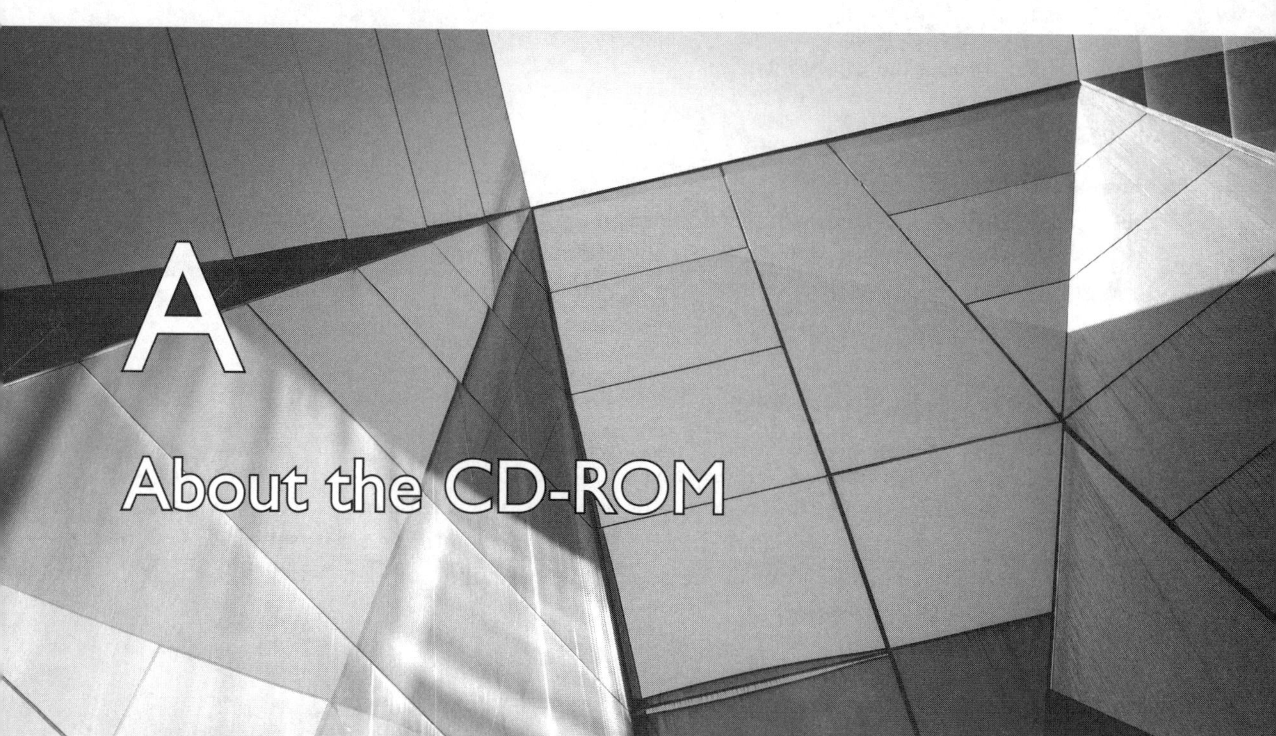

A

About the CD-ROM

The CD-ROM included with this book comes complete with Total Tester customizable practice exam software and a PDF copy of the book.

System Requirements

The software requires Windows XP or higher and 30MB of hard disk space for full installation, in addition to a current or prior major release of Chrome, Firefox, Internet Explorer, or Safari. To run, the screen resolution must be set to 1024 × 768 or higher. The PDF copy of the book requires Adobe Acrobat, Adobe Reader, or Adobe Digital Editions.

Total Tester Premium Practice Exam Software

Total Tester provides you with a simulation of the live exam. You can also create custom exams from selected certification objectives or chapters. You can further customize the number of questions and time allowed.

The exams can be taken in either Practice Mode or Exam Mode. Practice Mode provides an assistance window with hints, references to the book, explanations of the correct and incorrect answers, and the option to check your answers as you take the test. Exam Mode provides a simulation of the actual exam. The number of questions, the types of questions, and the time allowed are intended to be an accurate representation of the exam environment. Both Practice Mode and Exam Mode provide an overall grade and a grade broken down by certification objectives.

To take a test, launch the program and select the exam suite from the Installed Question Packs list. You can then select Practice Mode, Exam Mode, or Custom Mode. After making your selection, click Start Exam to begin.

Installing and Running Total Tester Premium Practice Exam Software

From the main screen, you may install the Total Tester by clicking the Total Tester Practice Exams button. This will begin the installation process and place an icon on your desktop and in your Start menu. To run Total Tester, navigate to Start | (All) Programs | Total Seminars, or double-click the icon on your desktop.

To uninstall the Total Tester software, go to Start | Settings | Control Panel | Add/Remove Programs (XP) or Programs And Features (Vista/7/8), and then select the Total Tester program. Select Remove, and Windows will completely uninstall the software.

PDF Copy of the Book

The entire contents of the book are provided in a PDF on the CD-ROM. This file is viewable on your computer and many portable devices. Adobe Acrobat, Adobe Reader, or Adobe Digital Editions is required to view the file on your computer. A link to Adobe's web site, where you can download and install Adobe Reader, has been included on the CD-ROM.

Note: **For more information on Adobe Reader and to check for the most recent version of the software, visit Adobe's web site at www.adobe.com and search for the free Adobe Reader or look for Adobe Reader on the product page. Adobe Digital Editions can also be downloaded from the Adobe web site.**

To view the PDF copy of the book on a portable device, copy the PDF file to your computer from the CD-ROM, and then copy the file to your portable device using a USB or other connection. Adobe offers a mobile version of Adobe Reader, the Adobe Reader mobile app, which currently supports iOS and Android. For customers using Adobe Digital Editions and an iPad, you may have to download and install a separate reader program on your device. The Adobe web site has a list of recommended applications, and McGraw-Hill Education recommends the Bluefire Reader.

Technical Support

Technical Support information is provided in the following sections by feature.

Total Seminars Technical Support

For questions regarding the Total Tester software or operation of the CD-ROM, visit www.totalsem.com or e-mail support@totalsem.com.

McGraw-Hill Education Content Support

For questions regarding the PDF copy of the book, e-mail techsolutions@mhedu.com or visit http://mhp.softwareassist.com.

For questions regarding book content, e-mail customer.service@mheducation.com. For customers outside the United States, e-mail international_cs@mheducation.com.

ACID Atomicity, consistency, isolation, and durability. Four characteristics that a relational database must be able to maintain for transactions.

ADDM Automatic Database Diagnostic Monitor. A tool that generates performance tuning reports based on snapshots in the Automatic Workload Repository (AWR).

ADR Automatic diagnostic repository. The default location for the alert log, trace files, and other information useful for fault finding. An always-on facility that captures errors in trace and dump files the first and subsequent times they occur.

ADRCI The automatic diagnostic repository (ADR) command-line interface accessed using the **adrci** command.

AES Advanced Encryption Standard. A widely used data encryption method.

AL16UTF16 A Unicode fixed-width, 2-byte character set, commonly specified for the NLS character set used for the NVARCHAR2, NCHAR, and NCLOB data types.

alias In Oracle Net, a pointer to a connect string. An alias must be resolved to the address of a listener and the name of a service or instance.

ANSI American National Standards Institute. A U.S. body that defines a number of standards relevant to computing.

API Application programming interface. A defined method for manipulating data—for example, a set of PL/SQL procedures in a package written to perform a related set of tasks.

ARBn Background processes that perform extent movement between disks in an Automatic Storage Management (ASM) disk group.

ASA Automatic Segment Advisor. An Oracle advisory tool that can recommend segments (tables or indexes) that are candidates for segment shrink.

ASCII American Standard Code for Information Interchange. A standard (with many variations) for coding letters and other characters as bytes.

ASH Active Session History. A category of information in the AWR that records details of session activity.

ASM Automatic Storage Management. A logical volume manager (LVM) provided with the Oracle database.

asmcmd A command-line utility used to query and maintain objects in an ASM disk group.

ASSM Automatic segment space management. The method of managing space within segments by use of bitmaps.

attribute One element of a tuple (aka a column or a field).

AWR Automatic Workload Repository. A set of tables in the SYSAUX tablespace, populated with tuning data gathered by the MMON process.

background process A process that is part of the instance that is launched at startup.

BFILE A large object data type that is stored as an operating system file. The value in the table column is a pointer to the file.

bind variable A named variable in a SQL statement that receives a value from a user process at statement execution time.

BLOB Binary large object. A LOB data type for binary data such as photographs and video clips.

block The units of storage into which datafiles are formatted. The size can be 2KB, 4KB, 8KB, 16KB, 32KB, or 64KB. Some platforms will not permit all these sizes.

BMR Block media recovery. An RMAN feature that recovers individual blocks instead of entire database objects to save time during recovery.

CDB_xxx views Data dictionary views that include metadata across all containers in a container database. Similar to the corresponding DBA_xxx views but has an additional column CON_ID to identify which container this row applies to.

CDB$ROOT The root container in a multitenant environment. All other pluggable databases share the resources defined in CDB$ROOT.

character set The encoding system for representing data within bytes. Different character sets can store different characters and may not be suitable for all languages. Unicode character sets can store any character.

check constraint A simple rule enforced by the database that restricts values that can be entered into a column.

checkpoint An event that forces the DBW*n* (database writer) process to write all dirty buffers from the database buffer cache to the datafiles.

CKPT The checkpoint process. The background process responsible for recording the current redo byte address—the point at which the DBW*n* has written changed data blocks to disk—and for signaling checkpoints, which force DBW*n* to write all changed blocks to disk immediately.

client-server architecture
A processing paradigm in which the application is divided into client software that interacts with the user and server software that interacts with the data.

CLOB Character large object. A LOB data type for character data, such as text documents stored in the database character set.

cluster A hardware environment in which more than one computer shares access to storage. A Real Application Cluster (RAC) database consists of several instances on several computers opening one database on a shared storage device.

column An element of a row. Tables are two-dimensional structures, divided horizontally into rows and vertically into columns.

commit To make a change to data permanent.

common privileges A system or object privilege granted to a common user in a multitenant environment and is therefore in effect for that user in all containers.

common profile A database profile that exists for all current and future pluggable databases in a CDB.

common role A database role that is granted to a common user and therefore is available to that user in all containers. Common roles begin with C## or c##.

common user A user account in a container database (CDB) that exists across all pluggable databases in a container database (CDB). The same user may have different privileges in each PDB. Non-Oracle-created common users begin with C## or c##.

complete recovery Following a restore of damaged database files, a complete recovery applies all redos to bring the database up to date with no loss of data.

connect identifier An Oracle Net alias.

CONNECT role A preseeded role retained only for backward compatibility. Oracle now adopts a minimal security policy at installation and database creation, allowing administrators better control over database security. Granting the CREATE SESSION privilege is the preferred way to allow users to connect to the database instance.

connect string The database connection details needed to establish a session: the address of the listener, the port number, and the service or instance name.

consistent backup A backup made while the database is closed.

consolidated database replay An enhancement to Oracle Database Replay to replay individual workloads from multiple non-CDBs and play them back within a single multitenant environment. Using Consolidated Database Replay helps to measure resource requirements for the new CDB.

constraint A mechanism for enforcing rules on data; a column value must be unique or may contain only certain values. A primary key constraint specifies that the column must be both unique and not null. Foreign key constraints ensure that a column value must exist as a primary key in a parent table.

container An object in a multitenant environment that hosts zero, one, or more pluggable databases (PDBs). Also known as a container database (CDB). A container is a single instance in a non-RAC environment.

container database See *container*.

control file The file containing pointers to the rest of the database, critical sequence information, and the RMAN repository.

CPU Central processing unit. The chip that provides the processing capability of a computer, such as an Intel Pentium or a Sun SPARC.

CTWR Change tracking writer. The optional background process that records the addresses of changed blocks to enable fast incremental backups.

data blocks The units into which datafiles are formatted, made up of one or more operating system blocks.

data dictionary The tables and views owned by SYS in the SYSTEM tablespace that define the database and the objects within it.

data dictionary views Views on the data dictionary tables that let the DBA query the state of the database.

Data Guard A facility whereby a copy of the production database is created and updated (possibly in real time), with all changes applied to the production database.

Data Pump A facility for transferring large amounts of data at high speed into, out of, or between databases.

database buffer cache An area of memory in the System Global Area (SGA) used for working on blocks copied from datafiles.

database event trigger An Oracle program code block that fires when a specific database event occurs such as startup, shutdown, or some other database-wide event. Database event triggers have been enhanced in Oracle Database 12*c* to automate the opening of pluggable databases when the root container (CDB) starts up.

database link A connection from one database to another, based on a username and password and a connect string.

Database Replay An Oracle monitoring feature that can help to assess the change in performance on a test system by capturing the workload on a production server and replaying the workload on a test system.

datafile The disk-based structure for storing data.

DBA Database administrator. The person responsible for creating and managing Oracle databases—this could be you.

DBA role A preseeded role in the database provided for backward compatibility that includes all the privileges needed to manage a database, except the privilege needed to start up or shut down.

DBCA The Database Configuration Assistant. A GUI tool for creating, modifying, and dropping instances and databases.

DBID Database identifier. A unique number for each individual database, visible in the DBID column of the V$DATABASE dynamic performance view.

DBMS Database management system. This is often used interchangeably with RDBMS.

DBNEWID A command-line utility (usually **nid**) that can change the value of the DBID for a database.

DBWn or DBWR The database writer. The background process responsible for writing changed blocks from the database buffer cache to the datafiles. An instance can have up to 20 database writer processes, DBW0 through DBW9 and DBWa through DBWj.

DDL Data Definition Language. The subset of SQL commands that change object definitions within the data dictionary: CREATE, ALTER, DROP, and TRUNCATE.

deadlock A situation in which two sessions block each other such that neither can do anything. Deadlocks are detected and resolved automatically by the DIA0 background process.

DHCP Dynamic Host Configuration Protocol. The standard for configuring the network characteristics of a computer, such as its IP address, in a changing environment where computers can be moved from one location to another.

DIA0 The diagnosability process that detects hang and deadlock situations.

DIAG The diagnosability process that generates diagnostic dumps.

direct path A method of I/O on datafiles that bypasses the database buffer cache.

directory object An Oracle directory. A, object within the database that points to an operating system directory.

dirty buffer A buffer in the database buffer cache that contains a copy of a data block that has been updated and not yet written back to the datafile.

DML Data Manipulation Language. The subset of SQL commands that change data within the database: INSERT, UPDATE, DELETE, and MERGE.

DMnn Data Pump master process. The process that controls a Data Pump job—one will be launched for each job that is running.

DNS Domain Name System. The TCP mechanism for resolving network names into IP addresses. Runs on a machine called a DNS server.

domain The set of values an attribute is allowed to have. Tables have rows, and rows have columns with values; or, relations have tuples, and tuples have attributes with values taken from their domain.

DSS Decision support system. A database, such as a data warehouse, optimized for running queries with high I/O activity on large chunks of data, as opposed to online transaction processing (OLTP) work that accesses small chunks of data at a time.

DWnn Data Pump worker process. One or more of these will be launched for each Data Pump job that is running.

Easy Connect A method of establishing a session against a database by specifying the address on the listener and the service name, without using an Oracle Net alias.

Enterprise Manager Database Express A lightweight monitoring and query tool for an Oracle database instance on a single server. Replaces Enterprise Manager Database Control in Oracle Database 12*c*.

environment variable A variable set in the operating system shell that can be used by application software and by shell scripts.

equijoin A join condition using an equality operator.

fast incremental backup An incremental backup that uses a block change tracking file to identify only changed blocks since the last backup.

FGA Fine-grained auditing. A facility for tracking user access to data, based on the rows that are seen or manipulated.

flash recovery area A location on a file system or an Automatic Storage Management (ASM) disk group for all recovery-related files.

Flashback Data Archive A database container object that retains historical data for one or more database objects for a specified retention period.

Flashback Database A flashback feature that recovers the entire database to a point of time in the past using Flashback Database logs.

Flashback Database logs Changed database blocks that are stored in the flash recovery area and used for Flashback Database.

Flashback Drop A flashback feature that makes it easy to recover dropped tables if they are still in a tablespace's recycle bin.

Flashback Query A flashback feature that enables you to view one or more rows in a table at a time in the past.

Flashback Table A Flashback Query that recovers a single table and its associated objects to a point in time that has passed.

fractured block A database block that is simultaneously being read by an operating system copy command and modified by the DBWR process.

full backup A backup containing all blocks of the files backed up, not only those blocks changed since the last backup.

GMT Greenwich mean time. Now referred to in the United States as UTC, which is the time zone of the meridian through Greenwich Observatory in London.

grid computing An architecture for which the delivery of a service to end users is not tied to certain server resources but can be provided from anywhere in a pool of resources, linking multiple low-cost, independent commodity machines into a single, far more powerful grouped virtual platform.

GUI Graphical user interface. A layer of an application that lets users work with applications using a graphically driven screen interface, using both keyboard and mouse. The X Window System and Microsoft Windows are both GUI applications that provide GUI-driven access to other GUI applications.

HTTP Hypertext Transfer Protocol. The protocol that enables the World Wide Web (both invented at the European Organization for Nuclear Research in 1989). This layered protocol runs over TCP/IP.

HWM High water mark. The last block of a segment that has ever been used—blocks above this are part of the segment but are not yet formatted for use.

image copy A Recovery Manager (RMAN) bit-for-bit copy of a file.

inconsistent backup A backup made while the database is open.

incremental backup A backup containing only blocks that have been changed since the last backup was made.

instance recovery The automatic repair of damage caused by a disorderly shutdown of the database, either from a crash or from running SHUTDOWN ABORT.

I/O Input/output. The activity of reading from or writing to disks—often the slowest point of a data processing operation because it's the slowest piece of hardware when compared with CPU and RAM.

IOT Index-organized table. A table type in which the data rows are stored in the leaf blocks of an index segment. The table is effectively an index.

IP Internet Protocol. Together with the Transmission Control Protocol (TCP/IP), it's the de facto standard communication protocol used for client-server communication over a network.

IPC Interprocess Communications protocol. The platform-specific protocol provided by your OS vendor and used for processes running on the same machine to communicate with each other.

ISO International Organization for Standardization. A group that defines many standards, including SQL.

job A row in a scheduler table that specifies what to do and when to do it. The "what" can be a single SQL statement, a PL/SQL block, a PL/SQL stored procedure, a Java stored procedure, an external procedure, or any executable file stored in the server's file system.

job chain A database object that contains a named series of programs linked together for a combined objective.

job class A scheduler object that is used to associate one or more jobs with a Resource Manager consumer group and to control logging levels.

join The process of connecting rows in different tables based on common column values.

JVM Java Virtual Machine. The runtime environment needed for running code written in Java. Oracle provides a JVM with the Oracle binaries that executes Java code within the database. Typically, another version of Java is installed with your operating system and runs standalone Java applications.

large pool A memory structure within the System Global Area (SGA) used by certain processes, principally shared server processes, and parallel execution servers.

LDAP Lightweight Directory Access Protocol. The TCP implementation of the X.25 directory standard, used by the Oracle Internet Directory for name resolution, security, and authentication. LDAP is also used by other software vendors, including Microsoft and IBM.

level 0 incremental backup A full RMAN backup that can be used as the basis for an incremental backup strategy.

level 1 cumulative incremental backup An RMAN backup of all changed blocks since the last level 0 incremental backup.

level 1 differential incremental backup An RMAN backup of all changed blocks since the last level 0 or level 1 incremental backup.

LGWR Log Writer. The background process responsible for flushing change vectors from the log buffer in memory out to the online redo log files on disk.

library cache A memory structure within the shared pool that is used for caching SQL statements parsed into their executable form.

lightweight job A scheduler job that has many of the same characteristics of a standard job, except that a lightweight job is ideal for running many short-duration jobs that run frequently.

listener A server-side process that listens for database connection requests from user processes and launches dedicated server processes to establish sessions. The sessions become the connections between the user process and the database unless shared servers are in use, in which case a dispatcher process is used to share time to shared server processes.

LOB Large object. A data structure that contains a large amount of binary or character data, such as an image or a document. LOBs (Oracle supports several types) are defined as columns of a table but can be either physically stored in a separate segment or stored within the table segment itself.

local privileges A system or object privilege granted to a local user and is therefore in effect for that user in only a single container.

local profile A database profile that exists only in a single PDB and can be assigned only to local users.

local role A database role that is created in a single PDB and granted to a local user and therefore is available to that user in only one container.

local user A user account that is created and exists only in a pluggable database (PDB). The root container (CDB$ROOT) cannot have local users, only common users.

Locale Builder A graphical tool that can create a customized globalization environment by generating definitions for languages, territories, character sets, and linguistic sorting.

log switch The action of closing one online log file group and opening another (triggered by the LGWR process filling the first group) and then causing the recently closed log file to be archived.

logical backup A backup that reads a set of database rows and writes them to a file in the operating system or to another tablespace.

LRU Least recently used. An algorithm in which LRU lists manage access to data structures that are used infrequently in a sequence corresponding to the structure's frequency of use.

LVM Logical volume manager. A layer of software that groups physical storage areas (one or more disk partitions) all into groups or volumes. A single volume is then accessed to manage data on one or more underlying physical disks.

MMAN The memory manager background process, which monitors and reassigns memory allocations in the SGA for automatically tunable SGA components.

MML Media management layer. Software that lets RMAN make use of automated tape libraries and other SBT (system backup to tape) devices.

MMNL Manageability Monitor Light. The background process responsible for flushing Active Session History (ASH) data to the Automatic Workload Repository (AWR)—if the Manageability Monitor (MMON) is not doing this with the necessary frequency.

MMON The Manageability Monitor. A background process that is responsible for gathering performance monitoring information and raising alerts.

mounted database A condition in which the instance has opened the database control file and the online redo log files but not yet opened the datafiles.

MTBF Mean time between failures. A measure of the average length of running time for a database between unplanned shutdowns.

MTS Multithreaded server. Since release 9*i*, renamed Shared Server. This is the technique whereby a large number of sessions can share a small pool of server processes, rather than requiring one dedicated server process each. Dedicated server processes can often be the most efficient for anything other than the most extreme types of production environments.

MTTR Mean time to recover. The average time it takes to make the database available for normal use after a failure.

multiplexing To maintain multiple copies of files (particularly control files and redo log files). Previous versions of Oracle have used the terms *multiplexing* to describe control file duplication and *duplexing* to describe log file member duplications.

multitenant architecture An architecture that hosts many logical databases within one larger database instance to more efficiently use server resources such as memory, CPU, and I/O.

namespace A logical grouping of objects within which no two objects may have the same name.

NCLOB National character large object. A LOB data type for character data, such as text documents that are stored in the alternative national database character set.

NLS National language support. The capability of Oracle Database to support many linguistic, geographical, and cultural environments—now usually referred to as *globalization*.

node A computer attached to a network.

non-CDB A standalone database that cannot automatically be plugged into a CDB or can host PDBs. A non-CDB can be at any database version, but to convert to a PDB directly, it must be at version 12.1.0.1 or newer.

null The absence of a value, indicating that the value is not known, is missing, or is inapplicable. Null values are used in databases to save space and to avoid continually having to program zeros and space characters into empty columns in tables.

OC4J Oracle Containers for J2EE. The control structure provided by the Oracle Internet Application Server for running Java programs.

OCA Oracle Certified Associate.

OCI Oracle Call Interface. An API published as a set of C libraries that programmers can use to write user processes that will use an Oracle database.

OCP Oracle Certified Professional. The qualification you are working toward at the moment.

offline backup A backup made while the database is closed (completely shut down).

OLAP Online analytical processing. Selection-intensive work involving running large and intensive queries against a (usually) large database. Oracle provides OLAP capabilities as an option, in addition to the standard query facilities.

OLTP Online transaction processing. A pattern of activity within a database typified by a large number of small, short transactions as well as small queries.

online backup A backup made while the database is open.

online redo log The files to which change vectors are streamed by the Log Writer (LGWR), recording all changes made to a database, which ensures complete recoverability.

ORACLE_BASE The root directory into which all Oracle products are installed.

ORACLE_HOME The root directory of any one particular Oracle product, within the ORACLE_BASE.

Oracle Net Oracle's proprietary communications protocol, layered on top of an industry-standard protocol such as TCP/IP.

OS Operating system. Typically, in the Oracle environment, this will be a version of Unix (perhaps Linux) or Microsoft Windows.

parallelization Using multiple slave processes managed by a single coordinator process to perform queries or DML operations in parallel across multiple CPUs and I/O channels simultaneously. RMAN backups take advantage of parallelism by allocating multiple channels and improving backup performance by executing partitioned chunks of I/O in parallel.

parse To verify syntax and convert SQL statements into a form suitable for execution.

PDB See "*pluggable database*".

PDB$SEED A read-only pluggable database within a root container (CDB) used as a template to create new PDBs within the CDB.

PFILE A text-based file containing initialization parameters and initial values that are set when an Oracle instance starts.

PGA Program Global Area. The variable-sized block of memory used to maintain the state of a database session. PGAs are private to the session and controlled by the session's server process.

physical backup A copy of the files that constitute the database.

PL/SQL Procedural Language/Structured Query Language. Oracle's proprietary programming language, which combines procedural constructs, such as flow control and user interface capabilities, with SQL.

pluggable database Also known as a PDB. A logical database that exists within a container database and shares the memory, process slots, and other resources with other logical databases within the CDB but is isolated from all other logical databases in the same container. Pluggable databases can be unplugged (removed) from the container database and plugged back in later to the same or different container.

PMON The process monitor. The background process responsible for monitoring the state of user sessions against an instance.

primary key The column (or combination of columns), whose value (or values) can be used to identify each row in a table.

program A scheduler object that provides a layer of abstraction between the job and the action it will perform; it is created with the DBMS_SCHEDULER.CREATE_PROGRAM procedure.

RAC Real Application Cluster. Oracle's clustering technology that allows several instances in different machines to open the same database files with the objectives of scalability, performance, and fault tolerance.

RAID Redundant Array of Inexpensive Disks. Techniques for enhancing performance and/or fault tolerance by using a volume manager to present a number of physical disks to the operating system as a single logical disk.

RAM Random access memory. The chips that make up the real memory in your computer hardware versus the virtual memory presented to software by the operating system. RAM is the second fastest piece of hardware in your computer other than your CPU.

raw device An unformatted disk or disk partition.

RBAL Rebalance process. A background process in an Automatic Storage Management (ASM) instance that coordinates disk activity for disk groups. In an RDBMS instance, it performs the opening and closing of the disks in the disk group.

RDBMS Relational database management system. This term is often used interchangeably with DBMS.

recovery catalog Tables in a database schema that contain metadata and other backup information for RMAN backups of one or more databases.

recovery window An RMAN parameter and time period that defines how far back in time the database can be recovered.

referential integrity Rules defined in a relational database between primary and foreign keys, where the primary key must exist in a table for a row to exist on a subset table (in the foreign key) and defines one-to-many relationships.

relation A two-dimensional structure consisting of tuples with attributes (aka a table).

resource consumer groups Groups of users or sessions that have similar resource needs.

Resource Manager An Oracle feature that can allocate resources based on CPU usage, degree of parallelism, number of active sessions, undo space, CPU time limit, and idle time limit.

resource plan A set of rules in Resource Manager that assign various resources at specific percentages or relative priorities to a resource group.

resource plan directives Rules within Resource Manager that associate consumer groups with a resource plan and specify how the resources are divided among the consumer groups or subplans.

restore point A database object containing either a system change number (SCN) or a time in the past used to recover the database to the SCN or timestamp.

resumable space allocation An Oracle feature that suspends instead of terminating large database operations that require more disk space than is currently available. A suspended operation can be restarted from where it finished off, at a later point in time, when the space issues have been resolved. It saves time.

retention policy The number of copies of all objects that RMAN will retain for recovery purposes.

RMAN Recovery Manager. Oracle's backup and recovery tool.

root container The primary container in a container database that hosts pluggable databases. All initialization parameters are set in the root container and are inherited by each pluggable database unless overridden. Only a smaller subset of parameters defined in the root container can be changed in a pluggable database along with the default temporary tablespace.

Rowid The unique identifier of every row in the database, which is used as a pointer to the physical location of the row from logical objects such as tables and indexes. The rowid data type is proprietary to Oracle Corporation and is not part of the SQL standard, and it is not recommended for direct storage into tables because the values can change.

RVWR The Recovery Writer background process is an optional process responsible for flushing the flashback buffer to the flashback logs.

SBT System backup to tape. An RMAN term for a tape device.

schedule A specification for when and how frequently a job should run.

schema The objects owned by a database user; synonymous with a user from a physical perspective. A schema is a user who is used to store tables and indexes. Users are created to access that schema user as multiple application users of that centrally managed schema.

SCN System change number. A continually incrementing number used to track the sequence and exact time of all events within a database.

seed container Also known as the seed database in a multitenant environment. The seed container is a special instance of a pluggable database name PDB$SEED, is always read-only, and is used as a template for creating a new pluggable database in the current root container.

segment A logical database object within a schema that stores data.

segment shrink A database operation that makes the free space in a segment available to other segments in the tablespace by compacting and releasing the empty, unused data blocks in a segment.

sequence A database object within a schema used to generate consecutive numbers.

service name A logical name registered by an instance with a listener, which can be specified by a user process when it issues a connect request. A service name will be mapped onto a system identifier (SID) by the listener when it establishes a session. A service name is created by default for each PDB and is the preferred and primary connection method for database clients.

session A user process (application) connected through a server process that is connected to the instance.

SGA System Global Area. The block of shared memory that contains the memory structures that make up an Oracle instance.

share A portion of resources granted to a single PDB. Each PDB will have at least one share, and the total resources available to a PDB is based on the ratio of the PDB's shares to the total number of shares allocated to all PDBs within a CDB.

shared object An object created in the root container that is available to all current and new PDBs in the container. Only Oracle-supplied common users (such as SYS and SYSTEM) can create shared objects.

SID 1. System identifier. The name of an instance that must be unique on the computer on which the instance is running. Users can request a connection to a named SID or to a logical service and let the listener choose an appropriate SID. 2. Session identifier. The number used to uniquely identify a session that is logged on to an Oracle instance.

SMON The system monitor. The background process responsible for opening a database and monitoring the instance.

SPFILE The server parameter file. The file containing the parameters used to build an instance in memory. This is a binary form of the parameter file. A text form of the parameter file is called the PFILE.

SQL Structured Query Language. An international standard language for extracting data from and manipulating data in relational databases.

SQL Tuning Advisor An Oracle advisor that performs statistics analysis, SQL Profile analysis, access path analysis, and structure analysis.

synonym A pointer (named reference) to a database object, typically used to avoid fully qualified names for schema objects.

SYSASM A system privilege in an ASM instance that facilitates the separation of database administration and storage administration.

SYSDBA The privilege that lets a user connect with operating system or password file authentication and create, start up, and shut down a database.

SYSDG System privilege for Data Guard operations.

SYSKM System privilege for managing Transparent Data Encryption (TDE) keystore operations.

SYSOPER The privilege that lets a user connect with operating system or password file authentication and start up and shut down (but not create) a database.

SYSTEM A preseeded schema used for database administration purposes.

table A logical two-dimensional data storage structure, consisting of rows and columns.

tablespace The logical structure that abstracts logical data storage in tables from physical data storage in datafiles.

TCP Transmission Control Protocol. Together with the Internet Protocol (IP), TCP is the de facto standard communication protocol used for client-server communication over a network.

TCPS TCP with SSL. The secure sockets version of TCP.

tempfile The physical storage that makes up a temporary tablespace that is used for storing temporary segments.

TNS Transparent Network Substrate. The heart of Oracle Net, a proprietary layered protocol running on top of whatever underlying network transport protocol you choose to use—probably TCP/IP.

transaction A logical unit of work, which will complete in total or not at all.

TSPITR Tablespace point-in-time recovery. A recovery method that is ideal for recovering a set of objects isolated to a single tablespace.

tuple A one-dimensional structure consisting of attributes (aka a row).

UGA User Global Area. The part of the Program Global Area (PGA) that is stored in the System Global Area (SGA) for sessions running through shared servers.

UI User interface. The layer of an application that communicates with end users; nowadays, the UI is frequently graphical—a GUI.

URL Uniform Resource Locator. A standard for specifying the location of an object on the Internet (a web site name you type into your browser) consisting of a protocol, a hostname and domain, an IP port number, a path and filename, and a series of parameters.

user-managed recovery Using tools or commands outside of RMAN to recover a database or tablespace.

UTC Coordinated Universal Time, previously known as Greenwich mean time (GMT). UTC is the global standard time zone. All other time zones relate to it as offsets, which are ahead or behind UTC.

virtual private catalog A logical partitioning of an RMAN catalog to facilitate the separation of duties among several DBAs.

whole-database backup A database backup that includes all datafiles plus the control file.

window A scheduler construct that extends the concept of schedules by giving Oracle more freedom on deciding when to run a job within a specific start and begin time—for a single day or every day of the week.

X As in the X Window System, the standard GUI environment used on most non–Microsoft Windows computers.

XML Extensible Markup Language. A standard for data interchange using documents, in which the format of the data is defined by tags within the document.

INDEX

A

C

D

M

N

R

S

U

V

W

X

LICENSE AGREEMENT

THIS PRODUCT (THE "PRODUCT") CONTAINS PROPRIETARY SOFTWARE, DATA AND INFORMATION (INCLUDING DOCUMENTATION) OWNED BY McGRAW-HILL EDUCATION AND ITS LICENSORS. YOUR RIGHT TO USE THE PRODUCT IS GOVERNED BY THE TERMS AND CONDITIONS OF THIS AGREEMENT.

LICENSE: Throughout this License Agreement, "you" shall mean either the individual or the entity whose agent opens this package. You are granted a non-exclusive and non-transferable license to use the Product subject to the following terms:

(i) If you have licensed a single user version of the Product, the Product may only be used on a single computer (i.e., a single CPU). If you licensed and paid the fee applicable to a local area network or wide area network version of the Product, you are subject to the terms of the following subparagraph (ii).

(ii) If you have licensed a local area network version, you may use the Product on unlimited workstations located in one single building selected by you that is served by such local area network. If you have licensed a wide area network version, you may use the Product on unlimited workstations located in multiple buildings on the same site selected by you that is served by such wide area network; provided, however, that any building will not be considered located in the same site if it is more than five (5) miles away from any building included in such site. In addition, you may only use a local area or wide area network version of the Product on one single server. If you wish to use the Product on more than one server, you must obtain written authorization from McGraw-Hill Education and pay additional fees.

(iii) You may make one copy of the Product for back-up purposes only and you must maintain an accurate record as to the location of the back-up at all times.

COPYRIGHT; RESTRICTIONS ON USE AND TRANSFER: All rights (including copyright) in and to the Product are owned by McGraw-Hill Education and its licensors. You are the owner of the enclosed disc on which the Product is recorded. You may not use, copy, decompile, disassemble, reverse engineer, modify, reproduce, create derivative works, transmit, distribute, sublicense, store in a database or retrieval system of any kind, rent or transfer the Product, or any portion thereof, in any form or by any means (including electronically or otherwise) except as expressly provided for in this License Agreement. You must reproduce the copyright notices, trademark notices, legends and logos of McGraw-Hill Education and its licensors that appear on the Product on the back-up copy of the Product which you are permitted to make hereunder. All rights in the Product not expressly granted herein are reserved by McGraw-Hill Education and its licensors.

TERM: This License Agreement is effective until terminated. It will terminate if you fail to comply with any term or condition of this License Agreement. Upon termination, you are obligated to return to McGraw-Hill Education the Product together with all copies thereof and to purge all copies of the Product included in any and all servers and computer facilities.

DISCLAIMER OF WARRANTY: THE PRODUCT AND THE BACK-UP COPY ARE LICENSED "AS IS." McGRAW-HILL EDUCATION, ITS LICENSORS AND THE AUTHORS MAKE NO WARRANTIES, EXPRESS OR IMPLIED, AS TO THE RESULTS TO BE OBTAINED BY ANY PERSON OR ENTITY FROM USE OF THE PRODUCT, ANY INFORMATION OR DATA INCLUDED THEREIN AND/OR ANY TECHNICAL SUPPORT SERVICES PROVIDED HEREUNDER, IF ANY ("TECHNICAL SUPPORT SERVICES"). McGRAW-HILL EDUCATION, ITS LICENSORS AND THE AUTHORS MAKE NO EXPRESS OR IMPLIED WARRANTIES OF MERCHANTABILITY OR FITNESS FOR A PARTICULAR PURPOSE OR USE WITH RESPECT TO THE PRODUCT. McGRAW-HILL EDUCATION, ITS LICENSORS, AND THE AUTHORS MAKE NO GUARANTEE THAT YOU WILL PASS ANY CERTIFICATION EXAM WHATSOEVER BY USING THIS PRODUCT. NEITHER McGRAW-HILL EDUCATION, ANY OF ITS LICENSORS NOR THE AUTHORS WARRANT THAT THE FUNCTIONS CONTAINED IN THE PRODUCT WILL MEET YOUR REQUIREMENTS OR THAT THE OPERATION OF THE PRODUCT WILL BE UNINTERRUPTED OR ERROR FREE. YOU ASSUME THE ENTIRE RISK WITH RESPECT TO THE QUALITY AND PERFORMANCE OF THE PRODUCT.

LIMITED WARRANTY FOR DISC: To the original licensee only, McGraw-Hill Education warrants that the enclosed disc on which the Product is recorded is free from defects in materials and workmanship under normal use and service for a period of ninety (90) days from the date of purchase. In the event of a defect in the disc covered by the foregoing warranty, McGraw-Hill Education will replace the disc.

LIMITATION OF LIABILITY: NEITHER McGRAW-HILL EDUCATION, ITS LICENSORS NOR THE AUTHORS SHALL BE LIABLE FOR ANY INDIRECT, SPECIAL OR CONSEQUENTIAL DAMAGES, SUCH AS BUT NOT LIMITED TO, LOSS OF ANTICIPATED PROFITS OR BENEFITS, RESULTING FROM THE USE OR INABILITY TO USE THE PRODUCT EVEN IF ANY OF THEM HAS BEEN ADVISED OF THE POSSIBILITY OF SUCH DAMAGES. THIS LIMITATION OF LIABILITY SHALL APPLY TO ANY CLAIM OR CAUSE WHATSOEVER WHETHER SUCH CLAIM OR CAUSE ARISES IN CONTRACT, TORT, OR OTHERWISE. Some states do not allow the exclusion or limitation of indirect, special or consequential damages, so the above limitation may not apply to you.

U.S. GOVERNMENT RESTRICTED RIGHTS: Any software included in the Product is provided with restricted rights subject to subparagraphs (c), (1) and (2) of the Commercial Computer Software-Restricted Rights clause at 48 C.F.R. 52.227-19. The terms of this Agreement applicable to the use of the data in the Product are those under which the data are generally made available to the general public by McGraw-Hill Education. Except as provided herein, no reproduction, use, or disclosure rights are granted with respect to the data included in the Product and no right to modify or create derivative works from any such data is hereby granted.

GENERAL: This License Agreement constitutes the entire agreement between the parties relating to the Product. The terms of any Purchase Order shall have no effect on the terms of this License Agreement. Failure of McGraw-Hill Education to insist at any time on strict compliance with this License Agreement shall not constitute a waiver of any rights under this License Agreement. This License Agreement shall be construed and governed in accordance with the laws of the State of New York. If any provision of this License Agreement is held to be contrary to law, that provision will be enforced to the maximum extent permissible and the remaining provisions will remain in full force and effect.